Wend von Kalnein   *Architecture in France in the Eighteenth Century*

Translated from the German by David Britt

Yale University Press
New Haven and London

Some sections of this book were previously published as Part Two of *Art and Architecture of the eighteenth Century in France*, by Penguin Books Ltd, 1972

This edition first published by Yale University Press, 1995

Typeset in Linotron Ehrhardt by Best-set Typesetter Ltd., Hong Kong and printed by CS Graphics Pty, Singapore

Designed by Sally Salvesen

Library of Congress Cataloging-in-Publication Data

Kalnein, Wend von, 1914–
    Architecture in France in the eighteenth century/Wend von
Kalnein: translated from the German by David Britt.
        p.   cm. — (Yale University Press Pelican history of art)
Based on the architecture portions of W. Kalnein and M. Levey's Art and
architecture of the eighteenth century in France.
    Includes bibliographical references (p. 283) and index.
    ISBN 0-300-06013-0
        1. Architecture—France.   2. Architecture, Baroque—
France.   3. Architecture, Rococo—France.   4. Neoclassicism
(Architecture)—France.   I. Kalnein, Wend von, 1914–   Art and
architecture of the eighteenth century in France.   II. Title.   III. Series.
NA1046.K35   1994
720′.944′09033—dc20   93-49720
                                                        CIP

TITLEPAGE: Anges-Jacques Gabriel: Paris, Place de la Concorde (Place Louis XV), 1757–75.

Contents

Preface

This book differs from the first version in one fundamental respect: architecture is given a volume to itself, separately from painting and sculpture, and this means that the scope of the discussion is considerably expanded. A wider coverage of the theme is made possible, as its specific nature demands: for the eighteenth century was a period of radical change. Over the last few years there has been a growth of interest, reflected by a flood of scholarly publications. Research, mostly by English and French scholars, and a number of exhibitions devoted to individual architects, have brought to light facts and relationships that utterly transform our picture of the evolution of architecture in the period. By 1980 Allan Braham, in *Architecture of the French Enlightenment*, was able to give a well founded and fascinating summary of the second half of the century. Much of what was once *terra incognita* has become familiar and well-documented territory. All this has made it necessary to rewrite the book completely. Numerous points of fact have had to be corrected, and outdated conclusions rectified, so that little of the original text remains.

The centre of gravity lies in Paris, which was not only the seat of the Academy, and thus of the elite of French architects, but also the focus of ideas. The provinces have, however, been given their due wherever they have original achievements to show. French architecture outside France has been included only where a direct connection with Paris exists. In this field the standard works are still, for Germany, Pierre du Colombier's *L'Architecture française en Allemagne au XVIIIe siècle* and, for Russia, Louis Real's *L'architecture française en Russie de Le Blond à Ricard de Montferrand.* For further literature, see the Bibliography, which includes all important publications down to 1992.

As before, I must record my gratitude for help received from many quarters. Along with the Kunsthistorisches Institut in Salzburg, my thanks go first of all to the Zentralinstitut für Kunstgeschichte in Munich, whose unique library has given me invaluable assistance and has spared me more than one journey to Paris; also to the Bibliothèque Nationale, the Archives Nationales and the Musée Carnavalet in Paris, all of which sustained me in my laborious quest for original designs. Among individuals who helped me substantially with the production of this book I would mention gratefully first David Britt for his superior and subtle translation and the critical comments on my text as well as Sally Salvesen for the delightful co-operation in the technical production and Susan Rose-Smith for the excellent illustrations she managed to collect throughout Europe. Not least, I owe particular thanks to my wife, who has once more needed to summon all her reserves of patience.

Salzburg, April 1992

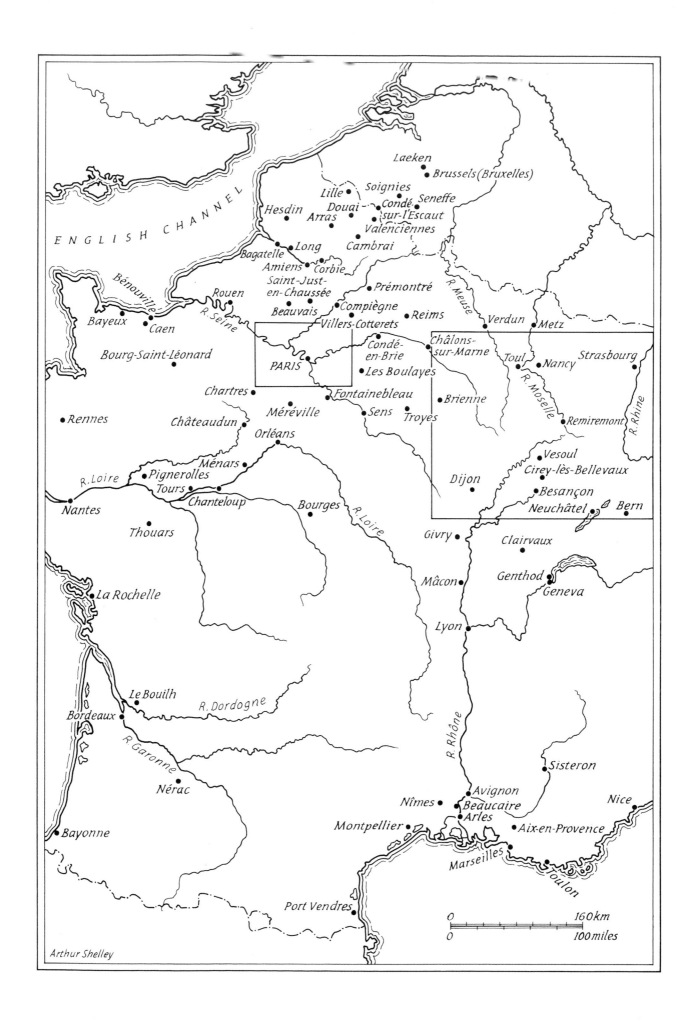

ENGLISH CHANNEL

Laeken
Brussels (Bruxelles)
Soignies
Lille   Seneffe
Hesdin   Douai   Condé-
Arras   sur-l'Escaut
              Valenciennes
Long   Cambrai
Bagatelle
Amiens   Corbie
Saint-Just-   Prémontré
en-Chaussée   R. Meuse
Rouen   Beauvais   Compiègne   Reims   Verdun   Metz
         Villers-Cotterets
Bayeux   Châlons-
Bénouville   sur-Marne   Toul   Nancy   Strasbourg
Caen   Condé-
Bourg-Saint-Léonard   en-Brie   R. Moselle
PARIS   Les Boulayes   R. Rhine
         Chartres   Brienne   Remiremont
                    Fontainebleau
Rennes   Méréville   Sens   Troyes
         Châteaudun
                    Vesoul
         Orléans   Cirey-lès-Bellevaux
Ménars   Dijon   Besançon
R. Loire   Pignerolles   Neuchâtel   Bern
         Tours
Nantes   Chanteloup   Bourges   R. Loire
         Thouars   Givry   Clairvaux

La Rochelle   Mâcon   Genthod
                                             Geneva

                                    Lyon

Le Bouilh   R. Dordogne
Bordeaux   Sisteron
         R. Garonne   R. Rhône
              Nérac   Avignon   Nice
                              Nîmes   Beaucaire
Bayonne   Montpellier   Arles   Aix-en-Provence

                                        Marseilles   Toulon
              Port Vendres

                              0   160 km
                              0   100 miles

Arthur Shelley

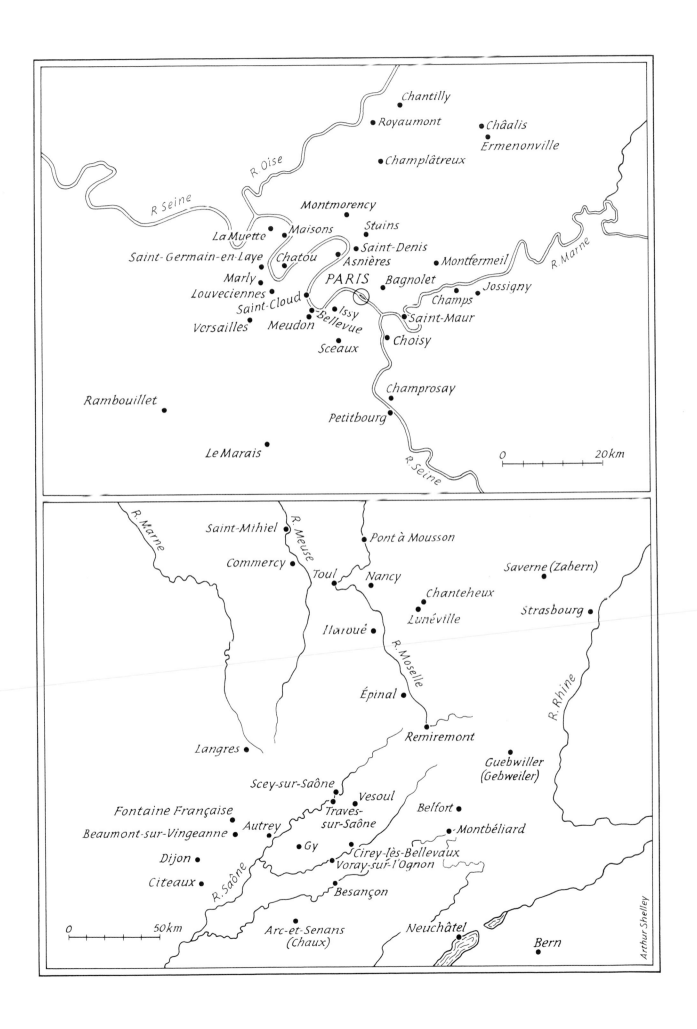

Top map (Paris region):

Chantilly
Royaumont
Châalis
Ermenonville
Champlâtreux
R. Oise
R. Seine
Montmorency
Maisons
Stains
La Muette
Saint-Denis
Saint-Germain-en-Laye
Chatou
Asnières
Montfermeil
R. Marne
Marly
PARIS
Bagnolet
Jossigny
Louveciennes
Champs
Saint-Cloud
Issy
Meudon
Bellevue
Saint-Maur
Versailles
Sceaux
Choisy
Champrosay
Rambouillet
Petitbourg
Le Marais
R. Seine
0   20km

Bottom map (Eastern France):

R. Marne
R. Meuse
Saint-Mihiel
Pont à Mousson
Commercy
Saverne (Zabern)
Toul
Nancy
Chanteheux
Strasbourg
Lunéville
Haroué
R. Moselle
Épinal
R. Rhine
Remiremont
Langres
Guebwiller
(Gebweiler)
Scey-sur-Saône
Vesoul
Fontaine Française
Traves-sur-Saône
Belfort
Beaumont-sur-Vingeanne
Autrey
Montbéliard
Dijon
Gy
Cirey-lès-Bellevaux
Voray-sur-l'Ognon
Citeaux
R. Saône
Besançon
0   50km
Arc-et-Senans
(Chaux)
Neuchâtel
Bern

Arthur Shelley

PART ONE

The School of Jules Hardouin-Mansart and the Goût Moderne

CHAPTER I

Introduction

Architecture ranks high among the products of the French genius: no less so than the arts of painting and sculpture. Indeed, it has tended to attract a wider public debate than either. In their day, the debates on the building of the Louvre and of the Place Louis-XV (now Place de la Concorde) in Paris exercised the minds of a whole generation. One manifestation of this conspicuous status was the existence of an Academy of Architecture; founded by Colbert a little later than the Academy of Painting and Sculpture, this was the only state institution of its kind anywhere in Europe. Its keenly fought annual competitions for the Prix de Rome were a national concern, funded by the state. The tradition of French architecture has always been a distinguished one; and if its first age of supreme achievement was the Gothic, its second was in the eighteenth century. This was the time when architecture defined the look of France herself, her cities, streets and bridges; and cities such as Bordeaux, Nantes and Rennes bear witness to this today.

French eighteenth-century architecture is distinguished from that of other countries by its quality of restraint and proportion, and by the inner consistency that it maintained from one generation to the next. People looked to it not for the supreme achievements of individual genius but for sureness of taste and a combination of outward grace, socially apt form and practical utility. Its hallmark is pragmatism: excess and exuberance are foreign to its nature. In the pragmatically minded age of the Enlightenment, this ensured its general acceptance, and in particular – where domestic architecture was concerned – gave it preference over Italian architecture. All the same, in this respect as in others, there is nothing monolithic about the eighteenth century: this was an age of cross-currents and directional shifts. It cannot viewed only in terms of Baroque and Rococo. The full artistic and social achievement of eighteenth-century French architecture can be seen only in terms of the clash between classical and anticlassical tendencies, and of the sheer diversity of the individuals who represented those tendencies.

For France, that eventful century opened with a catastrophe. The War of the Spanish Succession (1701–14) brought Louis XIV a series of unaccustomed and crushing defeats. From the heights of triumph the country was plunged into a profound crisis that ruined both its economy and its finances and left the people starving. 'The famine is so terrible,' wrote Madame (the king's sister-in-law, Lieselotte) to the Electress of Hanover, 'that people are to be seen everywhere dropping dead from hunger; there is lamentation and misery everywhere, from the highest to the lowest... Whenever you leave the house you are followed by crowds of the poor, black with hunger. Everything is paid for with slips of paper; there is no money anywhere.'

Along with the economic decline went a psychological and political crisis. People were weary of Louis XIV's despotic rule. Archbishop Fénelon of Cambrai, the tutor to the king's young grandson, the Duc de Bourgogne, had written a novel of education, *Télémaque* (1699), in which he had been the first to venture on a criticism, however muted, of the king's love of war and the misery that this inflicted on the people. The Church, too, had weakened its own position, and given ammunition to its critics, by its intolerance and also by its constant theological squabbles. Fontenelle, in his *Histoire des oracles* (1687), and Bayle, in his *Dictionnaire historique et critique* (1695–7), had been the first to attack the faith itself, by declaring reason to be the supreme authority and by requiring a rational explanation for every fact.

Even the court of Versailles lost its magnetic attraction. The short respite afforded by the Peace of Ryswick (1697), and the arrival of the young Duchesse de Bourgogne, had brought a brief revival of life and gaiety. The king's passion for building had flared up again, and his great building projects in Paris and at Versailles – the Place Vendôme, the Dôme des Invalides, and others – had been set in train once more. But this revival soon petered out under the increasing burdens of war and the bigoted rule of Madame de Maintenon. In 1712, the sudden deaths of the Dauphin, of his two sons, and of his daughter-in-law, the universally beloved Duchesse de Bourgogne, came as a severe blow to the king, who was confronted with the possible extinction of his whole line. 'The sadness that prevails here is not to be described,' wrote Lieselotte. The court relapsed into dull and sanctimonious gloom. Anyone who could afford it escaped from the desolate precincts of the gigantic Château de Versailles to the more intimate social life of Paris, where new artistic and intellectual centres were forming.[1]

When Louis XIV died, there were hostile demonstrations at his funeral; but the sense of liberation from his oppressive rule soon ushered in a regime of a very different kind. The new king, Louis XIV's great-grandson, who resided at first in the Tuileries was a minor. The country was ruled in his name by his uncle, the Duc d'Orléans, who acted as sole regent; this was in direct contravention of Louis XIV's will, in which he had named his nephew only as the chairman of a council of regency. The regent elbowed out the late king's legitimized bastard sons and saw to it that all the high offices of state were in his personal gift; but this could be done only at the cost of extensive concessions to the Parlement, which thus acquired influence in the running of the country for the first time. The business of government slipped out of the hands of the ministers and passed to numerous 'councils' or committees, mostly chaired by dukes friendly to the regent. In everything he did, the regent was driven to rely on the goodwill of the counsellors of Parlement and of their rivals,

Paris, Hôtel de Soubise, detail of Plate 55.

the dukes, who had no idea of official business and spent their time wrangling over questions of precedence.

There was the further danger of the intervention of Philip V of Spain, who laid claim to the French throne as Louis XIV's grandson. Moreover Louis XIV's eldest legitimized son, the Duc du Maine, conspired with Spain and plotted murder; to meet the threat, the regent was driven to arrest and imprison both Maine and his intriguing duchess. In a brief time, an ordered regime had turned into anarchy, in which everyone did as he pleased; and morals in general duly became more relaxed. It was some years before the councils were destroyed by their own incompetence, and the ministers returned to their posts.

The outstanding event of the Régence was the financial operation mounted by a Scot, John Law, the 'financial genius of the age', whom the regent had entrusted with the reform of the shattered state finances. Initially, all went well. Backed by the state taxation system, Law set up a state bank and issued shares in the East India Company and in the French colonies on the faraway Mississippi. This achieved his aim of bringing the hoarded money of the war profiteers and financiers into circulation; but the prospect of quick profits soon led to a speculative boom that ran out of control. The result was the spectacular collapse of Law's state bank. Numerous citizens were ruined, but at the same time others had made exorbitant profits.

All this had its consequences for architecture. The successful speculators, some of whom were of humble birth, built themselves luxurious town houses – hôtels – and advertised their new-found status by moving to the elegant districts of Paris. A number of the finest hôtels in the Place Vendôme and in the Faubourg Saint-Germain owe their existence to those speculative gains.

In 1723, after eight years of regency, Louis XV great-grandson of Louis XIV was declared to be of age. The regent died in the same year. But it was not until 1726 – after a brief and inglorious episode of government by the Duc de Bourbon – that the intelligent and cautious Cardinal Fleury finally gave the country the firm and consistent leadership that it so desperately needed.

This shift of political power had momentous consequences for architecture, and for the arts in general. With the death of Louis XIV, the court had given up the leadership of the arts; and the young king showed no sign whatever of enthusiasm for building. It is often alleged that he had been dissuaded by the dying admonitions of his great-grandfather; but it is more likely that he was simply not interested. This, at least, was to be Jacques-François Blondel's complaint as late as 1736.

At Louis XIV's death, the centre of gravity of the art world moved to Paris. There, in the town houses of the aristocracy and at the regent's court in the Palais-Royal – where Gilles-Marie Oppenord, Jean-Antoine Watteau, Charles Cressent and, briefly, Bernard Toro met in a unique forum for the avant-garde – the new taste took shape. This was the *goût moderne* or *goût nouveau* that was to set its mark on the entire first half of the century. In architecture, the orders, unchallengeable since the Renaissance, disappeared from sight. The old, grand style (*grand goût*), with its free-standing columns and its pilasters, was now regarded as a

'ceremonial form' (Sedlmayr) and accordingly confined to official or otherwise special contexts; external sculpture was limited to window cartouches and balustraded parapets. Walls were no longer to be articulated by sculpturally defined elements but by flat pilasters and strips (chaînages) in stone or stucco. Low roofs and large windows – especially the newly fashionable *portes-fenêtres* or French windows – deprived the wall of its apparent weight, so that it became no more than an outward skin. Inside, too, applied orders were permitted only in such ceremonial rooms as vestibules, staircases and state bedrooms (chambres de parade). Rooms that were actually lived in became more convenient, more intimate and – above all – more full of light. The painted ceilings that opened into illusory skies disappeared, to be replaced by elegant plasterwork.

Iconography also underwent a change. The gods descended from Olympus and assumed a human guise; painters and tapestry weavers were kept busy with recording their love affairs. Jupiter, Apollo and Hercules were joined, and indeed supplanted, by Diana, Pan and Venus. Antoine Coypel's painted ceiling at the Hôtel d'Argenton, *The Deities of Love Expel the Higher Gods from Olympus* (1708), must have seemed like a manifesto. Led by Watteau, artists set out to convey a hedonistic, Arcadian mood that had nothing whatever in common with the ideals of the *Grand Siècle*.

The keynote of this new taste was grace. Coypel, the court painter whom the regent employed to paint the Galerie d'Enée in the Palais-Royal, demanded in a public speech that the grand style should be softened by grace. Abbé Dubos voiced the new priorities when he wrote in his *Réflexions critiques sur la poésie et sur la peinture* (1719) that art must be governed by 'sensation', not by 'reason'.

The first mention of the advent of a new style was in 1713, when it was described (apropos of an interior decorated in 1704) as 'incomparably more convenient and more agreeable than that which was formerly pursued'.[2] It represented a total break with the past. What was emerging in France was not so much a kind of late Baroque, but a new approach to art. Its beginnings lay at Versailles, in the interior of the Grand Trianon, in the decoration of the Ménagerie for the Duchesse de Bourgogne, and in the mirrors at Marly. It was to culminate in the Rococo; and in between we find a steady progression towards freedom and lightness that assimilates Régence and Rococo into a greater unity, in which all distinctions are matters of degree.[3]

The advent of the new style was accompanied by an extensive theoretical literature. The most important manual for amateurs of architecture, and for amateur architects, was the *Cours d'architecture* (1691) by Jules Hardouin-Mansart's pupil Claude-Louis Daviler; by stating the architectural conventions of Mansart's day, Daviler defined the starting point of the whole evolutionary process. In 1710, a new edition, revised by Alexandre Le Blond, took account of intervening developments. Most of the other treatises, such as those by Sébastien Leclerc, Jean Courtonne and Charles-Etienne Briseux, concerned themselves mostly with questions of proportion, and of the connection between external and internal form. The new ideas were best formulated by Courtonne, in his *Traité de la perspective pratique* (1725), in which he called for a total harmony between exterior and interior, and in *L'Architecture moderne, ou l'Art de bien bâtir pour toutes sortes de personnes*, which the publisher Jombert brought out under his own name in 1728, and which heralds the Rococo. These theoretical works were magnificently complemented by the four engraved volumes of the *Architecture française*, issued by the publisher Jean Mariette from 1727 onwards; in over 400 plates, this supplies a comprehensive survey of the architecture of the first third of the century.[4]

The response of the Academy was mixed. Its allotted function was to act as the custodian of tradition. But in the wake of Claude Perrault's declaration that the proportions handed down by Vitruvius were not absolute but subject to changes in fashion, and of the ensuing controversy between the 'Ancients' and the 'Moderns' on the imitation of antiquity as a general principle, the Academy had split into two warring camps. Unable to agree on any binding formula, it adopted the principle of 'good taste' – and this was invoked at all its meetings. But what was good taste? For François Blondel, this still had meant no more and no less than the rules and proportions of antiquity; but later on its interpretation became increasingly subjective and individual. In his *Traité de proportion* (1714), Leclerc somewhat vaguely declared: 'By proportion we mean here not a rational relationship, such as the surveyors would establish, but an accord between the parts, founded on good taste.' Voltaire, who defined good taste as the 'consensus of educated people', wrote his own account of the subject, spiked with irony, in the poem *Le Temple du goût* (1735). What was expected of the architect was no longer genius but taste; and it was the task of the theorists to deduce from the ideal of taste some general rules for practical use.

For a building to display good taste, it must first satisfy three cardinal requirements. *Convenance* or decorum, which *François* Blondel still equated with the exact observance of the orders, came rather to stand for the consonance of all the aesthetic and practical qualities of a building, and for the precise differentiation of its parts. The building was seen as a unity, a synthetic organism, in which every part, including the garden, had a clearly defined place and a function; and from this function each part derived its location, its size, and its form of decoration.[5] *Bienséance* or fitness, on the other hand, concerned the building's suitability for the purpose for which it was built and, in particular, its appropriateness to the social status of the client, a matter of great importance in eighteenth-century life.[6] Finally, *commodité* meant practical convenience, not only that of the house as a whole but that of individual rooms and suites of rooms.

It was in this last area that the Régence made astonishing progress. The art of planning, the rational division (*distribution*) of space, was now developed to a perfection unheard of before or since; in this, France set an example to the whole of Europe. Jèan-François Blondel spoke of planning as a 'new art', invented at the turn of the century. However beautiful to look at from outside, earlier buildings had in his view been barely habitable within.

The verdict of the public at large on the 'good taste' debate is exemplified by the *Mémoires critiques* (1702) of the Parisian lawyer and president of finances, Michel Frémin. Describing the orders as the least considerable part of architecture, he freely maintained that what counted was to make a house suit its occupants' needs, the climate, the surroundings, and so on, before paying any heed to rules or good taste.

Less brusque, and more influential, was Abbé de Cordemoy's *Nouveau traité de toute l'architecture* (1706). Cordemoy, of whose personality we know nothing,[7] took Perrault as his starting-point, though he was clearly not uninfluenced by Frémin. Convinced that antique architecture had been simpler than the Renaissance theorists had been prepared to admit, he demanded not only truth and naturalness but a repertoire of simple, clear and self-contained forms unburdened by any decorative function. The main structural support was not to be the pier but the column and lintel. He condemned pilasters and broken entablatures. He had a passion for coupled columns, as used by Perrault in his design for the Parisian church of Sainte-Geneviève. Cordemoy was the first theorist to value Greek architecture more highly than Roman. But, like Frémin, he also admired the Gothic, for the lightness of its construction, its reduction of the built mass, and the tension of its structural system. Cordemoy saw the Greek temple and the Gothic cathedral as embodiments of the same principle: a rhythmic succession of tall, slender supports, in the intervals of which the space could unfold, untrammelled and undisguised, in the spirit of Perrault's ideal Sainte-Geneviève. His unspoken ideal was a church built on Gothic structural principles out of Greek architectural elements.

For a number of years, the military architect A.F. Frézier conducted a running battle with Cordemoy in the columns of the *Mémoires de Trévoux*, before ultimately accepting most of his views and even his enthusiasm for the Gothic. Cordemoy's main interest was ecclesiastical architecture. He had little or no following in his own day, but his work prepared the ground for the theories of Abbé Laugier, and for the church building of the second half of the century.

CHAPTER 2

The Last Works of Jules Hardouin-Mansart

Eighteenth-century French architecture begins with Jules Hardouin-Mansart. Chronologically, he belongs to the age of Louis XIV, but his shadow lies across the following decades. With his buildings for the king and for the Church, his châteaux and hôtels, he set the standard for following generations. In 1699 the king promoted him to the rank of Surintendant, a title otherwise confined to ministers and to nobles of high rank. This bound him to the court, where he was beset by malice and intrigue;[8] but no minister, courtier or senior official ever failed to turn to him for advice.

Behind J.H. Mansart stood the Service des Bâtiments du Roi, the king's office of works, which he himself reorganized in 1699.[9] This was a large body of architects, draughtsmen, inspectors, clerks of works and others, divided into a number of specialized offices. The central office had the responsibility for handing down the Surintendant's instructions and preparing the drawings. Its director, and thus the second man in the hierarchy, was Mansart's brother-in-law, Robert de Cotte. This efficient organization, with its highly qualified staff – all the king's architects, les architectes du Roi, were full Academicians – was able to cope promptly and smoothly with a vast range of work that covered the entire country. Although a number of projects, such as the Place Vendôme in Paris, were dealt with by individual architects, all had to be approved by the Surintendant; and so his style set the tone in all things.

However, Mansart's activities were considerably curtailed by the outbreak of the War of the Spanish Succession in 1702. From then on, projects in hand were completed, but no new ones were started. One exception was the Château Neuf (1706–9) at Meudon,[10] intended as a guest house for the Dauphin (Plate 1). Its garden front already revealed the new tendencies that were to mark the final years of the old reign. It was no longer dominated by columns and heavy cornices – that is, by architectural elements – but by decorative motifs, such as window surrounds and wrought-iron balconies on sculptured consoles. Only the court façade was enriched with a giant order; its prototype was the Place Vendôme, where the same mouldings, window surrounds and base forms appear, although at Meudon the order did not rest on a podium but directly on the ground.

The ground plan also had some very modern features. The long corridors gave access to a series of uniformly planned guest suites, each consisting of three rooms: bedroom, cabinet, and dressing room. These 'living units', which took account of the individuality of their occupants and allowed each of them a personal, secluded sphere of his own, had already been employed by J.H. Mansart – though less systematically and on a smaller scale – at Trianon-sous-Bois, the wing of the Grand Trianon intended for the princesses and ladies-in-waiting. Each incorporated a bed-alcove, an innovation that the Dauphin had introduced for his own use in the alterations to the main fabric of the

Château de Meudon itself, as early as 1699; this brought a great saving of space. The Appartement du Roi, the only state apartment in the Château Neuf, was entirely traditional, with a grand, double-height vestibule and staircase; but the gallery, which at Versailles and Saint-Cloud remained the most important display room, had become a rectangular hall inserted crosswise at the end of the right-hand wing, connecting the state bedchamber and the cabinet; and the two studies at the far end were even provided with low ceilings and entresols.

This departure from magnificence in favour of commodité, this leaning towards domesticity and intimacy, was characteristic of Meudon. The Dauphin had already demonstrated his modern views, which differed from those of the king, in the rebuilding of the main château and particularly during the construction of the wing known as the Aile des Marronniers (1702), with its Petit Appartement de Monseigneur. His influence is also unmistakably present in the Château Neuf, though the old king himself had commented on and approved the plans.

As well as this château, Mansart undertook two ecclesiastical projects: the lady chapel (Chapelle de la Vierge) at Saint-Roch in Paris, and the Primatiale in Nancy. The former was a large circular chapel, added to a church begun by Jacques Lemercier in the mid-seventeenth century but then still uncompleted.[11] With a diameter equal to the width of the nave, the chapel consists of two elements: an inner, double-height rotunda, which is the lady chapel proper, and a circular ambulatory intended for the administration of communion. Beneath is a crypt to serve as an ossuary for the cleared churchyard. The ambulatory leads into an additional small chapel at its east end. The functions of the two spaces were designed to be strongly differentiated, both in the painted decoration and in the furnishing. In the execution, which began in 1706, this idea was drastically watered down. The elimination of much of the decorative detailing, and the relegation of Masses to the small east chapel, destroyed the internal relationship between the spaces; and, when the windows of the east chapel were walled in, the ambulatory declined into a dark and meaningless appendage.

A similar fate befell the Primatiale in Nancy. Ever since the early seventeenth century, there had been plans to build the cathedral that Nancy had always striven after.[12] Finally, in 1700, after the Duke of Lorraine returned to his country from wartime exile, a new church was begun to a design by the Italian-born architect Jean Betto, who had made a name for himself as architect to the Benedictine Order in Lorraine. Work was halted after a short time by the emergence of a rival design by the duke's medallist, Ferdinand de Saint-Urbain. The cathedral chapter wrote to ask Mansart to submit the matter to the Academy in Paris for arbitration; but in 1706, without consulting the Academy at all, Mansart sent back a new design of his own.

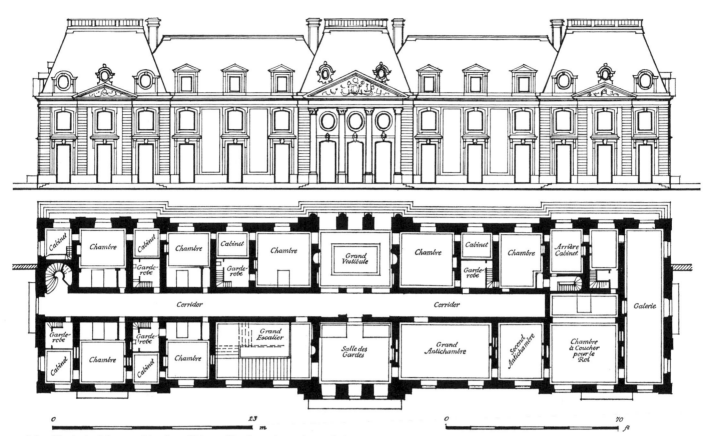

1 Jules Hardouin-Mansart: Meudon, Château Neuf, 1706–9, plan and elevation.

2 Jules Hardouin-Mansart: Nancy, Primatiale, plan, 1706.

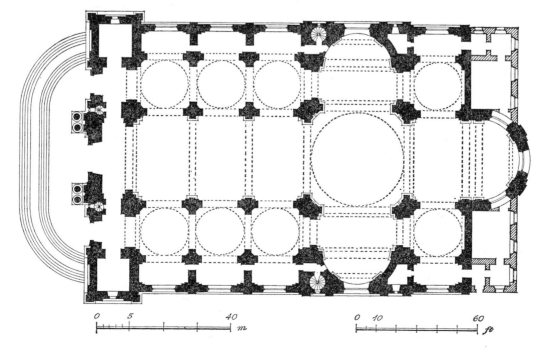

4 Germain Boffrand: Nancy, Primatiale, façade project, 1723, engraving by Anto

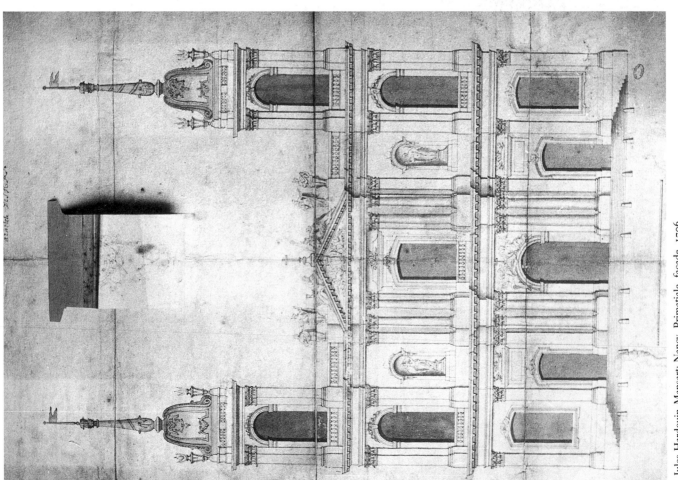

3 Jules Hardouin-Mansart: Nancy, Primatiale, façade, 1706.

5   Nancy, Primatiale, interior.

This was largely based on Betto, but converted from a cruciform to a rectangular plan by the addition of extra chapels along the aisles (Plate 2). Above all, however, Mansart changed the shape of the internal space. By enlarging the crossing, reducing the four bays of the nave to three and adding the linked side-chapels, he gave the interior a spacious quality, with continuous major axes, that goes far beyond Betto's design. The plan is based on a centralized principle that recalls François Mansart's Val-de-Grâce, with its little domes over the aisles; here, however, the Italianate, additive form of Val-de-Grâce has given way to a spatial synthesis.

For the façade, J.H. Mansart had to build on Betto's foundations, which were designed to support two towers; and so his design was unusually wide (Plate 3). In principle, however, it was a continuation of that of Notre-Dame at Versailles. The centre was emphasized by massive coupled columns and by statues on the skyline, and the towers provided a vertical accent. Mansart designed a pair of gilded, scrolling steeples, supporting crowned columns, which looked bizarrely like dining-table ornaments. The dome at the crossing, with its figured sculpture and its tall lantern imitated from that of the Dôme des Invalides, supplied a culminating and dominant accent.

Work recommenced in 1706, under Betto's supervision, and by 1719 all was complete except the dome. But from the start the design was coarsened and distorted. The chapels that lined the nave dwindled into shallow niches. The big windows in the apse, which were essential to light the choir, were walled in. Most disastrous of all, the dome was never built; and with it went not only the principal source of daylight for the interior but also the whole external effect. The central accent was lost; and in a frontal view the twin towers framed a void that the triangular pediment was wholly inadequate to fill. Even the efforts of Germain Boffrand, chief architect to the Duke of Lorraine, were not enough to save the dome. On his design in 1723 the towers were heightened by the addition of pavilion-like superstructures and topped with lanterns similar to the one that Mansart had designed for the dome. To balance all this, Boffrand designed a tall pyramid to go over the crossing, with a clock dial borne aloft by allegorical figures and a culminating terrestrial globe (Plate 4); the intrigues of local architects prevented this from being built. In 1734–6, after lengthy debates, a third storey was added to the central portion of the façade, thus finally ruining Mansart's conception and making the façade itself oppressively heavy.[13] Even so, through all its vicissitudes, the interior has retained much of its splendour (Plate 5).

CHAPTER 3

Robert de Cotte

PUBLIC BUILDINGS

J.H. Mansart died in 1709, and his post was taken over by his brother-in-law, Robert de Cotte (1656–1735). This was, as it were, preordained. De Cotte came of a long line of architects and had been excellently prepared for his task.[14] He had worked under J.H. Mansart since 1676, spending twenty years in the design office. His marriage to Catherine Bodin had made him the chief architect's brother-in-law and thereby advanced his career considerably. He became a member of the Academy in 1687, and two years later, at his brother-in-law's behest, he made a study trip to Italy, which left no detectable trace in his work.[15] In 1699, when the Service des Bâtiments was reorganized, he took over the central bureau in Paris, the nucleus of the whole organization. At the same time he became director of the Gobelins tapestry works and director of the Academy; in 1702 he was ennobled. He worked on all Mansart's projects, often as his representative, and attracted the king's attention at an early stage with his independent design for the colonnade of the Grand Trianon (1687).[16] De Cotte was thus Mansart's born successor.[17] He did not, however, receive the title of Surintendant, which the regent was eventually to give to the Duc d'Antin, a son of Madame de Montespan's by her first husband.

The appointment of Robert de Cotte ensured a continuity in the evolution of French architecture that transcended all changes of regime and fluctuations of taste. With the Service des Bâtiments behind him, he carried on his predecessor's work on the same scale as before. De Cotte's historical significance lies not so much in the invention of new forms as in the refinement and modernization of those he inherited from his predecessor. With his sound practical sense, his inimitable and unerring sense of proportion, and the generosity and elegance of his planning, he precisely satisfied the expectations of his time. What was more, he was both intelligent and amenable; so he became an unquestioned architectural authority. Princes and bishops vied for his services, and he set standards not only for France but for the whole of Europe.

De Cotte's reputation is now rather overshadowed by those of J.H. Mansart and Ange-Jacques Gabriel, and his name is not associated with any royal building of note; for this, history itself is to blame. In the Sun King's last years, the state coffers were empty; and in the first half of his reign the young Louis XV felt no inclination to build. For a quarter of a century, the French crown was not a patron of architecture. Its place was taken by foreign princes and bishops; and it was for them that de Cotte did some extraordinary work. He supplied designs to the Electors of Bavaria and Cologne, the king of Spain, Prince William of Hesse-Kassel, the prince-bishop of Würzburg, the bishops of Strasbourg and Verdun, and many others. In most cases he also made available an architect to supervise the execution on site. He left a vast quantity of plans and designs, which still exist, along with a voluminous correspondence that shows how close were his contacts with his foreign clients, and how closely his Paris head office was kept informed. Without ever leaving France, he kept the reins firmly in his own hands, and his spirit simultaneously presided over numerous construction sites. The creation of such a network, which extended all over Europe and as far afield as Turkey, has remained an unparalleled achievement.

De Cotte began working on his own account even before J.H. Mansart's death. It is probable that the Place Vendôme, in its second, present form, is his. Another important early work was the Abbey of Saint-Denis, a milestone in the latter-day development of monastic building in France. At Saint-Denis, by the 1690s, rebuilding could be postponed no longer. The medieval conventual buildings were in an advanced state of disrepair, and the monks had long been demanding relief. What was more, Saint-Denis was the most prestigious monastery in France, and the burial place of the French kings; its preservation was a dynastic concern. In 1696 Dom Arnould de Loo took office as grand prior – the title and dignity of abbot had been abolished in 1691 – and immediately asked de Cotte to prepare designs for a rebuilding. His initial design, which involved the demolition of all the existing fabric, was rejected by the chapter in favour of a cheaper and less radical rival design by Jean Bayeux, who had worked for the Benedictines on several occasions. The grand prior succeeded in overcoming the fierce resistance of the chapter, and imposing de Cotte's design, but only because he had the king's support (Plate 7).

The first stage of construction, 1700–25, covered only the east and south ranges, incorporating the chapter house, consecrated in 1717, and the refectory, completed in 1720. After de Cotte's death, the west wing was started by Jacques V Gabriel; and the great court or cour d'honneur planned by de Cotte was built only in 1774, by François Franque. The building was completed in 1782.

De Cotte's design gave this august foundation a completely different appearance. He enlarged it not only eastward, past the chevet of the Basilica of Saint-Denis, but southward, beyond its old boundary wall, and tidied the irregular quadrilateral of medieval conventual buildings into a clear rectangle with long façades. In front of the east range, in place of the old walled gardens, he laid out a large parterre with walks and fountains, and in front of the west range a small cour d'honneur.

The palatial east range was set aside for ceremonial purposes. Here, since time immemorial, the court and the princes of the blood royal had gathered for the funerals of the kings of France. Along with the chapter house, this range therefore contained the Grand Appartement, consisting of a vestibule and three salons. Above this was the lodging of the grand prior. The vast length of this range forced de Cotte to lengthen the west range to match, far past

Place Bellecour the character of a Place Royale. Initially based on the Place Vendôme, the façade designs evolved into an independent solution to satisfy the council's desire for an Italianate central block divided into five apartment houses (Plate 8).

With great skill, de Cotte reconciled the utilitarian purpose of the composition with the requirements of prestige. The extraordinary length of the façade, with its thirty-five bays and five entrance doors, enabled him to take command of the immense space; for the Place Bellecour, unlike the Place Vendôme, was no mere city square. Its size and its greenness made it more like a slice of landscape introduced into the town: like the later Place Louis-XV in Paris, it was 'a piece of countryside in the city, a palace garden open to the public'. Of the Place Vendôme the façades retain only the blind arcades, the giant order in the centre pavilion – but with pilasters instead of columns – and the central pediment; the end pavilions and the continuous arcades have vanished. Above the podium there are three storeys instead of two, with strong rusticated dressings, and instead of dormer windows the skyline is marked by balustrades with urns and trophies. This is what gives the façades something of the effect of an Italian palazzo.

A simplified version of de Cotte's design was put into execution in 1717 and completed in 1725; the equestrian statue of the king had been in place since 1713. In the Revolution, the statue was overturned and melted down, and the façades at either end were destroyed on the grounds that they, too, were symbols of the Ancien Régime. Only the river gods of Rhône and Saône, by Guillaume and Nicolas Coustou, were spared.[21]

PRINCELY RESIDENCES

It was the building of palaces and châteaux that made de Cotte's international reputation; and in this field he was far more important than his predecessor. Like François Mansart and Louis Le Vau before him, he created a definitive type that governed the building of princely residences for years to come. His plans and elevations were based on traditional patterns, but into these he absorbed the tendencies that had emerged with the new century. His work visibly differed from that of J.H. Mansart at every point. De Cotte's architecture was lighter, more elegant, and less laden with sculpture. His ground plans were marked both by generosity and by practicality. This gave him the advantage over the Italian formula, which was still wedded to long enfilades without secondary rooms, and marked him out as the great renewer of princely architecture in Europe.

Among his earliest buildings in France was the Château de Chanteloup (begun 1711), later famous as the seat of the Duc de Choiseul. It was built for the Princesse des Ursins, a woman of great ability who had acted as adviser to Philip V of Spain, and who was angling for the governorship of Touraine as a reward for her help with the negotiations for the Peace of Utrecht. The house was undoubtedly modelled on J.H. Mansart's Château de Clagny, though on a smaller scale. The princess's own apartment was on the ground floor of the *corps de logis*; the state apartments and gallery in one of the wings. All the rooms except those in the shallow *corps de logis* were accompanied by corridors or small antechambers. The elevation, too, was reminiscent of Clagny. The *corps de logis* was articulated by three pavilions, all breaking forward slightly and all with balconies; the centre was emphasized by columns, a pediment and probably also a dome. Chanteloup's most brilliant period was in the 1760s, when Choiseul, Louis XV's long-serving former minister, lived there in splendid exile from the court and had the house enlarged and remodelled by Louis-Denis Le Camus.[22]

Foreign commissions came in only after the Peace of Utrecht, in 1714; and by that time the new taste prevailed all over Europe. New châteaux and palaces were being planned everywhere. One of the first German princes to adopt French art as his ideal was Elector Max Emanuel of Bavaria. His initial choice as architect of his new palace at Schleissheim was Enrico Zuccali, from Grisons. But in 1704, three years after construction started, Max Emanuel sent emissaries to Paris to engage the services of Alexis Delamair. The outbreak of war prevented Delamair from travelling to Munich, and shortly thereafter Max Emanuel found himself in exile. In 1705, at Bouchefort, near Soignies in Belgium, he engaged Boffrand to built him a hunting lodge that was a purely French creation. Finally, from Saint-Cloud, where he spent the last years of his exile, he applied to the chief architect himself for a new design for Schleissheim. Max Emanuel's brother, Elector Joseph Clemens of Cologne, who was also in exile, made a similar request for his own palace in Bonn, which had also been begun by Zuccali before the war. The young, French-born king of Spain, Philip V, who wanted a new palace on his estate of Buen Retiro, just outside Madrid, also entrusted the planning to de Cotte. Designs for these three palaces – Schleissheim, Bonn and Buen Retiro – were ready almost simultaneously, although funds never materialized to build any of them. Even so, the designs deserve a close look; they are important documents both of de Cotte's style and of the post-Mansart period as a whole.

In his initial design for Schleissheim, which was probably completed in the early months of 1714, de Cotte paid absolutely no regard to the lie of the land (Plate 9).[23] He based himself on the overall form of Versailles, both in the park, with its axis marked by a grand canal, and in the palace itself, with its shallow *corps de logis*, projecting wings incorporating internal courts, and precisely defined sequence of forecourt and *cour d'honneur*. The Versailles complex however had been built in a number of stages at different times; in his design for Schleissheim, de Cotte tightened this, rationalized it and brought it up to date in order to reconcile the requirements of ostentation and practical use.

Together with a small theatre and a number of apartments, most of the ground floor was set aside for domestic purposes; court life took place on the first floor. The *corps de logis* contained the staircase, one large room lined with columns – presumably the guard chamber – and the apartments of the Elector and Electress (Plate 10). The wings contained a grand gallery, which ran between two oval corner salons, a chapel, an opera house and an oval concert room. The main entrance, unlike that of Versailles, lay in the centre of the *corps de logis*. From it, the grand staircase ascended in three flights, occupying the entire depth of the block. Two circular

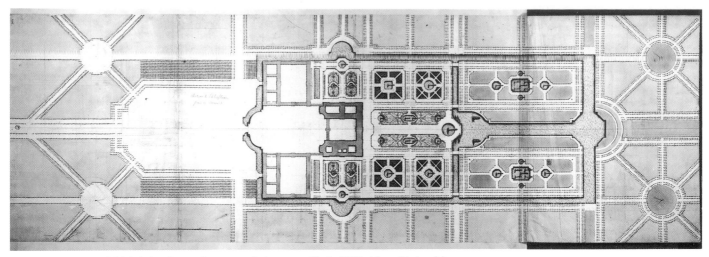

9   Robert de Cotte: Schleissheim, first project, general plan 1714 (Paris, Bibliothèque Nationale).

vestibules, ingeniously tucked into the oblique corners of the return façades of the wings, led through into the internal courts. The hallmarks of de Cotte's style – the smooth fit of the spatial forms, the calculated distribution of accents, the avoidance of hard edges and harsh transitions, the numerous lobbies and staircases – were already clearly apparent. On the exterior, the elevations were still long and punctuated by columned pavilions; but at the ends of the wings the compact, cubic block had already given way to a smoother transition into the *cour d'honneur*. One pencil sketch indicates that de Cotte intended to crown the *corps de logis* with a dome; like the open arcade that lined the *cour d'honneur*, this was a borrowing from the so-called Grand Dessein for Versailles, prepared by J.H. Mansart in 1679.

It was not until his second design that de Cotte took note of the existing buildings at Schleissheim, and of Zuccali's plans, which were sent to him from Munich, at the Elector's behest, in August 1714. Zuccali had planned a quadrangular building, of which the Altes Schloss of William V and Maximilian I was to form the west range; and the carcass of his own east range was already complete. To bring this design up to date, de Cotte proposed to open up Zuccali's quadrangle to the west by demolishing the Altes Schloss, to cut short the north and south wings to give the right proportions for his *cour d'honneur*, and to make a wider opening between the single-storey domestic blocks that flanked the forecourt, in order to reveal the return façades of the wings. In the planning he left Zuccali's east range intact except for the insertion of a central, double-height garden salon between the apartments of the Elector and the Electress. The north and south wings, however, had to be completely redesigned, both because they had to be cut off short and in order to deal with the side pavilions planned

by Zuccali. Perhaps because of the unduly low ceilings of Zuccali's upper floors, de Cotte moved all the state apartments down to the ground floor, which thus became the principal level and gave the whole palace something of a country-house feeling.

For financial reasons all this was cut back, and only the east range was completed, as a free-standing block, from 1719 onwards. The architect in charge was not de Cotte but Joseph Effner, a pupil of Boffrand's, who reverted to Zuccali's design.

The situation in Bonn was similar. There, too, in 1697, Zuccali had embarked on a large new palace for the Elector, in the same Italianate vein as Schleissheim. This was another quadrangular structure, with the Electoral apartments in the south range behind a monotonous garden front that overlooked the old fortifications. Like Schleissheim, it was still uncompleted when the Elector had to flee before the advancing imperial armies in 1702. In 1713, still in exile in Valenciennes, he contacted de Cotte and explained to him his ideas for changing the orientation of the palace.

The project which de Cotte sent to Bonn in spring 1714 opened up Zuccali's building by turning its arcaded inner court into a *cour d'honneur*, facing out towards the city and screened on that side by a semicircular colonnade with a circular central pavilion. On the other side looking towards the old fortifications, was to be a large three-wing palace, based on an idea sketched by the Elector himself (Plate 11). The side wing on the left of the court would consist of the completed portion of Zuccali's building, and the wing on the right would include the Elector's apartment.[24] The connecting *corps de logis* would be occupied, as at Versailles, by a single gallery running between two corner salons. The wings were further connected, two-thirds of the way along, by a

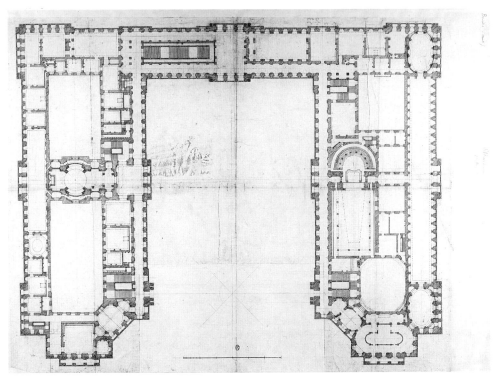

10   Robert de Cotte: Schleissheim, first project, plan of first floor.

11   Robert de Cotte: Bonn, Electors Palace, second project, 1714, plan of first floor.

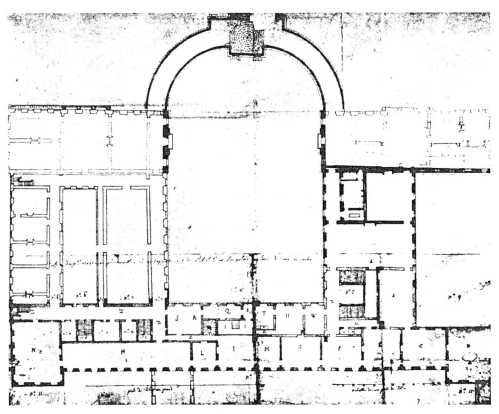

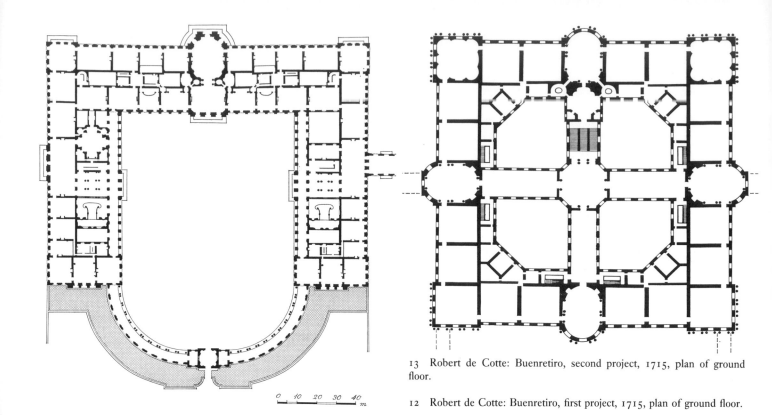

13 Robert de Cotte: Buenretiro, second project, 1715, plan of ground floor.

12 Robert de Cotte: Buenretiro, first project, 1715, plan of ground floor.

range containing the vestibule, the main staircase and two large flanking rooms, and separating the *cour d'honneur* in front from a garden court. From the *cour d'honneur*, a canal extended in a straight line to the villa of Poppelsdorf, outside the gates of Bonn, which played an important role in the composition as a view-stopper.

The right-hand wing, planned strictly in accordance with the French ceremonial sequence of rooms, was the nucleus of the palace. Its garden front, with rhythmically placed, columned pavilions, followed the precedent set by J.H. Mansart at Versailles. But a decisive innovation was the bowed projection of the double-height central salon, which set a dominant accent both internally and externally. The elevation, which at Versailles remains rigid, thus acquired a dynamic pull and a clear central emphasis. De Cotte took this motif from Le Vau, but tied it more firmly into the pavilion system by giving it a flat, columned frontispiece, so that it no longer looked like an appendage – as at Vaux-le-Vicomte – but lent an entirely natural swing to the façade as a whole.[25] The modernity of de Cotte's architecture is particularly clear from a comparison between this wing, with its clear and well-thought-out spatial sequence and its flexible use of lobbies and secondary rooms, and the opposite wing by Zuccali.

The Elector's will was thwarted by the Rhenish Estates, and neither of de Cotte's designs was built. The Elector had to content himself with a modest reworking of Zuccali's garden front, with blind arcades on the ground floor, an added attic as a central accent, and more elegant superstructures on the towers. Only at the west corner was he able to indulge his Francophile tastes by adding a horseshoe-shaped annexe, known as the Buenretiro, for which de Cotte designed the decor.

In designing for Madrid, de Cotte had more of a free hand; there was no existing structure to take into account.[26] The king had initially intended to modernize Philip II's old palace in the park of Buen Retiro. After a number of fruitless attempts, this idea had been abandoned and the decision taken to build an entirely new palace. In the winter of 1715, de Cotte sent to Madrid two designs approved by Louis XIV himself.

The first bore a general similarity to Schleissheim. From a large, circular forecourt, at the convergence of seven rides, a single axis ran through two courts, the palace itself and its gardens to a large pool in the distance (Plate 12). The kingly scale of this design was immediately evident from the forecourt that preceded the actual *cour d'honneur*. It was surrounded by six identical pavilions for the ministers and the guard, reminiscent in both form and function of those at Marly. The *cour d'honneur*, like that for Bonn, was fronted by a semicircular, colonnaded screen, which was prefixed in turn by a moat.

The palace itself was clearly a further development of Schleissheim and Bonn. To comply with Spanish court convention, the *corps de logis* had to have apartments for the king and queen both on the north and south sides, one for summer and one for winter. De Cotte accordingly placed a pair of apartments on either side, separated by a spine of closets and lobbies accessible from both directions. Once more, the focus was a central oval salon, which shared the longitudinal axis with the large vestibule. There was much here that recalled Versailles, including the great enfilades and the vestibules in the wings, which led directly to staircases; but the design as a whole was very much more practical and rational than its French prototype.

On the exterior, de Cotte followed classical precedents. On the court façade, with some variations, he repeated the

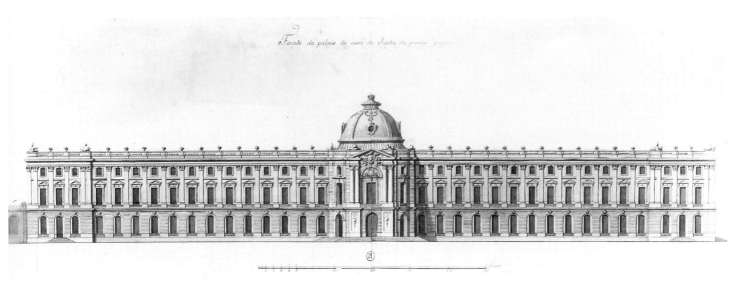

14 Robert de Cotte: Buenretiro, first project 1715, façade.

system of the Place Vendôme. The garden façade, however, had a different source: François d'Orbay's design for the south front of the Louvre. This design, prepared in 1666, contained all the elements of Buen Retiro; the ground-floor rustication, the giant order of the two upper storeys, the triangular pediments over the windows, and the flat roof. To these, de Cotte added an unwonted element of Baroque dynamism in the shape of a bowed centre, with giant coupled columns beneath a broken pediment bearing a massive coat-of-arms (Plate 14). This feature, with its slender proportions and elegant, sculpturally moulded dome, very different from the domes of J.H. Mansart, lightened the whole block and countered the long horizontals with a powerful vertical accent.

De Cotte's second design for Buen Retiro was highly unusual. Here the palace was a centrally planned, square structure with an inscribed cross (Plate 13). On the outside were four identical apartments, again one pair for summer and one for winter, while a string of secondary rooms, dressing rooms and ancillary staircases lined the central court and cut off its corners. Each of the four sides was conceived as a unitary composition; in each case an oval salon formed a bowed central projection, with the corner pavilions breaking slightly forward and emphasized with columns. The arms of the inscribed cross consisted of four gallery-like spaces that met in an octagonal central salon; on the ground floor these served as hallways, and on the upper floor as communicating passages between the apartments. The staircase, into which the chapel was inserted, lay on the entrance axis, and led up into the octagonal hall, crowned with a dome and a lantern, that formed the centre of the building.

The square plan, as used here, had always remained alive in France. In the *Livre d'architecture* (1559) of Jacques Androuet du Cerceau, it appeared in numerous variations that became part of the history of French architecture and were undoubtedly known to de Cotte. His immediate source was probably the design for the Louvre made by Nicodemus

Tessin in 1704. In this, four ranges were set around a circular court, and each contained a single apartment with a dominant central room. How much this idea interested de Cotte is evident from the fact that he made his own copy of Tessin's covering memorandum.

Neither of de Cotte's designs for Buen Retiro was executed; the Spanish king took an Italian second wife, and the French influence was eclipsed. De Cotte's son, who had been sent to Madrid with the plans, had to turn tail and bring them back to Paris, his mission unaccomplished.

One work that bears some relation to this group of designs is the small Schloss Poppelsdorf (Plate 15). This is a partial realization of what remained a dream at Buen Retiro: the ideal centralized plan. It is not really a Schloss or château at all, but a *maison de plaisance* or rural villa; originally some way outside the city of Bonn, it was connected with the Elector's palace by a canal and served the palace as a view-stopper.[27] It is square in shape; four identical ranges, articulated by pavilions, surround a colonnaded circular court. The centre pavilions of the four sides are crowned with square domes (Plate 16).

The first design that de Cotte sent to Bonn in 1715, after a lengthy correspondence with the Elector,[28] was two-storeyed throughout. It probably derived from a reworking of the second Buen Retiro design. Typologically, it marked de Cotte's closest approach to Tessin's Louvre design (Plate 17).[29] The interior arrangement was similar to that of Buen Retiro, except that the secondary rooms and the stairs were relegated to the curved corners of the circular court. One range was occupied by the chapel, another by the kitchens and domestic offices. It was a masterly solution to the problem of accommodating a princely household in a confined space and in a mathematically ideal form.

When this design had to be scaled down for reasons of cost, de Cotte dispensed with the upper storey of each range, between centre and end pavilions, except on the garden side, and compensated by giving more weight to the pavilions themselves with richer articulation and taller

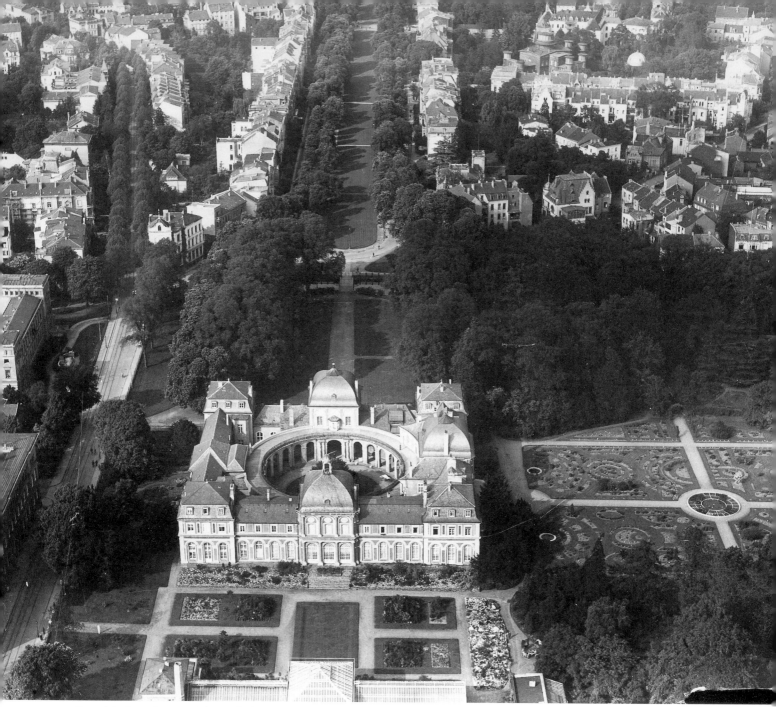

15 Poppelsdorf near Bonn, aerial view (before 1944).

domes. The animated skyline created by the tall pavilions and low intervening structures lent the whole a festive appearance, very much in the vein of garden architecture, which had not formed part of the original intention. In the garden front, de Cotte left the precedents set by J.H. Mansart decisively behind him. It was based, in principle, on Clagny, long regarded as a model of its kind; but the dominance of the central pavilion was enhanced by the use of an order on the upper storey, by rich detailing on the lunettes and dormers, and by a belvedere that added height to the dome; there is a marked crescendo of emphasis towards the centre.

Building work began in 1715. It was initially supervised by Benoît de Fortier, and, after his dismissal in 1716, by Guillaume Hauberat, one of de Cotte's ablest associates.

The constant shortage of funds led to a progressive impoverishment of the design, and most notably to the omission of the proposed roof balustrades; this impaired not only the slender effect of the domes but the look of the building as a whole. The carcass was complete on the Elector's death in 1723. Under the new Elector, Clement Augustus of Bavaria, one wing was demolished and eventually – in the 1740s – rebuilt to a design by Balthasar Neumann, so that the French character of the work was watered down still further. In the building as it now stands, it is hard to recognize de Cotte's masterpiece.

Another centralized design by de Cotte was for Tilburg in Brabant, where Prince William of Hesse-Kassel, then governor of Breda, wanted to rebuild a moated medieval castle. For this, de Cotte reverted to the Marly formula. On

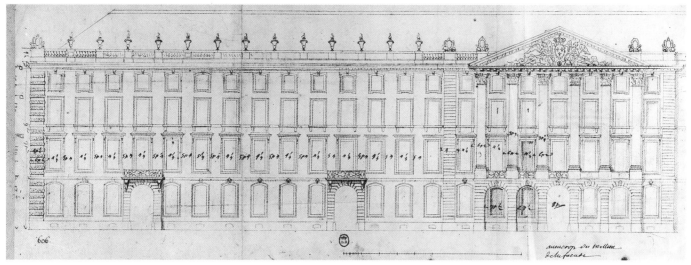

8 Robert de Cotte: Lyon, Place Bellecour, preliminary design, 1714 (Paris, Bibliothèque Nationale).

the south cross range that contained the refectory, kitchens and main staircase. As a result, on the south side of the composition, there came into being a large new court, with side wings ending in pavilions, not unlike the *cour d'honneur* of a château.

The façades are marked by long horizontals (Plate 6). In its interior court, the Hôtel des Invalides supplied a precedent for the pavilion articulation, the blind ground-floor arcades and the turret clock that surmounts the centre pavilion. What was entirely new at Saint-Denis was the elegance of the proportions and the general lightness that marked de Cotte's style from the very beginning. He initially meant to insert mezzanine windows above the ground-floor arcading of the east range, as in the guest range on the west side; but, as in this case the large rooms inside are vaulted, he converted the windows into framed, rectangular stone tablets, which lend the wall a somewhat monotonous relief pattern. In spite of such later concessions to changing fashions as the lavish Rococo detailing added to the end pavilions of the west range, de Cotte's overall design was maintained throughout the long building period, so that his conception has survived to this day.[18]

At Versailles, no major new commissions were forthcoming after the death of J.H. Mansart. The main concern here was the completion of the chapel, where decorative work dragged on until 1710, and of the Salon d'Hercule, which forms the transition between the chapel and the Grands Appartements. Only the wall articulation of the Salon d'Hercule was completed in the old king's lifetime, in 1712. Its majestic, marble-faced, coupled pilasters are in the tradition of the Galerie des Glaces; but the elliptical form of the chimney-piece, the masks on the brackets of the ceiling cornice, and the sweeping, concave curves of the picture frames are already signs of a new age.

Another major decorative undertaking for de Cotte was the remodelling of the choir of Notre-Dame de Paris. In fulfilment of a vow made by his father, Louis XIV initially intended to endow a new high altar; then, for reasons of prestige, he decided to remodel the whole choir. J.H.

Mansart prepared a design, but in 1708 this was discarded in favour of a new one by de Cotte. Besides the altar itself, there were new choir stalls, incorporating six large oil paintings; a new rood screen; a new marble casing of the piers, with inset bronze reliefs; and, fronting the piers, a set of life-size bronze angels on richly ornamented consoles, together with a new polychrome marble floor throughout. This vastly expensive ensemble, in which all the leading Versailles artists were involved, was completed in 1714. It was one of the most important decorative undertakings of the period.[19]

For the rest, de Cotte's official activity in Paris was on a modest scale, being largely confined to two structures that formed part of the city's water supply system: the pump house of La Samaritaine, adjoining the Pont Neuf (1711–15), and the Château d'Eau, or water tower, from which the water was distributed. This latter was dexterously concealed behind a palatial façade with rustication and a pediment, which also served to confer an impressive, scenic quality on the unprepossessing square in front of the Palais-Royal. Plans for a large barrack block for the royal musketeers on the Quai d'Orsay, and for a royal stable, remained unexecuted.

Among de Cotte's projects outside Paris, the Place Bellecour in Lyon deserves particular mention.[20] The brief was to create a suitable setting for the statue of Louis XIV that the city council had commissioned from Etienne Desjardins. He made a preliminary visit in the autumn of 1700, when a number of possibilities were considered, including a composition linked with the Loge au Change; but the final choice fell on the Place Bellecour, an irregular, sparsely developed expanse of land in the south of the city, between the rivers Rhône and Saône. In 1711–14, in the course of tough negotiations with the city council, de Cotte produced several designs for this site. These envisaged a regular development along three sides of a rectangular square, with trees along the fourth side. The main emphasis was on the two ends, which were designed to form an impressive setting for the royal statue and thus to give the

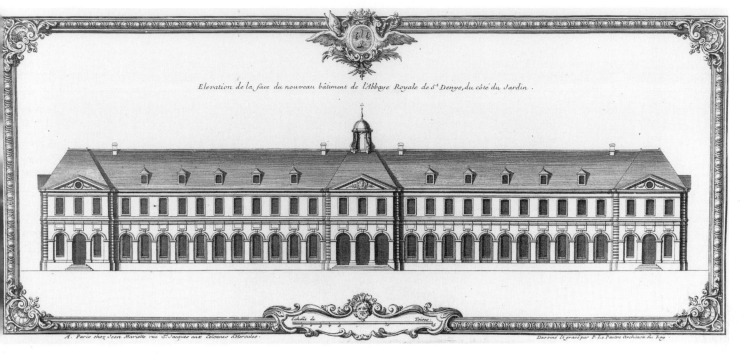

Elevation de la face du nouveau bâtiment de l'Abbaye Royale de St Denys, du côté du Jardin.

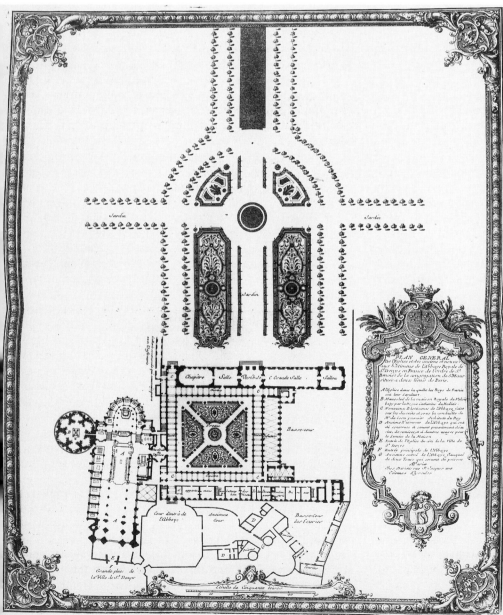

6 Robert de Cotte: Abbey of Saint-Denis, 1700–25, elevation of east wing.

7 Robert de Cotte: Abbey of Saint-Denis, 1700–25, plan. (Mariette, *L'Architecture Française*, pl. 26).

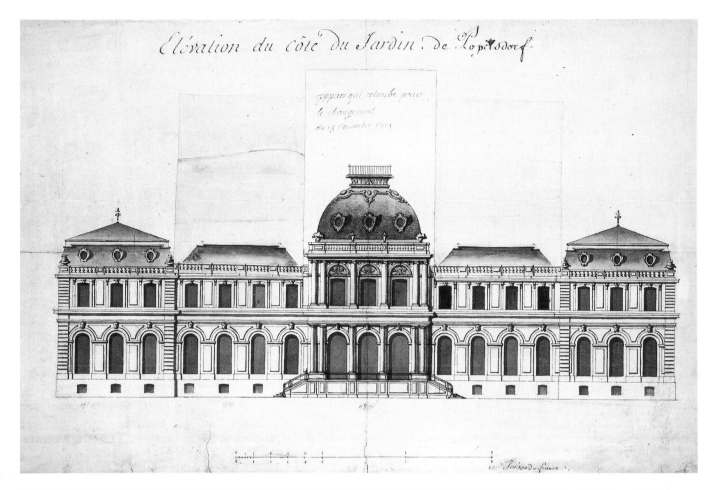

Élévation du côté du Jardin de Poppelsdorf

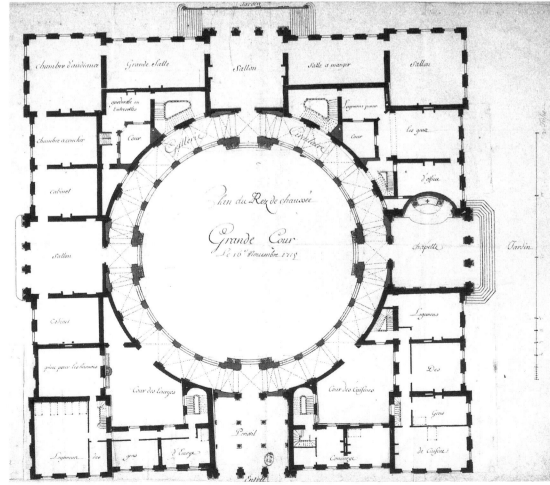

16 Robert de Cotte:
Poppelsdorf, plan of ground
floor, 1715.

17 Robert de Cotte:
Poppelsdorf, design for façade,
1715 (Bonn, Landeskonservator
Rheinland).

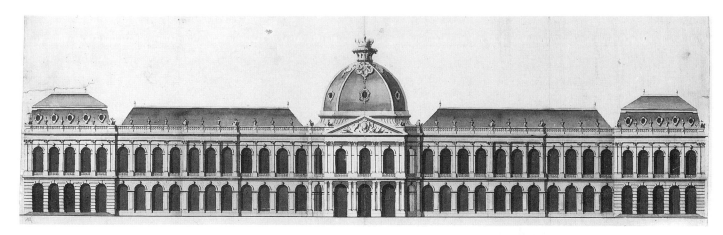

18   Robert de Cotte: Würzburg, design for façade, 1723 (Paris, Bibliothèque Nationale).

19   Robert de Cotte: Frankfurt, Palais Thurn und Taxis, 1727–40, Court façade (before 1944).

the approximately square medieval foundation he placed a cross, with vestibule and salon on the longitudinal axis, dining room and billiard room in the cross arms. All these rooms looked out across terraces to the surrounding moat, and were connected with the mainland by bridges aligned with the principal axis. Into the corners between the arms of the cross he tucked four small apartments, all with lofts containing servants' quarters and storerooms. As he pointed out in his covering letter, all available space was used, both horizontally and vertically. The four extremities were emphasized by pavilions with little domes, so that the allusion to the moated medieval fortress was maintained. The plans probably date from 1715 or so; it is, however, questionable whether they were ever carried out.[30]

In the plans for the Residenz in Würzburg, the last of de Cotte's major projects, his mature style was fully developed (Plate 18). Although intended for a bishop, this was not so much an episcopal as a princely palace, very much in the style of Schleissheim and Bonn – which is why its discussion belongs here. Construction began in 1719, to a design by Maximilian von Welsch; but a few years later, in 1723, Prince-Bishop Johann Philipp Franz von Schönborn sent his own architect, Balthasar Neumann, to Paris to solicit the opinions of de Cotte and Boffrand.[31] We know from Neumann's letters how diplomatically he managed this, in order to avoid becoming enmeshed in the rivalry between the two architects, and also how high the reputation of the chief architect was in France at that time.[32]

De Cotte criticized Welsch's plans as 'Italian with German features', by which he meant mainly the mezzanine windows on the façade and the extravagant use of space in the double staircase. The design that he sent to Würzburg was a further development of Schleissheim and Bonn. In it, notably, he established a consistent separation between principal and secondary rooms; a clear and rational definition of the spatial sequences; greater unity in the *cour d'honneur*; and the use of ovals with bowed projections to stress the axes. In the *corps de logis* he dispensed with the double staircase that Welsch had prefixed to the enfilade of the state rooms, enlarging the stair on the right and replacing that on the left with the palace chapel, which he brought in from its previously remote position. As at Schleissheim, the grand gallery, between its two corner salons, occupied the whole length of the right-hand wing.

The façade was similar to that of Buen Retiro I, but deficient in tension. The upper·storey, with its coupled pilasters, tended to overburden the arcaded ground floor, and the end pavilions were too narrow in relation to the whole. The centrepiece adopted the moulded dome of Buen Retiro, but with its low pediment it failed to hold the façade together. It was Buen Retiro without the Baroque rhetoric.

These plans, too, remained unexecuted. It was probably the chief architect's inflexibility, his uncompromising adherence to French convention, that led the prince-bishop to give his preference to the design submitted simultaneously by Boffrand.

With the Palais Thurn und Taxis in Frankfurt am Main, which was destroyed in the Second World War, de Cotte brought the French town house to Germany.[33] The Thurn und Taxis family owed its position and its wealth to the hereditary office of postmaster general to the Holy Roman Empire, which it had held since the sixteenth century. Since 1695 the head of the house had been a prince of the Empire, and they were keen to display their new-found status to the world. This was probably why Prince Anselm Franz turned to de Cotte when he came to transfer his own residence, and the Generaldirektion der Post, from Brussels to Frankfurt. He bought a plot of land there in 1724, and de Cotte sent in his plans in 1727; but, as Frankfurt, a Free Imperial City, hotly resisted the idea of a princely household, building work did not start until 1731. As usual, de Cotte sent a covering memorandum in which he explained the plan and, for the benefit of his foreign client, the function of the rooms.[34] The site architect was Hauberat, who had already shown himself a reliable deputy in Bonn and Poppelsdorf, and who was also now in charge of the palace at Mannheim. Work was probably completed in 1740 or so.

As the Frankfurt city authorities would never have accepted anything that looked like a palace, de Cotte had recourse to the less ostentatious type of the Parisian hôtel *particulier*, which he had used shortly before for the seat of the bishop of Strasbourg (the so-called Château des Rohan) (Plate 19). The two buildings were contemporaries, and the resemblance is close. This is particularly evident in the concave curve of the street front of the Palais Thurn und Taxis, with its pavilions, and the majestic portico of the court frontispiece, as also planned for Strasbourg. Again, the main entrance to the corps de logis was probably based on the two side doorways in Strasbourg, with their inset columns and flat lintels. The rest of the court elevation, with its profusion of pilasters, was already old-fashioned when it was built. It was reminiscent of the Parisian hôtels of the second decade

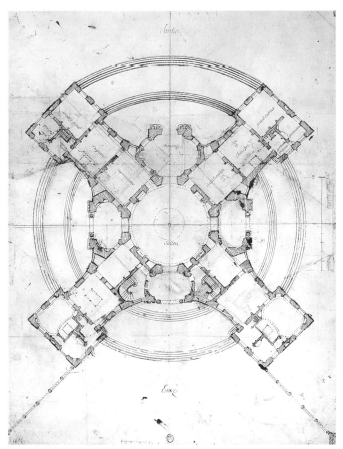

20 Robert de Cotte: Compiègne, plan of ground floor, *c.* 1730 (Paris, Bibliothèque Nationale).

of the century, such as the Hôtel de Torcy and the Hôtel de Montesquiou. De Cotte would never have got away with such a thing, if he had a client who knew anything about architecture. The garden front, on the other hand, was a masterpiece. By extending wider than the *cour d'honneur*, it served to disguise the narrowness of the site; and de Cotte used the bowed projection of the salon, with its array of pilasters and its surmounting dome, to endow the garden side with the princely character that he had so scrupulously avoided on the court side.

The ground plan was in accordance with Parisian custom. On the ground floor was the Grand Appartement, consisting of six rooms, 'where high society and the nobility customarily forgather' (de Cotte's memorandum). It was reached through the antechamber to the right of the vestibule, 'where the servants are usually to be found'. De Cotte had dispensed with a longitudinal axis. The first floor could be divided, as required, into one or two apartments, and there were further apartments in the attic, in the side wings that flanked the *cour d'honneur*, and in the gate pavilions. As at Poppelsdorf, de Cotte had provided accommodation for a great household within a limited space. The decoration was carried out by an Italian family firm of plasterworkers, the Castelli, who had already worked at Bonn and Poppelsdorf.[35] There was also the young and dynamic Paul Egell, from Mannheim, one of the leading Baroque sculptors in southern Germany, whose portal sculptures were a worthy counterpart to those in Strasbourg by Robert Le Lorrain.[36]

De Cotte received his only royal commission in France at the end of his life. This was for the Château de Compiègne, which Louis XV wanted to convert into a modern hunting lodge.[37] Accordingly, de Cotte's unexecuted design (1729–33) was not for a château but for a *maison de plaisance*, which he fitted into a grand composition of courts and parkland as the focal point of an extensive axial system (Plate 20). Around a triple-height central rotunda were four wings in the form of a cross, each containing a five-room apartment; between them were oval vestibules. The two wings on the garden side were intended for the king and queen, with smaller apartments for members of the court on the first floor. The flat, balustraded roofs were dominated by the drum of the central salon, with its curvaceous dome topped with a platform.

With its sweeping, late Baroque lines, this design was already very much in the Rococo spirit, far from de Cotte's point of departure, the restrained Baroque of J.H. Mansart. The stimulus no doubt came both from Boffrand's design for La Malgrange II, and from Marly. It was Marly that inspired the central salon and the vestibules, with the corner apartments here transformed into wings. De Cotte welded these influences into an original creation of great charm and originality, which shows him, in spite of his great age, retaining a sure mastery of his resources and keeping entirely up to date.

BISHOPS' PALACES

Episcopal residences form a group in their own right within De Cotte's work, occupying an intermediate position between the château and the urban hôtel. Most bishops were scions of great landed families, and as clerics they had no intention of depriving themselves of the style of life to which they had previously been accustomed. So it was that in the eighteenth century the ancient cathedral cities of France were adorned with town houses of a Parisian stamp that often looked decidedly out of place in their immediate surroundings. The individual parts of such a palace were no longer free-standing, as in earlier centuries, but subordinated to a rational system in which the bishop's apartment occupied the dominant position; even the chapel was now only one element among many. In this field, as in others, de Cotte set new standards.[38]

The sequence began with his design for the bishop's palace at Châlons-sur-Marne. This was begun in 1719, but the bishop died young, and it never progressed beyond the foundations. De Cotte's design was for a house on three sides of a court, with the staircase in one of the side wings and the chapel in the other. The lie of the land meant that the garden was a whole storey higher than the court, so that the building had two storeys at the front and only one – like a villa – at the back. The sole access to the bishop's apartment was by way of the staircase in the right-hand wing.

A much more important work was the bishop's palace in Verdun, which still exists. Here the concave court façade overlooks a long, entirely enclosed *cour d'honneur*, which gives the palace the look of a château (Plate 21). The planning was done in 1724–5, in close consultation with the bishop, who made a constant succession of new demands. De Cotte's designs, initially based on a horseshoe form, reveal a growing differentiation in the planning and a progressive harmonization of the court. The concave façade – for which the precedents lie not so much in Le Vau and Mansart as in Jacques V Gabriel's Château de Choisy or de Cotte's own Pavillon d'Orly – welds the *corps de logis* and the sides of the court into a single block.[39] At the bishop's request, de Cotte developed the vestibule and the garden salon into a powerful central axis. To the left of this, along the garden front and back along the left-hand side of the court, he put the assembly and reception rooms for the clergy; the bishop's private quarters occupy the right-hand half of the *corps de logis*. As at Poppelsdorf, de Cotte inserted the stair, secondary rooms and little light wells behind the curve of the court façade. The first floor was set aside for the bishop's retinue.

The overall effect is dominated by the court, closely tied to the *corps de logis*, both spatially and in its articulation. The two side wings carry equal weight, despite their different purposes: that on the right contains carriage houses, and in that on the left the bishop's private chapel is reached by way of a gallery that runs, as at Versailles, between two corner salons. With a range of buildings on every side, the court has the look of an enclosed room, particularly as the entrance is in one of the canted corners and there is therefore no central axis. The tall, slender blind arcades, with ornamental keystones, that surround the court as if it were a banqueting hall, are like an echo of the arcades forming the plain, markedly horizontal emphasis of the *corps de logis* (Plate 22). Construction began only in 1731 and dragged on until 1751; but de Cotte's plans were strictly adhered to, and this building may therefore be regarded as an authentic work of the 1720s.

This group culminates in the palace of the bishop of Strasbourg (1727–42). This is closely associated with the name of Cardinal Armand-Gaston de Rohan, France's richest and most aristocratic prince of the Church and a discriminating connoisseur and amateur of the arts. De Cotte had been working for him for many years: from 1712 onwards, he had enlisted the leading artists in France to work on a magnificent remodelling of the bishop's summer residence, the Château de Saverne.[40] This work lasted into the 1730s, culminating in the Salle des Colonnes and the Appartement de Parade, where the Cardinal received the young queen, Marie Leszczyńska, in 1725. De Cotte had thus succeeded in transplanting the art of the French court into the hitherto German cultural territory of Alsace. His subsequent commission to replace the ancient and inconvenient episcopal palace in Strasbourg thus emerged naturally from a long relationship of mutual professional esteem.[41]

This was a bigger and more important commission than Verdun. The Cardinal was not only bishop of Strasbourg and the king's representative but also a prince of the Holy Roman Empire. De Cotte therefore gave the palace a twofold aspect. On the town side it presents itself as a Parisian hôtel

on a grand scale; but on the side that overlooks the river Ill, with its gardens on the facing bank, it is a princely Schloss with a portico and a square dome. The plan, too, reflects this dual function (Plate 23). The deep *cour d'honneur*, oriented to face the south transept of the cathedral, is separated from the street by two three-bay pavilions, one for the diocesan administration and one for the kitchens, and a deeply incurved gateway screen. As at the Hôtel de Bourbon in Paris, the entrances to the building lie in the corner of the side wings. That on the left leads into a large oval vestibule, directly followed by the main staircase. That on the right, with its own columned vestibule, forms a separate entrance to the private apartments.

In the *corps de logis* the Verdun scheme is further developed. The clergy rooms adjoin the vestibule and staircase on the left; they are followed on the river side by the royal apartment, consisting of two rooms and an antechamber, and

on the court side by the apartment of the Cardinal. At the right-hand end is the chapel, completed only in 1736. Because of difficulties over land ownership, the chapel did not form part of the original plan, and so the central axis on the river side differs by two bays from that on the court side: a trick frequently employed in Paris hôtels to mask a discrepancy in the lengths of the two elevations. As at Verdun, the first floor was set aside for retainers and guests.

In the course of planning, the exterior went through some major changes. On the court side, de Cotte originally intended to have columns, which the Cardinal seems to have considered old-fashioned; they were replaced by pilasters. The façade was also enriched by rusticated dressings. On the river side, the base was initially smooth and unarticulated (Plate 24). As the planning progressed, it developed into a podium, with blind arcades and rustication. Above it, the original giant pilasters gave way to a giant order of columns,

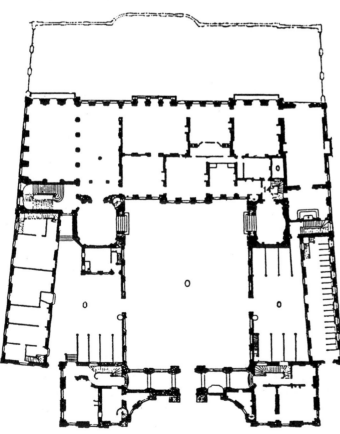

23   Robert de Cotte: Strasbourg, Château des Rohan, 1727–42, façade.

24   Robert de Cotte: Strasbourg, Château des Rohan, 1727–42, plan of ground floor.

25   Robert de Cotte: Strasbourg, Château des Rohan, the king's bedroom.

and the single roof was broken up into sectional roofs. Construction began in 1732, after the demolition of the old palace, and was supervised by de Cotte's representative, Joseph Massol. After de Cotte's death, and undoubtedly at the Cardinal's behest, Massol gave greater weight to the river front by heightening the pediment and adding a square dome of the shape designed for Versailles by J.H. Mansart.[42] Work was completed in 1743 with the construction of the great riverside terrace.

The Château des Rohan, as this palace came to be known, is richly decorated – as are all Rohan buildings – with sculptures based on a clearly defined programme. The sculptors were Robert Le Lorrain, who had already worked at Saverne and at the Hôtel de Rohan in Paris, and his assistants Johann August Nahl and Paul de Saint-Laurent. Le Lorrain himself did the portal sculptures and the figures of prophets on the keystones of the court façade; Nahl carved the masks of gods on the river front. The decoration of the interior is also of high quality; the Chambre du Roi (Plate 25) and Salon du Roi are among the crowning glories of the Rococo. Partly designed by de Cotte himself, the decor was executed only after his death, in 1735–41. Nahl, a German, who later won fame in Berlin, Potsdam and

Kassel, was responsible for the panelling; Saint-Laurent for the figurative cartouches in the corners, the ceiling in the bedchamber, with the four Times of Day, and that in the Salon du Roi, with the Four Seasons. These two rooms form a pendant to the almost contemporaneous interiors in the Hôtel de Soubise, for which the Cardinal's brother had engaged the services of Boffrand. In its artistic significance, the Château des Rohan is thus far more than an episcopal palace: it is a display of French art in the furthest eastern territories of the kingdom, on the border of the Holy Roman Empire.

The building of the Château des Rohan, and the presence of Massol, brought the Régence style to Strasbourg, where it enjoyed a long career. Among the numerous hôtels, the Hôtel Klinglin (1730) and the Hôtel de Hanau (1731–6; later Hesse-Darmstadt), with its deep *cour d'honneur* and its bowed centre piece, deserve particular mention. The Hôtel du Grand-Doyenné, built for La Tour d'Auvergne, the dean of the cathedral, by A.M. Saussard, is somewhat earlier. These buildings markedly altered the look of the city. Into the ancient town centre of Strasbourg, hitherto entirely German, they brought a breath of France that shifted the cultural focus westward.

CHAPTER 4

Germain Boffrand

Alongside Robert de Cotte, Germain Boffrand (1667–1754) was the dominant figure of the Mansart school; and Blondel, in his *Architecture française*, ranks him closest of all to the genius of J.H. Mansart. His rise to honour and influence took place without the benefit of an official post and a well-oiled organization, purely on the strength of his own personality and the sheer scope of his talent.

Boffrand was worlds removed from de Cotte's instinct for balance and harmony. In accordance with a tradition that flowed directly from François Mansart and Le Vau, he was interested in giant orders, in contrasts of masses, and in architecture as an undisguised three-dimensional presence. Although he never went to Italy, he often came close to the Italian way of seeing; and Andrea Palladio, in particular, influenced him deeply. It was Palladio who opened his eyes to the architecture of antiquity, to which, in his *Livre d'architecture*, he was one of the few members of his generation to pay admiring tribute; and he thus enjoyed an inner affinity with John Vanbrugh and with English Palladianism. Different though they were, Boffrand and de Cotte often worked for the same clients, and indeed tackled the same assignments, most notably at Würzburg. There was certainly a tacit rivalry between them, in which de Cotte, as chief architect to the crown, enjoyed the advantage.[43]

Boffrand was extraordinarily versatile. He interested himself in all kinds of technology; he was a bridge engineer, a contractor, a property speculator. In his youth he even wrote plays; his uncle was the poet Philippe Quinault, best known for his collaboration with the composer Jean-Baptiste Lully and for the classical purity of his diction. Boffrand himself wrote his theoretical treatise, the *Livre d'architecture*, both in French and in Latin.[44] In his youth, his uncle Quinault brought him to Versailles from his native Nantes and initially apprenticed him to the sculptor François Girardon. In 1685 he transferred to the office of J.H. Mansart; and there, first as a draughtsman and later as a clerk of works, he worked on the first version of the Place Vendôme. He left abruptly in 1699; presumably this was after a disagreement with Mansart, since in 1709, after Mansart's death, we find him back on the books of the Service des Bâtiments with the title of *architecte du Roi*. By that time, however, his career had taken a different and decisive turn.

Boffrand made his name with the Hôtel Le Brun, which he built in 1700 for the son of the celebrated court painter.[45] The unwontedly compact outline, the sculptured pediment set against bare walls and windows without surrounds, and above all the frontispiece on the garden side, which juts out through the main cornice without any attempt at covering the transition, were unprecedented in the architecture of the day. It was a first move away from Mansart and towards Palladio. His next work was the Hôtel d'Argenton (1704), built in the gardens of the Palais-Royal for the mistress of the Duc d'Orléans.[46] It was this commission that brought him into contact with Elector Max Emanuel of Bavaria and

with Duke Leopold of Lorraine, Orléans's brother-in-law.

First the Elector of Bavaria employed him to build a hunting lodge (1705) at Bouchefort, near Soignies in Belgium; for Boffrand, this meant a direct encounter with Palladio (Plate 26). His point of departure for Bouchefort was the Villa Rotonda, which J.H. Mansart had already reinterpreted twenty years earlier in the Pavillon Royal at Marly. At Bouchefort, however, the tranquil balance of the original gave way to a curious unrest. The square plan became an octagon, and the simple dome became an animated roof line. The mobility created by the breaks in the outline, and particularly by the canted bays to either side of each portico, also prevailed in the interior (Plate 27). The apartments were not relegated to the corners of a square but formed a ring round the outsize central salon. In place of the unbroken enfilades of Marly there were constant changes of direction and variations in spatial form. A monumental stair, in the manner of the Escalier des Ambassadeurs at Versailles, occupied one whole side of the octagon, although the upper floor contained nothing but bedrooms. The double-height octagonal salon was marked by a similar Baroque overstatement. It was a copy of the salon at Marly, but much taller. In designing the caryatids that supported the vault, Boffrand undoubtedly had those of Marly in mind, but also their prototypes, the signs of the zodiac at Vaux-le-Vicomte.

Bouchefort bore all the marks of a youthful work, though its Baroque excesses – and its grotesque lantern in particular – probably sprang from the Elector's insistence on having his own way. It was a decidedly Baroque composition. The house was at the centre of a large, circular space, and of a radial array of rides that alternated with blocks of domestic buildings, very much as with the Ecuries, the stables at Versailles (Plate 28). Bouchefort was all set to become a baroque version of the Villa Rotonda; but in the spring of 1706 the imperial armies advanced on Brussels, the Elector fled, and the building of his hunting lodge never progressed beyond the earliest stages. It was destined to have numerous successors; but these were in Germany and not in France.[47]

Boffrand's connection with Lorraine was very much more fruitful. The young Duke Leopold returned from exile after the Peace of Ryswick, in 1698. There then began a lively period of building activity, closely comparable to that which was taking place beyond the Rhine, at Darmstadt, Mannheim, Rastatt and elsewhere. Leopold was a prince of the Holy Roman Empire, closely related on his mother's side to the imperial house; but he married a French princess, the niece of Louis XIV, and thereafter inclined towards France. His court was modelled on that of Versailles, and Voltaire remarked that one noticed almost no difference when one travelled from Versailles to Lunéville.

The engagement of Boffrand thus heralded a new architectural age dominated by France that would rescue Lorraine from its provincial obscurity and place it in the limelight for half a century to come. The duke was ambitious, and keen to

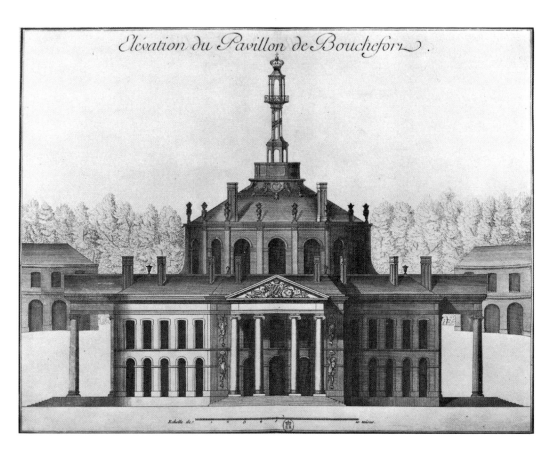

26 Germain Boffrand:
Bouchefort, 1705, elevation.

27 Germain Boffrand:
Bouchefort, 1705, plan of the
hunting pavilion.

28 Germain Boffrand:
Bouchefort, 1705, general plan.

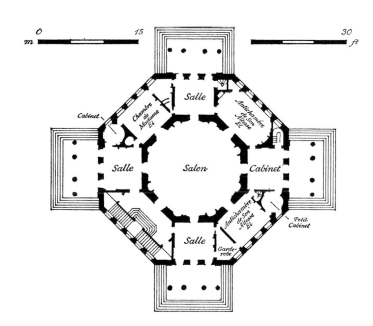

emphasize his position as a sovereign prince; for Boffrand, it was a perfect opportunity. The palaces of Lunéville, Nancy and La Malgrange, together with country seats and town mansions elsewhere, were to keep him fully occupied for fifteen years.

His first task was the Château de Lunéville. We cannot date this precisely:[48] he submitted his plans to the Academy in Paris in 1709, but his name does not appear in the Lorraine archives until 1711, the year in which he was named

chief architect to the duke. However, work had started by 1702 on the remodelling of the old ducal hunting lodge, where the duke had taken up residence after the outbreak of the War of the Spanish Succession and the French occupation of Nancy. Although there is much in the archives about this, it is impossible to gain a clear idea of the nature and extent of these early works. Certainly, the side wings on the outer court side were built then, and work started on the right-hand wing on the garden side, which contained

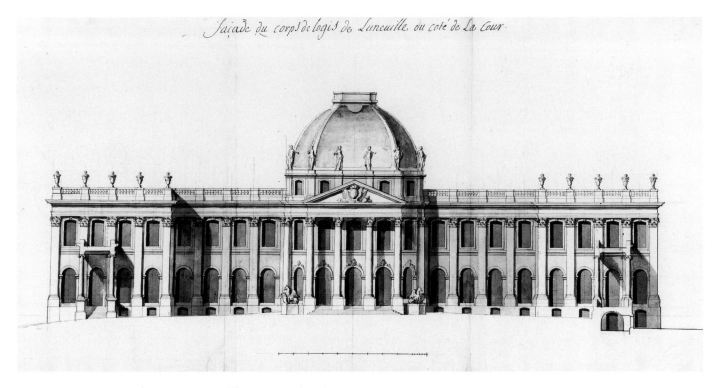

façade du corps de logis de Luneuille du coté de La Cour

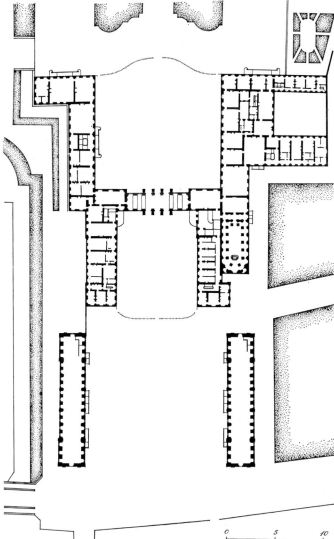

29 Germain Boffrand: Lunéville, (*above*) first project, 1709 – ?; (*opposite*) first project, side wings, 1709 (?) (Nancy, Service régional de l'inventaire général en Lorraine).

30 Germain Boffrand: Lunéville, 1709–15, plan.

the apartments of the ducal family. Additionally, some – presumably provisional – renovation work was done on the nucleus of the old château, which consisted of a shallow *corps de logis* and two massive, tall-roofed terminal pavilions. This was ready for occupation by 1705, so the work cannot have been very extensive. An undated design for the garden front, now in the library in Nancy, shows this *corps de logis* with an open loggia passing through the centre, flanked by giant columns and topped by a massive pediment: the essence, in fact, of Boffrand's eventual solution.[49]

Irrespective of such work on the old château as was already completed, or still in hand, the duke determined to build a new one. The successive phases of Boffrand's planning process can be reconstructed from surviving designs, although no precise chronology can be established.[50] The initial design – presumably the one that Boffrand showed to the Academy – was for a massive block, twenty-one bays long, with two internal courts, a bowed centre on an elliptical curve, and modest projections at either end (Plate 29a). The elevations were articulated by a giant order of pilasters. The bowed centre on the court side was fronted by a carriage porch on four free-standing giant columns, with a pediment adorned by a coat of arms. Above was an octagonal dome on a low drum. The frontispiece on the garden side was crowned by an attic, with statues on the skyline. The ornament was restricted to ornamental keystones on the arcades of the centre and end pavilions. The side wings of the *cour d'honneur*, of which the one on the right contained a chapel

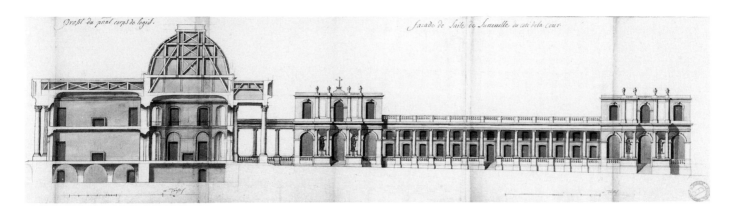

and a theatre, were flat-roofed, fronted by peristyles and linked to the *corps de logis* only by open colonnades (Plate 29b).

This design bore an unmistakable affinity with Palladio. The giant orders along the elevations, and the attic on the garden front, were reminiscent of Palladian palazzi; the giant columns of the portico recalled the church of S. Giorgio Maggiore in Venice. The flat-roofed peristyles of the wings were an echo of the long colonnades that flank Palladio's villas.

The plan was reminiscent of Vaux-le-Vicomte (Plate 30). As there, a strongly defined central axis was flanked by twin staircases, with small adjoining light-wells. The side elevations, however, were much longer than those of Vaux: one accommodated a suite of small apartments, the other a large banqueting hall. The garden front was entirely taken up with the ducal apartments.

This grand design – a continuation of the French seventeenth-century château tradition without any reference to Versailles or to the Mansart system, but with added Palladian touches – no doubt exceeded the duke's means; in any case, it remained on paper. In his second – or alternative? – design, Boffrand went back to the U shape, enlarging the *cour d'honneur*, connecting the wings firmly to the *corps de logis*, returning them outward at the ends, and adding an additional wing on the town side. The elevations lost their giant order, and the dome disappeared. Only the giant columns on the central porch remained. Here the motif of a triple archway made its first appearance; it was to remain a constant.

When this design too had to be scaled down, Boffrand restricted himself to the existing nucleus. The foundations of the shallow *corps de logis* of the old château, with its two corner pavilions, were retained, and two short two-storey wings, with one-and-a-half storey continuations, were added to flank the *cour d'honneur*. The main accent was provided by the triple archway, with its portico, now surmounted by a dome markedly simpler than the one in the first design. The ducal apartments were brought back from the side wings of the *cour d'honneur* into the right-hand garden wing. The chapel, too, was removed from the right-hand court wing, which was now narrower, and put into a chapel wing of its own on the far side of it.

The château as completed in 1715 was no doubt closely based on this third design but we do not know what it looked like, because it was severely damaged in a fire in 1719. It was presumably very like the present structure; for the rebuilding, which began at once, and of which Boffrand has left a record in his *Livre d'architecture*, was completed by 1723. Both the duke's financial situation and the shortage of accommodation for his court make it highly unlikely that the design was radically changed in the intervening time.

Even in its present, diminished form, Lunéville has retained a touch of magnificence (Plate 31).[51] Like Versailles, it is fronted by two courts: the old forecourt and the new *cour d'honneur*. The wings grow progressively taller towards the massive central portico, with its free-standing giant columns and its dome. This central feature is not actually the symbolic core of the palace – the ducal apartments were in the garden wing, so that the *corps de logis* consisted entirely of vestibules and antechambers – but only a passage into the gardens behind; and this lends the building a curiously transparent air, reminiscent of such garden villas as Le Brun's country house at Montmorency or the Grand Trianon at Versailles.

The chapel deserves special mention (Plate 32). It is characteristic of Boffrand's reformist approach. The first chapel, in a wing of its own behind the right-hand court wing, had been destroyed in the fire. The new one was built in 1720–2, directly abutting the right-hand wing and linked by a narrow vestibule to the main staircase in the short two-storey section of the wing. It shares with its counterpart at Versailles its tripartite division into nave and aisles and its two-storey design; structurally, however, it is utterly different. The space is dominated by a double Ionic order and an unbroken entablature; that is, a framework of verticals and horizontals. This is much more in evidence than the sparse decor of the walls, which consist largely of big windows. The formal apparatus is thus limited to simple, clear, autonomous elements.

The fundamental distinction between this and Versailles is shown above all in the treatment of space. Versailles has an upward impulse and a rapid rhythm of supports; Lunéville has a tranquil balance and a light-filled spaciousness that allows every column to make its full effect. The aisles are reduced to a minimum, so that the interior looks like a single, unified space. The proportions are so chosen that the height of the lower order is equal to the width of the central nave, and the height of the two orders together is equal to the width of the whole interior. In his *Nouveau Traité de toute l'architecture* (1706), Cordemoy had been the first to call for the abandonment of multiple recessions, and also of all piers

31   Germain Boffrand: Lunéville, 1709–15, general view and courtyard façade.

32   Germain Boffrand: Lunéville, chapel, 1720–22.

and arches, and to preach a plain architecture based on the column and the right-angle – in other words, the lintel. Boffrand, in his chapel at Lunéville, was the first architect to fulfil these demands. The column-and-lintel system had no precedents, except Perrault's design for Sainte-Geneviève and Gobert's for Versailles. Cordemoy's other demand, that coupled columns should be used as much as possible in church building, was adopted by Boffrand in the first chapel at Lunéville, before the fire. He was later to return to it in his design for Würzburg.

There is a close affinity between Lunéville and Boffrand's

subsequent designs for La Malgrange, a *maison de plaisance* for the duke, close to his capital city of Nancy. Work began there in 1712, and the carcass was completed in 1715. Then the duke lost interest – allegedly because of a critical remark by the Elector of Bavaria, but more probably for financial reasons – and left the house unfinished. In his *Livre d'architecture*, Boffrand published two versions. The first, La Malgrange I, belonged to the Vaux-le-Vicomte tradition and displayed a marked resemblance to the first project for Lunéville. This is particularly clear from a comparison of the garden front of La Malgrange (Plate 33) with the court front

of Lunéville, although at Lunéville the Palladian elements were much stronger. There, the giant pilasters extended across the whole façade, whereas in La Malgrange I, as at Vaux-le-Vicomte, they were restricted to the end pavilions. The detached wings of La Malgrange I were an almost literal repeat of the colonnaded wings designed for Lunéville. The two ground plans, too, were very similar. La Malgrange I (Plate 34), like Lunéville, was a single block around a pair of inner courts; a lengthwise central axis passed through one rectangular and one oval room; one end was developed as a suite of apartments, the other as a single large room –

probably a dining room – with secondary rooms; the ducal apartment occupied the garden front. It therefore seems likely that, in planning La Malgrange I, Boffrand reused the discarded first plan for Lunéville, with slight variations. At La Malgrange he replaced one of the two staircases with the chapel and brought the vestibule further forward, so that both the staircase and the chapel opened out of it.

The source for La Malgrange I lay in the designs for the Castello di Rivoli, in Piedmont, that were prepared in J.H. Mansart's office, probably by de Cotte, in 1702 or there-abouts. These designs have survived among de Cotte's

33 Germain Boffrand: Malgrange I, 1712–15, garden façade (Boffrand, *Livre d'architecture*).

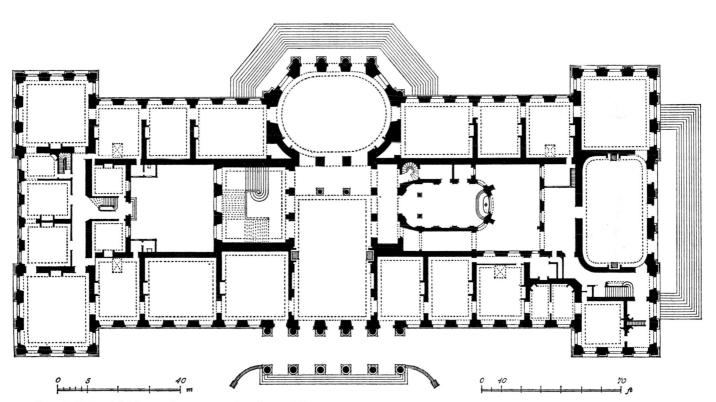

34 Germain Boffrand: Malgrange I, 1712–15, plan of ground floor.

papers, and may well have contributed to the planning of Lunéville too, although they are closer to La Malgrange.[52]

In contrast to Malgrange I, La Malgrange II had the look of ideal architecture (Plate 35). Its plan was X-shaped.[53] From a core that consisted, as at Bouchefort, of a triple-height, circular hall with an internal peristyle, four long wings projected like the sails of a windmill; each contained a single apartment. The entrance hall, the vestibule, the staircase and an oval room, probably the dining room, were inserted into the acute angles of the X. We do not know where Boffrand got the inspiration for this unusual form,

which Filippo Juvarra took up decades later for the Palazzina di Stupinigi; however, the source might well have been a Viennese one, in the work of Johann Bernhard Fischer von Erlach. His pleasure villa or *Lustgebäude* for Count Althan, of 1690, featured the X-shaped plan as well as the central drum.

The Viennese connection was strong in Lorraine. These were years of military failure for France, and the duke was looking increasingly towards his imperial connections in Vienna. In 1707, moreover, he summoned Francesco Bibbiena to build an opera house in Nancy. Bibbiena had

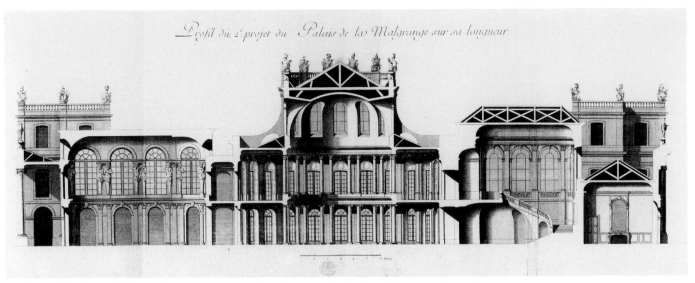

35 Germain Boffrand: Malgrange II, *c.* 1712, courtyard façade and section (Boffrand, *Livre d'architecture*).

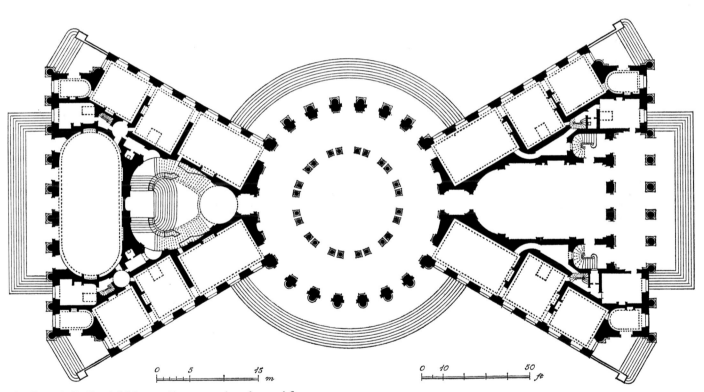

36 Germain Boffrand: Malgrange II, *c.* 1712, plan of ground floor.

built the Vienna Opera shortly before, and the Nancy Opera contains many echoes of it. This opera house thus introduced to Lorraine not only the Italian but also the Viennese Baroque. Bibbiena was an important source of the fanciful and decorative *style lorrain* that now emerged.[54]

In La Magrange II, however the baroque spirit of the Viennese model has been remarkably increased (Plate 36). The giant columns and the curvaceous flying buttresses of the central drum gave it a Roman monumentality. The ends of the wings were stressed by pavilions, and the drum, with its elaborate decor of trophies, loomed like a great crown

over their flat roofs. The ground plan, too, had been monumentalized. A single axis ran through the whole building, from the wide portico at one end, through the two-storey vestibule and the three-storey central salon, to the vast and well-lit staircase on the far side, with its two curved flights rising to the upper floor from a wide half-landing. It was a grand, Italianate sequence of visual contrasts,[55] and a spatial effect unequalled even at Stupinigi.

In the ducal capital itself, Nancy, nothing had happened meanwhile. On his initial, brief return in 1698, the duke had decided on a modernization of the old château and had

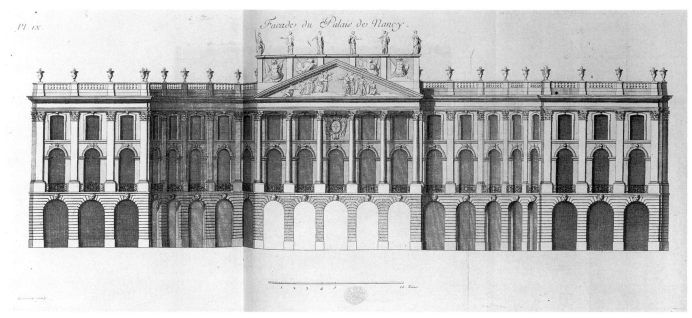

37   Germain Boffrand: Nancy, Ducal Palace, 1717–22, façade.

applied to J.H. Mansart, who had come to Nancy in 1700 – at least partly at the behest of Louis XIV himself – to provide designs for a new building that would incorporate the old while leaving it largely intact. The main façade was to be switched from the busy, ancient city centre to the tranquil and patrician Place de la Carrière; behind, a large formal garden was to stretch as far as the ramparts. But all this came to nought when Nancy was reoccupied by French troops and the duke withdrew to Lunéville. It was not until after he returned to his capital after the peace of 1714 that he took up the plan once more and employed Boffrand to carry it out.

In his design, which was ready by 1715, Boffrand proposed to demolish the old château and replace it with a completely new palace that would abandon the traditional link with the ancient city of Nancy. Like Mansart, he set its main entrance on the Place de la Carrière, a former tournament ground.[56] The palace was to consist of four massive ranges around a rectangular court; and by this the duke, who hankered after the title of king, undoubtedly intended an allusion to the Louvre in Paris. The concave entrance façade, between end pavilions, repeated the elevation of the Place Vendôme, with giant pilasters above an arcaded podium (Plate 37). The five-bay frontispiece was emphasized by a giant order of columns and a wide pediment; above, as in the first design for Lunéville, was an attic crowned by statues. Five archways beneath the frontispiece led to the court, in which the entrance to the grand staircase was sited. In contrast to the entrance façade, the court itself had a curiously jejune look, as if taken straight from a treatise on the orders of architecture. The centre pavilions on its four sides, each with three superimposed orders, were reminiscent of Palladio's Convento della Carità.

The lifelessness of the court elevations was repeated in the plan. A monotonous succession of large rooms ran from the main stair on the left-hand side of the court to the ducal apartments, which occupied the entrance range and were the

only part of the whole to display any richness of variation. Secondary rooms were used very sparingly. The grand gallery was inserted, inorganically, along the right-hand side of the court, with the theatre tacked on to the end. The chapel, abutting the left-hand wing, was lined with columns, as at Lunéville, but with a dome to provide a strong central emphasis.

This project, the Louvre of Nancy, suffered much the same fate as La Malgrange. Work began in 1717 and was halted in 1722. The rebuilding of Lunéville had exhausted the ducal coffers. When Lorraine was later handed over to King Stanislas of Poland, there was no longer any need for a ducal residence on such a scale, and all that was ever built – the entrance range – was pulled down in 1745.

One echo of this vanished palace is the Hôtel de Beauvau or de Craon, the finest town mansion in Nancy, which Boffrand constructed on the Place de la Carrière. Its six-bay frontispiece, taller than the plain wings, is a faithful reproduction of the end pavilions of the ducal palace; with it Boffrand was already planning the wider connection with the Place de la Carrière as a whole.[57] Directly opposite the Hôtel de Craon, in 1752, King Stanislas built the Bourse des Marchands in the same style, thus setting a scale for the square and keeping alive the memory of the grand design that had once existed.[58]

For the Château de Commercy, the seat of the Prince de Vaudemont, a relative of the duke's, Boffrand supplied a design for the *corps de logis* (c. 1712); this probably bore some relation to the early planning stages of Lunéville. However, it is impossible to say whether, or to what extent, Boffrand's design was altered in the execution by Nicolas d'Orbay.

The most important of the châteaux that Boffrand built for the nobility of Lorraine is Haroué (1712–13) (Plate 38). Like the Hôtel de Beauvau, it was built for Marc de Beauvau, Prince de Craon, whose wife was said to be on intimate terms with Duke Leopold. It was not a completely new structure but a remodelling of a moated medieval castle,

38 Germain Boffrand: Haroué, 1712–13.

retaining the moat, the corner towers, and the plain external walls.[59] In rebuilding this austerely rectilinear block, Boffrand introduced a highly fashionable Parisian touch by removing one side of it to create a *cour d'honneur* of a lively and festive appearance. He doubled the depth of the *corps de logis* and gave it a court frontispiece with two superimposed orders. The side wings – again following Palladio – have galleries with elegant wrought-iron balustrades supported by ranks of slender columns. The garden front is a reminiscence of the Hôtel de Lorge. Haroué occupies a special position in that it shows Boffrand, for once, following closely in the footsteps of Mansart. It illustrates how, when the situation demanded, he could handle his master's manner with perfect freedom, but that he studiously avoided the courtly style of de Cotte and was not prepared to sacrifice the interplay of masses to any consideration of harmonious balance.

This fundamental difference is most clearly evident in the rival designs for the Residenz in Würzburg.[60] On his visit to Paris in 1723, Balthasar Neumann had contrived to consult Boffrand without arousing the suspicions of de Cotte. Boffrand, indeed, showed himself to be the more amenable of the two, as he was less inclined to take his stand on principle and readier to consult the client's wishes. In criticizing the existing Würzburg designs, he agreed with de Cotte about the mezzanine windows, which were not customary in France, and the restless form of the *cour d'hon-*

neur. However, he altered little of Welsch's ground plan. In his design, which he published in his *Livre d'architecture*, he kept the double staircase, with the addition of landings all round and an additional storey. The chapel, too, retained its place in the centre of a side wing. In it, he further developed the combination of longitudinal and centralized planning that was already evident in the court chapel for Nancy. The length of the nave, which occupied a connecting range flanked by two internal courts, was balanced by a dominant, centralizing element in the shape of the wide, domed oval that projected in the centre of the right-hand side elevation. As in the first chapel at Lunéville, the nave and aisles were separated by coupled columns. In terms of spatial variety, however, and in the practical segregation of principal and secondary rooms, Boffrand's plan lacked the flexibility achieved by de Cotte.

Of Boffrand's Würzburg façade designs the one now in the Kunstbibliothek in Berlin, differs from those by de Cotte principally in replacing the large first-floor arcades with relatively small rectangular windows and thus increasing the mass of the wall; additionally, the side and intermediate pavilions were fronted by identical columns. By contrast, the design published by Boffrand in the *Livre d'architecture* (Plate 39) shows an impressive pyramidal increase of height towards the centre, created by the two tall stairchambers and the heightened central hall between them, and a conventional

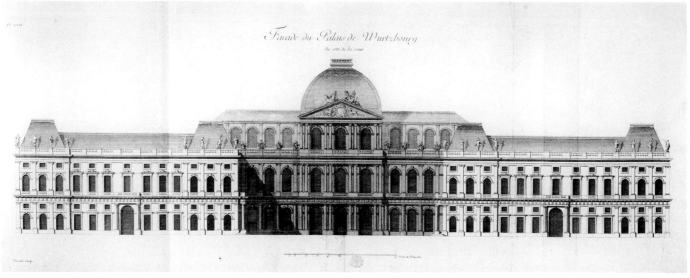

39   Germain Boffrand: Würzburg, design for façade, 1724 (Boffrand, *Livre d'architecture*).

academic superimposition of three orders on the frontispiece. It would never have occurred to de Cotte to create this kind of interplay of masses; it would have offended his sense of proportion.

It was probably Boffrand's altogether more biddable attitude that led the prince-bishop to prefer his design and invite him to Würzburg. When he arrived in Germany, in 1724, Boffrand was able to revise his designs for the Residenz, and for the Schönborn chapel in the cathedral, and to design the plasterwork decor for the north wing in conjunction with the seasoned *stuccatore* Johann Peter

Castelli, who had already given proof of his abilities at Bonn and Poppelsdorf; he was also able to visit the Schönborn residences in Franconia, such as Pommersfelden. There he would have had ample scope for his genius, had not the prince-bishop unexpectedly died in the same year. Boffrand's commission lapsed, and his contacts with Würzburg were broken off. In subsequent building work on the Residenz, little remained of his ideas. Only one of the two staircases was built, with the upper landing proposed by Boffrand, but without the upper range of windows that would have flooded it with light.

53 Bullet de Chamblain: Champs, 1701–7, garden façade.

fully projecting and slightly taller central bow, with its tall, narrow windows and continuous rustication; decoration is reduced to one wrought-iron balcony on high, curved consoles.[80] In this façade, as in the ground plan, Bullet de Chamblain shows himself to be a representative of the new age, influenced by J.H. Mansart. His plan, which is the same on both floors, is remarkable not only for its clarity but for its respect for the practical requirements of domesticity. All the rooms are nearly square, to ensure an even distribution of light.

Although Champs stands at the very beginning of the century, it is a key work, with all the modern features. It proved particularly significant in the evolution of the *maison de plaisance*, a type based on the pursuit of uncluttered elegance and improved comfort, which sought to combine the architectural conventions of the urban hôtel with the requirements of country life.[81] Not only is its influence visible in numerous villas in the Paris area; through the agency of Bullet de Chamblain's pupil Carl Hårlemann, it also took root in Sweden.

One of J.H. Mansart's most faithful followers, although never a member of his office, was Alexandre Le Blond (1679–1719). Le Blond worked in Paris for only ten years; but this was enough to establish his reputation both as a practitioner and as a theorist. In 1710 he brought out a new and up-to-date edition of Daviler's *Cours d'architecture*, incorporating the major new developments in the planning and decoration of hôtels. His own *Traité d'architecture* was held back by his publisher, Jombert, and published only in 1765, under Jombert's name. His practical work included two town houses – Hôtel de Vendôme (1706, enlarged 1714–16)[82] and Hôtel de Clermont (1708–14) – and two country houses near Paris. All share a free treatment of the Mansart repertoire of forms. But, for all his formal borrowings, Le Blond had a resourceful imagination of his own and was fully in tune with modern developments. At the Hôtel de Clermont he used the newly fashionable, broad, low roof à *l'italienne*; and at the Château de Regnault, at Châtillon-sous-Bagneux, he used a Mansart pilaster order on the porch beneath a low upper storey, in unexpected con-

articulated design and reducing his intended broad elevation to a narrow and somewhat cramped-looking façade.[75]

A few years later, for the Prince de Rohan, son and heir to his initial client, Boffrand designed a *maison de plaisance* at Saint-Ouen, near Paris (1714–17), with which he created a considerable stir. On a small terrace at the central focus of an extensive park, he built a single-storey villa between lower, detached wings (Plate 51). The *cour d'honneur* was flanked by a kitchen court and a stable court, and behind the house was the park. In spite of the reduced scale, the resemblance to Marly is unmistakable: the central pavilion corresponded to the Salon du Roi, and the wings to the guest pavilions. The formal prototype, however, was the Château du Val, a much-admired early work by J.H. Mansart; as there, the house stood on a raised terrace, and its interior consisted of a central salon flanked by two small apartments.

Saint-Ouen showed Boffrand at his most charming. The building was ephemeral in its lightness, open on every side through doors and windows. It was fronted by a portico; at the back, it was articulated by pilasters and enlivened by ornate window surrounds. In the tradition of Marly, Boffrand had created a new villa type, 'in a new and entirely individual style' (Germain Brice), which was never intended to be anything more than a setting for a relaxed stay in the country, a place where a small party could enjoy gaming and entertainment within easy reach of the city.

Alongside the leading players, Lassurance, de Cotte and Boffrand, a whole phalanx of architects were involved in the early eighteenth-century building boom. Most of their names and works are recorded in the engravings of Mariette's *Architecture française*, an invaluable source for the architecture of the first third of the century.[76] To capture, at least in outline, the variety of production and the character of this transitional period, it is worth reviewing the most important of them: Bullet de Chamblain, Le Blond, Dulin, Cartaud and Delamair.

Jean-Baptiste Bullet de Chamblain (1665–1726) was long overshadowed by the reputation of his father, Pierre Bullet. In Paris, his work was confined to the Hôtel Dodun and designs for the façade of Saint-Roch; his one historic contribution to architecture is the Château de Champs, to the east of Paris (1701–7). In this house, built for the rich financier Poisson de Bourvalais in a vast expanse of parkland, he created a new château or villa type derived from Vaux-le-Vicomte and the tradition of Pierre Bullet.[77] At Champs, the *corps de logis* reverts to the form of an isolated block, with short stub wings on the court side and a bowed projection on the garden side for the oval salon (Plate 52). The vestibule shares the central axis with this salon, and the two halves of the house display bilateral symmetry. The main staircase, however, is to one side of the vestibule and not – as at Vaux-le-Vicomte – beyond it, thus accommodating a full-width vestibule while allowing the salon to be stretched to a lengthwise oval.

A long succession of designs enables us to trace the evolution of this ground plan from Pierre Bullet's Château d'Issy (1681). One design in particular, probably made on a previous occasion for another owner of Champs, comes extraordinarily close to Issy both in plan and in elevation.[78] Pierre Bullet himself was involved in the design of Champs, as a number of drawings in his hand demonstrates; and the exterior, too, reveals typical characteristics of his art: rusticated window and door surrounds, segment-headed windows, the shape of the roof, etc. The court frontispiece, above all, with its superimposed orders of Tuscan columns and Corinthian pilasters, its busts, and its wide pediment, is almost identical to that of Issy.

Bullet de Chamblain's achievement lay in his interpretation of the sources, both in the well-balanced ground plan, in which by adding the wings he has transformed the model of Issy into that of Vaux-le-Vicomte,[79] and above all in the garden front (Plate 53). Its effect lies entirely in the power-

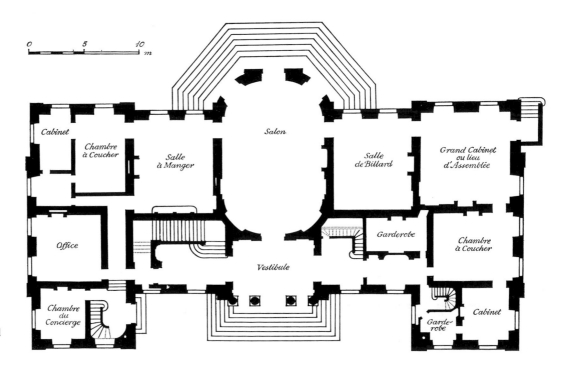

52 Bullet de Chamblain: Champs, 1701–7, plan of ground floor.

CHAPTER 5
Domestic Architecture in and outside Paris

THE LAST YEARS OF LOUIS XIV

Such private building activity as survived the economic catastrophe was concentrated in Paris, where Louis XIV's last years witnessed the emergence of a style that formed the transition to the new era. Its origins lay not only in the drift of polite society away from Versailles but also in the changes in society at large that accompanied and followed the War of the Spanish Succession. A new class of financiers, military contractors and profiteers appeared alongside the nobility and the upper bourgeoisie, and were joined by those who had made their pile as a result of Law's financial reforms. All were keen to put their money into houses and land, and to take their place within established society as quickly as possible. The old caste barriers, which had been showing signs of weakness even in the seventeenth century, crumbled still further, and a new public took over the dominant role in the evolution of taste.

The urban planning measures that had been taken by the crown – the building of the Place Vendôme, the opening up of the left bank of the Seine through the building of the Pont-Royal and the Hôtel des Invalides – acted as a powerful stimulus to private building activity. The world of high finance settled around the Place Vendôme, the nobility and senior officials in the new Faubourgs Saint-Germain and Saint-Honoré. These new suburbs on the edge of the city, with their greenery and fresh air, were sought after by all who desired to escape from the noise, noxious atmosphere and cramped conditions of the ancient city centre. The pace of development in the faubourgs was breathtaking. A comparison between the Gomboust (1652) and Turgot (1734) town maps will make this clear. The hôtels that were built there for the nobility are among the most precious inheritances that the eighteenth century has bequeathed to modern Paris.

The town mansion or hôtel *particulier* – the term hôtel was reserved for the residences of the nobility, and that of *palais* for princes of the blood royal – was not a new creation. As a building type, it had existed since the Renaissance, and there had been many important examples. In the eighteenth century, however, it was reorganized and rationalized: its layout was firmly defined and adapted both to the ceremonies of social life and to the practical needs of its inmates. The prototypes were supplied, above all, by J.H. Mansart – and by Daviler's *Cours d'architecture* of 1691, the most-consulted architectural manual of its day.[61]

The most popular formula was what was called the hôtel *entre cour et jardin*, built between a front court and a back garden. The court was flanked by side wings that contained the kitchens, stables and carriage houses. It was closed off from the street, and from the eyes of the public, by a high wall, interrupted only by the main gateway. The dwelling itself, the *corps de logis*, was built in strict accordance with a plan that reflected the rank of the owner. This involved three categories of accommodation: the *appartement de parade*, in which official receptions were held; the *appartement de société*, in which family and friends were entertained; and the *appartement de commodité*, where one could be alone with one's immediate family, or to which one withdrew in winter or in case of illness.[62] The *appartement de parade* was not on the first floor, as in an Italian *palazzo*, but at ground level, with direct access to the garden; the private rooms were on the first floor or in entresols, which were easier to heat in winter. Only such exalted persons as the royal princes had their state apartments on the first floor.

The ideal formula for the plan of such a house, as laid down by Daviler in 1691, retained its validity until the Régence. In the course of the century, however, the hôtel *particulier* underwent considerable changes, so that the ideal plan supplied by Jacques-François Blondel in his article for the *Encyclopédie* in mid-century already differed markedly from that given by Daviler.[63]

In Daviler, a short lengthwise axis led from the court, through the vestibule, into the salon and then to the garden. There were two parallel transverse axes: one, on the court side, takes in the staircase, vestibule and dining room; the other, on the garden side, was composed of the suite of rooms that made up the *appartement de parade*. The centrally placed salon, distinguished by its size and the richness of its decor, was a grand reception room, also used for such events as concerts and balls; and here the double-height salons beloved of the seventeenth century disappeared, to be replaced by the square or bow-fronted *salon de compagnie*. Galleries, too, tended to disappear, except in princely households. The most notable practical innovations were the provision of secondary rooms and closets and the new institution of a permanent dining room. The kitchens, storerooms and servants' quarters, which occupied the side wings of the court in larger houses, were in the basement in smaller ones.

For façades, Mansart set an enduring example with his Hôtel de Lorge (1697).[64] There, for the first time in a private house, he employed the coupled columns and the floor-length, arched windows that had previously been confined to châteaux and palaces, thus successfully endowing the house with a patrician air. Only a year later, the Swedish Minister in Paris, Nicodemus Tessin, sent a drawing of this façade to Stockholm; and in 1699 it was imitated in the Hôtel Buisson in Geneva.[65]

The round of new building in the Faubourg Saint-Germain was opened by Pierre Cailleteau, known as Lassurance the Elder (*c.* 1660–1724). Lassurance had been J.H. Mansart's draughtsman and right-hand man for sixteen years (1684–1700), and the Duc de Saint-Simon, who loathed Mansart, alleged that Mansart and de Cotte had kept him under lock and key (*sous clef*), and that he had given them all their ideas. Once Lassurance had acquired the title of *architecte du Roi* and opened his own practice, he became

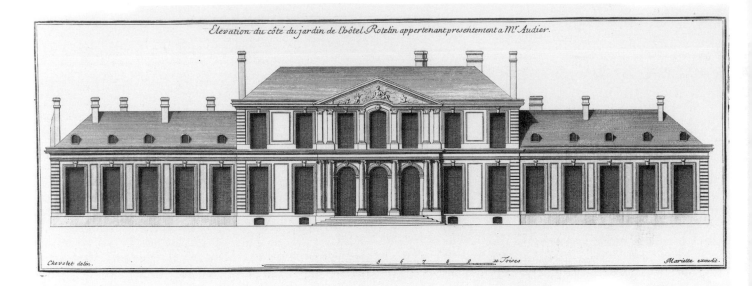

Chevotet delin.   6   6   7   8   9   10.*Toises*   *Mariette excudit.*

40   Pierre Lassurance: Paris, Hôtel de Rothelin, 1700, garden façade (Mariette, *L'Architecture Française*, pl. 182).

41   Pierre Lassurance: Paris, Hôtel Desmarets, 1704, garden façade.

42   Pierre Lassurance: Paris, Hôtel Desmarets, 1704, plan of ground floor.

43   Robert de Cotte: Paris, Hôtel d'Estrées, plan of ground floor (Mariette, *L'Architecture Française*, pl. 176).

one of the most important and most sought-after Parisian architects of his day.

Lassurance pursued the tradition of J.H. Mansart virtually unchanged: the long enfilades first used by Mansart in the Hôtel de Noailles in the town of Versailles; the low, markedly horizontal façades; the frontispieces adorned with pilasters and columns; and the divided roofs (Plate 40). Examples include the Hôtel de Rothelin (1700), the Hôtel de Maisons (1708), and the Hôtel de Béthune (also 1708). Similarly, his Château de Petitbourg (*c.* 1715), for the Duc d'Antin, harked back twenty years to Mansart's Château de Boufflers; the interior was a modernized form of the Château Neuf de Meudon, with a similar apartment for the king and guest apartments arranged along corridors on the first floor. One innovation of Lassurance's was the use of tall, narrow, compressed-looking windows, which became a stylistic hallmark of the Régence. He also departed from Mansart's precedent by using extra-high central windows and broken pediments.

After the Hôtel de Rothelin, an early work, Lassurance found his classic form in the Hôtel Desmarets (1704), in which he adhered closely to Daviler's formula (Plate 41, 42).

The two transverse axes of the *corps de logis* are now equal in depth, which alters their proportional relationship; and the relationship between the garden side, with five rooms, and the court side, with three, is more balanced. Two rooms that belong to the court enfilade in the Hôtel de Rothelin are here transferred to the side wings. On the garden side, the salon is clearly emphasized as a central feature; the room sizes progressively decrease from the centre outwards. The ground plan has thus become a clear, rhythmically articulated organism, into which secondary staircases, closets and small light-wells are integrated.

Such an ideal arrangement was rare. Mostly, Lassurance was forced into compromise either by the nature of the site or by his clients' wishes. But it was precisely the flexibility of his planning – as best exemplified by the Hôtel de Bêthune, where he had to put the *corps de logis* at right angles to the axis of the vestibule – that was the foundation of his fame and ensured that he never went short of work, even in his old age.

A true stylistic shift became apparent only in the work of Robert de Cotte. His importance as a builder of hôtels was long underestimated: only one of his town houses, the Hôtel

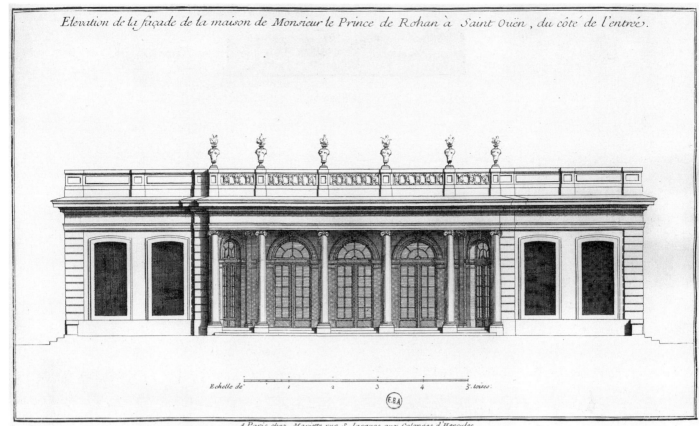

Elevation de la façade de la maison de Monsieur le Prince de Rohan à Saint Ouën, du côté de l'entrée.

Echelle de   1   2   3   4   5. toises.

E.B.A

A Paris chez Mariette rue S. Jacques aux Colonnes d'Hercules

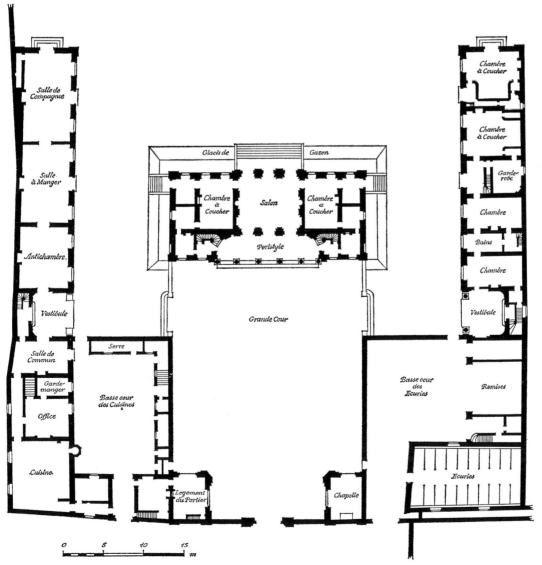

51 Germain Boffrand: Saint-Ouen, 1714–17, elevation and plan of ground floor.

Salle de Compagnie

Salle à Manger

Antichambre.

Vestibule

Salle de Commun

Garde-manger

Office

Cuisine.

Logement du Portier

Serre

Basse cour des Cuisines

Glacis de

Chambre à Coucher

Salon

Perlstyle

Gazon

Chambre à Coucher

Grande Cour

Chapelle

Basse cour des Ecuries

Chambre à Coucher

Chambre à Coucher

Garde-robe

Chambre

Bains

Chambre

Vestibule

Remises

Ecuries

0   5   10   15
     m

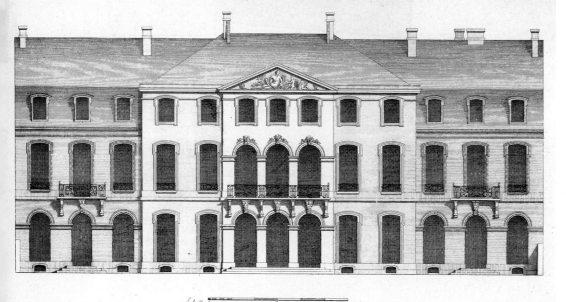

49 Germain Boffrand: Paris, Hôtel Amelot de Gournay, 1712, court façade.

50 Germain Boffrand: Paris, Hôtel de Torcy, c. 1715, garden façade.

right-hand wing, and the apartment reduced to essentials; it looks very much as if the two architects were working to completely different briefs.

The river front of the Arsenal (1715–25), the residence assigned by Louis XIV to the Duc du Maine, grand master of the artillery, is a composition of blocks animated only by a row of balconies. The decoration is concentrated in the roof zone; there, in lieu of a pediment, Boffrand employs a massive frieze, with metopes enriched with military emblems, and above it a balustrade crowned with stone cannons. The contrast between the sculptural enrichment at the top and the sobriety of the wall beneath lends the façade an unexpected tension that aroused the admiration of contemporaries.[74]

Finally, a special place in Boffrand's oeuvre is occupied by his work for the house of Rohan, one of the noblest and most artistically inclined families in France. Boffrand entered their circle in 1707 and maintained the connection through every phase of his creative life. One of his first assignments for them, in 1709, was the completion of the façade of the church of La Merci; in its unfinished state, this was spoiling the view from their newly built Paris residence, the Hôtel de Soubise, just opposite. Boffrand planned a completely new church, with a portal based on the formula devised by J.H. Mansart for the Dôme des Invalides, but had to rest content with reworking what there was of the seventeenth-century façade and building the upper storey in a more up-to-date style – thus losing the balanced effect of his own richly

47 Germain Boffrand: Paris, Petit Luxembourg, 1709–13, staircase.

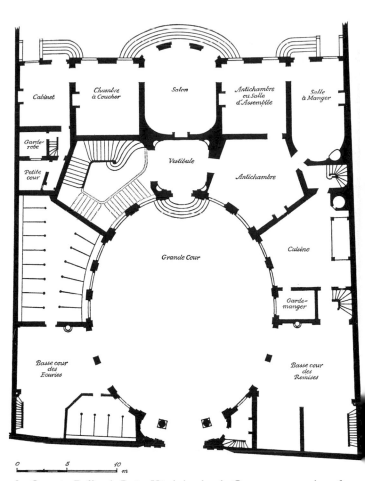

48 Germain Boffrand: Paris, Hôtel Amelot de Gournay, 1712, plan of ground floor.

Boffrand pioneered in hôtel architecture, is a model of the economical use of space (Plate 49); the concave court façade is complemented by rooms with curved and polygonal plans that were unfamiliar in Paris. These, once more, hark back to the Baroque phase of French architecture, to Le Vau and the young J.H. Mansart, creator of the Château du Val.

The Hôtel Amelot had no successors. In his other hôtels, Boffrand adhered to the rules; but even there he took his own line. The contrast between him and de Cotte found positively exemplary expression in his Hôtel de Torcy (1713–15), a building set apart from its fellows by its size and by its prominent position on the bank of the Seine (Plate 50).[73] Boffrand bought the site in 1713 and sold the house, almost finished, to the Marquis de Torcy, a nephew of the great minister Colbert. De Cotte also prepared a design for Torcy, although it is by no means certain that this was for the same site. Boffrand's house is a rectangular block, articulated only by the way in which the lateral parts fall back, in almost imperceptible steps, with increasing distance from the centre. Smooth and sparsely decorated, the wall surfaces abut with nothing to mark the transitions. On the garden side, as at the Hôtel Amelot, the seven-bay centre pavilion is one storey higher than the wings, and its diminutive pediment is restricted to the three middle bays.

This disproportion is entirely intentional, as is proved by the Hôtel de Seignelay (1716), built later on an adjoining section of the same estate but sold separately: there, with a similarly tall five-bay garden frontispiece, the pediment has disappeared altogether. In de Cotte's rival design, by contrast, the *corps de logis* was preceded by a *cour d'honneur* framed by two short transverse wings and two entrance pavilions; the entrance was emphasized by columns, the walls were animated by reliefs, and a large and well-proportioned pediment capped the façade.

In Boffrand's design the crescendo towards the middle is achieved not through decoration but by architectural means alone – in this case, through the multiple projections of the centre. No columns or pilasters are used at all. The decoration is limited to wrought-iron balconies on ornate consoles and ornamental keystones over the central windows. This sparseness of decoration, combined with the gentle curve of the heads of the windows, which counteracts the rigidity of the wall, lends Boffrand's façades a brittle elegance that impressed even de Cotte – as can be seen from the decorated keystones of the Hôtel du Maine.

In its plan, Boffrand's design is more generous than de Cotte's. The central axis, which leads by way of several sets of steps and through two large rooms, is strongly emphasized, as in his château designs; the staircase on the right-hand side is effectively displayed. On the first floor the central axis is occupied by a gallery. With de Cotte, by contrast, all was plainer and more intimate. The staircase was moved to the

axis, and no connection between the vestibule and the central salon, so that the visitor was compelled to take the long way round. This may well have been a precaution against unwanted callers; it certainly served to enforce the ceremonial sequence of the apartment.[68] The façade articulation retained some Mansart-inspired motifs (Plate 45), all of them probably derived from the Hôtel de Lorge, with its columns and coupled pilasters; by comparison with the Hôtel d'Estrées, this was undoubtedly a step backward.

One of de Cotte's few executed buildings of the same period is the Hôtel de Réauville (now Hôtel de Caumont) in Aix-en-Provence, which he designed for the President of the Parlement of Provence.[69] Its unusual square plan and its tallness are explained by the narrowness of the site. For the same reason, the staircase occupies the centre of the house, and the *appartement de parade* is arranged round it, while the ground floor is traversed by an axis that runs through a vestibule, the stair, and a light well behind. The court façade is very like that of the Hôtel de Torcy, although the old-fashioned pilaster articulation on the second floor is something that de Cotte had already dispensed with in his Parisian buildings. The design, which dates from 1714, was considerably altered in the course of building – presumably by the local architect in charge, George Vallon – so that it is hard to detect de Cotte's handiwork in it.

Among his most important hôtel commissions were the Hôtel du Maine (1716–19) and the Hôtel de Toulouse (c. 1715–19), both examples of the kind of princely town residence that came into fashion after the death of Louis XIV and the dissolution of the court of Versailles. Here de Cotte was in his element. The Hôtel du Maine, which had been started as a house for the Princesse de Bourbon-Conti, was sold before completion to the Duc du Maine, the eldest of Louis XIV's legitimized natural sons. It was an enlarged and princely version of the Hôtel d'Estrées. As the young Claude Mollet was also engaged on the project, it is not always easy to identify de Cotte's work; however, the plan of the *corps de logis* was certainly his. The *appartement de parade*, with its chapel, was on the first floor, and there were two other five-room apartments on the ground floor. The two floors were linked by a grand staircase, with its own hallway leading into the vestibule. On the façade, as at Meudon, the orders had entirely disappeared, to be replaced by a balcony on sculptured consoles. Only the decor of busts was reminiscent of Versailles.

The Hôtel de Toulouse was the splendid house of the second of Louis XIV's legitimized sons, the Comte de Toulouse. It was not a new building but a remodelling of François Mansart's Hôtel de la Vrillière; and it is now the headquarters of the Banque de France.[70] As the exterior was not to be altered, de Cotte confined himself to rebuilding the interior and redesigning the main court, where he replaced the original entrance with a closed frontispiece and flanking columns. Into François Mansart's building he inserted two state apartments, one on the ground floor and one on the first floor, linked by a magnificent staircase, thus proclaiming the owner's exalted rank.

As grand admiral of the fleet, chairman of the council of the navy, master of the royal hunt and governor of Brittany, the Comte de Toulouse held some of the greatest offices of state. This showed itself not only in the state apartment on the first floor (Plate 46) – guardroom, grand antechamber, state chamber, grand salon, bedchamber, cabinet, council chamber with built-in chapel – but also in the iconographic programme that ran through the house, dominated by the dual themes of seafaring and the chase. It dominated the vestibule and staircase, with symbols of the four continents surrounded by grappling irons and hunting trophies above the doors, and also the Salle des Amiraux, with its portraits of seventy-three French admirals. There were even model ships scattered through the rooms. Here, for the last time, a complete iconographic programme in the Baroque sense was achieved. On the ground floor, the Salle des Rois alluded to the owner's royal parentage. Although the regent was always at pains to keep Louis XIV's bastards away from the business of state, he was unable to prevent Toulouse from making an unequivocal political demonstration in his own house.

Boffrand, too, was an important builder of hôtels; and in these, as in châteaux, he was the polar opposite of de Cotte. He countered linear harmony with solid blocks, continuous rhythm with contrast. He worked mostly for the Parisian aristocracy of office-holders, but also occasionally for the upper nobility, whom de Cotte also counted among his clients; so it sometimes happened that both were involved with the same project. But since Boffrand had more time to concentrate on private commissions, he built considerably more than his rival.[71] He built many houses on his own account, as speculations; and he was among the most active participants in the property speculation of the postwar years, in which the entire Mansart school took part.

As a builder of hôtels, Boffrand was both more imaginative and more inventive than de Cotte, and did not shrink from the Baroque effects that the Mansart school generally avoided. Prime examples include the Petit-Luxembourg and the Hôtel Amelot. At the Petit-Luxembourg (1709–13), which he transformed from a plain sixteenth-century hôtel into a princely residence for the Duchesse de Bourbon-Condé, the tripartite vestibule has for a backcloth a magnificent staircase (Plate 47), inspired by Saint-Cloud, which is the true nucleus of the house.[72] The first-floor apartment is arranged around this, and leads on into an elegantly arranged *appartement de commodité*. The oval dining room, adjoining the staircase, harks back to Le Vau. Its ring of eight internal columns, each backed by a pilaster, is a straight lift from the corner salons of Le Vau's 'envelope' design for Versailles (1669).

The Hôtel Amelot (1712), by contrast, has the oval as its basic form (Plate 48). All the parts of the house are arranged around an oval court, in a graduated progression from the open arcades of the side courts by way of the low wings to the dominant *corps de logis*, the stages in the progression being defined by massive horizontal cornices. The *corps de logis*, with a giant order of pilasters, looms abruptly over the wings without benefit of pediment – an unheard-of departure for the Mansart school – and forms a compact block that anticipates the Hôtel de Craon in Lunéville. Both the oval court and the giant pilasters are borrowings from Le Vau, who had used them similarly in the Hôtel de Lionne. But, as so often in Boffrand's work, we are also compelled to assume that he had looked at Bernini.

The annular layout of the *corps de logis*, a feature that

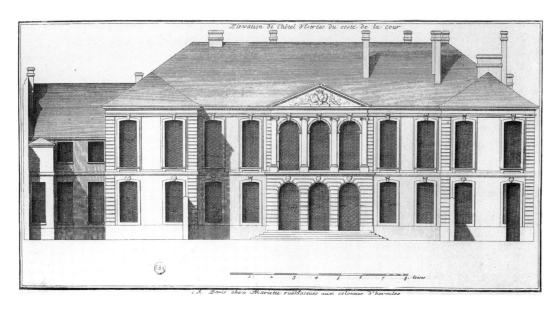

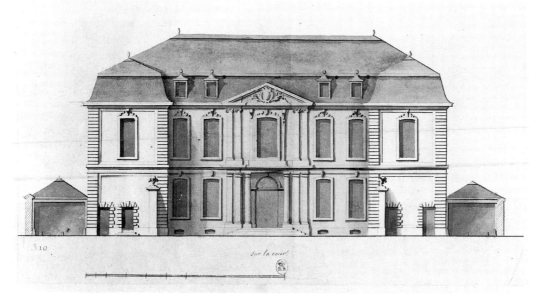

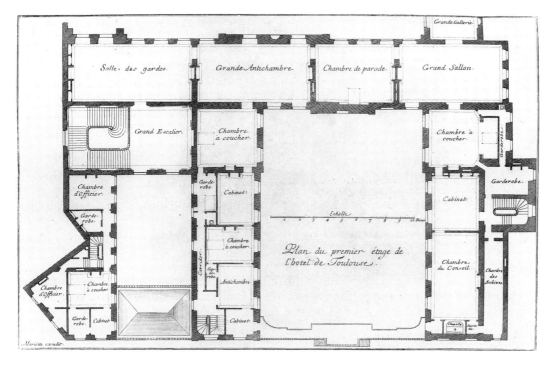

44 Robert de Cotte: Hôtel d'Estrées, 1715, court façade.

45 Robert de Cotte: Paris, Hôtel de Torcy, *c.* 1715, design for courtyard façade, *c.* 1715 (Paris, Bibliothèque Nationale).

46 Robert de Cotte: Paris, Hôtel de Toulouse, 1715–19, plan of first floor (Mariette, *L'Architecture Française*, pl. 112).

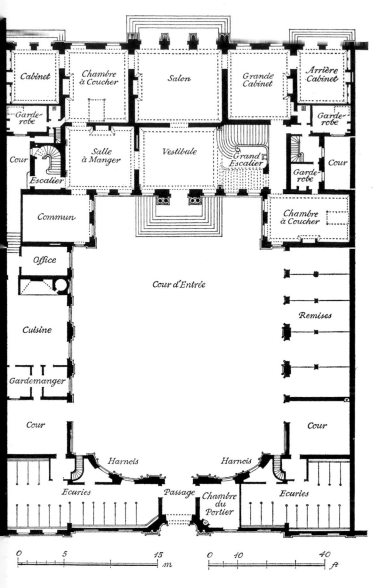

Cabinet — Chambre à Coucher — Salon — Grande Cabinet — Arrière Cabinet
Garde-robe — Garde-robe
Cour — Salle à Manger — Vestibule — Grand Escalier — Cour
Escalier — Garde-robe
Commun — Chambre à Coucher
Office
Cuisine — Cour d'Entrée — Remises
Gardemanger
Cour — Cour
Harnois — Harnois
Écuries — Passage — Chambre du Portier — Écuries

0 5 15 m · 0 10 40 ft

The court-side transverse axis of the *corps de logis* thus ran to its full length. A concern for *commodité* was revealed, on the other hand, by the closets at both ends of the apartment, with their backstairs access to the servants' quarters. A pointed allusion to the owner's exalted rank was the installation of a second *appartement de parade*, complete with chapel, on the first floor.

In its dignified restraint, the façade (Plate 44) illustrates the gulf that separated de Cotte from Lassurance, but also from Mansart. The columns have disappeared, and the ground floor is completely devoid of ornament; the first floor has a simple pilaster motif. Narrow strips of rustication express the structure of the building. The street frontage, too, derives a rhythm from rustication, and from a pair of pavilions to house the coachman and the porter. The front wall of the court curves inward to create a stage-like forecourt which neatly masks the oblique placing of the house in relation to the street and simultaneously protects the gates from damage.

Most of de Cotte's hôtel designs were of the same type. One group of *c.* 1715 that calls for special mention is exemplified by his design for the Hôtel de Torcy, done in competition with Boffrand.[67] All followed the formula of the hôtel *entre cour et jardin*, with abbreviated side wings of the kind customary in château building, and a plan resembling that of the Hôtel d'Estrées. In this group, however, the main entrance was mostly placed in the *corps de logis*, where it and the staircase formed a spatial entity. There was no lengthwise

d'Estrées, is still standing, and even this has been altered. But the countless plans and designs that he left behind him at his death bear witness to intensive activity in this field.[66] His position and his great experience meant that his advice was sought on all sides. Accordingly, there are numerous alternative designs by him for works designed by other architects – including, for instance, the Hôtel de Torcy and the Palais Bourbon. His main field of operation was Paris, but he also supplied designs for the provinces, including the Hôtel de Grammont in Besançon (1714) and the Hôtel de Caumont in Aix (1720). Schooled in the atmosphere of Versailles, his style was marked by stately façades, imposing enfilades and grandiose staircases. He therefore became, primarily, the architect of the nobility and of royal princes.

His first work, the Hôtel du Lude (1710), still looked very old-fashioned, with its long enfilades in a shallow *corps de logis*. But only three years later, at the Hôtel d'Estrées (1713), he achieved the tranquil equilibrium that stamps all his later work (Plate 43). The plan harked back to the Hôtel Desmarets; however, the main staircase, prefaced by an antechamber, had moved to the left-hand wing, and the right-hand wing, opposite, contained the subsidiary entrance.

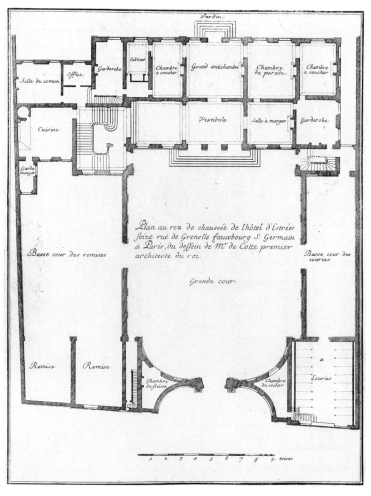

Jardin
Garderobe — Cabinet — Chambre à coucher — Grand antichambre — Chambre de parade — Chambre à coucher
Salle du comun — Office
Cuisine — Vestibule — Salle à manger — Garderobe
Gardemanger
Basse cour des remises
Plan au rez de chaussée de l'hôtel d'Estrées seize rüe de Grenelle fauxbourg S. Germain à Paris, du dessein de M. de Cotte premier architecte du roi.
Basse cour des écuries
Grande cour
Remise — Remise — Chambre du suisse — Chambre du cocher — Écuries
1 2 3 4 5 6 7 8 9. toises

junction with narrow, modern windows, a broken pediment and elegant keystones.

In 1716 the Russian General Lefort, in Paris as the emissary of Peter the Great, recruited Le Blond as chief architect to the Czar. In that capacity, despite the extensive plenipotentiary powers that the Czar devolved upon him, he achieved little. His ambitious plan for the expansion of St Petersburg fell foul of the powerful Prince Menshikov, who forestalled him with a plan of his own. His designs for Strelna also remained unexecuted, and his premature death in 1719 prevented him from completing his palace of Peterhof; his design was later altered to the point of unrecognizability by Bartolommeo Rastrelli.[83]

Another who was slow to break away from the Mansart model was Nicolas Dulin. Mariette credits him with two hôtels, the Hôtel d'Etampes and the Hôtel Sonning (c. 1711), and two country houses; but contemporary tourist guides reveal that he built far more. He, too, combined traditional elements of façade design – tablets, busts, large pediments – with modern roofs à l'italienne. His ground plans, practical in their arrangement and rendered flexible by the use of secondary staircases and closets, were surprisingly modern. In his Maison Dunoyer, for the first time, the kitchen was brought into the corps de logis alongside the dining room, a revolutionary innovation. In the Maison Galepin, a villa at Auteuil, almost square in plan and with pediments on all four sides, the ground floor was made up of four reception rooms, and the first-floor rooms were grouped around the central, top-lit, double-height salon à l'italienne. These innovations, including the salon in the centre of the first floor, were carried to Geneva by Dulin's pupil, Jean-François Blondel, when he was invited to move there in the 1720s. The town and country houses that he built there – Maison Mallet, Maison Lullin, Maison Cramer, and others – are based on the French formula.

One of the members of the Roman-minded entourage of the Duc d'Orléans, the future regent, was Silvain Cartaud (1675–1751). Cartaud made his name by working for the banker and art collector Pierre Crozat, known – to distinguish him from his far wealthier elder brother, who built the Hôtel Crozat on the Place Vendôme – as 'Poor' Crozat. In Italy, the younger Crozat had acted for Orléans in purchasing the collection of paintings that had once belonged to Queen Christina of Sweden; and, like the duke, he maintained close contact with modern artists. On his return from a visit to Rome in 1704, Cartaud built him a house that incorporated an art gallery; Piganiol de la Force praised it as one of the pleasantest and most remarkable in Paris.

It was built like a Roman palazzo around a small court: Jacques-François Blondel thought this a 'stroke of genius'. It was nevertheless prefixed by a cour d'honneur, but this was one to which the house turned not its longer but its shorter side, so that the whole length of the building, articulated by very slight projections in lieu of wings, could extend into the garden. The ground plan was correspondingly oriented lengthwise (Plate 54). A wide central axis traversed a stately vestibule, articulated by wall piers and niches, and a stair-chamber, to the inner court. To either side lay an apartment, reduced to three rooms, neatly graded in size to express their relative importance, and all with a view of the garden.

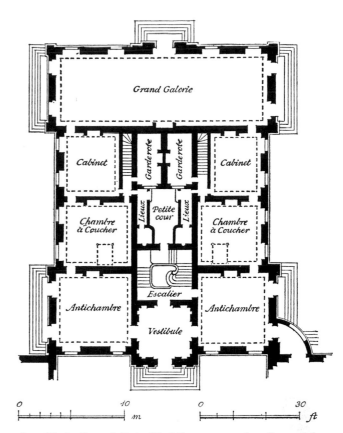

54 Jean-Silvain Cartaud: Paris, Hôtel Crozat, 1704, plan of ground floor.

Small secondary rooms were arranged around the court, so that the living rooms remained undisturbed by domestic activity. A gallery ran across the full width of the far end, to accommodate Crozat's celebrated collection. The first floor included two further gallery rooms, and numerous guest rooms for the artists who enjoyed the hospitality of the house: Lafosse, Oppenord, Watteau and others lived there for years.

Also for Crozat, Cartaud built a château on the estate at Montmorency that had formerly belonged to the painter Le Brun; the banker bought it in 1709. This was to look like a Roman palazzo, so Cartaud gave it a compact rectangular form without wings, and with a giant order all round, as on Michelangelo's Capitoline Palaces. The façades were broken by a polygonal projection for the vestibule, on the court side, and a wide bow for the transverse oval of the central salon, on the garden side. The interior had a Roman grandezza. The double-height garden salon was similar in design to that at Vaux-le-Vicomte. It had the same pilaster articulation, with caryatids supporting a painted dome. The upper floor was split into two halves by a long spinal corridor; like that of Crozat's town house, it consisted of numerous guest rooms for artists.

The brilliance of these two buildings earned Cartaud a commission from the regent to undertake extensive rebuilding work at the Palais-Royal, on which he was kept busy for the rest of his life. He still undertook some private commissions, but without ever achieving the originality of his earlier works.

55 Alexis Delamair: Paris, Hôtel de Soubise, 1704–7, court façade.

A final representative of this period between *la magnificence* and *le goût moderne* was Alexis Delamair (1676–1745), a talented artist who once seemed to have a great future, but who was the victim of his own obstinacy and cantankerousness. A product of de Cotte's office, he never ceased to live in the world of Louis XIV. This is already apparent in his first work, the Hôtel de Chanac-Pompadour (1704), with its façade burdened by columns, mural busts and trophies. Elector Max Emanuel of Bavaria invited him to Munich, but war supervened, and he never went. Delamair's big chance came with the remodelling of the historic Hôtel de Guise into the Hôtel de Soubise, one of the grandest of the patrician mansions that stood in the heart of Paris.[84] Prince François de Rohan-Soubise bought the large site in 1704, and (apparently after first consulting J.H. Mansart) he followed the recommendation of his younger son, Armand-Gaston, the future Cardinal, and gave the commission to the youthful Delamair.

In order to keep as much of the old Hôtel de Guise as possible, while replacing the old Gothic west gateway with a new and dignified front, Delamair turned the direction of entry through ninety degrees, placed the new *cour d'honneur* on the site of the old riding school to the south, and set a new façade in front of what had been the side elevation of

the Hôtel de Guise (Plate 55). To reduce the size of the court, he inserted a wide colonnade with a hemicycle at the gate end, like the one designed by Pierre Delisle for the Hôtel de Souvré (the seat of the Grand Prior of the Knights of Malta, in the Temple quarter). Such a colonnade was already old-fashioned, and Delamair was able to keep it only against the determined opposition of the princess. He continued its rhythmic motif of coupled columns across the façade, where those of the lateral bays support plinths on which Robert Le Lorrain's figures of the *Four Seasons* sit enthroned. In the centre, the coupled columns form the lower tier of a double portico on a regal scale. With its array of columns and sculptures – which originally included a coat-of-arms on the pediment – this composition of court and colonnade, rounded off by an equally ornate street gateway, is a showpiece of the first order. It was much admired in its own day, when it served to proclaim the wealth and magnificence of the house of Rohan; but it did so in the style of an earlier age.[85]

Inside the house, Delamair was not to be deflected from his idea of inserting into the *corps de logis* of the old Hôtel de Guise, which lay end-on to the new façade, a single, long enfilade with central doors and a view through to the garden beyond. In this, however, he was opposed by his client's

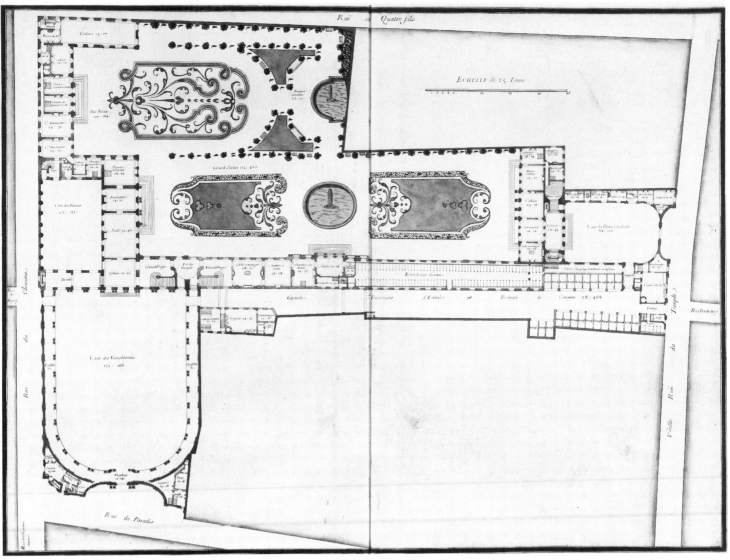

56 Alexis Delamair: Paris, Hôtel de Soubise and Hôtel de Rohan, project to connect the two properties, *c.* 1705. (Munich Staatsbibliothek, *Recueil Delamair*, 1714).

eldest son and heir, Hercule Mériadec, who, as a member of the younger generation, detested long enfilades on the Versailles pattern. Delamair had already incurred the wrath of the princess with his colonnade, and these planning proposals were the last straw. Discharged in 1707 on the grounds of invincible obstinacy, he was replaced by Boffrand, whom he never forgave.

Delamair's work was not confined to the Hôtel de Soubise. His protector, Armand-Gaston de Rohan, had simultaneously entrusted him with the building of his own house, on the same Paris estate. This is the Hôtel de Rohan, later celebrated for its library, which became the favoured resort of the scholars of the day. Here, again, Delamair supplied a façade that must have looked decidedly old-fashioned, with its decor of columns and urns. The Hôtel de Rohan (1712) was intended to form the point of departure for a further grand design that was to join the whole estate into a unified whole (Plate 56). The garden front of the Hôtel de Soubise, which was at right angles to the court front, was to be matched in height and in proportions to the Hôtel de Rohan, which faced it across a large formal garden consisting of a parterre with a central pool. In line with the garden front of the Hôtel de Soubise, but beyond a line of trees, an almost identical façade was to be built in order to pull together the irregular elements of the old Hôtel de Guise, otherwise known as the Hôtel de Clisson. This in turn would be fronted by a similar garden. A long, two-storey range containing a gallery, an *appartement d'apparat* and – at the junction with the Hôtel de Soubise – an additional staircase, was to connect the two family hôtels, the Hôtel de Soubise and the Hôtel de Rohan, and round off the composition. Its central portion would bear a slightly modified repetition of the two garden fronts. The result would have been a magnificent architectural complex, as large as the Palais-Royal, and unmatched anywhere in Paris. But it was never executed.

Even after his dismissal from the Hôtel de Soubise, Delamair retained the Cardinal's confidence, and thus also the responsibility for completing the Hôtel de Rohan. He was not employed either at Saverne or in Strasbourg, but he worked for years on the extension of the stable block at the Hôtel de Rohan, for which Le Lorrain provided the celebrated groups of horses. But he never again worked on a major building project. He dedicated a compilation of his works to the Elector of Bavaria, but nothing came of it. Embittered, unemployed, and clearly suffering from a persecution complex, Delamair devoted the rest of his life to attempts at self-justification. In his books, *Procuration curieuse* (1731), *Le Songe et le réveil d'Alexis Delamair* and *La Pure*

57 Gilles-Marie Oppenord: Design for the stables of the Duc d'Orléans, *c.* 1720, façade (*Grand Oppenord*).

Vérité (1737), he denounced everyone in sight, and Boffrand and de Cotte in particular, for intrigue and ignorance; but the truth was that he himself had failed to comprehend the needs of the age.

RÉGENCE ARCHITECTURE

In the second decade of the eighteenth century, a new generation appeared on the scene and defined the style of the Régence. A series of major artistic undertakings gave the *goût moderne* a sharper and more independent profile, so that the example of J.H. Mansart gradually faded. The system as a whole was still the same, but it was increasingly accompanied by new forms. The salient feature of the Régence is therefore its transitional character. By the 1720s, the structural pattern of the building had begun to dissolve into optical and decorative effects, and the result was the *style pittoresque*.

One of the principal representatives of the Régence, though more as a decorator than as an architect, was Gilles-Marie Oppenord (1672–1742), an outsider who added an entirely new component to the Parisian art scene. Oppenord was a member of the entourage of Pierre Crozat, which formed the opposition to the conservative Mansart school. The son of a Dutch cabinetmaker,[86] he had lived in Rome in his youth. When he took service with the regent he was already forty-three years old, though he had achieved nothing worthy of mention. Overshadowed during the lifetime of J.H. Mansart, he found himself suddenly in the limelight at the opening of the new reign.[87]

Oppenord's name is principally associated with the remodelling of the Palais-Royal. Cartaud was nominally in charge, but his artistic contribution was negligible; Oppenord's was incomparably greater. He made the Palais-Royal into the starting point of a new trend, and this not only defined the look of the Régence period but founded a new 'Orléans style', entirely independent of the king's court.

Oppenord had formed his style in the course of his seven years in Rome; but there the crucial influence was not the art of antiquity but Francesco Borromini and the Roman Baroque. He had also absorbed the influence of North Italian Mannerism, and that of Pellegrino Tibaldi and Galeazzo Alessi as well as of Palladio. Back in France, he combined this inheritance with the French tradition; the resulting style was a highly idiosyncratic mixture of French and Italian elements.[88] Oppenord's background did not lie in architecture but in craftsmanship; and so what interested him in Borromini was not so much the architectural as the decorative and sculptural aspect. From Northern Italy he took the use of layered recession, the combination of organic and inorganic forms, and the often harsh, block-like quality that brought his drawings and buildings close to the *style rustique*. An example of his use of multiple recession was the unexecuted design for the regent's stables (Plate 57), in which rough rustication alternated with classical architectural members, a basket arch cut deep into the sculptures on a pediment, and lions lurked in dens hollowed out beneath the balcony. This was a concentrated expression of the anticlassical thread that ran all through Oppenord's work. Similarly, his numerous designs for garden architecture, most notably for the Elector of Cologne,[89] had a curiously hybrid look, with their contrasts between French elegance and Italian monumentality, and their liberal use of columns, pilasters, domes and curved roofs.

Oppenord's influence was greater in decoration than in architecture. With its constant interplay of natural and mineral, animate and inanimate forms, his ornamental style reduced monumentality to playfulness, setting the seal on the Régence and paving the way for the Rococo (Plate 58). He was a draughtsman of genius; Blondel called him 'one of our greatest draughtsmen'. His extant designs run into thousands,[90] but in most of them architecture gets short

58 Gilles-Marie Oppenord: *Grand Oppenord*, title page, *c.* 1710.

59 Gilles-Marie Oppenord: Paris, Palais Royal, design for the corner salon, 1719–20.

shrift. His strength lay in decoration and in ornamental composition, as exemplified by his designs for the celebrations held at Villers-Cotterêts on the occasion of Louis XV's return from his coronation in Reims.

At the Palais-Royal, Oppenord's principal responsibility was for the remodelling of the interior. He added two rooms to the regent's personal apartment: these were a circular study and the so-called Galerie en Lanterne, for the collection of paintings. At the same time (1716–17), he gave a new look to J.H. Mansart's Galerie d'Enée by adding a suitably grand conclusion in the shape of a huge, richly draped, mirrored overmantel above a marble chimneypiece, flanked by two obelisks hung with trophies.

Two years later, in 1719–20, he created the celebrated corner salon (Plate 59). This room, known to contemporaries as the Salon d'Oppenord, or, because of its top lighting, the Lanternon, occupied the right angle between the Grands Appartements of the *corps de logis* and the Galerie d'Enée; in it, as in Le Vau's Salon Oval in the Louvre, two spatial axes met. Oppenord made it into an oval, so that it pierced the line of the external walls, with one end jutting out on a console over the Rue de Richelieu – a piece of structural audacity that attracted much attention.[91] With its markedly

smaller upper storey, the sides of which had to be made straight for structural reasons, this oval was no doubt a reminiscence of Borromini's interiors. The basket arches of the window heads also had precedents in Borromini, and in the architecture of Northern Italy; this was a form that had been extinct in France ever since François Mansart had used it in the Chapelle des Minimes and in his design for Blois.

Despite his fame and success, Oppenord had no luck with his buildings. A sizeable extension to the Hôtel Crozat, which he built around 1720, caved in. His crossing tower at Saint-Sulpice overloaded the vault, and he had to demolish it. None of his executed work of the 1720s was significant, or bore comparison with that of other architects.[92] The trouble with Oppenord was that statical calculations were not his forte; nor did he have much respect for the stringent rules of taste. As a result, he never stood a chance in open competition.

In the building of Parisian hôtels, the Régence period laid particular weight upon variety of planning and on the development of *commodité*; and in this the lead was taken by three members of the younger generation, Mollet, Courtonne and Aubert. Armand-Claude Mollet (*c.* 1670–1742) descended from a family of gardeners, and had held the post of a comptroller in the Bâtiments du Roi under J.H. Mansart. He made his name with the stately Hôtel d'Evreux (1718) (Plate 60), which he built for the son-in-law of 'Rich' Crozat, one Louis-Henri de la Tour d'Auvergne, Comte d'Evreux (this house is not to be confused with the Hôtel d'Evreux on the Place Vendôme, by Pierre Bullet). Brice called Mollet's Hôtel d'Evreux one of the most splendid in Paris, one that combined grandeur with *commodité* and exemplified the perfection of French architecture. In 1753 it was acquired by the Marquise de Pompadour; under the name of Palais de l'Elysée, it is now the official residence of the President of the French Republic. The *corps de logis* has only short, pavilion-like wings, but there is a vast *cour d'honneur*, with kitchens tucked away on one side and large stables and carriage houses on the other. The weighty decoration of the court façade is markedly reminiscent of Champs, probably because of the first owner's historic connection with Bullet de Chamblain. The round-arched window openings of the end pavilions are very different: the mouldings that run round them without imposts are an innovation on Mollet's part, and a sign of the incipient disintegration of the structural articulation of the wall. At the Galerie Neuve (now a part of the Bibliothèque Nationale), which Mollet started in 1719 for John Law and his bank, but which was abandoned when the client went bankrupt, these same mouldings recur throughout the façade.[93]

The interior of the Hôtel d'Evreux reveals the same coexistence of disparate styles. While the sequence of the rooms in the *corps de logis* was still designed to be entirely traditional in character, and thus purely for show – the two antechambers were themselves preceded by a Grande Salle – the left-hand pavilion was adjoined by a small, comfortable private apartment with a garden and entrance of its own. This was not the first time this had been done: at the Château de Stains (1714), which had the same short stubs of wings as the Hôtel d'Evreux, Mollet had placed self-contained three-room apartments on the first floor. Tradi-

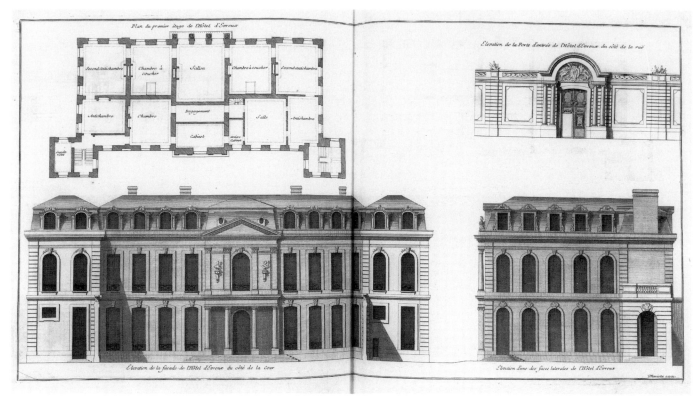

60 Armand Mollet: Paris, Hôtel d'Evreux, 1718, plan and elevation (Mariette, *L'Architecture Française*, pl. 117).

61 Jean Courtonne: Paris, Hôtel de Matignon, 1720–4, plan of ground floor.

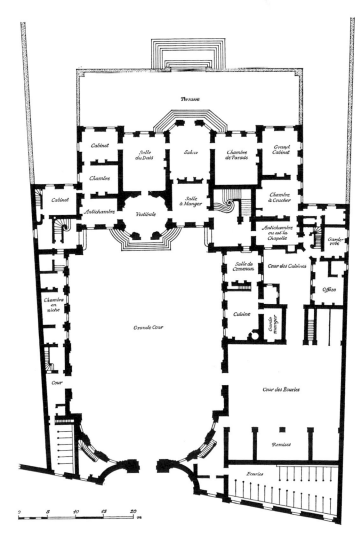

tionally, the bathroom had been sited either in the orangery or near the kitchens, for convenience of heating; in the Hôtel d'Evreux it was in an isolated position near the stables. In the Hôtel d'Humières (1715), for the first time, Mollet placed it close to the bedrooms.

Mollet was very much the practical architect; by comparison, his contemporary Jean Courtonne (1671–1739) was more of a theorist. Mariette mentions only two hôtels by him: the Hôtel de Noirmoutier and the Hôtel de Matignon. There are also a number of extant designs for interior decoration and a theoretical work, *Traité de la perspective pratique avec des remarques sur l'architecture* (1725), which embodies Courtonne's extensive theoretical knowledge. In 1730 he took a professorial appointment at the Academy. At the Hôtel de Noirmoutier (before 1720), he was fettered in every respect by the instructions of his client, so that he could contribute little of his own. Shortly afterwards, in the Hôtel de Matignon (1720–4), he had more of a free hand; and the result was one of the finest mansions in the *noble faubourg*.[94]

Matignon is most remarkable for its plan (Plate 61). To cope with the irregular site and the large stable block, which did not permit a symmetrical layout, the centre of the narrow court façade is two bays to the left of that of the wider garden front. Courtonne made use of this axial displacement to create an interlocking rhythm in the two façades, each with its own strong central accent: the oval vestibule on one

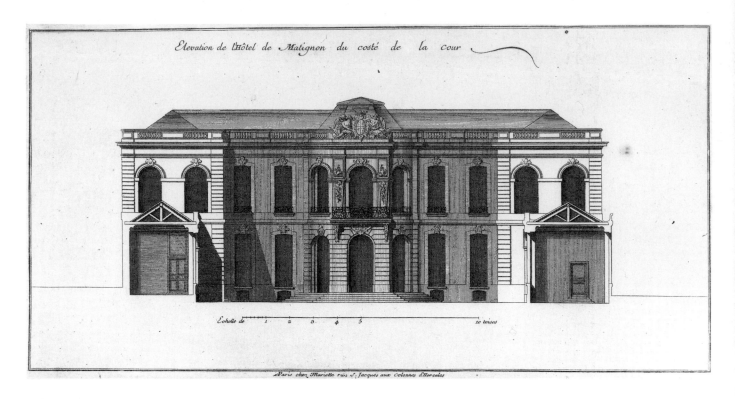

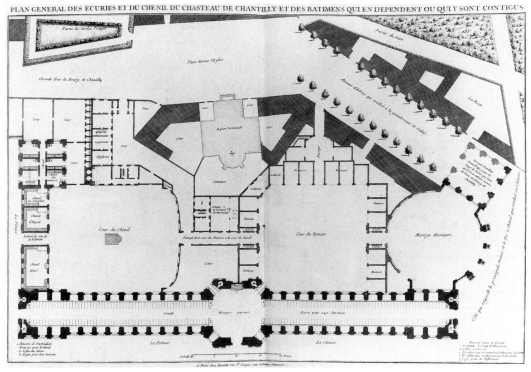

62 Jean Courtonne: Paris, Hôtel de Matignon, 1720–4, courtyard façade (Mariette, *L'Architecture Française*, pl. 204).

63 Jean Aubert: Chantilly, stables, 1721–35, plan (Mariette, *L'Architecture Française*, vol. v).

64 Jean Aubert: Chantilly, stables, 1721–35, façade.

side and the salon with its polygonal projection on the other. The ground plan compensates for this displacement through an ingenious division of space: next to the vestibule is a dining room that also serves as an antechamber both for the staircase and for the salon, and thus interlocks the two parallel lengthwise axes.

The major features of the plan are reflected in the elevations, as Courtonne himself demanded in his *Traité de la perspective pratique* (Plate 62). The exterior is an array of tall, narrow windows; and a comparison with Champs reveals how much lighter architecture had become in the intervening

twenty years. Another modern feature of the elevations is the sculptural decor, here concentrated on the court frontispiece, where it takes the form of balcony consoles, elaborate balcony grilles, festoons on the wall piers, and large armorial cartouches on the roof balustrade. Sculpture thus takes on an entirely new significance, usurping the role formerly played by architectural articulation. This is particularly evident in the baluster-shaped panels above the balcony, in which a structural solid has turned into a decorative plane, without a vestige of its load-bearing function.

This gradual spread of decoration, and the invasion of the

wall by decorative keystones and balcony consoles, is typical of the architecture of the 1720s. It is already apparent in the small town house in the Faubourg Saint-Germain that the Swiss banker Hoguer employed François Debias-Aubry to build for the actress Charlotte Desmares in 1720; here the 'classical' articulation of the court façade contrasts with the modern decorative garden façade.[95]

Outside Paris, there is another excellent example at Beaumont-sur-Vingeanne (1724), in Burgundy, a villa built by a (presumably) Paris-trained architect for Abbé Claude Jolyot. The articulation of the façade is reduced to rusticated strips, and the real accents are provided by the keystones, the pediment and the massive and richly sculptured consoles, which take the place of pilasters.[96]

The most successful architect of the younger generation was Jean Aubert (c. 1680–1741), whose name is principally linked with the house of Condé. Aubert had worked as a draughtsman under J.H. Mansart, on whose recommendation he had been admitted to the Academy at an early age. After the Surintendant's death, however, he left the Bâtiments du Roi and entered the service of the Duc de Bourbon-Condé, for whom he began by supervising re-modelling work at Chantilly.[97] His great moment came when the duke made a huge speculative profit on Law's shares and embarked on a major programme of improvements at Chantilly that included both the interior remodelling of the Petit Château and the building of a new stable block. Aubert had all the right qualifications for the Petit Château, in that he was an expert draughtsman and had presumably been employed on decorative work at the royal châteaux. His

remodelling of the Petit Château, to which we shall return later, is one of the outstanding decorative achievements of the Régence.

The stable block, the Grandes Ecuries (1721–3), pre-sented a vastly greater challenge, and one that demanded a sure sense of proportion. The irregular ground plan of the main château itself, and its moat, meant that the stables could not simply be integrated with its domestic offices, and so they had to be built as a detached building on a separate site. They also had a prestige function to perform. Bourbon-Condé was the president of the council of regency, one of the most powerful men in France, and a grandson of Louis XIV. There was thus an element of rivalry with Versailles. Aubert rose to the occasion; and the stables at Chantilly are the most monumental creation of the Régence period, anywhere in France.[98]

The plan is a combination of a rectangle and a trapezoid (Plate 63). It links two courts, one for the kennels and one for the carriage-houses, with an open riding circuit or Manège. The common lengthwise axis is aligned on the position of the Grand Cabinet du Duc in the now-destroyed Grand Château, just as the Grandes and Petites Ecuries at Versailles are aligned on the Chambre du Roi. The riding circuit swings out at one end of the trapezoid in a grand, curved, open arcade, lavishly adorned with statuary, which Aubert used as a monumental frontispiece to face the château. The long external elevations, with their rustication, their array of uniform, recessed, round-headed windows, and their balustraded parapet, are reminiscent of the Orangerie at Versailles, from which they differ only in the

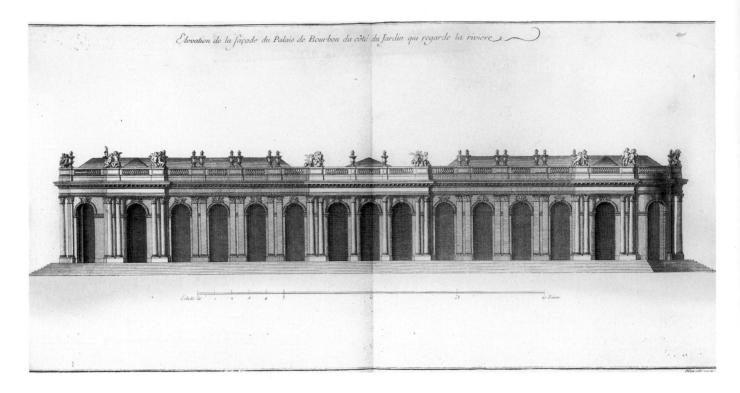

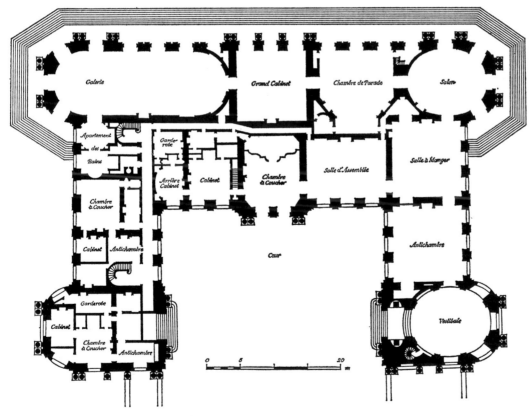

65   Pierre Lassurance and Jean Aubert: Paris, Palais Bourbon, 1722–5, garden façade.

66   Pierre Lassurance and Jean Aubert: Paris, Palais Bourbon, 1722–5, plan of ground floor.

67   Jean Aubert: Paris, Hôtel de Biron, 1728–30, garden façade.

high mansard roofs used for servants' quarters (Plate 64). The wings are held together by a vast centre pavilion modelled on the rear pavilion of the Versailles stables. It was originally crowned by an equine sculpture in lead, the *Cheval de la Renommée* or 'Horse of Fame', an imitation of Antoine Coysevox's figures at Marly; inside is a large, circular hall that was used as an indoor riding-school.[99] The tunnel

vaults of the wings, resting on transverse arches, are another borrowing from the Orangerie at Versailles.

The decoration is an essential part of the look of the exterior. It is concentrated on the centre pavilion, the riding circuit arcades, and the entrance to the kennel court. The principal motifs are of horses and hounds; the lively and spirited designs are by Aubert himself, and the execution

by Rémy-François Bridault. This decor endows the huge building with a liveliness and elegance that by far outdoes its counterpart at Versailles. It was a contemporary quip that there were monarchs in Europe who were worse housed than this duke's horses and hounds.

Aubert also had a hand in the magnificent town house of the dowager duchess, the Palais Bourbon (1722–9). Several architects had worked on this remarkable, open site on the banks of the Seine; the building has nothing but its name in common with the present home of the French parliament. Initially, in 1722, the duchess employed an Italian, Giovanni Giardini, with instructions to imitate the most modern palazzi of Florence and Rome. When Giardini died in the same year, she turned to Lassurance the Elder, who himself died two years later, and also consulted de Cotte, several designs by whom exist.[100] Aubert took over in 1726; and, 'unfortunately,' as Piganiol de la Force remarked, 'the best came last.' The building contracts show that he was responsible only for the execution, not for the design.

However, it is impossible to tell exactly what it was that Aubert inherited from his predecessors. Brice observed that Giardini's project, unlike the palace as built, was two-storeyed; and so the street elevation, with its pair of flat-roofed, two-storey gatehouses, may well have been his. However, the layout of the forecourts and the overall form of the building were undoubtedly the work of Lassurance. This is confirmed not only by the literary evidence of Mariette and Blondel but by the form of the façade, with an articulation of columns and pilasters very similar to that of the Hôtel de Pussort, built a few years earlier. The single-storey garden front (Plate 65), with its coupled pilasters and its balustraded parapets and urns, was reminiscent of the Grand Trianon at Versailles, a building that the duchess – very much the daughter of Louis XIV – would have known since childhood. Aubert's hand is visible in the lavish use of statuary, and in the large lunette above the projecting

frontispiece on the court façade; this corresponded to that on the centre pavilion at Chantilly, and incorporated the emblem of the Sun King, a rising sun with the signs of the Zodiac.

Preceded by two courts with extensive stables, this was a palace on a royal scale throughout.[101] Its plan (Plate 66), with the four projecting ovals that mark off the *corps de logis* from the side wings and transform the ends of these into independent pavilions, was unusually animated for Lassurance and extremely progressive for its time. The internal planning, in which Aubert will have had the principal say, was a masterly reconciliation of princely ceremonial with domestic comfort. The entrances were in the ends of the wings, as prescribed by de Cotte in both of his designs. The magnificent *appartement de parade* occupied the whole of the right-hand wing and the river (garden) side of the *corps de logis*, where it terminated in an elongated oval gallery. Both changes of direction were covered by ovals. On the court side, a parallel transverse axis led from the dining room into the apartment of the duchess herself – whose bedchamber lay, as at Versailles, in the centre of the court façade – and was given external emphasis by coupled columns and by Aubert's lunette. The whole left-hand wing was occupied by private apartments. It was a neat mosaic of bedrooms, cabinets, closets, and backstairs, including a 'bathing apartment', and included the usual entresol for the servants above. A long, narrow corridor was inserted between the two principal axes of the *corps de logis*, so that the domestics did not need to pass through the state rooms. Every scrap of space was used to the full. Even in the triangular spaces at the corners of the salons there were little stairs and closets. Such were the innovations that led Blondel to regard the Palais Bourbon as the birthplace of modern domestic arrangements, and as the glory of French architecture.[102]

Like an echo of its great prototype, the delightful little Hôtel de Lassay (1726–9) was built by Aubert next door for the Duchess's constant companion, the Marquis de Lassay. It was later known as the Petit Bourbon, and is now the Speaker's residence, the Présidence de la Chambre des Députés. Devoid of columns and pilasters, and indeed of all historical allusions, this small house, with its combination of display and domesticity, its simple, clearly articulated elevations, its single-storey structure and its parapet statuary, was more like one of the newly fashionable villas, pavilions or *folies* than an hôtel *particulier*. The later addition of an upper storey utterly destroyed its character.

The tendency to dissolution of outline, already visible in the Palais Bourbon, is maintained in the Hôtel de Biron (1728–30), one of the most celebrated houses in the Faubourg Saint-Germain (it is now the Musée Rodin). This, too, belonged to the Condé circle: Aubert built it as a status symbol for a former wigmaker called Peyrenc de Moras, who had enriched himself on the stock market, had risen to become *chef de cabinet* to the Duchess, and now felt himself to be a part of the princely house of Condé.[103] The house, which has now lost its *cour d'honneur* and side wings, betrays the influence of the Palais Bourbon. There the wings terminated in pavilion-like, projecting bays: here the garden front does the same (Plate 67). By providing a counterweight to the ornate frontispiece, which breaks forward only slightly, these bays lend movement to the whole elevation. As at the Hôtel de Lassay, and at Chantilly, the continuous rustication helps Aubert to gloss over the underlying structures, blurring the hard edges of the terminal pavilions to give the effect of soft curves. This lends added prominence to the decorative

accents: the balcony with its large consoles, the relief in the pediment, and – originally – the statuary along the cornice. The architectural emphasis is becoming optical and decorative rather than functional.

As at the Hôtel de Matignon, the plan can be read off from the façade. It exhibits bilateral symmetry: to either side of the central axis formed by the vestibule and salon, an apartment extends in the prescribed sequence along the garden front and back along the side of the house. The two suites meet in the large central salon, and, as at the Palais Bourbon, oval salons in the corner pavilions ease the change of direction. With its rhythmic variations in the size and shape of the rooms, this is a supremely rational piece of apartment planning.

The Hôtel de Biron stands on the threshold between the Régence and the Rococo; it also marks the end of the first period of hôtel-building in Paris. In 1731, the year of its completion, the Faubourg Saint-Germain reached the city boundary, beyond which no building was permitted.

Aubert's last work was the rebuilding of the Cistercian Abbaye de Châalis, where he took up the tradition of the great eighteenth-century Benedictine monasteries. Intended as a large quadrangular composition, Châalis never progressed beyond the palatial entrance wing that contained the abbot's lodging. Begun in 1739, the works were halted in 1745 for lack of funds and never resumed. What now exists conveys a very imperfect idea of the magnificence of the composition planned by Aubert, which was reminiscent of Chantilly in many ways.

CHAPTER 6

Decoration

LEPAUTRE AND BOFFRAND

In eighteenth-century architecture, decoration counted for more than ever before. In France, however, it was concentrated on the interior; only in the final phase of the *goût moderne* did it invade the external elevations, and then not to the same extent as in southern Germany or in Austria. In eighteenth-century France, interiors actually became far more important than exteriors. They manifested not only the true character of the house but also – and more importantly – the social standing of its owner. Theorists – Blondel foremost among them – were at one with practising architects of the rank of de Cotte, Boffrand, or Oppenord in paying the closest attention to interior decoration; and no architectural history would be complete without it.

As the *goût moderne* took over, the orders disappeared from interiors, along with high, painted ceilings and marble revetments. The walls were now lined with wooden panelling, with carved ornaments. The articulation consisted in a system of wall panels – *panneaux* – that embraced the doors as well as window embrasures and chimneypieces. The harmony of white and gold on the walls, the white plaster ceilings, and the tall windows, made the rooms seem airy and light. Dark corners were regarded as a crime against good taste.

In interior decoration, as in all else, the *goût moderne* began at Versailles. In setting up the Ménagerie for the young Duchesse de Bourgogne, Louis XIV stipulated not only a rejuvenation of thematic content but a looser and more rhythmic panel system for the walls. To this was added, from the turn of the century onwards, a widespread interest in Jean Bérain's arabesque and ribbonwork ornament. A pupil of Le Brun's, Bérain had been the leading master of decorative arabesque since the 1680s.[104] As *dessinateur de la chambre et du cabinet du Roi*, in charge of commissioning the craftsmen employed by the King's Revels or Menus-Plaisirs, he exerted a decisive influence on the style of court decoration. His engraved designs circulated all over Europe and provided an inexhaustible fund of ideas for architects and decorative artists. Bérain had pruned back Le Brun's luxuriant formal vocabulary to a linear interplay of curves consisting of an elegant pattern of tendrils with figurative scenes interspersed. A prime feature of his ornamental style was the C-scroll (the so-called *bec de corbin*, or billhook), which he developed out of the fleshy acanthus growths of Le Brun.

The decisive step of translating Bérain's ribbonwork ornament into three dimensions, and incorporating it into the panelled structure of the wall, was taken in several different contexts. The pioneer was Pierre Lepautre (*c.* 1648–1716), son of the engraver Jean Lepautre and a nephew of the architect Antoine Lepautre. The crucial turning point, which marked the advent of the new style in decoration, came in 1699, when J.H. Mansart took Lepautre into his office as a draughtsman and engraver. Lepautre was no longer a young man; he had already worked for Perrault, Daviler, Bérain and others. But this was his chance to inaugurate a new stylistic epoch.

Lepautre caused an immediate stir with his very first designs for chimneypieces at Versailles and Marly (1699), and his decorations for the Grand Trianon (1702–3); they were imitated at once.[105] In the Marly chimneypieces (Plate 68) he appropriated Bérain's formal repertoire – the C-scroll, mirror frames with concave, volute-like curves, delicate plant tendrils curling over the tops of mirrors, scrolled ribbonwork rising palmette-like at the ends of pilasters, as well as central rosettes and mosaic backgrounds in the flat of the wall. By adding three-dimensional relief to all these previously two-dimensional forms, he injected a new rhythm into the existing system of mural decoration. At Versailles, surviving examples of the origins of the style are the Chambre du Roi, the Salon de l'Œil-de-Boeuf (Plate 69), and parts of the Cabinet du Conseil (*c.* 1700).[106]

The keynote of the Salon de l'Œil-de-Boeuf is set by the deep, gold mosaic coving, with its playful putti; but the new arabesque and ribbonwork style is in evidence on the doors, in the wall panels under the large paintings, and in the soffits of the arched window embrasures. Other signs of the general relaxation of form are the concave corners of the mirror frames and the wide arches of the shallow chimneypieces, which have replaced the strict, boxlike shape. Only the window reveals still have the plain white panels previously customary.

In Lepautre's Trianon designs (1703), the new style emerged for the first time as a coherent system (Plate 70). The framework was formed by narrow, ceiling-high wall panels over a low skirting, thus creating a new vertical emphasis that was to prevail in wall articulation until the end of the century.[107] These panels alternated with windows, mirrors and paintings in a carefully judged rhythm; and the linear structure thus set up was relaxed somewhat by a relief decoration of patterns derived from Bérain. In the centre of each panel was a large rosette; in the corners and on the short sides were arabesques and C-scrolls, spreading out across the flat surface. The round heads of the windows and mirrors, and the oval frames of the paintings, caught up the whole wall system in a rhythmic undulation that also embraced the mirror frames beneath the paintings.

In the choir stalls of Orléans Cathedral (1702–6), carved by Le Lorrain and Jules Degoullons but probably designed by Lepautre, this system is transferred into religious art. The small wall panels are adorned with reliefs of liturgical subjects, and paintings have been replaced by oval medallions with effigies of saints. The cornice above is supported not by pilasters but by consoles that flank the round-headed panel frames. The novelty of this decoration lies in the dominance

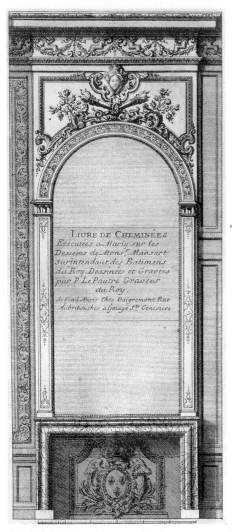  

68   Pierre Lepautre: Design for three chimney-pieces for Marly, 1699.

of the oval medallions and the consistent rounding of the panels, with their relief ornament, so that a chain of curves, accompanied by delicate arabesques and floral festoons, runs through the whole choir.

The further course of this development can be traced in the chimneypiece designs by Lepautre that Le Blond published in his new edition of Daviler's *Cours d'architecture* in 1710. Here the surround mouldings have become thinner and lighter, and the straight lines are mingled with curves. The decorations over the mirrors, developed from Bérain's baldachin motifs, have dwindled into segmental arches with concave corners. In the wall panels above, cartouches entwined with tendrils and festooned with flowers are framed by graceful, often curvilinear mouldings. The chimneypieces themselves have also become lighter, and their marble mantels and consoles have joined in the play of curves.

Until his death, Lepautre remained the leading decorative designer of the Service des Bâtiments. Both J.H. Mansart and de Cotte recognized his outstanding abilities, and he was entrusted with all the major decorative commissions of the age. As both were indifferent draughtsmen, Lepautre was responsible for the actual designs, so that his influence on the decorative side was far greater than that of his principals.

Among his masterpieces is the organ case in the palace chapel at Versailles (Plate 71). In formal terms, this is a novel creation in every way. Although the main features of its decoration had been established by the turn of the century, it acquired its true character and its real value only through the statuary that was added in 1709–10. Lepautre might have found a source for his seated genii in the military church of Saint-Louis des Invalides; and the David playing his harp in the central panel derives from an engraving by Antoine Lepautre after Domenichino (1689). What was entirely new, however, was the palm trees that adorn the corners, and which here make their first appearance in decorative art. In its sculptural emphasis and its exuberant decoration, this organ is a shining example of the *goût nouveau*.

At Versailles, enrichments still tended to be on the heavy side (as with the carved door panels of the chapel); but in Paris and its environs there appeared a number of decorative ensembles of great lightness and elegance. This applies in particular to the (now destroyed) decorations of the Château de Bercy (1712–15).[108] There the wall panels were overlaid with a delicate linear pattern, and Bérain's loops of ribbon-work had given way to delicate tendrils, which increasingly reached out from the edges of the panel towards the centre

69   Pierre Lepautre: Versailles, Salon de l'Œil-de-Boeuf, 1701.

82   Jean Aubert: Chantilly, Petit Château, 1722, Salon de Musique.

the achievement of a younger generation: Oppenord, Aubert and Jacques V Gabriel. Oppenord's works have already been described. Jacques V Gabriel, in his hôtels on the Place Vendôme – Hôtel de Parabère (1719–21) (Plate 81), Hôtel Peyrenc de Moras (1723–4), and others – combined Lepautre's panels with Boffrand's arcading and a system of decorative detailing that had the capacity to wrap itself round corners. As a result, the unity of the room as a whole was maintained, but the wall surface as such set up a new rhythm, held in a state of suspended tension, that was the exact opposite of Lepautre's equilibrium. The ascending arabesques of the wall panels, taken over from Oppenord, and the floral festoons in the spandrels, direct descendants of Boffrand's C-scrolls, were unprecedented in their lightness. At the Hôtel Peyrenc de Moras,[126] the wall panels were painted with grotesques by Audran and Nicolas Lancret, set in ornate surrounds that looked like mirror frames in reverse. As Gabriel here had at his disposal the Versailles woodcarving team of Degoullons, Pierre Taupin and A.J. Le Goupil, his decorations were of a distinctly superior quality.

A first step in the direction of asymmetry was taken by Bullet de Chamblain at the Hôtel Dodun (c. 1722), where,

in the Grand Cabinet, he arranged his wall panels in pairs, in such a way that their upper edges combined into a single concave curve, which was filled by a large oval medallion.[127]

After all the alteration and destruction that has taken place at the Palais-Royal and in the Galerie Dorée, Aubert's schemes at Chantilly and in the Hôtel de Lassay are the best-preserved decorative ensembles of the Régence. At Chantilly, the decoration of the Petit Château was begun in 1718 and was ready to receive the young king after his coronation in Reims in November 1722. In this, presumably in deference to instructions from on high, Aubert toed the Service des Bâtiments line. He adhered to the conventional system of wall division, with its unbroken linear continuity (Plate 82). But, as at the Hôtel de Bourvallais, the panels have become large, continuous surfaces, the central rosettes and medallions have developed into autonomous motifs, gilded arabesques reach far out across the panel from both sides, and the mirror and door frames are softly curved. The coving, above all, has undergone a fundamental change; the decoration has sprouted beyond it. In the corners, and half-way along the walls, the massive cornice is surmounted by magically light cartouches and medallions made up of gilded

70 Pierre Lepautre: Trianon, design for the king's apartment, 1703.

71 Pierre Lepautre: Versailles, chapel, the organ, 1709–10.

72 Pierre Lepautre: Bercy, 1712–15, grand salon.

(Plate 72). The general relaxation of form had also overtaken the surrounds of the panels, which acquired an aesthetic value of their own through subdivision into thin, parallel mouldings that bounded the ornamental zone and eased the transition between one plane and another. The panel itself now advanced towards the viewer in multiple levels of relief, culminating at the centre in either a rosette or the frame of a medallion.[109]

This stratification of relief, and the tension between three-dimensional ornament and plain surface, constitutes the essence of this decorative style, and the fundamental distinction between it and anything Italian. The only point of comparison is not the Italian Baroque, with its sculptural consistency, but the similarly stratified French ornament of the late Gothic and the Renaissance.[110] At Bercy, the architectural pattern of the wall was maintained, but the faces of the pilasters were recessed and ornamented: a first sign of impending dissolution. The traditional ceiling cornice with modillions – as still used in the Salon d'Hercule at Versailles – had given way to an ornamental coving, with friezes of putti and the newly fashionable female masks.[111]

The transposition of Bérain's decorative style into three dimensions was not exclusive to Lepautre but common to the whole generation of the school of Mansart, although no other designer achieved equal prominence. In this as in much else, Boffrand took a decidedly individual line, and his style is clearly distinct from Lepautre's.[112] For Boffrand, the unit was not the wall but the whole room. In his major decorative ensembles of the early years of the century – the Petit-Luxembourg (1710), the Arsenal (c. 1715), La Malgrange (after 1711) – great arcades pulled the space together and subordinated doors, windows and mirrors

to a regular rhythm.[113] He applied the same system to the restoration of Lunéville after the fire.[114]

Boffrand located the focus of his decor not – as Lepautre did – in the centre of the wall panels but in the spandrels between the wall arches. This was a principle first applied by J.H. Mansart in the gallery at the Grand Trianon. A string of ornate spandrels runs around the Salon at the Petit-Luxembourg like a wide band of gold above the red velvet of the wall hangings (Plate 73). At the Arsenal, where the windows are wider apart, Boffrand converted this into a wide band of relief, with connected scenes from the life of Alexander the Great, and incorporates the semicircular overdoors into the arcading. The unity thus achieved is further emphasized by rounded corners and a slightly vaulted ceiling. With few exceptions, Boffrand never adopted Lepautre's use of panels but maintained the seventeenth-century practice of keeping the actual wall surface, above its low dado, free for hangings, tapestries or paintings. Taken as a whole, his system of decoration – Mariette speaks of his 'masculine taste' (goût mâle) – is architecturally oriented and more rigorous than de Cotte's.

In his choice of motifs, too, Boffrand went his own way, very much closer to Bérain than to Lepautre. Not only his principal motif – the linked C-scrolls entwined with palmettes and festoons, which fill the spandrels at the Petit-Luxembourg and the covings for La Malgrange – but also the figurative motifs, the winged sphinxes and fabulous beasts seated on pedestals, the herms and female heads of the mirror frames at La Malgrange, all derived from Bérain's repertoire of forms. Boffrand probably came closest to him in the large areas of painted arabesque that he used both in the Cabinet of the Petit-Luxembourg and at La Malgrange.

73 Germain Boffrand: Paris, Petit Luxembourg, 1710, Grand Salon.

By contrast, he made very sparing use of the large central rosettes beloved of Lepautre and de Cotte, and he never used gold mosaic at all. In his hands, the cornice, which de Cotte accentuated with modillions or female faces, became a running ornamental frieze; only in an early work, the staircase of the Petit-Luxembourg, was this punctuated – as in the Salon de Mars at Versailles – by helmets above the pilasters.

There is little trace of stylistic evolution in Boffrand's decorative work. His mouldings became thinner, and the mirror frames richer; they began to incorporate segmental arches with concave curves in the corners, surmounted by lofty C-scrolls; but his wall panels remained flat and rectilinear, and the linear flow remained continuous. Even at La Malgrange, the precedents of the Grand Siècle still held good. In the double-height salon (Plate 74), the atlantes with heraldic shields that supported the upper balconies were straight out of Bérain's and Le Brun's repertoire; they are to be found in an almost identical form on the ceiling of the

Galerie d'Apollon at the Louvre. In a feminine guise, they reappear on the arcading at the Arsenal. Again, the compact, pendant trophies that adorned the walls of the upper storey, each beneath a light floral festoon, were taken from Le Brun. This was a grand but conservative style, which treated decoration as subordinate to architecture. It was only with great hesitation that Boffrand followed the contemporary trend towards the dissolution of visible structure.

RÉGENCE DECORATION

With the Régence, the *goût moderne* entered a new phase. Two new factors were decisive here: firstly the painted grotesque ornament of Watteau, Claude Audran III and Claude Gillot, and secondly the influx of new artistic talent from the Mediterranean countries, which brought with it a strong sense of three-dimensionality and an interest in figurative representation.

The protagonists here were Oppenord, working for the

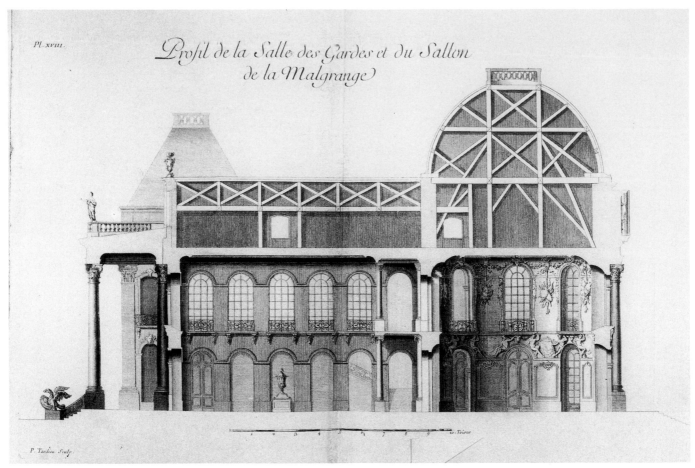

Pl. XVIII.

*Profil de la Salle des Gardes et du Sallon
de la Malgrange*

P. Tardieu Sculp.

74 Germain Boffrand: Malgrange I, Grand Salon, decoration, 1711
(Boffrand, *Livre d'Architecture*, pl. XVIII).

regent and his circle, and François-Antoine Vassé (1681–
1736), working for the Service des Bâtiments. Oppenord
was a product of the Rome of Borromini; Vassé was from
Provence. In Toulon, the birthplace of Pierre Puget, he had
worked on the Arsenal; he was employed on the decoration
of the Versailles chapel from 1706 onwards, and a few years
later on the remodelling of the choir of Notre-Dame de
Paris. In 1713 he became *dessinateur général de la Marine*; in
1723 he became a member of the Academy.[115] Another
Provençal was the ornamental and figurative woodcarver
Bernard Toro (1672–1731), who lived in Paris for a number
of years. His volumes of engravings, published there in
1716 under the title of *Dessins à plusieurs usages*, included
cartouches, trophies and – for the first time – rocailles, in
wildly animated, swirling forms of great sculptural vigour.[116]

Those closest to the regent were unanimous in their
enthusiasm. But the abandonment of the hitherto prevalent
two-dimensionality was also accepted by de Cotte; and in
1708 Vassé entered the Service des Bâtiments, initially under
Lepautre and, after the latter's death, as the leading
decorator. Vassé and Oppenord were responsible for the
most important decorative ensembles of the Régence. Both
exerted a strong influence on subsequent developments, with
the result that two separate streams came into being, and
these persisted until the advent of the *style rocaille*.[117]

Oppenord's first decorative works were designs for altars
in the choirs of Notre-Dame (1699) and Saint-Germain des

Prés (1704). These remained entirely under the influence of
their Roman prototypes.[118] Later – in his altars for Amiens
and for Saint-Jacques de la Boucherie in Paris (1712) –
Oppenord reverted to French patterns, but he never adopted
Lepautre's system. At the Hôtel de Pomponne (1714), his
first major private commission, he filled the wall panels with
scenes of rustic life and the chase, constructed on purely
pictorial, still-life principles, which were worlds apart from
the contemporary decorative work of de Cotte, as exemplified
by the Hôtel de Grammont in Besançon. Oppenord's ornaments were basically grotesques and arabesques after Audran
and Gillot, translated into relief. The panel system of the
wall remained intact, but the ornament had completely
emancipated itself from the geometrical structure. There can
be no doubt that it was this seemingly magical freedom in
Oppenord's work, as well as his currently fashionable Roman
background, that made him so attractive to the regent.

Oppenord made his public debut at the Palais-Royal,
where at first the Italian influence was still clearly detectable,
not only in individual elements – the strong mouldings,
the distinct levels of relief, the strongly three-dimensional,
sharp-edged cartouches,[119] the lavish use of statuary – but
also in the generalized, monumental quality of the work.
This culminated in the end wall of the Galerie d'Enée
(1717) (Plate 75), where a pair of trophy-hung obelisks
flanked a chimneypiece surmounted by a huge mirror;
on the mantel, groups of putti supported many-armed can-

Tom. V.   Pl. LV.

DECORATION DE LA GALLERIE DU PALAIS ROYAL, VUE DU COTÉ DE LA CHEMINEE.

Blondel del.   le Roi Sculp.

Echelle de 1   2 Toises.

75 Gilles-Marie Oppenord: Paris, Palais Royal, Galerie d'Enée, 1717.

76 Gilles-Marie Oppenord: Paris, Palais Royal, Grands Appartements, 1720, detail of a design for boiseries (*Grand Oppenord*).

Porte pour le Sallon cotté · IV.   Huquier Sculp.

delabra. Above the mirror, two genii bore aloft an armorial cartouche from which a gathered curtain was draped. The entablature, supported by fluted pilasters, was adorned with three-dimensional spread eagles. Roman memories also surfaced in the designs of the Galerie en Lanterne and the Salon à l'Italienne, with their cartouches, obelisks and statuary; here Toro's cartouche designs may well have exerted an influence.

Still at the Palais-Royal, Oppenord's slightly later remodelling of the Grands Appartements was more restrained and more French in character (Plate 76). The ornaments became more delicate and more two-dimensional, the outlines more animated and more nervous. Here the outspread bat wings, the figurative medallions and the general preponderance of natural elements, unmistakably reveal the influence of Gillot's and Audran's grotesques. From the same source came the panel and medallion frames made up of festoons of tendrils and flowers, or of undulating, curved mouldings, that relaxed the architectural rigidity of the panelling system. Mirrors and fireplace surrounds were adorned with female heads, the so-called *têtes en espagnolette*.[120] Taken together, these features represented a major proportion of the Régence ornamental repertoire. Finally, a foretaste of the Rococo appeared in the transformation of shellwork into rocaille, which was done either by hollowing out and relaxing the Louis XIV shell form or by inflating mirror and panel surrounds into shell-like forms reminiscent of grotesque ornament.

Vassé's answer to the Galerie d'Enée at the Palais-Royal was the Galerie Dorée at the Hôtel de Toulouse (1718–19), in which he showed himself to be Oppenord's greatest rival.[121] The Galerie Dorée was the final phase of the

remodelling of the Comte de Toulouse's Paris residence: it was his picture gallery, housed in a range specially built by François Mansart, and it marked the climax of the iconographic programme of seafaring and hunting that ran through the entire house (Plate 77).

This was Vassé's major work, albeit one in which he had yet to shake off the influence of Oppenord. As far back as his first individual commission, the choir of Notre-Dame, the angel figures at either end had been imitated from Oppenord's angels at Saint-Germain des Prés. In the case of the Galerie Dorée, the prototype was the Galerie d'Enée. Vassé has imitated it by giving an oval termination, articulated by pilasters, to Mansart's originally rectangular gallery. In the Baroque opulence of the scheme, and in the distribution of the sculptural accents – such as the horn-blowing huntsmen in the canted corners, or the many-armed candelabrum – he follows Oppenord's example. His drawings show that at the far end he initially intended to repeat Oppenord's large heraldic cartouche of Bourbon fleurs-delis, and to flank this with fluted pilasters and pendant trophies of seafaring and hunting. In the event, he replaced the cartouche with a ship's prow and the trophies with figures of two of the Seasons, in niches. The other two Seasons occupy corresponding positions at the entrance end of the gallery, which is devoted to the chase. The leaves of the door are carved with hunting trophies, and the overdoor lunette is filled with leaping hounds, in the round. Above, a set of antlers project into the room and the entablature originally featured recumbent figures of Diana and her nymphs.

The sides of the gallery (Plate 78), and the vault, are occupied by paintings trimmed to fit the built-in frames. Along the walls, which are articulated by tall pilasters, the paintings alternate with windows on one side and with mirrored niches on the other. The effect is overwhelming; the succession of huge, doubly incurved frames sets up an all-pervading, vibrant rhythm that embraces the paintings and fills the whole room.

This gallery was not an isolated case. The alternating arrangement and the doubly incurved frames were a frequent combination in de Cotte's work; they appear in the design for the Buenretiro wing of the Schloss in Bonn, in a gallery design for the Landgrave of Hesse – possibly for Tilburg – and in another for the Salon du Grand Maître at Versailles. However, the formula was never used to such effect as here. The carved cartouches with their hunting trophies, and the large medallions of the Labours of Hercules, are of extraordinary sculptural power; and even the swelling at the bases of the pilasters reveals a new sculptural feeling. The Galerie Dorée is the last of the great French galleries. In its overall arrangement it is related to the Galerie d'Apollon at the Louvre; but with its advanced ornamental forms – especially in the cartouche frames and on the pilaster bases, where rocaille forms already appear – it stands between the Régence and the Rococo.

In the Galerie Dorée, Vassé – who must take the credit for the design – had shown himself to be a match for Oppenord. And in the long run it was Vassé, with his firmer roots in French tradition, who was the more influential of the two – in the Service des Bâtiments, at any rate.[122] On the other hand, Oppenord enjoyed the protection of the

77 François-Antoine Vassé: Paris, Hôtel de Toulouse, Galerie Dorée 1718–19, chimney-piece (Mariette, *L'Architecture Française*, pl. 447).

regent, and so he initially enjoyed the larger commissions. He supplied decorative designs to the Elector of Cologne for his palace in Bonn and later for his hunting lodge of Falkenlust, near Brühl (1728). At Saint-Sulpice he provided elegant interior plasterwork for the transepts and sacristy. Of all his numerous private commissions in Paris, only one has survived: this is the Hôtel d'Assy (1719; now part of the Hôtel de Soubise) (Plate 79). There, many features of the Palais-Royal reappear; but the wall articulation, with its arcading and its emphasis on the spandrels, comes close to Boffrand, though markedly more advanced than Boffrand's contemporaneous work.[123] Not only do the spandrels, with their points rounded off, set up a regular undulating movement in the upper zone of the walls; the overdoors, framed in palm fronds and contracted into a trefoil shape, have detached themselves from the encircling arches to become autonomous elements of airy lightness. Oppenord's influence can be seen not only in the Hôtel de Villeroy (c. 1720), by

78 François-Antoine Vassé: Paris, Hôtel de Toulouse, 1718–19, Galerie Dorée, wall decoration (Mariette, *L'Architecture Française*, pl. 448).

79 Gilles-Marie Oppenord: Paris, Hôtel d'Assy, Salon, 1719 (detail).

80 Robert de Cotte: Paris, Hôtel de Bourvallais, Grand Salon, 1717.

81 Jacques Gabriel: Paris, Hôtel de Parabère, Grand Salon, 1718–20.

Claude Guillot-Aubry – an almost literal repeat of the Hôtel d'Assy system – but also in the Hôtel d'Evreux (1723), where the splendid trophies in the Grand Salon, designed by Jules-Michel Hardouin and carved by Michel Lange, are very close to his style.[124]

By contrast with Oppenord's profusion of ideas, Vassé's later work seems comparatively conventional. In this, however, one must bear in mind the conservative attitude of de Cotte, who laid down the guidelines for the decorative work. As far as the Service des Bâtiments was concerned, Lepautre's formula held good. It governed the decorative work that was done in the Buenretiro wing in Bonn (1717), at Saverne (1721–2), at the Hôtel de Bourvallais (c. 1717) and even in de Cotte's own house (1721–3).

The sole surviving example is the Hôtel de Bourvallais, which de Cotte remodelled and redecorated in 1717, when it became the Chancellerie de France (Plate 80); it has the same pilasters with recessed ornament as at Bercy, five years earlier, and the same S-curved tops to the mirror frames as at the Hôtel de Lauzun (c. 1709). Some stylistic evolution is visible, however, in the larger scale of the wall divisions, the amalgamation of the panels into large surfaces, the greater autonomy of the large, central rosettes and the softer curves. The overdoors, too, have broken free of their rectangular setting, although they are far from equalling the freedom of Oppenord's. At ceiling level, the cornice supported by modillions has given way to a coving with arabesques and putti;[125] the corners are emphasized by winged cartouches.

The final demise of the Lepautre system and the move into the Rococo did not take place under de Cotte but was

83 Jean Aubert: Paris, Palais Bourbon, 1722–5, Grand Cabinet (Mariette, *L'Architecture Française*, pl. 477).

84 Jean Aubert: Paris, Hôtel de Lassay, *c.* 1728, Grand Salon.

tendrils, flowers and chimaeras that reach out across the empty space of the ceiling. In the Grande Galerie, these are linked above the cornice by a lacy border; and the separating function of the cornice itself is thus entirely abolished.

The decoration of the Palais Bourbon, which represents the official style of the mid 1720s, is known to us only through the engravings of Mariette (Plate 83). In its Grand Cabinet, the narrow wall piers between the casement doors on the garden side were entirely covered with damask or with large mirrors, and the zone of ornament was confined, as with Boffrand, to the spandrels of the arcading. These were filled with loose, entirely curvilinear tendrils in restless, darting forms that already come very close to the Rococo, albeit with no rocaille. Finally, all the current decorative tendencies are epitomized in Aubert's work at the Hôtel de Lassay (Plate 84). The central rosettes of the large wall panels, together with the arabesques on both end walls, have resolved themselves into figurative relief medallions. The cornice is now swamped in decoration throughout its length, and the central and corner cartouches – now in the form of

figured medallions – swell or even interrupt it. Lacy rosettes stretch out towards each of them from the centre of the ceiling, so that the distinction between wall and ceiling almost disappears. There is also a mixed system of wall decoration. Lepautre's panels are combined with Boffrand's arcading and with his freely decorated spandrels. The ceiling, filled with naturalistic and irrational motifs derived from Oppenord, spreads a kind of golden net over the covings. Amid this profusion of ornament, the individual motif loses its significance, and the impression conveyed is that of an infinite wealth of forms.

The Hôtel de Lassay – we know nothing of the decoration of the Hôtel de Biron – marked the end of the Régence style in interior decoration, as in architecture. The Lepautre system, based on the autonomy and rhythmic organization of individual parts, and subordinating the decor to the structure of the wall, had now disintegrated. Ornament was no longer a decorative accessory but an autonomous element of imagery, equal in status to painting. The way was clear for the advent of the Rococo.

The Rococo

Introduction

The Rococo was the ultimate expression of the *goût moderne*: the result of nearly fifty years of evolution towards ever greater freedom and relaxation of structural form. At the same time, however, it needs to be seen as a style in its own right. Its inherent anticlassical bias, its distinctive repertoire of forms, and its inner homogeneity, set it apart not only from the earlier Louis XIV style but from the Louis XVI style, which is Neoclassicism; although it remains closely akin to the Régence. With its wealth of invention and its harmonious forms, this is one of the most original and most delightful expressions of the French genius.

The Rococo marked the triumph of ornament, which now no longer restricted itself to interiors but took possession of architecture itself. Pierre Patte was to pass a Neoclassical verdict on this:

Lajoue, Pineau and Meissonnier had led architecture astray. In decoration, only eccentric outlines were allowed; there was nothing to be seen but a chaos of randomly arranged objects and ornaments, the creatures of a disordered fancy. One saw absurd accretions of oblique cartouches, rocailles, dragons, reeds, palms, and every possible fancy plant, and these long remained the showpieces of our interiors, so that sculpture held absolute sway over architecture. (*Mémoires sur les objets les plus importante de l'architecture*, Paris 1769)

But there is more to the Rococo than mere ornament. Only when architecture, painting, decoration and furniture harmoniously combine does its true character emerge: a playful lightness of touch, a cultivated taste, the enchantment of precious materials and the sheer grace that the Goncourt brothers were the first to hail as the 'inner law' of the Rococo.[1]

The Rococo derives its name from rocaille, the species of grotto and shellwork ornament that presided over its birth. The term 'Rococo' itself first came into use, in a decidedly pejorative sense, in Parisian artists' studios at the close of the eighteenth century; it entered official usage only in the 1842 edition of the *Dictionnaire de l'Académie française*.[2] Contemporaries referred to it as the *style pittoresque* or the *genre pittoresque*.[3] The long-held view that the Rococo was a terminal phase of the Baroque, imported from Italy, has been untenable since the researches of Weigert and Kimball, if not for longer:[4] the style may have been enriched by Italy, but its basic structure was unequivocally French.

The Rococo was the dominant style in France from about 1730 to about 1755; so its reign was not exactly coterminous with that of Louis XV. The term *style Louis-XV*, which is in current use in France alongside *style rocaille*, is therefore misleading. Nor did the Rococo hold exclusive sway: in

official architecture the *grand goût* (i.e. the classical orders) still prevailed and town planning on a large scale with brilliant results was going on in cities like Rennes, Bordeaux, Nancy and others. Its principal domain however was in private residential building. From the 1730s onwards, it spread beyond the borders of France to conquer the whole of Europe, where it either evolved into discrete local styles – as at Potsdam, in Bavaria or in Venice – or, more often, allied itself as a purely decorative style with the indigenous traditions of the late Baroque.

The Rococo coincided with one of the most peaceful and prosperous periods that France had ever known, that of the administration of Cardinal Fleury. Fleury, who was Louis XV's former tutor, held no public office; but he was a cautious and skilful mentor and guide to the young king, and for all practical purposes his prime minister. The political and economic rebuilding of the kingdom was his work, and that of his closest associates, Philibert Orry and Le Pelletier. Among his first measures, in 1726, was the establishment of a stable relationship between gold and silver currency; in the same year, having thus stabilized the value of money, he went on to reform the system by which revenue was collected through the tax farming authority, the Ferme Générale. Orry, one of the best brains in the administration, and much hated for his unyielding rectitude as finance minister, succeeded in balancing the budget for the year 1739 – a feat that was never again accomplished until the Restoration period.

Fleury's greatest long-term success was in foreign policy. In 1735 the War of the Polish Succession was concluded by the Peace of Vienna. France had taken part as a lukewarm ally of the deposed king of Poland, Stanislas I Leszczyński, who was Louis XV's father-in-law; and in the Peace her reward was the reversion of Lorraine. The rightful duke, Francis III, ceded his country to King Stanislas, and received in return the grand duchy of Tuscany, where the Medici line had just died out. This was on condition that, on Stanislas's death, Lorraine would pass to France as the inheritance of his daughter. Without firing a shot, the Cardinal thus gained for France a frontier province that had been fought over for centuries, while at the same time banishing from her eastern frontier the implicit Austrian threat raised by the marriage between Duke Francis and the emperor's daughter and heiress, Maria Theresa.

This happy interlude ended all too soon, with Fleury's death in 1743. By then, in 1741, France had embarked on another war, that of the Austrian Succession; the Cardinal had opposed this, arguing that France had nothing to gain by it, and history was to prove him right. The efforts of Marshal Belle-Isle, including a brief occupation of Prague, prevented neither the accession of Maria Theresa in Austria nor the coronation of her consort, Francis of Lorraine, as Holy Roman Emperor. Even the brilliant victories of Fontenoy and Rocourt in the Netherlands brought no profit. At the Peace of Aix-la-Chapelle, in 1748, France came away empty-

Versailles, Cabinet de la Pendule, see Plate 143.

handed. She was compelled to give the Netherlands back to Austria and lost important overseas possessions to the British.

To cover the enormous war debt, and reform the public finances once for all, the finance minister, Jean-Baptiste Machault d'Arnouville, decided to introduce an income tax, which was to apply to all, including the privileged clergy and nobility. Although the rate was to be no more than five per cent, the king was unable to overcome clerical opposition to it. This was the beginning of the financial decline that increasingly limited the government's options and brought the crown to its final impasse.

The monarchy faced another peril in the shape of the Enlightenment, which stood for individual freedom and freedom of thought against all state and clerical interference. As early as 1721, in his *Lettres persanes*, Montesquieu produced a trenchant satire on France under the Régence. In his *Esprit des lois* (1748), he used the form of a treatise on jurisprudence to express his admiration of the English system of government, and contrasted the doctrine of the separation of powers, which guaranteed the rights of the citizen, with the absolutist form of government that prevailed in France. Daring as this was, the *Lettres philosophiques sur les Anglais*, which Voltaire published in 1734 after a three-year stay in England, were more so: they were an open challenge to the state, and were received as such. With many contemporary allusions, Voltaire contrasted English liberty with life in France under the sway of a mindless despotism and a bigoted Church. The book was publicly burned, and its publisher was thrown into the Bastille; Voltaire himself took refuge in Lorraine. But the authority of the regime had already been severely undermined. By the time Voltaire returned to Paris, such was his literary fame that he had nothing more to fear. At the instance of Madame de Pompadour, he became a member of the French Academy and even a chamberlain to the king, before in 1750 he accepted an invitation from the king of Prussia to go to Potsdam.

In the king's mistress, Madame de Pompadour, the Enlightenment had a friend in high places. The Goncourts called her the 'Queen of the Rococo'. She first appeared at court in the capacity of official mistress, *maîtresse déclarée*, in 1745. Of plebeian origins – her father had been a supplier to the military, condemned to death at one time for fraud – but highly educated and extraordinarily beautiful, she made an early marriage with a prosperous tax-farmer named Lenormant d'Etioles and attracted philosophers, writers and artists to her country estate. Once at Versailles, she succeeded in keeping the bored and restless king entertained and thereby established for herself a strong position at court. She took an interest in artists and philosophers, and it was thanks to her that the crown recovered its former leading position as a patron of the arts, and public architecture came back to life. She also induced the king to confer the office of director of the Bâtiments du Roi – previously held by the finance minister, Orry – on her uncle, Le Normant de Tournehem, with her brother as his designated successor. But her political ambitions, and her attempts to influence appointments to the high offices of state, damaged both the effectiveness of government and the reputation of the king, and played their part in discrediting the regime as a whole.

Rococo architecture was a private rather than an official phenomenon, with a marked tendency towards smallness and intimacy.[5] Few large châteaux were built; even princes now wanted small rooms to live in. The king himself, at Versailles, no longer resided in Louis XIV's Grands Appartements but in what were called the Petits Appartements, where things were done with less ceremony. Social life transferred itself from the châteaux and hôtels of the nobility to the salons, where people practised elegant conversation as an art in its own right, subject to a system of rules based on mutual consideration and respect. The *courtisan*, or courtier, had become an *homme du monde*, a man of the world. Long enfilades, which had unhappy associations with Versailles, disappeared. Rooms became more intimate and were ingeniously grouped. There were many more of what were called *dégagements*, small, mostly concealed lobbies and passages that permitted the servants to go about their business noiselessly. Every spare corner was used to the full.

The perfection of the art of planning, however difficult the site, was one of the major architectural achievements of the Rococo. French architects took particular pride in it. Jacques-François Blondel, in his *Traité d'architecture dans le goût moderne, ou de la distribution des maisons de plaisance* (1737), spoke of planning as a new art which had already reached its peak of perfection. Patte, in his *Discours sur l'architecture* (1754), concluded his discussion of the Rococo with these words: 'The principal feature of the evolution of architecture during the present reign is the art of the ground plan. Previously, dwellings were designed purely for display, and nothing was known of the art of living in comfort, for one's own benefit. It is the pleasing distribution of space in the hôtels of the present day that transforms our dwellings into abodes of charm and delight.' Aubert's Palais Bourbon, and François Franque's Palais Abbatial at Villers-Cotterêts, are proof that this pride was not misplaced.

Externally, architecture was marked by its simplicity. Even the aristocracy made no attempt to show off its rank. The outer wall was now no more than an envelope that enclosed the interior. It lost all dynamic tension: an important distinction between Rococo and Baroque. Its articulation was limited to a low relief, which derived its rhythm from horizontal cornices and from vertical *chaînages* or stone dressings. Ponderous rustication was banished, except for the podium of a public structure such as the Fontaine de Grenelle. Sculpture, too, was employed sparingly, in the form of balcony consoles and decorated keystones for doors and windows.

Interiors were a totally different matter. There, the only rules that counted were those of taste; and there the *style pittoresque* unfolded in all its splendour. A network of gilded curves twined across the walls; putti and birds disported themselves in the covings; paintings of Arcadian and mythological scenes surmounted the mirrors and doors. The light that flooded in through the tall French windows was reflected by large mirrors and refracted through Venetian chandeliers: by night, as these stirred in the draught, their cut-glass prisms 'transfigured the candlelight and scattered it in a shower of sparks' (Sedlmayr).

There was a marked loss of interest in exteriors, as against interiors.[6] Everyone who thought he was anyone had his apartment redecorated, or even – like the Duc de Villars

with his gallery – added a new room to it. The building fever of the Régence gave way to a decorative mania that cast its spell even on the architects.[7] Blondel's *Traité ... de la distribution des maisons de plaisance* (1737), a practical handbook of villa building that enjoyed great success, contained no discussion of the orders. According to Blondel, the beauty of architecture resided solely in the harmony of the proportions inherited from antiquity; but the beauty of interiors lay in their elegance and comfort. The grandeur and opulence of the façade was beside the point. Blondel went on to warn his readers against excess and overcomplication in ornament, and pleaded for it to be well adapted to the room and to its purpose.

But the danger of excess was inherent in the prevalent decorative mania. Ornament not only swamped interiors but – especially in town houses built for rent – began to encroach on façades. Dragons and other monsters positioned themselves beneath balconies and on door panels; foliated ornament, of a kind that contemporaries called *chicorée*, proliferated above doorways and around windows. Cornices and balconies began to develop curves and countercurves. The critics entered the fray, dismissing all this as a crime against good taste for which they blamed Borromini. The first writer to mock the general decorative obsession was Voltaire, in his *Temple du goût*;[8] Blondel, too, castigated the 'ridiculous jumble of shells, dragons, reeds, palm-trees and other plants that is the be-all and end-all of modern decoration'. But not even the hostility of the theorists and the mockery of Voltaire could moderate the popularity of the *genre pittoresque*.

Of all the theorists and critics of the day, the most important was Jacques-François Blondel (1705–74).[9] A nephew of Jean-François Blondel, the Mansart pupil who had made a name for himself with his buildings in Geneva,[10] Jacques-François had worked in his youth on the engravings for Mariette's *Architecture française*. In 1743, against some initial opposition from the Academy, he founded the Ecole des Arts, a private school of architecture that was a great success. Based on modern principles, its curriculum was very different from the Academy's. It included architectural theory, practical draughtsmanship and – a noteworthy innovation – the study of modern buildings in and outside Paris. Among its students we find such celebrated names as those of William Chambers, Charles de Wailly and Claude-Nicolas Ledoux.

Blondel's theoretical works not only served to spread knowledge of architecture but also helped to educate public taste. In the earliest, *Traité ... de la distribution des maisons de plaisance* (1737), he was still firmly on Rococo ground; but in his *Architecture française* (1751–6) – an expanded republication of Mariette's work, with a full accompanying text – he took up the cause of classical architecture, which he declared to be superior to contemporary work. The influence of Boffrand's *Livre d'architecture* (1745) is unmistakable;[11] Blondel had clearly taken to heart Boffrand's ideas on the comparability of music and architecture, as well as his warnings against the tyranny of fashion and against excessive decoration.

By contrast, *L'Art de bâtir les maisons de campagne* (1751), by C.E. Briseux, was a practical textbook with numerous examples. Used in conjunction with Blondel's earlier work on *maisons de plaisance*, it made an important contribution to private villa building in the Rococo style. Much of what Briseux had to say had already been current in the Régence; but the emphasis had now shifted to the smoothing of transitions: whether in coved recesses for gateways and doorways, or in a general rounding of corners, or in the use of bowed projections for vestibules and garden salons.

Whatever might be going on in practice, the theoretical controversy on matters of taste continued unabated. The most important contribution was made by Père André in his *Essai sur le beau* (1741).[12] Rather than take his stand on any fixed canon of beauty, André distinguished between *le beau essentiel*, the essential beauty of immutable architectural principle, and *le beau arbitraire*, the arbitrary beauty of those principles that were founded on proportions. This compromise, which lent itself to a definition of taste, was well received by an age that had strong reservations about classical models. From the dogmatic wing of the Academy, Briseux hotly contested André's thesis in his *Traité du beau essentiel* (1752), but was unable to undermine it effectively.

On the nature of taste itself, no consensus was never arrived at. For Boffrand, good taste consisted in *juste convenance* or decorum; for Voltaire it consisted in *bienséance* or fitness. In his *Temple du goût*, which was largely devoted to literature, Voltaire made the highly elitist statement that taste arose from the consensus of educated society as to the rules of beauty. He thus excluded all classes but the gentry, *les honnêtes gens*, from any possibility of contributing to the formation of taste.

It must nevertheless be remembered that leading architects, though they might bend the rules, never disavowed the classical discipline and never doubted the validity of its maxims. Pierre Vigné de Vigny was the only architect who welcomed the relaxation of the classical rules and took the view that the new freedom in decoration would liberate architecture, too, from the shackles that had hitherto restricted its freedom. 'Our architects', wrote Vigny, 'are in a kind of servitude: for they force themselves into an exclusive adherence to the model of the ancient buildings of the Greeks and Romans. To set them free would require a genius such as Borromini, who, with others in Italy, set out on new paths.'[14]

Vigny's colleagues all subscribed to the classical rules. They nevertheless took the view that, although the Rococo had produced nothing significant in the field of architecture, planning (*distribution*) was the one exception: they regarded the ground plans of their own day as superior to anything produced by antiquity, or by the *Grand Siècle*.

Jacques V Gabriel and Public Building

The death of Robert de Cotte in 1735 did not mark a clean break. He had been blind for several years, and had retired from office in 1734. His successor was his kinsman, Jacques V Gabriel (1667–1742), only a few years younger, who had already taken over much of his work.

A nephew of J.H. Mansart's on his mother's side, Jacques V Gabriel belonged to a close-knit clan of architects who had occupied the leading positions in the Service des Bâtiments for generations.[15] He came of a Norman family. His father, Jacques IV, had worked under J.H. Mansart and had made his name by building the Château de Choisy for Louis XIV's cousin, La Grande Mademoiselle. The son's career was thus assured by professional and family connections. After a study trip to Italy with Robert de Cotte in 1689–90, he entered the office of J.H. Mansart, who valued his advice and taste – or so we are told by the Swedish architect Daniel Cronström[16] – and saw to it that he received preferment. In 1699 he became an Academician, second class, and outdoor surveyor at Versailles; in 1709 he additionally became indoor surveyor. This meant that he was involved in all building work on the palace, and that he was under the king's eye. In 1716 he was appointed chief engineer of bridges and highways, and in the next year Academician, first class. He had been elevated to the nobility in 1704. After a rise that followed the same pattern as de Cotte's, his appointment as chief architect came as a surprise to no one. The years that followed saw him appointed director of the Academy and inspector-general of the Bâtiments du Roi. This was the top of the tree. He, too, stood firmly within the tradition of the Mansart school, although his relationship to classical form differed from his predecessor's.

When Jacques V Gabriel succeeded de Cotte at the age of sixty-seven, he already had a considerable career behind him, mostly in urban planning. At thirty-three, seven years after entering J.H. Mansart's office, he built the bishop's palace at Blois (1700–3). This unusually early commission would have been unthinkable without the intervention of his protector. The building itself bears all the hallmarks of Mansart's handiwork – the restrained projections, the use of corner dressings to mark the articulation, the ground-floor rustication on the model of the Orangerie at Versailles, the richly sculptured pediments, the Baroque dormers, and finally the difference in the height of the two façades caused by the sloping site, an anticipation of the Château Neuf at Meudon. The interior, too, with its double-height *salon à l'italienne*, and its magnificent enfilade through the bishop's apartment, recalls compositions by Mansart.

In the continuing absence of major crown commissions, Gabriel turned his attention first of all to private developments in Paris, where he built a number of mansions – among them the Hôtel de Varengeville (1704) and the Hôtel de Blouin (*c.* 1718) – and became deeply involved in speculative building for John Law. The centre of all this was the Place Vendôme, where five of the hôtels are known to be his.[17] For the interiors of these he took advantage of his official position at Versailles to bring to Paris the team of decorators who worked under him there, Degoullons, Taupin, Le Goupil and the rest. Of these buildings, the only survivor is the Hôtel de Parabère, the home of the Regent's mistress.

Jacques V Gabriel's appointment as chief engineer of the department of Ponts et Chaussées brought not only a widening of his scope but a marked enhancement of his prestige. This newly created office involved supervision of roads and bridges all over the kingdom; and the chief engineer was responsible for the design and building of any new structures that became necessary. Of all his numerous bridges, it was the one over the Loire at Blois (1717–26) that most enhanced his reputation.[18] This is a masterpiece of engineering, and since his day it has withstood not only floods but wars. It is a saddle-backed bridge on eleven arches; at the crown of the central arch is a great cartouche, and above this is a tall

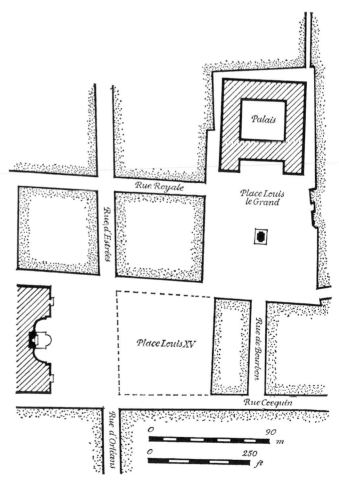

85 Rennes, Place Louis-le-Grand and Place Louis XV, layout.

86 Jacques Gabriel: Rennes, Présidial, preliminary design, 1728.

Elevation du Bâtiment du Presidial et de la Tour de l'Orloge du côté de la Place.

pyramid on an inscribed base, surmounted by an orb and cross.

Public responsibilities continued to dominate Gabriel's working life. His technical knowledge qualified him particularly well as an urban planner. Among his projects were the rebuilding of Rennes after a fire, the design of the Place Royale in Bordeaux, the siting and erection of a statue of Louis XIV in Dijon and the building of the Halles or covered market in Nantes.

Three-quarters of the city of Rennes had been burnt to the ground in November 1720. For the rebuilding, the celebrated military engineer Robelin, after a long career building fortifications in various provinces of France, submitted a plan that replaced the maze of crooked lanes in the old town by a grid system of straight streets with uniform façades and monumental vistas. He also planned to lay out two large squares, and to embank the river Vilaine as it ran through the city.[19]

Robelin's plan showed the influence of his military background, but it also reflected the most modern urbanistic notions of the day, with their concentration on light, air and general well-being: 'everything must be calculated with an eye to convenience and the public interest' (Lavedan). It was approved by the city council, but there was vociferous public opposition to its proposals to redistribute land and standardize building heights. Robelin's inflexibility and the citizens' determined resistance led to a heated dispute and finally to Robelin's dismissal.

In 1725, therefore, Jacques V Gabriel was sent to Rennes and put in charge of reconstruction. He adopted Robelin's plan in principle, but was more flexible than his predecessor and was prepared to make compromises over building heights; and so he succeeded in coming to terms with the citizens. Rebuilding then went ahead, at least in the half of the city north of the Vilaine, in accordance with prescribed and only slightly varied house types. It was continued after Gabriel's death by his son Ange-Jacques, and work on the southern half of the plan continued far into the nineteenth century.

The crucial changes that Jacques V Gabriel made to the plan in 1725 concerned its two large squares, the Place du Palais and the Place Neuve (Plate 85). The Place du Palais (now the Place du Parlement de Bretagne) lies in front of the Parlement building by Salomon de Brosse. The idea of doubling the size of the square was Robelin's; Gabriel transformed it into a Place Royale by surrounding it with uniform façades based on the Place Vendôme, by levelling the sloping surface, and by adding an equestrian statue of Louis XIV. To give due weight to this, he sacrificed the great flight of steps and perron in front of the Parlement and replaced it with a new, smooth, continuous façade that served merely as a foil for the image of the king. Behind the façade, on the court side, he built a new staircase, open to the air on one side; this is a work of great transparency and elegance, remarkable not only for its coupled Ionic columns, derived from the Grand Trianon, but for its beautiful mascaroons on the ground floor.

The other monumental square, the Place Neuve (now

87 Jacques Gabriel: Rennes, town hall, 1731–62.

Place de la Mairie), was markedly smaller and almost entirely enclosed by buildings. To avoid competing with the Place Royale, Gabriel countermanded Robelin's order that the façades should be a uniform height of three storeys. His initial idea was to make the square smaller by inserting four L-shaped blocks in the corners and a free-standing clock tower in the centre. On second thoughts he gave it two facing blocks, one consisting of the Présidial (the law courts) and the clock tower (Plate 86), the other consisting of an hôtel for the governor of Brittany. As the available space turned out to be too narrow for this, he produced a third and final design in which he turned the axes of his blocks through 90 degrees and combined Présidial, clock tower and city hall (Plate 87) into a single block, with the governor's hôtel on the other side of the square. The work dragged on for over thirty years (1731–62), and the gubernatorial mansion was never built; its intended site was eventually used for the theatre.

The composition that now dominates the Place de la Mairie is a prime example of Gabriel's mature style. It derives from his second design (1728),[20] in which the main stress was on the clock tower, which stood free on three sides; the long bulk of the Présidial, with its flat, uneventful façade and its side wings breaking forward at right angles, supplied a setting for it. Optically, the tower combined with the façade behind it to form a unified whole, with the base of the tower simultaneously doing duty as the frontispiece of the façade. In his sure mastery of proportions, his impeccable handling of cornices and mouldings and his discreet use of

ornament, Jacques V Gabriel manifested all the virtues of the Mansart school. There was much in this design, including the tall, closely arrayed windows with their ornamental keystones and the elegance of the forms, to recall the architecture of the Parisian hôtels, and notably the late work of Lassurance. The secure and confident design of the tower, though undoubtedly influenced by the town halls of Flanders, was entirely unprecedented.

At this stage the Intendant of Brittany intervened, and Gabriel was forced to cut down both the height and the sculptural enrichment of his project. At the same time, he took the opportunity to shift the emphasis. By bringing the city hall under the same roof and relaxing the rigidity of his great block, he created a composition in three parts – Présidial, clock, city hall – and thus gained not only in significant content but in scenic effect. The city hall and the Présidial became matching pavilions with a horizontal emphasis, tied together by the vertical element (convex in plan) of the clock tower. Both in articulation and in sculptural detail, the matching portals of the wings echo the monumental frontispiece, with which they combine to form a unity. These portals are all the more important in that the wing façades are otherwise virtually devoid of ornament.

The central focus lies at the base of the tower, with its proscenium-like recess (possibly a reminiscence of S. Agnese in Rome). This formerly served as a triumphal arch to frame the niche containing Jean-Baptiste Lemoyne's statue of Louis XV. The whole architectural complex thus became a setting for the figure of the monarch; and even the tower

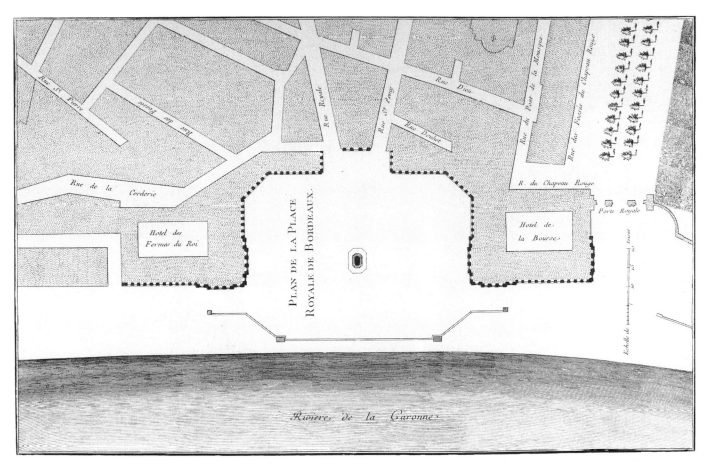

88 Jacques Gabriel: Bordeaux, Place Royale, 1731–55, layout.

89 Jacques Gabriel: Bordeaux, Place Royale, 1731–55, elevation of
central pavilion.

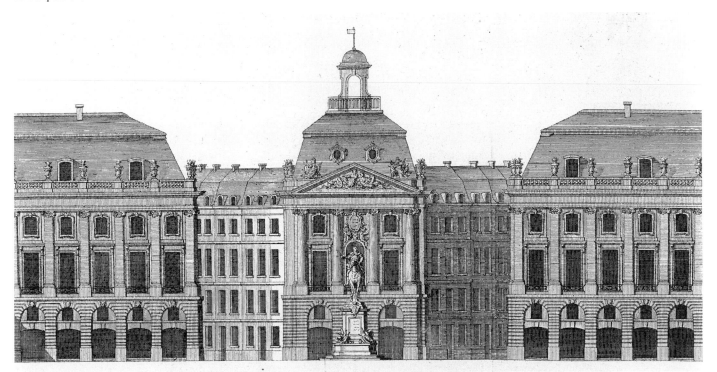

above, conceived as an emblem and a landmark for the city, assumed the function of a baldachin. This, too, changed its form in the third design, and it now has two instead of three open, lantern-like storeys. The onion dome, an unusual form in France and possibly an import from Lorraine, was already present in the 1728 design. It is wittily matched to the outline of the tower by the way in which, without interrupting the stepped diminution of the storeys, it brings the process to a gentle conclusion. It is this softness of outline, the concavity of the centre of the block and the loose, even playful relationship between the parts, that constitutes the unique character of the whole composition and makes it, despite the classicism of its formal repertoire, into one of the principal works of Rococo architecture.

The relationship between the two squares in Rennes reveals a considerable imaginative insight on the architect's part into the structure of the city. They are not linked directly but by a narrow length of street between the corners of adjoining blocks, so that each square first meets our gaze in a surprising oblique view. It was to stress the differences between them, and to avoid monotony, that Gabriel reduced the Place Neuve to half the size of the Place Royale and turned the axis of its dominant composition – the clock tower and the governor's mansion opposite – at ninety degrees to that of the Parlement building. Additionally, however, the effective articulation of the clock tower group, with its concave centre, enshrined the idealized royal presence in a very different setting from that of the uniform façades that encompassed Louis XIV, the *Roi Soleil*, as he stood in solitary state in the Place Royale. Gabriel's conception was never fully realized; the absence of the governor's mansion left the Place Neuve as a torso.

In Bordeaux, Gabriel faced a very different situation. There he had to lay out a square on the bank of a river. The peculiar difficulty was that the tightly packed, ancient city, which had retained its medieval street pattern, was shut off from its lifeline, the river Garonne, by fortifications, and that the citizens had no intention of permitting these to be removed. The idea that Bordeaux should follow the example of other cities and erect a statue of Louis XIV in a suitable setting had always been blocked by this. Eventually, in 1726, the Intendant of Guyenne, Boucher, asked the local architect Héricé for a design, and he submitted a proposal for an oval plaza outside the city walls, combined with a new embankment along the Garonne. However, Héricé's mediocre design found favour neither with the provincial Parlement nor with the Surintendant, the Duc d'Antin, who passed it to his chief architect, de Cotte, for revision. In his design (1728), de Cotte transformed the oval into a rectangle, set the king's statue in the centre of it, and surrounded it with uniform façades, with blind arcading on the ground floor and a continuous giant order of pilasters, replaced by applied columns on the pedimented frontispieces. When the city council persisted in rejecting this plan, and the breach in the walls that it would entail, Jacques V Gabriel was sent to Bordeaux.[21]

His plan (1729) embodied guidelines for the further development of the city, including the building of the later Allées de Tourny and the square in front of the theatre. As finally approved in 1730, it provided for a square open to the Garonne, with a pair of canted corners on the landward side, like those of the Place Vendôme, and a riverside terrace terminated at either end by figures personifying the Garonne and the Dordogne (Plate 88). The façade type was that proposed by de Cotte, except that his flat roofs were replaced by mansard roofs with balustrades and urns (Plate 89). The terminal pavilions that overlooked the river became more massive and solemn, each with pediments on two sides. In the centre of the landward side, Gabriel designed another small square, divided from the main square by a moat and a drawbridge; from it led a pair of divergent streets separated by a large, three-bay pavilion with giant columns and a pediment. This was the only breach in the walls that Gabriel could persuade the city fathers to accept.

To set the scene for the new square and win over the citizens of Bordeaux, work began in 1731, under the direction of the local architect André Portier, on building the end pavilions facing the Garonne.[22] The Hôtel des Fermes, the revenue office on the south side of the square, was ready by 1738; the Bourse on the north side followed in 1741–7. The equestrian statue of Louis XIV – another work by Lemoyne, and regarded as the century's finest equestrian statue – was set up in 1745. For his architectural sculpture, Gabriel called in his old associate from Versailles, Jacques Verberckt; together with his fellow-Fleming van der Woordt and six assistants, Verberckt undertook all the pediment sculptures and the rest of the stonecarving work: capitals, keystones, mascaroons, urns and trophies. He was succeeded by another member of the Versailles team, Claude Francin, a nephew of the Coustous'. These sculptors from Versailles were responsible for the outstanding quality of the work; they brought the newest Parisian taste to Bordeaux.

After Jacques V Gabriel's death, the work was carried on by his son Ange-Jacques, who adhered closely to his father's plans. By this time the development of Bordeaux was in the hands of a new Intendant, Aubert de Tourny. It was his wish to give a new and welcoming look to the city, and to this end he extended Gabriel's Bourse façade northward, saw to the completion of the pavilion on the town side, with its two diverging streets (1750–5), and built outside the walls a new and generous network of streets that defines the character of the city to this day.

The Place Royale (now Place de la Bourse) became the point of departure for the remaking of Bordeaux; it was a spectacular achievement and a great credit to Jacques V Gabriel. Architecturally, however, it contained nothing new: it was a repetition of the thirty-year-old Place Vendôme. The architectural framework is de Cotte's, but the decorative enrichment, and therefore the scenic effect, are Gabriel's. It all goes to show that what counted, in this final phase of the Mansart tradition, was not so much the architectural conception as sheer stagecraft and richness of effect.

Jacques V Gabriel's decorative abilities are shown to their best advantage in Dijon, where, for the Estates of Burgundy, he had to build an archive wing and a chapel onto the Palais des Etats. The wing was to run along the Rue de Condé (now Rue de la Liberté) and would contain the provincial archive, offices, and reception rooms for the deputies, as well as a grand staircase leading to the debating chamber, as a replacement for the external steps by J.H. Mansart that would have to be demolished.[23]

90 Jacques Gabriel: Dijon, Palais des Etats, Archives wing, design of façade, 1731.

91 Jacques Gabriel: Dijon, Palais des Etats, staircase, 1731–6.

In Gabriel's design of 1731, the right-hand portion of the new wing, adjoining the existing fabric of the Palais des Etats, is occupied by the archive and the stair (Plate 90), and the left-hand portion by offices for the deputies. The link between the two, a domed, oval vestibule, gives access to the staircase and incorporates a carriage entrance into the court. In the course of execution the last two bays on the left-hand side were omitted for reasons of cost, so that the wing became asymmetrical, much to Gabriel's distress.[24]

The most interesting feature is undoubtedly the staircase (1731–6) (Plate 91). Its design is governed by the fact that the archive is housed underneath it. The two tribunes between which it ascends form roof terraces, as it were, over the vaults of the Archive below. Gabriel uses them to achieve an extraordinarily effective composition of space and light that bears comparison with the great staircases of the South German Baroque. What brings it all to life, however, is the decoration. This is a brilliant example of the *style rocaille*, as practised in the Service des Bâtiments du Roi; and here the changes from the first design (1731) to the second (1735) reflect the stylistic shift from Régence to Rococo. The first design was still firmly within the tradition of de Cotte: simple central medallions and sheaves of palm fronds around the edges of the panels, cartouches with festoons of flowers above the windows. In the second design, the panels are filled with pendant trophies, and the crowns of the window arches are filled with large rocaille motifs.[25] The decor of the vestibule is unchanged, but in the stairchamber nothing remains of the first design but the cornice, with its modillions, and the four niches tucked into the rounded-off corners at either end.[26] The wrought-iron balustrades, too, have been modernized. A simple pattern of parallel horizontal bands with C-scrolls has given way to a web of curves and counter-curves into which the royal arms and those of the Duc de

92 Jacques Gabriel: Dijon, Palais des Etats, Chapelle des Elus, 1737.

Bourbon-Condé, governor of Burgundy, are interwoven.

The street façade of the new wing was completed somewhat later. It derives its rhythm from Jacques V Gabriel's typical large, round-headed windows, but its significance from its ornate decorated door-way. This, again, was entirely composed of decorative elements. It was flanked by two slightly projecting, giant pilaster strips, in the form of simple wall-panels, dominated by enormous pendant trophies. The semicircular arch above, rising into the roof area, may well have been inspired by Aubert's Grandes Ecuries at Chantilly.[27] The trophies themselves – 'modernized' by comparison with those of 1731 – were endowed by Gabriel with allegorical significance. Justice and Prudence, with their attendant blessings, were introduced – along with Fortitude, Concord, Sciences and Arts in the stairchamber – to put the Estates in mind of their duty. Above them were trophies of war and, on the extrados of the arch, allegories of Temperance and Fortitude. The tympanum was adorned with the arms of Burgundy and a tablet inscribed 'Palais des Etats'.[28] With this façade, and the only slightly earlier staircase, the Rococo in its courtly form made its first appearance in Dijon; however, the slipshod execution was not at all to the liking of Gabriel, who had intended to set an example of contemporary architecture.

Immediately after the completion of the staircase wing, the Estates decided to build a chapel for members' use and employed Gabriel's associate, Pierre Le Mousseux, to design it.[29] The available space was extremely ill-suited to the purpose, as it had to match the height of the Palais des Etats but was squeezed between the back end of the building and an adjoining private property, so that all its light had to come from above the roof line of that house. In his design, Le Mousseux used a double order of pilasters, with blind arcades below and large windows, alternating with pilasters on tall bases, above. The Estates turned this down, and in 1737 Gabriel amended it by masking the join between the storeys:

above the Corinthian pilasters on the ground floor he set a deep, richly articulated and strongly projecting entablature that absorbs the bases of the upper pilasters and thus conceals the true height of the space (Plate 92). The rhythm set up by this continuous entablature and by the ornate, sculptured wall arcades serves to create a unified and uncommonly effective space; the harmony between the sculptural enrichment of the walls and the richly carved doors distracts the visitor's attention from the excessive height of the chapel.

For the decoration, Gabriel once more called in the best workers. The woodcarvings on the doors and windows are in the same style as the contemporaneous work at Versailles. The woodwork in the choir, which was completed only in 1743 – a large crucifix with orant angels, several candlesticks, and the picture frame above the altar – is by Verberckt. Like Rennes, Dijon exemplifies the distance that separates Jacques V Gabriel's fundamentally anticlassical style from that of de Cotte.

The leading personality in public building, aside from Jacques V Gabriel, was Boffrand. In the first two decades of the eighteenth century, his name was principally associated with Lorraine and with the Parisian hôtel; but in the second half of his career the emphasis was on public works, in which he was an acknowledged authority. In this, his technical experience stood him in good stead. Like Gabriel, he was employed by the Ponts et Chaussées, for which he worked as a bridge builder, and in which he succeeded Gabriel as chief engineer from 1743 onwards. He built bridges at Villeneuve-sur-Yonne, Pont-sur-Yonne, Sens and elsewhere, which became celebrated for their ingenious solid geometry.

However, his reputation as a technician was primarily based on the waterworks that he built at Bicêtre (1733) for the Hôpital Général. This powerful institution was the central administration of the Paris hospitals. The position of its architect, which Boffrand held from 1724 onwards, and which he combined with that of a director, was an onerous and many-sided one. The decrepitude of the hospital buildings constantly presented new problems, whether in the provision of new buildings, in engineering works or in such larger urban questions as the completion of the Salpêtrière complex begun by Le Vau.

The Hospice de Bicêtre had suffered for years from a chronic lack of water. To solve the problem once and for all, Boffrand sank a well fifty metres down to the level of the river Seine, and constructed a pumping mechanism that transferred the water into a large reservoir. The technical audacity of the engineering, and the solid construction of the reservoir, earned the admiration of his contemporaries and gave Boffrand just cause for pride. In his *Livre d'architecture* he presented the project under the heading of 'Great Works of Architecture'.

This connection with the Hôpital Général was the occasion for Boffrand's last major work, the Hôpital des Enfants-Trouvés, the foundling hospital of Paris, which became the principal source of his posthumous fame.[30] This venerable institution, which occupied a number of buildings on the Ile de la Cité, urgently required a new, single home. The shortage of space on the overcrowded island in the Seine, the tradition of respecting the existing street layout, and the close proximity of another hospital, the Hôtel-Dieu, which

was independent of the Hôpital Général and did not take kindly to competition, made the planning vastly more difficult. In such a situation Boffrand saw that he had no chance of creating a grand modern building by conventional means. His design of 1745 therefore had two aspects. He proposed not only a rebuilding of the Enfants-Trouvés but at the same time a programme of improvement and 'regularization' of the whole quarter, involving a generous enlargement of the square before the Cathedral, the Parvis de Notre-Dame, and also the widening and straightening of the street that led into it, the Rue Neuve Notre-Dame (Plate 93).

At the near end of this street, facing the Cathedral, he designed twin porticoes, one on the right for the Enfants-Trouvés and one on the left for the Hôtel-Dieu. The short lateral wings along the Parvis were to accommodate the chapels of the two institutions. The total width of the porticoes, with the street in between, matched that of the west front of Notre-Dame, to which, if only symbolically, they would form a counterpoise. Twin porticoes of this kind, a motif derived from Palladio, had already been used by Sir Christopher Wren for his Royal Naval Hospital at Greenwich, which Boffrand might have seen in the *Vitruvius Britannicus*. But then, the same architectural accent sets off the beginning of the Corso in Rome, with its pair of flanking church porticoes.[31]

With this design, Boffrand was tackling one of the most-discussed problems in Paris: the clearance and rebuilding of the ancient city centre.[32] The clergy had long wanted to improve access to Notre-Dame and to clear a way for religious and royal processions. Delamair, in his *Livre des embellissements de Paris* (1731), had proposed a radical restructuring of the Ile de la Cité, with an enlarged Parvis surrounded by a double colonnade based on those built by Bernini before St Peter's in Rome. Boffrand's design covered a smaller area and was markedly more balanced, with clear architectural accents.

The only part of the programme to be executed was the Enfants-Trouvés, a building of monumental dignity (1746–51; lost in the nineteenth-century redevelopment of the Ile de la Cité) (Plate 94). Its massive street frontage was held together by the uniform ground-floor arcade and by the entablature zone, which – like that of the Arsenal, of thirty years before – derived a special weightiness from its sheer size and from the alternation of modillions and windows. With its tranquil, rather ponderous forms and its tall, separated roofs, this façade harked back to seventeenth-century classicism. The lateral pavilions, with their giant order, were a repeat of those at Le Vau's Collège des Quatre Nations.

The chapel was particularly important. Consecrated in 1751, it had a highly unconventional scheme of painted decoration (Plate 95).[33] This consisted of a complete system of fictive architecture, within which Charles-Joseph Natoire had painted a procession of Shepherds along one side and another of Magi along the other; these met at the altar to adore the Christ Child. The figures of spectators looked down on the processions from the arcades of the upper storey. The architectural setting itself, which was painted by the father-and-son team of Gaetano and Paolo Antonio Brunetti, bore every sign of dilapidation and decay. Half of

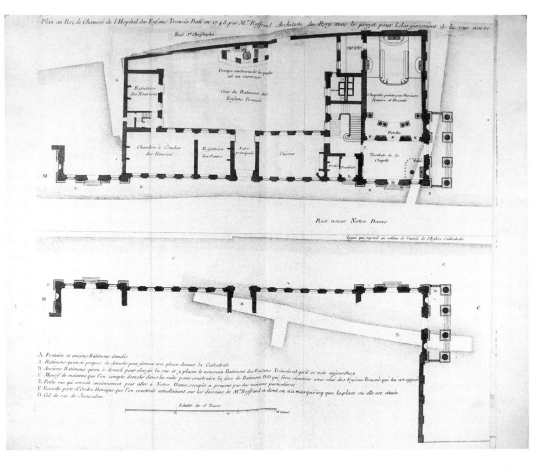

93 Germain Boffrand: Paris, Orphanage, 1746–51, layout (Boffrand, *Livre d'Architecture*).

94 Germain Boffrand: Paris, Orphanage, 1746–51, elevations (Boffrand, *Livre d'Architecture*).

95 Germain Boffrand: Paris, Orphanage, chapel, 1746–51, paintings by Natoire and Gaetano Brunetti (Paris, Bibliothèque Nationale).

the ceiling appeared to have caved in, and exposed beams hung perilously in mid-air. The desperate poverty of this Bethlehem stable was an allusion to the nature of the establishment as a hospital for waifs and strays.

The decor was a sensational success, reviewed at length in the *Mercure de France* and praised by Abbé Laugier as 'a grand idea and a very fine invention'. Although the Brunettis' trompe-l'oeil decorations were familiar, the transformation of a whole church interior into a ruin was something quite new. Such an extreme of Baroque illusionistic painting was the last thing anyone would have expected to find behind Boffrand's classical façade. But it was precisely this breadth of grasp, encompassing both classical form and the *goût nouveau*, rigour and levity, that distinguished Boffrand from all his contemporaries.

Of de Cotte's pupils, only one ever designed a notable building. This was Pierre Vigné de Vigny (1690–1772), the architect of the Hôpital Général in Lille (begun 1738, destroyed in the Second World War).[34] He planned it as a vast rectangle with five courts and a centrally placed, cruciform church, but only the entrance façade, the *cour d'honneur* directly behind it, and the two courts to the left were built; the church never advanced beyond the early stages, and none of the courts on the right was ever built. In its cool elegance, the noble river front looked more like a château than a hospital. It was 140 metres or 460 feet long and reflected de Cotte's style both in its horizontal emphasis and in its use of a central frontispiece with a giant order under a triangular pediment. The centres of the long wings were marked out like frontispieces by narrow strips of rustication. However, Vigny divided de Cotte's continuous, rusticated

podium into tall, individual pedestals for the giant pilasters, and reduced the ground-floor arcade to simple arches over the windows. This fragmentation produced a restless effect, unknown in de Cotte's own buildings, which marked the dissolution of his system.

Of the theatres built in this period, the only one worth mentioning is the Comédie in Metz, a large, transverse rectangle with a strongly projecting, polygonal frontispiece. Situated on an island in the river Moselle, it was begun in 1738, but the carcass was not completed until 1749. The intended prototype was the theatre in Strasbourg; but neither its builder, the Metz city architect, Oger, nor the architect who took over in 1751, Roland de Virloys – a self-styled 'Architect to the King of Prussia' who had very little idea of his business – was able to construct a stage that would work. After Virloys had spent two years on the job, amassed considerable debts, and decamped, a committee was called in from Paris to redesign the interior and make it usable. In 1755 two end pavilions were added, and these and the existing convex façade were fronted by an arcade; the resultant pattern of undulation has ever since dominated the Place de la Comédie and given the theatre its character.[35] Germain Soufflot's theatre in Lyon, which was based on an entirely new architectural conception, is discussed in its wider context below.

One of the distinctive features of French public architecture in the early and mid eighteenth century was a change in function: buildings ceased to be isolated single objects, and became elements in a larger urban organism. It is significant that Boffrand got his plans for the Enfants-Trouvés accepted only after the council of state had classified them as a measure for the embellishment of the Parvis de Notre-Dame. The improvement and modernization of the French cities was one of the great tasks facing Louis XV's government. The city was no longer seen as a mere accumulation of houses but as a rationally designed organism, subject to established rules. There can be no doubt that the fortress architecture of Vauban, with its chequerboard town plans derived from Italy, had set a precedent: Rennes is a good example of this. However, the process of general change can only have been prompted by the rise of Enlightenment ideas, which brought with them a new sense of social responsibility. And so Delamair described his book *Le Songe et le réveil d'Alexis Delamair* as 'An Architectural Treatise such as will promote the glory of the King, the interests of the Church of France, the healthfulness, embellishment and convenience of Paris, the relief of the poor and the progress of art'.[36] It was the craving for hygiene, for wholesome water and healthy air – in short, for general well-being – as expressed by Voltaire in his *Etablissement de Paris* (1749), that led to the paving of the streets, the introduction of street lighting and public drainage, the reform of hospitals and monastic buildings. The provincial Intendants made it their ambition to give the cities of their own bailiwicks a modern and welcoming appearance, often in the teeth of strenuous opposition from the city fathers: Bordeaux was the most compelling instance of this. In Paris, the task of rescuing the city from its medieval congestion and its traffic chaos was undertaken in the *Plan général* of Pierre-Louis Moreau (1762–9).[37]

The architects, for their part, saw architecture no longer *en maçon*, as masons, but *en philosophe*, as thinkers: they turned it into a social and societal concern. This is evident not only from the theoretical writings of the day – Delamair's *Livre des Etablissements de Paris* (*c.* 1730) and Patte's *Monuments érigés à la gloire de Louis XV* (1765) and *Mémoires sur les objets les plus importants de l'architecture* (1769) – but from the plans that were made for the redevelopment of whole quarters.

This impulse to renew the urban fabric came from the crown. Under Louis XIV, Paris, Lyon and Dijon had acquired grand and imposing new squares. Under his successor, as Patte tells us, Bordeaux, Nancy, Lunéville, Besançon, Metz, Rennes, Tours, Dijon, Nîmes and many other towns entirely transformed themselves. The city laid itself open to the surrounding country. A general sense of security made the old city walls redundant; they were replaced by open parks and walks. Houses on the bridges were demolished, rivers were embanked with stone promenades, and in urban planning France became the most advanced country of the age.[38]

A decisive role in all this was played by the Places Royales, which were among the distinctive features of French cities. In these, the late Bourbon monarchy created a lasting memorial to itself.[39] Unlike the early squares laid out under Henry IV – the Place Royale (now Place des Vosges) and Place Dauphine in Paris, or the Place Ducale in Charleville – these Places Royales were intended not only to adorn the cities concerned but also to enhance the prestige of the state and of the monarchy. To this end, they were surrounded by public buildings, and markets and shops were excluded. They were not built for commerce or for traffic; their purposes were primarily political and aesthetic.[40] In the seventeenth century they remained isolated locations; but in the eighteenth they became the focal points of new street networks, fitted into unbroken axial alignments, each of which ended in a view-stopper – a church, a town hall, or whatever. Already visible in Rennes, this new type finds its fullest expression in the Place Royale in Bordeaux, which is open not only to the city and along the Garonne embankments but to the river itself. The pattern continues in the Place Louis-XV (now Place de la Concorde) in Paris, and in the squares of Nancy and Reims; an equally grand composition projected for Rouen never left the drawing board. The Places Royales were the aesthetic touchstone and the pride of every city that possessed one; the royal monuments that adorned them were by the best sculptors in the country. Patte published them in his book of engravings, *Monuments érigés à la gloire de Louis XV* (1765).

Of the public parks and gardens of the day, the 'Promenades' that appeared all over the country and greatly improved the appearance of the cities, I will mention only one; but it is one that excels all the others. This is the Jardin de la Fontaine, in Nîmes.[41] Around a Roman sacred spring, two local architects, Esprit Dardalhon and Jean-Philippe Maréchal, created a kind of water garden in which nature and architecture are intimately united. The balustrades constructed along the ancient canals, which had been restored or re-excavated, and the rich sculptural ornament suggest a comparison with the Villa Lante near Orvieto. But here all this is integrated into a great axial system, at the end of which, above the Roman bath and alongside the so-called Temple of Diana, wide steps and terraces ascend a hillside crowned with the ruins of a Roman temple.

CHAPTER 3

Court Art and the Early Work of Ange-Jacques Gabriel

After losing its leading role at the death of Louis XIV, the court resurfaced as an artistic force in the 1730s; but by then the atmosphere had changed. As contemporary observers unanimously testify, Louis XV was a man of artistic interests and a man of taste;[42] but when it came to architecture he tended to be erratic and indecisive. His first priority was to find accommodation for his large family, rather than to create great art or to enhance his own posthumous reputation. In his palaces alterations were constantly in progress, and so he spent vast sums of money without having anything really permanent to show for it.[43]

At Versailles, the work was mostly decorative: the completion of the Salon d'Hercule (c. 1730), the Appartement de la Reine (1730–5 and 1746–7), the Petits Appartements du Roi (1735–8) and the apartments of the Dauphin and Dauphine in the left-hand wing (1746–7). Each time, some remodelling took place. The most radical change was the insertion of the Petits Appartements in the right-hand wing in the 1730s. There the young king, who had no desire to go on living in his great-grandfather's apartments, staked out a territory of his own.

Starting in the 1720s, the so-called Cabinets du Roi had been installed on the first, second and even third floors around an internal court, the Cour des Cerfs. The result was a warren of small and intimate spaces – card rooms, laboratories, libraries, summer and winter dining rooms, closets, bathrooms, staircases, and the rest – the number and decor of which were constantly changing, and in which the king gradually took up residence.

This displacement of the central focus of Versailles was then made official and permanent by the building of the Petits Appartements. The parts affected were mainly the previously untouched Louis XIV rooms facing the Cour de Marbre and the Cour Royale. First the Cabinet du Billard was enlarged, by the addition of a bed alcove, into the new royal bedchamber, the Chambre du Roi or Chambre Louis-XV. Then came the apsidal Salon des Jeux (later Cabinet des Pendules) and the Cabinet d'Angle or Cabinet Intérieur, which, with its fashionably canted corners, led into the existing Salon Ovale. The adjoining Petite Galerie, once decorated by Pierre Mignard, still served as a picture gallery, and was kept for the present, but with a new wall and ceiling decoration (Plate 96).

The result was an artistically coherent suite of rooms, which theoretically formed the *appartement de société* (the rooms upstairs, to which only the king's personal guests were admitted, being the *appartement de commodité*); but even these, with the exception of the bedchamber, suffered from the king's chronic inability to leave well alone. The apsidal end of the Cabinet des Pendules was replaced by straight walls, as were the canted corners in the Cabinet d'Angle; in 1753 the Petite Galerie was subdivided and its paintings removed. In 1755 the Salon Ovale disappeared altogether.

As work on the Petits Appartements continued under Louis XVI, their original state can be reconstructed only with difficulty.[44]

Much the same happened at La Muette, the château in the Bois de Boulogne that the king loved because he had spent the happiest days of his childhood there.[43] In 1737, Jacques V Gabriel rebuilt the court front, and in 1739 the garden front, in the style of a hôtel *particulier*. But as early as 1746 there was another remodelling, this time with a majestic *dôme à l'impériale* as a central accent (Plate 97). The garden front was crowned with a typically Gabrielian segmental pediment; but the coupled pilasters and broken pediment on the court side were more reminiscent of Lassurance the Elder, and of his Hôtels and Desmarets in particular.

The only major undertaking that confronted Jacques V Gabriel was at Fontainebleau. Here his task was to remodel the king's relatively modest apartments overlooking the Jardin

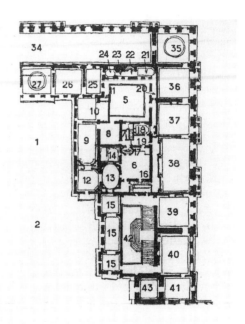

1. Cour de marbre. — 2. Cour royale. — 3. Cour de la Reine. — 4. Cour dite de Monsieur. — 5. Cour des Cerfs. — 6. Petite cour intérieure du Roi. — 7. Degré du Roi. — 8. Antichambre dite des Chiens. — 9. Salon-ovale ou Cabinet des Pendules. — 10. Nouvelle Chambre du Roi ou Chambre de Louis XV. — 11. Cabinet de Garde-robe. — 12. Cabinet à pans ou Cabinet-intérieur (Cabinet d'angle). — 13. Ancien Salon-ovale de Louis XIV. — 14. Cabinet en niche. — 15. Petite Galerie avec ses deux salons. — 16. Degré d'Épernon. — 17. Escalier ovale montant aux Cabinets du second étage. — 18. Chambre des Bains. — 19. Pièce des Cuves. — 20. Corridor. — 21. Cabinet-doré. — 22. Escalier demi-circulaire. — 23. Cabinet de Chaise. — 24. Petit Cabinet particulier du Roi. — 25. Cabinet des Perruques. — 26. Cabinet du Conseil. — 27. Grande Chambre ou Chambre de Louis XIV.

96 Versailles, Petits Appartements, plan (from Verlet, *Versailles*, 1961).

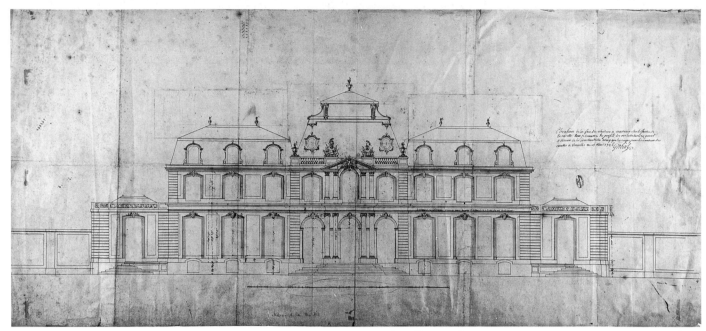

97 Ange-Jacques Gabriel: La Muette, design for court façade, 1746 (Archives Nationales).

98 Jacques Gabriel: Fontainebleau, Gros Pavillon, façade project, 1740 (Archives Nationales).

99 Ange-Jacques Gabriel: Fontainebleau, Gros Pavillon, 1750–4.

de Diane, to add a new wing for the princes, and to enlarge the whole château to accommodate the regular visits of the whole court. The king had decided to demolish the venerable Galerie d'Ulysse, a key work of early Renaissance architecture, with frescoes by Primaticcio that were said to be in a ruinous condition. In its place he wanted a long wing of apartments along the south side of the Cour du Cheval-Blanc (now the Cour des Adieux). Then the left-hand side wing of the Cour de la Fontaine – the Aile des Reines-Mères or Aile de Mesdames – was to be lengthened and terminated with a large pavilion directly overlooking the lake; this became the Gros Pavillon (Plate 98).

The Galerie d'Ulysse was demolished in 1738, and in the following year Gabriel embarked on the building of the Aile Neuve (Aile Gabriel) along the Cour du Cheval-Blanc. His simple, two-storey elevation, with its alternation of brick and ashlar, shows due respect for the façades opposite, which date from the reign of Francis I. He added more weight only in the centre pavilion, with its sculptured pediment and its tall, set-back roof; the elliptical arch over the doorway, with its Borromini-like cartouche, lends a Rococo touch. The link with the existing east range of the Cour du Cheval-Blanc is formed by a three-bay pavilion that matches the storey height, fenestration and pilaster ornament of the sixteenth-century façade.[46]

Jacques V Gabriel's 'Grand Projet', of which these works formed the first stage, was intended to give a new dimension to the Château de Fontainebleau and put an end to its perennial shortage of space.[47] The Cour du Cheval-Blanc was to be entirely rebuilt, to match the Aile Neuve, with a pair of new terminal pavilions on the entrance side modelled on the Gros Pavillon. The Cour de la Fontaine was to be regularized by making its two side wings a better match, with the Gros Pavillon at the lake end and a duplicate at the end of the matching wing, together with a new façade for the old Galerie de François Ier. All this would have made Fontainebleau consistent, but at the expense of much of its picturesque charm. Work was in full swing in 1742, when

100 Ange-Jacques Gabriel: Trianon, Pavillon Français, 1749.

Jacques V Gabriel died. He was succeeded in the post of chief architect, as a matter of course, by his son Ange-Jacques, who had been closely involved in all his projects.

Ange-Jacques Gabriel (1698–1782) had been groomed to succeed his father. Thanks to the best of family connections, he had rapidly climbed the ladder of advancement in the Bâtiments du Roi, where his father had trained and systematically promoted him. In 1728 he had taken over his father's post of surveyor general; in 1735, when the latter became chief architect, he took over as surveyor at Versailles, with sole responsibility for the decorative work. On de Cotte's death in the same year, he was promoted to the first class of the Academy. He also enjoyed the particular confidence of the king, who had come to share his predecessor's interest in architecture and now spent many hours poring over plans and designs with the younger Gabriel.[48] The king's good opinion did a great deal to strengthen his position, and was to give him a considerable advantage in dealing with his director-general, whether this was Madame de Pompadour's uncle, Le Normant de Tournehem, or her brother, the Marquis de Marigny. For thirty-three years Ange-Jacques Gabriel worked – unlike his father – exclusively for the king.[49] Almost every piece of building work that was done personally for Louis XV was his. He thus became a central figure in French architecture.

The 'Gabriel style', named after Ange-Jacques, is characteristic of Louis XV's reign. It leads from Rococo to Palladio and Neoclassicism without a break, flexibly adapting itself to the trends of the day. Ange-Jacques Gabriel was an acute observer who had no inhibitions over appropriating the new ideas of his day, including those of younger colleagues, and absorbing them into his own style. The criticisms that were levelled at him sprang largely from the belief that his appointment – not to speak of his father's – was the result of an abuse of family connections, tantamount to a dynastic principle, and that this had deprived many others no less gifted of the opportunities that were their due. Ange-Jacques Gabriel, always mistrustful of his professional colleagues, serenely ignored all this, and used his position as the heir to a grand style to pursue the ultimate in proportion, balance and elegance. His art was the noblest embodiment of French taste: 'Gabriel lacked the genius of an innovator, but he had the qualities of a great master: nobility and simplicity of design, elegance of detail, a monumental sense.' (M. Gallet)

His artistic individuality first asserted itself at Fontainebleau, when work resumed there after the Peace of Aix-la-Chapelle. As the king was particularly interested in the remodelling of the Cour de la Fontaine, the Aile Neuve was not completed at once, but a start was made on the Gros Pavillon. Jacques V Gabriel's design for this had been in existence since 1740; but its execution by Ange-Jacques (1750–4) clearly points to the differences between father and son (Plate 99). While retaining the overall proportions, the son shifted the points of emphasis. On the ground floor he confined the rustication to the three central, arched bays, and on the first floor he emphasized the centre with a projecting portico. He replaced the segmental arches on the second floor with flat lintels, and the pediment with a horizontal balustrade. The wall also gained a degree of relief from the replacement of his father's wrought-iron balcony by another stone balustrade. In all this, Ange-Jacques Gabriel was harking back to seventeenth-century classicism: he turned away from the façade mentality of the Rococo to a sculptural conception of the building as a solid in space. His Gros Pavillon is a reminiscence of Le Vau's garden front at Versailles, although the tall roofs disguise this at first sight. But the trophies and flaming urns on the balustrade, which appeared in the design and at one time on the building itself, were a clear allusion.

The reversion towards classicism is also shown in the numerous pavilions that Ange-Jacques Gabriel built at this time. Among the earliest was the Ermitage (1749), built for Madame de Pompadour outside the park of Fontainebleau. This was a commission that came his way in spite of having been initially assigned to Lassurance the Younger. The plainness of the exterior was in keeping with the taste of its intended occupier. It was a regular block of three bays, at the end of a long *cour d'honneur*, with a centre breaking slightly forward between rusticated dressings. Curves were eliminated, and the horizontal ruled supreme. Only the segmental pediment softened the outline and relaxed the rigour of the system. This was also the only feature to have any sculptural ornament; the window keystones were barely discernible.

An even clearer departure from the Rococo is apparent in the Pavillon Français at the Trianon (1749) (Plate 100). This charming little building was originally the centre of a *ménagerie* built by the king for Madame de Pompadour, and was intended as a gaming room. The exterior, with its alternation of banded and smooth wall, its rectangular windows and its minutely detailed cornice, is very like that of the Ermitage at Fontainebleau. The building consists of an octagonal central salon with four cabinets arranged in a cross around it. For this Ange-Jacques Gabriel had older precedents, such as the Pavillon de Sceaux or the pavilion designed by de Cotte for Compiègne.

Light and elegant though it is, the Pavillon Français clearly reveals that by the time it was built the full-blown Rococo, as expressed for example in the Pavillon du Dauphin at Versailles (1736, by Jacques V Gabriel), was a thing of the past. The forms no longer merge into each other but are plainly distinguished. Curves have given way to straight lines; the flat-headed window has replaced the segmental arch. The door opening is no longer a coved recess but a right-angled reveal. The pyramidal form has also disappeared, and the skyline is defined not by a pediment but by balustrades crowned with putti and urns. The interior decoration, on the theme of the flowers and birds of the *ménagerie*, is of the greatest refinement. But here, too, architectural elements predominate. As in the Salle des Colonnes of the Grand Trianon, built sixty years earlier, Corinthian columns mark the corners of the salon and conduct the octagon, by way of a massive cornice, into the circle of the dome.

The pendant to the Pavillon Français was the now-vanished, square Salon Frais, which was used as a dining room. This was entirely overgrown with trellised plants and was flanked by arcades, also trellised and filled with orange and linden trees trimmed to a perfect sphere. Here, in the window lintels and roof balustrades and in the recessed doorway with its sharp mouldings, the straight line and the angular contour prevailed.

This emphasis on sharp edges as distinct from rounded corners, and the accompanying tendency towards cubic form, point the way to Gabriel's mature style. This is already evident in the Pavillon du Roi at Choisy church (1743),[50] but above all in Louis XV's numerous hunting lodges, scattered all over the forests of the Ile-de-France.[51]

The Pavillon du Butard (1750–1), for instance, consists of a rectangular block with a polygonal projection at the rear to accommodate a round salon (Plates 101, 102). The entrance front breaks forward only slightly in the centre, which is emphasized by a pediment. The external articulation is limited to strips of rustication. A columned porch, flanked by stags' heads on the wall, was deleted from the design during construction. The only piece of decoration on the building is the pediment, with a relief of a wild boar hunt.[52]

The consolidation of architectural form that manifests itself here is also seen in the increasing use of architectural rather than decorative ornamental motifs. At Le Butard, for example, the previously customary acanthus brackets are replaced by triglyph brackets: a motif, derived from Michelangelo, that is rare in French architecture. This goes along with a new form of garland, no longer suspended from the brackets but threaded through them.[53] All this reveals that even before the antique revival Ange-Jacques Gabriel was paving the way for Neoclassicism.

The king's new-found enthusiasm for building was certainly influenced by Madame de Pompadour. Her role at Louis XV's court as a patroness of the arts was undoubtedly an important one; her background in the world of finance had accustomed her to the idea of spending money on expensive pastimes – a category that certainly included building. The habit of acquiring châteaux and hôtels, for which she was much denounced by her critics, sprang not merely from the desire to keep her royal lover amused, and thus attach him more firmly to herself, but also from personal inclination. Contrary to the opinion of the Goncourt brothers, however, she had no time for the excesses of the Rococo. It would be quite wrong to associate her with the origins of the style: her influence came to bear only after the Rococo had passed its peak, at a time when its early formal exuberance had dwindled, leaving behind only the harmony of the soft and curvaceous line.

Although she had secured considerable influence over the Service des Bâtiments du Roi through her uncle and her brother, her own architect was not Ange-Jacques Gabriel but Jean Cailleteau, alias Lassurance the Younger, the son of the Régence architect Pierre Lassurance. He was responsible not only for her new buildings, such as Bellevue, but also for the remodelling of those that she received as gifts from the king, or bought for herself – Montretout, La Celle-Saint-Cloud, the Hôtel d'Evreux in Paris – or simply rented, like Champs.

The Château de Bellevue (1748–50) was the first house

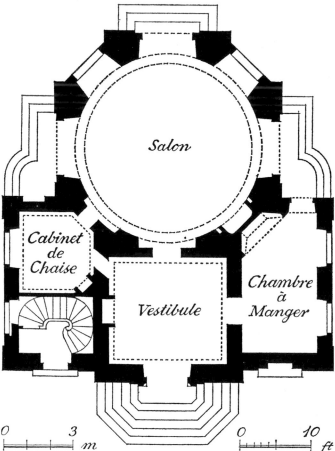

101 Ange-Jacques Gabriel: Pavillon du Butard, 1750–1.

102 Ange-Jacques Gabriel: Pavillon du Butard, 1750–1, plan.

that the royal favourite built for herself. It became famous not only for its position overlooking the Seine valley, with a garden designed by Garnier de l'Isle, but for its costly furnishings. It revealed Lassurance the Younger as a conventional architect, firmly ensconced in the Mansart tradition. The château was an isolated block, nine bays long by six bays deep, surrounded by low domestic buildings. All the elevations were articulated in the same way: rusticated frontispiece with pediment, segment-headed windows, Baroque œil-de-boeuf windows in the mansard roof. They also shared the same sculptural decor of marble busts, which appeared both as window keystones and in between the windows; this was a reminiscence of such houses by Lassurance the Elder as Petitbourg.

Even after the king bought Bellevue from the marquise in 1757 and handed over the direction of the work to Gabriel, the same obsolete but – to the king – familiar style persisted through all the successive enlargements of the 1760s and 1770s. However, the interior acquired a Neoclassical decor, dominated by pseudo-antique reliefs and large areas of arabesque. Until the Revolution, Bellevue was the residence of Louis XV's daughters; in 1823, much of it was demolished and the remaining parts altered beyond recognition.

CHAPTER 4

Emmanuel Héré and Architecture in Lorraine under King Stanislas

Lorraine has a place of its own among the French provinces. It was extremely active artistically under its own dukes; and during the reign of King Stanislas it produced a brief blaze of architectural pyrotechnics that vanished as suddenly as it had appeared. The first great architectural period, dominated by Boffrand, had ended with the death of Duke Leopold in 1729. His son and successor, Francis III, for whom Leopold had secured the hand of Archduchess Maria Theresa of Austria – the marriage took place in 1736 – lived in Vienna and took little interest in his duchy. In 1731 he left his mother, Elisabeth Charlotte, in charge as regent; and in 1737, even before the formal conclusion of the Peace of Vienna, he renounced his own titles in order to become the successor of the Medici in Florence. In the same year, King Stanislas arrived in Lorraine and took up residence at Lunéville. The duchess regent moved to Commercy, where she continued to enjoy the honours due to a sovereign princess until her death in 1744.

King Stanislas's own sovereignty was more apparent than real. In return for an annual pension of two million livres, he had relinquished both the governance and the revenues of his duchies; administrative authority rested with the French Intendant. This was no more than a nominal reign, a device to ease the transition from sovereign state to French province. However, it lasted longer than either Vienna or Paris had expected: Stanislas died at a ripe old age in 1766.

By way of compensation, and to win the affection of his new subjects, the king assumed the only role that remained open to him: that of a patron of the arts. He embarked on a building programme that went far beyond all the efforts of his predecessors. It had very little in common with the classicism of Boffrand. The king's taste had been formed by the Italian and German Baroque, and he had also garnered some Turkish inspiration in Bessarabia, where he had spent some time in the camp of Charles XII of Sweden. Endowed with a lively imagination and abundant energy, even late in life, Stanislas was tireless in the improvement both of his own residences and of his adopted country. He was actively involved in the planning and execution of all his projects.

His architect was Emmanuel Héré (1705–63), a man as fertile in ideas as himself and well able to satisfy his often eccentric wishes.[55] Of Héré's origins and training we know little. Few of his buildings have survived; and the vanity of the king, who liked to assume the credit for his work, ensured that his name was not mentioned too often; indeed, he sank into oblivion. Modern researchers labour under the additional handicap of the loss of most of the archives of Lorraine.

Héré's father had accompanied Duke Leopold on his return to Lorraine from exile in Tirol (though this does not necessarily mean that he was himself of Tirolese origin), and had then worked in the ducal office of works. Emmanuel Héré himself was on the payroll, in a subordinate position, from 1720 onwards; and after Stanislas's arrival in 1737 he was appointed governor (*capitaine et concierge*) of the royal Château de Lunéville. This was a position with excellent prospects. He may or may not have studied in Paris; there is no documentary evidence either way. He probably learned his business at Lunéville, first under Boffrand and then under Boffrand's successors, Nicolas Jadot and J.N. Jennesson, who successively dominated architecture in Lorraine after his departure.

Nothing is known of Héré's work at this stage of his life. He owed his meteoric rise to the fact that the king fell out with Jennesson, who had succeeded Jadot as chief architect, but who refused to demean himself by building a Turkish kiosk. Héré, who had no such scruples, seized the opportunity and designed the building. In 1748 he succeeded Jennesson as *Premier architecte et inspecteur des hôtels et maisons de Sa Majesté* and moved into an apartment in the Château de Lunéville; in 1751 he was raised to the nobility and styled himself Héré de Corny after his own recently acquired château. His work for the king is recorded for us by two large books of engravings that he published on the king's behalf.[56] He died after a long illness in 1763, some years after retiring from practice.

Héré was a phenomenon. Obviously poorly trained, and promoted chief architect without any practical experience, he rapidly developed into an original and imaginative artist who handled the formal inheritance of Boffrand with a light and almost playful touch and created a resplendent setting for the new court. The hectic pace of his work for the king left him little time to reflect on aesthetic or theoretical problems. It would therefore be unfair to measure him against a figure of Boffrand's stature. But for the relaxed, Rococo tone of Stanislas's court he was precisely the right man. His buildings formed the setting for a society that looked to architecture not for classical rules but for grace and delicacy.

The work at the Château de Lunéville with which his career began was of no profound significance. It consisted in internal remodelling, together with comprehensive redecoration and refurnishing; the last duke had taken everything with him. The only external feature that Héré changed was the shape of the roof, replacing Boffrand's separate roofs and central dome with a single roof and truncated pyramid. This gave the palace a more unified look; but the balustrades that he added half-way down the roof slopes reveal little understanding of Boffrand's conception. They introduce a restless and frivolous note that is out of key with Boffrand's building.[57]

At Commercy, too, which Stanislas took over after the death of the duchess regent in 1744, Héré left Orbay's building essentially unchanged,[58] adding only a forecourt and a water garden linked with the château on its high terrace by a pair of curved flights of steps. Orbay had connected the town with the château by a straight road; some

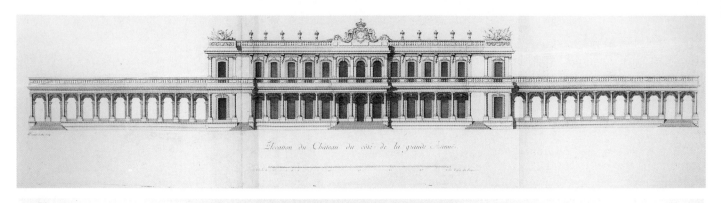

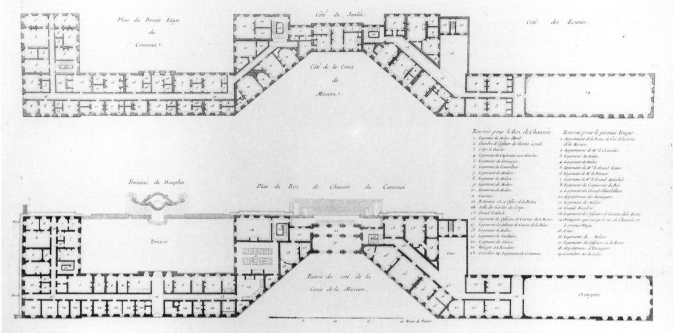

103 Emmanuel Héré: La Malgrange, château, 1739–40, elevation
(Héré, *Recueil* T.I fig. 37).

104 Emmanuel Héré: La Malgrange, Communs, *c.* 1740, plan
(Héré, *Recueil* T.I fig. 39).

way before entering the *cour d'honneur*, this expanded into a horseshoe-shaped space. The forecourt was between this horseshoe and the side wings of the château itself. It had originally been enclosed by plain, low walls; Héré replaced these with single-storey stable blocks, which he attached to the horseshoe by curved communicating wings. Having thus welded the enclosed forecourt and the *cour d'honneur* into a single unit, he divided it with a great, curved, wrought-iron fence that mirrored the line of the horseshoe. The low wings, with their rustication, shallow blind arcades, and roof balustrades adorned with urns and trophies, were an anticipation of the slightly later Basses Faces in the Place Royale in Nancy.

Stanislas built only one important château, that of La Malgrange (1739–40). This was the king's favourite creation. It stood not far from the site of its unfinished predecessor, Boffrand's La Malgrange, demolished in 1738; but it was more of a sumptuous villa – a *maison de plaisance* – than a château (Plate 103). The main block, which was reserved for the exclusive use of the king and Queen and a few guests, consisted of a long, two-storey *corps de logis* with balustraded roofs and a parapet cartouche. Its principal feature was its interminable colonnade, which not only ran along both main elevations but marched on, far beyond, into

the gardens on either side. The only articulation of the façade was a frontispiece with columns below and a projection of the main structure above, flanked by a pair of separate, small stair pavilions.

La Malgrange was planned with a view to informal living. A small vestibule flanked by two antechambers – the smallest room in the house – led into the grand Salle de Marbre that occupied most of the garden front and adjoined the bedchambers of the king and queen. The secondary apartments, with little differentiation and of modest size, were placed around the ends of the wings and continued along the court side as far as the vestibule zone. Behind the projecting frontispiece of the upper storey was another royal apartment, with the bedchamber in the centre of the façade, and this was flanked by two pairs of guest apartments, symmetrically arranged. Small side pavilions, communicating with the *corps de logis* only through the colonnades, contained the chapel and the kitchens. The exterior was entirely clad with faience tiles, which gave it its fairytale, exotic look. In the gardens behind the château, hidden by the landscaping, were long, narrow domestic blocks and garden houses, including the celebrated 'Salle à Manger' converted from an orangery.

This palace of faience was utterly different from Boffrand's creation. It took no account either of the orders or of the requirements of decorum: even the stairs were accessible only by way of open galleries. It was the product of a princely caprice untrammelled by any rules, whether of aesthetics or of protocol: worlds apart, in fact, from the ambitious mind of Duke Leopold, obsessed as he was by rules of precedence. Its prototypes might have included garden houses such as the Grand Trianon and Saint-Ouen, both of which Stanislas had seen, but also Italian villas. Héré might have derived the colonnade motif from Boffrand, who had used it in very much the same way in his first design for Lunéville. There, a colonnade ran the full length of the side wing containing the chapel, between two flat-roofed end pavilions; and, as here at La Malgrange, it was roofed by a balustraded terrace.[59] This does not explain the lateral colonnades, which can only have been pure garden architecture, like J.H. Mansart's so-called Colonnade in the park at Versailles. At La Malgrange, they formed a kind of optical screen between the front and back gardens of the château. Nor was there any European precedent for the faience tiling of the walls. The Trianon de Porcelaine no longer existed in Stanislas's day, and in any case its faience tiling had been confined to the roof. Memories of Turkish kiosks and pavilions must have played a part here.

The Communs, the building for the royal household, which Héré added in ensuing years, was as unusual as the faience palace itself (Plate 104). At right angles to the palace, it formed a barrier between this and its park, which lay to one side. On the château side it appeared to be divided into three almost detached blocks, with terraces, steps and fountains. On the park side, however, it formed a single block more than 200 metres or 650 feet long. To relieve this uniformity, Héré made the centre swing inwards in a canted recess to an open vestibule, like that at Lunéville. Above the arches were the queen's private quarters, the Petits Appartements de la Reine, with a pilastered frontispiece on the château side; the rest of the elevations were plain. The overall look of the Communs reflected Héré's love of stagecraft. The central recess relieved the monotony of the building; but in the wings, for the sake of symmetry, he flouted all the rules of *convenance*. The exterior articulation of the right-hand wing gave a completely false impression of the orangery within; and the fenestration of both wings included a number of blind windows with no rooms behind them at all.

Héré used the central recess and archway of the Communs to mark an axis that ran across the park from the queen's apartment, by way of flights of steps and box-hedged parterres, to the Croix de Mission, a large processional cross surrounded by the twelve Stations of the Cross.[60] There, within sight of the château and in the midst of some highly secular fountains, a place of pilgrimage sprang up, fostered by the pious king through the foundation of a miniature Capuchin friary.

The king's main interest, at La Malgrange and at his other *châteaux*, was in the gardens. There he could give free rein to his imagination. At his behest there arose Turkish kiosks, Chinese pavilions, toy hermitages, summer dining rooms, water pavilions, and so forth, which became famous and much-admired tourist sights. All of them were recorded in paintings in his gallery at Einville. For Héré, who became *Directeur des jardins, parcs et jets d'eau* on the departure of

Leopold's landscape architects, Yves des Hours and Louis de Nesle, this offered a new field of activity that suited his talents perfectly, and in which he could vie with his master in ingenious invention. These *fabriques*, as they later came to be called, were the earliest examples of exotic architecture in Europe. They were built some years before Kew Gardens and the Chinese pavilion designs of Chambers, which are generally described as the first examples of such architecture. The enthusiastic response of Abbé Laugier shows how well attuned they were to contemporary taste.[61]

Stanislas's predilection for building these ephemeral garden structures, rather than massive châteaux, was not solely a consequence of his limited means. It was also a matter of personal taste and life-style. Ever since Tschifflik, the house he had built during his exile at Zweibrücken, he had loved exotic pavilions, which he used to show off to his guests, and in which he often used to let them stay.

The first of his pavilions in Lorraine was the Turkish kiosk that he ordered for the park at Lunéville, soon after his arrival, thus precipitating the breach with Jennesson. The building that Héré then duly supplied betrayed the fact that this was still unfamiliar territory for him; he probably had to work on instructions from the king. But he was an apt student; and within a few years he was a master of fantasy architecture. One proof of this was the Trèfle, a Chinese pavilion in the shape of a clover-leaf, which he built in the same park at Lunéville a few years later (Plate 105). This consisted of a circular salon to which were appended two curved miniature apartments, each consisting of a bed-chamber and a small closet, and a third group of rooms, also curved, consisting of entrance lobby, closet, bathroom and stairs to the upper floor. The whole thing was ringed by a gallery in the same trefoil shape and roofed with curved 'Chinese' roofs. In the furniture and fabrics, Chinoiserie

105 Emmanuel Héré: Lunéville, Trèfle, *c.* 1742, plan (Héré, *Recueil* T.I fig. 21).

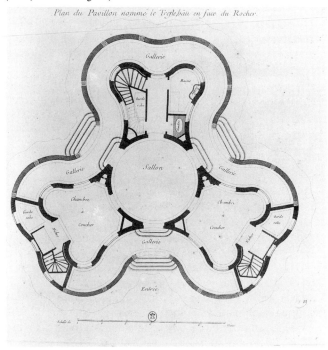

Elevation de la façade du Pavillon de Chanteheux vu côté de l'Entrée

prevailed throughout. Stanislas was in the habit of offering summer quarters in the Trèfle to particularly favoured members of his entourage. In a simplified form, it was the model for Frederick the Great's Japanisches Teehaus in the grounds of Sanssouci. There, the curvilinear plan of the Trèfle has been reduced to two concentric circles, leaving no room for living accommodation.[62]

A further attraction was the Salon de Chanteheux, a *maison de plaisance* built in three square tiers of diminishing sizes (Plate 106); with its terraces, it rose above the surrounding buildings like a fairy castle. This was Héré's second essay in this vein, built only three years after the Kiosk, but already showing supreme assurance in both planning and construction. The ground floor was occupied by a salon in the shape of a Greek cross, with porticoes at the ends of all the arms. The angles of the cross were fitted out as small apartments, accessible from the porticoes; the staircase and the tiny chapel adjoined the main entrance. In the central hall, sixteen columns sustained a complicated vaulting system that spanned both the central space itself and the aisles between columns and wall. The upper part of the pavilion was occupied by a single, double-height hall, the Salon itself. In this the Greek cross gave way to an octagon, the abbreviated cross-arms being screened off with columns to form secondary spaces. As on the ground floor, the intervening angles were occupied by small apartments. The interior was lit by eighteen large, round-headed windows on each side, so that there was little solid wall to be seen.

The external articulation was reduced to horizontal cornices and a few corner dressings in an alternating rhythm, but these were in any case visually swamped by the decorative forms that proliferated on every available surface. In the spandrels of the windows there were probably stucco ornaments; the descriptions speak of white and gold. Grisaille paintings occupied the intervening wall piers. Then there were the urns and groups of putti – the later probably cast in lead – on the balustrades and, to crown the whole, a clock in

an ornate cartouche. This luxuriant decoration, which would have been unthinkable on the façade of a *corps de logis*, made it clear that this was not a residence but a purely festive piece of architecture; hence the name of Salon de Chanteheux, used by Héré in his published collection of engravings.

The interior was entirely in keeping. The ascent from the lower hall, with its vault, its fountains and its dim lighting – like a *sala terrena* – into the brilliance of the double-height salon, with its two tiers of windows, was a magnificent piece of Baroque stagecraft in itself, especially at night, in the blaze of thirty-six chandeliers and fifty-two sconces. This was matched by the bewildering splendour of the decor: the simulated polychrome marble of the walls, the marble floor with its glittering floral inlay, the chimneypieces with their wall-high mirrors and inset paintings, the statuary in niches, the gilded capitals and the gilt balustrade of the minstrels' gallery. It was an enchanting sight, which inspired Louis XV, on a visit to Chanteheux, to utter the (authenticated) exclamation: 'My Father, there is only one Chanteheux in the world!'[63]

This 'salon unique in its beauty', as one anonymous visitor called it, was not at all a 'pasteboard palace' (*palais de carton*), as it has since been called.[64] On the contrary, it was a solid and well-though-out piece of architecture in stone. Its formal origins lay at Marly. That was the source of its plan, a central octagon inscribed in a square, with small apartments in the angles of the square. The Greek cross of the ground floor was simply a further development of the octagon, in which the spaces screened off above became proper wings below; its function was merely that of a base to the structure above.[65] The stepped cubic outline that the pavilion presented from the outside was, however, undoubtedly a quotation from Johann Bernhard Fischer von Erlach's imagined Tower of Babel, as illustrated in his *Entwurf einer historischen Architektur*. Fischer's tower has a larger number of steps, but it too is dominated by large, round-headed windows and surrounded by balustraded terraces.[66] We can

107 Emmanuel Héré: Commercy, Pavillon Royal, 1745–50 (Héré, *Recueil* T.II fig. 14).

Elevation en perspective du Pavillon Royal situé au bout du Canal de Commercy

safely assume that Stanislas possessed a copy of Fischer's book; and this would have made it accessible to Héré. This pavilion was much more than an eye-catcher, to complete the prospect from Lunéville and its gardens; it was a viewpoint in its own right, from which one could see as far as the Vosges. Even for so prominent a monument, the comparison with the Tower of Babel was absurd, of course; but it was symptomatic of the king's imagination and of his aspirations.

The parks of King Stanislas in Lorraine owed their fame not only to their exotic buildings but to their watercourses and fountains. These were remarkable not only for their scale and imaginative resource but for their sophisticated engineering. Stanislas loved hydraulic toys and kept a staff of mechanics and machinists to maintain his automata and fountains. In these gardens and buildings, water was an omnipresent source of animation, which also supplied the motive power for such hydraulic devices as the celebrated 'Rocher' on the banks of the grand canal at Lunéville, an artificial landscape with a miniature village whose human and animal inhabitants were water-driven automata. Nor was this all: both at Lunéville and at Commercy, there were great moated pavilions in which water became a constituent of the architecture itself.

The Pavillon Royal at Commercy (1745–50) was an entirely original showpiece (Plate 107). It formed the end of the grand axial canal that Héré had laid out as a continuation of the water garden below the château. Its façade was an integration of water and architecture. In its overall appearance the pavilion recalled the wide, single-storey form of the Grand Trianon, except that the central portion had an extra storey. This contained a mezzanine apartment for the king and a large upper salon, with doors onto the roof terrace. At the back, twin flights of stairs led to a first-floor landing fronted by coupled columns, as at the Trianon, with a view of the gardens beyond. Each of the lateral pavilions, linked to the main block by open arcades, had a short rear annexe to house kitchens and servants' quarters.

The Pavillon Royal owed its fame to its 'water columns': the hydraulic device whereby columns were formed by water jets directed downwards between thin metal rods. The six columns of the portico were not made of stone but of water, which discharged from the bases through lion masks. Contemporaries were unanimous in their admiration of this original feat of engineering. In his *Cours d'architecture*, Blondel described the effect as that of *un corps de cristal*: a crystalline solid.

The same technology was used – again at Commercy – in the Colonnade Hydraulique, a bridge some twenty metres long, aligned with the central axis of the château, and flanked on both sides by columns and piers of water surmounted by an ornate wooden entablature. The water was pumped up into the entablature, formed itself into columns and piers in its descent, and ran off through masks of river gods in the bases. With a column height of approximately four metres or thirteen feet, this was a hydraulic masterpiece.

Conjured forth, as if by magic, in the space of a few years, these châteaux, pavilions and hydraulic devices – which also included a kiosk that had 'curtains of water' instead of windows – were fated not to last. After the king's death in 1766, his châteaux were pulled down on the orders of Louis XV and the contents sold off. By then, the country's financial plight had become desperate, and the French crown was hard put to it to maintain its own châteaux, without adding more. Lunéville and Commercy were turned into barracks. The exotic pavilions, most of which were only made of wood and plaster, fell into disrepair.[67] Nothing remains of the waterworks that once aroused the astonished admiration of contemporaries. On the other hand, many of Héré's public buildings have survived. In Nancy he built a number of buildings for religious orders, including the Missions Royales for the Jesuits (1743) and – the only one still standing – a Maison des Frères de Saint-Jean de Dieu (1750–2) that is the purest example of his style, with its pilaster strips and its window arches in strong relief.

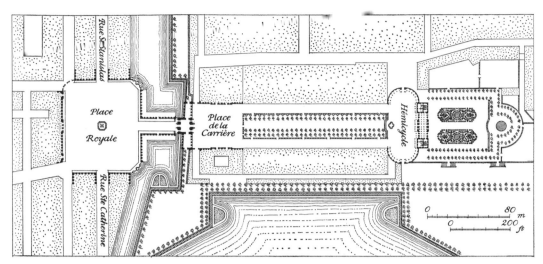

108 Emmanuel Héré: Nancy, Place de la Carrière and Place Stanislas, 1752–5, layout.

109 Jean Lamour: Nancy, Place Stanislas, gilded iron grating, c. 1755 (Héré, Recueil).

110 Emmanuel Héré: Nancy, Place Stanislas, town hall, 1752–5.

Élévation devélopée d'une Grille et Fontaine posée en tour creuse aux angles de la Place Royale de Nancy.

His last and by far his most important work is the grand sequence of squares with which he linked the old and new parts of the city of Nancy, and which culminates in the Place Royale (1752–5; now Place Stanislas) (Plate 108).[68] In spite of the disparity of its component parts – Hémicycle, Place de la Carrière, Place Royale – this grand axis forms an entirely coherent unity, with which Héré gave a new face to the capital city and at the same time established the framework for its subsequent development.[69] In building it, King Stanislas also had another motive: to prepare the population of Lorraine for union with France. He decided to erect a statue of his son-in-law and heir, the king of France, and to combine it with a Place Royale. This was a highly unusual idea: it was commonplace for a monarch to erect a statue of his or her predecessor, but Stanislas was the only one who ever paid the same compliment to his successor.[70]

The principal obstacle to the king's long-cherished plan was the need to breach the fortifications of the old city, an idea that France stubbornly resisted on military grounds. After lengthy negotiations, work finally began in 1752. Where the street crossed the moat, Héré replaced the old city gate with a triumphal arch modelled on the Arch of Severus in Rome.[71] He thus formed a link between the old city and the new one separating at the same time the Place de la Carrière and Hémicycle from the Place Royale. As the latter was flanked by the old fortifications, which by agreement with France would have to remain in being, Héré shifted the centre of gravity of the Place Royale to the far side, where he built the city hall that now dominates the square, with its massive façade and triangular pediment (Plate 110). Its internal staircase, which rises up at the end of the vestibule by way of a half-landing and two elliptically curved return

flights to the Salon Carré on the first floor, is a masterpiece of Baroque spatial effect.[72] The short sides of the Place Royale, bisected by a new cross-route – the Rue Saint-Stanislas and Rue Sainte-Catherine – continue the architecture of the Hôtel de Ville, but their subordinate status is marked by the absence of pediments. The resulting four blocks were used to house the theatre, the Bourse, the Intendance, and the financial and judicial administrations. Gilded wrought-iron gates, by the celebrated metalworker Jean Lamour,[73] close off the square from the neighbouring streets.

On the side nearest to the old, walled city, Héré masked the fortifications and the moat with large Baroque fountains framed by more gilded wrought iron (again by Lamour), in the form of triumphal arches (Plate 109), and with a pair of low galleries, the Basses Faces, topped by a rich assortment of statuary and returning across the moat to the triumphal arch. With this novel and unconventional composition, Héré created a Baroque square with a decidedly festive air, in total contrast to the ceremonious gravity that normally prevailed in such places. The centre was occupied by Barthélemy Guibal's statue of Louis XV, who was seen looking west towards France, his marshal's baton pointing east. Four bronze medallions on the plinth, modelled by Paul-Louis Cyfflé, symbolized the progress of the association between Lorraine and France.[74]

Inside the city walls, Héré imposed uniform façades on the long, narrow Place de la Carrière. By planting linden walks and a central strip of lawn, and installing more balus-trades, fountains, sculptures and gilded grilles, he transformed this old tilting yard into an elegant promenade, a *jardin public*. At the end nearest to the triumphal arch was Boffrand's Hôtel de Craon, which the king had purchased and made into the Palais de Justice; Héré faced it with a matching building, the Bourse de Commerce, and supplied the necessary end range for the Place de la Carrière by linking both to the arch with arcades. At the far end, he put a facing pair of square terminal pavilions with ground-floor porticoes. The Carrière thus acquired a well-defined and unified shape.

The north end of the Carrière is filled, not with Boffrand's demolished Louvre, but with the imposing bulk of the Hôtel de l'Intendance, the seat of the French Intendant (Plate 111). The elongated oval in front of this, known as the Hémicycle, performs two functions: it is both the forecourt of the Intendance and the old-city end of the Carrière. In place of the semicircular walls prefixed by a rank of columns, which now join the Intendance to the corner pavilions of the Carrière, Héré originally planned to have open arcades. The composition was to be rounded off by a public garden, visible and also accessible through the open central vestibule of the Intendance.

The sequence thus established, Place Royale – Carrière – Hémicycle, is a masterpiece of urban planning, in which squares and streets, architecture and nature, alternate in a harmonious rhythm. Its influence is detectable in the great squares that were subsequently laid out in Reims, in Brussels and – though only on paper – in Rouen.

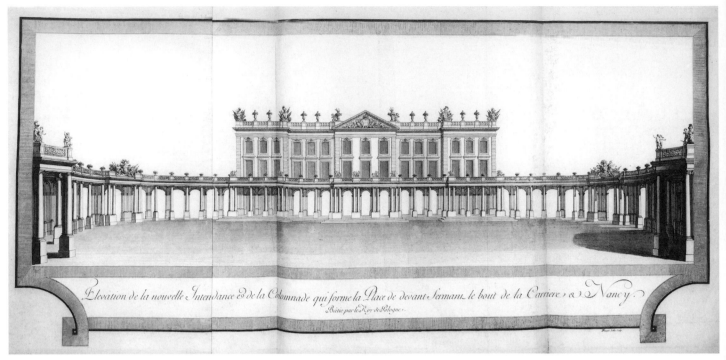

111   Emmanuel Héré: Nancy, Intendance, project *c.* 1752 (Héré, *Recueil*).

There can be no doubt that Héré was strongly influenced by Boffrand, whose memory was still very much alive in Nancy. The theme of giant pilasters on a rusticated base, first sounded in Boffrand's Hôtel de Craon, is echoed everywhere: in its articulation, the Hôtel de Ville readily betrays its derivation from Boffrand's Louvre, demolished as recently as 1745. But the differences are significant. Above all, the relationship between wall surface and opening has changed. With Héré, the mass of the wall has shrunk, and the windows have grown larger. In the terminal pavilions of the Carrière they occupy most of the wall, into which the inset columns and pilasters seem to have been pressed. The wall thus loses its sculptural character. The façades of the Place Royale seem flat and devoid of depth, with articulation applied to the surface. Here, again, decoration assumes a new importance. Héré makes it into a constituent, and occasionally a dominant, part of the architecture. The roof line, in particular, with its luxuriant crop of urns, trophies and figure groups, goes far beyond Boffrand's simple row of urns and lends the built mass a restless, darting silhouette. All this endows Héré's façades with a theatrical quality, like elements in a spectacular stage set.

The only building that impairs the unity of the composition is the Intendance. The last part of the sequence to be built (1753–7), this is not by Héré but by his successor in office, Richard Mique. Héré had designed the façade as a pendant to the Hôtel de Ville, with the same number of storeys, the same centre and end pavilions (albeit in a different rhythm), and a triangular pediment. Rusticated dressings and narrow, closely spaced windows were to counteract the horizontal emphasis. Ground-floor colonnades eliminated the need for an order. Presumably on the instructions of the French Intendant, Mique drastically modified this design, overloading the façade with coupled columns and pilasters. The result was to throw the whole thing off-balance. The deep cornice between the two upper storeys tends to make the façade look even longer than it is. The top storey, which has lost a part of its intended height, looks like an afterthought, especially as at this level the frontispiece does not break forward and the pediment has disappeared. The last vestige of Héré's lightness of touch vanished with the closing of the open archways of the vestibule. The view through to the gardens was blocked off, and a building that should have been light and airy became a solid block.

The building of the Place Royale was a grand urban gesture; Stanislas and Héré saw it as a chance to remodel the city. From the Place Royale, new streets were laid out and new residential districts were built. The strong transverse axis through the square – Rue Sainte-Catherine and Rue Saint-Stanislas – was developed with uniform façades; and at the ends there were new city gates, the Porte Sainte-Catherine and Porte Saint-Stanislas, designed to welcome the traveller while drawing attention to the new layout of the city. Another street that issued from the Place Royale, aligned for reasons of symmetry along the left-hand side of the Hôtel de Ville, afforded a view of the Primatiale, the principal church of the city. Not far away, in a new quarter to the east, the king personally subsidized the construction of the regular façades of the original Place Stanislas; smaller and more modest than the then Place Royale, this was not named after the king himself but after his patron saint. In 1756, on the occasion of the treaty between Louis XV and Empress Maria Theresa that reconciled the former ruling house of Lorraine with France, this square was renamed Place d'Alliance and adorned with the obelisks that had previously stood in the fountain in front of the Intendance.

Even after the deaths of Héré and the king, their plans were adhered to. In the east the barracks and the Pépinière, a large public park adjoining the Hémicycle, and in the west the Cours Léopold, another connection between the old and new parts of the city, were completed in the 1760s. The reign of the Polish king had proved to be a blessing beyond all expectations, and had set its seal on his capital city.

Héré did little ecclesiastical work. One of his earliest buildings was the little church of Notre-Dame du Bon Secours, on the site of an ancient pilgrimage chapel on the outskirts of Nancy (1738–41); Stanislas had chosen it as his own burial place.[75] This well-preserved, aisle-less church is an exotic implant on the soil of Lorraine. The four tall columns that adorn the façade were taken from Boffrand's demolished La Malgrange; they lend it a Roman gravitas. The interior, with its Baroque tombs for the king and queen, has a similarly Italianate quality. The inside walls are faced with simulated polychrome marble, the ceiling bears a faded fresco, and a plaster curtain is draped aloft between nave and choir. There is nothing French about any of this. Here, undoubtedly, the king was expressing his personal taste, and Héré was merely the executant.

In Héré's other church, that of the Abbaye de Saint-Jacques in Lunéville, his contribution was again a limited one; he was responsible only for the tower lanterns and for the interior. But the result is Héré at his best (Plate 112). The building history of this important Lunéville landmark is rather complicated and has yet to be fully clarified.[76] Originally known as Saint-Rémy, the abbey had adopted the patron saint of the demolished parish church of Saint-Jacques. Duke Leopold had laid the foundation stone in 1730. The plan and elevations were probably by his chief architect, Jennesson, who had built the very similar church of Saint-Sébastien in Nancy – another hall-church with tall columns – not long before (1720–31). However, the massive, pedimented portico and the lower parts of the towers are by Jadot, clearly inspired by Borromini's S. Agnese in Rome.[77]

When Héré took over in 1743, work had been suspended for several years. Whether he found Jadot's towers already built or completed them himself, we do not know. The lanterns that he added are highly reminiscent of those designed by Boffrand for the Primatiale in Nancy. They are a perfect match for the towers – more slender but almost as tall again – and pursue the rhythm of the large openings and balustrades below. Their culminating figures of St Michael and St John Nepomucene are visible far and wide.

The tall superstructure above the pediment, with its clock supported by Chronos and attended by soaring angels, is crucial to the success of the façade. Héré built it to correct the infelicitous proportions of Jadot's over-tall towers and to relax their grandiloquent rigidity. The interaction between the clock superstructure, the animated pediment figures and the playful lanterns creates a highly pictorial composition that is typical of Héré's style. This impression is maintained in the interior, which was completed in 1745. With its delicacy of spatial effect, its excellent plasterwork, its frescoes by Jean Girardet and its theatrical-looking organ case, this interior holds a special place among the churches of Lorraine.

112 Lunéville, Saint-Jacques, 1730–47, façade.

CHAPTER 5

Private Building

The middle years of Louis XV's reign were marked by vigorous private building activity, in town and country alike. The general economic recovery made itself felt here as elsewhere; and it was accompanied by a change in the style of life, with a greater emphasis on informality, prettier surroundings and healthier living. Many of the cities lost their medieval aspect and assumed a modern, more welcoming look. Streets became wider, and new development was governed by strict regulations. Timber framing was prohibited, as were oriel windows and drains discharging into the streets. Countless old houses were pulled down and replaced by new ones. In many cities, whole new quarters appeared, uniform in appearance, with light, cheerful façades enlivened by curvilinear balconies, ornamental window keystones and rocaille enrichments. Examples include the long, straight Cours in Bordeaux, the Rue Royale in Orléans, the area around the Quai de Fosse in Nantes and the quarter centred on the Rue Saint-Ferréol in Marseille.

Paris was no exception; but there the emphasis had shifted. Now that the city limits had been reached, and the nobility was back at Versailles, the building of hôtels was no longer the main concern. Among the last stragglers from the great hôtel boom of the Régence were the Hôtel de Rouillé, by Jean-François Blondel, and the Hôtel de Janvry, by Cartaud. In 1734, for the finance minister, Gaudion, Oppenord designed a house with theatrical perspectives, façade sculptures, and a climactic, grandiose staircase swinging round a colonnaded landing, that was entirely within the tradition of Borromini; but in all likelihood also this was executed only in part.[78] In subsequent years, a number of existing hôtels were remodelled, mostly in conjunction with a redecoration of the interiors (Hôtels de Villars, de Roquelaure, de Mazarin, de Villeroy and others). Most of these projects are connected with the name of Jean-Baptiste Leroux (c. 1677–1746), whom Jacques-François Blondel called 'one of the busiest men of his day'.

One such undertaking was the two-storey pavilion that Boffrand erected in 1735 at the end of the garden wing of the Hôtel de Soubise, and which, in order to preserve the enfilade within, he caused to project far beyond the line of the existing façade: a feature that distinguishes it from all of its predecessors, and most notably from Le Vau's Salon de Mars in the Louvre. The architectural autonomy of this pavilion, with its broken outline and its rich ornamentation of keystones and brackets, is matched by its interior, which is one of the supreme achievements of the Rococo. In order to balance Boffrand's pavilion, with its high roof, the Prince de Rohan engaged Pierre Contant d'Ivry to add a two-tier portico (1752) to the middle of the façade, which by comparison, looks rather ponderous; it reveals that the Rococo was running out of steam.[79]

While the building of hôtels stagnated, the bourgeois dwelling house gained in importance;[80] and this was where the Rococo came fully into its own. In eighteenth-century Paris the rebuilding of the ancient city centre was in full swing; medieval and later houses were demolished and replaced by new ones, many of them designed to be rented out for multiple occupation. Blondel scornfully dismissed all this as *architecture subalterne*; but his publisher, Jombert, more clearly saw the importance of the houses that were going up all around him day after day. In his *Architecture moderne* he published numerous specimen designs, remarking that no orders were required: what mattered was good planning, not the proportions of columns. And, indeed, these were not houses to which academic criteria could be applied. The narrowness of the old sites often made any façade development impossible and compelled the builder to go up as far as eight storeys; and five-storey houses appear among Jombert's designs. The owners, mostly merchants or industrialists with no artistic pretensions, tended to leave the execution in the hands of building contractors or of architects who had no higher education and were untroubled by the rules of taste. In order to satisfy the universal craving for beauty, which by now had reached the middle and lower orders of society, these men applied to their façades either an excess of ornament or – as in the case of the Hôtel de Jaŭcourt – technical tricks that invoked the critical wrath of the Academy. At times, however, even relatively unknown architects created façades of great charm and distinction through the use of balconies and console ornament. Examples are the Hôtel du Grand Veneur (1734) (Plate 113), by Jean-Baptiste-Angustin Beausire, and the Hôtel d'Albret (c. 1740), by Jean-Baptiste Vautrains, with a façade that is very much in the vein of Oppenord. The role of the sculptor or decorator in such façades was a major one – greater, in many cases, than that of the architect, who tended to stick to his ground plans and leave the rest to the decorator.

Parisian Rococo architecture was not, however, limited to these minor masters – the 'petits maîtres de l'architecture' whom Frémin had mocked in his *Mémoires critiques* (1702). Some well-known Academy names were involved, including Pierre Vigné de Vigny, Jacques Hardouin-Mansart de Sagonne, Pierre Boscry, Jean-Baptiste Leroux and Michel Tannevot.

The most important of these was certainly Pierre Vigné de Vigny (1690–1772), a pupil of Robert de Cotte's.[81] In his youth, de Cotte had sent him to Constantinople to build a new French legation to the Sublime Porte. On the way back, he had spent a considerable time in Rome, studying the Roman Baroque, and he had been an admirer of Borromini ever since. Back in Paris, he extended his admiration to Oppenord, whose influence is evident in his early works, whether at the Hôtel Chenizot (1726), where his portal with its alternate rough and smooth courses of stone recalls Oppenord's design for the Regent's stables, or in the dragon consoles of the Hôtel de Saint-Albin (1723), or in the Cour du Dragon (1728–32).

113 Jean-Baptiste-Augustin Beausire: Paris, Hôtel du Grand Veneur, façade.

114 Pierre Vigné de Vigny: Paris, Cour du Dragon, 1730, entrance.

Now demolished, the Cour du Dragon was a large residential and commercial complex, built for the wealthy banker Crozat. Entirely in the classical tradition, Vigny conferred a monumental quality on its sober façade by using a classical porch motif, which he carried up through three storeys in order to counter the width of the block with a vertical accent. The Rococo asserted itself, nevertheless, in the deep concave curve of the portal itself – which was actually stipulated by the client, in view of the steep slope of the street – and also in the façade sculpture, which was highly reminiscent of Oppenord. Above the *porte cochère* was a gracefully curvilinear balcony; beneath this lurked the dragon that gave the name to the whole complex, and the crown of the arch above supported an enormous cartouche, half head, half foliage (Plate 113). The sculptor was Paul-Ambroise Slodtz.

Vigny's early work – initially passed on to him by de Cotte – was mostly for Paris financiers; but after 1740 he worked largely for the clergy and nobility, including one individual who stood very close to the throne, the Duc de Luynes. His major work, the Hôpital Général in Lille, in which he reverted to the style of his master, de Cotte, has already been mentioned.

Vigny's great reputation, uncontested even by Blondel, earned him election to the Royal Society in London, for which he wrote a reception essay, the *Dissertation sur l'archi-*

tecture (published 1752), a historical survey on the lines of Fischer von Erlach's *Entwurf einer historischen Architektur*. In spite of his classical schooling, Vigny was one of those who refused to take the classical system of architecture on trust. He considered that the present day had more to learn from Borromini than from antiquity; and he was one of the first to advocate the use of Gothic for religious architecture. In later years he retired from practice and devoted himself to his artistic interests.

Mansart de Sagonne has left us one perfect, surviving example of Rococo architecture in the shape of the convent of the Dames de Saint-Chaumont (1734). Here the whole façade is dominated by curves and countercurves (Plate 115). The convexity of the *corps de logis* is answered by the concave curves of the wings. This Borrominesque use of curvature – by no means the only example in Paris – was intended, as Père Estève put it in his *Essai des Beaux-Arts* (1753), to offer all parts of the façade to the eye at once; the incurved ends to the wings are intended as points of repose. This façade is a cooperative effort: the sculpture and the wrought-iron balconies are by Nicolas Pineau. When this celebrated decorator was employed for an interior, his services were also retained, as a matter of course, for the façade as well. Few of his works have survived, but we know that he worked not only for Mansart de Sagonne but for Jean-François Blondel, Antoine-Mathieu Le Carpentier, Leroux, Boscry

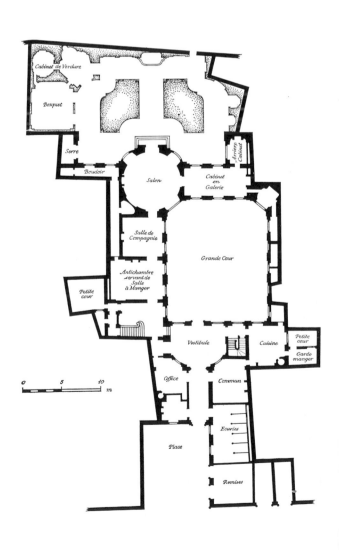

115 Jacques Hardouin-Mansart de Sagonne: Paris, House of the Dames de Saint Chaumont, rue Saint-Denis, 1734.

116 Thomas Lainée: Avignon, Chapelle des Pénitents noirs, 1739, façade.

117 Jean-Baptiste and François Franque: Avignon, Hôtel de Villeneuve, c. 1740, plan of ground floor.

118 François Franque: Villers-
Cotterêts, Abbot's Palace, 1765,
plan of ground floor (J.B. Blondel,
Cours d'architecture T.4, pl. XLVI).

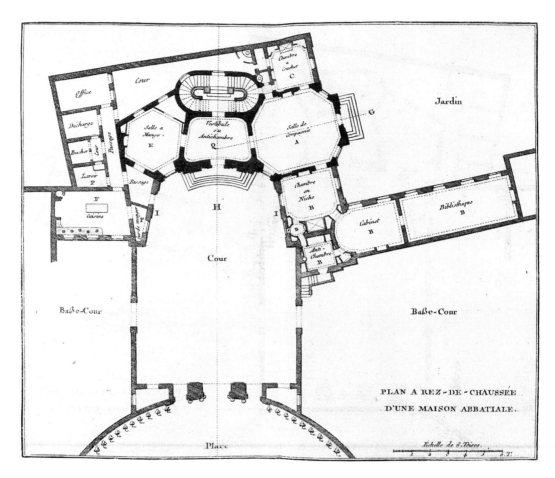

and others. In the same way as Oppenord, Pineau set the tone of architectural ornament in Paris: slanting, asymmetrical window keystones; rose-garlands, seashells and wings on balcony consoles; sweeping curves and floral and shellwork ornament on balcony and window grilles.

In the south of France, acceptance of the Rococo was slow and grudging. In Provence, especially, the influence of neighbouring Italy was strong, and the Baroque died hard. In Aix, that most genteel of Provençal cities, which still bore the mark of the architectural dynasty of Vallon, giant orders and the *grande manière* held sway until the middle of the century. Not until the Hôtel de Villeneuve d'Ansouis (1754), with its curvaceous balconies, mascaroons and ornamental keystones, did the Parisian Rococo come into its own.[82]

In Avignon, unlike Aix, the Italian habit of placing façades directly on the street had been abandoned by the end of the seventeenth century. Here, too, façade design was more sober. It was the arrival of Thomas Lainée (1682–1739), a product of the circle of J.H. Mansart and Robert de Cotte, that set things moving in a new direction.[83] Lainée started by undertaking decorative work in a number of hôtels, and went on to introduce the Parisian style to Avignon in a succession of his own buildings: the theatre (1735) and the chapels of the Pénitents-Rouges (1736–7, destroyed) and the Pénitents-Noirs (1739). The Pénitents-Noirs, with its highly unusual façade (Plate 116), is a design by Lainée that was built after his death by Jean-Baptiste Franque. Its Rococo temper, an utter novelty for Avignon, shows itself not only in the cavalier treatment of the orders on the façade – Tuscan pilasters above Corinthian – and the large central

relief of John the Baptist's head on its charger in a glory, but also in the salon-like interior, with its numerous paintings and its Rococo coving.

Jean-Baptiste Franque (1698–1758), who had welcomed and employed Lainée on his arrival in Avignon, absorbed much of his style – and particularly the Parisian conventions of planning and decor – in his own hôtels, including the Hôtel Forbin de Sainte-Croix, Hôtel de Beaumont and Hôtel de Villeneuve-Martignan; but he maintained the pedimented windows and balustraded flat roofs of the local style.[84] Franque's most important town house is the Hôtel de Villeneuve-Martignan (now Musée Calvet), which he built in 1741 in collaboration with his son François; this is a masterpiece, both in its proportions and in its planning (Plate 117).[85] The ambitious rebuilding of the Abbaye de Montmajour, which Franque took over from Pierre Mignard in 1726, was never completed owing to shortage of funds. All that was finished was the east range, adjoining the old cloister, and the central block; these collapsed in the nineteenth century, and all that remains of them is a shapeless ruin.

Whereas Jean-Baptiste's activities were confined to Provence, François Franque (1710–86) far outgrew the confines of his native region. Moving to Paris, he entered the Service des Bâtiments du Roi, became a member of the Academy and worked all over France, principally for the clergy but also sometimes for the nobility. The list of his buildings is imposing.[86] It includes twelve churches and twelve abbeys – including Corbie (*c.* 1740), Soissons (1741), Saint-Benoît-sur-Loire (1746) and Villers-Cotterêts (1765)

119 Jacques Hardouin-Mansart de Sagonne: Paris, Asnières, Le Château, 1751, upper storey of the façade.

120 Antoine-Mathieu Le Carpentier, Pavillon de la Boissière, 1751, plan and elevation.

– as well as seminaries in Bourges (*c.* 1742) and Avignon (1749), palaces for the bishops of Viviers (1732) and Carcassonne (1743) and a number of hôtels, châteaux and villas. Blondel regarded him as a paragon of good taste, and published in the *Encyclopédie* his design for the patrician Abbaye de Penthémont in Paris, with a stately, three-storey conventual building combined with a church in the same way as the Dôme and Hôtel des Invalides. When it came to the actual building (1743–56), however, Contant d'Ivry was brought in, and he whittled down Franque's grand spatial effects and varied façades to the point of unrecognizability.

François Franque was celebrated for his ground plans. An outstanding example is the Palais Abbatial at Villers-Cotterêts (Plate 118), in which he had to combine two axes that met at an obtuse angle. He managed this by welding together two differently oriented blocks around a *cour d'honneur* to give two façades – a garden front and a court front – whose axes intersected in the vestibule. The slight kink in the transverse axis is masked by the spatial geometry of the enfilade, and on the longitudinal axis, which led straight to the elliptical staircase, it is not even perceptible.

A group of traditionalist architects, of whom François Franque was one, carried on the style of the Mansart school past mid-century without ever falling under the spell of Neoclassicism. Such was Franque's reputation that his name was attached to a large number of buildings which he had no part at all. The most important of these is the palatial residence of the abbot of Prémontré; with its continuous giant order running round the whole building, this is much more likely to be by Jean Bayeux of Rouen, the architect of the city hall of Beauvais.

In the south, Montpellier, with its celebrated university, occupied a special position. Daviler had brought the style of J.H. Mansart to the city at the close of the seventeenth century, and it had been independent of Italian influence ever since. Jean Giral (1679–1753), who was to be the

founder of a local architectural dynasty, introduced the *goût moderne* to Montpellier with such buildings as the Hôtel de Cambacêrès and Hôtel des Trésoriers de la Bourse. In these, the classical orders disappeared, and architecture became less rigid and more animated. The doors and windows had segmental arches – *davilertes* – with masks of female faces as their keystones. The local idiosyncrasy of staircases open to the courtyard was, however, maintained.

One house in the Parisian Régence vein was the Château Mosson, near Montpellier, which Giral built for the rich textile manufacturer Joseph Bonnier in 1723–9. The façade boasted columns and a pediment, and the garden front, with its bowed projection, had a double order of pilasters. The interior, too, was in the grand manner of a Parisian *maison de plaisance*, with a large garden salon as the climax of the composition. The sculptures in the park were by the youthful Nicolas Sébastien Adam.[87]

Jean Giral's nephew and successor in practice, Jean-Antoine Giral, was also entrusted with some major commissions. One noteworthy building of his is the Hôtel de Saint-Côme, built as an anatomy lecture theatre for the university of Montpellier in 1752–7 and still standing today. To comply with the terms of the trust fund involved, this had to be a copy of the Hôtel de Saint-Côme in Paris, an octagonal, domed building of the late seventeenth century. Giral made it into a showpiece. Above a low, balustraded base, he combined the ground floor and drum of his Parisian original into a single tall storey, curved the faces of the octagon deeply inward between the corner piers, and lined them with an order of tall pilasters. Above this, and within a continuous balustrade, he set a tall, ribbed dome with richly sculptured oculi. His domed theatre stands some way back from the street, and on that side he has given it an elegant if somewhat old-fashioned hôtel façade. Giral's most important work was Le Peyrou, which is discussed below.

In the countryside, architecture enjoyed more scope. Away

Pavillon de la Bossiere, Rue de Clichy, bâti par Carpentier, Architecte

Pl. 55.

Coupe

Plan du Rez-de-Chaussée, N° 1.

from cramped sites, building regulations and the constraints of prestige, the individual imagination could unfold more freely. From the Régence onwards, country life in general came to be better thought of. This was manifested not only in the numerous *maisons de plaisance* and *pavillons* that were built in the environs of Paris but in the rustic motifs that appeared amid the decorative grotesques of Audran and Watteau. Never, perhaps, since the Italian Renaissance, had country life and rustic diversions been more in vogue than they were in eighteenth-century France.

The Rococo spirit manifested itself not so much in châteaux as in the smaller *maisons de plaisance* and *pavillons*, where people met to dine, to hear a concert or to cultivate the art of conversation. These garden buildings represented surely the most cultivated and refined form of sociability, and they afforded every freedom: they were subject to no architectural rules whatever. There, no one was likely to take exception to mixed or wrong orders. Very little of all this has survived; but Jacques-François Blondel's earliest publication, the *Traité . . . de la distribution des maisons de plaisance* (1737), in which he remained wholly under the spell of the Rococo, serves to illustrate the extent of the contemporary demand.

Naturally, traditional châteaux were still built, both because old buildings were being replaced by new and because the rising *noblesse de robe* – such hereditary magistrates as the presidents of the Parlements, Cours des Comptes, and the like – and the rich merchants liked to assert their status by building entirely new country seats. Traditional forms did not disappear, though they were often combined with a less rigid outline and a softer linear flow, with rounded corners and coved doorways. In most cases, the château now had a flat façade, with little by way of pavilion articulation, but with a triangular pediment and a mansard roof; sometimes a dome was added, as at Brienne (Aube) and Fontaine-Française (Côte d'Or). With its giant order, Rollancourt (Nord) is an exception, presumably influenced by Bayeux's city hall in Beauvais, not far away. Few châteaux are purely Rococo in character; one such is Long (Somme), which is remarkable for its bowed pavilions, its restless roof line, its rounded corners, and its frontispiece crowned by a gently curving arch adorned with consoles and garlands.

A more unified and a more modern effect could be achieved in *maisons de plaisance* and in *folies*, small pavilion-like houses in gardens or outside city walls, which derived their name from the sheltering foliage in which they nestled, and which belonged to a tradition that went back to Marly and the Trianon. It was here that the Rococo spirit found its most direct expression. Perfect examples away from Paris included Bagatelle (Somme), a gracious *folie* with a bowed centre and very few rooms, built by a rich textile manufacturer from Amiens in 1754,[88] and the small villas of the South, such as L'Engarran or La Piscine, near Montpellier. At L'Engarran the façade is dominated by the gentle curves of the frontispiece and by the porch, at La Piscine by the large reliefs of pendant trophies that flank the door, and by the pilaster strips that simulate end pavilions.

The environs of Paris were especially rich in buildings of this kind. Among the few that survive, we should mention the charming Château de Jossigny (c. 1743), which is Rococo in the gentle curves that relax the solidity of the block, in the use of rounded or chamfered corners throughout, in the restless roof line with its pediment entirely made up of curves, and in the ornamental consoles of the porch; and the Château d'Asnières (Plate 119), which Mansart de Sagonne built in 1751 for the Marquis d'Argenson, Louis XV's minister of war. This is a château in name only; it is really a courty type of *maison de plaisance*, sited within easy reach of the capital, with a conventional pilaster articulation, consoles presumably intended to carry ornamental busts, and an attic crowned with urns by way of allusion to the client's official status.[89]

The last of the Parisian *folies* was the Pavillon de Hanovre (now transferred to Sceaux), which the Duc de Richelieu, a noted rake, employed Jean-Michel Chevotet to build for him in 1757 on the edge of his large estate on the Boulevard des Italiens. It was paid for, or so it was said, out of the spoils that Richelieu had brought back from Hanover as a military commander in the Seven Years War.

The most sumptuous *folie* of all was the Pavillon de la Boissière (Plate 120), built by Le Carpentier in the grounds of a house in the Rue de Clichy in 1751. With its ingenious grouping of round and octagonal rooms – summer salon, winter salon, stucco salon, and so on – and its large windows, this achieved an optimum combination of variety, splendour and domestic comfort, with the added dignity of an external order.

CHAPTER 6

Church Architecture in the First Half of the Eighteenth Century

More churches were built in eighteenth-century France than is generally supposed. Almost all the architects of the day worked on ecclesiastical as well as secular commissions: Brice recorded in 1752 that several million livres' worth of church buildings had been erected in Paris since 1716 or so. Much the same applied to the provinces, where the abbeys, in particular, were not slow to bring their way of life up to date and to replace medieval simplicity and austerity with splendour and comfort.[90] Among others, the abbots of Prémontré (c. 1740), Remiremont (1750), Saint-Ouen in Rouen (1753–9) and Saint-Just-en-Chaussée (1758) lived in palatial dwellings that looked for all the world like secular châteaux. In church building as such, however, rigid adherence to an early seventeenth-century formula, and the ingrained French aversion to painted and sculpted decorations in church, had led to a sterility that was deplored both by Abbé de Cordemoy and by Père Laugier.[91] Only on the periphery of France did autonomous solutions spring from local traditions.

In Paris, numerous new churches had been started in the wake of the religious revival of Louis XIII's reign and then left unfinished. The first task of eighteenth-century ecclesiastical architecture was therefore that of completion. The scale of the task can be gauged from the fact that between 1690 and 1755 twenty-four façades were added to existing church and chapel buildings, at a time when new starts were almost non-existent. This last fact did nothing to stem the flow of theoretical writings on church architecture.[92] The fundamental work was the *Cours d'architecture* of an Academy professor, Antoine Desgodets, based on a lecture course delivered between 1720 and 1728.[93] In this, Desgodets provided numerous church designs clearly based – plans and elevations alike – on the seventeenth-century tradition of Lemercier, François Mansart and Pierre Bullet. The two-storey Italian façade type introduced by Lemercier – five bays below and three above – survived intact into the eighteenth century; and so François Mansart's Feuillants became the model for Saint-Roch and for Notre-Dame des Victoires, and his Visitation the model for the Abbaye de Penthémont.

Alongside these traditional forms there also appeared new types of façade: the rectangular screen wall with an equal number of bays above and below, possibly derived from S. Luigi dei Francesi in Rome – as in Boffrand's La Merci and in Bullet de Chamblain's designs for Saint-Sulpice and Saint-Roch – and the façade with twin towers. This last, formerly reserved for bishops, became popular among eighteenth-century parish priests as a way of asserting their independence. J.H. Mansart's Notre-Dame de la Victoire, at Versailles, can stand as the prototype of such façades. The range of possibilities that this formula offered can be seen from the competition designs for Saint-Sulpice. As well as Bullet de Chamblain's screen wall with its short lantern-towers – a wider version of the façade design for Saint-Roch – there were twin-tower façades by Oppenord and Jean-Nicolas Servandoni. Hybrids and overlaps between the two types – as in Servandoni's second design for Saint-Sulpice, or the anonymous design for a three-storey screen wall with two tall, free-standing towers – were frequent, and indeed characteristic of the first half of the century.

Then there was the Roman Baroque tendency. The façade of the Chapelle des Irlandais, by Boscry (1738), was an almost literal repeat of Bernini's S. Andrea al Quirinale. Juste-Aurèle Meissonnier's design of 1726 for Saint-Sulpice (Plate 121) – which is the most original of them all, despite its distinct resemblance to a centrepiece for a dinner table – had a façade indebted to Borromini's S. Carlo alle Quattro Fontane, and to a design by Andrea Pozzo for S. Giovanni in Laterano. His imposing but impracticable design for an ecclesiastical complex for the Order of the Holy Ghost, opposite the Ile de la Cité (c. 1730), combined reminiscences of S. Agnese in Rome and of the Versailles palace chapel.[94] Also in the Borromini tradition is the façade of Saint-Louis du Louvre (1740), by the goldsmith Thomas Germain, with the undulating projections and recessions of its portal area. Here the fabric of the building becomes as yielding as clay, and plastic qualities prevail over structural ones.

These Baroque solutions remained exceptional in France, where they fell foul of the native taste for clarity and logic. Nor, indeed, is there any evidence of a response to the ideas of Cordemoy, except in the communion chapel of Saint-Jean-en-Grève (1735), by Jean-François Blondel, where the nave and aisles are divided by columns supporting lintels.

The most important building works in Paris were those at Saint-Roch and Saint-Sulpice. At Saint-Roch, de Cotte had completed Lemercier's nave in 1719–23. For the façade, Bullet de Chamblain prepared a design in the 1720s that recalled Boffrand's La Merci, with the addition of some strongly Baroque features (Plate 122).[95] The design as executed (Plate 123) is by Robert de Cotte, built under the supervision of his son, Jules-Robert, and work was completed in 1738 (or, according to Brice and Argenville, in 1736). The façade of Saint-Roch is a logical continuation of J.H. Mansart's formula. Its arrangement admittedly owes something to François Mansart's Feuillants, but in the use of columns and multiple recession it exactly corresponds to the Dôme des Invalides. There is, however, greater spatial depth. The doorways are deeply recessed, and the pediment and cornices project strongly. The interplay of advancing and receding breaks in the cornices, and the constant alternation of spaces, columns, and zones of shadow, create an unrest that runs counter to all the laws of classicism.

Here, de Cotte has gone far beyond his master, and has developed a dynamism in which the Baroque interplay of forces is fully resolved. In his original design, a rich sculptural decor reinforced the impression of the façade as a

121 Juste-Aurèle Meissonnier: Paris, Saint-Sulpice, design for façade, 1726 (Paris, Bibliothèque Nationale).

122 Jean-Baptiste Bullet de Chamblain: Paris, Saint-Roch, design for façade, c. 1730 (Stockholm, Nationalmuseum).

123 Jules-Robert de Cotte: Paris, Saint-Roch, façade, finished 1736 or 1738.

three-dimensional, sculptural whole. And yet a comparison with such Roman Baroque churches as Rainaldi's S. Maria in Campitelli immediately makes it clear how firmly Saint-Roch is wedded to a network of proportions. Horizontally, the façade is held together by the similar arches of the entrance doors; vertically, the arch motif is repeated above in the central window. Unity is preserved, and not even the massive force of the coupled columns can disrupt it.

The building history of Saint-Sulpice is more complicated.[96] In the course of the seventeenth century, the building of a replacement for the medieval church had been entrusted to a succession of architects, ending with Daniel Gittard. Nothing had been done since 1676. In 1719 an ambitious and influential parish priest, Père Languet du Gergy, engaged Oppenord, then at the height of his fame, to continue the work. Oppenord adhered to Gittard's design, while giving the interior an elegance unusual in Parisian churches, with fluted pilasters in the nave, Corinthian columns at the transept ends, and lavish plasterwork. But he was let down by his lack of structural expertise. His crossing tower threatened collapse and had to be demolished in 1731. He was removed from the direction of the work and replaced by Servandoni, who had been working on the decoration of the lady chapel since 1729.

At the same time, a competition for the façade was announced, and there were entries from Oppenord, Bullet de Chamblain, Meissonnier, Servandoni and others. The winner of this contest, the most important in eighteenth-century Parisian church architecture, was Servandoni. His design (Plate 124) was not uninfluenced by Oppenord, but was ultimately based on St Paul's in London. Like St Paul's,

it had two superimposed orders with broken entablatures, a centre emphasized by open porticoes (the upper storey was to contain the parochial library, and was consequently lit by arched openings) and by a comparatively small pediment, and twin towers (these last rather clumsy by comparison with those proposed by Oppenord).[97] Work on the façade began in 1733; but soon afterwards – Patte gives the date as 1736 – Servandoni made radical changes to his design (Plate 125). He extended the central porticoes by two bays each and widened the pediment accordingly, so that its ends were under the bases of the towers. This made the porticoes into the dominant element and gave the façade a strong horizontal emphasis, especially as the lack of space in front of the church made it necessary to have the entrance steps inside the ground-floor portico. The towers, too, became lighter and less restless in form. By 1745, when the church was consecrated, the façade was complete to just below the pediment; work started on the towers in 1749. In 1751 Servandoni replaced his wide pediment – which had been condemned by an architectural commission including both Ange-Jacques Gabriel and Lassurance the Younger – with a balustrade; not long afterwards, he replaced this in turn with a third storey, like that of the Primatiale in Nancy.[98]

Whatever Blondel and Laugier may have supposed, it was no part of Servandoni's intention to pave the way for Neoclassicism. Born to a French father and an Italian mother in Florence, and a pupil of Giovanni Paolo Pannini and Domenico Rossi, Jean-Nicolas or Giovanni Niccolò Servandoni (1695–1766) was anything but a Neoclassicist. One glance at the wrought-iron balustrade on the staircase of his own house would make this abundantly clear. On the contrary, he was a man of Baroque imagination and versatility: architect, painter, stage designer and above all decorator.[99] In Paris, where he arrived in 1726 and made a name for

himself with stage sets and decorations for festivities, he was chief scenic artist at the opera and the Academy of Music. A man of great charm and spirit, he was a welcome visitor to the courts of London, Lisbon, Dresden and Vienna. The ideas that he brought to his architecture were not those of Neoclassicism but those of the later Roman Baroque. This is apparent not only in the overall rhythm of his orders but in his deep porticoes, for which abundant Roman precedents exist in such churches as S. Maria Maggiore, S. Giovanni in Laterano and S. Maria in Via Lata. The open double portico with entablature and classical frieze, though unknown in Rome, appears – as already mentioned – at St Paul's Cathedral in London. It had also been illustrated in Desgodets' *Traité des ordres d'architecture* (1711), which Servandoni undoubtedly knew. But by contrast with the flat church façades of Paris, it was a revolutionary innovation.

When Servandoni died in 1766, the Academy accepted a suggestion from Patte that his third storey should be demolished and the wide pediment reinstated; two years later, this was struck by lightning and destroyed. Again on the recommendation of the Academy, Oudot de Mac Laurin embarked on a remodelling of the towers, only to succumb to a devastating barrage of criticism as soon as the south tower was complete.[100] Finally, in 1776, another architect was called in: this was Jean-François Chalgrin, a pupil of Servandoni's, who had made his name with the new church of Saint-Philippe du Roule. He gave the façade its present unity and polished elegance by fluting all the columns and crowning it with a balustrade (Plate 126).[101] He went on to remodel the north tower, with columns instead of pilasters, a square base with prominent triangular pediments, and a circular upper storey that looks rather like a gazebo. Its superiority to Mac Laurin's south tower is manifest; but the latter was never rebuilt.

Languet du Gergy had had the idea of fronting his church with a suitable *parvis* or square, and of demolishing the seminary that blocked the view of the façade. This was never done in his lifetime, but Servandoni seized on the idea as his chance to create a lasting memorial for himself in Paris. He designed a great open space (1752) with long façades on every side of the church, pierced by four incoming streets and swinging outwards to form crescents opposite the transepts. The west front would be faced by another crescent, with a triumphal arch in the centre as the main entrance to the square. This project was scaled down several times before building work began in 1754, only to be abandoned not long afterwards for lack of funds. All that ever was built was one house: Servandoni's own.[102]

Two other major churches that came within the Parisian sphere of influence were the cathedrals of Versailles, by Mansart de Sagonne, and La Rochelle, by Jacques (and Ange-Jacques) Gabriel; though widely separated on the map, they are closely related in form.[103] In them, J.H. Mansart's grandson and nephew respectively adopted the ground plan

124 Giovanni-Niccolo Servandoni: Paris, Saint-Sulpice, first design for façade, 1732.

125 Giovanni-Niccolo Servandoni: Paris, Saint-Sulpice, second design for façade, 1736.

126   Jean-François-Thérèse Chalgrin: Paris, Saint-Sulpice, façade, 1776.

127 Jacques Hardouin-Mansart de Sagonne: Versailles, Saint-Louis 1743–54.

of his Notre-Dame de la Victoire, Versailles. The difference is in the elevations.

Saint-Louis (1743–54), now the cathedral of Versailles, is a direct successor to Saint-Roch; it marks the final stage of the Baroque (Plate 127). Here the animation that is confined to the façade at Saint-Roch has spread to the whole building, in a way that is unusual in France: the low flanking towers, the ends of the transepts and the curiously squashed dome all seem to pulse with life. There is a pictorial impulse here that is entirely characteristic of this last phase of the Baroque – as seen at Saint-Jacques in Lunéville, at Langres Cathedral, and elsewhere. In the interior, which has the grandeur of all Mansart churches, the elegant plasterwork by Pineau comes as a surprise, particularly in the cartouches above the nave arches, with their delicate floral festoons.

By contrast, La Rochelle (begun 1742) was more soberly conceived from the start. The towers were designed to be one storey higher than those at Versailles, and adorned with diagonally arranged columns and balustrades; but for the interior Jacques Gabriel chose an austere Doric order and, as his only concession to ornament, scrolled brackets as keystones of the arches. Perhaps he thought that this spareness was in keeping with the city's Huguenot traditions. Delayed by lack of funds and by difficulties over land owner-ship, the cathedral was a long time in the building; at its consecration in 1784 it was still unfinished. The choir and apse were built in the nineteenth century; the towers and sculptural decoration are still missing to this day.

Away from Paris, only the northern and eastern provinces have any native achievements to show. There, as in the neighbouring Netherlands, the tradition of the hall church was firmly established. Notable northern examples are Saint-Géry in Cambrai, Saint-Maurice in Lille, and Saint-Pierre in Douai; in Lorraine there are the three great monastic churches of Saint-Mihiel, Autrey and Pont-à-Mousson. Saint-Mihiel (1696–1710) and Autrey (1711–14) remain under the spell of a tardy Gothic derived from Saint-Clément, Metz.[104] In both, the additions made to the existing medieval nucleus retain a late Gothic form, and – as in Metz – only the antique detailing of the piers reveals that a new age has dawned. The same Gothic verticality prevails in the Premonstratensian abbey church of Pont-à-Mousson (1705–16), although there the architect to the Order, Nicolas Pierson, has translated the entire Gothic formal repertoire into classical terms. Here in one of the finest church interiors in eastern France, the overall effect is dis-tinctly that of a Gothic hall church, though one with huge Corinthian columns (Plate 128).

This tradition survived even the building of the Primatiale in Nancy. Before that church was completed, Jennesson built Saint-Sébastien, Nancy (1720–31) as another hall church: one in which the pronounced entasis of the columns, and the ornate and curved façade, manifest a native Baroque temperament quite uninfluenced by the Primatiale. Saint-Jacques in Lunéville, already discussed, belongs to the same tradition; both in its plan and in the form of its supports, it is very close to Saint-Sébastien.

A separate group in eastern France is formed by the Jesuit churches of Epinal (1724–5), Verdun (1731–5) and Langres (1746–60). All use columns instead of piers, wide pilasters to give emphasis to the choir, no transepts and a continuous façade, without subdivisions, surmounted by a segmental pediment. This whole group, which included other churches now lost, was the work of a Jesuit, Père René Maugrain, whose inspiration came from the hall churches of Flanders. The connecting link here was the Jesuit church at Hesdin in Picardy (1714–15).[105]

In the province of Franche-Comté, where the hall churches are distinguished from those in Lorraine by their more rigid ground plans, the leading architects were Jean-Jacques Galezot and Nicolas Nicole.[106] In his invariably

128 Nicolas Pierson: Pont-à-Mousson, Premonstratian Abbey, 1705–16, interior.

129 Nicolas Nicole: Besançon, Sainte-Madeleine, 1746–66, interior.

transeptless churches – including Saint-Georges, Vesoul (1736), and Scey-sur-Saône (1733–61) – the little-known Galezot used tall piers bearing stilted arches; the result is an impression of particular lightness. Far more important was Nicolas Nicole (1702–84), who formed the link with Paris. He studied there for two years, in 1737–9, and was in contact with Jacques-François Blondel during the latter's stay in Besançon. The first fruits of his studies came in the Chapelle du Refuge (now Chapelle de l'Hôpital) in Besançon, in which he combined the prototype of Le Vau's Collège des Quatre Nations with Desgodets' published design for a monastic church.

Nicole's masterpiece however is the Madeleine in Besançon (1746–66), which is not only the most important church in Franche-Comté but one of the most important eighteenth-century churches anywhere in France (Plate 129). The plan, like that of the Primatiale in Nancy, is a cross inscribed in a rectangle; and Nicole has developed this into a work of the greatest originality, combining the fluted, coupled columns and pilasters, the massive entablature and the richly moulded archivolts of Blondel's manner with the stilted arches of the local hall-church tradition. The result is a striking contrast between the weight of the classical members and the soaring weightlessness of the space and its domes. Here ten years before Sainte-Geneviève, Nicole drew on local tradition to anticipate Soufflot's idea of combining the structural lightness of the Gothic with the dignity of the antique orders. Nicole's façade design – executed, with modifications, in the nineteenth century – resembles Servandoni's first design for Saint-Sulpice; in its day, it started a widespread tradition of its own, as the prototype of the twin-towered façades of Saint-Christophe, Belfort, and Notre-Dame, Guebwiller.

The picture in the south of France was far less coherent. Of the few churches that rose above mediocrity, most were in the Rhône valley. The most important is undoubtedly the Carthusian church of Saint-Bruno, in Lyon, the final achievement of the Baroque in a city whose artistic sensibilities were attuned to those of neighbouring Italy. Little is known of the architect, Ferdinand Delamonce (1678–1753). Born in Munich, where his father was in the service of the Elector of Bavaria, he accompanied the Elector to Paris and there worked for engravers as an architectural draughtsman. On the death of Louis XIV, like many artists unsustained by an appointment in the Bâtiments du Roi, he left Paris. After thirteen years in Italy, he returned to France in 1728; in 1733 he settled in Lyon, where he worked for both public and private clients. Saint-Bruno des Chartreux was his principal work in that city.[107]

The church had been begun in the seventeenth century, but by the time when Delamonce took over, in 1733, all that had been built was the choir and half of the crossing. In the successive designs (Plate 130) that he submitted to the Carthusian Order the idea of a trefoil-shaped crossing within the width of the transepts appeared very early on; the principal question was whether to keep or demolish the choir. The resulting church, on which work started in 1734, is a compromise (Plate 131). Delamonce has retained the existing choir; a pair of apsidal bays replace the transepts, and the third lobe of the trefoil, towards the choir, is marked by segmental corners. The legend on Delamonce's design reveals that his source was the Dôme des Invalides, of which he had prepared drawings for the engravers of Félicien d'Avaux's *Description de l'Hôtel royal des Invalides* (1710), and in which J.H. Mansart had faced a similar problem in linking his centrally planned space with the nave of the existing military church. There are further likely echoes of the Invalides in the dome of Saint-Bruno, though it is not a twin-shell construction. In choosing the final design, the city council was decisively swayed by the argument that the dome would be a particular ornament to the city.

When Delamonce withdrew from the project in 1738, the church was basically complete; further work was supervised by the young Jacques-Germain Soufflot. The Italian character of Saint-Bruno is evident in restless cornices, un-French plasterwork and the vast reliefs of prophets in the crossing. The idea of casing the interior with marble, which Delamonce loathed, was never proceeded with. The central

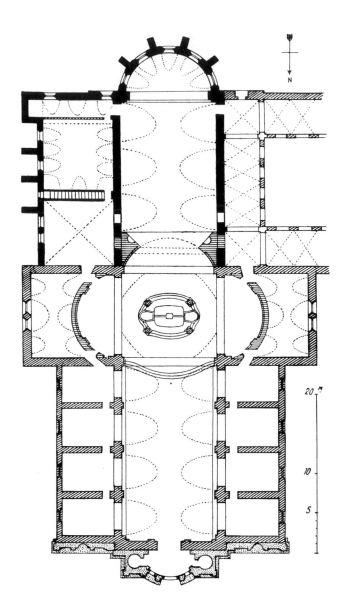

accent is the monumental baldachin or ciborium over the high altar, by Servandoni. Delamonce himself made three designs for this; he regarded it as particularly important because – aside from its decorative effect – it offered the advantage of masking the unduly low chancel arch, which would otherwise have spoilt the effect of the crossing. The ciborium itself, a late Baroque version of the one that Bernini designed for St Peter's in Rome, is a characteristic work by Servandoni, who used the stage decorator's trick of soaking real draperies in plaster. With its ornate and massive presence, it underscores the dramatic effect of Delamonce's architecture. We have Soufflot to thank for making the completed crossing into a coherent composition, which maintains the interplay of allied arts through paintings by Pierre-Charles Trémolières, in ornately carved frames of Soufflot's own design, and a large, double-sided marble altar.

In Provence, the ecclesiastical centre was Avignon. The fraternity chapels of the Pénitents-Rouges and Pénitents-Noirs, by Thomas Lainée, have already been mentioned. Another exotic implant was the Oratoire, built as a replacement for an older church belonging to the Oratorian Fathers. This unusual building had been begun by an unidentified

130 Ferdinand Delamonce:
Lyon, Saint-Bruno, 1734–8,
plan.

131 Ferdinand Delamonce:
Lyon, Saint-Bruno, 1734–8,
interior.

architect in 1713 or 1714; after a long hiatus, it was carried up to a height of six metres by Delamonce in 1729–32 and completed in 1741 by J.B. Péru, of Avignon. Its decoration took another nine years.

The plan, an oval inscribed in a rectangle – the foundations of which were already in place when Delamonce took over – derives from Pierre Puget's Chapelle de la Charité in Marseille (1682–1702), a work whose influence can be traced all over Provence: in the Eglise des Carmelites in Aix, in the Chapelle de la Miséricorde in Nice, at La Turbie and elsewhere. However, the Avignon interior differs from Puget's. His oval is surrounded by ambulatory-like spaces; in Avignon these are replaced by an array of T-shaped side chapels. The alternation between continuous and double-height chapels, combined with the polychrome

decor – red columns, plaster pilasters with gilded capitals – sets up a rhythm of movement and light that comes to rest only in the circular space that surrounds the altar. The decoration is the work of an Oratorian from Marseille, which goes to confirm the close connection between the two churches.[108]

The leading architect in Avignon, François Franque, was not involved in any of this work; his principal ecclesiastical commission was elsewhere, at Beaucaire. There, it had been decided to replace the Romanesque Notre-Dame des Pommiers with a large, new church to accommodate the pilgrims who flocked to the annual Masses. The design submitted by Franque, who enjoyed the support of the archbishop of Arles, was opposed by the Consuls of Beaucaire, who preferred that of their own candidate, the provincial engineer,

Guillaume Rollin. The result is a remarkable compromise. Franque's austerely Baroque interior, which echoes the Romanesque tradition in its three apses and shallow dome, is prefixed by Rollin's curved, Italianate façade.[109]

The easterly coastal strip of Provence belonged entirely to the Italian sphere of influence, especially Nice with its two Baroque churches, Saint-Pons (1705–13) and the Chapelle des Pénitents-Noirs or Chapelle de la Miséricorde (c. 1740, by the Genoese architect Bernardo Vittone). These are centrally planned churches on an oval plan, with vigorously curved façades and sumptuous marble and plaster decoration.

Finally, a special case: the great project of rebuilding the Gothic cathedral of Orléans. In France, in spite of all the Academy's efforts to establish the canon of the antique orders, the Gothic had never been entirely forgotten. Local traditions apart, this was to the credit of the Benedictines of Saint-Denis, Saint-Germain des Prés and Saint-Maur, who painstakingly recorded the history of their own abbeys and kept alive the memory of the achievements of the Gothic. The feeling that Gothic was the true religious style had deep roots. For Notre-Dame de Bonne-Nouvelle, Orléans (c. 1718), Guillaume Hénault submitted his design in two versions: one was classical, on the model of the Versailles chapel, but the other was Gothic – quaintly so, in parts.[110]

Even in the most exalted circles, moreover, the Gothic was still valued and could hold its own against the *goût moderne* – as is clearly shown by the example of Orléans Cathedral.[111] Severely damaged by Huguenot action in the sixteenth century, this had been gradually restored in the late Gothic style of the surviving portions. Already in 1623, in the deliberations on the reconstruction of the totally destroyed north transept, Gothic prevailed over the style of the day, as championed by Salomon de Brosse, Jean Androuet du Cerceau and others. When the same issue came up again in 1707, over the rebuilding of the façade, it was King Louis XIV himself who rejected a classical school-of-Mansart design in favour of the one submitted by Hénault and most probably approved by Robert de Cotte (1708) 'in the Gothic order'.

This design of de Cotte's, was broadly based on Notre-Dame de Paris; but the true Gothic feeling had clearly been lost, as can be seen in the gratuitous repetition of the rose windows and the overall horizontal emphasis. After de Cotte's death the work came under the supervision of Jacques V Gabriel, who made great efforts to expedite matters and had a wooden model of de Cotte's design made in 1736 (Plate 132); even so, the foundation stone was not laid until 1742. Under Loriot, who succeeded Gabriel in Orléans, progress continued to be slow, and by 1765, when Louis-François Trouard took over, it had gone no further than the portals. This remarkable fidelity to the Gothic was sustained throughout the second half of the century.

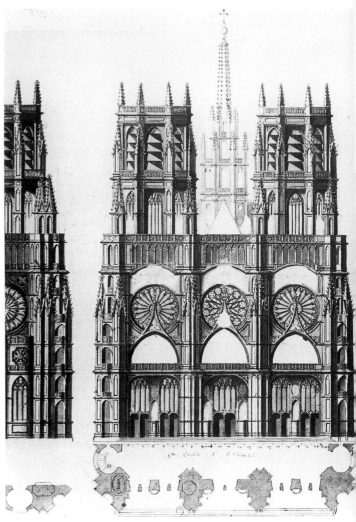

132 Guillaume Hénault: design for the façade of Sainte-Croix in Orléans, 1736.

CHAPTER 7
Decoration

Nowhere did the Rococo so clearly manifest itself as in decoration; there its qualities were displayed to the full. The style was in its true element indoors. Its decorative system, with its articulation of walls into panels, its rosettes and medallions, its proliferation of arabesques and tendrils, had taken shape in the Régence; and all of this survived. An all-embracing, animated rhythm, such as we find in Germany or in Italy, remained exceptional in France; all that happened was that the structure became less rigid. No longer rectilinear, the panels acquired curves and responded to each other's shapes. Curves were everywhere. Unity was no longer based on structure but on the interconnection of all the parts through a loose network of lines. Even the firm separation between wall and ceiling disappeared. Decoration began to flow, and the eye no longer found a point of repose. On all sides there was a ceaseless 'metamorphosis of forms' (Hubala), a constant transition from figure to ornament, from plant form to outline. To this was added one momentous innovation: asymmetry, which abolished axial relationships.

Thematic content also changed. Motifs imported from Italy – the Borghese dragons, Borromini's seraphs, Oppenord's giant cartouches – remained as fashionable as before. But these were now supplemented by the unmistakable hallmark of the Rococo, the jagged, asymmetrical, shell-like form known as rocaille. Ornamental design as a whole was overtaken by a wave of uninhibited naturalism. Bérain's abstract line was translated into plant forms. The edges of wall panels were no longer marked by mouldings but by reed stems and branches of olive and laurel. Palm fronds sprouted up the sides of mirrors. The Arcadian world of Watteau and Lancret stepped out of the picture frame and spread itself across the walls.

Decoration however was subject to strict rules. It grew more elaborate, in a precisely calculated gradation, as one approached the climax of the scheme, in the central salon or in the *chambre de parade*. The vestibule and staircase retained their traditional, ceremonial character; thus, the vestibule of the Hôtel de Luynes (1748) featured a painted architectural prospect by the Brunettis, with coupled columns in the Versailles manner. The most imaginative decoration was not to be found along the main enfilades but in the essentially private spaces that were known as cabinets. Only there was it acceptable to depict singeries and chinoiseries (very few of which have survived). Not that these rules were always obeyed; indeed, it was the uncontrolled proliferation of ornament in the wrong places that invited criticism and tended to discredit the style itself.

The true creators of the Rococo were probably Juste-Aurèle Meissonnier, Jacques de Lajoue, and Nicolas Pineau. All three were members of the Accademia di S. Luca in Rome: Meissonnier as an architect, Lajoue as a painter and Pineau as a sculptor. Blondel calls them the three prime inventors of the *genre pittoresque*.[112] The most versatile and ingenious of the three was Juste-Auréle Meissonnier (1695–1750), who was goldsmith, painter, draughtsman and architect, all rolled into one. Blondel called him 'one of the greatest men, as far as talent goes' (*un des plus grands hommes pour le talent*), adding that he was good at everything: fireworks, festive decorations, splendid ceilings, goldsmith's work and more besides.[113] Born in Turin to a Provençal goldsmith father and an Italian mother, Meissonnier grew up in Italy and moved to Paris in 1720. A trained goldsmith, he was appointed goldsmith to the king in 1724 and designer for festive occasions three years later, thus becoming the most influential ornamental designer at court.

As an architect he was blocked by the king's own architects and never made his mark; his designs for Saint-Sulpice (façade 1726, lady chapel 1727), and for a number of altars in Parisian churches, were altogether too reminiscent of Borromini and Guarini to be accepted. He therefore worked mainly for foreign clients. For the Polish Count Czartoryski he created the Grand Salon at Pulawy, near Warsaw, and for Marshal Bielinski the decor of a cabinet for the Palais Bielinski in Warsaw itself (1734; Plate 133); this went on show at the Tuileries before being sent to Poland. For the Marshal's sister, who had moved to France on becoming Madame de Besenval, he designed a whole apartment.[114] His only building in France is the Maison Brethous (1733), in Bayonne, where he has fitted octagonal and oval rooms into a difficult, trapezoidal ground plan.

In his decorative work, Meissonnier adhered to the Piedmontese Rococo but exaggerated it to an extreme. His wall panels and mirror frames are all curves; his cornices positively swirl. Asymmetry runs wild and negates the structure of the building. The ceilings, with their painted balustrades and their central accumulation of figures, are a reversion to the system of Pietro da Cortona. Four years after Meissonnier's death, Claude-Nicolas Cochin, that implacable judge of all things Rococo, saw very clearly what the essence of Meissonnier's style was when he wrote, full of indignation:

> Meissonnier took to destroying all straight lines ... He curved his cornices upwards and downwards, forward and back ... He invented contrasts, which means that he banished symmetry. It was he who created the fashion for all those marvellous double curves; he used them everywhere. Truth to tell, all his designs, even those for buildings, were nothing more or less than a concatenation of such forms, strung out in all directions.

Meissonnier played a leading role in the dissemination of the *style pittoresque*. The starting point of this process can be traced to one candelabrum that he made, as a goldsmith, in 1728. In it, for the first time ever, asymmetry appeared as a constitutive element in association with rocaille. Not that he

133 Jules-Aurèle Meissonnier: Design for a Cabinet for Marshal Bielinski.

134 Jules-Aurèle Meissonnier: *Œuvres*, c. 1735, title page.

was the inventor of either: asymmetry had been used by Toro in his cartouches,[115] and rocaille – not to be confused with regularly formed shellwork (coquille) – was first hinted at by Vassé in the Galerie Dorée.[116] But this had remained an isolated episode; and it was Meissonnier who was regarded as the father of rocaille.

In his engravings (Plate 134), which found their way to every part of Europe – the *Livre d'ornements*, the *Livre de légumes* and others – rocaille is the dominant figure, the symbol of the Rococo. These images open up a fantastic world, unreal in every particular. The title page of his *Œuvres* is dominated by a huge rocaille that rears up like a wave and at the same time supports the balcony of a château. Rocaille functions both as architecture and as ornament. The ornament may transform itself into fountains, ruins and stairways; but always, before we know it, the image of reality has turned into ornament again. In the cabinet of Marshal Bialinski all structure is abolished; one sphere of reality flows into another. The visual restlessness is accentuated by all the running water that ascends in a fountain or cascades out of the architecture. In reviewing Meissonnier's first suite of engravings (1734), the *Mercure de France* gave what was almost certainly the earliest contemporary definition of the *genre pittoresque*, while correctly pointing out the affinity with Stefano della Bella.

Close on the heels of Meissonnier's engravings came those of Jacques Lajoue (1686–1761). This highly regarded architectural painter, with clients among the aristocracy and at court, was a regular exhibitor at the Salon.[117] He first made his name with a perspectival scheme of decoration in the Bibliothèque Sainte-Geneviève (1731–2), and with the library and cabinet of curiosities that he decorated for the collector Joseph Bonnier de la Mosson (1734).[118] The engravings from his cycle of paintings for the Duc de Picquigny, later Duc de Chaulnes, were among the most-used source documents of the period. In his effective architectural vistas, interiors and buildings in a contemporary style are set within Arcadian landscapes clearly derived from Watteau and Lancret.

In his own engravings (Plate 135), published from 1735 onwards, Lajoue comes close to Meissonnier (Plate 136). Here, too, in wave after wave of crests, swirls and troughs, rocaille forms itself into craggy pedestals, fountain basins, elements of architecture and frames for fragments of landscape. Here, too, a world of grotesques takes shape 'in which ornament and image mingle without negating each other' (Sedlmayr). Time and again, ornament evaporates into pure illustration. More than in Meissonnier, streams of water, garlands of flowers and rustic idylls breathe life into the abstractions of rocaille and integrate it with nature. Lajoue

135 Jacques de Lajoue: *Livre nouveau de divers morceaux de fantaisie*, 1736, design.

136, 137 Jules-Aurèle Meissonier: *Livre d'Ornaments*, two designs.

138 Nicolas Pineau: Paris, Hôtel de Villars, Galerie, 1733.

carries his architectural distortions to an ultimate conclusion in his *Quatre livres d'architecture, paysages et perspectives* (1740). His lighter and looser compositions are a French answer to Meissonnier's Italianate dynamism and solidity.

In terms of practical work done, the pre-eminent decorator was Pineau, whom we have to thank for the finest and most finished decorative ensembles of the Parisian Rococo.[119] Nicolas Pineau (1684–1754) had gone to Russia with Le Blond in 1716, and on the latter's death he had succeeded him as director of works to the Czar; his carved woodwork at Peterhof is among the loveliest products of Régence decorative art. He seems to have left Russia in 1727, although it is not known when he arrived in France. In Paris, where he saw no chance of finding work as an architect, he concentrated entirely on the design of ornamental woodcarving. 'Since he was a good draughtsman, and design came easily to him, he enjoyed an extraordinary success in this field.' (Cochin, *Mémoires inédits*, 1880.) He took a leading role in the remodelling, enlargement and redecoration of numerous Parisian hôtels during the 1730s and 1740s, and enjoyed a particularly close association with Leroux, with whom he worked on his first scheme, the Galerie de Villars (1732) (Plate 138). Others who set great store by his services included Briseux, Le Carpentier, Tannevot and Mansart de Sagonne. Of his numerous works in Paris, few have survived:

139 Nicolas Pineau: Paris, Hôtel de Roquelaure, Salon rouge, 1733.

140 Nicolas Pineau: Paris, Hôtel de Villeroy, Salon oval, c. 1746 (Mariette, *L'Architecture Française*, pl. 468).

the Hôtel de Roquelaure (1732–3) (Plate 139), Hôtel de Marcilly (*c.* 1738), Maison Tannevot (*c.* 1740) and Hôtel de Maisons (*c.* 1750). Some other work, including that done for the Hôtel de Rouillé and Galerie de Villars, is no longer in situ but dispersed in French and foreign collections.[120]

Pineau's decorations are typified by their extraordinary lightness and inventiveness. Tendrils and garlands, interspersed with flower vases, swarm up the walls, in defiance of gravity, and fill the covings. Rocaille and ribbonwork loop themselves around mirrors and wall panels in irrational forms reminiscent of grotto decoration. Everything undergoes a metamorphosis into plant form; and there are times when the wall looks like some ephemeral piece of garden architecture. Asymmetrical grotesques on door or wall panels evoke surprising associations (Plate 140).[121] At times, even the horizontal demarcation line of the dado is abandoned and the upper and lower panels are interlinked. Curves rule supreme. In the Galerie de Villars, the cornice below the

coving of the ceiling is the one and only straight line in the room. This, again, was described by Cochin in another inimitable attack on Pineau in the *Mercure de France* in 1755:

In his hands, cornices and mouldings – in which Oppenord and Meissonnier sought to retain what they described as a masculine quality – became altogether insubstantial. He manipulated them with such delicacy that they almost entirely vanished from view; within a given space, he was able to multiply their number six-fold. He very soon set behind him the law that those others had so much taken to heart: namely, that ornaments should always be connected. He separated them, divided them into a thousand pieces, all of which ended in the scroll that has always been our most important decorative element . . .

'He forswore the straight edge and the compasses, once and for all. Symmetry was already banished; but he went one step further. If ever he so far forgot himself as to make two similar wall panels, he placed these symmetrical figures so far

141   Germain Boffrand: Paris, Hôtel de Soubise, Salon de la Princesse, 1736–9.

apart that only the most attentive scrutiny would reveal their similarity . . . He instituted the practice of eliminating all flat ceilings and instead instructing the carvers to apply pretty little lacy motifs in relief, at very little cost; the success of these led to the sagacious decision to do away with the covings of all domestic rooms and to fill them in with these charming lace patterns.

His contemporaries were enthusiastic; Pineau was the height of fashion. Such engravers as François-Thomas Mondon, P.E. Babcl and François de Cuvilliés disseminated the new style all over Europe. It is true that in 1737, Blondel complained in the *Traité . . . de la distribution des maisons de plaisance* of the absurd accretions of shellwork, dragons, reeds, palm fronds and other plant forms that had become the principal attraction of interior decoration; but by 1754 he was writing, admiringly:

Never before has such elegance of form, such beauty of execution and such richness of material been handled with

such sureness of taste. For this degree of perfection we are indebted today to Pineau, Lange, Verberckt and others, who have helped to make our houses deserve the admiration of other, less experienced nations.[122]

There was no one to resist Pineau's influence. It is as much in evidence in Ange-Jacques Gabriel's work for Versailles as in the late decorations done by Oppenord for his old patron, Gaudion, at La Grange-du-Milieu.[123] Even Boffrand was not immune. His interiors at the Hôtel de Soubise are like a deliberate answer to Pineau, though in them the Baroque tradition is still alive, and all the arts are enlisted to reinforce the effect.

The occasion for this scheme was the second marriage of Prince Hercule Mériadec de Rohan-Soubise to a young and beautiful bride, Sophie de Noailles. Boffrand, employed to refurbish the Hôtel de Soubise, extended the garden front by adding the oval pavilion already mentioned. His decorative work (1736–9) embraces two complete apartments, one for

142 Jacques Verberckt: Versailles, Grand cabinet intérieur de la Reine, 1737, design of boiseries.

143 Jacques Verberckt: Versailles, Cabinet de la Pendule, 1737–8.

the Prince on the ground floor and one for the Princess on the first floor (Plate 141).[124] Here Boffrand is at his gracious and resourceful best. Influenced by Pineau, though characteristically more conservative, he avoids asymmetry entirely and sets firm sculptural accents by using large, figured cartouches, by grouping figures in the round on the cornices and by emphasizing picture and mirror frames with strong mouldings. In keeping with the accepted rule, each of the two apartments rises to a climax in its last room: that is, in the room contained in the new, oval pavilion. As in the grand salon at La Malgrange, the principal emphasis lies in the spandrels between the arches of the window and door openings. In the Salon du Prince, these are filled in with figurative medallions in high relief, allegories of the Prince's virtues; in the Salon de la Princesse, immediately above, they are filled with paintings by Natoire of the legend of Cupid and Psyche. Above these is a light, pergola-like dome, supported by perforated balusters, with a large rosette in the centre. The opulence of the ornament, and the harmonious enmeshing of the arts, make these rooms into a supreme manifestation of the Parisian Rococo. But in this particular decor the architectural articulation remains intact; it is evident that the guiding hand has not been that of a decorator but that of an architect.

Decorative work at court in the same period was also of high quality, and was executed by the best ornamental carvers in France. Work at Versailles started in 1725, with the king's wedding. De Cotte was still in charge, with the practical execution entrusted to Vassé and his seasoned team of

Degoullons, Taupin and Le Goupil. They created the chimneypiece and the two massive picture frames in the Salon d'Hercule (c. 1730), as well as the large mirror frames and overdoors in the Queen's bedchamber (1730). In these the forms are Régence, and well within the tradition of the Galerie Dorée, though the palm trees entwined with olive branches are an innovation.

The Cabinet du Roi, in what is now the Bibliothèque Nationale in Paris, was also decorated at this time.[125] In this, the former salon of the Hôtel de Lambert, the king's collection of coins and medals was to be housed. Work started under Robert de Cotte at some time after 1724, but it was finished only in 1746, by his son Jules-Robert, in a style close to that of the Hôtel d'Assy. An undulating rhythm runs through the room, initiated by the deep spandrels between the elliptical window arches. These spandrels are adorned with large trophies in relief, the wall piers beneath them with paintings by Natoire. The impression created is similar to that of Boffrand's work at the Hôtel de Soubise. The end walls are dominated by François Boucher's life-size portraits of Louis XIV and Louis XV, attended by allegories of the Sciences; the frames continue the undulating line that runs through the rest of the room. The date of 1730, known from Robert de Cotte's inventory of the furnishings, would seem likely to apply to the decorations as well.

With the retirement of Robert de Cotte and the gradual disappearance of his associates from the scene, the true Rococo found its way into the decor of Versailles. Ange-Jacques Gabriel, who took over the direction of works at

Versailles not only to reduce his father's work-load but on the strength of his own outstanding draughtsmanship, had already worked for some years under de Cotte. Vassé's successor, Jacques Verberckt (1704–71), a highly gifted ornamental carver of Flemish origins, was another who had belonged to the same team.[126] There is accordingly very little to choose between his early work and that of Degoullons or Le Goupil all the more as Verberckt had married the niece of Degoullons and after her death the daughter of Le Goupil.

At Versailles, the new decorative spirit made its first appearance in the Queen's bedchamber (Chambre de la Reine, 1735–7) and in adjoining rooms (Plate 142). There it manifested itself in the increased delicacy of the mouldings, in the growing prevalence of plant motifs, in the irrational curves of the mirror frames – with their floral festoons hanging clear of the surface of the glass – and above all in the wall panels. These reveal the same marked tendency towards concentration as those at Chantilly and in the Hôtel de Lassay. The ornamental focuses – the gilded rosettes above, in the centre and below, around which the tendrils and arabesques twine – are cut loose from the edges of the panel and gathered into large, quasi-pictorial compositions, which may be either shell-like rosettes with serrated outlines or figurative reliefs like those at the Hôtel de Soubise. Here the influence of Pineau is not to be ruled out.

The richest decor is naturally to be found in the Petits Appartements in the right-hand side wing, the living quarters of the king. These originally extended through three floors, of which the two upper ones were kept simple, with coloured lacquer painting in *vernis Martin* in place of gilding. The full splendour of gold manifests itself only in those first-floor rooms that formed the heart of the whole palace in Louis XV's day. Subject to constant alteration from the very start, these no longer present anything like a coherent whole. All that survives of the first phase of decoration, in 1737–8, is the Chambre du Roi, the Cabinet de la Pendule (Plate 143), the so-called Antichambre des Chiens, and parts of the Cabinet d'Angle or Cabinet Intérieur (Plate 144).[127] These are very similar to the Queen's bedchamber, but stronger and more emphatic. In the wall panels, as at the Hôtel de Lassay, the lower rosettes have turned into figured reliefs and the upper ones into sizable seashells. As with Pineau, the mirror frames have dissolved into a kind of latticework, interlaced with rocaille, in which playful putti disport themselves. Total informality also prevails in the ceiling covings, in which, with no regard for cornices or for symmetry, birds flutter amid a tangle of plant shoots and rocaille.

There is not much that is different in the later rooms, dating from 1753–5, including the so-called Arrière-Cabinet, the Cabinet Intérieur de Madame Adelaïde (now the Salon de Musique) and Verberckt's large wall panels in the Cabinet d'Angle.[128] To an even greater degree than before, figure has taken over from ornament. The wall panels are dominated by scenes in relief, or by large pendant trophies; these last are veritable masterpieces on Verberckt's part, of which the finest are the compositions of musical instruments in the Salon de Musique. The arabesques around the medallions have now been entirely replaced by flowering fronds, tied with bows of ribbon.

forms (Plate 145). Along with much reused material, its wall panels incorporate a sequence of large framed relief compositions consisting of carved pendant trophies and allegorical reliefs from the antique. This was the first major commission undertaken by the youthful Antoine Rousseau, who took Verberckt's large panels as his model but gave them greater sculptural weight by using a more substantial frame and adding freely pendant garlands. Both rocaille and asymmetry, still present in the Salon de Musique, have disappeared. For all the freedom of the detailing, the forms are once more fitted into the architectural framework. The flow of movement no longer runs across the entire wall but is held within the individual panel.

The decorations at Fontainebleau resemble those at Versailles. The phases of work were the same: 1736–9, 1746–7, 1751–4; and so were the executants. The lion's share of the work once more fell to Verberckt. The style, even so, is freer, and less weighed down by tradition; and the winged cartouches bearing heraldic fleurs-de-lis or crowns, which are *de rigueur* at Versailles, are rare at Fontainebleau.

The Cabinet de Retraite du Roi (1737) (Plate 146), immediately adjoining the Cabinet du Conseil, has a lightness of touch worthy of Pineau himself.[129] In contrast to Versailles, the surrounds of the wall panels curve inwards to link with the large central medallions, thus annulling the architectural articulation of the wall and creating a state of suspense that is echoed in the mirror-head, with its floral surround, and in the rocaille overdoors. The vegetable kingdom has taken over to such an extent that even the palmettes at the panel edges have turned into flower vases.

At Fontainebleau, this free handling of form culminates in the covings of the Gros Pavillon (1751–4). The Grands Appartements, on the other hand – the Chambre du Roi, Chambre de la Reine, Cabinet du Conseil – suffer from a certain ponderousness; for here Ange-Jacques Gabriel had to cope with coffered ceilings, doors and chimneypieces dating from the reigns of Henry II and Louis XIII, which the king wished to preserve out of respect for his forebears. There is therefore no carved relief on the walls of the Cabinet du Conseil, which is decorated with painted grotesques; the massive coffers of the ceiling were painted by Boucher. However, on one wall of the Chambre du Roi (1752–4), there are large, carved and framed trophies that recall the Cabinet du Conseil at Versailles, and indeed excel it, both in quality of invention and in delicacy of execution.

The carved wall panels at Rambouillet, the seat of the Comte de Toulouse (c. 1735), can also be discussed under the heading of court art. No names are recorded, but the quality of both invention and execution strongly points to Verberckt.[130] Here, again, the influence of Pineau is evident. The delicate network of ornament that runs over the panels, and the constant disruption of the frame outlines, recall the Hôtel de Rouillé and the Galerie de Villars. The panels in the boudoir of the Comtesse de Toulouse are framed not with mouldings but with reed stems, in root-like clusters, lined by a string of curves and countercurves (Plate 147). On the coving, gods and putti disport themselves freely amid waves and rocaille curves. The other rooms are more conventional, but have the same sparkling vivacity.

The only surviving example of decorative work done for

145 Antoine Rousseau: Versailles, Cabinet du Conseil, 1755–6.

A similar style prevails in Verberckt's decor for the Dauphin's apartment, on the ground floor of the left-hand wing of the Cour de Marbre (1747), and in the queen's rooms directly above. Here, the panel frames have oval heads, a relic of the paintings that formerly occupied the same location; this novelty was to be of importance for later work.

The Petits Appartements represent the climax of the Rococo at Versailles. They betray no diminution of its power, although the second campaign of decorative work coincides with Cochin's attacks and Marigny's change of taste. Only the Cabinet du Conseil, the last room in the sequence to be remodelled and enlarged (1755–6), reverts to more restful

144 Jacques Verberckt: Versailles, Cabinet intérieur du Roi, 1737–8.

146 Jacques Verberckt:
Fontainebleau, Cabinet de retraite
du Roi 1737, design (Archives
Nationales).

147 Jacques Verberckt:
Rambouillet, Boudoir of the
Comtesse de Toulouse, c. 1735.

the circle of Madame de Pompadour is at the Château de Champs (*c.* 1747). It is probably by Lassurance the Younger; in it, the *genre pittoresque* is as imaginative and charming as ever, but without ever disrupting the architectural frame-work.[131]

Alongside carved decoration, there was a considerable role for painting, whether genre, grotesque, or illusionistic. Gilding generally appeared only in state apartments, while colour schemes in other rooms followed successive changes of taste. Little of all this has survived. The most celebrated examples of genre painting are the Cabinet des Singes at Chantilly (before 1740), Champs (1748) and the Hôtel de Rohan (*c.* 1750), in which comedy scenes and grotesques are combined.

Illusionistic painting served very different purposes. It was used to heighten and enlarge the room, thus conveying to the beholder an impression of dignity and grandeur. The Brunettis worked in the Italian manner, adorning mainly staircases – as for example at the Hôtel de Luynes (1748) and the Hôtel de Soubise (*c.* 1750) – with architectural fantasies that afforded a view of spacious halls and gardens. At Condé-en-Brie, Servandoni painted the garden salon with great fluted pilasters alternating with prospects of the most celebrated garden sculptures of Versailles. The out-standing achievement of this kind was the perspective of ruins that the Brunettis painted for Boffrand in the chapel of the Enfants-Trouvés, with its life-size processions of Shepherds and Magi to the stable at Bethlehem (Plate 95).

PART THREE

Early Neoclassicism

CHAPTER I

Introduction

The peaceful evolution that marked the early part of Louis XV's reign came to an end in mid-century. The popularity of the monarchy reached its peak in the 1740s with the victory of Fontenoy and the Peace of Aix-la-Chapelle. There ensued a political and intellectual crisis that endangered the existence of the state itself. The ineptitude of the French generals made the Seven Years War (1756–63) into a disaster; and the naval war against Britain (1755–63) cost France her maritime supremacy, as well as important colonies in America and India. At home, the long-smouldering conflict between the crown and the Parlements broke out openly, and led in 1771 to the dissolution of the Parlement de Paris, the country's supreme court of jurisprudence, and the banishment of its members from the capital; Parlements in the provinces, too, openly defied the central power. The clergy aroused public hostility by clinging to their privileges and resisting all attempts to reform the taxation system; it thus furnished welcome ammunition to the propagandists of the Enlightenment. Public resentment focused on the Jesuits, whose influence was believed to underlie all the actions of the court. In consequence, in 1764, the Society of Jesus was dissolved, its assets were confiscated, and its schools, some of the foremost educational institutions of the day, were closed.

In such circumstances the prestige of the monarchy inevitably suffered. Louis XV took the blame not only for general reluctance to reform but for the unhappy outcome of the Seven Years War. In 1770 the foreign minister, the Duc de Choiseul, who sympathized with the unruly Parlements, was dismissed and banished to Chanteloup; the ovations that greeted him on the way were tantamount to public demonstrations against the king.

The intellectual crisis, too, grew ever more acute. The Enlightenment presented a united front and moved to occupy the moral high ground. With the critical writings of Voltaire – the *Essai sur les moeurs* (1751), a universal social history with a distinct anti-monarchist bent, the *Traité sur la tolérance* (1763) and the *Dictionnaire philosophique* (1764), which was publicly burned on account of its anti-religious polemic – and with Rousseau's *Discours sur l'origine de l'inégalité* (1753), but above all with the twenty-eight volumes of Diderot and d'Alembert's *Encyclopédie* (1751–272), which made everything from Atheism to Zoology subject to rational explanation, the Enlightenment undermined the very foundations of the absolute monarchy and of the Church. Voltaire described d'Alembert's 'Discours préliminaire' for the *Encyclopédie* as 'a magnificent and intelligent introduction to this repository of knowledge, but one that gives due notice to envy and ignorance that they must arm themselves'.

The utilitarian character of Enlightenment thinking had profound consequences for architecture. Beauty gave way to Utility and Necessity, and the aesthetic principle was in retreat.[1] The Encyclopaedists measured beauty by reason alone; they called for architecture to be subordinated to the laws of structural solidity and logic. Robert Morris in England, and Carlo Lodoli and Francesco Milizia in Italy, argued the same principles. The transition from Rococo to Neoclassicism is therefore more than a stylistic shift: it is a far-reaching change in attitudes to art as a whole.

The fight against the Rococo was fought on two fronts: by the traditionalists, who sought to perpetuate the tradition of the *Grand Siècle*; and by the antiquarians for whom salvation resided exclusively in the revival of the ancient world. Both these parties united in demanding a return to good taste.[2] Blondel, in his *Traité . . . de la distribution des maisons de plaisance* (1737), had decried the 'absurd accretions of oblique cartouches, rocailles, dragons, reeds, palms, and every possible fancy plant' that were all the rage in the decoration of his day. From the 1740s onwards, the criticisms grew harsher.[3] In his *Lettres d'un Français*, written in England but later (1745) published in France, Abbé Leblanc mounted the first public onslaught on the Rococo, its asymmetry, and the disorder and confusion of scale in its ornament. He was followed by Pierre-Jean Mariette, with a vitriolic obituary of Meissonnier in the *Mercure de France* for December 1750, in which he wrote:

> M. Meissonnier avoided every kind of symmetry, even in ornament; and, as an example of the abuses to which imitation can lead, we have seen his imitators putting up their brackets and keystones crooked, even though these must by their very nature be vertical.

The decisive turning point came in 1749–51, with the Italian tour undertaken by Tournehem's designated successor as director-general of the Bâtiments du Roi. This was Madame de Pompadour's brother, Abel Poisson (1727–81), later Marquis de Vandières, but best known by the title he received in 1754, that of Marquis de Marigny.[4] Once the king had promised him the post, his sister sent him to Italy on a preparatory study tour. As his companions she sent her own adviser on purchases of works of art, Abbé Leblanc, the young architect Jacques-Germain Soufflot, who had made a name for himself with his Hôtel-Dieu in Lyon, and the draughtsman and engraver Charles-Nicolas Cochin, an employee of the Menus-Plaisirs.[5] Marigny spent nearly two years touring northern Italy, Rome and Naples, and returned as a sworn adversary of the Rococo. However, it was not until some years later, in the salon of Madame Geoffrin, the intellectual centre of Parisian life, that he became a convert to the Greek revival, the *goût grec*.

Tournehem died in 1751, and Marigny took up his appointment in the same year. His travelling companions

Versailles, Petit Trianon, see Plate 172.

remained his life-long friends. In 1755 Cochin became chief painter to the king and permanent secretary to the Academy; Soufflot became surveyor to the Bâtiments du Roi for Paris. The new course was set.[6]

In the *Mercure de France* for December 1754, shortly after Pineau's death, Cochin published his ironic *Supplication aux orfèvres* ('A Petition to the Goldsmiths'), in which he called on architects to look at ancient buildings, and to build houses with right angles instead of rounded corners and with rectangular instead of octagonal rooms:

> We shall not demand of them any restraint in the use of the palm fronds that they cultivate in such profusion in our dwellings ... But at the very least we may reasonably expect them not to distort those things that might well be square, and not to foist S-curves on the upper parts of mirror frames, which can perfectly well be round.

In the following year Cochin wrote an equally ironic defence of the *genre pittoresque*, in which he put into the mouth of a fictitious Rococo architect the claim that, since he and his colleagues were universally admired, all objections were beside the point; after all, anyone who could afford to build regarded himself *ipso facto* as an authority on architecture.

Witty and spirited, though with a touch of polemical overstatement, these articles had their effect; however, the *genre pittoresque* survived well past the death of Pineau. Marigny himself, presumably influenced by his sister, firmly allied himself with the new tendency, but his own taste tended to waver. In 1756 he instructed the Academy to set the interior decoration of châteaux as the principal task for the candidates for the next Prix de Rome, 'in order to improve the poor taste in ornament that still prevails'. But as late as 1760 he remarked to Soufflot, apropos the commissioning of picture frames: 'I want neither modern *chicorée* nor strict antique, but half one, half the other.' (Letter to Soufflot, 18 March 1760)

Illogical though it may seem, the major element in the anti-Rococo reaction was not love of antiquity but nostalgia for France's recent past. Blondel's generation looked back admiringly to the *Grand Siècle* and its buildings, and compared the current dearth of new public building in Paris with the great building programmes of the seventeenth century. It was in this frame of mind that Blondel himself wrote his fundamental article on architecture for Diderot's *Encyclopédie*;[7] and Voltaire, in his *Histoire de Louis XIV* (1751), glorified the reign of the Sun King as one of the great ages of human history. Such admiration went hand in hand with a generalized inferiority complex. Vasari had seen Michelangelo and his contemporaries as the acme of artistic perfection, after which decline was inevitable; and in much the same way the majority of mid-eighteenth-century intellectuals saw themselves as latecomers, witnesses to a universal decline of taste that was comparable only with the artistic decadence that followed the Augustan age in Rome. Viewed in evolutionary terms, this is precisely the kind of situation that leads to historicism.

The architecture of the 1750s and 1760s therefore consciously harked back to seventeenth-century precedents. Ange-Jacques Gabriel, in his façades for the Place Louis-XV (Place de la Concorde) in Paris, and Soufflot, in the colonnades of Sainte-Geneviève, both had Perrault's façade of the Louvre in mind; the young Etienne-Louis Boullée, in his interiors, used the vocabulary of J.H. Mansart. In 1765 the publisher Jombert brought out a pocket manual of classical architecture for the use of young architects, with 350 designs by Vignola, Palladio, Scamozzi and other classics. Blondel, the great theorist and influential Academy professor, never tired of drawing his students' attention to the exemplary status of the great masters of the past, above all François Mansart, the 'god of architecture'.

In the long run, however, the look of Neoclassicism was defined not by Blondel's conservatism but by the antique – and with it by Palladio. France took its place within a general current that flowed through the whole of Europe.[8] This was not by any means the first antique revival; but what distinguished eighteenth-century Neoclassicism from the Renaissance in all its previous versions was the moral aspiration that it expressed. The antique was more than an aesthetic prototype: it was a moral criterion. According to the doctrines of Johann Joachim Winckelmann, it represented goodness and beauty, human greatness and meaning. To these values, the philosophes of the Enlightenment added those of plain living, moral virtue and public spirit. The architect, as an artist, was entrusted with an educative, social function: it was his task to cite antique prototypes and thereby to influence the modern world. Architecture thereby acquired a moral dimension. Instead of uniting the visual arts in a synthesis or *Gesamtkunstwerk*, as Boffrand had done at the Hôtel de Soubise, the Neoclassicists set out to segregate them. Their ideal was an architecture liberated from colour and ornament, an expression of timeless grandeur. The term 'Neoclassicism' itself was originally a pejorative one, coined in the nineteenth century to denote the resuscitation of a lifeless and depersonalized antiquity. The word was unknown in the eighteenth century; what we call Neoclassicism was regarded by contemporaries simply as the one and only 'true' style. It was regarded not as a mere fashion but as the revival of the arts and the revelation of timeless verities.[9]

Public interest in the ancient world was stimulated, and the antique monuments were rendered generally accessible, by a number of books of engravings that appeared in mid-century. In 1748 Piranesi published the first of his *Vedute di Roma*, and in 1756 his *Antichità romane*, thus bringing the grandeur of ancient Rome before the eyes of the public. The first volume of the *Antichità de Ercolano* appeared in 1757. Concurrently, in England, there were *The Ruins of Palmyra* (1753) and *The Ruins of Balbec* (1757), by Robert Wood. Then came a new factor: the discovery of Greek architecture. Here the most important work was the book of engravings by David Le Roy, *Les Ruines des plus beaux monuments de la Grèce* (1758), followed in Britain by *The Antiquities of Athens*, by James Stuart and Nicholas Revett (1762). For the first time, the Greek temple became a known quantity, and Greece became a magnet to the cultivated world. Although Stuart and Revett were more accurate than Le Roy, he did have the advantage of publishing first, and this earned him universal attention and decisively influenced the genesis of the *goût grec*. The scope of archaeological interest had now been greatly widened; and the controversy as to the priority of Greece or Rome, kindled by Piranesi's book *Della magnificenza ed architettura de' Romani* (1761), was therefore conducted on a wide front. In France, the cause of Rome was vigorously championed by Mariette.

In France, the collectors and students of antiquities (or *antiquaires*) tended to gravitate to the circle of the Comte de Caylus, an influential grandee with connections all over Europe, who collected antique objects of every kind. Caylus had travelled in Asia Minor as early as 1716, and had rediscovered the ancient technique of encaustic painting; his *Recueil d'antiquités égyptiennes, étrusques, grecques et romaines*, in several volumes (1752–7), became a standard work.[10] He had nothing in common with the *philosophes*. His circle included the Duc de Choiseul and Abbé Leblanc, already mentioned; Abbé Barthélemy, curator of the Cabinet des Médailles; and Mariette, the celebrated collector and acerbic obituarist of Meissonnier.

Caylus also gathered around him the youthful winners of the annual Prix de Rome, as they returned to Paris from their time in Italy; these were the pioneers of Neoclassicism. In Rome they had become acquainted with the world of antiquity and had acquired precise archaeological knowledge by making measured drawings of ancient buildings. Thanks to Caylus's patronage, they became the true purveyors of antique forms, whether working for the Bâtiments du Roi, or for the city of Paris (like Pierre-Louis Moreau-Desproux), or at foreign courts.

The antique revival did not happen all at once, but in successive stages or waves. The first wave consisted of the Prix de Rome winners of the 1740s. It was characterized by a joint admiration of antiquity and of the Renaissance, and its tenor was not so much archaeological as eclectic. In the 1750s and 1760s Paris was swept by a vogue for the *style grec*; in the absence of any genuine knowledge of Greek art, anything that looked antique was labelled *grec*.[11] Baron Grimm reported in 1763:

> For some time now, the preference has been for antique ornaments and forms. The effect on taste has been salutary, and the vogue has become so general that nowadays everything is *à la grecque*. The internal and external decoration of buildings, furnishings, textiles, jewellery of all kinds: everything in Paris is *à la grecque*.[12]

The practical consequences of this first wave were limited; it coincided with the Seven Years War, which put a stop to all building activity.

The second wave, which reached Paris in the 1760s, was vastly more important. Its concerns were archaeological. It brought with it antique temple porticoes and circular, 'thermal' rooms. The seminal publication that launched this phase of Neoclassicism in Paris was the *Œuvres d'architecture* of Marie-Joseph Peyre; its publication in 1765 marked the conquest of architecture by the antique. In the previous year however, at the church of Saint-Symphorien, Montreuil, Trouard had already combined the antique temple portico with the form of the Early Christian basilica. By the accession of Louis XVI in 1774, as François-Joseph Bélanger's bath pavilion in the garden of the Hôtel de Brancas in Paris demonstrates, the antique formal vocabulary had been absorbed complete.

Neoclassicism was closely bound up with the name of Palladio. Somewhat eclipsed by Vignola in the seventeenth century, he was triumphantly resurrected in the second half of the eighteenth. Blondel remained unshaken in his allegiance to his own idol, François Mansart; but his pupils were covert admirers of Palladio, 'the most ingenious of modern architects', as Peyre called him. For the returning Rome scholars, who were privileged to meet Palladio's biographer, Tommaso Temanza, a detour to Venice and Vicenza became a prime duty. Peyre's *Œuvres d'architecture* included the first, much admired examples of Palladian architecture in France, both at the Hôtel de Neubourg – 'for which there are many precedents in Palladio' – and in many church designs conceived as compact, cubic, temple-like blocks.

Then there was the influence of Britain, where Palladianism had been dominant since the 1720s. Successive volumes of *Vitruvius Britannicus*, published from 1715 onwards, constituted a prime source of information. For Ledoux and Bélanger, the foreign country from which they brought back inspiration was not Italy but Britain. William Chambers's visit to Paris in 1749, and his period of study under Blondel, also led to a number of cross-Channel friendships.

Even so, French Palladianism is not comparable with the English variety. In France, with few exceptions, Palladio was imitated only in detail; the overall character of the building remained French. The rare instances of direct imitation include Moreau-Desproux's Pavillon Carré de Beaudouin, modelled on the Villa Ragona, and Ledoux's Pavillon Hocquart, after the façade of William Wakefield's Atherton. However, individual Palladian features are an inseparable part of the look of Neoclassical architecture. They made their first conspicuous appearance in the town house of Marigny, by Soufflot (1768), with its façade dominated by the Palladian motif of the *serliana* or Serlian window: an arch springing from a pair of short entablatures, each supported by two columns. The *serliana* and the fluted Ionic column now gained currency on private houses, churches and chapels.

The French architect who made the freest and most lavish use of the Palladian formal vocabulary was Ledoux. He worked with the same simple stereometric forms and used effects of light and shade to emphasize the volumes. He modified the cubic form of the Palladian villa, as already developed in England, in a bold way, by transposing some of its parts and by making an ingenious, thoroughly French use of the habitable area within. However, it was not until the ensuing period that Palladian architecture was totally appropriated and absorbed.

Blondel's system came under fire from another quarter, also close to Neoclassicism. In 1753 Abbé Marc-Antoine Laugier published his *Essai sur l'architecture*, in which he raised the demand for an architecture purged of all decorative accessory forms. Laugier was a Provençal Jesuit who had made a name for himself as a preacher both in Paris and at Versailles. At the same time he was a typical *homme de lettres*, a man who moved in Parisian literary circles and set down his ideas with a practised pen. On leaving the Society of Jesus he became the editor of the *Gazette de France*, and he served briefly as French *chargé d'affaires* at the court of the Archbishop-Elector of Cologne. Laugier published a number of books on history, art and music, but only one of them was epoch-making: the *Essai sur l'architecture*. In this, he proclaimed that no architectural member should be purely ornamental, and that its functional significance should always be clear. He based his argument on the primeval wooden hut, as supposedly built by human beings in a state of nature. This consisted of corner posts, a ridge, and a roof to afford shelter from snow and rain while admitting light to the full. 'I see only columns,' says Laugier, 'a covering or lintel and a pitched roof that forms a gable at either end. There is no vault, still less an arch; no base, no attic, not even a door or a window.'

From this he drew the conclusion that the only essential parts of any order were the column, the lintel and the gable, and utterly rejected the pilaster ('the bastard of architecture') and the arch, as well as niches, relief panels and all other devices for articulating wall surfaces. The wall was a protective skin, to keep the weather out, not an autonomous component with an aesthetic function of its own. With this, Laugier called in question the whole traditional system of architecture; nor did he exempt the orders from his strictures. As all the parts of the building were structural elements, and none should serve purely decorative purposes – to the extent that it should be impossible to take any part away without the whole structure collapsing – the orders, too, must vanish.

This was inevitably regarded as sacrilege. Since the Renaissance, the orders had been an inseparable constituent of architecture. In his *Cours d'architecture* of 1671, François Blondel had gone so far as to describe them as the noblest and most important part of architecture, while leaving such qualities as *solidité* and *commodité* out of the reckoning altogether. Laugier was the first writer to take a stand against this oft-lamented prejudice. By reducing the components of a building to the column and the lintel, he reverted to the first principles of Greek architecture. In this, he was in full agreement with the *antiquaires*, and with the Comte de Caylus in particular, even though the term 'Greek' was still rather a nebulous one.

Laugier was not (as might at first be supposed) a functionalist. He demanded solidity, plainness and clarity, but he also – and above all – demanded elegance and lightness, columns in place of piers, and as little wall surface as possible. There was nothing fundamentally new about all this. Cordemoy had made similar demands, condemning the irrationality of pilasters and calling for the replacement of piers with columns. Boffrand's chapel at Lunéville, and to

some extent Perrault's design for Sainte-Geneviève (1676), had exemplified the same principle. Laugier's *Essai* therefore did not come entirely unheralded; all the same, its appearance unleashed a storm. Written with a light and arrogant touch, brilliantly formulated, albeit often provocatively subjective and logically suspect, the book was as enthusiastically hailed by the young, and by the progressive intelligentsia, as it was denounced by architects.[13]

In his *Observations sur l'architecture* (1765), Laugier responded to massive counterblasts from such architects as A.F. Frézier and C.A. Guillaumot by modifying some of his demands, but he stuck to his basic principles. His influence was immense, mainly – though not exclusively – in church building, and above all at Sainte-Geneviève, later the Panthéon.

Early Neoclassical theory found its expression in the eight volumes of engravings published by an architect from Liège, Jean-François de Neufforge, under the title of *Recueil élémentaire d'architecture* (1757–68).[14] Neufforge was strongly influenced by Jean-François Le Lorrain, with whom he had worked on the engravings for *Les Ruines des plus beaux monuments de la Grèce*, by Le Roy. The early volumes of the *Recueil* therefore included all the characteristic forms of the *style grec* and of the first wave of the antique revival – porticoes, relief panels, heavy festoons, even top-lit galleries – along with constant references to the High Renaissance as well as to antiquity.

However, in Neufforge's later volumes, and in his two supplementary volumes (1772 and 1780), this eclecticism vanished. In both plans and elevations a new tendency began to appear: cubic house types, prostyle porticoes, window openings without surrounds, centrally placed staircases and emphatic, double-height, central salons. Neufforge had come under the dual influence of Peyre and Palladio; and he also made some unmistakable borrowings from English Palladianism. The cubic house type, the flat, unrelieved wall, the prostyle portico and the Renaissance detailing were customary in England and could be found in the *Vitruvius Britannicus* and in Chambers's *Treatise on Civil Architecture* (1759). The cube, a recurrent feature of Neufforge's designs, was treated as the basic form in Robert Morris's *Lectures on Architecture* (1734–6). The existence of a direct English influence on French Neoclassical architecture has been proven several times over;[15] it was, however, principally confined to landscape architecture and decoration. In most other cases, there is no need to look any farther than the mediating role of Neufforge.

CHAPTER 2

Blondel and the Traditionalists

The leading champion of classical tradition was Jacques-François Blondel. After a distinguished career as director of the Ecole des Arts and editor of French standard texts on architecture, he became a professor at the Academy in 1762. With him, the Academy acquired a classical doctrine with a strong French flavour. In his article on architecture for Diderot's *Encyclopédie*, he laid great stress on *convenance* and *bienséance*, on proportion and on the orders. His illustrations are classic examples of the practical application of these principles, and of good taste as he understood it. Among examples worthy of imitation, he cited works by François Franque, Contant d'Ivry and Le Carpentier and a design of his own for a large hôtel.

Blondel's teaching methods, which he carried over from the Ecole des Arts to the Academy, and his principles in general, were most clearly set forth in the six volumes of the *Cours d'architecture* (1771–3), a compilation of his lectures edited by his student, Pierre Patte.[16] He admired the great masters of the seventeenth century, and principally the 'god of architecture', François Mansart. This admiration was made patently evident in his own designs for a city hall for Strasbourg, an archbishop's palace for Cambrai, and other projects. But in the course of his twelve years' tenure at the Academy he saw the younger generation turning more and more towards Palladio and the antique, and regarding Mansart's style as obsolete. Both Graeco-Roman forms and English Palladianism were incompatible with his system. His last publication, *L'Homme du monde éclairé par les arts* (1774), betrayed both a sense of disappointment and a reluctant admiration for the works of his own pupils.

Blondel himself built very little. In 1767 the abbot of Saint-Arnould summoned him to Metz to build the Collège Royal de Saint-Louis, an institution for young ladies. He published his designs in the *Cours d'architecture*; and in fact they look for all the world like illustrations to his lectures, being an anthology of details from the famous churches that he admired. Building started in 1771 but never progressed beyond the initial stages. A more important commission came from the governor of Metz, to lay out a parade ground, or Place d'Armes, on the south side of the cathedral (Plate 149). Here, Blondel saw his chance to replan the whole quarter, he included the Hôtel de Ville, the Corps de Garde (guardhouse), the Parlement and the arcaded south wall of the cathedral in a monumental ensemble with a unified rhythm that lent both unity and dignity to the Place d'Armes (1764–75). On the unfinished west front of the cathedral itself, he added a portal (1763–6) that neatly chimed with the Gothic forms, and went on to front this with a Parvis flanked by the bishop's palace on one side and the Parlement on the other. On the north side of the cathedral he laid out a terrace, from which two flights of steps descend to the Place de Chambre, further down the slope. There is a chilly, academic quality about Blondel's buildings, but as an en-semble they bear imposing testimony to his gifts as an urban planner.[17]

For Strasbourg, a city that had become French in the comparatively recent past, he provided Choiseul with a plan intended – partly for military reasons – to rationalize the still largely medieval layout of the city, to resite its public buildings and to accentuate the nodal points.[18] But, like Robelin before him in Rennes, he came up against the entrenched opposition of the citizens and of the city's own architects. He pursued the project for a number of years, and included it in the *Cours d'architecture*, but all that was ever built was the Aubette (1766–7), on the main square of the city (now Place Kléber); this is a vast building, originally intended for military purposes, which repeats the articulation of the Hôtel de Ville in Metz. Blondel was unable to impose uniform façades on this central square, or to give it the intended polygonal end.

Blondel's plan for Strasbourg is a revealing specimen of Enlightenment city planning. It was a general aspiration to 'improve' cities by straightening old streets and driving through new ones, by laying out regular squares and by building new city halls, market halls, theatres and the like, and thus to rationalize them down to the last detail. Whereas most plans of this sort were drawn up by engineers with primarily utilitarian ends in view, Blondel's plan for Strasbourg was largely governed by aesthetic considerations. His cautious approach, and his respect for existing structures and for the aesthetic impression evoked by every change of scene, set his plan apart from all others of its kind and endow it with genuine artistic value in spite of its abortive outcome.

Among the fashionable architects of Paris, it was Contant d'Ivry, Le Carpentier and Jean-Michel Chevotet, above all, who represented Blondel's line. All three were active in building hôtels as well as châteaux, and all were deluged with commissions.

The most eminent of the three in terms of official status, but artistically the most questionable, was Pierre Contant d'Ivry (1698–1777). He was a talented architect, but stylistically he tended to fall between two stools. In his youth, like Blondel himself, he had practised the *style rocaille*. In his project for the Place Louis-XV he modelled himself on Le Vau; in his design for the church of Saint-Eustache (1749), which he published in his own *Oeuvres d'architecture* (1758), he harked back to François Mansart's Visitation and the whole formal repertoire of the seventeenth century. He took Neoclassicism on board, but only half-heartedly; he used its forms, but its spirit remained alien to him.

By 1750, when he entered the service of the Duc d'Orléans, Contant already had a successful career behind him.[19] In 1741 he had designed the Château de Bizy, near Vernon, for the Maréchal de Belle-Isle, and magnificent gardens and terraces at Heilly in Picardy for the Marquis de Gouffier; in Paris, in 1743–7, he had made his reputation

149 Jacques-François Blondel: Metz, Place d'Armes (view towards town hall and *corps de Garde*).

150 Pierre Contant d'Ivry: Paris, Palais Royal, staircase, 1766–8.

with the remodelling of the Hôtel Crozat and the Hôtel d'Evreux, and had gone on to direct the building of the patrician Abbaye de Penthémont (conventual buildings 1747 onwards, church 1753 onwards). There, as before at Bizy, he used the Catalan technique of roofing with flat clay tiles, thus vastly improving fire-resistance.

By this time he had already worked for the Orléans family, and had cemented his ties with them by building two pavilions in the park of Saint-Cloud (the Belvédère, 1743, and the somewhat later Pavillon de la Gaîté). When his patron, Louis, Duc de Chartres, succeeded his father as Duc d'Orléans in 1750, Contant was drawn into the rebuilding of the Palais-Royal under the direction of Cartaud, and succeeded him as chief architect to the house of Orléans in 1752. It therefore fell to him to carry out the extensive remodelling of the Palais-Royal that the young duke had decided to undertake.

The first task was the building of a new, right-hand wing, adjoining the then Opera on the Rue de Valois, to contain the new apartment for the Duchess (1752–60). For this he revived an unexecuted project of his own for the Hôtel d'Evreux by extending the salon with a polygonal projection in which rocaille forms somewhat clumsily mingle with Neoclassicism influenced by Gabriel. After the Opera burned down in 1763, it became necessary to build a new staircase (1765–8); and this is a masterpiece of the Baroque manipulation of space (Plate 150). At the end of a low vestibule lined with columns – the first Parisian example of the shallow vault *à la catalane*, for which Contant was famous – the stair abruptly soars into the dome above, flooded with light. As at the Hôtel d'Evreux, which he had used as a test-bed, Contant abandons rectilinearity and straight flights and develops his staircase, in a space restricted by the proximity of the Opera, as an oval, with twin flights diverging laterally and leading back to an upper balcony – one of the most magnificent spatial effects in eighteenth-century Paris. To enhance the impression of space, he engaged Pierre-Antoine de Machy to paint the flat side walls with views of an outdoor scene through a colonnade. The grandeur of the effect is enhanced by ornate wrought-iron balustrades and by luxuriant palm stems on the landings, originally intended to hold candelabra.

The external elevations of the Palais-Royal now bear only traces of Contant's handiwork. The court façade was reworked by Moreau-Desproux after the 1763 fire. However, the superimposed columnar orders and the segmental pediments in the attics of the two entry pavilions are based on ideas by Contant and actually figure in his *Œuvres d'architecture*. On the garden front, the central frontispiece is Contant's; with its attic figures, it looks curiously old-fashioned, like a variation on the garden front of Versailles. Here, again, tradition outweighs contemporaneity. Contant's major work, the church of the Madeleine, is discussed below.

Antoine-Mathieu Le Carpentier (1709–73), a native of Rouen, was praised by Patte for his flexibility and open-mindedness. He worked on the Cour des Comptes under Jacques V Gabriel and made his name by building and remodelling aristocratic hôtels in Paris before being awarded a number of château commissions in the 1750s: Courteilles (Eure), La Ferté-Vidame (Eure), Ballainvilliers (Seine-et-Oise) and others. From 1765 onwards, for the Prince de Condé, he enlarged the Palais Bourbon by adding two long, projecting side wings in conventional forms and closed off the court with a triumphal arch.[20]

What would have been Le Carpentier's major work was doomed to remain unexecuted: the city hall and Place Royale of Rouen. The city council had long been petitioning the governor of Normandy, the Duc du Luxembourg, for a new city hall. On the Governor's recommendation they applied to Le Carpentier, and in 1750 he submitted a vast plan that went far beyond the building of a city hall. In it, he proposed not only to transform the ancient marketplace that fronted the Hôtel de Ville into a Place Royale but to remodel the whole quarter by straightening the neighbouring streets and piercing new axial thoroughfares. The elevations of the Place Royale itself were in the usual form: rusticated ground

floor, giant order of pilasters, attic storey with œil-de-boeuf windows. The Hôtel de Ville was articulated by columns, but the storey heights matched those of the rest of the square. As in Contant d'Ivry's design for the Place Louis-XV, the influence of Le Vau is clear. To the rear, two long side wings flanked a deep *cour d'honneur* that was prolonged by a large formal garden as far as the octagonal Place du Luxembourg; from this, another axis led to the Hôtel-Dieu of Rouen, outside the city wall. The plans were approved in 1757, but work progressed slowly, and in 1763 funds ran out, and it was abandoned. Neither the city hall nor the new street layout ever materialized.

Jean-Michel Chevotet (1698–1772), a winner of the Prix de Rome and a member of the Academy, was another architect whose practice lay among the nobility and senior officialdom. Not far from Paris, he built the Château de Champlâtreux for President Molé of the Paris Parlement. This has superimposed orders on the entrance front (Plate 151), in the style of the early eighteenth century – Chevotet had supplied measured drawings of the Hôtel de Soubise for Mariette's *Architecture française* – and, on the garden front, a polygonal projection reminiscent of Champs. The *toit à l'impériale* of the frontispiece recalls Gabriel's remodelling of La Muette. It may well have been Chevotet's elderly and status-conscious client who attached importance to these bygone forms. It was for another member of the older generation, the Duc de Richelieu, that Chevotet built the Pavillon d'Hanovre, an entirely Rococo building, on the Boulevard des Italiens, then at the very edge of Paris.[21]

In the provinces the school of Blondel survived until well into the 1770s. In Dijon its main representative was Samson-Nicolas Lenoir (1733–1810), known since his stay in Rome as Lenoir-le-Romain. Among his numerous works – Hôtel Bouhier de Lantenay, and Hôtel Barbisey in Dijon, Château de Longecourt-en-Plaine, Abbaye de Cîteaux and others – the outstanding achievement is the palatial hôtel that he built for President Bouhier de Lantenay, of the Parlement of Dijon (1756–60). Within a conventional layout, this incor-porates an array of novel features. The contrast between the banded rustication of the court front and the smooth garden front with its concave and convex curves; the flat-roofed attic over giant pilasters; the main cornice supported by lion-faced brackets: all are signs of an impending stylistic revolution.[22]

Lenoir-le-Romain's forward-looking style is even more apparent in the slightly later, but far more advanced, new conventual building at Cîteaux (begun in 1760), of which only two ranges of the planned quadrangle were built. The strict horizontal and vertical articulation of the façade, the rough rustication of the ground floor and the heavy brackets under the main cornice make a strong contrast with such earlier, entirely Rococo abbeys as Prémontré, Penthémont and Saint-Just-en-Chaussée. It was presumably this reversion to austere sobriety that prompted Voltaire to call the youthful Lenoir to Ferney to rebuild his own château and the village church.

In Champagne the mid-century style was perpetuated by Nicolas Durand, as city architect of Châlons-sur-Marne and later as provincial architect. Durand designed most of the public buildings in Châlons: Intendance (1759–71, from a design by Legendre), Porte Sainte-Croix (1770), theatre, city hall (1772), barracks (1784). In Reims he built the theatre (1773) and in Langres the city hall (1781) and barracks (1783). These bear all the hallmarks of academic classicism: correct proportions, symmetry, fitness for purpose, but also chilliness and aridity.

In Nantes, a pupil and long-serving associate of François Franque, Jean-Baptiste Ceineray, became city architect in 1760. Before the year was out, he had devised an improvement plan that led to a large-scale modernization of the city. His façades along the Quai Brancas and Quai Fesselles have all the balance and harmony of his master's work. They retain the traditional formula of a giant order with blind arcading in the podium. Only in the Cour des Comptes (1763–77), his major work, do the columns and pilasters reflect the stylistic shift that took place in mid-century.[23]

CHAPTER 3

Legeay and the Genesis of Neoclassicism in Rome

The antique revival was set in motion by the Rome prize-winners of the 1740s. Since 1720, the students at the Academy of Architecture had competed for an annual state prize, the Prix de Rome, which consisted of a three-year scholarship to reside as *pensionnaires* in the Académie de France in Rome; this was a privilege previously confined to painters and sculptors. There they came under the supervision of an Academy director who reported on their work to the director-general of the Bâtiments du Roi in Paris.

Rome in the mid-eighteenth century was an international focus and a marketplace of ideas, where artists learned from the works of art that surrounded them 'to despise and cast aside their national prejudices' (Charles-Louis Clérisseau). Among the architects who met and exchanged impressions and discoveries in Rome we find the names of Piranesi, Legeay, Le Lorrain, Clérisseau, Adam, Chambers, Erdmannsdorf, Winckelmann and others; a network of friendships took shape, and influences subsequently flowed across national boundaries. Clérisseau and Robert Adam, whose work reveals a particular degree of affinity, set out together from Rome to Split (Spalato) to survey the Palace of Diocletian.

In such company, under the influence of the monuments of antiquity and of the Roman painting of ruins, there emerged a new understanding of the antique.[24] These young men gained their sense of the grandeur and historical significance of ancient architecture at first hand, by surveying antique buildings and by travelling together to the excavations at Pompeii and Herculaneum. The great mediator here was Giovanni Battista Piranesi. He had set up shop as an engraver next door to the Académie de France and was on friendly terms with the young *pensionnaires*, who witnessed at first hand the production of his works: *Prima parte di architetture e prospettive* (1743), *Carceri* (1745), *Antichità romane* (1748). They were deeply impressed by his gigantic halls, with their ranks of columns, coffered ceilings, staircases and statues, his bridges with their colossal arches, and his sheer passion for the buildings of antiquity. Through Piranesi they discovered a new dimension in architecture, a way of seeing it in terms of effects of light and shadow that did not treat the building in isolation but placed it within a wider context.

Following his example, the young Rome scholars turned to the most varied sources. In their designs, antiquity mingles with the Baroque of Juvarra and the rigour of Michelangelo. Stiflingly overloaded, theatrical compositions alternate with precisely constructed, free-standing monuments in landscape settings. Other sources included Fischer von Erlach's *Entwurf einer historischen Architektur*: thus, Nicolas-Henri Jardin's design of 1747 for a 'Sepulchral Chapel' based on the Pyramid of Cestius (Plate 152) is indebted to Fischer's 'Pyramid of Thebes'; and his 'Triumphal Bridge' of 1748 derives from Fischer's 'Pons Augusti'.

Those French Rome scholars of the 1740s who began to make direct use of the forms of antiquity – among them Jardin, Le Lorrain, Dumont, Moreau-Desproux and Challe – were anticipated by a slightly earlier fellow-scholar, Jean-Laurent Legeay (died 1788). Legeay was in Rome from 1737 to 1742, and there worked with the celebrated engraver Vasi; he was the first French scholar to embark on shared projects with such local architectural bodies as the Accademia di S. Luca.

We know little of his work in Rome.[25] The director of the Académie de France, Jean-François de Troy, credited him with great talent and described his drawings as showing 'fire and genius' (*du feu et du génie*). From a copy preserved in the sketchbook of Chambers, who visited Legeay in Paris before 1749, we know of one ideal design from this period (Plate 153). Its ground plan, inspired by Baldassare Peruzzi's design for St Peter's and expanded by rotundas like those at S. Constanza and in the Roman baths, is highly reminiscent of Baroque studies by members of Juvarra's circle. What was new is the care with which everything is worked out in detail. The relationships of the spatial forms, their intersections, and the lavish use of columns, have no precedents in French classical architecture. It is worth noting that the same apsidal colonnades, and the same antique stage scenery, are to be found in the work of Piranesi: for example, in the 'Antique Mausoleum' of 1750. Piranesi and Legeay had worked together for Vasi, and so in this case it is by no means certain who influenced whom.[26]

Jean-François Le Lorrain and Michel-Ange Challe – both of whom were really painters – were the first to derive inspiration from Piranesi; they were followed by Jardin and Ennemond Petitot. In Le Lorrain the transition from Roman Baroque to Neoclassicism can be traced through his decorations for the annual Festa della Chinea.[27] His triumphal arch of 1745 is still influenced by Galli and Bibbiena (Plate 155a); but the cloud-girt temple of 1746, with its porticoes, reliefs and laurel garlands, already shows Piranesi's influence, as in the antique relief of sacrifice in the frieze of the drum (Plate 155b). In the following year he devised an antique rotunda on the lines of the Temple of Vesta at Tivoli, with a statue of the goddess in the centre; and here the antique is fully developed (Plate 155c).

This generation was not influenced by antiquity alone, but also by the Renaissance and the Baroque. Gabriel-Pierre-Martin Dumont, in his 'Temple of the Arts' (1746), uses the porches of Michelangelo's Capitoline Palaces, with their inset columns (Plate 154); Jardin, as we have seen, borrows a pyramid from Fischer von Erlach. Nor is the generalized stylistic influence of Juvarra to be underestimated. All in all, these artists' works have an eclectic air, very unlike that of the second wave of the antique revival.[28]

On their return to France they brought with them not only

Elevation en Perspective d'vne Chapelle Sepulcrale.

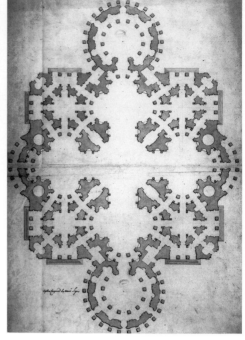

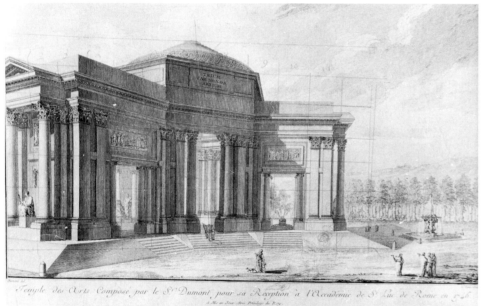

Temple des Arts Composé par le S.' Dumont pour sa Reception à l'Accademie de S.' Luc de Rome en 1746.
Mis au Jour Avec Privilege du Roy.

152 Nicolas-Henri Jardin: Chapelle sépulcrale, 1747.

153 Jean-Laurent Legeay: Plan of ideal architecture (copy by William Chambers) (London, R.I.B.A.).

154 G.-P.-M. Dumont: Temple of the Arts, 1746.

antique forms but the vision of Piranesi; and the young students still at the Academy found their horizons perceptibly widened. Legeay played a major part in this. He was teaching at the Academy in the years 1743–8, and had been very close to Piranesi, although not during the latter's purely Neoclassical period. Legeay shared Piranesi's delight in monumental effects, his interest in archaeology and his love of inserting antique fragments into his compositions; however, the comments of his students reveal a different, even a divided personality. On one hand, he was constantly in pursuit of architectural perfection; on the other, he was fascinated by all things singular, bizarre and overblown. This aspect of Legeay's nature is particularly evident in his late engravings, in which the architecture – very unlike that of Piranesi – is devoid of proportion and logical coherence and teems with iconographic and morphological monstrosities. The individual motifs are arbitrarily combined in an 'obviously perverse delight in pursuing an anti-Vitruvian, man-

nerist method of composition' (John Harris) and negate all the fundamental criteria of balance.

Legeay's arrival in Paris transformed not only the Academy's teaching but its spirit. All the major architects of the second half of the century – Peyre, de Wailly, Moreau-Desproux and Boullée among them – were among his students, and their biographers unanimously report that his teaching had a decisive impact on them. Without concentrating on the antique to the exclusion of all else, he made them feel the need to engage with it; he also taught them a new form of architectural drawing that did not confine itself to presenting the building as a purely linear structure in plan and elevation but captured its three-dimensional reality, with all the concomitant effects of light and shade, and thus made it appear larger. 'He was the first', wrote his pupil De Wailly in a posthumous tribute, 'to lay aside the compasses and the straight edge and compose architecture freehand, with the brush.' Of particular significance in this context is the verdict

155   J.-F. Le Lorrain: Decorations for the
Festa della Chinea, Rome, 1745–7.

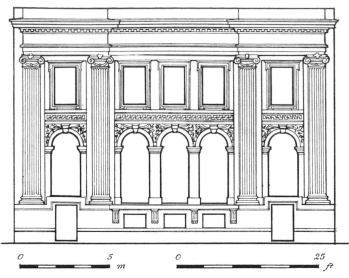

156 Pierre-Louis Moreau-Desproux: Paris, Hôtel de Chavannes, 1758, elevation.

157 Louis-Joseph Le Lorrain: Writing table and filing cabinet, made for La Live de Jully, c. 1757 (Chantilly, Musée Condé).

of Cochin, who in his *Mémoires inédits* ascribes more importance to Legeay's return from Italy even than to Marigny's: 'The advent of an improved taste may be dated from the arrival of Legcay, an architect who had been a *pensionnaire* in Rome. He was one of the finest architectural geniuses that ever lived, but without restraint and, so to speak, without reason ... Be that as it may, Legeay had excellent taste, and he opened the eyes of many people. The school of architecture underwent a perceptible change, to the great astonishment of all the older architects of the Academy.' Under Legeay's influence, his students designed larger buildings with a view to monumental effects.[29] Above all, their designs were filled with columns. A positive column mania characterizes the Academy designs of the 1750s, and prevails even in Chambers's design (1751) for the Mausoleum of the Prince of Wales.

The practical consequences of this initial wave of antiquarian enthusiasm were limited. On their return from Rome, the progressives found no commissions that would have allowed them to put their ideals into practice. Little was being built in Paris during this period, and Marigny, Gabriel and Blondel were dead set against too much imitation of antiquity. In his *Cours d'architecture*, Blondel fulminated against the 'false ideas' of imitating works dug out of the bowels of Rome and the ruins of Greece, without reference to native, French custom and practice. Among the few new buildings of the period were the Hôtel de Chavannes by Moreau-Desproux (Plate 156), Trouard's own house (both 1758) and François-Dominique Barreau de Chefdeville's façade for the church of Saint-Nicolas, Nérac (begun 1762). Servandoni's design for the house fronts in the Place Saint-Sulpice, and especially the triumphal arch that was begun in 1754 but never finished, might also come under this heading.

It follows that the major role open to the former Rome scholars was that of influencing public taste. In Rome, where the age of major building projects was past, they had participated in a culture of taste that sprang from an academic, intellectualized approach to architecture. This culture, a distillation not only of the antique but of various branches of the Baroque, was an interdisciplinary one. It laid equal emphasis on architecture, painting and decoration; and it lent the work of the French Rome scholars a decisively cosmopolitan strain that was entirely free of provincialism and nationalism.

Its first manifestation in France was the so-called Cabinet Flamand that Barreau de Chefdeville, just back from Rome, created in 1756–7 for the art collector Ange-Laurent La Live de Jully, a member of Caylus's circle, with furniture designed by Le Lorrain (Plate 157).[30] Two years earlier, on Caylus's advice, Le Lorrain had created his own first Neoclassical decorative scheme in the dining room of Åkerö Castle, in Sweden for Count Tessin: a painted decor of antique columns, with vases and statues of gods in the intercolumniations. The furniture, made to his specifications, was 'in admirable taste and entirely novel, such as no one had ever seen, let alone constructed'.

Le Lorrain's furniture for La Live de Jully was also 'entirely novel'. It had straight lines, heavy fluting, Greek keys and heavy, rope-like festoons like those in Le Lorrain's own Roman architectural drawings; Cochin scornfully referred to

158   Jean-Laurent Legeay: Potsdam, Neues Palais, Communs, designed 1763.

these last as 'well-ropes'.³¹ Although these pieces owed a great deal to Boulle furniture of the seventeenth century, they looked extremely modern. The praise of Caylus and his circle – and notably that of the salon of Madame Geoffrin – gained them an unexpected popularity and made them one of the sources of the *style grec*: Greek, or Grecian, in the general sense of 'classical'.

This Greek fashion was the first reaction to the rediscovery of the antique. By the 1760s, as La Live de Jully remarked, it was the done thing to look Greek: 'that style of work *à la grecque* is now absurdly used for everything: for tableware, jewellery, fabrics, hairstyles and the like, and even for shops, which now almost all have signs *à la grecque*.' In 1764, with English Palladianism in mind, Horace Walpole mockingly wrote: 'They suppose themselves to have made a discovery, when they are taking up something that we have had for twenty years... Everything must be *à la grecque*.' And once Blondel himself, in the *Encyclopédie*, had hailed Greece as the cradle of 'good' architecture, the architects, too, wanted to build 'Greek'. There was certainly nothing Greek about Gabriel and Soufflot; but they were credited with the purity and dignity of Greek architecture, and so their works, too, were described as *à la grecque*.

Not all the young architects who returned from Rome found scope for their talents in France. Moreau-Desproux was appointed city architect of Paris, and Dumont became a professor at the Ecole des Ponts et Chaussées and edited numerous sets of architectural engravings; but the rest went off to seek their fortunes abroad, most of them armed with recommendations from Caylus. Le Lorrain went to Russia, and Petitot to the Spanish Bourbon court of Parma. In 1754 Jardin received a summons to Copenhagen, together with the sculptor Jacques-François Saly, to build the Frederikskirke (now Marmorkirke).

This church had been begun by Niels Eigtved; Ange-

Jacques Gabriel, too, had sent drawings for it. In his design (1754–6), Jardin retained Eigtved's basic form, a tall rotunda with two free-standing bell towers, but gave it a weighty, markedly Neoclassical look by using a multitude of columns and introducing elements of antique and Renaissance origin. Building was halted at an early stage. Among the private commissions that Jardin carried out in Denmark the most important was the remodelling of the Palais Moltke; there, in the dining room (1757), he created the earliest Neoclassical ensemble by a French architect to have survived to the present day.³²

Legeay, the most promising of all these alumni of the Prix de Rome, fell victim to his own overconfidence and lack of self-discipline.³³ His practical career got off to a promising start in 1747, when he was invited to Berlin to build the Hedwigskirche. For this a design already existed, prepared by Frederick the Great himself in association with Georg Wenzeslaus von Knobelsdorff. Legeay reworked this to bring it closer to the form of the Roman Panthcon, with a temple frontispiece and an interior lined with niches, but he added a lantern to the dome and called for the interior to be painted throughout, in the manner of Roman Baroque churches.

In 1748, just when the foundations were being laid, he turned his back on Berlin and went as chief architect, and from 1752 as director of works, to the court of the Duke of Mecklenburg-Schwerin. His good relations with the duke did not last long, however, and he proved inadequate to the tasks he was asked to perform, including the building of Schloss Ludwigslust. Legeay was always going too far, both in his personal presumptions and in the sheer scale of his designs; and in the end his position became untenable. In 1755 he was back in Berlin as chief rural architect to the king of Prussia; but there, too, he squandered his chances by falling out with the king over the building of the Neues Palais in Potsdam. Although his design for the main façade

159   Jean-Laurent Legeay: Engraving from 'Tombeaux', 1768.

has not survived, we have his design (1763) for the Communs, the block that forms the grand street façade in front of the *cour d'honneur* (Plate 158). Legeay's design is a syncretic amalgam of English Palladianism – the two lateral pavilions have precedents at Wrotham Park and elsewhere – with Roman Baroque (Juvarra and Bernini, in particular) and early Neoclassicism. In its eclecticism and in the effective, theatrical grouping of the individual components, this is a reflection of the first, experimental wave of Neoclassicism in France; it is also Legeay's major work, although he himself had no hand in its construction, which was supervised by Karl Philipp Christian von Gontard.

Legeay's precipitate departure from Prussia marked the end of his career. Before returning to Paris in 1769, he spent several years in London, where he met up with Chambers again and angled vainly for a recall to Schwerin. The sets of engravings that he published there are redolent of Piranesi (Plate 159);[34] but these are perverse forms, oppressive compositions of antique spoils and sepulchral monuments, filled with distortion, caricature and a Romantic gloom that no doubt reflects the artist's state of mind. In Paris he found no openings: time had passed him by. After fruitless attempts to secure an appointment, or at least patrons for his often utopian technical projects, he died in Rome in 1788, impoverished and forsaken.

CHAPTER 4

Ange-Jacques Gabriel: Mature Work and Followers

PUBLIC BUILDINGS

In spite of the exhortations of Blondel and the prevailing enthusiasm for the *style grec*, official architecture in the second half of Louis XV's reign was dominated by Ange-Jacques Gabriel and by Soufflot; in a synthesis of true genius, these two created an independent and thoroughly national style. By virtue of his position, Gabriel was the more influential of the two; personally, too, he was closely associated with Louis XV himself, and his retirement came shortly after the king's death in 1774. He will therefore be discussed first.

When the conclusion of the Peace of Aix-la-Chapelle in 1748 afforded France a brief respite from war, the king, encouraged by Madame de Pompadour, reverted to dynastic tradition by embarking on an extensive programme of building works, public as well as royal, which transformed the face of Paris through the completion of the Louvre and the building of the Place Louis-XV (Place de la Concorde) and Ecole Militaire. For Gabriel, who had hitherto worked only for the king in person, this opened a new field of activity. It was now his responsibility to create new landmarks and open new prospects within the capital city.

The most important public building involved was the Palais du Louvre. This had lost much of its former splendour. Since Louis XIV had moved out to Versailles, the great palace had stood unfinished, packed with artists' studios, academy chambers and private dwellings, hemmed in by a warren of houses and narrow streets, and disfigured by unsightly annexes, the so-called Baraques du Louvre, built in its great court (the Cour du Louvre) to house artists, artists' widows and architects. A plan published by Blondel in his *Architecture française* shows that in 1752 three-quarters of the palace was still unroofed. Its state had been deplored in print by Voltaire and by the art critic La Font de Saint-Yenne.[35] There had been various proposals to clear the court and build a square to front the colonnade, but nothing had happened. Then, in 1754, parts of the colonnade collapsed, and young Marigny took the opportunity to make his mark with the public by including the Louvre in his programme for action. In 1755 he instructed Gabriel to restore the colonnade and prevent any further deterioration.

In 1750, to find a new use for the Louvre, it had been decided to revert to an old plan of de Cotte's and install the royal library in the south range. Then in 1754, the king assigned the east range as the official home of the Grand Conseil, a newly created body that was to oversee the execution of decisions made by the king and the Parlement. With these objectives in mind, Gabriel designed a monumental staircase that would give access to a public hall on the colonnade side of the east range (Plate 160). In this he took up the motif of the Escalier des Ambassadeurs at Versailles, which he had been compelled to destroy not long before. It was in the course of these new works that Soufflot

made his first appearance on the scene; on succeeding to the surveyorship of Garnier de l'Isle at the latter's death, he had been assigned to the Louvre as his special field of activity.

With Soufflot's support, Gabriel overcame considerable resistance, both from the general public and from Marigny, and added a third storey to the ranges around the Cour du Louvre, with the exception of Pierre Lescot's west range, which already had an attic.[36] This addition was made to the east range and the eastern half of the north range in 1755–8, maintaining the rhythm of the coupled columns on the colonnade side. The pediment sculptures overlooking the court, the Corinthian capitals of the coupled columns and the medallions on the north wing are the work of Guillaume II Coustou. At the same time, Marigny ordered the Baraques to be cleared from the court. A royal decree concerning the 'completion' of the Louvre ordained the placing of a public square between the east front and the church of Saint-Germain-l'Auxerrois, with regular house fronts and a central axis aligned on the centre of the colonnade. Barbier tells us that land clearance for this had already begun when the Seven Years War broke out and brought all work to a temporary halt.

When the war ended in 1764, the coffers were empty, and Marigny could no longer find the necessary funds. In 1768 the plan of accommodating the Conseil Général in the east range was abandoned. In 1770 Marigny gave up all hope of adding the pediment sculptures above the colonnade and ordered the scaffolding to be struck. The east range and the western half of the north range were still unfinished; in the south range, where Marigny had already had the central dome removed, the third storey had reached no more than half its height. All projects for the use of the building, including the installation of the library, came to nought. It was the tragedy of Marigny's career that he never succeeded in restoring the majesty of the Louvre.

For Gabriel, the encounter with the Louvre and its *Grand Siècle* architecture was nevertheless highly significant: it armed him for his next major projects, the Place Louis-XV and the Ecole Militaire. The Place Louis-XV cannot be understood in isolation from the prehistory of its making, even though this takes us back to the previous period.[37] Unlike the provinces, Paris had had virtually no new public architecture since the death of Louis XIV: only de Cotte's Château d'Eau and Edme Bouchardon's Fontaine de Grenelle (1739–45), which is more of a vehicle for sculptural ornament than a true work of architecture. In 1749 the general resentment found expression in a pamphlet, *L'Ombre du Grand Colbert et la ville de Paris*, in which, in the form of a dialogue between the shade of Colbert and a personified Paris, La Font de Saint-Yenne indignantly reproached the crown with having done nothing for its capital city and drew unflattering comparisons with the age of Louis XIV.

It therefore caused a considerable stir when, after the

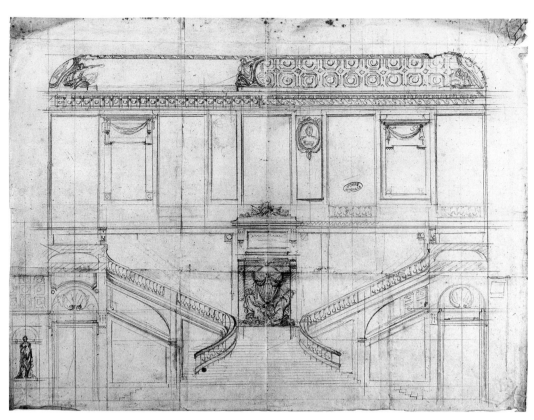

160 Anges-Jacques Gabriel:
Louvre, Grand degré, 1754
(Archives Nationales).

161 Claude Guillot-Aubry:
Project for a Place Royale, 1748.

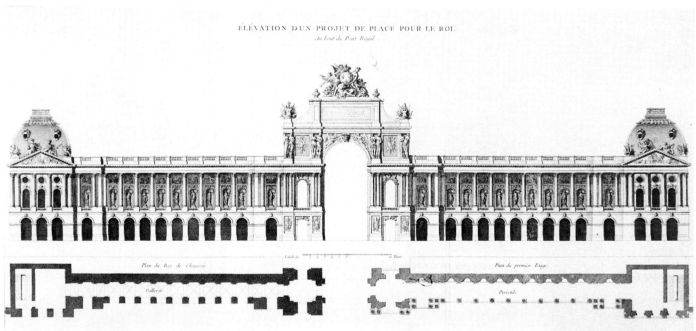

ÉLÉVATION D'UN PROJET DE PLACE POUR LE ROI.
Au bout du Pont Royal

Peace of Aix-la-Chapelle (1748), the merchants of Paris decided to pay loyal tribute to Louis XV by erecting an equestrian statue of him. Simultaneously, but independently, Lenormant de Tournehem, in the king's name, requested the members of the Academy to submit proposals for a Place Royale. The response was overwhelming. Not only Academicians but other architects, engineers and amateurs of all kinds submitted proposals, and a torrent of designs – well over one hundred – poured onto Lenormant's desk. It was probably the biggest architectural competition of all time.[38] It became evident that the *grand goût* was alive and well, despite all the vagaries of the Rococo, and that all this time people had been waiting for an opportunity to try their hands at classical architecture. As Voltaire had urged, almost all the projects were connected with the redevelopment of one or other of the city's ruinous and chronically congested older quarters. The designs look like an anthology of 'unbuilt French architecture'; they must be seen as the result of half a century of architectural reflection within the Academy.

Some were of outstanding quality. For a site on the left bank of the Seine, opposite the Tuileries, Guillot-Aubry had designed a pendant to the royal palaces in the shape of a

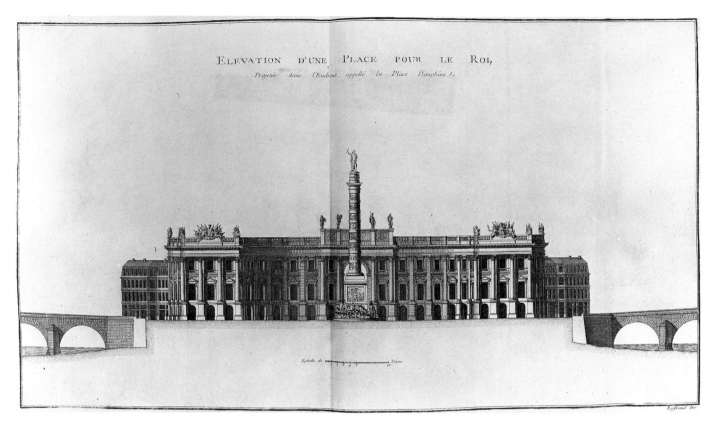

ELEVATION D'UNE PLACE POUR LE ROI,
Projetée dans l'Endroit appellé la Place Dauphine 2.

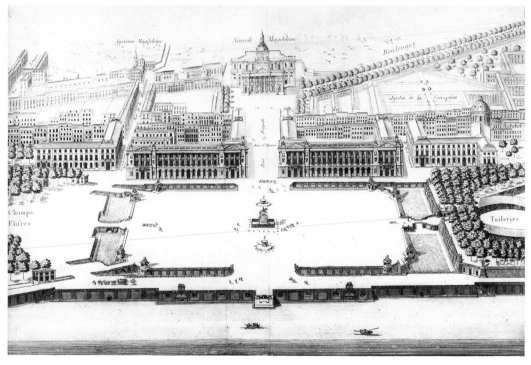

162 Germain Boffrand: Project for a Place Royale at the Place Dauphine, 1748.

163 Anges-Jacques Gabriel: Project for a Place Royale outside the Tuileries (actually Place de la Concorde), 1753.

columnar screen derived from the east colonnade of the Louvre, in two halves, with a grand triumphal arch in the centre (Plate 161). Contant d'Ivry faced the Grande Galerie du Louvre with a massive city hall complex in the manner of Le Vau, with colonnaded galleries and concave wings.

The grandest ideas were those of Boffrand (Plate 162). His three designs reveal him at the height of his powers, despite his great age: he was over eighty years old. They were composed of large blocks articulated by giant orders and superbly sited as elements of the urban scene. His 'Forum des Halles' embraced a succession of three squares,

linked by great colonnades, with the king's statue in the central one. His project for the Place Dauphine set the city hall at one end of the triangular plaza in the form of a huge block with a concave façade forming a hemicycle, again with a giant order, and with a street passing beneath a triumphal arch at its centre. In front of this, as in Fischer von Erlach's engraving of Trajan's Forum, was a column wrapped in bands of bas-relief: a Colonne Ludovise.[39]

After all this effort, the competition proved abortive.[40] The king balked at the enormous cost of tearing down so much old property and made available a piece of his own

164 Anges-Jacques Gabriel: Paris, Place de la Concorde (formerly Place Louis XV), north side, 1757–75.

land at the end of the Tuileries Gardens and opposite the Palais Bourbon: it was the site that had been selected by Lassurance the Younger.[41]

In 1753, to put an end to the countless intrigues in which the project had become enmeshed, Marigny announced a new competition for the chosen site, restricted to members of the Academy. The sole stipulation was that the view of the Champs-Elysées, the Tuileries Gardens and the Palais Bourbon should not be obstructed: a demand that was symptomatic of a growing cultural appreciation of nature. Gabriel submitted a design that incorporated a concave façade at the north end, with an opening on the central axis; at the opposite end, nearest to the river, he placed horseshoe moats with a pavilion at either end. Boffrand proposed a very similar formula, except that his square had a straight north end consisting of three blocks. As Marigny could not make up his mind between these two designs, the king ordered Gabriel to prepare a new design that should combine the advantages of all the others – a procedure that was grossly unfair to the other contestants.

In the same year, Gabriel modified his design accordingly. The moat that ran around the square became rectangular,

with the king's equestrian statue in the centre flanked by two fountains; the north side became straight, in accordance with Boffrand's design, with the columnar façade proposed by Guillot-Aubry. The result was thus a conflation of several designs, in which individual contributions become difficult to distinguish. In 1755 Gabriel adjusted it once more, to deal with site problems and enhance the visibility of the statue by reducing Boffrand's three blocks to two. By so doing he restored his own original central axis, which became the Rue Royale, and locked the square into the future street network. The view-stopper at the end of the Rue Royale was to be the portico of Contant d'Ivry's new church of the Madeleine, a far-off continuation of Gabriel's colonnades (Plate 163).

The Place Louis-XV thus took shape not as an administrative or ceremonial centre, like the other Places Royales, but as an open promenade, surrounded by parks and bordered on one side – like the Place Royale in Bordeaux – by a river, and deriving its significance solely from the equestrian statue of the king.[42] It was crossed by an existing east-west axis, but in his earliest as well as in his final design Gabriel inserted a north-south axis that was intended to be prolonged by a bridge across the Seine.

The execution began in 1755 with the moat, its balustrades and the eight little sentry-boxes, which were complete by 1758. Of the four customs posts that were intended to be built to flank the entrances to the Cours la Reine at the southwest corner, and the corresponding road to the north-west, only two were built.

The façades on the north side (Plate 164) were begun in 1757 (the western half) and 1758; they were completed in 1765 and 1766, respectively. In designing them, Gabriel harked back to the colonnade of the Louvre, which he himself had restored a few years previously, and which was regarded as the quintessence of French classical architecture. From it, he took not only the giant inset columns, the continuous entablature and the corner pavilions, with their applied order that wrapped round the corner into the Rue Royale, but also the decorative detailing: the garlanded oval medallions, the statuary niches, the antique dentils and the palmettes on the frieze. And yet this work is not a copy but an autonomous creation; while adhering precisely to the Academy's stipulations as to height and girth of shafts and capitals, depth of entablature, height of pediments, and so on, Gabriel contrived, by altering the proportions and in-troducing effects of light and shade, to express the spirit of his own time. The use of single instead of coupled columns, and an arcaded rather than a solid podium, lends the façades a supreme lightness; the increase in the number of bays – from seven to eleven – and the low pediments of the corner pavilions create a horizontal emphasis. Guillot-Aubry's de-sign, of which Gabriel certainly made some use, was closer to the prototype; Gabriel's solution was more independent and more full of contrast.

Even after the façades were built, their use remained undecided. At length, in 1768, the king decided to use the eastern half, towards what is now the Rue de Rivoli, for the crown furniture repository, the Garde-Meuble de la Couronne (it is now the navy ministry). The western half was destined first for the royal mint, then for a barracks for the king's musketeers. Ultimately, in 1775, it was sold off (as the Hôtel de Coislin, later the Hôtel Crillon). Jointly with Soufflot, Gabriel was also in charge of the interior design of the Garde-Meuble; the decor probably dates from the late 1770s.

The Place Louis-XV, roundly castigated by Lenoir and enthusiastically praised by Eugène Viollet-le-Duc,[43] is still Baroque in its overall layout, but in the clarity of its lines and its sparing use of sculptural decoration it is the first great example of the swing in Parisian taste back towards the ideals of the Grand Siècle. In contrast to the city squares of Italy, where statuary subordinates itself to architecture, this Place Louis-XV was entirely tailored, both in size and in building height, to the statue of the king. The erection of the present obelisk by Louis-Philippe was thus grotesquely mis-conceived. Even worse was the planting of colossal female figures – symbols of the cities of France – on Gabriel's elegant sentry-boxes. They destroy the proportions completely.

Along with the Place Louis-XV, the Ecole Militaire is the other great example of Louis XV public architecture. It shows the next stage in Gabriel's evolution towards Palladianism and towards the antique. The Ecole Militaire was a school for young nobles, built to accommodate 500 students together with their instructors, officers, chaplains, doctors and the like.[44] The idea came from a financier, Pâris Duverney, who had made a fortune out of supplying the army. In 1750 he put forward a memorandum proposing the foundation of a *collège académique* to educate young noblemen for the service of the state; in a second memorandum he limited the scope of this to a military academy, alleging the ignorance of the officer corps and the lack of discipline in the army. Madame de Pompadour, who was an old friend of Duverney and of his brothers, gave strong support to the idea.[45] She wanted to create a parallel to the institution for young ladies that Madame de Maintenon had created at Saint-Cyr. The king, for his part, saw it not only as an opportunity to reward the nobility for its services in past wars but as an ornament to his reign, something to set alongside his great forebear's Hôtel des Invalides. As a result, the institution officially came into being as early as 1751.

Pâris-Duverney, who knew the army well from his own background, had not only drawn up a curriculum for the school but had also proposed a site for it, on the left bank of the Seine, on the road from Paris to Versailles, and not far from the Invalides, so that the traveller's first view of Paris would embrace both institutions at once. Gabriel's first design was rejected by Duverney as too costly; his second, basically similar design, of 1752 (probably the one published in an engraving by Lerouge in 1754) matched Duverney's programme down to the last detail (Plate 166).

A first court, the Cour Royale, was embraced on three sides by a vast building, the château, which contained a great hall, staff headquarters, secretariat, archives and rooms for pupils, teachers and officers. Refectories, kitchens, stables and riding schools were grouped around the second court. At the far end of this, as at the Invalides, stood the church, linked to the adjacent ranges by quadrant colonnades, just as in J.H. Mansart's 1702 design for the Dôme des Invalides. Behind these again, symmetrically placed, were an infirmary on one side and a court for the laundry and bakery on the other. The façade towards the Champ de Mars was that of a château. The massive central block, with its forceful centre and end pavilions and its square dome, the symbol of the royal presence, was flanked by further courts and wings terminated, again, by large pavilions. In all this, Gabriel harked back to a classical prototype – Le Vau's south front for the Louvre, which de Cotte had already used for Buen Retiro – but modified it by enlarging the attics of the pavilions and inserting entresols above the first floor. In the initial design, with a rusticated ground floor and no entresols, the resemblance was even closer.

Work began on the infirmary and domestic offices, which were to provide temporary accommodation. From the outset, however, funds were inadequate. Several times, Madame de Pompadour had to rescue the project by putting in money from her own pocket. During the Seven Years War, work stopped altogether. By the time it was resumed in 1765, half of the student body had been hived off to the former Jesuit college at La Flèche. It became clear that Gabriel's de-sign could not be carried out. It was abandoned, and the architectural office set up for the purpose was closed down.

All that stood of the intended complex was the rear

165 Ange-Jacques Gabriel:
Ecole Militaire, façade, 1768–73.

166 Ange-Jacques Gabriel:
Ecole Militaire, project, after
1754, engraving by Le Rouge.

167 Ange-Jacques Gabriel:
Paris, Ecole Militaire, 1768–73,
Cour Royale.

168 Anges-Jacques Gabriel:
Ecole Militaire, chapel, c. 1770.

domestic block, with a number of wings projecting irregularly from it. Gabriel was compelled to give up not only his church but his monumental façade, the heart of the whole complex. Instead, it was decided that the existing part of the composition was to be closed off on the side facing the Champ de Mars by a pair of pavilions at the outer ends of the two quadrants, linked by a simple gallery and a wrought-iron gate.

Gabriel appealed to Choiseul, who held ministerial responsibility for the school, and was able to scotch this proposal, which would have turned the school into a mere barracks, and to salvage the idea of a château, albeit in a much reduced form. In a new design, dated 1767, he replaced the two detached pavilions with a large *corps de logis* and brought this so far forward towards the Champ de Mars that it aligned with the existing wings on either side (Plate 165). The massive pile that now faces the Champ de Mars occupies some two-thirds of the length of the château as originally intended. Behind the frontispiece is the great hall – originally known as the Salle du Conseil – with its secondary rooms and the spacious main staircase, with one of the finest of all wrought iron balustrades; the left-hand wing contains the chapel.

Without the second court and the church, the composition had to be completely reoriented. The rear of the château became the entrance front. Gabriel laid out the Cour Royale in front of this, and flanked it with low, open colonnades (Plate 167). The king's statue stood in the centre. The carcass of the château was completed in 1773, and the interior decoration in 1775. The last stage of the project was the levelling of the new grounds to the south and the demolition of the buildings that obscured the view of the Cour Royale from that side. Gabriel did not live to see this done; he retired from the direction of the project in 1780, at the age of eighty-two, and was succeeded by Boullée and, two years later, by Alexandre-Théodore Brongniart. The school was closed down in 1788.

Even in its diminished state, the Ecole Militaire is one of the outstanding buildings of the eighteenth century. The initial design, with its pavilion system and its continuous giant order, was entirely within the tradition of the French Baroque château; but the design that was finally executed, that of 1767, looks above all to Palladio. He is present in the north front of the building, towards the Champ de Mars: in the single block with its columned portico, and its contrast between free-standing columns and flat wall surfaces, but also in the lateral pavilions, with their echoes of the Palladian villa. Only the square-based dome is a relic of Gabriel's original conception.[46]

For the south front of this same block, Gabriel had initially intended two superimposed arcades, as in the Cour d'Honneur of the Invalides; in 1768 he replaced these with piers with engaged columns and an entablature, possibly an echo of the Michelangelesque motif that Soufflot was using concurrently for Marigny's house. The quasi-antique colonnades to right and left of the Cour Royale appear in volume 1 of Neufforge's *Recueil élémentaire*.

The chapel has a strong antique-revival flavour (Plate 168). Like the basilica described by Vitruvius, it is lined with giant columns – eight along each side and four at each end.[47] The walls do not look like a spatial enclosure so much as a lightweight screen between the columns. The decoration, too, recalls the Augustan epoch of classical art. Like everything in this building, it is of extraordinary elegance and finesse in detail, whether in capitals, entablatures or coffering. Taken as a whole, the Ecole Militaire exemplifies Gabriel's style of transition between Baroque and strict Neoclassicism, with its unique stylistic synthesis of old and new.

ROYAL PROJECTS

Most of Gabriel's time was taken up with work for the king. Since Louis XV had discovered the pleasure of building, there was no end to his projects: not only at the great royal residences, such as Versailles, Fontainebleau and Compiègne, but also at small hunting lodges, 'hermitages' and *maisons de plaisance*, which the king loved for their greater intimacy. However, quite unlike Louis XIV, he seldom achieved a lasting result. His smaller buildings, above all, were always changing their appearance, endlessly being improved and enlarged. Whatever was begun as a simple hunting box invariably ended as a fully fledged château.

Characteristic examples of this are Choisy and Saint-Hubert. Choisy, built for the Grande Mademoiselle by Gabriel's grandfather, Jacques IV, was acquired by the king in 1739; in the 1740s, Gabriel added wings to house the royal retinue and also enlarged the Cour Royale. In 1752 the width of the *corps de logis* was doubled to make room for a new staircase, and the concave hemicycle of the court façade – probably the prototype for de Cotte's episcopal palace in Verdun – was destroyed.[48] A theatre wing and further domestic wings followed in the next few years. In the park, in 1754–6, Gabriel built a separate house, the Petit Château, to which the king withdrew with his intimates: a small, single-storey building with few but lavishly appointed rooms, articulated by two short side wings on the court side and a projecting, octagonal salon on the garden side. Its dining room contained the celebrated *table volante* or flying table, which rose out of the basement to make the presence of domestics unnecessary. There was even a church, built in 1748–55, and one of the earliest examples of Gabriel's mature style, with its clear reference to the classicism of Mansart.[49]

The same process took place at Saint-Hubert, a hunting lodge in the Forest of Rambouillet (1755–7); originally intended to accommodate the king, Madame de Pompadour and a few favoured guests, it was constantly enlarged by the addition of new pavilions and forecourts and was finished only in 1774, the year of the king's death.[50]

Among the major royal residences, Compiègne was the only one where the king's intentions were fully carried out. It was a palace that he particularly liked, because of its vast expanse of forest, but by the late 1730s it was both antiquated and cramped. At that point Jacques V Gabriel and Nicolas d'Orbay embarked on a makeshift programme of improvement and extension, but despite the addition of several new wings it remained an irregular complex of buildings old and new, wedged into the acute angle between the town of Compiègne and the line of the old fortifications. A number of drawings show, however, that the idea of a complete rebuilding in the grand style, and on the eventual scale, was already under consideration.[51] Planning reached a decisive stage only with the Dauphin's marriage in 1747; he now urgently required more space, and at the same time the king wanted to make more room for Madame de Pompadour.

Ange-Jacques Gabriel's first design, of 1747, was entirely a product of the school of Mansart. It involved regularizing the great entrance court – the Cour Royale – and building a long façade, articulated by pavilions, to face the town. The Cour Royale was to be followed by a second court, the Cour de la Chapelle, bounded on the right by the anomalous, oblique line of the range containing the old royal apartments.[52] Level with this, to the left, were two further courts, separated by a large chapel. The overall symmetry was disrupted by the alignment of the royal apartments with the old moat, which could not be built over.

This 'Grand Projet', none of which was ever executed, was first revised in 1751 (Plate 169). Gabriel opened the Cour Royale out to face the Place d'Armes (Place du Palais), bounded it on that side only by a columnar screen, and gave greater weight to the end pavilions of the side wings by enlarging them to five bays each. The sequence of courtyards on the left was extended by the addition of a third, the Cour de l'Orangerie. On the right, he turned the obliquely aligned central range, which had been an anomaly in the earlier design, into the principal motif of the whole vast garden front by extending it to the full length of the palace. As a result, the palace took on the form of a vast right-angled triangle, with its shortest side facing the town and its longest and principal façade facing the park.

The façades completed the move away from the Mansart school (Plate 170). The ground floor arcading in the Cour Royale was replaced by a vigorous rustication with rectangular windows; the dormers in the mansard roof lost their segmental heads and lateral volutes and acquired triangular pediments and triglyph brackets; the side wings of the Cour

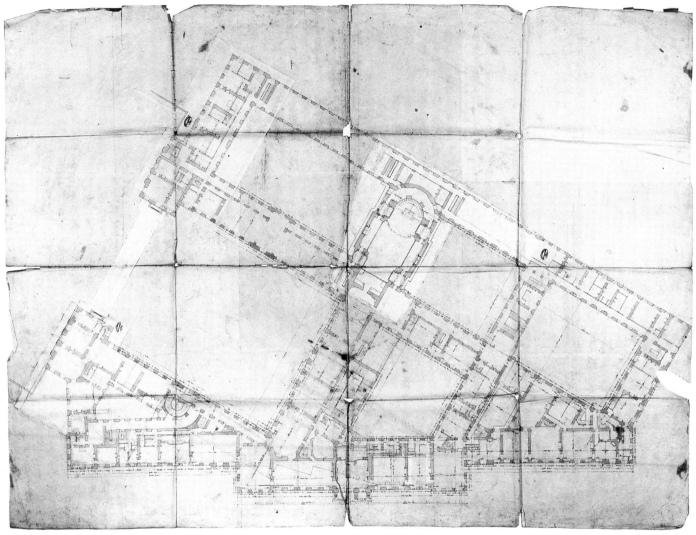

169 Ange-Jacques Gabriel: Compiègne, Grand project, plan of ground floor, 1756 (Archives Nationales).

Royale acquired centre pavilions articulated by garlanded stone plaques.

The same change affected the garden front, on its elevated terrace. The two-storey pavilions and tall roofs disappeared. A giant order for the king's centre pavilion, block rustication for the pavilions on the Dauphin's wing, and continuous flat roofs with balustrades reveal the emergence of a new spirit. This was the same stylistic transition that was taking place almost simultaneously on the Gros Pavillon at Fontainebleau. As Gabriel himself proudly remarked,[53] this new 'simplicity and nobility' was a deliberate reversion to seventeenth-century good taste (*le bon goût du siècle précédent*). It involved not only the elimination of all curvature but the imposition of a new set of decorative forms, such as stone plaques and oval medallions surrounded by garlands. Gabriel intended these as a pattern for the whole of the rest of the building.

The first stage of actual construction, in 1752–6, embraced the left-hand side of the Cour Royale – the Aile de Mesdames – and the range for the Dauphin on the park side. At the same time, Gabriel embarked on the building of a Petit Château (1753–5), a square pavilion with two short wings, for the king and Madame de Pompadour, which stood in its own grounds adjoining the great park.[54] During the Seven Years War, work was suspended; and during this time the Grand Projet underwent a second transformation. Gabriel's new design of 1763, on which construction work began in 1764, bears distinctly Palladian features. The end pavilions of the Cour Royale have taken on a cubic shape; the court façade is emphasized by alternating window pediments and giant pilasters (columns on the frontispiece). The mansard roof is replaced throughout by an attic surmounted by a balustrade. This design has set its seal on the whole of the rest of the building.

In 1768 the left-hand end pavilion was ready. Then progress began to flag, as funds became more and more scarce. It was not until 1774 that Gabriel began building the range for the king and Queen, overlooking the park. When he retired in the following year, the palace was still unfinished. His pupil and successor as architect in charge, Le Dreux de la Châtre, nevertheless overcame great financial difficulties and succeeded in completing it by 1789. In general, despite some departures in matters of detail – as can be seen, for instance, from the harsh outlines of the park front – he maintained Gabriel's conception of 1751, as modified in 1763, and thus preserved the unity of the composition.[55] Of

170 Ange-Jacques Gabriel: Compiègne, façade to the Place d'Armes, 1752–6.

171 Ange-Jacques Gabriel: Versailles, Petit Trianon, first project, 1761.

172 Anges-Jacques Gabriel: Versailles, Petit Trianon, 1762–4, garden façade.

face sur le Potager

all the royal châteaux, Compiègne is the only one to have been completed before the collapse of the Ancien Régime, and the only one that bears the mark of a single artist.

At Versailles, Ange-Jacques Gabriel's name is associated with three important pieces of work: the Petit Trianon, the Opera, and the Grand Projet. The most perfect of these is undoubtedly the Petit Trianon. It embodies Neoclassicism in its most elegant and spirited form, before it succumbed to the lure of antiquity. Built to terminate the extension of the Nouvelle Ménagerie du Roi, at the end of an avenue that starts from the Pavillon Français, it stands on a terrace that commands views in four directions: back along the avenue, across the botanical garden, across the so-called flower garden, and towards the Pavillon Français. For each of these views it has a different façade, with or without podium, and with or without terrace; all are variations on the theme of the tetrastyle portico. Their consummate harmony conceals the complex genesis of the building.

The earliest design, of 1761 (Plate 171), showed a pavilion with the same decor of pilasters and columns, but only three bays wide; the effect was ponderous and out of balance. In 1762 Gabriel found the ideal solution by increasing the

width to five bays (Plate 172). Then the proportions fell into place; the excessive central emphasis gave way to a tranquil balance, in which the consistent horizontal of the window cornices counterbalances the vertical impulse of the giant orders. The interior, too, has gained in brightness and comfort from the widening of the building. There is more room for the staircase, and two lateral staircases are fitted in. The carcass was built in 1762–4; work on the superb interior, the work of Honoré Guibert, went on until 1770. The sober forms of the detached chapel belong to Gabriel's late style; it was not completed until 1776.

The Petit Trianon is not an isolated phenomenon in French architecture. It had its precedents in English Palladianism;[56] and Neufforge had published the same type in his *Recueil* (Plate 173). It was certainly no coincidence that the project set by the Academy for its Prix de Rome competition in 1758 was a 'pavilion on the bank of a river and at the top of a terrace', and that the winning design, by Mathurin Cherpitel and Jean-François-Thérèse Chalgrin, contained almost all the elements of Gabriel's final design, right down to the paired flights of steps in front of the portico. Marigny had copies of this made for his own use.

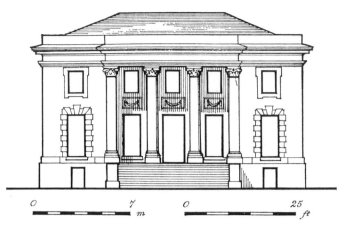

173 François de Neufforge: Design for a country house, (*Recueil d'architecture*).

The idea was in the air; Gabriel had no need to invent it. But the use to which he put his sources in his solution, the crescendo of the portico motif on the four façades, from a plain row of pilasters to free-standing columns with terrace and steps, is masterly. Madame de Pompadour, for whom the king intended the villa, did not live to see it completed; she died in 1764. But it was her spirit that governed its style. At her death, the main lines had been established, including those of the interior; and the progressive attitudes that she stood for all her life are clearly detectable. In the Petit Trianon, the strict Palladianism of the basic form is perfectly blended with French classicism and eighteenth-century elegance. To this is added the inimitable touch of discretion and dignity that appears in all Gabriel's works.

A further instance of a successful synthesis of Palladianism and French tradition is the Opera at Versailles.[57] For this, Gabriel reverted to an old design by J.H. Mansart and Gaspare Vigarani: the Salle des Ballets, at the far north end of the château, which had been abandoned at the outbreak of the War of the Spanish Succession. The terminal pavilion of the north wing, intended for this, had been carried up to its full height only on the garden side; on the street side it had advanced no further than the foundations. In the 1740s, with a Dauphin's wedding imminent, the need for an opera theatre inside the château became apparent. Initial designs were submitted, and Gabriel built the connecting range alongside the so-called Gros Pavillon; but the Opera itself was built only in 1764–5. In it, he mostly followed the intentions of his great predecessor, Mansart; but on the street side, where Mansart had intended to have a distinct façade, he matched the elevation to that of the Gros Pavillon, from which it differs only in the rustication of the ground floor. On the north side, towards the Réservoirs, he replaced Mansart's segment-headed windows with rectangular ones, and the pilasters of the frontispiece with columns; here, too, he rusticated the ground floor.

His real problems began with the interior. Numerous, often mutually contradictory plans and sketches bear witness to Gabriel's intensive concentration on this issue and to his constantly changing ideas of the shape of the auditorium.[58] The prototype, in general terms, was Benedetto Alfieri's new court theatre in Turin, which was regarded as the most modern in Europe. But the confined space available for the Versailles Opera – the garden side of the building was still occupied by private apartments – compelled Gabriel to re-

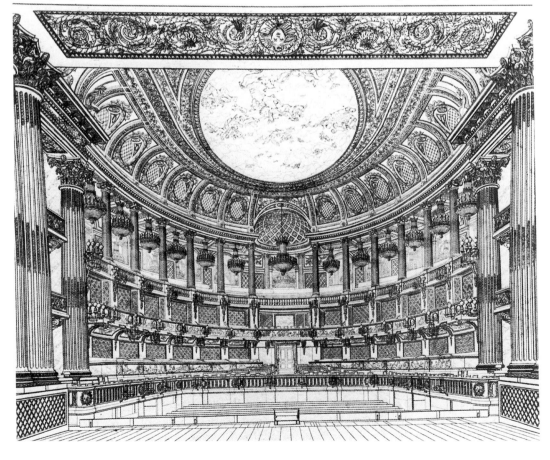

174 Anges-Jacques Gabriel; Versailles, Opera, auditorium, 1765–70, engraving by Hibon.

think his design over and over again and to make new proposals ranging from Vigarani's original U form to a circle. It was not until the king ordered the private apartments to be cleared, in 1765, that the whole building became available, and Gabriel was able to complete the planning process.

The auditorium now takes the form of an elongated oval (Plate 174), and a wide, double-height foyer has been inserted on the garden side. A momentous innovation, made in the same year, was Gabriel's decision to replace the second and third tiers of boxes with a colonnade. This echo of Palladio's Teatro Olimpico in Vicenza sets the tone for the whole interior, including the royal box. This does not project into the auditorium as a separate oval under a high baldachin, as in previous designs, but forms a semicircular niche in the colonnade, which swings round behind it. The coffered half-dome above its concave entablature is the work of de Wailly, who has introduced a theme derived from the decoration of Roman baths. The proscenium, which frames the stage and stage boxes between giant columns, forms a grand conclusion to the auditorium; it has a Palladian look of its own, though the column motif as such is a legacy from Vigarani's Salle des Machines and is present in the earliest designs. In Gabriel's hands – as at the Ecole Militaire – the columns have taken on an antique splendour and grandeur.

The decoration is sparing and sober by comparison with earlier designs, and largely consists of architectural elements. Gabriel, who knew he could expect to come under fire from the ambitious winners of the Prix de Rome, was careful to enlist the aid of younger artists. De Wailly provided not only the royal box but the decoration of the foyer; Augustin Pajou was responsible for the sculpture, providing reliefs on the aprons of the boxes and large groups in the foyer. By comparison, painting plays rather a subordinate role. In the overall decorative scheme, once more, Gabriel keeps close to tradition. The oval medallions, with their garland and ribbonwork ornament, and the pilasters and vault of the foyer, are derived from the Grand Siècle, and from J.H. Mansart and Le Brun in particular.

Of course, the Versailles Opera is not the exclusive work of Gabriel. Quite apart from Pajou and de Wailly, an important contribution was made by the experienced technician Arnoult, who built the stage area, with its complicated machinery, drawing on the latest advances in Italy. The architecture of the foyer, which is highly progressive in style, is largely the work of the head of Gabriel's office, Nicolas-Marie Potain. But it was the Premier Architecte himself who held all the threads in his hands and took every decision (including, on several occasions, the decision to revert to a previously discarded idea, as with the shape of the auditorium and the design of the royal box). The Versailles Opera must therefore definitely be regarded as his work. The interior was completed only from 1768 onwards, under severe financial constraints. Nevertheless, the Opera was finished in 1770; and in the same year it was inaugurated with the nuptials of another Dauphin, the future Louis XVI.

Gabriel succeeded in finishing the Versailles Opera; but his 'Grand Projet', which was intended to confer an unified aspect on the entire château, never progressed past its earliest stages.[59] Even Louis XIV had realized that the rather piecemeal court frontage of Versailles did not meet the

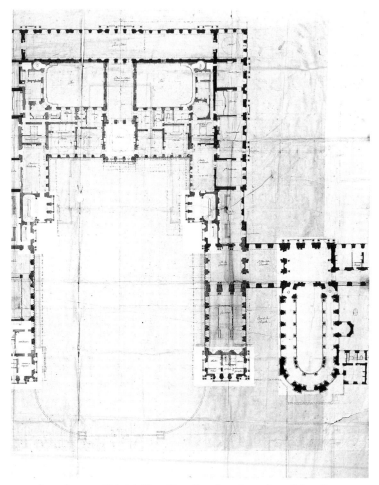

175 Ange-Jacques Gabriel: Versailles, Grand project, plan of first floor, c. 1743 (Archives Nationales).

requirements of a royal palace; but he had never been able to bring himself to embark on building a new one. Louis XV, who had great respect for his great-grandfather's work, would have ignored the criticisms of Voltaire, Blondel and others and left everything as it was, had not his hand been forced by the growing shortage of space and the decrepitude of the right-hand wing.

The condition of this wing, known as the Aile du Gouvernement, and especially that of the staircase known as the Escalier des Ambassadeurs, gave rise to considerable anxiety. Both the colonnade on the return façade of the wing and the roof structure of the celebrated staircase, which had to bear the weight of its lantern, were in imminent danger of collapse. Furthermore, since the building of the Salon d'Hercule, the Escalier des Ambassadeurs had lost its function as an introduction to the Grands Appartements and was less and less frequently used. In 1752 it was therefore demolished,[60] along with a small theatre (the Théâtre des Cabinets) built for the use of Madame de Pompadour, who occasionally appeared there in person. Most of the space thus vacated was taken up with the apartment of Madame Adelaïde, the king's favourite daughter.

The need to provide a new ceremonial staircase, and to rebuild the whole of the right-hand wing, prompted consideration of a general programme of rebuilding that would

176 Ange-Jacques Gabriel: Versailles, Grand project, elevation, 1759.

embrace and unify the court and garden fronts of the château. The essentials of this Grand Projet were already contained in Gabriel's design of 1749 (Plate 175) (itself partly based on an earlier, undated and unsigned design).[61] The new main staircase, the Grand Degré, was at the near end of the right-hand wing and rose along it, occupying the entire width of the wing, in two parallel flights to the first floor, where it gave access to the Grands Appartements through the Salon d'Hercule on the right, and to the Petits Appartements on the left. The greatest change affected the central *corps de logis*. This was extended forward across the Cour de Marbre – as far out as the Salon de Mars – and separated from the Galerie des Glaces by new internal courts. The king's apartment lay on the right, the Queen's on the left. The central axis was formed by a domed gaming room and an adjoining music room, which later became a picture gallery. Contrary to possible expectations, the external dome thus had no symbolic significance.

In the elevations, Gabriel kept to the formula of the garden front: continuous arcading on the ground and first floors, punctuated by Corinthian pilasters on the first floor; above, an attic articulated to match. He created a strong central emphasis, as J.H. Mansart had intended to do, by means of a triangular pediment and the massive dome, while the side wings retained Le Vau's articulation and his tall roofs. An entry in Argenson's journal confirms that there was a firm intention to start work in 1749. But, as always, the king vacillated, and the execution was postponed.

At the next stage of planning, in 1759,[62] Gabriel gave the two upper storeys a giant order that continued round the whole court (Plate 176). He gave added emphasis to the frontispiece of the *corps de logis*, and to the entrances to the staircases, by using free-standing Corinthian columns, and on the return façades of the side wings he placed balcony-like open colonnades: a variation on Le Vau's original colonnades, without the familiar roof lanterns. The tall mansard roofs disappeared, to be replaced by flat roofs with a balustraded parapet. It was a majestic, highly Palladian

177 Ange-Jacques Gabriel: Versailles, Grand projet, final design for staircase, 1774 (Archives Nationales).

178   Ange-Jacques Gabriel: Fontainebleau, Cour du Cheval Blanc, project for closing screen, 1773 (Archives Nationales).

composition into which J.H. Mansart's chapel would have fitted perfectly. But it was not until 1771, when the existing right-hand wing (which had been threatening collapse ever since 1765) was finally pulled down, that Gabriel could make a start on his Grand Projet. Always deeply attached to the Versailles tradition, the king resisted to the last; and, as late as the summer of 1771, designs were prepared for the rebuilding of the right-hand wing exactly as Le Vau had left it. Then, in the autumn of that year, Louis XV suddenly gave in and agreed to the Grand Projet, in a spirit more of resignation than of conviction. This change of mind on his part was probably the doing of Madame de Pompadour's successor, the Comtesse du Barry, another sympathizer with the avant-garde, who contributed a considerable sum from her private fortune to speed the work.

The new right-hand wing was built in 1772–5; it was the only part of the Grand Projet that was built. Gabriel entrusted its decoration to his own close associates, Potain, Jean-François Heurtier and Le Roy. For the elevations, he abandoned the enrichments he had envisaged as late as 1771 – a hexastyle portico for the frontispiece, distinct pavilions at the corners of the court and another hexastyle portico on the return façade of each wing – and reverted, no doubt partly for reasons of economy, to the sobriety of his 1759 design. However, the Grand Degré within the new wing was designed to make a vivid contrast with this outward plainness. More sumptuous than any previous design, with its decor of trophies and reliefs and the pilasters that marched with the flights, its final version (1774; Plate 177) would have made an ascent entirely worthy of the importance of the château, and a noble example of Gabriel's late style.

The Aile Gabriel, or Aile Neuve, has remained a fragment, an alien presence that markedly disrupts the proportions of the château as a whole. Nor is this greatly remedied by the matching left-hand wing, begun by Napoleon and continued by Louis-Philippe. The Grand Projet came too late to set a convincing new visual entity against the familiar outline of Versailles. What is more, Gabriel's style had by now grown over-rigid. He had reduced architecture to a mere framework, wholly dependent on proportions for its effect, and inadequate as a vehicle for the wealth of the French tradition.

Fontainebleau had a Grand Projet of its own, designed to transform both the Cour de la Fontaine and the Cour du Cheval-Blanc: but this suffered much the same fate as its counterpart at Versailles.[63] The remodelling of the Cour de la Fontaine never progressed beyond the building of the Gros Pavillon, already discussed. The new façade for the Galerie François-Ier, planned by Gabriel in the 1760s to pull the court together and discreetly modernize it, with a frontispiece incorporating a giant order, and with ground-floor rustication to match that on the Aile de Mesdames, was never built.

As for the ambitious planning of the Cour du Cheval-Blanc, which would have transformed this into a Cour Royale, all that was completed (in 1772–4) was its south wing, the Aile Neuve (Aile Louis-XV), begun by Jacques Gabriel. At the west end of this, Jacques Gabriel had intended to build a symmetrical match for the Gros Pavillon; this in turn was to be matched by another on the north side of the court, and linked with it by a single-storey screen wall, with a central entrance gate in the form of a triumphal arch. When this project had to be cut back on grounds of cost, the terminal pavilions were redesigned (1773). The reference to the Gros Pavillon disappeared, and their court façades were matched to the transitional pavilion at the east end of the Aile Neuve (Plate 178). For the return façades, which look out towards the town, Ange-Jacques Gabriel reverted once more to the motif of the corner pavilions of the Place Louis-XV: a columnar portico with lateral niches and oval medallions. On the other hand, the central gateway – presented in three variants in the finished drawing – already possessed the rigorous, quasi-antique character of the Louis XVI style that was to supplant that of Gabriel. In his turn, the young Louis XVI could not make up his mind, and this ambitious project remained on paper.

With the death of Louis XV, Gabriel's work was done.

One year later, in 1775, half blind and laden with honours, he retired from the royal service. It was the end of an epoch.

THE FOLLOWERS OF GABRIEL: POTAIN, MIQUE, ANTOINE, BARRÉ

Gabriel was such a strong personality that few escaped his influence. His style was continued, most notably, by Potain, Antoine, Barré and Mique; Ledoux, too, owed him a great deal. The architect closest to Gabriel was his own *chef de bureau*, Nicolas-Henri Potain (1713–91), winner of the Prix de Rome in 1738; at the end of Potain's time in Rome, Gabriel had commissioned him to make a study tour of the Italian theatres. Potain was in charge of the works on the Place Louis-XV, where he built the Hôtel de Saint-Florentin, to Gabriel's design, to effect the transition between the new square and central Paris. However, his principal interest was in theatre and church building.[64] A theatre design that he produced in 1763 was innovative enough for Neufforge to include it in his *Recueil*, and for Cochin to claim it as his own. The building is square, but the main internal division is diagonal. The oval auditorium is wider than it is long, and to improve the view from the boxes (there are no stalls) it is diagonally placed, with the staircase in the front corner. The main stage is flanked by two smaller stages so that the spectators could enjoy plays without interruption. On the exterior, the diagonal is marked by two unpedimented prostyle porticoes, placed across the corners of the external walls. Potain probably took these from an engraving in Neufforge, where they appear for the first time in this form. His part in the building of Rennes Cathedral is discussed below.

An architect who moved in court circles, unlike Potain, was Richard Mique (1728–94), a native of Lorraine, whom Queen Marie Leszczyńska brought to Versailles after her father's death in 1766. A pupil of Blondel, and chief engineer of bridges and highways in Lorraine, Mique had built the Intendance, the Porte Saint-Stanislas and the Porte Sainte-Catherine in Nancy and had succeeded Héré in 1763 as director of works to King Stanislas, but the appointment had lapsed on the king's death. At Versailles, the Queen used a legacy from her father to commission Mique to build a convent school for fifty undowered girls, a private foundation on the lines of those at Val-de-Grâce and Saint-Cyr.[65] The result was a monastic-looking complex of dormitory ranges grouped around three courts, with a chapel on the main axis flanked by two pavilions to serve as parlours.

When the Queen unexpectedly died in 1768, the carcass of the conventual buildings was just completed. Madame Adelaïde, the king's energetic daughter, resolved to continue her mother's work and confirmed Mique's appointment as Intendant de la Reine, independent of the king's chief architect, so that he had a free hand. In his first design for the chapel (1768), Mique envisaged it as a basilica, lined with columns and tunnel-vaulted, with narrow side aisles, an oval, domed choir for the nuns at the east end, and a big gallery for their charges over the west door. The façade, with its tetrastyle portico and its relief decoration, bore a striking resemblance to that of Saint-Philippe du Roule, by Chalgrin, for which the designs were also completed in 1768. Above the pediment, with its figured sculpture, was a tall cross. In a second version, designed after the Queen's death, Mique accentuated the segregation of nuns and pupils by placing them in two separate, flanking choirs, one to either side of the nave, each with its own façade and small dome; at the same time, he prolonged the nuns' choir eastward to form a long rectangle.

His third and final design, as built, shows clear signs of the influence of Soufflot. Abandoning the basilican plan altogether, he makes the nave into a Greek cross inscribed in a square; above the crossing is a dome, supported – as at Sainte-Geneviève – by free-standing columns. The choirs for nuns and pupils have become large circular halls, divided from the nave only by grilles, and flanking the round apse; Mique combines these with the arms of the cross – also round-ended – into a block from which the entrance bay and portico strongly project. This prominent portico, together with the conversion of the cubic lateral pavilions into a pair of angled forms, enables Mique to break up the rigidity of the initial design and infuse some pulsating life into

179 Richard Mique: Versailles, Couvent de la Reine (now Lycée Hoche), 1768–72.

180 Jacques-Denis Antoine: Paris, Mint, 1771–7, façade.

this aspect of the composition (Plate 179). With the careful balance and uniform articulation of his elements and the gravitation of emphasis towards the centre, where the crossing dome soars behind the cross on the pediment, he has created an ensemble of great vigour and sure taste; and all of it, including the accommodation block behind the façade, is highly reminiscent of Gabriel.

The same closeness to Gabriel is visible in the decoration. The elegant portico, with its fluted columns, statuary niches and oval medallions, the coffered internal vault with its rosettes, and the handling of the capitals and cornices: all this has extraordinary refinement and elegance. Antiquity and eighteenth-century tradition are perfectly blended. On its completion in 1772, the building was handed over to the Ursuline Order, and in the following year it was opened as the Couvent de la Reine (now the Lycée Hoche).

A decade or so later, in 1780–4, Mique erected a similar chapel for the Carmelite convent (now the Justice de la Paix) at Saint-Denis, to which another daughter of Louis XV, Madame Louise, had retired. Here, too, the plan is a Greek cross with short arms and a central dome. The exterior takes the form of an antique temple; only the elegant columns of the portico, which is reached by a tall flight of steps, betray that this is an eighteenth-century building. This chapel is more massive and more powerful than its predecessor at the

Couvent de la Reine; but, with its rich interior articulation, its coffered ceilings, its Ionic capitals, and the sheer elegance of all its stonework, it resembles it so closely as to leave barely a trace of the lapse of time that separates the two works.

The most important of all Gabriel's successors was undoubtedly Jacques-Denis Antoine (1733–1801). He began his architectural career as an outsider – he was the son of a joiner – but his integrity and reliability made him one of the most sought-after practitioners of his day. His very first work, the Hôtel de Fleury in Paris (1768; now the Ecole des Ponts et Chaussées), shows both originality and sureness of taste. The street façade is articulated by four tall pavilions, the central doorway being flanked by Doric columns; the façade ornament – stone balconies on consoles, moulded window architraves, banded ground-floor rustication – is sparing and crisp and evidently influenced by Gabriel.

Antoine's major work is the Hôtel des Monnaies (1771–7), the Paris mint, one of the major public buildings of Louis XV's reign. Plans for a new mint had existed for years. Originally intended for the Place Louis-XV (the site for which Antoine made his initial design), the project was transferred in 1767 to the left bank of the Seine, on the site of the old Hôtel de Conti. In the following year a competition was announced; Boullée was one of those who prepared

181 Jacques-Denis Antoine: Paris, Mint, Salon (Cabinet de l'Ecole des Mines), finished 1785.

182 Jean-Vincent Barré: Le Marais, c. 1770.

designs.[66] Building work started on Antoine's winning design in 1771 and was completed in the incredibly short space of six years.

The entrance façade (Plate 180) faces the river, with workshops and coining presses arranged around courts behind. Antoine has given it the impressive appearance required by its location opposite the Louvre, and by its status as a symbol of the national wealth. In its proportions, this façade is entirely within the French tradition; the influence of Gabriel is visible in the central pavilion, with its majestic colonnade above a low, arcaded ground floor. Antoine's detailing – banded rustication and balustrades between the columns – recalls the façades of the Place Louis-XV; but here all is more rigorous and cubic. The wings have no terminal pavilions or pilasters; deprived of an inner rhythm,

they stretch out in an unrelieved horizontality that is further emphasized by the deep cornice.[67] One crucial innovation is the absence of a central pediment and of a dome. For the first time in any conspicuous location, a columnar frontispiece is surmounted only by an entablature and an attic, and a basic principle of classical architecture has been abandoned. To set off his façade, and to relieve the heaviness of the attic, with its figured sculpture, Antoine originally intended to build up the Seine embankment into a podium with two ramps, but this was never done. The side elevation, on the Rue Guénégaud, rusticated throughout and surmounted by a dome, and the central court with its rounded end, once more reflect a closeness to Gabriel and to his design for the Cour du Cheval-Blanc at Fontainebleau.

The interior reveals the influence of Soufflot, especially in

the central doorway, with its coupled columns reminiscent of Palazzo Farnese, and in the monumental staircase with its coffered dome, very like that of Soufflot's Hôtel-Dieu in Lyon. The large central salon on the first floor finished only in 1785 (Plate 181) is opulent to a degree that by no means reflects the true state of the French state finances in the 1770s. The walls are adorned with large arabesques and reliefs. A large order runs round the room, and above it is a gallery, which bridges the diagonal corner niches above. The ceiling itself consists of a wide coving of gold mosaic, as used by Gabriel at the Ecole Militaire, with a large ceiling painting in the flat of the vault. These are all features that recall seventeenth-century classicism rather than the antique.

Antoine's success at the Hôtel des Monnaies brought him numerous public and private commissions. Jointly with Pierre Desmaisons, he succeeded Joseph-Abel Couture in charge of the rebuilding of the Palais de Justice in Paris, destroyed by fire. The form of the *corps de logis* had been established by Couture; but the two side wings that flank the Cour du Mai, the right-hand one of which contains the grand staircase, are Antoine's, as are the steps in the court itself and the great lobby or Salle des Pas-Perdus (1782–5).

Antoine's other public buildings are the façade of the new city hall in Cambrai (1786; a joint project with Jardin on the latter's return from Denmark) and the mint in Bern (1790). In these, and in his numerous châteaux and hôtels all over France, Antoine never offended against convention or good taste. In them, segment-headed windows, attic statues, square-based domes, and the banded ground-floor rusti-

cation beloved of Gabriel and Blondel, survived without a break. One particularly fine example is the Château de Herces (Eure-et-Loir), begun in 1772.

Only in his ecclesiastical buildings did Antoine depart from convention; and here he developed a surprisingly progressive style. He built the church of the Couvent de la Visitation in Nancy (1785) like those illustrated in Peyre's *Œuvres d'architecture*, as a windowless rotunda, with banded rustication throughout, a dome and a pedimented portico; in the tympanum above the doorway is a group of figures very similar to those on that of the Hôtel des Monnaies. In the roughly contemporaneous portal of the Hôpital de la Charité, in Paris, Antoine set out, in the words of Legrand and Landon, 'to convey an idea of the Propylaea [of the Acropolis in Athens], of which David Le Roy had spoken in his lectures'. It was a tetrastyle Greek temple portico with baseless, fluted Doric columns, among the first of its kind in France.

Jean-Vincent Barré (*c.* 1730–after 1788) was mostly employed in building châteaux (Le Marais, Montgeoffroy, Le Lude, and others), in which he continued the tradition of Gabriel. This is particularly evident at Le Marais (*c.* 1770), where the dome and the general form recall the Ecole Militaire, and the diminutive lodges recall the sentry-boxes of the Place Louis-XV (Plate 182). However, the monumental articulation of the salon, with its detached columns, goes far beyond Gabriel; this is an early example of the architecturalization of interior decoration in the 1770s. Barré's most important commission was the planning of a

183 Etienne Giral: Montpellier, Le Peyrou, begun in 1767.

Place Royale for Brussels, incorporating the existing church of Saint-Jacques de Coudenberg (1774–9); his design was executed, with minor modifications, by Guimard.

Le Peyrou, in Montpellier, belongs to the same context (Plate 183). There, in the late 1760s, was built one of the most beautiful promenades in France and, at the same time, one of the last of the Places Royales.[68] An aqueduct had been constructed to supply the city with water, and this terminated on the outskirts at Le Peyrou, where the Estates of Languedoc decided to develop a Place Royale. In so doing, they were reviving a project previously mooted by the provincial Intendant but abandoned as too remote from the city centre.

The commission was first offered to Soufflot, who declined; and then the Estates submitted a number of rival designs to the Academy in Paris for a decision. There an ad hoc committee selected the design by Jean-Antoine Giral, the nephew of Jean Giral and architect of the Hôtel Saint-Côme. He had taken advantage of the unique location to design a Place Royale surrounded only by balustrades, thus offering an unimpeded view of nature, very much in the contemporary spirit. He based himself closely on the Place Louis-XV in Paris, from which he took the canted corners,

the little sentry-boxes, the terraces with rusticated retaining walls punctuated by large stone plaques, and even – initially – the moat between the Place Royale itself and the belvedere at one end of the platform.

In 1767, after reworking his designs, Giral began the terracing work in association with his son-in-law, Jacques Donnat. On an upper platform, level with the aqueduct, he laid out an open, tree-lined square, in the centre of which he placed the statue of Louis XIV that had long been waiting for a site. At the end, on the axis of the existing triumphal arch, Daviler's Porte du Peyrou, he erected an open-sided, hexagonal temple with coupled Corinthian columns; this serves as a belvedere and also as a water-tower for the aqueduct. At a lower level, he surrounded the square with wide terraces planted with trees, the crowns of which were not to rise above the balustrade above. The resemblance to the Place Louis-XV is unmistakable; and the spirit of Gabriel also lives on in the hexagonal temple, the 'Fountain-head and Source of Water', which is adorned with the emblems of the liquid element – heavy fishing-nets, bundles of reeds, masks of river gods, and the like – and which, in the freshness of its imagery, reveals a trace of the antique spirit of nearby Provence.

CHAPTER 5

Jacques-Germain Soufflot

WORKS IN LYON

Alongside Gabriel, the dominant personality in Neoclassicism was Jacques-Germain Soufflot (1713–80). Soufflot was not only an influential stylist but a bold innovator in matters of construction, and he set new standards in church building with his major work, Sainte-Geneviève – the Panthéon – in Paris, which is one of the universal masterpieces of architecture. He differed from Gabriel in his monumental rigor, in his habit of thinking in blocks, and in his sparing use of decoration. Soufflot was an outsider. He was not a scion of the Parisian architectural establishment: his father was a lawyer in a small town in Burgundy. In 1731 he defied his father, who intended him for a legal career, and travelled to Rome, where he applied himself to the study of architecture and the antique with such enthusiasm that he came to the attention of the French Minister, who secured him a scholarship at the Académie de France. In Rome he made a number of influential friends from Lyon, and on his return to France he settled in that city, where he swiftly became the leading local architect.[69]

The fifteen years that Soufflot spent in Lyon, 1739–55, were fundamental to his later career. They were filled with practical activity, both in building and in urban planning. Lyon was one of the great cities of France, a centre of the silk industry and an important staging post on the way to Italy. Its intellectual centre was the Academy of Fine Arts. There Soufflot developed his theories on the art of architecture and presented the celebrated *Mémoire* of 1741, on the advantages of the Gothic and of its constructional principles, which he later put into practice in the building of Sainte-Geneviève. He was entrusted with important public works and planning responsibilities, and remained involved with the modernization and improvement of the city for the rest of his life, so that in 1775 he was awarded the title of 'Surveyor General of Buildings and Improvements to the City of Lyon'.

Soufflot's buildings in Lyon are full of reminiscences of the Roman Baroque. The multiple recessions in the block of Communs for the Hôtel Lacroix-Laval recall Filippo Raguzzini's Piazza di S. Ignazio; the rigorous geometry of the porticoes in the court of the archbishop's palace recalls the ends of Bernini's colonnades at St Peter's. Also when he built the Loge au Change for the Consuls of Lyon in 1748–50, and was required to save money by retaining the existing seventeenth-century Doric arcading; he transformed this into a ground-floor loggia with a great hall above, very much on the lines of a north Italian city hall, which he proceeded to translate into Roman terms through a lavish use of columns.

Soufflot's major work in Lyon was the Hôtel-Dieu, in which he revealed himself as an innovator of genius and an artist of far more than local significance.[70] The Hôtel-Dieu was a venerable institution, a hospital open to patients from all countries, and had long been a model of its kind. But as its old buildings fell short of the increasingly exacting hygienic standards of the eighteenth century, its board of Rectors had decided on an ambitious programme of expansion, with a view to giving every patient a separate bed and segregating fever patients from surgical cases. The new complex was to incorporate parts of the old, and would extend along the bank of the Rhône, to which it would present a unitary façade with provision for shops at ground level (hence the ground-floor arcading). Delamonce had devised an overall plan in 1733, but construction was delayed by the Consuls' determination to start by building an embankment for a riverside promenade.

By the time Soufflot arrived in Lyon in 1739, work was in progress on the foundations of the north wing. Only the façade remained an open question. A design prepared for the Rectors by Etienne Lebon had not met with the approval of the Consuls, and no agreement had been reached.[71] But Soufflot's friends had been active on his behalf. He submitted designs; both the Rectors and the Consuls liked them; and within three months the commission was in his pocket, with both Delamonce and Lebon cut out completely. The foundation stone was laid in 1741. By 1748, when work had to be suspended for lack of funds, the central portion was complete except for its square dome. When work began again, in 1756, Soufflot was no longer available; by then, Marigny had summoned him to Paris and would not release him. The dome was essential, not only for the ventilation of the wards – it was designed to work as a huge air-shaft – but because it was intended to house the chapel; and so, on Soufflot's recommendation, the Rectors engaged the architects Munet and Toussaint Loyer to execute his designs. The dome was completed in 1761,[72] and the south wing followed. The north wing was not completed until after the Revolution.

Soufflot's façade was fated to remain unfinished in his own lifetime; but this did not prevent it from becoming an instant sensation (Plate 184). In 1748 Blondel published it as an engraving, and Soufflot was not slow to send signed copies to all his patrons and fellow-Academicians. The façade, constitutes the essence of Soufflot's achievement. For the Hôtel-Dieu, with all its successive inner courts, is not laid out in the customary cruciform pattern but subordinated to a single façade that runs for 375 metres (a quarter of a mile) along the bank of the Rhône. What gives this façade its importance is the generosity and sureness of touch revealed by its articulation and detailing. The long horizontals are broken by the massive accents of the centre and end pavilions, and pulled together by the dome.

The overall pattern is that of the south façade of the Louvre – and, in particular, that of the unexecuted design by François d'Orbay that de Cotte also used. However, there are considerable divergences of detail (Plate 185). The great central pediment has been replaced by an attic enriched (in the design) with statuary; and the giant pilasters have been replaced, except on the end pavilions, by discreet pilaster

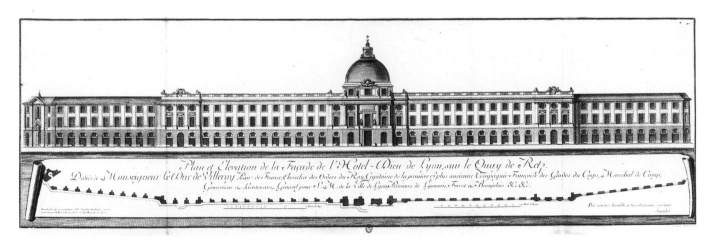

Plan et Elevation de la Façade de l'Hôtel-Dieu de Lyon, sur le Quay de Retz.

Elevation de l'avant corps du Milieu de l'Hôtel Dieu de Lyon.

184 Germain Soufflot: Lyon, Hôtel Dieu, façade, 1748; enraving by Blondel.

185 Germain Soufflot: Lyon, Hôtel Dieu, façade; central part, design by Autrechy (Paris, Bibliothèque Nationale).

strips. The rhythm of the fenestration is also different. Even so, Soufflot has unmistakably used a classical source. Even the sparingly applied decoration derives from classical precedents, although Soufflot employs an entirely idiosyncratic vocabulary that has French as well as Italian roots. The large, elliptical windows, draped with laurel garlands, and the statues on the attic are borrowed from the Louvre, but the drapery swags above the central first-floor windows derive from sixteenth-century French architecture. The stepwise progression from pilasters on the outer bays of the frontispiece to columns on the inner bays is an Italian motif; the lantern originally planned above the dome was a reminiscence of S. Carlo al Corso. Again, the severely plain capitals, with

their emphatic astragals – so different from those of the Mansart school – are Roman forms. The only Neoclassical elements are an afterthought on Soufflot's part: the lion mask and rope-like laurel garlands above the central window.

If we compare this façade with the contemporaneous ones of the Hôpital Général in Lille, or the Place Royale in Bordeaux, it is immediately evident how much more block-like and monumental it is. The soft, linear flow of the Mansart school has disappeared. At the Hôtel-Dieu, Soufflot shows himself to be thoroughly Baroque; just as, in his concurrent work on the decoration of Saint-Bruno, he makes use of the *style rocaille*. But his is the academic Baroque of Gianlorenzo Bernini, Andreas Schlüter or Christopher Wren. The same monumentalism is evident in the interior of the central pavilion, both in the vestibule with its inset corner columns – another Roman motif – and in the chapel above. This extends up into the dome (Plate 186), and is lined with fluted pilasters, alternating with arched openings into the wards. The balustraded balconies within these arches reflect the double-height form of the wards. Above, flooded with light from ten windows, is the dome itself, with a perspectival coffered ceiling. All this is both supremely grand and replete with quotations from the past. In his use of pilasters and his delicately carved garlands and festoons, Soufflot is harking back to the late work of J.H. Mansart; in the coffering, his reference is to the antique. No wonder Blondel included the Hôtel-Dieu in his article on architecture for the *Encyclopédie*, and Lafont de Saint-Yenne described it in ecstatic terms. This work paved the way for Neoclassicism; it also undoubtedly played a part in persuading Madame de Pompadour to select its architect as companion and mentor for her brother, the future Marquis de Marigny, on his tour of Italy in 1749–51.

In designing a theatre for Lyon (1754–6), Soufflot once more broke new ground. He started building before he moved to Paris, and the theatre was then completed by Munet in accordance with his designs. This was the first modern theatre in France and the first fruit of Soufflot's

186 Germain Soufflot: Lyon, Hôtel Dieu, interior of the dome.

tour with Marigny – which had the study of Italian theatres as one of its avowed purposes. At that time the most modern theatre in Italy, by common consent, was the Opera in Turin (1738–40), in which Alfieri had pioneered the use of the horseshoe ground plan; and it was from this that Soufflot took the shape of his auditorium, an elongated oval, the end of which was cut off by the proscenium. But instead of the Italian system of boxes stacked like honeycombs, 'which do not deserve the name of architecture' (Cochin), he surrounded the auditorium with continuous balconies, each containing raked rows of seating.

In the course of his tour with Marigny he had stopped off to visit Paestum with his friend Dumont and to survey the temples there;[73] this had sharpened his eye for the antique, and for the theatres based on antique precedents in Parma and Vicenza. In 1753, in the paper in which he presented his theatre design to the Academy in Lyon and reported on his impressions of Italy, he made the first reference to this connection and to its practical significance.[74] By applying the methods of antiquity, but without a colonnade, he had created a theatrical interior that was defined, for the first time, not by its decoration but by its architecture, and in which all the seats commanded a clear view of the stage; this was the prototype of the Neoclassical theatres of Versailles and Besançon.

Unlike the interior, the exterior failed to give a unified impression.[75] It was designed as a palace façade, with much use of relief decoration and figured sculpture on the roof line, and combined reminiscences of Rome with Neoclassical forms from the repertoire of Neufforge. But it possessed neither monumental quality nor any clear reference to the fact that it was a theatre. Soufflot's building was replaced by a new Opera in 1826.

The Lyon theatre gave Soufflot the reputation of an ex-

pert. But, although he was constantly consulted and solicited for designs – for Paris, Bordeaux, Versailles and elsewhere – he never designed another theatre. Even Marigny could not prevail on him to provide a new theatre for the Comédie-Française; this was later done by Peyre and De Wailly.

Another building of Soufflot's Lyon period is the Charité, in Mâcon (1752–61), a quadrangular hospital building confined to a cramped and poorly located site. Its chapel is a remarkable achievement, nevertheless. It represents the earliest revival of the Gothic principles of vault construction. An oval interior within a polygonal structure, it consists entirely of an open array of piers, rising through three storeys and affording direct access to the wards. The piers continue upwards as vaulting ribs and combine to form a dome amazingly reminiscent of a Gothic stellar vault.[76]

WORKS UNDER THE PATRONAGE OF MARIGNY

In 1755 Marigny summoned his former travelling companion to Paris to build Sainte-Geneviève. Behind this call stood Marigny's desire to create a countervailing force to the all-powerful Gabriel and to present himself to the public as a champion of the return to good taste. For Soufflot it was the chance of a lifetime. It admitted him to the inner circle of the leading architects of France and entrusted him with one of the most important architectural commissions in the realm. He arrived with something of an established reputation and soon gravitated to the Neoclassically minded salon of Madame Geoffrin, already frequented by Marigny and Caylus. The tastes of this circle were reflected in his earliest Parisian commissions, such as the (vanished) Sacristy of Notre-Dame.

Marigny initially secured him a post as surveyor at Marly. But in 1756, on the death of Garnier d'Isle, he succeeded him in an equivalent post in Paris,[77] and there he was appointed to oversee the completion of the Louvre and to act as an assistant to Gabriel. Marigny wanted the Louvre to do two things. As a masterpiece of classicism, it was to promote his own Neoclassical ideals; and it was also to assist in creating a new public image for the king himself. Louis XIV had abandoned his palace on the spur of the moment; his successor intended to restore its identification with the crown, and Soufflot accordingly regarded himself as the successor of Perrault.

Gabriel remained in overall charge; but, at the instance of Marigny, Soufflot was given a large measure of autonomy within his own sphere, both in the restoration of the colonnade, which he took over from Gabriel, and in the clearance of the Cour du Louvre and of the square to the east of the palace. The two architects worked together without much friction, despite Marigny's occasional efforts to curtail Gabriel's authority. Soufflot's major independent contribution lay in planning the allocation of space between the academies in the north and the royal library in the south – and, after the Grand Conseil idea was dropped in 1768, also in the east. Finally, by clearing the Grande Galerie and making the first designs for it to be top-lit, he paved the way for the eventual conversion of the Louvre into a museum. In connection with the library plans, he designed a staircase for the east range, based – like Gabriel's design some years earlier – on the

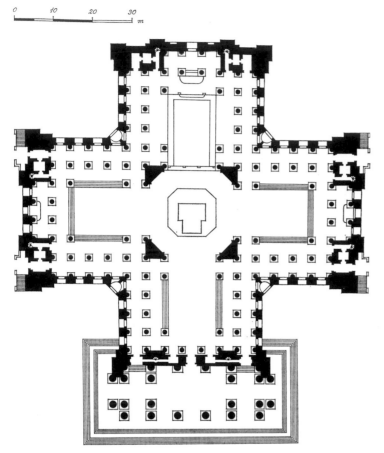

destroyed Escalier des Ambassadeurs at Versailles. Here, once more, Soufflot's more rigorous, architectonic approach and greater sobriety in detailing are already evident. Very little of what Soufflot designed for the Louvre was ever realized; not even the clearance of the Cour du Louvre was completed. Thwarted in the eighteenth century by the catastrophic state of the national finances, the Louvre project was to be accomplished only in the nineteenth.

Another ill-fated project was the Place Royale that Soufflot designed for a prominent street intersection in Reims.[78] At one end was to be a screen wall with the king's statue in its centre; on the other three sides an arcade 'in the manner of the Roman forums' was to enclose an inner, traffic-free area. This plan was approved, and work began. However, the execution (1756–60) was entrusted not to Soufflot but to the provincial engineer, Legendre, who departed from Soufflot's design by leaving out the arcade and surrounding the whole square with shops, so that it became a focus of traffic and commerce. In place of the screen wall he erected the Hôtel des Fermes, a sober, functional building despite its giant order. The utilitarianism of the Enlightenment had prevailed over the aesthetic norms of the *Grand Siècle*.[79]

Soufflot's crowning achievement, one that links him for ever with Paris, was the new church of Sainte-Geneviève.

187   Germain Soufflot: Paris, Sainte-Geneviève, plan, 1757.

188   Germain Soufflot: Paris, Sainte-Geneviève, 1757–90, interior, engraving by Poulleau, 1775.

189 Germain Soufflot: Paris,
Sainte-Geneviève, elevation, 1764
(Archives Nationales).

189 Germain Soufflot: Paris, Sainte-Geneviève, elevation, 1764 (Archives Nationales).

This, the largest and most important Neoclassical building in France, represents the summation of decades of thought and effort directed at the reform of ecclesiastical architecture.[80] The Abbaye de Sainte-Geneviève, which was the headquarters of the powerful Augustinian Congregation, was among the most venerable religious foundations in France. It contained the shrine of St Genevieve, who was reputed to have saved Paris from a Norman assault in 885, and who was held in great honour. The ancient abbey church had fallen into disrepair, and in 1697 this had inspired Perrault to design an ideal replacement. The idea was revived in 1744, when Louis XV fell ill in Metz and made a vow to rebuild the church. But it was not until 1754, when its collapse was imminent, that the king made up his mind to proceed with the rebuilding, which was to be financed out of the receipts of a lottery. Marigny had Soufflot in mind for the job all along, and to eliminate any possible rivals he circumvented the public competition that would normally have been held for so large a commission.[81]

Soufflot had his design ready in 1756 (Plate 187), and work began in 1757. But unexpected difficulties arose in the digging of the foundations, so that the king was unable to lay the foundation stone until 1764. On that occasion, to convey an idea of the finished building, Soufflot had the lower part of the outside walls built up in plaster and set up a scaffold on which he hung a life-size painting of the façade as it would be.

In his 1756 design he adopted a Greek cross plan, which was unprecedented in France, although in Italy both Bramante and Michelangelo had envisaged it for St Peter's, and Wren had used it in his Great Model for St Paul's. The portico, with its giant Corinthian columns and its surrounding steps, was very much in the manner of an antique temple, and formed a distinct structure at the end of the western arm of the cross.[82] The four arms of the cross were four domed compartments, as in an inscribed-cross church, with saucer domes above pendentives, each surrounded by four short sections of tunnel vault and supported at each corner by four columns in a square: it was a system very like that of St Mark's in Venice. Around the arms of the cross ran flat-roofed ambulatories, also lined with columns. The wide crossing was intended to accommodate the shrine of St Genevieve, beneath a low drum and a hemispherical dome to serve as baldachin. The central space, which extended into the arms of the cross, was five steps lower than the rest of the floor, so as to create daises for those who watched the ceremonies at the shrine. On four sides of the external drum, above the corners of the crossing, were four enthroned figures of Fathers of the Church. The dome was surmounted, in the manner of an antique temple, by a figure of the saint herself, so that Soufflot's church very soon became known as the Temple de Sainte-Geneviève.

The interior was – and still is – dominated by columns (Plate 188), shorter and more slender than those of the portico; and these do not support arches but a continuous entablature. There were two celebrated precedents for this, of which Soufflot made use: Perrault's Louvre colonnade and the chapel at Versailles. Undoubtedly, however, he also had in mind the ranks of columns in the temples of Paestum, which he had studied at first hand. The columns were fluted, and on the wall opposite each was not a pilaster but, as Laugier had demanded, a half-column. The walls themselves were perfectly smooth. This amounted to a total rejection of all existing schemes of wall articulation.

The wide intercolumniation, and the bright light through the low windows, lent the interior an extraordinary lightness and spatial transparency. At the crossing, applied half-columns disguised the triangular piers that supported the dome; boldly, Soufflot had reduced the mass of these piers to an unprecedented degree, to maintain the space intact. Outside, too, pilasters were avoided, and the walls became smooth surfaces, animated by window openings and relief

190 Germain Soufflot: Paris, Sainte-Geneviève (Pantheon) (from the south-west).

carvings; around the top ran a frieze of garlands, like that on the tomb of Caecilia Metella. Only the corners were emphasized by pier-like strips; and at each of them a flight of external steps afforded access to the transept through a side door.

Soufflot combined this composition, derived from classicism and the antique, with Gothic constructional principles; reduction of the mass of the wall and a complex system of load distribution. Behind the entablatures was a system of relieving arches and iron ties, and the massive external walls concealed flying buttresses. Poulleau's engraving of 1775 gives an idea of the ideal of *clarté* and *légèreté* that Soufflot had in mind. It was his aim to combine the clarity and grandeur of antique architecture with the lightness of Gothic construction: in other words, to combine the classical orders with modern techniques of vaulting.[83]

Soufflot's design caused a sensation, and was regarded as the beginning of a new age of ecclesiastical building. Laugier called it 'the first model of perfect architecture'. But this was an ideal design. The wishes of the clergy, and changes in taste over the years that followed, enforced a succession of changes. The western cross arm and the choir had to be lengthened, two flanking bell towers had to be added, the high altar had to be moved back from the crossing to an eastern apse (1758–9), and there had to be a crypt (1763). In designing this, Soufflot proposed fluted Doric columns, of the kind that he had seen at Paestum; but he was not yet ready to use them unadulterated, without bases.[84] In the crossing, which now had to accommodate the steps down to the crypt, Soufflot placed a high pedestal supporting the sculptural group of Four Virtues, by Germain Pilon, which bore the reliquary itself.

In its initial version, in 1756, the exterior of the dome had been based on that of the Dôme des Invalides, with four pairs of coupled columns diagonally arranged around the drum. In 1764, under the influence of the *goût grec*, Soufflot ringed the drum with half-columns, thus giving the effect of a temple (Plate 189), and emphasized the diagonals with pedimented porches, while converting the outer dome into a stepped cone, like an antique tomb, with the statue of the saint at the apex. This was a direct reference to Dumont's 'Temple of the Arts' design of 1746, in which the same porches and the same stepped cone appear, albeit separated by an attic.[85]

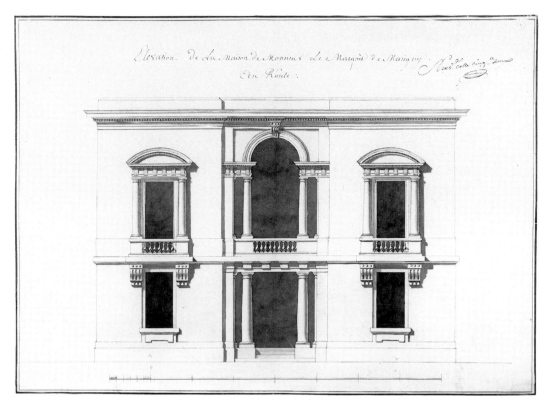

191 Germain Soufflot: House for Marigny, design for façade, 1769 (Paris, Musée Carnavalet).

In 1769 a public onslaught by Patte on the constructional system of Sainte-Geneviève, and on the alleged inadequacy of the crossing piers in particular, led Soufflot to check his calculations and alter the construction of the dome.[86] In order to distribute the load more evenly, he replaced the previous two shells with three and added an attic, so that the springing line of the dome no longer coincided with the windows of the drum. He stretched the dome vertically, opened it internally through an oculus in the lowest shell – with a view through to a painted ceiling above, as at the Dôme des Invalides – and replaced the saint on top with a lantern. On the base of the drum he replaced his four Church Fathers with a free-standing colonnade, which performed a statical function and also bulked out the silhouette of the dome itself. In 1777, after some vacillation, this colonnade acquired its present circular form (Plate 190), on the model of St Paul's in London. The colonnade – a very much calmer and less tense form than anything that had gone before – created a weighty effect, very unlike the lightness of the initial design; but it was an exemplary solution for its day, and it found imitators far and wide, from St Petersburg to Washington.

Patte's onslaughts, which were vindicated by the cracks that appeared in the crossing piers in 1776, unleashed a torrent of pamphlets, expert opinions and counter-opinions, from which – with the support of such eminent experts as Jean-Baptiste Rondelet, Emiliand Gauthey and Jean-Rodolphe Perronet – Soufflot eventually emerged victorious. In a centrally planned, octagonal church at Givry, Gauthey demonstrated just how far one could go in reducing the mass of masonry;[87] like Soufflot, he hollowed out the abutments of his vault to create galleries.

When Soufflot died in 1780, the church was vaulted, except for the transepts, and the drum had been carried up

to the circular base of the dome. The direction of the work was taken over by Soufflot's long-standing associate, Maximilien Brébion, aided by the great technician Rondelet and by Soufflot's nephew, Soufflot-le-Romain, as inspectors. In spite of great financial difficulties, which sometimes brought the work to a halt, the carcass was completed by the outbreak of the Revolution. The external dome was finished in 1789, and the lantern was topped out in 1790. The building was complete, except for its internal decoration.

In 1791, after the death of Mirabeau, the National Assembly resolved that the church of Sainte-Geneviève should become the 'Panthéon des Grands Hommes', and a new programme of sculptural decoration was decided upon. The metamorphosis into a Panthéon had the consequence of marring much of Soufflot's work. The proposer of the new sculptural programme, Quatremère de Quincy (Antoine-Chrysostome Quatremère, 1755–1849), was a dry-as-dust theorist and writer on art whose interests were primarily archaeological; he regarded austere rectitude, sobriety of outline and economy of ornament as the sole appropriate qualities for a church, and deplored what he saw as the undue levity of Soufflot's architecture. By walling up the windows, he deprived the building of its abundance of light; by destroying the sculptures, including the relief on the pediment, he robbed it of its festive air; by reinforcing and thickening the crossing piers, he took away its spaciousness and transparency. Even the east towers were torn down. Finally, after new cracks had appeared in the crossing piers, Rondelet, who had been appointed supervising architect in 1801, had to build new and massive piers to replace all the corner columns of the arms of the cross, thus cramping the space still more. Dim, chilly and overcrowded with tombs, the Panthéon of the present day has little in common with the Sainte-Geneviève that Soufflot designed.

Soufflot did not conceive his church in isolation, but set it in an urban context. The open space within which it stands forms a hemicycle facing the west front, and from it a wide street runs west to the Jardin du Luxembourg. The quadrants thus created were meant for the façades of schools of law and theology; of these only one, the Ecole de Droit, on the right as seen from the church, was built (1768 onwards). Its pendant was added in the nineteenth century. The giant portico of the Ecole de Droit is a reflection of that of the church; and the houses to either side were meant to be similarly treated, so that the entire Place Sainte-Geneviève would have been lined with columns.

The demands of his official duties left Soufflot very little time for private commissions, so that these played only a minor role in the second half of his career. The most important of them was the town house of his patron, Marigny (1769), which clearly reflected the director-general's eclectic taste. It was a pavilion-type structure at the end of a narrow *cour d'honneur*, with its block-like, Palladian compactness, it was a novelty in the Parisian architecture of the 1760s. The façade, dominated by six openings, consisted entirely of quotations (Plate 191). The flanking first-floor windows were lifted almost intact from the Palazzo Farnese; the recessed centre was filled by a *serliana* motif from Palladio's Basilica in Vicenza, in which Soufflot had avoided a direct copy by adding triglyphs to the entablature. For the main entrance, at Marigny's express desire, he designed 'a masculine, square doorway in the manner of Michelangelo' (*une porte mâle et carrée à la Michel-Ange*), which he took from the Palazzo dei Conservatori. This composite image of the Renaissance must have evoked memories of his youth for Marigny, though it does not seem entirely appropriate for a Directeur Général des Bâtiments.

At Ménars, too, the country seat on the Loire that Madame de Pompadour had left to her brother, Marigny employed Soufflot to enlarge the house by adding two pavilions and a connecting gallery on the court side, and to improve the gardens.[88] Here, too, in one of the most beautiful gardens of the eighteenth century, the Renaissance returned to life in the shape of a circular Temple of Abundance, a Grotto, a Temple of Apollo, and a number of other small buildings, most of which have since vanished. These works of garden architecture, built in 1768–9, were little masterpieces of perfect proportions, derived not so much from antiquity as from Italian Mannerism. The Temple of Abundance, intended as a link between the newly built orangery and the château itself, is a rotunda on Tuscan columns, projecting between two abbreviated wings. The grotto – 'piccola ma garbata', small but sweet, as Marigny called it – has an interior in the shape of a Greek cross, centred on a pool of the same shape with four columns at the corners, like a baptistery, and a dome above. The columns – safely underground, like those in the crypt of Sainte-Geneviève – were among the first anywhere in France to be built without bases. When Marigny asked him to build a Chinese pavilion, Soufflot flatly declined.

In 1775, by which time his relations with Marigny had cooled considerably,[89] Soufflot designed his last work; it was another grotto, in the country seat at Chatou, by the Seine, of the former Intendant of Lyon and future comptroller of finances, Henri-Léonard Bertin.[90] A semicircle of cinctured Tuscan columns – also without bases – encloses a pool roofed by a large vault in the form of a shell. Here – by contrast with the grotto at La Rivette, near Lyon, built in the 1740s and still entirely Baroque in its curves and counter-curves and its kidney-shaped pool – antiquity is a strong presence. Soufflot's prototypes at Chatou were the nymphaea of the ancient world, but probably also such French grottoes as Wideville or La Bastie d'Urfé, with their partiality for rusticated columns. The extensive vault, by Rondelet, is a masterpiece of three-dimensional geometry. For the polychromatic banding that gives this grotto its distinctive character, Soufflot used iron waste from the gun foundry that Bertin owned in Périgord.

The Pioneers of Antiquity: Peyre the Elder, De Wailly, Gondoin, Louis, Clérisseau, Le Camus de Mézières

The second wave of the antique revival was archaeologically oriented. Its prime movers were the Rome scholars who returned to France in the 1750s and 1760s. They, too, were under the influence of Piranesi; but they had an altogether clearer idea of what they mean by antiquity. Accurate surveys had given them a precise knowledge of the monuments; and this they brought home and used in a frontal assault on the French tradition. The exponents of this new understanding were Peyre, De Wailly, Gondoin, Clérisseau, and to some degree also Victor Louis. In their work temple façades, coffered vaults and 'thermal' halls modelled on the Roman baths made their entry into French architecture.

Marie-Joseph Peyre (1730–85), a pupil of Blondel's, arrived in Rome in 1753. He entered a competition at the Accademia di S. Luca with a design for a cathedral, complete with archbishop's palace and canons' residence, which was a conflation of St Peter's and the Roman Pantheon, full of prostyle porticoes and interminable colonnades, and still strongly influenced by Legeay. Conceived on the gargantuan scale that had become popular at the Roman Academy but had never before been seen in France, this design made its public point when Peyre published it in his *Oeuvres d'architecture* (1765): it was he who brought to France the megalomania that was to become the hallmark of late eighteenth-century French architecture. Peyre's exclusive preoccupation with the antique led him, jointly with De Wailly and Moreau-Desproux, to survey the Baths of Diocletian and Caracalla. These were the source of his designs for a gigantic academy complex – a strictly symmetrical arrangement of domed rotundas, apses and colonnades (Plate 192) – and for a palace in which he grafted the apsidal halls and colonnades of the Roman baths onto the French convention of a *corps de logis* with two projecting wings. Among his engravings, Peyre published a number of Roman tombs; and that of Caecilia Metella was the source of his own design for a funerary chapel.

Peyre's *Oeuvres d'architecture*, in which he published these designs in 1765, became a founding document of Neo-classicism. This was the first appearance in France of the temple porticoes in front of blank, windowless walls, the giant columns articulating internal walls and the coffered domes that filled the younger generation with enthusiasm and transformed the face of French architecture. Nor was the *Oeuvres d'architecture* by any means an isolated work: it was an entirely logical consequence of the cult of genius that had held sway in the 1740s. The link between the two is best exemplified by Chambers's design for a Mausoleum for the Prince of Wales, of 1751. In his commentary, Peyre declared open war on 'so-called French architecture' (by which, without saying so, he meant Blondel).

Peyre himself built relatively little. The house he built for Madame de Neubourg on the outskirts of Paris was a Palladian villa, the first ever seen in France: he himself called it a *maison de plaisance*. Everything about it was new and unconventional. The unadorned exterior, the decentralization achieved by the omission of the central pediment, the windows cut in without surrounds (Plate 193), and also the plan – entrance at one end and a succession of interconnecting rooms without corridors or lobbies – flouted every French convention. It was, in fact, precisely its plainness and its unconventionality that made this highly Palladian house so popular; it appeared in numerous books of engravings and pioneered a new residential type that gained wide currency in the late eighteenth century.

A more conventional project, designed at much the same time, was the design for the Hôtel de Condé that Peyre presented to the Academy in 1763. His youthful client, the Prince de Bourbon-Condé, the owner of Chantilly, was just back from the Seven Years War. More interested in the arts and sciences than in court life at Versailles, Bourbon-Condé was one of the few members of his class prepared to entrust himself to a progressive architect whose innovations must have struck a man like Marigny as nightmarish. However, Peyre's design kept to the rules. He combined the house, the stable block and the gardens into a unified composition; he fronted the *cour d'honneur* with a public square in which he placed a fountain richly adorned with statuary, like those of Rome. In the circular stable court, and in the strictly symmetrical entrance block, there is a distant echo of the Roman baths. The antique is present, above all, in the profusion of columns; although Neufforge, drawing on the same sources, had anticipated the Tuscan colonnades of Peyre's *cour d'honneur* and his use of a colonnade as a screen. Only the triumphal arch, already present in an earlier design by Peyre for a royal palace, here made its first appearance in a design intended for execution.

One revolutionary innovation was the combination of vestibule and staircase (Plate 194). These had always been kept strictly separate in classical French architecture, which regarded the staircase as an important ceremonial feature. Peyre now combined them into a circular space with perfect radial symmetry and led the stairs round the walls, behind a ring of columns crowned with a coffered dome. This idea was already present in a design of 1763 for a funerary chapel, based on the tomb of Caecilia Metella in Rome.

It was in that very year that Bourbon-Condé became the owner of the Palais Bourbon and transferred his interest to that; so Peyre's Hôtel de Condé was never built. Peyre did, however, publish the design in his *Oeuvres d'architecture*, and it rapidly gained currency as a source of inspiration for the younger architects. The idea of the circular staircase, above all, was taken up, and by the end of the century it had become an established domestic feature.

We know nothing of Peyre's intentions as to the interior decoration. But it is apparent from descriptions of the sumptuous interiors that he devised for the hôtel of the Duc de

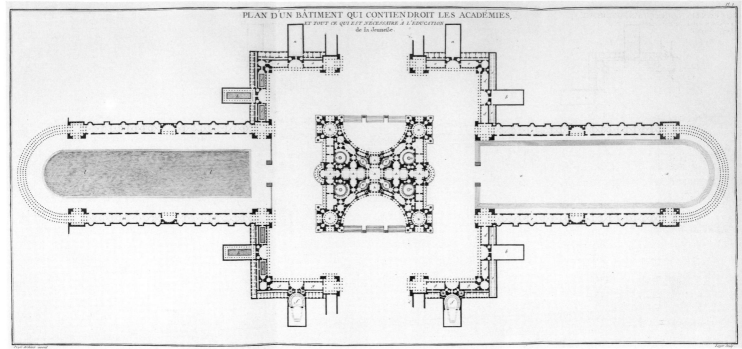

PLAN D'UN BÂTIMENT QUI CONTIENDROIT LES ACADÉMIES,
ET TOUT CE QUI EST NECESSAIRE À L'ÉDUCATION
de la Jeunesse.

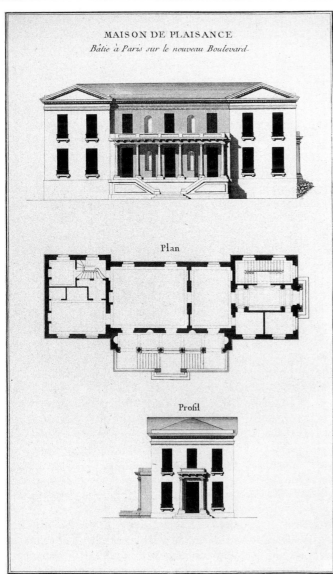

MAISON DE PLAISANCE
Bâtie à Paris sur le nouveau Boulevard.

Plan

Profil

192 Marie-Josèphe Peyre: Design for an academy building, *c.* 1755 (Peyre, *Œuvres d'architecture*).

193 Marie-Josèphe Peyre: Paris, design for the Hôtel de Neubourg, *c.* 1762, façade (Peyre, *Œuvres d'architecture*).

Nivernais, a former French Minister to the Holy See and a man of taste, that Peyre did not regard himself as in any way constrained by a austerely plain exterior. When he lined the Nivernais dining room with free-standing Ionic columns, he was the first architect to introduce this antique element into a French interior.

Although Peyre's Hôtel de Condé remained on paper, it served to secure its designer a part in the building of the new Comédie-Française (now the Odéon), which was erected on the same site and became the most important Parisian theatre of the Ancien Régime. There, in collaboration with his friend De Wailly, Peyre for once had the opportunity to realize his ideas in a public building.[91]

By contrast with Peyre, Charles De Wailly (1730–98) enjoyed one of the most brilliant architectural careers of the day.[92] He was not only an architect but also a painter and a talented draughtsman, who regularly showed his drawings at the Salon; in 1771 he was elected to the Academy of Painting and Sculpture, a rare honour for an architect. Through his work for foreign clients, and his German and Russian pupils (Jussow, Bazhenov, Starov), he became one of the major conduits for the spread of Neoclassicism across Europe. His obituarist remarked in the *Mercure de France* in 1799 that with a little more stylistic purity (i.e. with more classical rigour) he might have been the Palladio of the eighteenth century. De Wailly's catholic sympathies make it difficult to fit him into any one category; his work is distinguished by a bold application of archaeological knowledge, allied with great technical competence, but also by eclecticism and a deep affinity for the Baroque.[93]

194 Marie-Josèphe Peyre: Design for the Hôtel de Condé, c. 1763, detail of plan showing staircase (Peyre, *Œuvres d'architecture*).

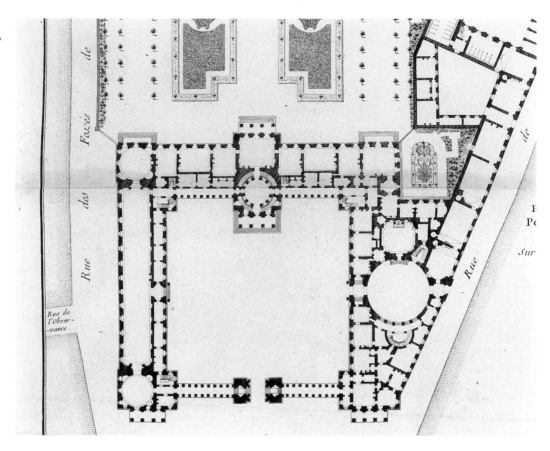

De Wailly initially studied with Blondel before transferring to Legeay, whose free and pictorial manner of composition particularly appealed to him. Legeay probably found him the most congenial of all his pupils. His successful competition design for the Prix de Rome (1752), the façade of a château with forecourt and side wings, with its profusion of columns, is a pure product of the school of Legeay – although the stagy composition and lighting are more likely to stem from his friendship with Servandoni, another important influence on his artistic personality.[94] In Rome, where he lived in 1754–6, De Wailly eagerly set to work, with his friends Peyre and Moreau-Desproux, to survey the Baths of Diocletian and of Caracalla and Hadrian's Villa at Tivoli; but he also took an interest in 'modern' buildings, notably St Peter's, and in the work of Bernini, whom he revered all his life. Back in Paris, he exhibited views of Roman monuments and squares, influenced by Legeay and Piranesi, which revealed him as a brilliant and effective draughtsman.

In the first few years after his return from Rome, De Wailly worked on stage design as a member of Servandoni's workshop, and then on designs for furniture, urns and other decorative elements, in which he established his own version of the *style grec*, a blend of antique and Baroque forms. He published some of these in a *Première suite de gravures de vases*. Then his career took off. In 1762 he became Contrôleur Adjoint at Versailles, where he worked under Gabriel on the building of the Opera; in this, his apprenticeship with Servandoni and his sound knowledge of Italy and of antiquity stood him in good stead. So highly did Marigny value De

Wailly that in 1767, against the wishes of the Academy, he had him promoted to Academician first class, without first passing through the second class and the customary election procedure; the result was a serious conflict between the Academy and the director-general. De Wailly also worked for Marigny in the park at Ménars, alongside Soufflot, Potain and Trouard (1768–72). There, among other things, he built the Chinese pagoda that Soufflot had refused to build, borrowing from Chambers's *Designs of Chinese Buildings* (1757).

De Wailly's exceptional talent was evident in his earliest works – the remodelling of the Hôtel d'Argenson (1762–70) for his patron, the Marquis de Voyer d'Argenson, and the building of the Château de Montmusard (1765–70) for the President of the Parlement of Burgundy, Fyot de la Marche. The Hôtel d'Argenson (formerly d'Argenton) was an early work by Boffrand (1704), alongside the gardens of the Palais-Royal; de Wailly's work on it reflects the profound shift in taste that accompanied the second wave of the antique revival. A small building, and in its day an early example of the *goût moderne*, it now changed its appearance utterly. De Wailly replaced the curves of Boffrand's segment-headed windows with straight lines, rusticated the façades throughout, and added porticoes front and back. The garden-side portico had classical Ionic capitals modelled on those of the Erechtheion in Athens, as shown by Le Roy in the engravings of his *Ruines des plus beaux monuments de la Grèce*. De Wailly also filled in the arches of the end pairs of windows on the garden front with sculptured tympanum reliefs. The new style was already apparent in the gateway to

the court, with its conspicuous statuary niche and its coffered vault, like the entrance to a Roman Renaissance palazzo.

The old interior decoration, too, was replaced, with the exception of such major items as the ceiling painting by Coypel. With assistance from Fragonard, Natoire, Pajou and Pierre Gouthière, De Wailly made the house into one of the sights of Paris. On his visit to Paris in 1774, Chambers drew the interior, with its combination of rocaille and antique decor, its colossal caryatids, military emblems, mirrors and mirror effects: 'All gold and glass' was the reaction of Mrs Thrale on her visit to Paris.

Montmusard, by contrast, was a new creation, in which De Wailly was not constrained by an existing fabric. Jean-Philippe Fyot, Marquis de la Marche, was a member of a landed family of office-holders in Dijon and president of the Parlement. Outside the city gates, Fyot's father and pre-decessor in office had laid out a celebrated garden, with canals, grottoes, waterworks and the like, and had thrown it open to the public. The building of a new château was to be the final step in the family's progress, asserting both its own status and the intellectual pretensions of the *noblesse de robe*.[95] Having rejected a traditionalist design by the young Dijon architect Charles Saint-Père, Fyot no doubt felt that the best way to acquire a suitably splendid new house was to employ a famous metropolitan architect.[96]

De Wailly's first design (*c.* 1762) was produced in ignor-ance of the lie of the land; it was not really a château at all but a *pavillon*, a villa consisting of two wings joined by a circular vestibule-cum-staircase borrowed from Peyre's design for the Hôtel de Condé.[97] The circular stairwell was surmounted by a highly antique circular temple, with an open peristyle and a coffered dome. This design had its shortcomings: the wings communicated with each other only through the vestibule, which was highly inconvenient. No doubt largely for this reason, the client turned it down.

In 1764, after a visit to Dijon to look at the site, De Wailly submitted his second design, which was accepted and built (Plate 195). This, too, was more of a large pavilion than a château. In it, he took his cue from his client's literary and poetic ideas. The president was a lover of Italy and the antique, who surrounded himself with a circle of equally enthusiastic artists and intellectuals. He had no desire to have just another run-of-the mill château. Inspired by the associations of the name Montmusard (*montagne des Muses*, Muses' Mount), he resolved to dedicate his house to Apollo and the Muses; and this was the symbolic, mythological and poetic programme on which de Wailly based both the ground plan and the decor of his audacious design.

The central axis of the house ran through two circular spaces, linked by a columned vestibule (Plate 196). One circle, the Temple d'Apollon, formed an open court; the other, the Salon des Muses, was walled and domed and

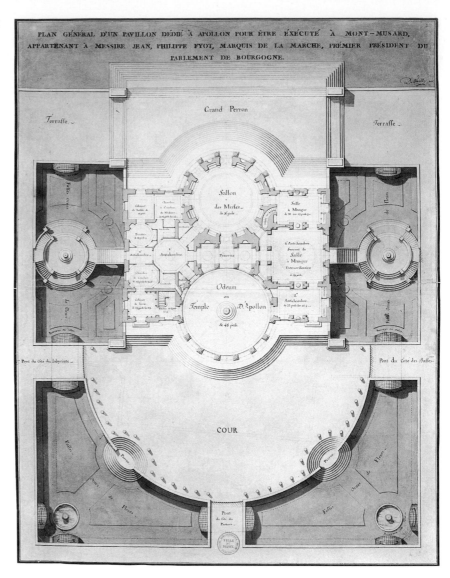

PLAN GÉNÉRAL D'UN PAVILLON DÉDIÉ À APOLLON POUR ÊTRE EXÉCUTÉ À MONT-MUSARD,
APPARTENANT À MESSIRE JEAN, PHILIPPE FYOT, MARQUIS DE LA MARCHE, PREMIER PRÉSIDENT DU
PARLEMENT DE BOURGOGNE.

formed the garden room. In the court stood a statue of Apollo, by the Dijon sculptor Claude-François Attiret; and in the Salon the dome contained a large fresco depicting Apollo and the Muses on Mount Helicon. The window spandrels contained paintings of episodes from the legends of Apollo. On the colonnade that ringed the Salon des Muses stood life-size figures of the Nine.

To the right and left of this axis lay the rectangular wings, containing the *appartement de société* and the *appartement de commodité*. The double-circle motif, which was repeated in the adjoining gardens, was taken from the baths of Rome, as were the vast hemicycle of the *cour d'honneur* and the compact symmetry of the whole design; but the internal planning of the wings belonged to the French tradition. It was an exemplary fulfilment of the Neoclassical ideal of a marriage between antique and modern architectural conventions.

However, at Montmusard De Wailly was setting himself up in opposition to official art and all its rules. In reckless defiance of the theories of Blondel, according to which the centre was to carry the main weight of the design, so that the importance of any element diminished in direct proportion to its distance from the centre, the centre here was dominated not by an *avant-corps* but by a void: the circular forecourt as a negative correlative to the Salon des Muses. The idea won general admiration, but Blondel never forgave his former pupil.

Construction began in 1765, and De Wailly entrusted the supervision to his own pupil Bernard Poyet; but a member of the president's circle, one Abbé Fabarel, took it out of Poyet's hands from the start and carried it on alone, so that the foundation stone does not even bear De Wailly's name. His protests were unavailing. The president was deeply in debt, and in 1772, one year after his death, the château had to be sold. In 1799 its new owner had it demolished, all but one tiny remnant.

De Wailly harked back to his design for Montmusard on two subsequent occasions: in the Temple of Minerva for Catherine the Great of Russia, and in the Temple of Diana for the Landgrave of Hesse. For her garden at Tsarskoe Selo, the Empress had expressed a desire to have a house in the antique manner, 'an abstract of the age and of the country of the Caesars and the Augusti' (*un résumé du siècle et du pays des Césars, des Augustes*). In 1772 De Wailly sent her his design, describing it as a *Palais des Sciences et des Arts*. This was Montmusard set on a rusticated podium, with large niches for the river gods of the Volga and the Neva, and a gigantic semicircular flight of steps up to the open colonnade, plus an attic storey with pitched roofs and bowl-like chimney pots such as he had already used in the gallery of the Hôtel d'Argenson. The open colonnade was dedicated to Minerva. The design for the Landgrave of Hesse is discussed below.

Another bravura performance that helped to make de

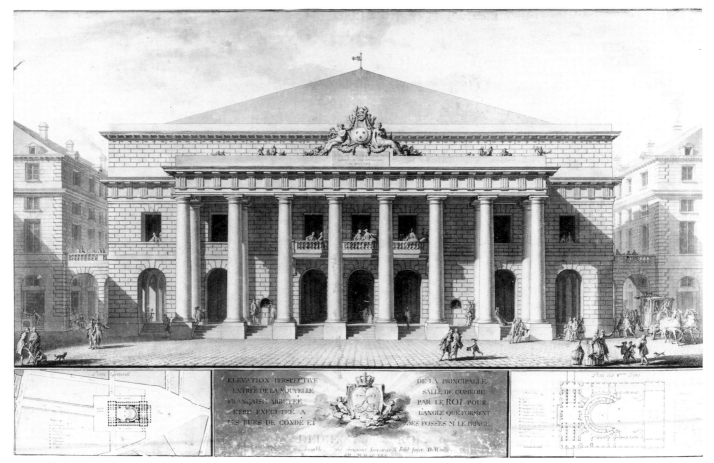

197   M.J. Peyre and Ch. de Wailly: Paris, Comédic Française, elevation, design, 1771 (Paris, Musée Carnavalet).

Wailly's name was the remodelling of the grand salon at Palazzo Spinola in Genoa – the former Palazzo Serra, by Galeazzo Alessi – for Marchese Spinola, Genoese Minister to the court of Versailles (1772–3). This was not a building commission, but the modernization of a large reception room that had hitherto been left as Alessi first designed it. Here, De Wailly proved himself to be both a brilliant decorator and a true pupil of Servandoni. He maintained to the hilt the principles of the Hôtel d'Argenson: the synthesis of the arts, the use of costly materials, the exploitation of mirror effects. Above a marble dado, fluted Doric three-quarter columns supported a massive entablature, on which in turn caryatids sustained a lofty vault containing a large oval ceiling painting depicting the apotheosis of the military commander Ambrogio Spinola. In an echo of the fantasies of Piranesi, the side walls were dominated by the Palladian motif of the *serliana*, repeated into infinity by the use of mirrors. This room, which had no direct precedents, was a masterpiece of Baroque stagecraft, which it combined with reminiscences of such antique imperial buildings as the Palace of Diocletian at Split. It very shortly became one of the sights of Italy, specially after de Wailly exhibited a suite of large drawings of it at the Salon of 1773 and subsequently published them in volume 7 (1777) of the *Encyclopédie*.

Domestic architecture did not form a major part of De Wailly's practice, but all his houses are remarkable for their originality. They included one for Voltaire, whom he had met on a visit to Ferney, one for his friend Pajou and one for himself. All had annular staircases, of the kind that he several times showed at the Salon. Voltaire's house, above all, was celebrated for its oval flying stair, similar to the one that De Wailly had built for Les Ormes, the château of his patron, Argenson. In his own house, too, he linked the tall *corps de logis* with the low street frontage not by a court but by a circular staircase that surrounded a colonnaded, temple-like rotunda with a fountain in the centre; it was surmounted by a skylight and a roof terrace. The rotunda was open to the street behind a columnar screen. The interlocking spaces thus created – the union between exterior and interior, circular temple and staircase, peristyle and interior spaces – are reminiscent of Baroque compositions. Pajou's house next door made comparable use of interlocking spaces: on the first floor of the façade was a large apsidal niche, deeply recessed and fronted by a terrace.

De Wailly's major work was the Comédie-Française, on which he worked in close collaboration with Peyre.[98] Here he touched on a central public theme. Never before had the theatre been so important as it was in the age of the Enlightenment; and, since Marigny's Italian tour and the publication of Cochin's *Voyage d'Italie* (1758) there had been a constantly growing interest in modern theatrical architecture. In 1768 the Academy set the design of a theatre as its Prix de Rome exercise.

The Comédie-Française was playing in a seventeenth-

century theatre by François d'Orbay that was now too small and too modest; the general enthusiasm for theatre-going that prevailed at the end of the Ancien Régime had led to a demand for a new, modern and comfortable playhouse on a grand scale. The construction of this became a national concern almost as momentous as that of Sainte-Geneviève. Initially, in 1763, Marigny wanted to engage Soufflot for this; he was too busy, though there is an unsigned and undated design in the Bibliothèque Nationale that is probably his: it combines a domed, colonnaded, rotunda with a rectangular stage block. There followed a succession of designs by other architects. But a decision was constantly deferred by the difficulty of finding finance and of securing the site, a process that involved not only the city of Paris but the Menus-Plaisirs, the players themselves and the owner of the chosen site, the Prince de Bourbon-Condé. These problems still confronted De Wailly and Peyre when Marigny put them in charge in 1767. Like Soufflot's theatre in Lyon, the new Comédie-Française was to become the nucleus of a whole new quarter of Paris; and this brought the property speculators onto the scene.

Peyre's and De Wailly's first design, of 1769, was based on a circle. The semicircular auditorium was preceded – as in the design attributed to Soufflot – by a semicircular façade. Short wings contained vestibules and, on either side, a café. Their second design, of 1770, which bore a marked resemblance to Poyet's prizewinning Academy design of 1768, took account of the intended enlargement of the public square and the desire for a larger foyer (Plate 197). For Marigny's benefit, De Wailly added a detailed commentary. The building had now become a compact oblong, with a tall slate roof, its antique austerity relieved only by a classical cornice. The ground-floor arcades to either side of the main entrance were intended for servants waiting for their employers; the intention, according to de Wailly, was to keep them out of the neighbouring taverns and billiard rooms. The temple-like façade, with its massive prostyle portico, had grown both in size and in dignity. Such a portico had been seen in theatre designs by Neufforge, but never actually built. Its Tuscan order was dedicated, in De Wailly's words, to Apollo as the protector of the arts; this reference was maintained in the sculptural group on the centre of the attic, a lyre flanked by the muses of Tragedy and Comedy. A pair of two-arched bridges led to the neighbouring buildings; this was to afford covered boarding and setting-down points for carriages, as well as a means of access to the cafés that were an essential social requirement of a modern theatre.

The project was beset by intrigues and speculative pressures. New proposals flooded in from all sides, including designs by Antoine and by Louis. In 1773, after Marigny's retirement, his short-lived successor, Abbé Teray, transferred both the planning and the execution of the work to Moreau-Desproux. Moreau moved the theatre to the opposite end of the Condé site, facing the Jardin du Luxembourg, and started to build.[99] In the following year – with De Wailly now in England – the finance minister, A.R.J. Turgot, halted the work because he wanted to build on the other side of the Seine. It was only after Turgot's fall that a new director-general of the Bâtiments du Roi, the Comte d'Angiviller, revived the project and re-engaged De Wailly and Peyre.

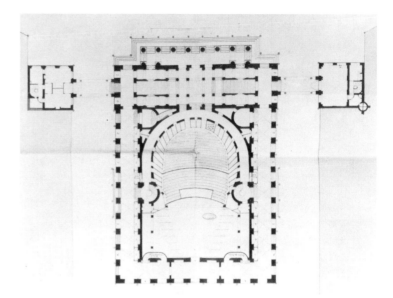

198   M.J. Peyre and Ch. de Wailly: Paris, Comédie Française (Odéon), 1779–82, plan (Paris, Bibliothèque de L'Histoire de la Ville de Paris).

Their third design, of 1779 (Plate 198), which maintained Moreau-Desproux's building site and involved only minor amendments to the interior, was the one actually built; and in three years it was finished. The new Comédie-Française opened with Racine's *Iphigénie* in April 1782.

With their Comédie-Française, Peyre and De Wailly had created a new theatrical prototype for the future. The exterior is a rectilinear block, with arcades on all sides and a portico dominating the square in front. In the third design, the auditorium, initially conceived as a circle, became an oval, with a slight narrowing at the proscenium. The giant columns in the proscenium were matched by giant piers that lined the auditorium and bore the load of the dome. Not a trace of gilding anywhere: the interior was white and grey throughout. For the first time ever, the pit was filled with seating. The receding balconies were divided into boxes only by dwarf partitions, and in the lowest tier these were absent altogether – an important step towards the undifferentiated seating systems of the future. The house was lit by a chandelier, which was raised and lowered through a large round opening in the ceiling. As De Wailly had pointed out in his commentary, this was customary in Italian theatres; but the similarity to the oculus of the Roman Pantheon was unmistakable.

The most important innovation was undoubtedly the way in which vestibule (Plate 199), stairs and foyer – hitherto treated as mere accessories – were formed into a self-contained ensemble. The façade was no longer simply tacked on to the auditorium, as in Soufflot's theatre in Lyon, but organically connected with it by way of the vestibule. A composition based on continuous axes welded the individual components into a larger unity. The portico led directly into a vestibule that formed a grand spatial sequence, unprecedented in any previous theatre: from a colonnaded ground-floor space with a central opening to the roof, wide stairs diverged to either end of the first floor, where promenades lined with columns led back to the central opening. There a great octagon of coupled columns supported a continuous

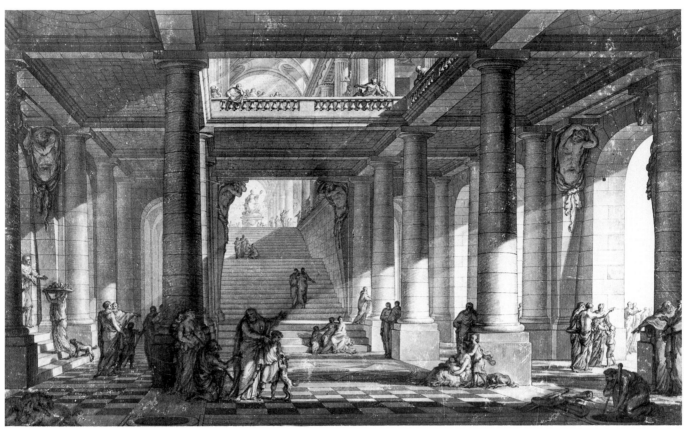

199 J.M. Peyre and Ch. de Wailly: Paris, Comédie Française, vestibule,
1771 (Paris, Musée du Louvre).

gallery, an arcade and a painted dome. The contrast between
the decorative virtuosity of this Baroque vestibule, which
De Wailly recorded in large, finished drawings and showed
at the Salon in 1781, and the classical austerity of the
exterior must have come as something of a shock to contemporaries.[100]

It will always remain difficult to distinguish between the
two architects' individual contributions to this building,
especially in view of the unusual unanimity of their ideas on
architecture. However, it is plausible to ascribe the spatial
planning and interior decoration to De Wailly, and the
austere, forward-looking, block-like exterior, 'the fine proportions and the fine masses' to Peyre – with each architect
working to moderate the other. Circumstances also combined to make De Wailly the more prominent partner: a
theorist and a brilliant draughtsman, he took sole charge
after Peyre's death in 1785.

In 1793, a plan to move the Opera to the new Comédie-
Française building led him to prepare some new designs,
including some conspicuous changes to the façade. Above
the main cornice he added a lofty, temple-like superstructure
with a central *serliana*; and in front of this, on the portico, a
pair of diminutive pavilions with segmental pediments. He
thus gave a historicist slant to Peyre's austere block. However, events took their course, and these designs remained
unexecuted.

The architecture of the Comédie-Française should not
cause us to overlook its place in the urban scene. It became

the focus of a radial street layout, on which, after years of
wrangling, agreement was finally reached in 1782, and then
only after the king's brother, the Comte de Provence – who
had taken over the Palais du Luxembourg and part of the
Hôtel de Condé site in 1779 – had taken a hand and
asserted his authority. In front of their theatre, Peyre and De
Wailly laid out a semicircle, which formed the centre of the
new quarter, and on which five streets converge. The lateral
arches fitted the theatre into the curve of the square, and the
axes of the incoming streets intersect not in the centre of the
square but at the proscenium. The inward form of the building thus radiates far and wide – an early instance of an intimate connection between architecture and urban planning.

De Wailly continued to interest himself in theatrical architecture. He submitted designs not only for the Théâtre des
Arts in Paris but also for the Théâtre de la Monnaie in
Brussels (1785–91) and the theatre in Strasbourg; and he
radically remodelled the structure and decoration of the
Comédie Italienne in Paris. In the park of the Château de
Seneffe in Belgium, he built a small theatre that still stands
to this day; from the outside it looks like a piece of garden
architecture, a landscaping *fabrique*, but inside it is complete
with a tiny square auditorium, two side rooms and a deep
stage flanked by perspectively foreshortened Doric colonnades. The absence of all ornament, the austerity of the
columns, and the unbroken whiteness of the walls, give the
building an uncommonly consistent, Palladian look that
anticipates the next stage of Neoclassicism.[101]

It is De Wailly's church buildings – all minor projects – that most clearly reveal the split in his artistic personality. In the Chapelle du Reposoir in Versailles, built as a resting-place for the Corpus Christi procession (1769), and in the crypt of Saint-Leu-Saint-Gilles in Paris (1780), the antique prevails: both are dominated by circular forms. The Reposoir has a rotunda of free-standing Ionic columns inside a temple-like, windowless cube, with a projecting, semicircular Doric portico and a dome.[102] The crypt of Saint-Leu-Saint-Gilles was intended to replace the demolished Chapelle du Saint-Sépulcre as a meeting-place for the Knights of the Holy Sepulchre; here, the ribs of the vault are borne by baseless Doric columns – the first in France.[103]

By contrast, De Wailly's lady chapel and pulpit at Saint-Sulpice are decidedly Baroque.[104] The chapel, with its decor by Servandoni, Lemoyne and the Slodtz brothers, had been damaged by the fire at the Foire Saint-Germain of 1762. De Wailly, who was recommended by Servandoni to undertake the restoration, gave it a completely new and Italianate look. He set a dome over the lofty entrance bay that led into the chapel from the choir ambulatory and put a new saucer dome into the chapel itself, with an oculus through which Lemoyne's restored ceiling fresco could be seen. The worshipper's attention is focused on Pigalle's figure of the Madonna, in its elaborate, columnar niche behind the altar, into which light falls from an unseen source (1774–8). This is the same principle that Bernini used in his *Ecstasy of St Theresa* in S. Maria della Vittoria and *Blessed Ludovica Albertoni* in S. Francesco in Ripa. The decoration, with its rich gilding, coloured sham marble, paintings, putti and plaster festoons, is among the richest in Paris, and its unveiling was greeted with equal measures of admiration and censure. De Wailly intended it as a kind of abstract of all the finest churches of the Roman Baroque.[105] The pulpit, too, which he built in the very last years of the Ancien Régime as a gift from the Duc d'Aiguillon (1788–9), is an astoundingly late manifestation of Bernini's influence in France. Iconographically and formally, it derives from the *Cathedra Petri* in Rome. This connection is clearly evident in a group of four sketches, dating from before 1781, that were discovered a few years ago in the Hermitage in St Petersburg. The key elements are the presence of the Fathers of the Church as supporters of the edifice of faith and the soaring lightness of the throne that they bear aloft. The idea gradually evolves, so that the scrolled feet of the original become steps, and the Church Fathers – still clearly present in the first sketch – give way to a pair of figures of Faith and Hope, seated on massive plinths. The prototype has thus been entirely absorbed; De Wailly has taken the given sculptural motifs and found his own way of translating them into architectural terms.

In the far south of the kingdom, De Wailly found himself confronted with an unusual urban planning task. In 1779 he was called to Port-Vendres, where work had begun on building a seaport and naval base in a large natural inlet.[106] He drew up a comprehensive development plan (1780), involving a grid street pattern in the shape of a semi-hexagon, fitted round two semicircular harbour basins, and with the principal intersections marked by public buildings; but this took no account of the lie of the land. What he actually built was

relatively insignificant: an esplanade, on a terrace above the harbour, intended as a Place Royale and centred on an obelisk adorned with bronze reliefs and surrounded by trophies on plinths.[107] In alignment with this, there was to be a chapel in the form of an antique temple, framed by tree-lined avenues; three years later, De Wailly replaced this with a large warehouse building on a U-shaped plan. The development of the town began in earnest – and virtually unregulated – in 1784, but by that time De Wailly was no longer involved.[108]

It was at this time that De Wailly's fame began to decline. His Baroque sympathies and decorative inclinations were utterly out of keeping with the austere rectitude of the 1780s. Finding few commissions in Paris, he concentrated on the many that still came flooding in from abroad. His most important client was Landgrave Frederick II of Hesse-Kassel, for whom he designed two new palaces: a replacement for the Stadtschloss in his capital, Kassel, and Schloss Weissenstein (now Wilhelmshöhe), above the city.[109]

For Weissenstein we have three detailed designs that are among the most important documents of Neoclassical château building. These are monumental ensembles of terraces, ramps and pools that rise to the palace itself, with a mountainside and the celebrated cascade as a backdrop. In its sequence of circular forms, this is a development of De Wailly's reconstruction of the Jerusalem Temple (1766), and reflects a knowledge of Fischer von Erlach's projects for Schönbrunn and for the palace of Frederick I of Prussia.

In his third design (Plate 200), De Wailly fronted his concave façade with a round court, a semicircular outer screen of columns and a central statue of Diana. This was the final transformation of Montmusard: from temple of Apollo and the Muses to temple of Diana. But here the relation between the circle of the court colonnade and that of the garden salon had changed: the court had grown and the salon had shrunk, so that from being spatial and iconographic equivalents they had become autonomous spaces.

One remarkable feature of this design was its rooftop theatre. In the second design, the theatre had filled one of the corners between semicircle and horseshoe; but the third was smaller, with no room to spare on the ground floor, so De Wailly put his theatre on the roof instead. The auditorium fitted inside the central dome, and the narrow stage – a repeat of the one at Seneffe, with its ranks of Doric columns – formed a rectangular excrescence that would have created a decidedly odd skyline. None of this was executed, as the Landgrave unexpectedly died in 1785, before the designs had even arrived in Kassel.

Of De Wailly's numerous projects in Belgium, none matched Kassel in importance. Most were small buildings of the pavilion type, schemes of interior decoration or garden structures, some at Seneffe, some at Laeken near Brussels, and others in the neighbourhood of Antwerp. A large château designed for the Duc d'Arenberg at Enghien (1782), with extensive grounds full of antique temples and *fabriques*, remained on the drawing-board, as did an 'Assembly Hall for Lovers of Liberty and Equality' (*Salle d'Assemblée des Amis de la Liberté et de l'Egalité*) for Brussels (1793), a tribute to the Revolution.

De Wailly's reputation also stood high in Russia. Aside

Coupe par le milieu du Temple de Diane, du grand Salon et du Théâtre

200 Charles de Wailly: Weissenstein, 1785, third project, section (Potsdam-Sanssouci, Schlösser- und Gartenverwaltung).

201 Jacques Gondoin: Paris, Ecole de Chirurgie, 1769–76, façade.

202 Jacques Gondoin: Paris, Ecole de Chirurgie, lecture hall (London, Courtauld Institute of Art).

from his villa design for Catherine the Great, which brought him an offer of the presidency of the Academy of Architecture in St Petersburg, and his designs for Kuskovo outside Moscow, the country seat of Count Sheremetev, his ideas found currency through the work of two of his pupils, Vasily Ivanovich Bazhenov and Ivan Yegorovich Starov.

Jacques Gondoin (1737–1818) was only a few years younger than Peyre, but he was far more radical in his views. A gardener's son from Choisy, he was trained by Blondel and subsequently – without winning the Prix de Rome – was sent to study in Italy for four years, under the king's personal patronage. In 1764 he entered the Service des Bâtiments and became inspector of furniture to the crown, officially responsible for designing furniture for the court cabinetmakers. This brought him into contact with Germain Pichault de la Martinière, the king's personal surgeon and a man of some influence; and in 1769, when the need arose for a larger replacement for the existing, seventeenth-century anatomy theatre (the Amphithéâtre de Saint-Côme), he secured the commission to build a new school of surgery. This, Gondoin's only building of note, is not only a milestone in stylistic evolution but a sign of the new status of surgery itself, which had now separated itself from medicine and

pharmacy to become a science and a subject of general interest in its own right.[110]

Gondoin's Ecole de Chirurgie (1769–79) is built like a nobleman's hôtel, around a *cour d'honneur* closed off on the street side by a double screen of paired Ionic columns and dominated by a massive hexastyle temple portico (Plate 201), behind which is the anatomy theatre, the heart of the building. A subsidiary lower order of Ionic columns runs round the court, and this flouts the rules by threading its way through behind the giant Corinthian order, so that the viewer is left uncertain as to the function of the portico. In the screen on the street side, Gondoin was harking back to the colonnaded courts of antiquity, but also aiming to make the rather shallow court appear larger than it really is, and to enhance the effect of the temple portico beyond. From the outset, he was criticized for using too many columns; he defended himself by pointing to the character of the school as a monument of royal munificence, and to the students who flocked to it from every land, and to whom it must be made open and accessible.[111]

The Ecole de Chirurgie was a declaration of war on the French tradition. In it, Gondoin has set out to realize his won conception of Greek architecture: contrast, symmetry and plainness. The contrast is largely provided by the relationship between the two orders and the buildings around the court; the symmetry lies in the planning of the interior; the plainness in the absence of all ornament. A further novel feature is the street frontage, which is dead straight, with no breaks either forward or back, and has a simple, continuous entablature without any architrave or subsidiary mouldings. Proportions are subordinated to a dominant horizontal; rhythmic accentuation and demarcation give way to endless repetition. Only in the centre of the screen does a set of relief panels, depicting the compassion and magnanimity of the king, furnish a hint of a triumphal arch.

The interior is a triumph of rationalism. At the centre is the anatomy theatre (Plate 202), the 'Temple of Aesculapius', as it soon came to be called. This is a cross between an ancient theatre and the Roman Pantheon. The seating, for 1200, rises in semicircular rows, affording everyone an adequate view of the dissecting table in the centre: a plan far superior to that of the earlier anatomy theatre, which is octagonal. Above the bare, unadorned walls rises a mighty, coffered half-dome; and, as in the Pantheon, the light enters from above through a central opening. The vast lunette formed by the entrance wall formerly bore a fresco showing the king encouraging Progress and rewarding Zeal.

Gondoin's spatial formula was a resounding success. First conceived for an anatomy theatre, this design was later taken up as a model for parliamentary debating chambers. It is the prototype of the Salle des Cinq Cents at the Palais Bourbon, and of the later National Assembly at the Luxembourg. Adjoining the theatre, and in the wings, were male and female hospital wards, a small lecture theatre for midwifery, an experimental laboratory, a chemical laboratory, and so on; on the first floor were a conference room, a room for the instrument collection, administrative offices and – in the range above the entrance screen – the library. The planning was novel and convincing. In spite of its positively shocking antitraditionalism, the Ecole de Chirurgie was unanimously

203 Jacques Gondoin: Paris, Ecole de Chirurgie, perspective view of forecourt (London, Courtauld Institute of Art).

hailed by the critics as an outstanding architectural achievement – even, indeed, as 'the classic monument of the eighteenth century'.[112]

In 1780 Gondoin published a far more extensive project (Plate 203), of which the Ecole de Chirurgie was to form only one part. Across an open square, it was to be confronted by a prison. For this embodiment of grim severity, Gondoin designed a cubic, almost windowless façade, with bare expanses of wall interrupted only by narrow bands of lettering and by a large central relief, beneath which a fountain in a large rectangular recess would discharge between baseless Tuscan columns. At one end of the square, the choir of the Franciscan friary church (the Cordeliers) was to be remodelled into a church of St Cosmas and St Damian, the patron saints of surgery, with a new façade by Gondoin, windowless and rusticated throughout, and a Doric portico. Gondoin explained that he intended this composition to convey an impression of utter solidity and public security: an early example of 'message' architecture, *architecture parlante*.

This plan was never carried out, but the intention itself is noteworthy. This was the first attempt to introduce an uncompromising rigour and absence of ornament, and to endow modern architecture with something of the expressive force that Piranesi had sought to capture in the architecture of antiquity. It thus went far beyond anything that had been thought of in the 1760s, and foreshadowed the utopian intransigence of the final decades of the century.

Though a near contemporary of the architects just discussed, Victor Louis (1731–1800) was never such a consistent champion of the antique. He can, however, be numbered among those whose work defined the look of French architecture in the second half of the eighteenth century.[113] Louis was a Parisian, but his practice was equally divided between the capital and Bordeaux, and it was in that city that he built his major work, the Grand Théâtre. He was a difficult character, cantankerous, arrogant and egotistic, and he made many enemies. As divided in his inclinations as de Wailly, he was his equal in generosity of planning and sense of decorative effect, though not in invention. While in Rome, on a study grant awarded in spite of his disqualification by the Academy, his arrogance lost him Marigny's favour and thus any prospect of a post in the Service des Bâtiments. But he had a marked talent for turning the social opportunities of his day – the Parisian salons, the clergy, Freemasonry – to his advantage and finding himself the right patron, so that he eventually far outstripped the court architects in importance.

In the salon of Madame Geoffrin, the twenty-three-year-old Louis came into contact with Stanislas II Poniatowski, the last king of Poland, who was making ambitious plans for his own palace, and who invited him to Warsaw. There, in 1765, the king commissioned him to design and furnish the official council chambers and also his own private apartments. The designs for these, most of which Louis prepared in Paris in 1766, had a decisive influence in bringing Neoclassicism to Poland. He built nothing for Stanislas II, but in the late 1770s he was still sending furniture and fittings for the palace, made in Paris to his specifications.[114]

204 Victor Louis: Besançon, Intendance, 1770–8, garden façade.

Like de Wailly, Louis had developed an interest in the Baroque during his years in Rome. An early sign of this was his design for the Warsaw palace forecourt, surrounded by colonnades derived from Bernini's at St Peter's; another is the still extant Chapelle des Pénitents, at Sainte-Elisabeth in Paris (c. 1764), where he enlisted Brunetti to paint a trompe-l'œil decor representing an antique basilica, complete with reliefs and marble statues in niches.

His first major commission, the Intendance in Besançon (1771–8), is another building that stands between tradition and Neoclassicism.[115] The Intendant of Franche-Comté, Charles-André de la Coré, was an enlightened spirit with a reputation for fostering art and literature, who was to employ Ledoux to build the Besançon theatre, and who took a lofty view of his own status. He had every intention that his official residence should express this; and so the Intendance is a building of some grandeur. At the front, the *cour d'honneur* swings out in a semicircle, which is entered through an bulky triumphal arch with Neoclassical trimmings. The *corps de logis* is articulated throughout by a continuous order of pilasters – a favourite motif of the architect's, which he uses in all his buildings to enhance the slender elegance of his tall, narrow window openings. In the court frontispiece, the pilasters give way to fluted, free-standing columns beneath a wide pediment; the result is a full temple façade, similar to that of Gondoin's contemporaneous Ecole de Chirurgie though more refined. The plan however centres on an oval salon that projects far out into the garden, like an anticipation of the Hôtel de Salm in Paris (Plate 204). The interior is coolly elegant. The oval salon has a pilaster articulation, with large mirrors and an antique-looking cornice. The window aprons of the garden front have delicate, carved laurel festoons, another hallmark of Louis's domesticated variety of Neoclassicism.

Deputing Nicolas Nicole to act for him in Besançon, Louis devoted his personal attention to his masterpiece, the Grand Théâtre in Bordeaux (1772–80). His patron was the Duc de Richelieu, whose town house he had remodelled in Paris (Chevotet had built the Pavillon de Hanovre in its grounds). As governor of Guyenne, the duke had his official residence in Bordeaux. There the old theatre had burned down in 1755, and plans for a replacement had been under discussion ever since. The duke went over the heads of the city councillors – who had engaged the local architect François Lhote – and called in Louis, who, supported by the duke, had just submitted an unsuccessful design for the Comédie-Française.

In 1773 Louis took his designs, prepared in the previous year, to Bordeaux, where they were approved by the duke and by the city council. His work there was made very much more difficult by a shortage of funds, by the rivalries between governor, Intendant and council, and not least by the hostility of the local architects – even though he had taken the precaution of appointing one of them, Bonfin, as his site architect. In 1774 the death of Louis XV and the resulting change of administration brought the undertaking to a total

halt. However, Louis eventually prevailed upon the new finance minister, Turgot, to authorize the resumption of work, on condition that the city council relinquished control of the theatre: a stipulation that was abandoned under Necker, a few years later. By 1776, when the Duc de Chartres officially laid the foundation stone, the building was well advanced and had become one of the sights of the city, shown to such distinguished visitors as the king's brothers or Emperor Joseph II of Austria. In 1780, two years before the Comédie-Française, the Grand Théâtre opened its doors; it was the grandest as well as the biggest theatre of the eighteenth century.

Externally, the Grand Théâtre is a free-standing monument, though without the antique, monolithic compactness of the Comédie-Française. The walls are pierced by windows and arcades; the individual forms are softer and more traditional. Along its lengthy side elevations, with arcades intended for shops, Louis has repeated the pilaster articulation of Besançon; but here it is prolonged to the point of monotony. The portico, too, follows the same principle of interminable repetition. It extends without additional emphasis across the entire façade and entirely lacks the tension of the portico by Peyre and de Wailly.

The real importance of the Grand Théâtre lies in its interior. This is made up of three units – concert room, staircase and theatre auditorium – which Louis has combined to magnificent, cumulative effect. The central focus is the staircase (Plate 205). A first flight on the main axis rises to meet a wall articulated with pilasters and statuary niches, between which a doorway flanked by caryatids leads straight ahead into the auditorium (originally into the city councillors' box). Dividing at the landing in front of this doorway, the stairs rise in a pair of matching flights to the colonnaded return galleries on either side of the central space; these lead to the concert room, which occupies the front of the building, above the vestibule. Above the staircase is a sail vault, and high up under its arched openings are more galleries, affording a glimpse of small relieving domes beyond. To build so opulent a staircase in a theatre was decidedly unorthodox; its general prototype was probably Gabriel's design for a monumental staircase for the Louvre. But Louis's own Warsaw staircase also contains much that is brought to maturity here: the placing of a staircase against a wall articulated by three entrances and two statuary niches; the central door framed by figures on plinths and a pediment, and surmounted by armorial bearings and trophies; and the rustication of the ground floor, a form of detailing otherwise reserved for exteriors. All these – though not the 'aisles' created by the flanking colonnaded galleries – were anticipated in the designs for Warsaw. The opulence and superb workmanship of the stairs, cornices and capitals is in perfect harmony with the splendour of the architecture.

The auditorium – which was to be entirely remodelled in the nineteenth century – was circular, and smaller than that of the Comédie-Française, but it employed a support system that was highly influential. A giant order, similar to that on

the external portico, ran round the entire space. The boxes projected strongly between the columns, but in such a way that the columns always remained visible. The boxes for the governor and for the Intendant, unlike their equivalents in Paris, were brought forward to the proscenium arch. The dome, again, was supported by a complex vaulting system, above four shallow crossing-arches, and buttressed by semi-domes with sail vaults. The vaulting of both the staircase and of the auditorium was a technical triumph that would have been inconceivable without a knowledge of Soufflot's vaulting system at Sainte-Geneviève.

The Bordeaux theatre was a challenge to de Wailly and Peyre; as a design the Comédie-Française took precedence, but Bordeaux was completed sooner. Nor were Louis's effects less powerful than De Wailly's. Even so, the two undertakings were different. In Bordeaux, the central feature is not the front-of-house area as a whole but the staircase. By concentrating so heavily on this and flanking it with galleries, Louis gave the audience an incomparable opportunity to see and be seen; the same need, already strong in Louis's day, was to prompt Charles Garnier, in his Paris Opéra, to follow the Bordeaux precedent. The Grand Théâtre marked a decisive turn in Louis's career, and in Bordeaux it led on to a large body of work that was to keep him in the city for many years.

Charles-Louis Clérisseau (1727–1820) occupies a special position in the architecture of the period.[116] After studying with Boffrand and winning the Prix de Rome, he arrived in the Eternal City in 1749. He was a *pensionnaire* of the Académie de France for five years and remained in Italy, paying his own way, for another thirteen. An intimate of Piranesi, he was friendly with Winckelmann and Cardinal Albani, and initiated Chambers, the brothers Robert and James Adam and Friedrich von Erdmannsdorf into the world of antiquity and the art of recording it in drawings. In the drawing of the antique, in antique ornament, and in the study of the great buildings of the Renaissance, he was Robert Adam's principal teacher. In 1757 he went with Adam to Split to survey the Palace of Diocletian, which Adam published under his own name in 1764 – without mentioning Clérisseau – as *Ruins of the Palace of the Emperor Diocletian at Spalato in Dalmatia*. His long residence in Rome, and his friendships and connections on every side, made Clérisseau into a key integrating figure in international Neoclassicism. His influence was extensive, and can be traced in the work of Chambers and of the brothers Adam, as well as in the decorative work of Erdmannsdorf at Wörlitz and of Charles Cameron at Tsarskoe Selo.

Clérisseau did not succeed in his intention of bringing out a new edition of Desgodets's *Les Edifices antiques de Rome* during his stay in the city, but he made a name for himself both as a painter of ruins and as a precise delineator of ancient buildings derived, not from reality, but from his own imagination. His painted decoration of the study cell of Père Le Sueur, at S. Trinità dei Monti, as a ruined antique temple (before 1767), became one of the sights of Rome and was several times imitated.

One echo of Clérisseau's studies of the antique was the publication, on Winckelmann's recommendation, of his survey of the Roman antiquities of Provence,[117] of which only

205 Victor Louis: Bordeaux, theatre, 1772–80, main staircase.

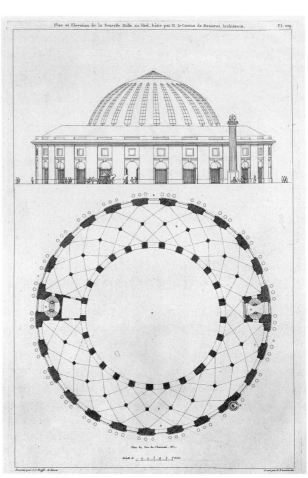

206 François-Joseph Bélanger: Paris, Pavillon de Brancas, 1769, façade (Paris, Musée des Arts Décoratifs).

207 Nicolas Le Camus de Mézières: Paris, Halle au Blé, 1763–6, plan and elevation.

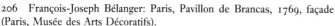

the first part, covering the monuments of Nîmes, appeared (1778). This accurate and substantial work is one of the most important products of the Roman revival.

In France, to which he returned in 1767, Clérisseau built little. His design for Château Borély in Marseille, dating from that year, was executed in a much-altered form by Esprit-Joseph Brun. In Metz, in 1778–9, he built the governor's palace (now Palais de Justice). This is a weighty, U-shaped building, articulated only by shallow projecting bays and massive cornices, and screened from the street by a wall as high as the ground floor. There is a touch of antique grandeur and austerity about the expanses of solid wall, adorned with historical reliefs. The large trophies on the projecting, sculptured porch are derived from Piranesi's engraving *Trophy of Octavian Augustus*.

Clérisseau's only architectural employment in Paris was as a consultant to François-Joseph Bélanger on the building of the so-called Pavillon de Brancas (Plate 206). This bath pavilion for the Comte de Lauraguais (later Duc de Brancas) was intended to be the acme of modernity; the result was a triumph of the antique. On Clérisseau's advice, Bélanger sent to Rome for a young sculptor, Nicolas-François Lhuillier, a pupil of Piranesi and Winckelmann. The Pavillon was built in the form of an antique temple, with an Ionic portico, reliefs and statuary niches; the portico was crowned, in Palladian style, with statues. Bélanger likened it to the temple

of Fortune Virilis in Rome, 'or one such as Palladio describes, which exists at Pola in Istria'. Inside there was no painted decoration except for the fresco in the dome. The circular salon that preceded the actual bath chamber was ringed by free-standing, coupled Ionic columns supporting a classical architrave; the intercolumniations, other than doorways, contained statuary niches and – in the upper zone – reliefs. The lunettes above the doors were occupied by allegorical figures and by heraldic medallions bearing the owner's initials.

Clérisseau sold his Italian drawings, more than a thousand of them, to Empress Catherine the Great of Russia, who rewarded him with an appointment as her chief architect. He had earlier sent her designs for a Roman House and for a triumphal arch for St Petersburg, which had vexed her by their excessive size and ponderousness. His designs for the Schloss in Weimar (1794), prepared in response to a personal request from Goethe, also remained unexecuted. His style had had its day.

The strong pull of antiquity was also felt by architects who had never been to Rome. The best example of this was the Halle au Blé (1763–6), the Paris corn exchange and the only major work of the otherwise obscure Nicolas Le Camus de Mézières (Plate 207).[118] It was built in the form of the Colosseum, in response to the growing desire to emulate Rome by erecting public buildings in the antique manner.[119]

This was the very purpose that it was to serve during the Revolution: a venue of the Fête de la Fédération in 1790, it subsequently became a republican amphitheatre, giving rise to constant references to its Roman prototype.

Built round a circular court, the Halle au Blé consisted of an annular arcade, two bays deep, to accommodate the retail trade, and an upper storey that was used for wholesale dealing and for storage. It was the first entirely circular secular building ever constructed in Paris. Le Camus's reasons were partly practical. His rotunda combined two traditional market formulas: the open marketplace surrounded by buildings and the covered market hall. One of his principal aims was 'to form two markets in one'; he also wanted to let light and air into a type of building that was generally regarded as unhealthy. Another innovation consisted in the two oval stairchambers, each with a double spiral stair to allow the simultaneous upward and downward movement of goods. This was an invention of Philibert de l'Orme's.

In the course of a few years, around the Halle au Blé, in the grounds of the former Hôtel de Soissons, there arose a new quarter of Paris, with streets in the radiating star pattern that had become familiar from the various Places Royales. The Halle au Blé itself soon turned out to be too small, and trade began to spread out of the covered market into the open court; as early as 1769, Le Camus was planning to cover the court with a dome. In 1782–3, after a competition in which Antoine and Rondelet also took part, and in which Bélanger – presumably as a result of his visit to England – proposed a cast iron dome, the court was roofed with a wooden dome by Jacques-Guillaume Legrand and Jacques Molinos that obviated the need to reinforce the existing annular building. It was based on an extraordinarily ingenious system of combining short horizontal timbers – another invention of de l'Orme's – and incorporated large sheets of glass, so that the rotunda was well lit. One of the architectural triumphs of its day, this dome turned the building into another Roman Pantheon. It was a sight that had to be seen by all foreign visitors – Thomas Jefferson called it 'the most superb thing on earth' – and there were numerous imitations,[120] from the circular salon of the Hôtel de Salm (1783), by Pierre Rousseau, to the Capitol in Washington, D.C. (1803), by Benjamin Latrobe.

CHAPTER 7

Domestic Architecture in Paris and the Early Work of Boullée and Ledoux

Private architecture in the second half of Louis XV's reign was dominated not so much by any strong evolutionary line as by the private tastes of its clients; as a result, it was far more disparate than official architecture. The structure of society was unchanged, and traditions died hard; even the most progressive client wanted *commodité* above all things. There was also the hiatus in building activity caused by the Seven Years War. The 1750s were largely a Rococo period, the last manifestations of which included the right-hand wing of the Palais-Royal, on the Rue de Valois side (1752–6), by Contant d'Ivry, and the Pavillon d'Hanovre (1757), built by Chevotet for a survivor of an earlier age, the Duc de Richelieu.

The first wave of the antique revival was largely a matter of interior decoration. In architecture the *style grec* did not appear until 1758, in the Greek key friezes and fluted pilasters of Trouard's house and Moreau-Desproux's Hôtel de Chavannes, combined in the latter case with decorative olive branches.[121] This period produced very little that has survived. The Seven Years War brought private building activity to an almost total standstill, and little of note was built until 1763.

When peace came at last, work began again with renewed vigour. After driving through Paris in the company of Soufflot in 1767, the Duc de Croÿ wrote: 'There was building in progress all over the city. It was clear that money was plentiful, and that the return of peace was greatly welcomed.' Encouraged by economic recovery, and by new legislation intended to protect clients from shoddy workmanship, Paris transformed itself into one vast building site. Cranes loomed on all sides, stone, timber and slates were landed all along the banks of the Seine, and massive wagons and stone-saws blocked the streets. To the west, the Faubourg Saint-Honoré merged into the Faubourg du Roule; to the north, the built-up area reached the Grands Boulevards; to the east, extensive blocks of houses sprang up around the Temple. In 1785, Sébastien Mercier estimated that one-third of the buildings in Paris were less than thirty years old.

This new start coincided with the second wave of the antique revival.[122] The running dogs and Greek-key friezes of the *style grec* were supplemented by such antique and Palladian elements as the columnar portico, the strict Doric doorway and the window pediment. The exterior of the Pavillon de Brancas (Plate 206), by Bélanger (1771), was a model of Neoclassicism. It changed the familiar look of domestic architecture. Expansive form gave way to cubic compactness; the central pediment vanished, to be replaced in many cases by a simple acroterion bearing the owner's coat of arms; and the taste for giant orders established itself, not only for churches but – in defiance of Blondel – for private houses as well. Relief panels played a special part. As a decorative element of antique origin, these had emerged as part of the *style grec*, and they soon invaded the façades of houses. Blondel put it vividly in his *Cours d'architecture*: 'Some years ago, an architect of taste introduced panels above the windows of a public building, in which he placed figures in relief. This was intended to catch on, and so it did. In six months, Paris was full of it.'

Meanwhile, ground plans became simpler and less restless. Polygonal rooms disappeared, and only the oval maintained its popularity. There was an increasing use of circular rooms, derived from the Roman baths.

Among the architects of the day, Boullée and Ledoux deserve pride of place, although numerous others – among them, notably, Cherpitel, Celerier and Brongniart – were involved in the remodelling of Paris. For all of them, the prime objective was to revive not so much the antique as the classical good taste of the previous century. It was an age of reaction. In this, they were entirely in tune with official architecture. Until well into the 1770s, the perceived incompatibility between *grandeur* and *commodité* led to a certain mistrust of Palladianism in domestic architecture; and so Boullée never quoted directly from Palladio until 1774, at the Hôtel de Brunoy.

Etienne-Louis Boullée (1728–99) was one of the most notable figures of the late eighteenth century. As a pupil of Blondel and Legeay, he initially came to the fore as a reformer of 'good taste' – of the classical tradition, that is. But after some years of this he gave up his private practice and concentrated on making designs for public buildings (opera house, library, museum) on the monumental scale that became fashionable under Louis XVI. Finally, after 1784, he turned his back on tradition to become the champion of what has since become known as 'revolutionary architecture'; some of the grandest projects in this vein are his, and these, above all, have been the source of his subsequent reputation.[123]

Boullée's early work has only recently been investigated, and it turns out that he holds an important place in the architectural history of the Parisian hôtel. Initially he wanted to be a painter, but his father insisted that he leave the studio of his teacher, Jean-Baptiste Pierre, a future chief painter to the king, and change over to architecture. Boullée was torn between painting and architecture for the rest of his life; and this influenced his architectural vision, as manifested in his late book, the *Essai sur l'art*. His practice was relatively small; according to his biographer, Villar, this was because of his unbending probity in dealing with his clients. His true vocation was teaching. To his students at Blondel's Ecole des Arts, where he taught from an early age – they included Chalgrin, Brongniart, Girardin, Crucy and Durand – he was a devoted and popular teacher and ally. In the dissemination of his ideas, he showed himself to be one of the great architectural theorists of the eighteenth century.

In official architecture Boullée never made his mark. In the competition for the Hôtel des Monnaies he was defeated by Antoine, in that for the remodelling of the Palais Bourbon he was defeated by Barreau de Chefdeville. His tenure of office as Contrôleur des Invalides (from 1778) and at the Ecole Militaire (from 1780) was brief; he resigned both posts in 1782. His ecclesiastical contribution – the decoration of the Chapelle du Calvaire at Saint-Roch, jointly with his former teacher, Pierre – was of no significance. But in hôtel building he was highly successful, and showed himself as an inventive architect, with imagination and taste, and with never a hint of the gargantuan scale of his late designs. It was with Boullée that the giant order began to prevail over the division of elevations into storeys.

His success began with the remodelling of the Hôtel de Tourolles in 1762, which established his reputation as a reformer of taste. He articulated the walls of the grand salon with fluted Ionic pilasters, linked by arches – an old motif of J.H. Mansart's that Contant d'Ivry had revived, minus the arcading, at the Palais-Royal. Above the garlanded capitals was a cornice with a narrow frieze of entwined laurel leaves; the overdoors and ceiling vault were adorned with paintings. In the court, de Machy had painted a perspectival view of a colonnade with a triumphal arch.[124] This decorative scheme was much admired; it earned Boullée his membership of the Academy and set his style for the next ten years.[125]

At the Château de Chaville (c. 1764), for the Comte de Tessé, the system took on its definitive form. The square salon was articulated by a blind arcade, with three bays to each wall, separated by ceiling-high Ionic pilasters and enclosing richly moulded doors, windows and mirrors. Above the narrow cornice was a painted ceiling vault. The exterior of this now-vanished building – or at any rate its court façade – is reproduced in the contemporaneous (and still surviving) Hôtel Alexandre in Paris. At Chaville, four giant Ionic columns, with shafts fluted only in the upper two-

thirds of their height, formed an open portico, with round-arched doors on the ground floor and carefully profiled rectangular openings on the first floor. Above the lateral doors were oval medallions with garland ornaments, a motif derived from Gabriel. The flat roof terrace was surrounded by a balustrade that was interrupted on the court side by an attic with festoons in relief. The windows inside the portico, too, were surmounted by reliefs. On the garden side, by contrast, the top floor was present in full, and giant pilasters articulated the second and third floors. An elegant festoon motif above the windows formed a common feature of both elevations.[126] In these early buildings of Boullée's the influence of Gabriel is unmistakable.

In the Hôtel de Monville (1764), which formed part of a complex of hôtels to the west of the Madeleine, the hallmarks of Boullée's style, as exemplified at Chaville and in the Hôtel Alexandre, were fully developed (Plate 208): the

208 Etienne-Louis Boulée: Paris, Hôtel de Monville, 1764, garden façade, engraving by Sergent et Guyot.

209 Etienne-Louis Boullée: Paris, Hôtel de Brunoy, 1774.

210 Claude-Nicolas Ledoux: Paris, Café Militaire, 1762, wall decoration (Paris, Musée Carnavalet).

211 Claude-Nicolas Ledoux: Paris, Hôtel d'Hallwyl, 1766–8, court, section, engraving by Ledoux.

212 Claude-Nicolas Ledoux: Paris, Hôtel d'Uzès, 1768–9, court façade.

cour d'honneur was flanked by long, narrow side wings, one of which contained the main entrance. Once more, the grand salon was a composition in triple time, with a painted ceiling vault. The garden front had an open ground-floor arcade with narrow, creeper-clad wings, which seemed to reach out and merge with their surroundings, its central giant portico bore a stepped, pyramidal temple roof surmounted by a statue of Flora, a compliment to the lady of the house.

The garden dropped away in a succession of terraces to the Champs-Elysées. Boullée had made such skilful use of his confined space, by planting trellises and lowering the level of the front rows of trees, that the 'Temple of Flora' arose like a vision from its setting of greenery; passers-by invariably stopped dead in their tracks. The symbiosis of house and garden which Boullée always pursued, and which he had tried to achieve through his English gardens at Chaville and the Hôtel d'Evreux, was here accomplished. In the temple form of the house, with its pyramidal roof, he was drawing upon antique motifs for the first time, surely influenced by Soufflot's temple-like design for the dome of Sainte-Geneviève (1764). The ultimate source was the Mausoleum of Halicarnassus, which remained a recurrent motif throughout the eighteenth century. The Hôtel de Brunoy marked the end of Boullée's career as a builder of town houses. His designs for public buildings, and his utopian inventions, will be considered in the following chapter.

The most creative spirit in hôtel building was the young Claude-Nicolas Ledoux (1736–1806). There is a tendency to see this audacious innovator exclusively as the creator of revolutionary architecture – all the more so since that was precisely how he wanted to be seen.[127] In reality, however, there were two faces to Ledoux. For nearly two decades he was the pampered, fashionable architect of Paris society, with an inimitable gift for reconciling tradition with the innovations of the day. It was only later that he shifted onto the monumental and utopian plane that he was to share with Boullée.[128]

Ledoux came from Champagne and studied under Blondel and Trouard. He never went to Italy, but probably derived his knowledge of Palladio and the antique from Trouard. In his youth he worked as a civil engineer for the state forestry authorities and built bridges and village churches in Burgundy: an activity to which he attached no particular importance. In 1762 he made a spectacularly successful Parisian debut by designing the interior of the Café Militaire (Plate 210). In this coffee house, principally frequented by officers, he lined the walls with mirrors and trophies and set up bundles of pikes entwined with laurels and surmounted by plumed, serpent-crested helmets – for all the world as if this had been a camp, where warriors returning from the field had stacked their victorious arms.

monumental frontispiece with its dominant attic and giant portico, the row of French windows on the ground floor with no central emphasis, the entresol windows blocked by relief panels, the roof terrace with its balustrade. The plan eliminated many of the secondary rooms that had once been such a highly praised feature of hôtel building. The Hôtel de Monville was celebrated for its exotic luxury. One salon was fitted out as a *bosquet* or grove, another as a windowless Turkish saloon, lit from above and furnished exclusively with ottomans and mirrors. The doors slid back into the walls at the touch of a button.

Of the considerable body of work that Boullée did for the wealthy tax farmer and banker Beaujon, at the Hôtel d'Evreux (now the Palais de l'Elysée) and at Issy, little has survived. At the Hôtel d'Evreux, where he rebuilt the left-hand court wing – the Petits Appartements – and replaced parts of the decor of the reception rooms, there are still a few overdoors, mirror frames and door leaves that bear witness to his activity. They are couched in a delicate, almost Rococo classicism, without a hint of the antique.

Boullée's masterpiece in this vein was the Hôtel de Brunoy (Plate 209), which he built in 1774; his client, a friend of Madame du Barry's, was the wife of the lunatic Marquis de Brunoy. Here Boullée's pictorial gifts came to the fore. He transformed the narrow site, which faced the Champs-Elysées, into a front garden from which the house rose like a temple. It formed a compact block; on the far side a deep

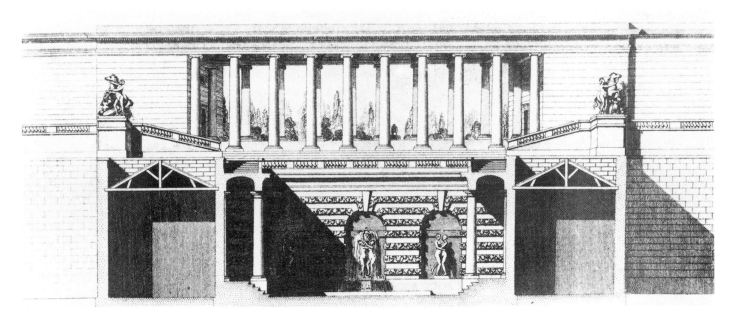

Ledoux was an engaging young man with excellent manners, and soon found his way into the very highest Parisian circles; it was not long before major commissions began to come his way. His first houses – the Hôtel d'Hallwyl (1766–8) and the Hôtel d'Uzès (1768–9) – still reveal his dependence on Blondel in such features as the subtle use of recession on the façades, the alternation of smooth walls and rustication and the use of round-headed windows. His occasional references to seventeenth-century classicism are also the fruits of his schooling with Blondel; examples include the doorway of the Hôtel d'Uzès, which was based on the Porte de Saint-Denis ('the prime miracle of our architecture', according to Blondel), with trophy-hung columns in place of the obelisks of the original.

In the garden behind the Hôtel d'Hallwyl, Ledoux strikes a fresh note: the open Doric colonnades on either side stem from the Neoclassical repertoire (Plate 211). Not long previously, Barreau de Chefdeville had created a similar atrium-like court in the nearby Folie de l'Intendant Boutin.[129] Ledoux went on to have the wall of the Carmelite convent across the street painted with a prospect of an antique colonnade with a garden beyond, so that the painted vista combined with the real colonnades to create the image of an antique court.

In remodelling the Hôtel d'Uzès, for which Cherpitel and Rousset had already submitted designs, Ledoux used giant orders for the first time: four Corinthian columns on the court side (Plate 212) and six fluted Ionic pilasters on the garden side, beneath an attic adorned with six life-size statues. This suggests the influence of Neufforge, in whose *Recueil* Ledoux would have found the giant orders, unpedimented porticoes, statues in the attic and windows without surrounds that he used here. Successive designs for this building record his gradual swing away from Blondel and towards Neufforge;[130] and he consequently found himself in trouble with Blondel, the implacable champion of the Mansartian system, who considered the giant order 'absurd', dismissed the magnificent and widely admired gateway as a lift from Contant d'Ivry, and denounced his former pupil for offences against convention, proportion and the elevated style.[131] The novel, tall panels of the salon (now in the Musée Carnavalet), which run from floor to ceiling unbroken by a dado moulding, along with the equally grand door panels with their allegories of the four continents, are among the most significant works of the period. In the motif of trees hung with trophies, Ledoux shows himself capable of an unconventional freshness and inventiveness unmatched since Oppenordt.

Ledoux's other great exemplar was Gabriel, whom he both admired and imitated. He regarded the elevations of the Place Louis-XV as the truest embodiment of the spirit of French architecture, although he also considered that the detailing was too minute for a distant view. His indebtedness is apparent in numerous details, such as the fluting of columns and pilasters, the delicate mouldings and dentils, the window balustrades, and the contrast between flat wall and vigorous articulation. Ledoux went further by turning the smooth walls, which Gabriel had used as a background, into positive architectural forms in their own right – as Peyre had done in the Hôtel de Neubourg – and cutting his window openings out of them without cornices or pediments.

He paid his last tribute to Gabriel in the Hôtel de Montmorency (1769–71), with its columnar frontispieces derived from the corner pavilions of the Place Louis-XV. Built on a corner site, and certainly conceived in full knowledge of Potain's theatre design of 1763, this house had two façades at right angles to each other (Plate 213). The main entrance was on the canted corner between them, with a heraldic cartouche at roof level. The court and domestic offices were behind the house. The plan was based on a

213 Claude-Nicolas Ledoux: Paris, Hôtel de Montmorency, 1769–71, façade.

214 Claude-Nicolas Ledoux: Bénouville, (*left*) court façade, 1770–3; (*opposite*) engraving by Ledoux *c.* 1785.

diagonal, so that the house seemed larger than it really was. On the ground floor, the diagonal axis led from the gateway through a circular lobby (from which carriages could proceed through a direct passage to the court) and on into an oval vestibule. The upper diagonal led back from the second antechamber in the far corner, through the oval first antechamber, to the circular salon above the entrance lobby. The reception rooms lay along the street frontages, so that their axes intersected in the circular salon. In the Hôtel de Montmorency, with its twin façades and its ingenious planning, in which no two rooms were alike, Ledoux had succeeded in creating a princely dwelling on a confined site; it was the making of his career.

An important turning point came with Ledoux's visit to England, which took place at some time during the period 1769–71. There he encountered English Palladianism and realized the challenge that it presented to Blondel's system. Without exactly imitating the style, he took from it the use of simple solids (cubes, half-cubes, cylinders), unfluted columns, sparing ornamentation and contrasts of light and shade. This lent his buildings dignity and monumentality, whether they were villas – the diminutive, temple-like pavilion in the Rue Saint-Lazare, the Pavillons Tabary and Guimard, Madame du Barry's Pavillon de Louveciennes – or châteaux, such as Bénouville. There can be no doubt that Palladianism suited his inclinations; this is manifest already in his borrowings from Neufforge. In one of his earliest works, the Pavillon Hocquart (1763–5), he had probably based himself on Atherton, a country house by William Wakefield that was published in the *Vitruvius Britannicus*; its plan however was an allusion to that of the Villa Rotonda.[132] But now there could be no more imitations of this kind. From this point on, the example of Palladio's own architecture stimulated him to compose not so much with individual forms as with the relationships between solids and surrounding space.

This is already evident in the Château de Bénouville, in Normandy (1770–3), which is based on the design of the Hôtel d'Uzès but is more massive and hard-edged through-

out (Plate 214a). The portico on the court side rises through three instead of two storeys; a tall, full-width attic lends a strong horizontal emphasis; and the towering giant orders, front and back, do not support pediments – as in Ledoux's early, Gabriel-influenced Château de Monfermeil – but straight entablatures. The court frontispiece is surmounted by a big heraldic cartouche; that on the garden side by an array of trophies, one above each pilaster, which allude to the owner's nautical interests by combining prows of ships with 'waving plumes and splendid arms and accoutrements'. On the central axis is one of the earliest and grandest of all Neoclassical staircases. Articulated with Ionic columns alternating with aedicules and surmounted by a lofty, coffered vault, it rises to the full height of the building.

At Bénouville, more than anywhere, it is easy to trace how radically, in his later years, Ledoux was to distance himself from his early work. In the engravings he prepared for publication, the façades lose their relief, and the attic shrinks into a bare block; the court frontispiece no longer breaks forward in two stages but displays a uniform rank of freestanding columns that have lost the elegant garlanding of their capitals (Plate 214b). Even the armorial cartouche has disappeared, so that the building becomes anonymous and historically meaningless. All references to living or 'Baroque' architecture have been eliminated. The craving for purity has led to sterility.

The 1770s were years of rapid professional advance for Ledoux, leading him from villas to the Saline de Chaux and to Besançon. It was his villas, above all, that made his reputation in Parisian society. They shared one common feature: an open, half-domed vestibule, recessed niche-like into the façade behind a screen of columns. This motif was derived from antiquity; it was the apse of the Roman baths, as published by Neufforge. It was a stroke of genius on Ledoux's part to transpose this into a façade. Presumably, inspired by Ledoux's engraving, an engineer pupil of Blondel's, François Lecreulx (1734–1812), used it for the façade of the church at Badonviller (1783).

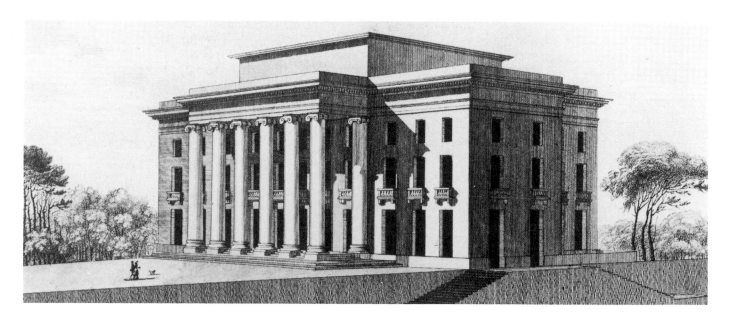

215 Claude-Nicolas Ledoux:
Paris, Pavillon Guimard, 1770–2,
engraving by van Cleemputte
(Paris, Musée Carnavalet).

216 Claude-Nicolas Ledoux:
Louveciennes, Pavillon de
Madame Dubarry 1770–1, water-
colour (London, British Library).

The motif appears three times in Ledoux's work. At the Pavillon Tabary (1770–3), for which he had originally intended a giant prostyle portico, the niche culminated in a recessed *serliana*, a motif rendered fashionable by Soufflot's use of it on Marigny's house. According to a drawing by Chambers, which conflicts with Ledoux's later engraving, the Pavillon Tabary had a pyramidal roof, its walls were not rusticated, and the spandrels of the *serliana* were unornamented.

The Pavillon Guimard (1770–2), by contrast, was more original (Plate 215). Marie-Madeleine Guimard was a celebrated dancer at the Opéra and the Comédie-Française, and princes and prelates frequented her house. Ledoux glorified her as Terpsichore, the Muse of the Dance; inspired by Robert Adam and the designs of Neufforge, he placed a group of *Terpsichore Crowned by Apollo* in the lunette of the frontispiece and displayed behind the screen a relief seven metres long of *The Triumph of Terpsichore*. The house was entered through a diagonally placed oval antechamber to the right of the porch. The dining room communicated, through a columnar screen, with a large winter garden; both were lit by skylights and lined with columns. In the intercolumniations were mirrors, painted to show a wooded landscape beyond a balustrade.

One particular attraction of the Pavillon Guimard was the miniature theatre in which the lady of the house danced for her guests. Ledoux built this above the *porte-cochère*, stables and carriage houses, in imitation of the theatre at Cramayel-en-Brie, which he had seen in the early part of his career. Like other private theatres of the period – Seneffe, Drottningholm and others – it had an auditorium ringed with a colonnade, in the manner of Palladio's Teatro Olimpico. It opened to a distinguished audience on 8 December 1772.

Ledoux's greatest success was the Pavillon de Louveciennes (Plate 216), which he built for Madame du Barry in the incredibly short space of nine months. It was the apex of his career. As he wrote later: 'I was universally known; I was at the height of popularity.' Madame du Barry made her court debut as the new royal favourite in 1769;[134] Ledoux had met her through the Montmorency family. As her residence, the king had given her the small Château de Louveciennes; her new Pavillon, not far from the house itself, was intended purely for receptions. De Wailly as well as Ledoux had been engaged to submit a design for this; where Ledoux placed his entrance niche, de Wailly proposed an open, colonnaded rotunda, as at Montmusard.

On the exterior, Ledoux used the same system as at the Pavillon Guimard, but improved the proportions by omitting the attic; he added dignity to the garden front with a giant portico and reliefs above the windows. The inside was on a kingly scale. The central axis was fully developed. Behind the porch was a transverse oval dining room, which led into the square Salon du Roi, with a magnificent view over the valley of the Seine. This was flanked by two other salons, elliptical on the left and apsidal on the right. Variety was all; no two rooms were alike. The central dining room was lined by pilasters with gilded capitals; between them were large mirrors and above them reliefs. Beneath a painted ceiling were little boxes for musicians. The salons were decorated with tapestries, mirrors and a cycle of paintings by Fragonard on the theme of Pastoral Love, which embodied transparent allusions to the mistress of the house. The banquet held in the presence of the king on 2 September 1771 to celebrate the completion of the house was recorded by Moreau-le-Jeune.

There is much to be learned about the evolution of taste from a comparison between the Pavillon de Louveciennes and its counterpart at Versailles, Gabriel's Petit Trianon, which was begun about ten years earlier. Louveciennes was more angular and replete with contrasts; there were no gentle transitions. The columns contrasted with the bare wall surfaces, into which the windows were set without surrounds. Relief panels appeared in the positions occupied at the Petit Trianon by mezzanine windows; and the relationship between wall and fenestration had changed throughout. The solid wall prevailed. The elements of articulation were fewer and had become detached from each other, as if spaces had formed around them. In its combination of austerity and luxury, antique form and French taste, the Pavillon de Louveciennes was an evolutionary milestone.

Ledoux's fame was at its height. Such was the press of curious visitors that no one could be admitted without a ticket signed either by Ledoux or by the Intendant of the Pavillon. The two circular temples in the grounds, which copy English models – one based on Sir John Vanbrugh's temple at Stowe, the other on Chambers's Temple of Aeolus at Kew – are believed to be the earliest circular temples in France; only the former is a documented work by Ledoux.

The Pavillon de Louveciennes has had a sorry fate in the twentieth century, and it now exists only in the form of a distorted copy.[135] However, it would have vanished from sight long since if only Louis XV had lived longer; for it would have been integrated into the left-hand terminal pavilion of the new Château de Louveciennes, which Ledoux designed for Madame du Barry and started to build in 1773. In this project, which was called off after the king's death in 1774, he returned to the atmosphere of Versailles, maintaining the pavilion system and the traditional set-back mansard roofs with gilded lead ornaments.[136] For the façades, the Pavillon de Louveciennes provided the module. It was repeated in the right-hand pavilion; for the centre pavilion Ledoux increased the number of columns from four to six. The increased depth of the new château made it necessary to double the ground area of the pavilion and abandon the niche-shaped porch; and so it became the apartment of the châtelaine herself. In the corresponding right-hand pavilion he installed a theatre. The centre was originally taken up by a circular hall and a walled garden later transformed into a grand salon. The connecting ranges, of which the left-hand one contained the apartment of the king, were fronted on the court side by the colonnades that are a common feature of Palladian villas.

Very traditional in appearance, with its pedimented portico surmounted by a central dome, the little Château de Saint-Vrain was designed by Ledoux for Madame du Barry after her banishment from court; he subsequently engraved and published it, though it is highly questionable whether it was ever built. The palace that he projected for her in Paris, with its positively orgiastic profusion of columns, also remained on paper.

The only building of Ledoux's for Madame du Barry that has survived is a group of buildings in Versailles that was intended to house her household and stables: the Hôtel des Equipages (1773). It consists of four ranges round a court, containing carriage houses and harness rooms, and a yard beyond containing the stables and a horse pond. The street façade is devoid of ornament except for a richly worked, quasi-antique cornice. Its central accent is a monumental gateway in the form of a recessed *serliana*, as used by Ledoux shortly before in the Pavillon Tabary. Here, however, the lunette is filled in with an armorial cartouche and the spandrels with reliefs of centaurs. In the building as it stands, the rustication of the flanking wall-piers is merely hinted at; in the subsequent engravings it is fully elaborated and indeed coarsened.

Next to this carriage and stable block stood the Hôtel de Binet, which Madame du Barry had acquired, and Ledoux incorporated this into the composition by placing a *cour d'honneur* between the two and repeating the façade of the Hôtel Binet, complete with portico, on the facing wing of the Hôtel des Equipages. The far end of the court was to be occupied by a menagerie, which Ledoux had planned in the form of a colonnaded rotunda inscribed in a square; this, however, was never built.[137]

217 Mathurin Cherpitel: Paris, Hôtel du Châtelet, 1770, courtyard façade.

In 1775 Ledoux took up an invitation from Landgrave Frederick II of Hesse-Kassel, who had admired the Pavillon Guimard on a visit to Paris, and travelled to Kassel. There he was appointed surveyor-general and – to the great annoyance of the court architect, Simon-Louis du Ry – entrusted with the design of a triumphal arch for a new square, the Friedrichsplatz, and of a library building, the Museum Fridericianum. The arch (1775), intended as a monument to the Landgrave himself and bearing the inscription 'Federico Secundo', took the form of a *serliana*, similar to that of the Pavillon Tabary. Its wide piers, like the façade of the Karlskirche in Vienna, were fronted by a pair of triumphal columns, and it was flanked by double colonnades with terminal pavilions. The Museum had already been begun by Du Ry, and it must have been a cruel affront to him to see his plans altered by Ledoux. However, the latter's design (1776) came too late to make much difference to the façade. He replaced Du Ry's lightweight roof balustrades with a heavy attic and crowned this with a lantern in the form of a tempietto, to illuminate the dark first-floor salon. The grand staircase at the rear harked back to the model of Bénouville. However, none of this was executed, and Du Ry paid very little heed to Ledoux's proposed amendments of detail.[138]

Lastly, we come to a body of work that stands very much apart: that of Mathurin Cherpitel (d. 1809). In his buildings, the giant order is combined with the older hôtel type. Cherpitel, who had won the Prix de Rome in 1757, first attracted Marigny's attention in 1758 – just like Chalgrin – with a pavilion design that came remarkably close to that finally adopted by Gabriel for the Petit Trianon. He became the architect to the great aristocratic families of the Faubourg Saint-Germain, who clung to the habits and forms of the past, defying the Neoclassical trend. And so, at the Hôtel du Châtelet (1770; now Ministry of Labour), the Hôtel de Rochechouart (1778; now Ministry of Education) and the Hôtel d'Harcourt he built richly articulated garden fronts in the style of the Régence. On the court side of the Hôtel du Châtelet (Plate 217), on the other hand, Cherpitel used his own rejected design for the Hôtel d'Uzès to create one of the most imposing façades of the day, with a giant order of four Corinthian columns, applied to a traditional elevation – complete with round-headed windows below and square-headed windows above – and displaying, with their smooth shafts, Cherpitel's admiration for the Roman façades of Carlo Maderna and Alessandro Galilei. At the Hôtel de Rochechouart, a giant order of pilasters lines the concave U of the façade. In both cases, as also at the Hôtel d'Andlau, the giant order is surmounted by a massive cornice, and the second floor is treated as a continuous attic.

These hôtels were equally traditional in their planning: the reception rooms in an enfilade, a spacious staircase leading off the vestibule, a variety of room shapes. Cherpitel became a member of the Academy of Architecture in 1776, and in 1801 he became a professor at its successor institution, the Ecole Nationale d'Architecture.

CHAPTER 8

Neoclassical Church Architecture

The *philosophes* were only partly successful in their campaign against the Church. In Paris, atheism and total indifference to religion became widespread; but in the provinces the religious faith of the masses remained largely intact, and church building went on unabated until the demise of the Ancien Régime. The most active regions were the northern and eastern provinces – and, indeed, the environs of Paris itself.[139]

In church façades, the traditional pattern of superimposed orders survived until the late 1760s. In Paris a straight line runs from Saint-Roch, by way of the Oratoire (1745) and the Temple des Billettes (1756), to Saint-Thomas d'Aquin (1769–70) – with a perceptible weakening of sculptural force on the way. In every detail, the design for Saint-Thomas d'Aquin by a certain Frère Claude is steeped in the spirit of the Mansart school. Outside the capital, a number of large ecclesiastical buildings perpetuate the Baroque mobility of Saint-Roch: among them are Langres Cathedral (1761–8), by Claude-Louis Daviler; Notre-Dame, Guebwiller (1766), by Beuque; and Saint-Vincent, Metz (1768–86), by Claudius Barlet, Victor Louis and Nicolas Lhuillier. Here the Baroque survives in the accumulation of columns and sculptural details, and in the projections and recessions that generate a play of light and shade.

The call for a change of formula came first from the traditionalist camp. In 1755 Patte published an article in the *Mercure de France* in which he criticized the traditional Italianate façade for its division into storeys and called for it to be replaced by a giant order modelled on the temples of antiquity; as he wrote this, Alfieri, the architect of the Turin Opera, was at work on the portico of Geneva Cathedral, with its six Corinthian columns (1752–6). Patte's own ideal design of a hexastyle portico for Saint-Eustache in Paris (c. 1754), probably conceived in full knowledge of the Geneva portico, still bore many Baroque features, but it was the first illustration of this idea. A conclusive example was then set by Soufflot's portico of Sainte-Geneviève, in which contemporaries were not slow to detect a similarity to Alfieri's work.

Thenceforward, the temple portico became the dominant façade motif of Neoclassicism. Initially the lateral portions were still adorned with statuary niches, windows or reliefs; but these disappeared in the late 1770s, so that the portico or the portal was set against a bare wall relieved only by rustication – as, for example, in Gondoin's design for the square in front of the Ecole de Chirurgie (c. 1775), or in Antoine's Chapelle de la Visitation in Nancy (1780–1). Further Parisian examples of this final phase included the Chapelle des Filles de Saint-Chaumont (1781) by Charles Convers, the Chapelle Saint-Nicolas by Nicolas-Claude Girardin and the Eglise des Capucins (1780; now Saint-

Louis d'Antin), by Alexandre-Théodore Brongniart (1739–1813).

Along with the outside, the interior system also changed. The demand for greater lightness and transparency had already been raised by Cordemoy, and had been taught at the Academy by Desgodets; it was Laugier who made it into a dogma. It was combined with a new attitude to the Gothic.[140] Boffrand and Soufflot had made no secret of their admiration for Gothic architecture; and Laugier's *Essai* found a ready audience. His ideal church had a tall nave carried on columns, in an approximation to Gothic proportions and a Gothic sense of space. In imitation of the Greek temple, he superimposed a second order on the columns of the nave; he roofed the nave with a barrel vault and the aisles with flat cells to match the intercolumniations. In the side chapels and in the clerestory, he resolved the wall surface into large windows. He thus sought to combine Gothic construction with antique form, using full daylight as a medium of spatial impression.

Contant d'Ivry and Soufflot were the first architects to put this idea into practice. Saint-Vasnon, at Condé-sur-Escaut (1751–6) and Saint-Vaast in Arras (begun c. 1755), both by Contant, are the earliest instances of columns with a continuous entablature (Plate 218). The use of columns corresponded to the still-vital local tradition of the hall-church, which Contant was obliged to take into account;[141] but it was his decision to replace the arches with a lintel. Unlike Condé-sur-Escaut, which still has some markedly Baroque features, Saint-Vaast is entirely conceived in Neoclassical terms. Massive columns divide the nave from the aisles, and two ranks of them line the choir. The crossing rests on four groups of three columns each, as in Soufflot's design for Saint-Geneviève; but Saint-Vaast, unlike Sainte-Geneviève, has one column in each group of three projecting into the nave. This creates four ressauts, each of which bears a tall, flaming urn instead of a second order – a restless interruption of the linear flow, which Laugier would never have sanctioned.

Contant's major ecclesiastical commission was the church of the Madeleine in Paris. Occupying a prominent site, as the view-stopper on the central axis emanating from the Place Louis-XV, it was intended as a pendant to Soufflot's Sainte-Geneviève. Contant's design of 1761 was not without a certain grandeur (Plate 219). The plan was a Latin cross; the side-aisles were lined with niche-like chapels, and the walls dividing these were fronted by half-columns and served as buttresses. As at Sainte-Geneviève, the bell towers stood on either side of the square-ended choir. For the crossing, Contant had devised a formula that earned him general admiration (Plate 220). In order to create a more spacious impression without having to increase the diameter of the

218   Contant d'Ivry: Arras, Saint-Vaast, begun 1755, interior.

219   Contant d'Ivry: Paris, La Madeleine, begun 1764, plan, engraving from Patte, 1765.

220   Contant d'Ivry: Paris, La Madeleine, interior, section.

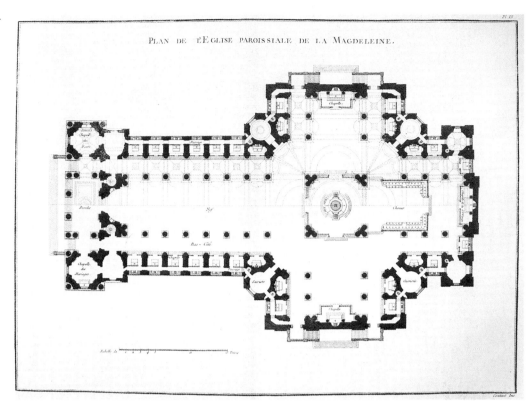

PLAN DE L'EGLISE PAROISSIALE DE LA MAGDELEINE.

dome, he ringed the crossing itself with a wide, octagonal ambulatory, in the centre of which the dome hung like a baldachin above the high altar. He reduced the crossing piers to clusters of three columns sharing a slender nucleus of masonry, and these supported the dome. The supports of the ambulatory as it crossed the nave, choir and transepts were free-standing columns; and at each corner of the crossing was a pier, hollowed out to form a circular sacristy. The baldachin idea first appeared at Saint-Vaast in Arras, where Contant had intended to place a second order on the four projecting columns of the crossing. The immediate source is likely to have been the crossing of Saint-Géry (now Saint-Aubert) in Cambrai, built in 1738, which Contant undoubtedly knew.[142]

In many ways, Contant's Madeleine design resembled Sainte-Geneviève: in its general spaciousness, its fluted columns with their straight entablatures, its aisles that continued around the transepts, its use of clustered columns at the crossing, and also in its quasi-antique decoration, restricted to sculptures and reliefs. But the effect was ruined by restless breaks in the cornice, by side chapels with elevated tribunes, by the faulty integration of the ambulatory with the arms of the cruciform plan and, finally, by the form of the exterior. The façade, with its massive portico, was an echo of Gabriel's façades in the Place Louis-XV; but with its projections and recessions, its contrasts of light and shade, and its giant pilasters framing statuary niches on either side, it looked – as can clearly be seen from the model in the Musée Carnavalet – more like Roman Baroque than Neoclassicism. Even the dome was out of scale with the rest of the building. There was an irresolute, indeterminate quality about the design that was criticized on all sides.

Construction began in 1764, but lack of funds meant that it made slow progress, and in 1774 it was halted completely in order to concentrate on Sainte-Geneviève. After Contant's death, the project was taken over by Guillaume-Martin Couture (1732–99). He enlarged the dome, lengthened the choir to accommodate the high altar and did away with the baldachin and ambulatory – ostensibly to save money, in reality because of the likely structural instability of the vaulting, already pointed out by Patte. He took up a later design by Contant, in which the portico extends right across the façade, and continued it back along the outside of the nave, as far as the transepts, thus coming close to the peripteral temple form of the church as it stands today.[143] This project, too, remained uncompleted. In 1790 work was halted again, until in 1806 Pierre Vignon, charged with the building of a Temple de la Gloire for the armies of Napoleon, tore down all the existing work, banked up the site and laid new foundations.

Sainte-Geneviève, on the other hand, had a widespread influence, in spite of all the criticisms.[144] Among its numerous offspring is the church of the Madeleine in Rouen (1764–81), by an architect who did much work in Rouen and elsewhere in Normandy, Jean-Baptiste Le Brument (1736–1804): originally intended as a chapel for the local Hôtel-Dieu, this is not centrally planned, though it spans a wide space lightly, with continuous entablatures.[145] Other derivatives of Sainte-Geneviève included the designs by Soufflot and Potain for Rennes Cathedral. At the request of

the Bishop of Rennes, Marigny had put Soufflot forward for this in 1754. Soufflot's design, which has not been preserved, left only the towers of the ancient Gothic fabric standing, while using them not to flank the entrance but at the opposite end, where they would not clash with the new portal. Soufflot was so overworked during the following years that Marigny commissioned Gabriel's *chef de bureau*, Potain, to work up the design. In his final version, approved in 1764, Potain retained the whole of the old twin-tower façade but replaced the Gothic piers of the interior with huge columns that were intended to maintain the impression of Gothic lightness while clearly supporting the dome. The transepts were vestigial; the choir was prolonged by a circular chapel, ringed with shallow niches, to contain the high altar. Funds ran short, however, and work was repeatedly postponed.

In the 1780s Mathurin Crucy submitted new designs in a basilican form. His initial design was rejected by the Academy in 1781 as too deficient in ornament; his second, in 1785, featured a wide nave with narrow aisles and an array of side chapels, rectangular transepts with screened-off sanctuaries at the ends, and a long choir with an ambulatory. Ionic columns, which continued along the choir, supported an entablature and a coffered tunnel vault; the crossing was surmounted by a dome on pendentives. Here, too, the decoration was limited to reliefs in the side chapels and in the transepts. Work began in 1787, only to be interrupted by the Revolution in 1790, and Crucy was able to resume it only in 1827. In the decoration, as elsewhere, he kept to his 1786 designs; the cathedral was eventually consecrated in 1844. Crucy's work has since been altered to the point of unrecognizability.

Soufflot's structural innovations found a response in the work of Emiliand-Marie Gauthey, a pupil of Dumont's. Gauthey worked in Chalon-sur-Saône as under-engineer of bridges and highways for Burgundy, where he had already made a name for himself by designing the theatre in Chalon and the town hall in Tournus. In the church at Givry (1771), centrally planned as an octagon with an appended oval lady chapel (Plate 221), he set out in his turn to demonstrate the structural stability of Gothic construction, and thus to sustain Soufflot against the onslaughts of Patte. He rested the central dome directly on the entablature of the inner colonnade, and pierced the pendentives above the columns with large oval medallions to prove that they had no structural function to perform. He also made a number of oval openings in the shell of the dome above the main octagon, and in that of the lady chapel (again supported on an internal colonnade), so that the mass of the whole vaulting system was reduced to a minimum. The same desire for lightness prevails in the dome constructions of a whole group of centrally planned churches in Burgundy. Of these, the most akin to Givry is Poncey-sur-l'Ignon (1785–7), the last centrally planned church to be built in France in the eighteenth century. This is not an octagon but a rotunda, ringed by side-chapels and with a rectangular choir; above each chapel the dome is perforated, as at Givry, and the load distributed onto the abutments formed by the divisions between the chapels.[146]

In Franche-Comté, Soufflot's ideas took on a markedly individual colouring.[147] The hallmarks of Neoclassical

221 Emiliand-Marie Gauthey:
Givry, 1771, plan of church.

222 Nicolas Nicole: Voray-sur-
l'Ognon, 1770, plan of church.

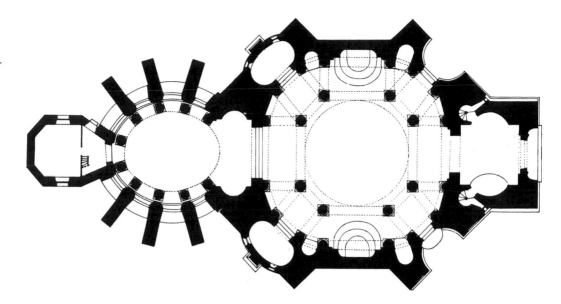

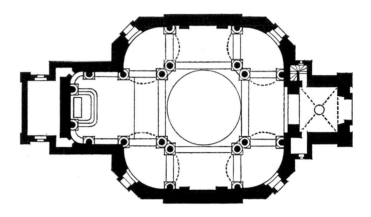

church architecture here are the Greek cross plan, columns supporting an entablature, and the central dome. The first columnar church interior, albeit still with arches, was built as early as 1747, at Traves-sur-Saône. The plan of Traves, a Greek cross with two bays to each arm and additional domes over the quadrants between the arms, was adopted by Nicole in 1770 at Voray-sur-Ognon (Doubs), where he shortened the transepts by one bay (Plate 222). For the central dome, he found a particularly elegant formula, setting the pendentives on four diagonally placed pairs of columns that mark out a square at the crossing. This church at Voray was the prototype for a succession of excellent centrally planned churches, of which Saint-Pierre, Besançon (1782–6), by Claude-Joseph-Alexandre Bertrand, and the tiny country church of Cirey-lès-Bellevaux are particularly finely proportioned.

The search for new forms of church architecture also led to a rediscovery of the Early Christian basilica, the starting point of all ecclesiastical architecture, to which Cordemoy and Desgodets had already drawn attention. It was in this form that Laugier's principles could most readily be put into practice, even though the tight spacing of its columns and the comparatively low tunnel vault made it impossible to achieve the lightness of Soufflot. The strong appeal of this form for the Neoclassical spirit is exemplified by the fact that, soon after work started on Sainte-Geneviève, no less than three basilican churches were built in the Paris area alone: Saint-Philippe-du-Roule in Paris itself, Saint-Symphorien at Versailles, and Saint-Louis at Saint-Germain-en-Laye.[148]

The largest of these was Saint-Louis (begun 1766), the former parish church of the royal Château de Saint-Germain. The design, by Potain, maintained a number of traditional features, including a string of side chapels and a pair of buttresses on either side of the portico, probably intended to support bell towers. At the east end of the nave, a pair of canted corner walls, bearing medallions, flanked a theatrical prospect of the light-filled lady chapel beyond, framed by two free-standing Doric columns. In spite of its antique garb, this design retains something of the courtly atmosphere that clings to the buildings of Gabriel and his school.

Saint-Symphorien, Versailles, although contemporary with this, already belongs to the next phase. In its uncompromising austerity and sobriety, it is more like an Early Christian basilica. The columns are fluted only half-way down, a form previously used only in vestibules; the entablature is smooth, without a triglyph frieze. Very much in Laugier's vein, the nave has a coffered tunnel vault, but without rosettes in the compartments except in the apse. The exterior is unornamented, except for a Palladian portico at the west end and another, smaller one at the east end, beneath the bell tower.

Louis-François Trouard (1729–94), the architect of Saint-Symphorien, built almost nothing but churches.[149] As the winner of the Prix de Rome in 1753, and a contemporary of Peyre, Moreau and de Wailly, he belonged to the second wave of the antique revival; his buildings reflect this, as does his influence on his pupils, the most distinguished of whom was Ledoux. As the central figure in a circle of artists and writers, he was one of those innovators who sought to bring architecture into line with the philosophical ideas of his day. As a member of the Service des Bâtiments, he was an exterior surveyor at Versailles and there came into contact with Marigny, for whom he worked at Ménars.

Trouard's career was dominated by his work for the Economats Royaux, a body that administered the property left behind by Protestant exiles and used the not inconsiderable proceeds to maintain hospitals and also to repair and build churches. In Trouard's time it was managed by the Bishop of Orléans, who divided the available building funds between his own cathedral and the churches of Versailles. One project at Versailles, concurrent with Saint-Symphorien, was the Chapelle des Catéchismes (now Chapelle de la Providence), attached to the north aisle of Saint-Louis. This is a long, rectangular structure, with bare outer walls adorned with reliefs; inside, it is screened off with columns into a central altar space and two wings, one for boys and one for girls. The only light comes from a round-headed window above the altar, and the whole thing looks like a protest against the Baroque opulence of the neighbouring cathedral. Of Trouard's work on the building of Orléans Cathedral we shall speak later.

The most important of these basilican churches is Saint-Philippe du Roule (1774–84), by Jean-François-Thérèse Chalgrin (1739–1811). It has been much altered, but the appearance of the original design is known from the engravings published by Chalgrin himself. The nave was lined, as it now is, with ranks of fluted Ionic columns (Plate 223); all along the walls, niches containing altars alternated with large statuary niches surmounted by oval medallions. To the right and left of the high altar, square chapels with inset columns and tribunes formed transepts of a sort, visible from outside as slight projections. The semicircular apse was built within the rectangle of the choir, leaving room behind it for a narrow passageway to connect the two lateral chapels (sacristy and catechism chapel) that continued the line of the nave aisles. As at the Madeleine, these chapels were meant to serve as the bases of the bell towers. The ranks of columns in the nave, as well as the statuary niches and medallions, continued into the choir and round the enclosed semicircle of the apse. Above was a continuous coffered vault with rosettes in the compartments. The result was a space with an antique sense of self-containment, lit by large windows and fulfilling all Laugier's demands.

When the church came to be built, Chalgrin had to dispense with his stone vault, for reasons of economy, and replace it with a wooden vault with the coffering painted on – and incorporating, on the model of the Halle au Blé, two large windows to light the altar. This, in turn, obviated the need for the flying buttresses shown in the design; he also had to dispense with the eastern bell towers. Like the statuary niches in the interior, the temple-like façade undoubtedly owes something to Peyre's *Œuvres d'architecture*. With its triglyph frieze, its heavy-shadowed cornice with large mutules, and its pediment relief, it has far more presence and volume than that of Saint-Symphorien.

The chapel of the Séminaire du Saint-Esprit (1768), tunnel-vaulted and without aisles, but lined with an elegant Ionic order of pilasters, echoes the Saint-Philippe du Roule design, which was almost literally replicated in the monastery chapel of the Capucins, Strasbourg (1774; destroyed), by Chalgrin's pupil Jean-Baphste Kléber.

Chalgrin was a member of the younger generation, but he was no radical reformer. A pupil of Servandoni and Boullée, he never abandoned the French tradition and retained a capacity for elegant and imaginative formal invention that lends an air of refinement to all his buildings and decorative work. In 1758 he won the Prix de Rome with the arresting pavilion design that probably influenced that of the Petit Trianon, and in the years that followed he became associated with Soufflot. His first major commission in Paris was the completion of the Hôtel Saint-Florentin, for which Gabriel had designed the external elevations. His work here was mostly concerned with the court façade, the staircase and the street frontage. In the austere Doric of the entrance screen, the unadorned entablature and the Palladian *serliana* motif of the arch, Chalgrin kept to Gabriel's preordained formula while revealing his own greater modernity and his closeness to Soufflot. In the Comte de Saint-Florentin, later Duc de la Vrillière, who was both secretary of state and minister of the royal household, Chalgrin gained an influential patron and protector. It was, however, Saint-Philippe du Roule that opened his way into the Academy and made his reputation as an innovator who had simplified the shape of the church interior and brought it closer to that of the temples of antiquity.

Chalgrin's part in the completion of the façade of Saint-Sulpice has already been discussed; but it remains to mention his concurrent work on the decoration of the two chapels under the west towers, which are an outstanding example of the combination of antique forms with the very French elegance of Gabriel. A fluted Corinthian colonnade runs all the way round each chapel, interspersed with projecting wall piers containing statuary niches, and with arched openings on four sides: entrance, side windows, altar. Detailing of the greatest delicacy – dentils, palmettes, festoons, and other motifs – adorns the cornices and other members, most notably the plinths and pediments of the niches. Little domes with foreshortened coffering suggest antique circular temples. The organ case of the same church (1776–81) is equally elegant: an concave Corinthian colonnade, with a tall entablature and a culminating profusion of sculpture.

In the provinces, the basilican formula made little headway: the few examples include Saint-Louis, Toulon (1767) and Saint-Martin, Morlaix (1773–8). In Paris, however, it became very popular. Cherpitel used it at Saint-Barthélemy (1778), Poyet at Saint-Sauveur (after 1778), Convers in the Chapelle des Filles de Saint-Chaumont (1781) and Brongniart at Saint-Germain-l'Auxerrois, Romainville (1785–7). Cherpitel was also the author of the unusual ground-plan of Saint-Pierre du Gros-Caillou (begun 1775), a basilica with a nave and two pairs of side aisles, for which Chalgrin had built a large, circular lady chapel in 1767. The façade resembled that of Saint-Philippe du Roule; and fluted Doric columns with shallow bases – of the Paestum type originally intended by Soufflot for the crypt of Sainte-Geneviève – were used for the wide hexastyle portico, and also for the four ranks of columns inside. Never completed, the church was torn down during the Revolution.

223 Jean-François Chalgrin: Paris, Saint-Philippe du Roule, interior.

224 Alexandre-Théodore Brongniart: Paris, Couvent des Capucins, 1780–2, façade, design (Paris, Bibliothèque Nationale).

225 Alexandre-Théodore Brongniart: Paris, Couvent des Capucins, cloister.

The last step in the simplification of the ground plan was the hall church, without aisles; and this first appeared in the late 1770s. One of the first was Saint-Louis at Port-Marly (completed 1778); the original design was probably by Trouard, and the execution was by Etienne-François Legrand. In the Palladian manner, the façade is joined by Ionic colonnades to two independent lateral pavilions, one for the presbytery, one for the director's residence. The interior is a plain hall, with banded rustication on the walls. The only accentuation is the entrance to the apse, a large Palladian serliana with foliated Ionic capitals borrowed by Legrand from Ledoux's chapel for the Saline de Chaux.

The same type is represented by Saint-Louis d'Antin, Paris; this formed part of the Capucins, the Capuchin friary that Brongniart built in 1780–2, at the instance of the Duc d'Orléans, to serve the new quarter around the Chaussée d'Antin (now the Lycée Condorcet).[150] This church, too, is innocent of ornamentation. The impressive space was lined simply with a Doric entablature (since removed), with the west apse separated from the nave by two Doric columns. The east apse, raised by a few steps, was reserved for the friars, and the high altar was brought forward to the last bay of the nave proper, fenced off by a curved balustrade.

The church forms the left-hand wing of the building, with a matching wing on the right intended for conventual uses. Facing the street, the identical, pedimented end façades of the wings are joined by a straight entrance block with the main doorway in the centre, flanked by columns. This austerely antique façade (Plate 224) was originally pierced only by a lunette above the central door. Brongniart turned down the friars' request for windows and instead offered them relief panels on either side of the lunette;[151] these, together with a row of statuary niches, formed the only contrast to the bare walls.

The cloister (Plate 225), which occupies the centre of the composition, is equally austere. Its particular significance lies in the fact that here, for the only time in any ecclesiastical building, Brongniart systematically used the Doric order without a base. His contemporaries were well aware of the momentous nature of this innovation, and regarded this cloister as a reduced imitation of the buildings of Paestum – although, in fact, Brongniart was giving a highly idiosyncratic interpretation of his archaic source. The reduction of the

forms – no fluting, no architrave – already reflects the simplifying and symbolic tendencies of revolutionary architecture. The Capuchins had a reputation for frugality, and Brongniart took this as his cue to adopt the rugged and weighty 'archaic' style as the setting for their daily life. Along the far end of the cloister, with equal disregard for convention, he surmounted his arcaded screen with a balustraded terrace to overlook the gardens – a sign that he was not thinking of a traditional cloister so much as of antique colonnades, like the one Ledoux had created behind the Hôtel d'Hallwyl. Brongniart here showed himself capable of a surprising modernity, matched in its radical logic only by Gondoin.[152]

The ideal reference to the antique temple lay either in a pure rotunda or in the combination of circle and square. De Wailly had provided the first example of this in his Chapelle du Reposoir at Versailles (1769). In larger churches this type had liturgical drawbacks, so it remained confined to the chapels of hospitals and religious orders. In 1780, influenced by de Wailly's chapel, Georges-François d'Arnaudin built the chapel of the Hôpital Civil, Versailles;[153] this stands in the centre of a large H-shaped building containing the wards of the hospital. The plan is a circle inscribed in a square, with four diagonally placed exedrae: a clear allusion to the architecture of the Roman baths. Around the inner ring of columns runs a circular ambulatory, as in the Chapelle du Reposoir, supporting a gallery that affords access to the wards. The whole is crowned by a coffered dome. The purest example of this type outside Paris is the church of the Visitandines, Nancy (1780–1), designed by Antoine as a rotunda inscribed in a cube. The rusticated external walls are unornamented except for the lavish portal, with its Ionic columns and its lunette relief.

Finally, something must be said about the revival of the Gothic.[154] In the event, despite laudatory remarks on all sides, the Neoclassical architects took a one-sidedly intellectual and technical view of the subject. They wanted the spaciousness and transparency of Gothic, and its structural system; but they had no feeling for the actual atmosphere of Gothic churches, or for the messages conveyed by subdued lighting, coloured glass or rich decoration. The Gothic sense of form, Goethe's enthusiasm for Strasbourg Cathedral (1772), and the national fervour of the Gothic Revival in

England, were entirely alien to them. So they embarked on a wave of modernization and purification, in which compound piers were plastered smooth, Gothic ornaments were chipped away, and altars, choir screens and stalls were swept away. The best example of this in Paris was Saint-Germain l'Auxerrois (1756), where the window tracery was replaced by iron glazing bars and the piers were converted into fluted columns. In many cases, medieval stained glass was sacrificed in order to let in more light. At the very least, the churches were whitewashed from top to bottom, to give them more dignity and grandeur. One of the most flagrant cases was Amiens, where, from 1755 onwards, at Laugier's suggestion, the cathedral chapter auctioned the fixtures and fittings and jibbed only at selling off the choir stalls. The desire to make everything better and more up-to-date, to correct the bases and capitals on classical lines, and to hack off the 'hideous' Gothic detailing, utterly destroyed the atmosphere and the true character of many Gothic churches.

On the other hand, when medieval buildings came to be restored, as with Notre-Dame in Dijon, the Eglise de la Toussaint in Angers, the choir of the Abbaye de Marmoutier or the west front of Orléans Cathedral, there was evidence of a new concern with stylistic authenticity. Gothic survival gave way to Gothic revival. The best example is Orléans Cathedral. In 1765, as architect to the Economats, Trouard had taken over the rebuilding of the façade, which his predecessors Gabriel and Loriot had carried up to the level of the top of the portal. Overall, de Cotte's conception still held good. But Trouard had made a careful study of other French Gothic cathedrals, and was able to draw on his superior knowledge to make the result more 'authentically' Gothic. He took the central doorways from Beauvais, the pinnacles on the buttresses from Amiens and Paris, the upper parts of the towers from Rouen and Toul. In so doing, he invented the Troubadour Gothic, a composite style that was 'correct' in detail but meaningless in context. It would never have occurred to de Cotte, in preparing his design in 1709, to copy parts of individual cathedrals and put them together to make a whole. With the advent of archaeological correctness, the Gothic entered a new chapter in its history. It was no longer a living tradition but a historical concept; and thus began the nineteenth-century Gothic revival.

Trouard's career came to an abrupt end after the Duc de Choiseul was disgraced in 1771. The Bishop of Orléans, as a close associate of Choiseul's, had to relinquish the direction of the Economats, and in 1773 Trouard lost his post, followed shortly afterwards by his position at Versailles. In Orléans he was succeeded briefly by Legrand and then by his own pupil Adrien Pâris, who continued the façade in accordance with his design and completed it in 1793.

CHAPTER 9

Decoration

In the field of decoration, as elsewhere, early Neoclassicism was a transitional phase.[155] The Rococo, which chimed so well with eighteenth-century habits of life, was long-lived. The so-called 'return to good taste' initially led to the emergence of a *style de transition*, in which curves and straight lines appeared in association. The full rigour of the Louis XVI style did not set in until the early 1770s. One excellent example of the survival of the Rococo is provided by Contant d'Ivry's decorative work at the Palais-Royal (1755–60). The play of curves persisted; the palm stems execrated by Laugier still framed the great wall mirrors; but the architectural framework had taken on greater solidity (Plate 227). Columns and pilasters articulated the wall; straight lines had returned to dado panels and coving, and each mirror was crowned by a coffered intrados. But the furniture, the chimneypieces, the candelabra, were all still pure Rococo (Plate 226).

Blondel illustrated these decorations in the *Encyclopédie* (1760) and in the *Dictionnaire des sciences* (1762) as a model of their kind, and in his *Observations générales sur la décoration* he referred to them as an ideal solution, a compromise between the massive Louis XIV style and the 'frivolous' Rococo. In his view, in spite of the modern architects' desire for a strict, 'masculine' style, interior decoration ought at all costs to remain 'agreeable': not ponderous, not over-symmetrical, and definitely not overdone. Purely architectural elements might be set off by other, contrasting motifs. This 'golden mean' was exemplified by the decorative work of Contant. With all their curves, the furnishings were strictly symmetrical, without a hint of rocaille, bat-wings, or anything of that sort. They made a contrast with the columns and pilasters, but they fitted into the same scheme of symmetry.[156] The same restraint was evident in Boullée's

early interiors, such as that of the Hôtel de Tourolles. Blondel and his contemporaries were all in favour of a return to order and 'good taste', but they were not prepared to sacrifice all the amenities of the Rococo.

The opposite viewpoint was represented by the Neoclassical extremists whom Blondel castigated in his *Cours d'architecture*; they meant to introduce the antique into interior decoration. It all started with Le Lorrain's designs for Åkerö (1754), which were followed by his furniture for La Live de Jully (1758 or 1759), 'composed in the antique style', the ultramodernity of which so annoyed Cochin. The influence of Le Lorrain and Challe was also evident in the highly progressive, if unsystematic, decorative compositions of Neufforge, which were published from 1756 onwards.[157] However, the impact of these new, 'masculine' forms, and of the La Live de Jully furniture, was restricted – as was that of the *style grec* as a whole – to a relatively small intellectual elite, and its consequences were negligible. Grimm's remark that in Paris everything was *à la grecque* should therefore be taken with a pinch of salt – as can be seen from the furniture depicted in paintings by Alexandre Roslin, François-Hubert Drouais and their like.[158] Cochin, Blondel, even La Live de Jully himself, dismissed the *goût grec* as absurd. By and large, the Rococo retained the upper hand until the early 1760s.

The mood at court was especially conservative. The personal taste of Louis XV, and the ambivalent attitude adopted by Marigny, meant that at Versailles, Choisy and Fontainebleau the Rococo remained alive into the late 1760s. The ornamental carvers Verberckt and Antoine Rousseau remained its principal exponents to the last. At Versailles, as late as 1767, Gabriel designed panelling and pendant trophies for the alcoves in the Salon de Musique de Madame Adelaïde, the king's daughter, in a Rococo style scarcely less effervescent than the earlier work alongside it, which dated from 1752. And in 1769, in the library of another daughter, Madame Sophie, on the ground floor, Chevallier created a plasterwork decor that was almost in the manner of A. Peyrotte and Christophe Huet. At the same time, constant alterations and a growing shortage of funds increasingly led designers to reuse parts of an old decorative scheme within the new.

The first sign of a shift in taste at Versailles – undoubtedly influenced by Madame de Pompadour – emerged at the Petit Trianon. Its decor is the most modern of its date (1763–7), and affords the best example of nascent Neoclassicism (Plate 228). Straight lines and right angles have displaced the curve. The panelling is once more rectilinear. Flat, unadorned areas once more begin to appear, although the overall character remains one of graceful lightness and elegance. In the Salon de Compagnie, the floral elements are as rich as those of the Rococo, but they are symmetrically matched to the architecture, and they are botanically correct. Nor are they intended as a contrast, but as an integral part of the room. Rococo motifs – C-scrolls and shellwork – do

226 Contant d'Ivry: Paris, Palais Royal, furniture, *c.* 1755, engraving by Blondel.

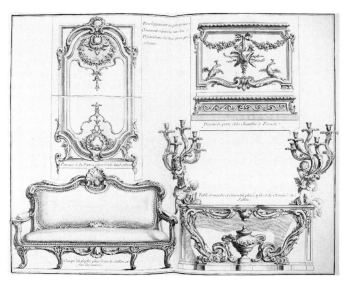

227 Contant d'Ivry: Paris, Palais Royal, interior decoration, *c.* 1755, engraving by Blondel.

228 Antoine Rousseau: Versailles, Petit Trianon, Salon de Compagnie, *c.* 1765.

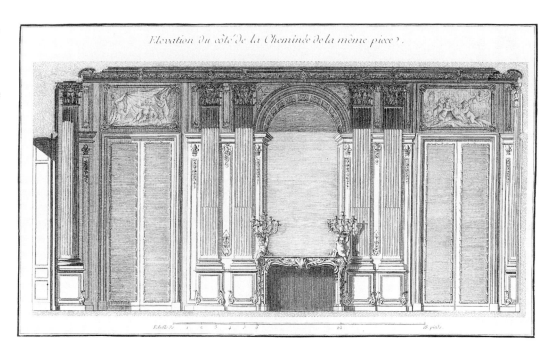

Elevation du côté de la Cheminée de la même piece.

229   Antoine Rousseau: Versailles, Petits Appartements, Cabinet des Bains de Louis XV, wooden panels, 1770.

appear, but these too are fitted into rectilinear frames. Amid the flowers, garlands, and trophies, antique motifs are as if playfully interspersed: palmetto friezes and modillioned cornices, urns and medallions, even an urn guarded by griffins. But the antique remains a literary conceit rather than a direct experience: it is all taken from engravings by Piranesi, with the probable addition of such English sources as Chambers's *Civil Architecture* (1759).[159]

This combination, which also incorporates late Louis XIV motifs, is characteristic of the *style de transition*. It also prevails in the furniture of the 1760s, in which rectilinear and curved forms, fluting and C-scrolls, are often to be found in one and the same piece.[160] One of the last examples of this style is to be found at Versailles, in the Cabinet des Bains in the Petits Appartements, with its four-colour gilt decor of reed-swathed medallions containing bathing scenes and figurative reliefs, all set in a delicate, quasi-antique architectural framework that translates C-scrolls into water-spouting

dolphins (Plate 229). The floral theme of the Petit Trianon became very popular, and reappeared in Henri Piètre's designs for the Hôtel Mélusine (1766), but above all in the designs supplied by Jean-Louis Prieur and Victor Louis for the royal palace in Warsaw (*c.* 1765), where it combined with Neoclassical forms.

Caylus had called for a return to the past; and this now made itself evident everywhere, not only in wall decoration but in ornament generally. Antique references were still confined to isolated motifs, but the reversion to the Louis XIV style was strongly marked. In the Salon de Compagnie at the Petit Trianon, Gabriel surmounted the mirrors with female masks of the kind that had been in fashion at the beginning of the eighteenth century. At the Ecole Militaire, he reverted to the wall decoration system of Lassurance the Younger, with its undecorated rectangular panels, and to such late Louis XIV motifs as the oval, garlanded medallions in the stairchamber, the bulky trophies on the chapel doors,

230 Ange-Jacques Gabriel: Paris, Gardemeuble (Ministry of Marine) Galerie Dorée, c. 1770.

231 Claude-Nicolas Ledoux: Paris, Hôtel d'Uzès, interior decoration, 1769 (Paris, Musée Carnavalet).

and the gold mosaic coving in the Salle du Conseil (now Salle des Maréchaux). At the Garde-Meuble, the wall and door panels of the Galerie Dorée (c. 1770), with their ponderous, isolated motifs, are well-nigh indistinguishable from seventeenth-century work (Plate 230). The grand salon in Antoine's Hôtel des Monnaies has a similarly backward-looking character; but here the gold mosaic coving has been translated into antique terms.

The private hôtel building of the 1760s was marked by a similar nostalgia. The interiors of Boullée, with their reminiscences of the seventeenth-century formal repertoire, have already been mentioned. This revival of the assertive mouldings of the past, the door architraves, the continuous upper cornice and the clear separation of the decorative elements, helped to stabilize and consolidate the system of wall decoration.

Ornament itself now reverted to its proper state of subordination to architecture. While retaining the lightness of the Rococo, it lost the asymmetry and abstract quality of that style and reverted to vegetable forms. Flowers and tendrils took possession of the panel, and Le Brun's motifs reappeared on all sides. This applied not only to the voluminous three-dimensional trophies of Ledoux's Café Militaire, with their echoes of Le Brun's trophies for Versailles, but also, and above all, to the arabesque decorations of Boullée, Antoine and others. Among the most significant inventions in this respect were the trophy-hung trees designed by Ledoux for the Hôtel d'Uzès (Plate 231), which rise from floor to ceiling, and his big arabesques of caryatids and tendrils for the Hôtel d'Hallwyl. Unprecedented in their sculptural vigour, these were immediately copied (Hôtel de Châtelet, Hôtel d'Argenson, Hôtel de Villette, and elsewhere).[161] Much more than in the late seventeenth century, motifs tended to be used in isolation; and this emergence from the ornamental undergrowth greatly enhanced their effect. At Versailles, in the last years of his

career, Gabriel harked back to Le Brun, both for the now-vanished first library of Marie-Antoinette (1772), the doors of which are now in the Versailles municipal library, and for the library of Louis XVI (1774). Here the *style de transition* has already been supplanted by grotesques and broad strips of twined, garland-like laurel foliage.[162]

It was only in the decorative work of the second wave of Rome scholars that the antique revival became dominant. An important source, here as elsewhere, was Peyre's *Œuvres d'architecture*, which finally brought columns inside the building. In the Rococo, decoration had migrated from the interior to the exterior; now, architecture transferred itself from the façade to the room. The articulation of interior walls became an architectural one, defined in terms of the classical orders. Coupled pilasters, separated by large arabesques, line the walls of the salon at the Hôtel du Châtelet (1770). At Le Marais (*c.* 1770), fluted, coupled Ionic columns are surmounted by a cornice complete with modillions and dentils (Plate 232). The salon of the Hôtel de la Monnaie, too, with its massive columns, reflects this new architectural emphasis. At the same time, the relief panel was introduced; and in the 1770s it conquered interiors as well as façades. Pictorial decoration was replaced by sculptural. A milestone in this respect was the *casin* of the Comte de Lauraguais, the Pavillon de Brancas (1771).

With Ledoux's Pavillon de Louveciennes, the new, antique-influenced decorative style made its court debut. The dining room contained all the new elements, and must have looked like a direct challenge to Gabriel. It was not

long, however, before Gabriel himself paid tribute to the new age. In his Grand Projet for Versailles, he lined the Cabinet du Conseil with a strict order of Corinthian pilasters (1771–2); and for the dining room at Bellevue (1773) he designed niches to contain figures of Apollo and the Nine Muses, little overdoor reliefs and, in an apsidal projection, a large relief on consoles – with the consequence that Louis XV made changes in his own hand to what must have seemed to him an excessively chilly decorative scheme.

The leading theoretical source of the day was a book of engravings by Charles Delafosse, *Nouvelle Iconologie historique*, which appeared in 1768; a supplementary volume followed in the early 1770s.[163] In this, for the first time, antique ornamental forms were published in a wealth of examples. An architect by profession, Delafosse (1734–91) was a professor at the Academy in Bordeaux; he was responsible for a number of buildings in Paris, including the Hôtel de Titon (1776–83). The architectural designs in the *Iconologie* – museums, theatres, fountains, tombs and so on – are both ponderous and heavily symbolic. His furnishings, urns, consoles and candelabra, with their ubiquitous rope-like festoons, are similarly encumbered with a symbolic programme that embraces the Seasons of the Year, the Sciences and the Qualities and Activities of Mankind and borders at times on the ludicrous. But Delafosse had success on his side, and within three years his book went into a new edition. Through the variety of his forms and the fertility of his imagination, Delafosse acted as a stimulus; his work set the decorative arts on a new course.

PART FOUR

The Second Phase of Neoclassicism

CHAPTER I

Introduction

The death of Louis XV in 1774, and the accession of his grandson, Louis XVI, not only marked a political break but coincided with a general change of direction in architecture. Marigny, who detested Madame du Barry, had resigned his post in 1773. In 1775 Gabriel, the personification of the age, retired from office. At the Academy, the archaeologist Le Roy succeeded Blondel as professor in 1774, and the conflict between French tradition and antique revival was settled once and for all.

From that moment on, the Academy stood at the cutting edge of progress, and the result was a change in architects' attitude to antiquity itself. Imperial Roman prototypes gave way to archaic rigour. There were more and more visits to Paestum, Segesta and Agrigentum. The antique took on a heroic tone. The Doric temples of Paestum and the Temple of Fortuna at Praeneste (Palestrina), at the top of its array of ramps and terraces – which Trouard surveyed in 1782, and which Louis-Jean Desprez sensationalized in a series of large drawings – were the key experiences that lay behind Louis XVI architecture. The baseless Doric column was first used by Ledoux, at the Besançon theatre (1778). Doric columns also dominated the chamber in which the Estates General were convened at Versailles in 1789. Then there were the interminable arrays of columns at Palmyra and Baalbek, as published in 1754 and 1757 respectively by Robert Wood; set off by bare walls, these reappeared in designs submitted to the Academy and in projects by Boullée (such as those for the royal library and for a museum).

The Academy students' designs grew bigger and bigger, and their columns proliferated out of control. In 1784 Peyre, De Wailly, Trouard and Le Roy criticized a design for a palace, by Antoine Vaudoyer, in these words: 'The beautiful monuments of the ancients were grand, noble and simple, and not weighty, frigid and monotonous; but unfortunately that is just what we often see in the designs of our pupils, who mistake weight for nobility and complication for ingenuity.' The Academy had a rule that Rome scholars should submit one major design of their own choice every year; but the resulting compositions were so 'gigantic and impracticable' that in 1787 the requirement had to be dropped.[1]

Along with the Doric, in France – though not in England – architects set great store by the unfluted Tuscan order, as promoted by Piranesi. He saw the Etruscans as the elder civilization, and therefore as the mentors of the Greeks: the massive walls of the archaic age were theirs, as were the massive vault and the smooth, baseless Tuscan column. This view, as put forward in his *Magnificenza ed architettura de' Romani* (1761), was vehemently opposed by both Mariette and Le Roy; but their attacks left Piranesi unmoved. In his *Parere sull'architettura* (1765), he dismissed Mariette's objections and made fun of the Grecian purists and of Winckelmann's theories in general.[2]

It was a measure of Piranesi's influence in France that so-called Etruscan architecture came to be regarded as the architecture of republican Rome. Venerated as the paragon of all those civic virtues that people desired to see in their own state, the Roman republic also became the ideal in architecture. The squat, baseless Tuscan column formed an intrinsic part of the new, 'Etruscan' style, as did cyclopean masonry, heavy cornices and ornamental motifs derived from Etruscan sarcophagi. Soufflot used Tuscan columns only in their proper place, which was underground, in the grotto at Ménars; but in 1774 Ledoux gave them their first public airing on the gatehouse of the Saline de Chaux. As a symbol of republican Rome, the baseless Tuscan column became a political statement in its own right. This is as true of the setting of Jacques-Louis David's *Oath of the Horatii* (1784) as it is of the Rue des Colonnes, in Paris, which was built under the Roman-minded Directoire as a model of an 'antique Roman' street.[3]

The ideas of the Enlightenment had by now taken firm root. The idea of a new and better world, a new social and moral order, had acquired a hold on people's minds. The new view of morality and of the human response to nature, as preached most notably by Rousseau, instilled a vein of sentiment into all the arts, architecture included. The classical norms were reappraised. Orders and set proportions lost their validity, as architecture became either an expression of emotional experience or else a component of a new social order. Architects were no longer content to see their buildings glorify the state, the monarchy, or one specific stratum of society: they aspired to create monuments that would celebrate human greatness, inculcate worthy remembrance, teach moral values. Beauty gave way to Sublimity.

As characterized by Jean-Louis Viel de Saint-Maux, the painter wrested from God the creative power whereby the wonders of nature appear before our eyes, and extended his art – in a fine, creative frenzy – to encompass the universe.[4] Architecture went the same way; it turned into 'visionary architecture', soaring above all earthly concerns into immeasurable, cosmic spaces. Rules could be ignored, for architecture was now the subjective creation of genius; and so it became Romantic. In Desprez's stage designs of the

Saline de Chaux, plan of the Ideal City, detail of Plate 279.

1780s there were motifs that anticipated Caspar David Friedrich; Jean-Jacques Lequeu's design for a castle on the seashore was a precursor of Karl Blechen's painting *Kastell am Meer*. What distinguished the Romantic Neoclassicism of the end of the century from the early Neoclassicism of the 1760s and 1770s was the Romantic ability to see architecture as subject to the natural processes of growth and decay, and the attendant historicism that looked to the past for historical remains, as well as for classical monuments.

The force of antique precedent had also been weakened by the encounter with exotic cultures; mediated principally by Britain, this was most evident in the sphere of landscape gardening. It led to a broadening of vision; ideas of beauty, which had hitherto been monopolized by the antique, started to become relative. Pride of place among these exotic cultures was held by China and Egypt; as early as 1772, Blondel was complaining that architects were imitating China in their interiors and the ponderous forms of Memphis in their exteriors.

First manifested in the Trianon de Porcelaine at Versailles, the Chinese fashion had been massively promoted by such works as Chambers's *Designs of Chinese Buildings* (1751) and *A Dissertation on Oriental Gardening* (1772) and Lerouge's *Jardins anglo-chinois à la mode* (1776–87). The first pagodas in France – one in the grounds of Chanteloup (1769), by Louis-Denis Le Camus, and one at Ménars (1770), by De Wailly – had been imitations of Chambers's pagoda in Kew Gardens. Now, with the publication of pattern books, anyone could learn the style, and by the end of the century there was not a park of any importance without its Chinese pagodas, pavilions or bridges.[5]

Much the same went for Egypt. The first wave of the Egyptian revival emanated from Rome, where obelisks, sphinxes and hieroglyphs had long been familiar sights.[6] There the young French Rome scholars saw them, and as early as 1752 an Egyptian temple, complete with hieroglyphs, was engraved by Jerôme-Charles Bellicard for the frontispiece of Blondel's *Architecture française*. Piranesi's *Diverse maniere d'adornare i cammini*, published in 1769, which presented for the first time a wide selection of Egyptian sculptures and decorative motifs, was brought to France by Lhuillier in that very year. By then, Egyptian architecture had already been discovered and described by the English writers Norden and Pococke: F.L. Norden's *Drawings of Some Ruins and Colossal Statues at Thebes in Egypt* was published in French translation in 1752; R. Pococke's *Observations on Egypt* (1743–56) appeared under the title of *Description de l'Orient* in 1772–3. These superbly illustrated accounts remained the standard works on the subject until Vivant Denon published his *Voyages dans la Basse et la Haute Egypte* in 1802; and they introduced sphinxes, obelisks and pyramids to French parks and gardens. It was, however, the Comte de Caylus who first recognized Egyptian art as a style with laws of its own. He viewed the Egyptians as a wise and enlightened people, whose austere and massive buildings made the Greek temples look, as he said, like dolled-up houses of cards.[7]

The designs for Egyptian tombs made in Rome by J.L. Desprez (*c.* 1780) were the first attempts to incorporate Egyptian art within Neoclassical architecture. When they were made, the major theoretical work on Egyptian architecture had just been written: this was the youthful Quatremère de Quincy's prize essay *De l'architecture égyptienne, considérée dans son origine, ses principes et son goût, et comparée sous les mêmes rapports à l'architecture grecque* (published 1785). The unbroken uniformity of the surfaces of Quatremère's Egyptian buildings, their colossal scale and their excess of solidity, seem to comment upon the utopian architectural fantasies of the Academy students.

Alongside these two principal tendencies, there was a profusion of other historical and exotic styles. Turkish, Tartar, Gothic and antique buildings were juxtaposed at random.[8] There were even some buildings – of which the Vauxhall on the Boulevard Saint-Martin was one – with a classical elevation at the front and a Gothic one at the back; others had roof gardens incorporating pyramids, antique ruins and Chinese bridges.[9] It was the first flowering of eclectic historicism. Chambers had set the fashion, around 1760, with his remodelling of the botanic gardens at Kew, near London, in which he cheerfully juxtaposed *fabriques* in the most varied styles: an antique temple, a Gothic church, a Chinese pagoda, the House of Confucius, and so on. His subsequent publication, *Plans, Elevations, Sections and Perspective Views of the Gardens and Buildings at Kew in Surrey* (1763), was an event of European significance.

In the long term, the major influence was the introduction of the English landscape garden. This radically altered the relationship between architecture and nature, which was no longer seen as a continuation of architecture but as an autonomous element with laws of its own. The change began in a modest way in the 1760s, when individual features of the English style were adopted in some of the smaller estates on the outskirts of Paris, such as Aunoy, Saint-Leu and Boulogne;[10] but the first systematic, large-scale composition was the park of Ermenonville (1766–76). The literary source for this was the 'Elysium' described in Jean-Jacques Rousseau's novel of education, *Julie ou la Nouvelle Héloïse*. The master of Ermenonville, the Marquis de Girardin, set out to realize Rousseau's conception by creating an Arcadia in which nature was elevated into a moral ideal, and from which the individual might go forth cleansed by solitude and meditation.[11] It was there that the celebrated philosopher spent the last days of his life. When he died in 1778, he was buried by torchlight on an island ringed with poplar trees. His sarcophagus set the seal of sanctity on the park and made it into a place of pilgrimage for persons of feeling.

Thus founded upon sentiment, the landscape garden and its temples, obelisks and pagodas rapidly caught on all over France. Among the major creations of this kind were the parks at Maupertuis, for which Brongniart and Ledoux designed a whole arsenal of *fabriques*, and at Méréville, where Bélanger and Hubert Robert created an artistic synthesis, or *Gesamtkunstwerk*, of architecture, water and planting. Even Marigny, who regarded himself as the custodian of good taste, wanted to embellish his own grounds at Ménars with exotic buildings and regretted that he had not a copy of Chambers to hand. Though Soufflot refused point-blank to build a Chinese kiosk, and suggested putting an antique Temple of Apollo in its place, there were others, including Potain and De Wailly, who were less squeamish.

233 Hubert Robert: *The Ruin in the Park of Betz*, *c.* 1780, engraving by C. Bourgeois.

234 François Barbier: The column in the Désert de Retz, 1780 (Le Rouge, *Jardins anglo-chinois*, cahier XIII).

Vue Perspective de la Colonne.

235   Bernard and Paris: Design for a Gothic windmill, *c.* 1785.

The landscape garden, with its cult of the past, was carried to its ultimate conclusion by Brongniart in his design for Père Lachaise, the first centralized cemetery in Paris (after 1804); he intended to fill it with antique sepulchres and Gothic chapels and to crown it with a tall pyramid.

In all this miscellany of styles, the Gothic was only one of many that were calculated to give the beholder food for thought and meditation; but it was one that proved to have a special relevance to the future.[13] The generation that responded with such enthusiasm to Rousseau and his *Nouvelle Héloïse* was drawn to Gothic not by its structural logic – as admired by the architects and the theorists – but by its atmospheric qualities: the poetry of ruins, the apotheosis of chivalry, the evocation of past closeness to nature. This interest in an indigenous historical past was an essential factor; it sprang from the same roots as Neoclassicism, as a response to mid-century nostalgia. It is no coincidence that garden *fabriques* in historical styles caught on at the same moment as the *goût grec*. Neoclassicism and the rediscovery of the Middle Ages sprang from the very same climate of nostalgia.

In utter contrast to the archaeological temper of Neoclassical architecture, the approach to Gothic in the building of *fabriques* was utterly undogmatic. Architects went medieval precisely because they wanted to emancipate themselves from academic norms and rules. In a telling contrast with Trouard's efforts in Orléans, the Gothic was viewed in terms of the Picturesque, and of an 'absence of rules'. Its forms were thought of as closer to nature than the normative language of the antique; Blondel called them enigmatic, and indeed there was an air of mystery about them. As the example of Lequeu shows, it was possible to air the most preposterous notions in Gothic guise without risking the accusation of 'bad taste' (Plate 235). The various building types to which Gothic was applied – chapels, towers, sentry boxes, even windmills – had no necessary relevance to actual function: in most cases the type was the merest historical fancy-dress, foisted onto a construction intended for entirely different purposes. Unity in this respect was not achieved until the nineteenth century. Even the reference to 'authentic' originals was vague in the extreme, usually going no further than pointed arches and battlements. Only in a few exceptional cases did this 'Gothick' vogue extend to actual houses; it mostly remained confined to gardens.

This preoccupation with time and transience, this nostalgic hankering after the goodness and truth embodied in nature, was the utter opposite of the heroic atmosphere of the revolutionary period. But both – the utopianism of visionary architecture and the sentimentalism of landscape gardening – were intrinsic components of the Romantic Neoclassicism that competed for supremacy with the strict antique throughout the last quarter of the century.

The fate of Neoclassicism, and of its exponents, was ultimately sealed by the political events that brought the Ancien Régime to an end; it was the Revolution that abolished all traditional criteria of judgment and laid the way open for the march of 'genius', in the person of Napoleon. The first signs of the political and psychological crisis that was to lead to the Revolution had become apparent in the 1750s. The crucial issues that confronted the monarchy

All these landscape gardens, with their memorials, grottoes and artificial ruins, were designed to edify, to uplift and to move the beholder.[12] What counted was not archaeological accuracy – although in practice these structures did serve as a test-bed for the Greek and Gothic revivals – so much as atmospheric quality, closeness to the constant flux of nature, and a sense of transience (Plate 233).

The symbol of that transience was the ruin, the sight of which was calculated to arouse contemplative and Romantic sentiments. The most original idea in this vein was undoubtedly the villa that François Barbier was employed to build for the whimsical and Anglophile Chevalier de Monville at the Désert de Retz in 1780 (Plate 234). This takes the form of the broken stump, thirty metres high, of a fluted column, with artificial cracks in the masonry to admit daylight to the inside. Each storey of the interior is elegantly laid out as a complete apartment, with living and sleeping accommodation made up of rooms with multiply curved plans. The central axis is occupied by a top-lit spiral staircase.

were, on one hand, the progressive collapse of the state finances, exacerbated by the obstructive behaviour of the Parlements, and, on the other, the growing agitation for a new and more liberal form of government. The *philosophes* stood in the van of that agitation, though most of the educated members of the population supported it. These were problems that would have taxed the abilities of a monarch of the stature of Louis XIV; the grandson of Louis XV, who ascended the throne as Louis XVI in 1774, was utterly overwhelmed by them. A man of personal integrity, with the best of intentions, the king lacked both the self-confidence and the energy to set the state to rights, and he had the additional misfortune of being married to a woman who was incapable of recognizing the magnitude of the task before her, and who never ceased to intrigue against him.

The seeds of the Revolution lay far back. It did not come from the people but from the interaction between the *philosophes*, the Parlements and the upper nobility. The king's greatest and most dangerous adversary was Philippe, Duc d'Orléans. Not only was Orléans richer than his crowned cousin but his residence, the Palais-Royal, was in the very heart of Paris, where all the threads of subversion came together. His network of conspiracy reached as far as the immediate royal entourage; it involved the king's brother, the Comte de Provence, as well as the queen, who was in constant touch with the disgraced Choiseul.

Louis XVI's reign got off to an encouraging start. Under the thrifty administration of Jacques Necker, the burden of debt was reduced, and the prestige of France was enhanced by her support and prompt recognition of the United States of America. Paris remained the cynosure of Europe; like every other city in the realm, it was engaged in a constant process of modernization and improvement. The king himself was popular. But disintegration had gone too far, and the ideas of Voltaire, Diderot and Rousseau had taken hold of the entire educated population of France. The *philosophes* remained a tightly knit group, pursuing the objective of a new order on the English model, both in the state and in society. Disunited and lacking all conviction, the champions of the old order stood no chance against them. In the Parisian salons where encyclopaedists rubbed shoulders with aristocrats and foreign visitors, anyone who spoke against absolute monarchy, or who praised England and its liberal system, was sure of a hearing. At the première of Beaumarchais's *Mariage de Figaro* in 1784, high society applauded to the echo the very ideas that spelt its ruin.

The state could have been saved only by a comprehensive economic and political reform programme. The king, who was well aware of the impending danger, was willing to undertake this; but the privileged classes were not. In 1787 the Assembly of Notables rejected all proposals for reform. The consequence was national bankruptcy and the convocation of the Estates General; and then it became apparent how far the king's authority had dwindled. He ordered the Three Estates to convene separately, but on 23 June 1789 they defied him, met in joint session, declared themselves to be a National Assembly and embarked on the drafting of a new constitution.

By then it was already too late. The monarchy had been systematically undermined, and all attempts to shore it up were thwarted by the half-heartedness and irresolution of the king himself. In 1792 the monarchy was abolished; the king was executed in 1793, and the queen later in the same year. The Terror ultimately destroyed every vestige of the old system without being able to put anything in its place. The ensuing anarchy was brought to an end on 9 Thermidor Year II (27 July 1794) by the fall of Robespierre and the advent of the Directoire, which opened the prison gates and attempted to restore the shattered structure of government. But only the coup of 18 Brumaire Year VIII (9 November 1799), and the personality of Napoleon Bonaparte, could construct a new state.

The Academy of Architecture followed the monarchy into oblivion.[14] It was the end of an institution that had bestowed international fame on French architecture; foreign princes continued to consult it to the last. In the eyes of the National Assembly, it was a school of servility, falsehood and jealousy; in a speech to the Convention, David alleged that it was a haven for aristocrats, riddled with *esprit de corps*, and that its teaching was reactionary and pernicious. In 1791 it was stripped of its oversight of the royal buildings; in 1793, together with the other Academies, including the Académie de France in Rome, it was dissolved by the Assembly, 'not so much for reasons of economy as in view of the fundamental ideals of the Revolution': by which was meant the principle of equality. In its capacity as the arbiter of architectural competitions, the Academy was replaced by a jury comprising painters, sculptors, civil servants, anatomists, actors and shoemakers, plus a few architects.

For the royal architects – or at least for those who did not ally themselves with the Revolution, as did De Wailly, Bélanger and Boullée – times grew hard. Almost all were treated as suspect persons and went in fear of their lives, because they had worked for the nobility and for the princes. Mique and Moreau-Desproux were guillotined. A number were imprisoned: Ledoux began the writing of his architectural *magnum opus* in a prison cell. Others managed to lie low until the Terror was over, as did Pâris in Normandy, Brongniart in Bordeaux, and Antoine-François Peyre in the uniform of a private soldier in the Army of the North. In the long run, however, their experience proved to be indispensable. When the Directoire reconstituted the ministries and reorganized the administration of public works, architects were once more in demand. Chalgrin, Rondelet and Brongniart had seats on the supreme building authority, the Conseil des Bâtiments. The inspectors in charge of the six subordinate 'classes' of that organization were also former Academicians. When those inspectors held their regular meetings with the three members of the Conseil des Bâtiments, the system of the last pre-Revolutionary year, presided over by the members of the Academy and a triumvirate of royal architects, was virtually reconstituted – except that formerly only the best architects in the country had belonged to the Academy, whereas now anyone, even a nobody, could be co-opted by ministerial fiat.

Former Academicians also took their places in the Institut de France, a body set up by the Convention to promote the progress of science and art by offering a forum in which all progressive thinkers might exchange ideas and display the results of their work. The Institut consisted of 144 members, divided into three classes: physics and mathematics; moral and political sciences; literature and art. These in turn were divided into sections. Unlike the former Academies, this was a union of artists on a purely theoretical basis. One of the eight sections in the third class was devoted to architecture; and its first members, elected without regard to their political sympathies, were Gondoin, De Wailly, Pâris, Antoine-François Peyre and Boullée. In 1803, when the visual arts were given a class to themselves, the number of architects was raised to ten; and these too were all former Academicians.

These former royal architects survived; but the break with the past was nevertheless total. The Revolution brought building activity to a complete halt; nor did the Directoire give it a new impulse. The royal architects were unemployed. Their former clients had either perished or fled the country, and ruin stared them in the face. Some, like Boullée and Ledoux, made use of the enforced leisure to put their theories into writing. Napoleon, for his part, took the view that the architectural profession had been the downfall of his predecessors, the kings of France; and initially, when he had anything to build, he gave the work to his engineers. His programme of public buildings started only in 1806, with the Arc de Triomphe and the Temple de la Gloire (now the Madeleine).

Nor was this all: the demise of the Academy had resulted in a horrific decline in architectural standards. As there were no longer any recognized qualifications, and everyone enjoyed the same rights, the profession was swamped with individuals who called themselves architects without having the least knowledge or experience. Many sheltered behind building contractors, in whose name they designed and built; equally, numerous contractors who were businessmen pure and simple nevertheless designed their own buildings. French architecture suffered a marked decline in quality: 'It was almost a good thing that no great monuments were built at that time; they would probably have been a disgrace to architecture and also, in a sense, to the nation itself.' (Viel de Saint-Maux)

CHAPTER 2

Court Art

Under Louis XVI, for the second time in the eighteenth century, the court relinquished its leading role in the pursuit of architecture. The financial situation had become desperate. Even that keen builder, Louis XV, had found that the growth of the public debt increasingly cramped his style; there was no money anywhere. Under the new king, whose tastes were modest and who had no love of ostentation, building activity came to a halt. There was also a change at the top. Marigny had already bowed to the inevitable and resigned in 1773; two years later, Gabriel retired from court office at the age of seventy-seven. It was the end of the era of grand projects that remains associated with his name.[15]

After a brief interregnum under Abbé Terray, the king appointed the Comte d'Angiviller to be Directeur Général des Bâtiments du Roi.[16] Charles-Claude de Flahaut de la Billarderie, Comte d'Angiviller, owed his appointment to the fact that from 1760 onwards he had been chamberlain to the royal princes. Louis XVI had thus been constantly in his company since his earliest youth, and this was his way of showing his gratitude. Unlike Marigny, who always remained approachable and never stood on his dignity, Angiviller was offhand and autocratic. He wanted everything under his own control and did not hesitate to pick a fight with the Academy by abruptly altering its statutes. Equally brusque and maladroit in his handling of artists, he forbade them to form cooperative associations and arbitrarily removed from the Salon any paintings that he found objectionable. In all these ways, he provoked the violent reaction that took place after the outbreak of the Revolution, when David founded the Commune des Arts.

Angiviller took more interest in painting, and history painting in particular, than in architecture. He instituted a series of statues of prominent men, of which Louis XVI ordered miniature copies to be manufactured in porcelain. It was his particular ambition to make his master into a great patron of the arts; he could hardly have picked a worse moment. A convinced amateur of the 'Etruscan' style, which came to the fore in the 1780s, he presented the Sèvres porcelain factory with a collection of Etruscan vases to use as models, and wrote to the directors to the effect that – even if they thought him, Angiviller, a barbarian – they were going to have to get used to the Etruscan taste.

Angiviller's architectural projects – a new Château de Rambouillet, a Place Louis-XVI on the left bank of the Seine opposite the Tuileries – were never realized. The remodelling of the Grande Galerie du Louvre, to accommodate the king's collection of paintings, also failed to progress very far, because it proved impossible to agree on the form of lighting. In 1778 Soufflot proposed blocking up the windows and installing skylights.[17] This idea was defeated by the cost, but it was several times revived, latterly by the Academy, which wanted top lighting *and* windows. The Revolution cut the debate short, and it was not until 1802

that Soufflot's idea was taken up again by the team of Charles Percier and Pierre Fontaine and put into execution.

The existence of the post of chief architect to the king was a thorn in Angiviller's side, and he was impatient for Gabriel to retire so that he could abolish it. In 1776 he reorganized the Bâtiments du Roi under a triumvirate of Intendants Généraux: Mique, Soufflot and M.B. Hazon. Among these, Mique, the queen's architect, who had briefly been Gabriel's successor, took precedence over Soufflot – who was furious at being passed over – and the insignificant Hazon. All major decisions had thenceforth to be taken jointly by this triumvirate. These authoritarian measures of Angiviller's also restricted the king's direct control over his own building works; they would have been unthinkable under Louis XIV or Louis XV.

Marie-Antoinette had confirmed Mique in his post as Intendant and surveyor-general of works to the queen, thus giving him a certain measure of independence from Angiviller; but there was not much for him to do in that capacity other than build a number of *fabriques* at the Petit Trianon and remodel the Appartements de la Reine in the main palace of Versailles.

At the Petit Trianon, which the king had given her, and where she felt less oppressed by the shadows of the past, the queen had created a realm of her own. She too wanted an 'English garden,' and so she instructed Mique to modernize the grounds. With Hubert Robert as consultant, Mique built her a small theatre, a miniature version of the Versailles Opera both in shape and in colour (1778), and a number of *fabriques* (1778–9). One of these, the Temple de l'Amour, an elegant dodecastyle rotunda with an exceptionally delicate frieze of plant tendrils, was inspired by the Sibylline Temple (Temple of Vesta) at Tivoli, a favourite motif of Robert's.[18] Another, the Salon du Rocher, was an octagonal gazebo – based on Chambers's Temple of Solitude at Kew – perched on the rocky shore of an artificial lake.

These creations are in the best Gabriel tradition; but just across the lake there stands a work of pure Romantic stagecraft: the Hameau (1783–5), a model hamlet of sham cottages along the shore, dominated by the lighthouse-like Tour de Marlborough (Plate 236). In this Marie-Antoinette was following the fashion of the age, which subscribed to Rousseau's gospel of the return to nature and the simple life. In preference to the exotic fancies of her contemporaries,[19] she chose a Norman village; its picturesque, timber-framed cottages ministered to her needs and also housed her own herds and some genuine peasants. Her models were the Hameau of the Prince de Condé at Chantilly (1774–5) and that of her aunts by marriage, Louis XV's daughters, at Bellevue (1779). In her hamlet, as in theirs, crumbling roughcast and rustic garb disguised interiors of luxurious refinement, and the ballroom was housed in a barn. The charm consisted in the contrast between real life and

game-playing, between courtly etiquette and spontaneous informality.

This union of classical antiquity and Rousseauesque enthusiasm for nature – still imperfect at the Trianon – was consummated in the Laiterie (Plate 237), the queen's dairy, at Rambouillet (1785–8).[20] Designed in accordance with the fashion of the day to supply milk to the queen and her ladies, both for drinking and for butter and cheese making, this remarkable building (like its counterparts at the Petit Trianon, Chantilly and elsewhere) consists of two rooms: a large, domed rotunda where crocks of milk stood on marble benches all round the walls, and a rectangular back room that ended in a huge, rocky grotto with water cascading down its walls. It combined the bucolic atmosphere of *Daphnis and Chloe*, the Arcadian notion of pastoral bliss and virtuous closeness to nature – as expressed in the rich relief decoration of the walls and niches,[21] and in the marble group of the nymph Amalthea and her goat – with the forms of a rigorous imitation of antiquity. The successive designs prepared by the architect Jacques-Jean Thévenin, a protégé of Angiviller's, reveal the evolution of taste away from the subtle classicism of Gabriel and towards the austere sobriety and block-like emphasis of the Louis XVI style. Both here and at the Trianon, however, the underlying idea stemmed from Hubert Robert, Piranesi's pupil. A Romantic influence is strongly apparent here: it was the painter, not the architect, who determined the siting and appearance of the temple.

Robert's services were also enlisted in the grounds of Versailles itself. The park had run to seed, and its remodelling is one of Louis XVI's genuine claims to fame. Over a period of ten years (1774–84) it was completely replanted, and the neglected *bosquets*, aqueducts and reservoirs were restored. In reaction against the prevalent fashion for English gardens, the king, supported by his Service des Bâtiments, adhered strictly to tradition and restored the park to the precise state in which it had been under Louis XIV. The sole exception was the 'Bath of Apollo'. Made for Louis XIV's Thetis grotto, this celebrated group was now placed in an entirely new and Romantic setting. Under Robert's direction, Thévenin created an artificial rocky scene that was half grotto and half ruin, with running water everywhere; tall trees surrounded the group and contributed to a Romantic mood that was utterly out of character with the château itself. It was the transposition of a painting into life, and the direct forerunner of the Rocher at the Trianon.

The reign of Louis XVI has left few traces in the architecture of Versailles. Gabriel's Grand Projet never progressed beyond the Aile Neuve. Not even the Grand Degré, the stair to the Grands Appartements, was completed; at the queen's wish, its place was taken by a theatre, built in 1785, which survived until Louis-Philippe's time. Another new project,

by Mique (1776), remained unexecuted. But the shortage of space remained acute. The queen, who felt that Gabriel's plans did not adequately reflect her needs, pressed the king to rebuild; Angiviller, too, was keen to set the seal on his career by supervising the building of a new Versailles. In 1780, after much hesitation, the king finally agreed to hold a competition for the complete rebuilding of the château, with just two provisos: that J.H. Mansart's garden front and the Grands Appartements should be retained, and that his own apartment should be moved to the entrance side.

As with the competition for the Place Louis-XV, the most celebrated architects in the country submitted entries, including Boullée, Potain, Mique, Pâris and Antoine-François Peyre.[22] Despite their utopian vastness of scale, the resulting designs are among the most magnificent château designs of the whole century. A comparison with Fischer von Erlach's designs for Schönbrunn and for a palace for Frederick I of Prussia, as well as his conjectural reconstruction of the Golden House of Nero, reveals an astonishing affinity in megalomania between the high Baroque and late Neoclassicism, before the latter began to operate in isolated blocks. All the Versailles designs set out to unify the vast pile and give it uniform façades, very much in line with Gabriel's ideas. In all of them, the Cour de Marbre disappeared behind a new façade that closed off the Cour Royale, level with the Salon d'Hercule. Louis XIV's château was left standing; but the picturesque character of its old elevations was lost to view within a vast new shell, uniform to the point of monotony.

236 Richard Mique: Versailles, Hameau, 1783–5.

237 Jacques-Jean Thévenin: Rambouillet, Laiterie, 1785–8, rotunda and grotto (*left*: exterior; *right*: interior).

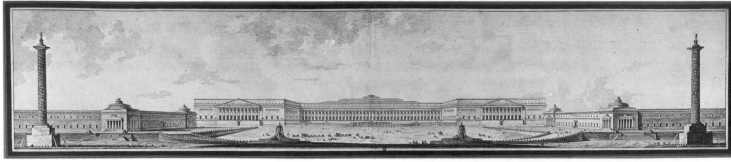

238   Etienne-Louis Boullée: Versailles, Grand projet, c. 1780.

239   Pierre-Adrien Pâris: Versailles, Hall of the Assemblée Nationale, 1789, engraving by Ponce after Bord.

In a number of the designs, including Boullée's (Plate 238), the approach to the château was to be flanked by massive blocks of ministerial offices with monumental, pedimented porticoes; the Cour Royale was to be widened; and the garden front was to be tripled in length, to provide an apartment for the king, with pavilions that projected far into the gardens. Others, like that of Peyre the Younger, enclosed the Place d'Armes with semicircular double colonnades and adorned it with fountains and Trajanic triumphal columns in allusion to Bernini's Piazza S. Pietro.

The design that kept closest to the shape of the existing fabric was that of Pâris (1785). He left the garden front unaltered and used the central portion of the château for two complete apartments – the king on the right, the queen on the left – ranged around a pair of inner courts and separated by the grand staircase; the external 'envelope' was to remain intact. The new façade would be dominated, as in the Place Louis-XV, by a continuous order of giant Corinthian columns, on a rusticated podium; the centre would be crowned by an attic, and the wings by an array of statues. The Place d'Armes, closed off by a hemicycle of barracks for the Swiss Guards and adorned with fountains and obelisks, became a gigantic forecourt to the colonnaded façades of the palace.

The king inclined towards this design; but since the financial plight of the state precluded any thought of putting it into practice, it and all the other designs were shelved, to await better times that never came. And so, ultimately, it was the Revolution that ensured the survival of Louis XIV's château to the present day.

Pierre-Adrien Pâris (1745–1819), just mentioned, was one of the last architects to work at Versailles.[23] A native of Besançon, he had been a pupil of Trouard's. He did not win the Prix de Rome, but Marigny arranged for him to spend five years in Rome, 1769–74, and there he devoted himself with such zeal to the study of antiquity that he was regarded as the leading expert on ancient art in Rome. His friendship with Trouard brought him into contact with the Duc d'Aumont, first chamberlain at court and director of the Menus-Plaisirs. His decoration of the Hôtel d'Aumont, on the Place Louis-XV (now Hôtel Crillon), a free interpretation of antiquity combined with Renaissance forms and Gabrielian elegance, chimed perfectly with modern taste. It earned him, on Challe's death, his post as *dessinateur du cabinet*, a key position within the Menus-Plaisirs that enabled him to display his extraordinary talent as a draughtsman. The king valued him highly and in 1784 appointed him architect to the Menus-Plaisirs. He thus became Gabriel's successor as personal architect to the king, and Mique was put in the shade.

Among Pâris's designs, which were mostly for theatrical shows and festive pageantry, were the structures known as the Baraques de Versailles.[24] These were temporary wooden buildings for ballet and theatrical entertainments, set up in the Cour Royale every year for the Carnival season, to relieve the lack of suitable performance spaces; after 1786, for the sake of tidiness, they were relegated to the south side of the palace. These Baraques, traditional items of court garden-party equipment, are known to us only from plans and drawings; they are interesting, nevertheless, as a courtly reflection of the last phase of Neoclassicism. In them, Pâris was able to give free rein to his archaeological expertise. Under the queen's influence, he initially deployed an 'upholsterer's style' (*style tapissier*), of exceptional elegance, all taffeta hangings, floral festoons, mirrors and costly chandeliers; but this soon gave way to a stricter style. The great ballroom used in 1787 was supported by Ionic columns, between which balconies for spectators were suspended, and ceiled with a massive coffered vault. The draperies already anticipated the Empire style and the work of Percier and Fontaine; the specially commissioned furnishings in Turkish and Gothic forms were avant-garde designs, far ahead of contemporary taste. The Salle d'Assemblée used by the Notables in 1787 was a similar temporary building by Pâris; but in this the austerity of the antique prevailed (Plate 239). Baseless, fluted Doric columns carried a classical entablature with a frieze of triglyphs; the walls were bare and unadorned, and the coffered vault opened, tent-like, in the centre.[25] The throne was placed above the entrance, in a proscenium-like opening surmounted by a large baldachin. Slightly modified, the same building served as the debating chamber of the Estates General in 1789, and thus became the birthplace of the French Revolution. Pâris was appointed architect to the National Assembly in 1790, but in the following year he was obliged to flee abroad to escape persecution.

CHAPTER 3

Public Architecture and the Late Work of Ledoux

In the teeth of a rapidly worsening financial situation, public building activity continued to the very end of the Ancien Régime, though many projects remained unexecuted. The greatly altered intellectual and social climate was not without its effect. The influence of the Enlightenment, and the growth of intellectual emancipation, had fed a demand for social and cultural institutions. The call was no longer for churches and affirmations of wealth and power but for theatres, libraries, hospitals, mercantile exchanges and the like. Within ten years or so, Paris witnessed the building of the Comédie Française (1779–82) by Peyre and De Wailly, the Théâtre des Italiens (1780–2) by Jean-François Heurtier, the Théâtre Feydeau (1789) by Legrand and Molinos and the Théâtre du Palais-Royal (1790) by Louis: six theatres in all. To these were added the major architectural projects of the crown: the completion of the Ecole Militaire, the building of a state bank, a new Opera, a royal library, the Hôtel-Dieu: of these, only the Ecole Militaire was completed, by Brongniart in 1788. A competition for the state bank was held in 1785; Ledoux, Antoine, Bélanger and Brongniart submitted entries, but no decision was taken.

The debate over the building of a new Opéra was particularly lively. The rebuilt Opéra in the Palais Royal had been burnt down in 1781. In the same year, and in the space of three months, Lenoir-le-Romain put up a temporary replacement at the Porte Saint-Martin. Since his youthful period in Dijon, Lenoir had built up an extensive practice in Paris, and he was one of the fashionable architects of the day, though not a member of the Academy; his theatre, mostly built in timber, was a creation of ponderous, quasi-antique but curiously inorganic forms.[26] But the idea of a prestigious, permanent opera house long remained a favourite discussion point among architects and within the Academy; however, no commission was ever awarded, and the scheme never got past the stage of a competition. Among the numerous entries, intended for the most diverse sites – including the Pont-Neuf, the rue Saint-Honoré, the gardens of the Palais-Royal and the Place du Carrousel – the most interesting were those of Boullée and Bélanger.[27]

Boullée (1781) designed a large, free-standing rotunda, ringed with forty-eight Corinthian columns, topped with an equal number of statues, a continuous attic and a shallow dome. This immense tholos stood on a high podium and was buttressed by four equidistant pedestals, on which were equestrian figures inspired by Coysevox's celebrated Horses of Marly in the Place Louis-XV. Between these, four wide flights of steps rose to the top of the podium, where every intercolumniation corresponded to a doorway. The interior was divided into two hemicycles, one for the auditorium and one for the stage area. The auditorium was lined with a giant Ionic order, on an unprecedentedly monumental scale, the entablature of which formed the third-tier balcony. Above

this – again for the first time in any theatre – there arose a vast, coffered half-dome; the balconies for the 'gods' were fitted into the lowest rows of coffers. A single immense arch, spanning the entire height and breadth of the theatre, framed the stage, which it did not compress but revealed to the full width of the building, removing the need for a proscenium.

The antique circular temple form, unprecedented in any opera house, was made possible only by relegating all the storage space into the cellars; it had been formulated in theory in Chaumont's treatise *Exposition des principes qu'on doit suivre dans l'ordonnance des théâtres modernes* (1769), in which the antique hemicyclic form was recommended for the auditorium, with particular reference to the advantage of having numerous identical exits, especially in case of fire. One concrete source was a design for the Comédie-Française, thought to have been prepared by Soufflot in the 1760s,[28] which Boullée developed on his own lines. Of all the locations that he considered for his new Opéra, the Place du Carrousel, in front of the Palais des Tuileries, had the great advantage that it would not entail the purchase of any land. Boullée therefore placed his opera house dead on the axis between the Tuileries and the Louvre, which he additionally emphasized by laying out a new road between the two palaces.

In his project (1781), Bélanger based himself on the same assumptions. He too placed the Opéra opposite the Tuileries, with which he linked it through two large exedrae in the form of colonnades, behind which were to lie the king's and queen's stables and subsidiary courts. After initially making his theatre rectangular, with a projecting octastyle portico, he changed the portico in a second design into a semicircular, pavilion-like vestibule, colonnaded like an antique temple and crowned with a dome.

Both these projects were ruled out by Angiviller, who saw any building on the Louvre-Tuileries axis as a threat to his never-abandoned Grand Projet. He gave his preference to the designs of Maximilien Brébion and of Marie-Joseph Peyre, both of whom wanted to set the Opéra close to the Tuileries but to one side of the central axis. The king's vacillation and the shortage of funds meant that no decision was taken, and all the projects stayed on paper.

A further, long-standing need was that of a suitable home for the royal library, after Marigny's and Soufflot's plans to move it to the Louvre had come to nothing.[29] The library needed not only new storage accommodation for its vastly increased holdings of books but – as it was a public library – a suitable reading room. The finance minister, Calonne, commissioned Boullée, who had already worked for him on the rebuilding of the Bourse,[30] to produce two alternative projects.

The first was a completely new building on the site of the convent of the Capucines, to the north of the Place

240 Etienne-Louis Boullée: Design for the Royal Library, 1785, lecture hall (Paris, Bibliothèque Nationale).

241 Etienne-Louis Boullée: Designs for the Royal Library, façade (*above*: first design; *below*: third design) (Paris, Bibliothèque Nationale).

Vendôme, in the shape of a gigantic rectangular block, with four internal courts arranged in a square around a central cruciform reading room. On the entrance side was a large exedra lined with colonnades and fronted by a fourfold columnar screen. The façade was entirely in the spirit of Gondoin. The central colonnade and the bare walls to either side were surmounted by a plain attic and a continuous cornice that pulled the whole together into a block. As at the Ecole de Chirurgie, there were no breaks and no crowning centrepiece. The emphatic tripartite structure, and the contrast between the light, transparent portico and the massive, solid expanses of wall to either side, were characteristic of Boullée's compositions of the 1780s.

This project (1784), with its total concentration on harmony of plan, without any regard for the practical requirements of a library, was too big and too costly even for Boullée, and he went on to concentrate on a second project (1785), no less grand, but confined to an adaptation of the existing building in the Rue de Richelieu. There, around an elongated, oblong court, the royal library was housed in the Palais Mazarin and adjacent buildings, which were understandably ill-adapted to the purpose. Where others had envisaged no alternative to total clearance and redevelopment of the site, Boullée now moved in the opposite direction. He left the old buildings untouched and used them for the book stacks; but he transformed the open court into a monumental reading room (Plate 240). He thus succeeded, despite the shortage of resources and the encumbrance of existing structures, in making the library practical without sacrificing its monumentality. This reading room was among Boullée's most magnificent designs. The long sides were tiered, with wide, man-high steps, on which books were stored. On the topmost step a colonnade ran the whole length of the wall, with more shelving behind it. At the end, the colonnade passed in front of a brilliantly top-lit, apsidal recess to form a kind of triumphal arch, suitable for the erection of allegorical figures. Above the colonnade was a

gigantic, coffered tunnel vault, reminiscent of the Roman basilicas. Here – as in the adjacent buildings, where the windows were to be walled up – all the light entered from above, just as Blondel had recommended in his *Cours d'architecture*.

This creation – it would have been the largest reading room in the world – owed its austere magnificence to a free interpretation of the antique; but its true prototype, as Boullée himself revealed in his *Essai sur l'art*, was Raphael's *School of Athens*. Here, as there, the sum of human knowledge was collected together beneath a massive vault that symbolized the universe: a telling indication of the span of artistic reference within Neoclassicism, and its ability to look beyond the antique and to make unprejudiced use of Renaissance sources.

Of Boullée's three designs for the entrance façade, the first was a paraphrase of the initial project, from which it borrowed the central portico, the attic and the continuous frieze with its relief (Plate 241a). Behind the columns, however, in the shadows of the vestibule, two flights of stairs could be seen – an inspired idea that Karl Friedrich Schinkel was to take up at the Altes Museum in Berlin. The second design had a solid wall broken only by a narrow Ionic portal and flanking statuary niches; and the third, somewhat later design (1788) was an example, of highly explicit *architecture parlante* (Plate 241b). The bare wall was relieved only by a frieze of festoons and by two inscriptions; the portal was flanked by a pair of Atlantean figures bearing an enormous globe – presumably an allusion to the two Baroque globes held by the library. Carved into the globe were the zodiacal constellations associated with autumn, as a symbol of the harvest of knowledge that is garnered here. This kind of decorative symbolism, which became general during the Revolution, was an exception in the work of Boullée, whose symbolism was otherwise strictly architectural.

The library project, which Boullée published in 1785, and for which he had a model made, was a great public success;

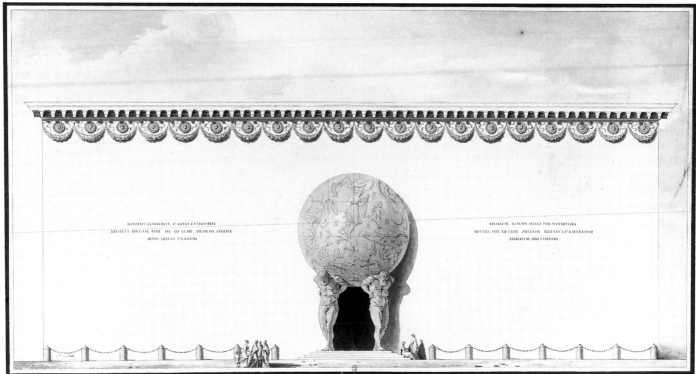

and in the nineteenth century de Laborde would still regard it as the best possible solution.[31] It had every chance of being realized, but the chronic indecision of the Ancien Régime authorities dragged matters out until the Revolution put an end to all projects.

Even more urgent than these cultural undertakings was the need to renew the provision of hospitals in Paris. The main problem here was the Hôtel-Dieu, where the conditions were inhuman and patient mortality was appalling; the building had also suffered a succession of devastating fires. Decisions were taken at different times to enlarge it, to divide its work among other hospitals, and to demolish it and

start again out of town; but nothing was done. A number of designs for a replacement were in existence. The most ambitious was by Bernard Poyet (1742–1824), a pupil of De Wailly's, who was Moreau's successor as city architect of Paris (1785); this looked like the Colosseum, but without the applied orders. The wards, 144 of them, occupied the outer circle and the connecting ranges that converged like the spokes of a wheel to a circular central court. Poyet's vast, three-storey building could have accommodated more than 3,000 patients. But as no one could decide the fundamental question – retain or disperse – the problem was still unsolved at the Revolution.

242   Mathurin Crucy: Nantes, Théâtre, Graslin, 1784–8, engraving by Hersan (Nantes, Musée du Château des Ducs de Bretagne).

What did happen was that a succession of smaller hospitals were built, organized on modern principles: wards classified according to diseases, a single bed for every patient, and so on. Thus, the financier Nicolas Beaujon employed Boullée's pupil Girardin to build the Hôpital Beaujon (1784) for the care of pauper children; and the chief architect to the Hôpital Général, a pupil of Chalgrin's, Charles-François Viel (1745–1819),[32] built the Hôpital Cochin (1780–2) with a conventional façade divided into centre and end pavilions and crowned with a triangular pediment above a Tuscan portico reminiscent of Brongniart's Capucins. After the rejection of his Hôtel-Dieu project, Poyet turned to the building of the Hôpital de la Roquette (1786) and the remodelling of the Hôpital Sainte-Anne, both model institutions of their day, which were completed after the Revolution.

The only public works that altered the appearance of the city at this time were the demolition, under Poyet's direction, of the houses that stood on the medieval bridges over the Seine, and the building by Jean-Rodolphe Perronet of the Pont Louis-XVI (1789–91; now Pont de la Concorde), which had been projected since 1777. Both undertakings contributed notably to the modernization of the city. In the Pont Louis-XVI, as in his earlier Pont de Neuilly,[33] Perronet applied his principle of equal arch heights – and thus a level roadway – together with a carefully calculated distribution of weight, as achieved by Soufflot at Sainte-Geneviève.[34] The great north-south axis, running through the Place Louis-XV, which Gabriel had in mind in his design for the square, was now a reality, and what is now the Place de la Concorde became the pivot of traffic movement in the western part of the city.

Outside Paris, it was Nantes and Bordeaux, above all,

that produced notable public works. At the very end of the Ancien Régime, Nantes not only implemented a comprehensive and well-thought-out urban plan but constructed a number of public buildings in no way inferior to those in Paris. For this the city had one of its own sons to thank: the architect Mathurin Crucy (1749–1826). Descended from a line of local timber merchants, a pupil of Blondel and a former Rome scholar, Crucy took up the work of Ceineray and transplanted the style of the Academy to Nantes.[35]

Modifying an initial plan drawn up by Vigny in 1761, Ceineray had devised an overall plan for the modernization of Nantes, the principal features of which were to be the razing of the city walls, the construction of new squares and embankments along the river Loire, the inclusion of the Ile Feydeau in the developed area, and the straightening of the streets in the ancient city centre: the same principles that had been followed by Gabriel in Rennes and by Blondel in Strasbourg. Nantes became one huge construction site. In 1779, after an Academy training under Blondel and Le Roy,[36] followed by four years in Rome, Crucy entered Ceineray's office (where he had probably served an initial apprenticeship before leaving Nantes). By that time the city walls had already been taken down, and the river embankments and adjoining streets were complete. In the following year he succeeded to Ceineray's position.

It was Crucy who introduced the rigorous Neoclassicism of the Greek revival to Nantes. He built the straight streets in the eastern part of the city – the Quartier des Cours – with their uniform façades, extended the promenades begun by Ceineray outside the walls (now the Cours Saint-Pierre and Cours Saint-André) and laid out the Place Louis-XVI (now Place Maréchal-Foch), at the end of the Paris road, dominated by the noble Palladian façade of the Hôtel de

Montaudouin. In the western part of the city he also designed an entirely new district, the Quartier Graslin. His façade designs for the Place de la Cour des Comptes (now Place Salengro) set the definitive house type for the whole development: three-storey apartment houses with a rusticated base, façades unadorned except for the balcony consoles, and a strong horizontal emphasis provided by continuous main cornices at roof level.

The Quartier Graslin was named after the rich speculator who had bought up the land piecemeal and had already started building houses for rent; at the same time, he built streets and squares and presented them as a gift to the municipality. Ceineray had incorporated all this in his plan in 1779, but planned development began only in 1781, under Crucy. He gave the quarter prestige by adorning it with two public buildings, the theatre (Plate 242) and the Bourse. The central feature, at Graslin's suggestion, was the theatre (1784–8). This moderately sized, beautifully proportioned building relies on the contrast between smooth walls and an octastyle Corinthian portico. The richly moulded classical entablature supports a low attic and statues above the columns; as in many Neoclassical churches, the middle four columns are duplicated behind. Then comes the vestibule, originally closed off from the outside only by a grille; it has a transverse tunnel vault and apsidal ends.

The Place Graslin, in front of the theatre, was originally intended to be an oval, but this was changed into a rectangle with rounded corners. As the meeting place of six radially placed streets,[37] it bears some similarities to the square in front of Peyre's and De Wailly's Comédie-Française in Paris, but is far more self-contained and better proportioned. The uniform façades, with their blind arcades on the ground floor and continuous first-floor and attic balconies, complement the portico, which chimes perfectly with its surroundings and sets the scale for the square. Eight years after opening, this theatre (which was the prototype for the theatre in Caen, built in 1787) burned to the ground; it was restored to its original form by Crucy in 1811.

For the Bourse, the city council had turned down Ceineray's design – and a subsequent one by Potain – on grounds of location and size. Crucy's proposal, of 1784, was to build a more modest Bourse in the Place du Commerce, the riverside commercial centre of the city, and this was accepted. His plans were ready by 1790, and construction covered the years 1792–1812. The resulting almost square building, much altered in the nineteenth century (it is now the Chambre du Commerce), has the same formal precision and air of distinction as the theatre. Classical pediments, consoles and window aprons are the only ornamental forms. Crucy gave the main façade a giant decastyle Ionic portico surmounted by statues; on the rear elevation he added a single-storey fore-building with a roof terrace supported by Tuscan columns. He gave over half of the interior to the great trading room of the Bourse itself, with a decor on revolutionary themes.

The theatre and Bourse in Nantes were among the last major Neoclassical buildings to be built in France; they are rare manifestations of the 'Greek' style, with its limited use of accents, that had prevailed at the Academy since Le Roy.[38] Of the public baths that Crucy built on the Ile

Feydeau (1802), a temple-like structure with statuary niches around the curve of the outer wall, nothing has survived.

The street layout of the new quarter, too, reveals Crucy's ordering hand. The centre is marked by the Place Graslin, with its theatre. From this, one axis runs eastward to the old city centre; there, Ceineray had intended to build a Place Royale in place of the old city gate, the Porte Saint-Nicolas, and in front of the eponymous church. The projection of the Quartier Graslin altered the function of this Place Royale. Crucy moved it away from the church, made it rectangular with one semicircular end and turned it into the point of articulation between the new and old towns, from which nine streets radiate. The buildings that frame this major intersection are surprisingly modest; this was a Place Royale in name only. Without a public building to suggest a ceremonial function, it is surrounded by four-storey apartment houses with uniformly sober façades. There is not a pediment, not a column, not a sculptural ornament to be seen: only two horizontal cornices. Nor is there now a statue of the king. The square has become the expression of a social function, in which all the citizens have a part.

The Cours Cambronne, a promenade planted with trees and lined with buildings, which Crucy laid out close to the theatre (begun 1792), is more conventional. Its particular attraction is the terrace-like podium on which the houses stand. Crucy articulated the continuous façades on the pattern already used by Ceineray: above a rusticated base – as used in the Allée Brancas and elsewhere – the two upper storeys are held together by giant Ionic pilasters, while the balconies and cornices match those of the Place Graslin. The development of the Quartier Graslin, in which Crucy continued to play a part after he ceased to be city architect, went on far into the nineteenth century.

In Bordeaux, the leading spirit was Victor Louis. Since the days of Intendant Tourny, the city had been engaged in a continuing process of modernization. Louis had marked a crucial accent with his new Grand Théâtre, on its pivotal site at the intersection of the Allées de Tourny and the Cours de l'Intendance and Georges Clémenceau, which form the framework of the new part of the city. Its counterpart in the historic city centre was the big archiepiscopal palace by François Bonfin (1776–8), based on a design by Etienne.

Louis's practice in Bordeaux was extensive, and included many private buildings. In the vicinity of his Grand Théâtre and elsewhere in the city he built numerous hôtels, most notably the palatial Hôtel de Saige (1775–7; now the Préfecture), which combines the Roman palazzo type with all the elegance and comfort of a patrician hôtel particulier.[39] Such works set a high standard for the architects of the following generation, including Louis Combes and Jean-Baptiste Dufart, and their influence was long-lived, so that Bordeaux became the centre of Neoclassical architecture in the southern part of France.

The area round the Grand Théâtre gained enormously in site values from the decision to raze the neighbouring fortress, the Château Trompette, on the banks of the Garonne, which had blocked the expansion of the city downstream. The proceeds were used to finance the building of the theatre. On the site of the Château Trompette itself, the Intendant decreed the building of a Place Louis-XVI or

243 Victor Louis: Bordeaux, Design for Place Louis XVI, 1785, watercolour (Paris, Musée du Louvre).

244 Victor Louis: Paris, Palais Royal, garden façade, 1781–3.

Place Ludovise, for which the local architect François Lhote submitted a plan as early as 1774. This was to be a Place Royale with a Colonne Ludovise modelled on Trajan's column in the centre. In 1784 Louis considerably expanded this design (Plate 243). He envisaged a huge hemicycle, receiving the streets that converged on it from the new quarter, and a matching curve at the end nearer to the river. For the façades he envisaged a low, arcaded base surmounted by a continuous giant order of fluted pilasters and, above these, a deep entablature with prominent modillions and a tall, balustraded attic. The endless monotony of the giant order was broken only by the attic-high triumphal arches through which the streets entered the square. The Place Ludovise was the last Place Royale ever projected in France; it was never finished. Work began in 1785, but such was the financial plight of the state that this grandiose scheme never progressed beyond a single block.

Of all the many works that Louis carried out in the environs of Bordeaux, one, the Château du Bouilh, begun in 1787 for the Marquis de la Tour du Pin, is of particular formal interest. A drawing now in the city archives in Bordeaux presumably represents a variant of the original design, though it looks more like an ideal project by one of the Rome scholars. The centre of the composition is occupied by a large, free-standing tempietto or circular temple, built to contain a chapel and the winery, the estate's principal source of income. Behind this is a hemicycle made up of pavilions with linking colonnades. Ramps curve round the base of the tempietto to give access to the wide terrace on which the whole composition stands. In the event, only one of the large end pavilions was built, and its detailing was never completed.

In Bordeaux, Louis had been introduced to Freemasonry by the Duc de Chartres, later Duc d'Orléans, who was one

day to become known as Philippe-Egalité.[40] Chartres was as great an enthusiast as the Comte d'Artois for all things English – notably horse-racing and betting – and in constant need of cash. In the teeth of a public outcry, he summoned Louis to Paris to plan the speculative development of the large garden behind the Palais-Royal. Louis proposed to line the garden on three sides with ranges of buildings over a continuous ground-level arcade that could be rented out as shops, cafés and restaurants; the upper floors would contain private apartments. His designs were ready in 1781, work began in the same year, and the development was completed in 1783.

The façades (Plate 244) bear a remarkable similarity to those that Louis designed at the same time for the Place Ludovise in Bordeaux. A continuous giant order of Corinthian pilasters, but here without a podium, rises through the arcaded ground floor and the floor above. Above the deep entablature, within which mezzanine windows are inserted between the pilasters, there is a set-back attic behind a balustrade adorned with urns. The constant repetition of an identical motif lends unity and a touch of grandeur to the façades that line the garden. Additionally, any sense of monotony is largely countered by the richness and delicacy of the relief ornament that runs across the spandrels of the arcades, the upper window zone and even the rhythmically punctuated entablature.

Louis originally envisaged a range of buildings at the near end of the garden, to form a link with the Palais-Royal itself and contain ducal apartments and a picture gallery; work started on this, but had to be abandoned for lack of funds. This end of the garden was eventually closed off by a double colonnaded screen. In spite of initial opposition, the Palais-Royal garden was a great success and became a popular rendezvous for all classes.

At the south end of the Palais-Royal complex, on the corner of the Rue de Richelieu, is the theatre (now the Comédie-Française), which Louis built in 1787–90 on the site of the burnt-out Opéra, after the Duke had failed in his attempt to have the new Opéra built at the Palais-Royal. The result reveals the limitations of Louis's formal repertoire. He has repeated the formula of his garden façades – the uniform giant order – on a confined site where it has no room to develop properly. With its vertical accumulation of orders – portico, giant order, attics and mansards – the theatre looks out of proportion, uninspired and ponderous. The auditorium is similar to that in Bordeaux, through less grand; and here, at least, Louis reveals his prowess as a technician. For the first time ever, he has used iron on a grand scale. Iron beams support the roof structure, the vault and the boxes: an inestimable advantage in reducing the danger of fire. Louis thereby prepared the way for Bélanger's iron dome over the Halle au Blé, while at the same time creating the most modern theatre in Europe.

The continuous giant order, Louis's major compositional principle, reappears several times in the *châteaux* of the 1780s. One example is Les Boulayes (1785), by Girardin. Another, and the most significant of all, is the Château de Saverne (Plate 245), the summer residence of the bishops of Strasbourg.[41] The old château burned down in 1779, and Cardinal Louis-René de Rohan (who was to be best known for his part in the affair of the queen's Necklace) employed the youthful Nicolas-Alexandre Salins (1753–1839) to build a new one.[42] Every inch the princely residence, the resulting palace covers more ground than the Neues Palais in

Potsdam. By 1790, when the Cardinal went into exile in Germany, the carcass was complete, without furnishings or fittings. Its garden front, with giant Corinthian columns in the frontispiece and pilasters along the wings, resembles Louis's façades in many ways, although it is more sharply accentuated. We know nothing of Salins's training, and it is unlikely that he knew Louis. But the inspiration for all these monotonous façades was no doubt the same everywhere: not English architecture, in which the proportions are different, but the Palladian château designs of Neufforge. At Saverne, Salins softens Neufforge's bleak formula through the elegance of his execution and the opulence of his sculptural decoration. The set-back attic above the frontispiece originally bore a wide strip of relief that must have considerably enlivened the façade.

The most important figure in public architecture was Ledoux. The pampered architect of Parisian high society, whose pavilion and villa designs had been such a sensational success, here showed himself capable of an unexpected monumentality and symbolic power that added a new dimension to architecture itself. His path towards utopian architecture can be traced through his public buildings; and the first step in this direction was taken at the Saline de Chaux.

Ledoux received this commission in 1774, during Louis XV's lifetime, and probably at the instance of Madame du Barry. For three years previously, he had acted as a royal commissioner, or inspector, alongside Perronet, who was inspector and engineer to the royal saltworks (Salines). The saltworks, in Lorraine and Franche-Comté, were subject

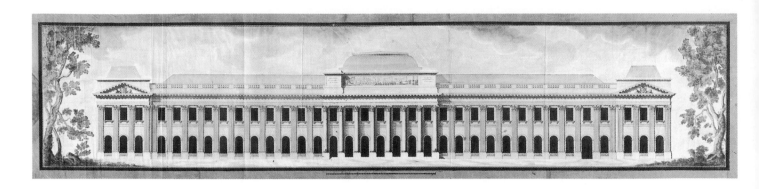

245 Nicolas Salins: Saverne (Zabern), château, 1785–90, design for garden façade.

246 Claude-Nicolas Ledoux: Arc et Senans, Saline de Chaux, plan, 1774.

247 Claude-Nicolas Ledoux: Arc et Senans, Saline de Chaux, 1775–9, House of the Director.

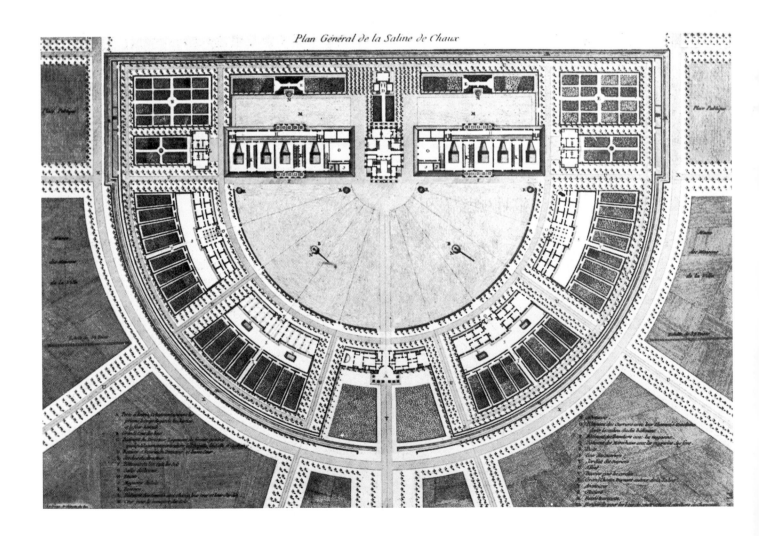

Plan Général de la Saline de Chaux

to the Ferme Générale, the tax-farming authority, which exploited them on behalf of the state. The monopoly salt trade was a profitable one, and a major source of state income. Salt production in Franche-Comté had declined considerably, and the sole remaining installation, at Salins, was no longer yielding sufficient supplies; the Ferme had therefore decided to divert the waters of its saline spring to a point close to the river Loue, between the villages of Arc and Senans, where there was to be a new Saline, fuelled with wood from the nearby Forest of Chaux.[43]

In his initial design (1774), which bears the signature of Louis XV, Ledoux envisaged a very Baroque, square complex of factory buildings and dwelling houses, with long, diagonal, colonnaded galleries to provide short cuts between the buildings. On sight of a rival design submitted by the Ferme itself, he revised his plan (Plate 246) into a semicircle with the director's house and the boiler houses along the base line, while the arc, divided into sectors by radial avenues, would contain the workshops and workers' housing, with an array of gardens beyond and the gatehouse at the point of bisection. The whole was surrounded by a fosse, or dry moat, and by tree-lined avenues. This design formed the basis of the execution, which began in 1775.

The plan itself was a novel one: structures that would previously have been scattered at random were subordinated to a strictly rational, hierarchical arrangement such as had previously been customary only in monasteries and palaces. Their form was still more of an innovation. Ledoux's massive, rusticated, symbol-laden architecture – something pre-viously quite unheard-of in industrial buildings – conveys a decidedly authoritarian message. The focal accent, to which all the rest is subordinated, is the residence of the director (Plate 247), the king's representative, with the works chapel on its first floor.[44] Ledoux's initial design showed a tall attic, haughty in its mien (*dans sa contenance altière*), with three large Palladian *serliane* along either side. The giant portico, of a size reserved for the Church and for the monarchy, is a forcible reminder of the presence of both these institutions. The ubiquitous rustication bears industrial and military con-notations, here realized on a gigantic scale. Massive rock-faced blocks spread across the wall surfaces and frame the windows and doors. The entrances to the carriage houses and office buildings have been made into immense *serliane*, on blocked columns; the gatehouse, which contains quarters for the gatekeeper, constable (*garde-champêtre*) and chaplain, takes the form of an archaic temple (Plate 248). The rusti-cation, with its partial reliance on random variations in the stone to create the vigorous interplay of light and shade that is particularly evident in the portico of the director's house, is an expression of Ledoux's lively response to nature, and of his sensitivity to pictorial effect: qualities on which he was to lay great stress in the text of his book, *L'Architecture*. In these buildings he was deliberately using Mannerist effects in order to counteract the tendency of space and light to dissolve form.

Among Ledoux's prime sources of inspiration were works by Palladio, including Palazzo Thiene, Palazzo Porto-Barbarano and the early villas, and the use of blocked rusti-

248 Claude-Nicolas Ledoux: Arc et Senans, Saline de Chaux, 1775–9, entrance.

249 Claude-Nicolas Ledoux: Arc et Senans, Saline de Chaux, decorative urn with petrified water.

cation in the work of English architects, notably Inigo Jones and Sir John Vanbrugh. There was, of course, also the precedent of ancient Greek architecture. The temples of Paestum, published in 1766, had brought to the fore an entirely new image of antiquity. The close spacing of the Paestum columns (one diameter apart) and their enormous height (six diameters) has been adopted by Ledoux for the porticoes of the gatehouse and of the director's house. But he has made some crucial changes to his antique prototype. The columns of the gatehouse are not fluted; the central intercolumniation has been widened; the bases have been reduced to thin discs, the capitals to shallow plates. The artificial grotto in which the visitor finds himself on entering the gatehouse portico is another departure from antique precedent. With its implication of delving into the salty interior of the earth, this is one more instance of the symbolic strain that runs through the whole composition, as seen in the ubiquitous urns from which petrified water flows (Plate 249). Again, the columns of the portico of the director's house, the drums of which alternate with square blocks, have a symbolic significance over and above their antique precedents: they represent the primitive, the unformed, the earthbound.

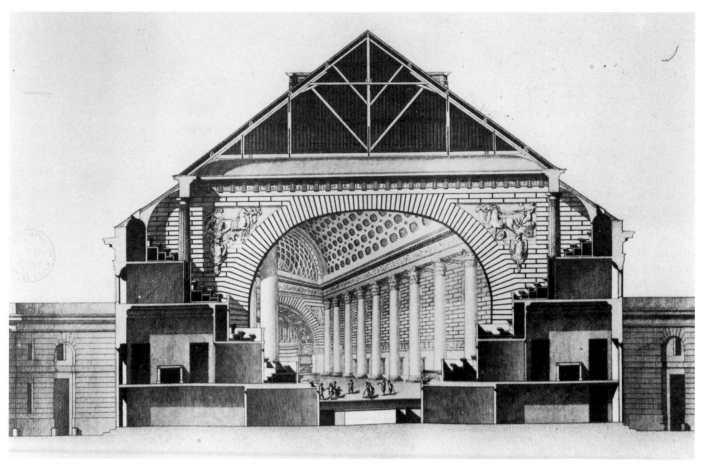

250 Claude-Nicolas Ledoux: Besançon, Theatre, auditorium, engraving by Sellier.

By 1775, at the latest, Ledoux had conceived a plan to extend the saltworks at Arc-et-Senans by adding a mirror-image of the initial hemicycle and elongating the whole into an oval. Around this, he planned to house the workers in a new city in which his social ideals would be realized. The planning of this utopia belongs to the late 1780s, however, and comes under the heading of revolutionary architecture, as discussed below.

Another project on the same monumental scale was the salt store (Grenier à Sel) that Ledoux built at Compiègne in 1775, once more for the Ferme Générale. In a manner typical of French trading practice under the Ancient Régime, this served a dual purpose: as a repository and as a court of justice, to try offences against the hated salt laws. Since the available site was very narrow and met the street at an angle, Ledoux resorted to a trick of genius. He faced the street with a huge, semicircular niche – thus masking the oblique angle – and ran a pair of matching flights of steps up the curve of the niche to the first floor, where the courtrooms were. The salt store was at ground level. He fronted his niche with a massive arch that is reminiscent of a Roman judicial basilica; the horizontal masonry joints of the bare walls are taken up and, as it were, echoed in the heavier, banded rustication of the base. The pediment, with its heraldic fleurs-de-lis, is supported by a massive cornice with prominent brackets. The niche itself, now destroyed, was

large enough to serve – as it still did within living memory – as a covered market.

In the same year, 1775, Ledoux was presented with the long-awaited opportunity to build a theatre. Through his wife's family he had connections with the court musicians at Versailles, and with the responsible authorities of the Menus-Plaisirs. And so, when the city architect of Besançon, Claude Bertrand, drew up a new city plan, and the question of a theatre arose, Ledoux received the commission through the good offices of Maréchal de Duras, who was both governor of Franche-Comté and principal chamberlain at court (and thus in charge of the Menus-Plaisirs). Bertrand was appointed as site architect, to supervise construction.[45] As usual, the new theatre was to be combined with a remodelling of the surrounding quarter; and the governor and the Intendant saw to it that the theatre was built next door to the new Intendance, then still under construction, and that the surrounding quarter would be a high-class residential one.

The Besançon theatre (1778–84), for which the final design was ready and engraved for publication in 1776, is a free-standing, cubic building with a prostyle Ionic portico of a Palladian type. Projections at either side contained the staircases and foyers. The originality of the design lay in the interior (Plate 250). Ledoux assigned to the stage – 'the true home of magical illusion in the theatre' – as much space as he did to the auditorium, and indeed extended the stage

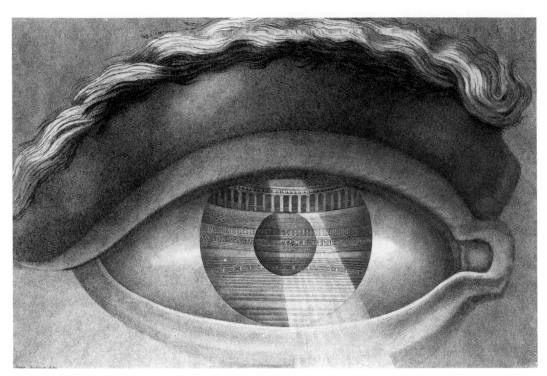

251 Claude-Nicolas Ledoux: Besançon, theatre, auditorium reflected in the eye, engraving by Ledoux.

forward by eliminating the customary proscenium area, with its flanking columns. For the first time, he dropped the orchestra into a pit between stage and audience, with a wooden baffle to direct the sound. The auditorium was not an oval but a hemicycle, widened by reverse curves, and ringed by a balcony and two tiers of boxes – for the officers of the garrison, the nobility and the bourgeoisie – with dwarf partitions. Above all this, as at the Teatro Olimpico and the Versailles Opera, a colonnade ran round the whole auditorium; and it was here that the baseless Doric column made its very first public appearance.[46] Ledoux abolished the standing-room in the pit, which was a constant source of disorder, replaced it with orchestra stalls for privileged theatregoers, and moved the holders of the cheapest tickets to the top, behind the colonnade, where he installed a stepped array of benches so that every member of the audience could be seated in comfort. He thereby alleviated social inequalities and made an attempt to be fair to every class of society; in 1794 he was to write, in his own defence, that he had built a republican theatre in an age of despotism. It was easier to effect such innovations in Besançon, where he had the support of Intendant Lacoré, than in Paris, where they were fiercely resisted, especially in court circles.

The need for economy meant that the marble and relief decor of the interior was executed in illusionistic painting. Even the huge, flattened proscenium arch, into which Ledoux reluctantly incorporated boxes for the Governor and the Intendant, had its coffering painted onto the intrados. The voussoirs painted on its face made it look like an arch of a Roman bridge, recollected from Piranesi. All this rough masonry inside the theatre must have come as something of a shock to the members of the audience.[47] The value that Ledoux attached to this theatre in the context of his œuvre can be seen from the important role he assigned to it in *L'Architecture*. In the first volume – the only one that was published – he described it as a place of communal life

and a temple of moral renewal, and showed it symbolically reflected in the iris of a human eye (Plate 251).

For Marseille, where a new theatre was mooted in the early 1780s, Ledoux designed an enlarged version of the Besançon theatre (1784), in which he sought to transfer a design adapted to the cramped conditions of Besançon to the scale appropriate to a great mercantile city, and to the more sybaritic habits of Southern living. The exterior resembled that of Besançon, but the portico was octastyle Corinthian instead of hexastyle Ionic, and was crowned by a quadriga. Along the sides, which were open to the outside through large *serliane*, there was a high-level terrace on which the audience could stroll during the intervals. The auditorium was designed to accommodate 3,000 people, and the café 2,000. But Ledoux's design arrived too late. The commission had already been awarded to Bénard, a former Rome scholar, who completed his theatre in 1787.

Ledoux's ambitious projects for Aix-en-Provence were also doomed. On the site of the ancient, tumbledown castle of the Counts of Provence he was commissioned to build a Palais de Justice, to house the Parlement and law courts of Provence, and a separate prison. Both were begun in 1787, but in 1790, after Provence had been divided up into Departments, work was halted with the walls no more than a metre above ground level.[48] It was a bitter disappointment for Ledoux. The buildings that now stand on the site have nothing of Ledoux about them, although his designs (initial version 1784, final version 1786) are important documents of his late style.[49]

The Palais de Justice, like Ledoux's theatre designs, was a combination of the square and the Greek cross. In spite of its immense size – it was to cover the best part of an acre – it was not built around an internal court but, as so often in the Louis XVI style, formed a solid block. It rose in a central pyramid crowned by a lantern in the form of a tempietto, which served to light the great central hall. It was to house a

252 Claude-Nicolas Ledoux: Aix, design for a prison, *c.* 1785, perspective view, engraving by Ledoux.

great variety of functionaries: the Chambre des Comptes on the ground floor, the Parlement and criminal court on the first floor, and the provincial court, provincial treasury and archive on the upper floors. The centre of the building was occupied by the great Parlement chamber, surrounded by giant Corinthian columns and by galleries; beneath this was the hall of the Cour des Comptes, less tall, and lined with heavy, baseless Doric columns. On the entrance front was a free-standing octastyle portico; behind this, a wide cere-monial staircase, framed on three sides by Ionic colonnaded galleries, rose to the Parlement chamber on the first floor. Along the axis of the staircase, beyond the Parlement chamber, was the chapel, a square, top-lit room with an internal peristyle and a sanctuary separately ceiled by its own coffered tunnel vault. All the walls were entirely un-decorated; the effect depended entirely on the contrast between plain surfaces and colonnades. The impeccable antique formal repertoire of the interior contrasts with the overstretched external elevations, with their monotonous fenestration and Manneristic porches. Here Ledoux gave full rein to the anticlassicism of his late period, with dis-cordant proportions and an oversized attic that bore down on the façades, reducing the pediments to insignificance.

The prison for Aix was an example of *architecture parlante*. The plan was a square with an inscribed cross, on the pattern that had been customary in hospital buildings ever since the Renaissance. The chapel occupied the crossing; the corner pavilions contained the infirmaries; the ranges between contained the cells. What really counted, however, was the external form, designed as an indication of the building's function. There was not a trace of humanity in it. Ledoux had made his prison into a deterrent, a frowning citadel of repressive power (Plate 252). The corner pavilions looked like antique sarcophagi; the entrances, oppressed by their pediments, looked like antique tombs; both spoke of departure from this life. This was an architecture based on

Piranesian visions, but infused with moralistic content and pressed into the service of a social utopia.

Until the end of his official career Ledoux remained in the service of the Ferme, with which his relations were good. In 1783 he embarked on the building of its Paris head-quarters, another cross inscribed in a square, with four courts; of this he was able to build only one range. Two years later he found his final great opportunity; the Barrières or customs posts of Paris. These marked both his last triumph and the end of his career. The *octroi* – the internal customs duty on the movement of foodstuffs and other goods into Paris – was an important source of income, not only for the Ferme Générale but for the municipality of Paris it-self. However, it was growing harder and harder to collect, because the demarcation line itself was ill-defined. The suburbs, outside the city limits, had a different tax regime; once the city outgrew its walls, and started to absorb the suburban villages, the distinction became blurred, and the smugglers had it all their own way. The Ferme therefore decided to build a new wall, to provide a clear demarcation between urban and suburban areas. At the crossing points there were to be customs posts built by Ledoux.

Work on the whole system began in 1785. It was not long, however, before the public became restive.[50] People were incensed not only by the sudden appearance of a new wall but also by the high cost of the posts themselves. For Ledoux took this commission, which many other architects would have spurned, and made it into something unique. He decided that the Barrières should be expressions of the greatness of the capital city, visible from afar. In his hands they therefore became autonomous monuments – temples, forts, towers – with no apparent relevance to their ostensible purpose. In 1787, to placate public opinion, Ledoux was relieved of his post by royal decree and placed under the supervision of four commissioners – all Academicians – whose task it was to scrutinize his designs and his costings. In the winter of 1788 he was reinstated; but eventually, in 1789, the king was compelled to shelve all further work and to dismiss Ledoux. The latter had seen this coming, and had driven the work forward so rapidly that almost all of it was already an accomplished fact. Of the sixty-five customs posts planned, sixty were built. They did not serve their initial purpose for long; for in 1791, to the delight of the people, the Ferme Générale was abolished.[51]

The Barrières or Propylaea of Paris – Ledoux modestly called them *bureaux* – were a classic instance of the metamor-phosis of classicism into its Manneristic opposite (Plate 253). In some cases the antique prototype was unmistakable: the archaic temples of Paestum for the Barrière de Courcelles, the circular Greek temples described by Pausanias for the Barrière de Reuilly and the Barrière de Chartres. The apsidal motif of the Roman baths was revived in the Barrière de Chopinette and the Barrière de Versailles. The influence of Palladio was even stronger, in the ubiquitous porticoes, *serliane* and square, temple-like buildings with pediments on all four sides. Even the arcades of the Barrière de la Villette and elsewhere, on their coupled columns, stem from Pal-ladio: they are an abbreviated variant – without the inter-vening half-columns – of the arched bays of the Basilica in Vicenza. But Ledoux was not concerned with classical forms

253 Claude-Nicolas Ledoux: Paris, Barrière des Bonshommes (Passy), 1785–9, demolished in 1860.

254 Claude-Nicolas Ledoux: Paris, Barrière de l'Etoile, 1785–9.

255 Claude-Nicolas Ledoux: Paris, Barrière de la Villette, 1785–9.

so much as with the long-distance effect; and for this the angular forms that he had used at Chaux were best suited. This applies, in particular, to the heavy rustication of his podia and columns, but also to the vigorous lateral outlines of the buildings; it was at its most explicit in the blocked columns of the Barrière de l'Etoile.

What distinguished these Parisian Propylaea from all of Ledoux's previous works was his use of simple geometric solids: cube, cylinder, semicylinder. These have taken such a hold that the antique forms in which they are encased often look like a mere disguise. At the Barrière de la Villette (Plate 255), the four ground-level porticoes are no more than a base for the dominant rotunda; at the Barrière de l'Etoile

(Plate 254) they were a mere disguise for the cylinder within. Antique proportions, too, had been invalidated. The pediments bore no relation to the height of the buildings; the doorways bore no relation to the walls. Ledoux went so far as to aver that it was a matter of choosing between the rigour of Paestum and the degenerate graces of Palmyra (by which he meant Soufflot and Mique); and yet it was a long way from these works to the archaic art of Paestum. In them, Ledoux devised a formal vocabulary of his own that went far beyond the antique and used entirely new resources. And one part of this was the smooth column shaft, which was regarded in the 1780s as the symbol of republican Rome. Revolutionary architecture was at hand.

CHAPTER 4

Domestic Architecture in Paris

While public works were completed only with the greatest difficulty, private building in Paris enjoyed a new flowering. Never since the Régence had the private mansion possessed so much importance as now, when the nobility and the big financiers were spending money freely, and the capital had wrested the intellectual and political leadership from Versailles.[52] The look of Paris altered visibly as it expanded to the north and northwest, where fashionable quarters sprang up in the Faubourg de la Poissonnière and around the Chaussée d'Antin. There, Neoclassicism and Palladianism dominated not only individual façades but whole streets; in the new districts one might have thought that one had been transported to Vicenza. Triangular pediments resting on heavy brackets, columned portals and unadorned window openings appeared on apartment houses and mansions. The danger of uniformity lay near at hand, but it was averted by the multitude of currents that flowed within Neoclassicism itself. Each architect's relationship to antiquity, to Palladio, to the Gabriel style or to the tradition of Blondel determined the character and style of his work.

Gabriel's line was most consistently pursued by Chalgrin. He maintained Gabriel's terse, accentuated formal vocabulary and his polished elegance, albeit in strict imitation of antiquity. Chalgrin's ecclesiastical works have been mentioned above. Of his secular buildings the Collège de France, which he rebuilt in 1780, deserves mention: one room, the Salle des Actes, comes close to the classical purity of the interior of Saint-Philippe du Roule. In 1775 he was appointed chief architect to Monsieur (the Comte de Provence, later Louis XVIII), and in this capacity he erected, amid the garden pavilions of Versailles, the captivating Pavillon de Musique de Madame (1784). It forms a Greek cross around a central rotunda painted within to look like a temple in a garden.[53]

Brongniart, by contrast, belonged to the tradition of Blondel, his teacher at the Ecole des Arts. At the same time, he was one of the pupils and protégés of Boullée, who kept him under his wing and secured his appointment as his own successor at the Hôtel des Invalides and at the Ecole Militaire.[54] Brongniart's elegant style, well attuned to the French tradition, and his winning ways soon made him one of the most fashionable society architects in Paris. As Poyet observed on his return from Rome in 1775: 'Chalgrin, Ledoux and Brongniart are currently the three most popular architects in Paris, where houses are to be seen springing up as if by magic.' By that time, Brongniart's reputation was already assured through his connection with the Orléans family.

Brongniart began his career in the quarter around the Chaussée d'Antin, which was the focus of modern development and of aristocratic hôtel building, but also of property speculation on an unprecedented scale. He himself had a hand in this: his first work, the Hôtel de Montesson (1770–

1), which he built for the Marquise de Montesson, mistress to the Duc d'Orléans, stood on a site that he himself had sold to her. Shortly afterwards the duke built himself a luxurious villa next door – probably not designed by Brongniart but by Piètre[55] – and secretly married Madame de Montesson; and so Brongniart established his Orléans connection. Madame de Montesson's salon was one of the meeting places of his future clients. His other chief area of activity was the developing quarter in the southern part of the city, adjacent to the aristocratic Faubourg Saint-Germain; and there, too, he engaged in speculation in a big way. The hôtels that he built in these two centres – Chaussée d'Antin and Boulevard des Invalides – in the 1770s and 1780s were among the best and most refined of all Neoclassical houses, and through them we can trace the general stylistic shift that took place within that period.

In the 1770s Brongniart showed himself to be an able pupil of Boullée, who, in his early hôtels, was himself a continuer of the Blondel tradition. The entrance façade of the Hôtel de Montesson was an almost literal borrowing from the outer bays of the Hôtel Alexandre, with their oval medallions and delicately worked ogee window architraves; its garden front (Plate 256) was like a variant of the Hôtel de Monville. In a number of other houses – the Hôtel de Bondy (1771), Hôtel de Monaco (1774–7), Hôtel de Sainte-Foix (1775–9) and Maison Dervieux (1777–8) – he adhered to the same model. All retained the same façade rhythm, the central emphasis created by an order of pilasters or columns, with unaccented lateral bays, the continuous row of French windows, the entresol windows replaced by reliefs and the flat roof terrace above an attic. The Hôtel de Bondy recalls the Hôtel de Brunoy, with pilasters in place of the giant columns. The high quality of Brongniart's hôtels, the care taken with proportions and with detailing, was particularly evident in the house he built for the dancer Mademoiselle Dervieux, the façade of which recalled the Petit Trianon (Plate 257).[56]

Around 1780 Brongniart changed his style. Concurrently with his monastery of the Capucins, he gave his hôtels, too, a more austere appearance; and there ensued a continual process of simplification. Even in the Hôtel de Bourbon-Condé (1781–2), built for a young princess, the bareness of the side walls of the court was interrupted only by a prominent scheme of relief decoration by Clodion, similar to the one executed simultaneously by the same artists for the façade of the Capucins;[57] on the completely plain garden front, the sole accent is the bowed projection of the central oval salon. The giant pilasters of Brongniart's earlier houses made one last appearance on the garden front of the Hôtel de Masseran (1787); but in general all such articulation disappeared. The walls, with banded rustication, were enlivened only by window consoles and a crowning classical frieze. Only the proportions – as in the Hôtel de Montesquiou

256 Alexandre-Théodore Brongniart: Paris, Hôtel de Montesson, 1770–1, garden façade, design (Paris, Musée Carnevalet).

257 Alexandre-Théodore Brongniart: Paris, Hôtel Dervieux, 1777–8, court façade, elevation.

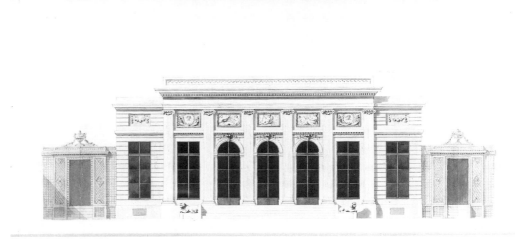

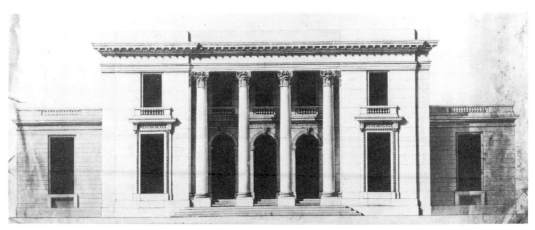

(1781) and Hôtel de Masseran – still reflect the old façade pattern, the hierarchy of frontispiece and side bays.

In planning, there was an increasing tendency towards circular rooms, but here Brongniart still largely adhered to tradition. One important innovation was the adoption of the Palladian oval staircase and its amalgamation with the vestibule, as seen for the first time at the Hôtel de Monaco. In decoration, Brongniart largely followed Boullée: the basic elements were fluted pilasters, a quasi-antique frieze, and semicircular arches over doors and mirrors, so that the traditional character of the interior remained intact. The pure antique surfaced only in such exceptional cases as the basement bathroom (or Nymphaeum) of the Hôtel de Chanac-Pompadour.

The block-like compactness and general sobriety that mark these last buildings of Brongniart's are characteristic of town houses in general at this time. The wings flanking the *cour d'honneur* had disappeared, giving the *corps de logis* a more monumental aspect. From the late 1770s onward, giant orders – initially, and correctly, treated as a central accent – increasingly spread across the whole façade. The last years before the Revolution were characterized by a habit of

'thinking in contrasts', as opposed to the earlier notion of symmetry; and this change found expression not only in the opposition between portico and bare wall but also in the relationships between advancing and receding planes. The columns, engaged at first, moved away from the wall. At the Hôtel de Gallifet (1775–92) (Plate 258) and the Hôtel de Jarnac (1784), both by Etienne-François Legrand, or at the Hôtel de Montholon (1785) by Soufflot-le-Romain, the portico – rather as in Ledoux's revision of his early work – formed a separate block, standing in front of the wall. Proportional relationships became subject to the same principle of contrast: a giant doorway would be set in a relatively low wall, as in Girardin's Hôpital Beaujon (1784) or Ledoux's Barrières. Again, plain wall and ornament were juxtaposed in order to bring out the decoration through an effect of contrast. This is what distinguishes Rousseau's Hôtel de Salm (1784) (Plate 259) from a pavilion of the Rococo period; the proportions and the domed, projecting centre of the delicately wrought garden front create a telling contrast with the classical, columned court side of the same building.

Another decisive change in the design of dwelling houses, including those built for rent, affected the planning. Ledoux

258 Etienne-François Legrand: Paris, Hôtel de Gallifet, 1775–92, court façade.

259 Antoine Rousseau: Paris, Hôtel de Salm, 1784, garden façade.

260 Louis Le Masson: Abbaye de Royaumont, Abbot's Palace, 1785–9, plan of ground floor.

had already centralized the ground plan and replaced breadth by depth. De Wailly had followed suit in a group of three houses in the Rue de la Pépinière. With the younger generation – men like Bélanger, Soufflot-le-Romain, Jean-Jacques Huvé and Jacques Cellerier – this principle became a rule. The circle became the basic shape. It appeared in the hall, in the staircase and in the projecting bow of the salon, and the other rooms were fitted round it. What is notable is how skilfully these un-French shapes were adapted to native habits of living. The most striking example of a plan of this sort is the abbot's palace at Royaumont (1785–9) (Plate 260); here Louis Le Masson used the experience he had gained as a pupil of Ledoux in the construction of town houses to combine the French system of apartments with the passion for circles, within the shape of the Villa Rotonda.[58]

The outstanding figure of the younger generation was François-Joseph Bélanger (1744–1818), whose brilliant career exemplifies the situation at the end of the monarchy and gives a remarkably clear idea of the Anglophile tendencies that existed in France at the time.[59] Bélanger studied under Le Roy and was probably also a member of Caylus's circle; but from the outset he was interested in natural science as well as in archaeology. In 1765, after a number of unsuccessful attempts to win the Prix de Rome, he went to England for two years. There he laid the foundations of his later work as a landscape gardener, notably at Lansdowne House, the London home of Lord Shelburne. Then his career took off. In 1767 he became draughtsman, then inspector to the Menus-Plaisirs, working on stage sets for the opera at Versailles; in 1770 he became Intendant des Bâtiments to the Comte de Provence, and in 1777 chief architect to the Comte d'Artois (later Charles X). His lively personality earned him the friendship of the celebrated opera singer Sophie Arnould (who created the title role of Gluck's

Iphigénie en Aulide in 1774), and through her he gained access to her circle: the Prince d'Hénin, captain of the Comte d'Artois's guard; the Prince de Ligne, 'every philosopher's friend', for whom, at Beloeil, he laid out one of the first 'English gardens' in Belgium; and the Comte de Lauraguais, for whom, with Clérisseau, he built the celebrated bath pavilion in the garden of the Hôtel de Brancas, the first complete antique revival building in Paris (1769).

Lauraguais, later Duc de Brancas, was well known for his eccentric scientific activities – which included dissolving diamonds – and for his Anglomania. Not only was he the pioneer of the English garden in France, but he also kept a racing stable in England and organized the first horse race in France. It was he who first drew Bélanger's attention to the English garden. Bélanger himself seems to have crossed the Channel several times, and is known to have called on Chambers; he chronicled one visit in detail in a sketchbook, the only extant record of a tour of England by a French architect, which depicts not only buildings but manufactures, then considerably more advanced than those in France. It was, however, not Lauraguais but Hénin who obtained for him the commission that secured his future: the building of a barracks at Versailles for the Comte d'Artois's guard.

In 1774 Bélanger's patroness, Sophie Arnould, who was envious of the dancer Guimard's villa on the Chaussée d'Antin, the 'Temple of Terpsichore' by Ledoux commissioned a house in the 'Greek' style, of equal size. In its pediment was a figure of Euterpe, the Lyric Muse, bearing her features. Mostly, however, Bélanger worked for the Comte d'Artois: the large stables in the Faubourg du Roule (*c.* 1780–8), the decoration of the Petits Appartements in the Temple (1777–85), improvements at the Château de Maisons (*c.* 1780),[60] and plans for a gigantic replacement for

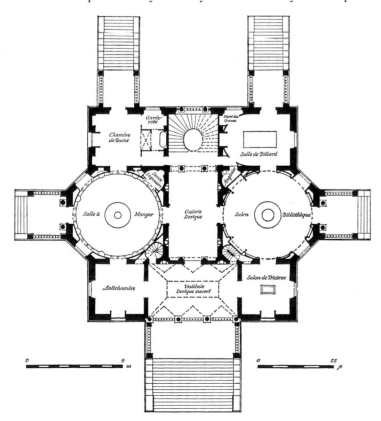

the Château de Saint-Germain (1777–84), which the king had given to his brother; of this, only the terraces were executed.

His most spectacular success was the construction of the Pavillon de Bagatelle (1777). This graceful villa (Plate 261) was built – in pursuit of a wager with Marie-Antoinette – within the space of sixty-four days.[61] It is not only an example of Bélanger's supremely confident approach to both design and execution, but also of a princely *folie* in the late Louis XVI style, just outside the gates of the capital. Less extravagant than Ledoux's Pavillon de Louveciennes, it is just as refined in plan and interior organization.

On its nearly square site, Bagatelle is strictly symmetrical. It combines everything necessary for an elegant week-end house: circular salon, dining room, billiard room, two boudoirs on the ground floor and two further bedrooms above. In accordance with the new fashion, the staircase is in the centre. The most conventional part is the elevation facing the little formal garden, where the circular salon projects to form a central bow with arched window openings. The court façade looks like a smaller version of the house of Sophie Arnould, with a columned doorway and a lunette above, smoothly incised statuary niches on either side and, instead of a pediment, a low attic bearing a long relief tablet – all designed in the graceful and concise 'Greek' style of Le Roy. The villa formed part of an axis of courts, lawns and domestic buildings, the latter with a concave façade facing the entrance to the villa.

Artois wanted to have an English garden of his own, like that of the Duc de Chartres at Monceau. So he called in the Scottish landscape gardener Thomas Blaikie to work under the supervision of Bélanger (whose ideas Blaikie testily described as 'ridiculous'). The grounds were overrun with winding pathways, artificial rocks and waterfalls, and preposterous *fabriques*: a Gothic pavilion on top of a waterfall, known as the Pavillon du Philosophe; a Chinese tent with a temple on top; a bridge with a pagoda on it; the Tombeau de Pharaon, which was an antique tombstone next to a barbarian tent and a Druid hut.

The gardens of Bagatelle were promptly eclipsed, however, by a rival park that Bélanger designed for a rich

261 François-Joseph Bélanger: Paris, Bagatelle, 1777, court façade, design.

262 François-Joseph Bélanger: Paris, Folie de Saint-James, 1777, elevation of garden façade (Paris, Bibliothèque Nationale).

263 François-Joseph Bélanger: Paris, the artist's own house, c. 1786, street façade, coloured engraving by Sergent (Paris, Bibliothèque Nationale).

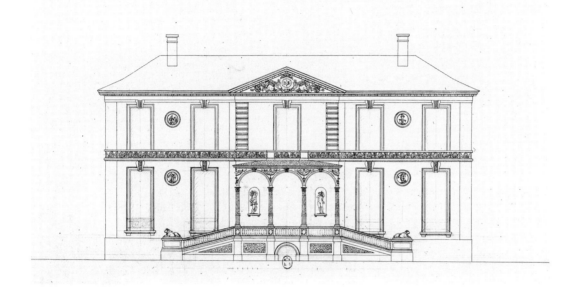

and empty-headed neighbour, whom this *tour de force* had rendered sleepless with envy. Claude Baudard de Saint-James, treasurer-general to the navy, was flattered to have a prince's house next to his own, but he meant at all costs to surpass it in splendour. He engaged Bélanger to build him a house and English garden, giving him a totally free hand, with the sole stipulation that the house should be expensive.

Stylistically, the Folie de Saint-James is a curious mixture of Régence and Neoclassical. On the garden side it has a terrace with a sort of Renaissance portico, in which Bélanger used columns for the first time as supports for arches (Plate 262). The lavish ornamentation of the shafts, spandrels and mouldings, including the deep frieze that runs across the façade appears to be borrowed from Piranesi's *Diverse maniere d'adornare i cammini*. The extensive grounds, packed with *fabriques* and sculpture groups, ran down to the banks of the Seine: 'It would be very fine,' remarked the Prince de Ligne, 'if only there were not too much of it.' In addition to kiosks and grottoes, this garden contained the most expensive and the most celebrated *fabrique* of the day, the Grand Rocher. This was a rocky cavern flanked by terraces, with steps leading up and monsters spouting jets of water. Beneath the arch of the cavern stood – and still stands in part – a

portico of four baseless Doric columns, with entablature and triangular pediment. Behind the columns, water came rushing out from a large opening in the rock, to fall into the pool in front of the temple. Here architecture was overwhelmed by nature: a common idea in the landscape garden, and a foretaste of Romanticism.

The most important of Bélanger's landscape creations, however, was Méréville. An opulent banker, Jean-Joseph de Laborde had bought this estate near Etampes in 1784. He employed Bélanger to enlarge the existing château, and entrusted the design of the grounds, which were his principal interest, jointly to the two leading authorities in the field, who were Bélanger and Hubert Robert. The two worked as a team, with Bélanger presumably responsible for the *fabriques*. The park at Méréville cost a fortune. A river runs through it, and Bélanger took this as his cue for watermills, waterfalls, islands and numerous bridges, some in wood but some in iron. Among his park structures (now moved to nearby Jeurre) were a marble memorial to the explorer Captain James Cook; a dairy; a rostral column, also in marble, in memory of the owner's two sons, lost at sea; and most notably, on top of a hill, the Grand Temple designed by Lhuillier, Bélanger's closest associate (1786–92). This cir-

cular marble temple, with its eighteen six-metre columns, based on the Temple of Vesta in Rome and the similar Temple of the Sibyl at Tivoli, is the finest of all Neoclassical round temples. The domed cella contained, in a niche, a statue by Pajou (completed 1792) of the owner's daughter Natalie, resting her left hand on a medallion bearing a profile bust of her father. Méréville was a creation of admirable taste, without exotic follies and maintaining a true proportion between nature and architecture. It was one of the most beautiful gardens ever made in France.

In Paris, Bélanger concentrated his activity in the emerging Quartier des Porcherons, north of the Chaussée d'Antin, in which he rightly saw a great future; a rapid succession of hôtels appeared there from the 1770s onwards. Among the hôtels and *folies* that he built or remodelled in the area and where he continued the early style of Ledoux – the Hôtels de Mirepoix, de Neukerque, de Weymerange, the Maison Dervieux, the Folie d'Adeline Colombe, and others – one, the Folie du Comte d'Artois, in the Rue Neuve des Capucins, close to Brongniart's Capuchin friary, stood out by virtue of its size and the novelty of its decoration. Around the wall of the salon were low, projecting pedestals bearing slender, free-standing, coupled wooden columns with bronze capitals; between these were sofas (beneath large mirrors) or statues. The façade (Plate 263) was an interesting example of the softening effect exerted on rigorous Neoclassicism by the eclecticism of the *fabriques* and by the intrusion of Renaissance and Mannerist influences. Above a heavy, rusticated podium, the centre opened out to form a three-arched loggia on four columns. Between their capitals and the entablature above was a contrasting, rusticated arcade zone. The frieze, with its decor of paterae, was Bélanger's invention. The unity of the pediment was disrupted by a resumption of the rustication within the tympanum, where it framed a shallow lunette reminiscent of the architecture of the Roman baths.

After the Revolution, Bélanger competed unsuccessfully for public commissions. To make the most of his time, he laid out another English garden, with numerous *fabriques* – a Chinese bath pavilion, a Temple of Bacchus, eccentric bridges and the like – on his own estate at Sanceny, east of Paris.

His only major work was the new dome of the Halle au Blé, erected in 1809–13 as a replacement for the wooden dome by Legrand and Molinos, which had been destroyed by fire in 1802. Bélanger employed cast iron ribs tied by wrought-iron rings to create the first iron dome ever built. His use of this system, admittedly anticipated by bridge builders in England, Germany and America, marked an epoch in French iron construction. With its successful neutralization of stresses, its light weight and its transparency, this dome marked the culmination, as it were, of Soufflot's and the Neoclassicists' efforts to re-establish Gothic vaulting techniques. It lacked the light and airy quality of its predecessor by Legrand and Molinos; but Fontaine described it as the most important work of the era of Napoleon. Its successors were the Halles au Blé at Alençon and Le Mans, and even the Corn Exchange in Leeds. When the Bourbons were restored, Bélanger resumed his old court offices as chief architect to Monsieur and architect to the Menus-Plaisirs, but he made no further influential contribution to architecture.

The greatest attraction in the quarter around the Chaussée d'Antin, which was not lacking in new and original buildings, was undoubtedly the Hôtel de Thélusson (1777–81), built by Ledoux for the widow of a Swiss banker, and one of his few private commissions at a time when he was almost entirely occupied with public works.[62] This was a building of outstanding quality, and a proof of the respected status enjoyed by Swiss Protestant financiers in France at this period. The owner's foreign nationality, the size of her inherited fortune and her social position outside the aristocracy enabled Ledoux to give free rein to his imagination, untrammelled by the conventions that still applied to the aristocratic hôtel.

As the site was not deep enough to place the *corps de logis* between front court and back garden, Ledoux reversed the relationship. What the visitor saw first was not the court but the garden front, which Ledoux had transformed into a stage set (Plate 264). In lieu of a proscenium there was a monumental triumphal arch, half sunk in the earth, which afforded a prospect of a mansion in the picturesque setting of an English garden. Two parallel carriage drives led to the house; between them, Ledoux placed a 'sunken' garden ending in a real rock-face that formed a base for the semicircular, bowed frontispiece of the house. This, with its colonnade, thus took on the character of an antique temple, standing on rocks in a natural landscape.

The gateway arch, built over a subterranean grotto and containing the porter's lodge and a water reservoir, served both as a defensive portal and as a garden feature. Modelled on the triumphal arch of the Circus of Maxentius, which was then half buried by an accumulation of rubble, it was the first example of the 'sunken architecture' (*architecture ensevelie*) that was to be one of the favourite themes of the Revolutionary period.[63] However, the idea probably stemmed from Piranesi, perhaps from his 'Entrance to an Antique

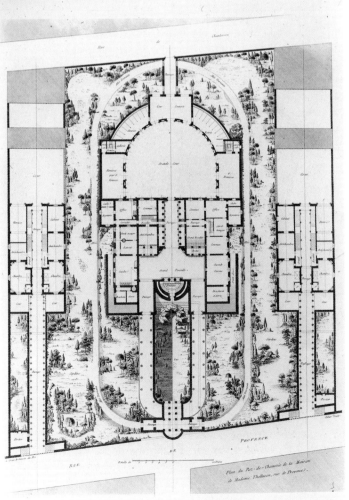

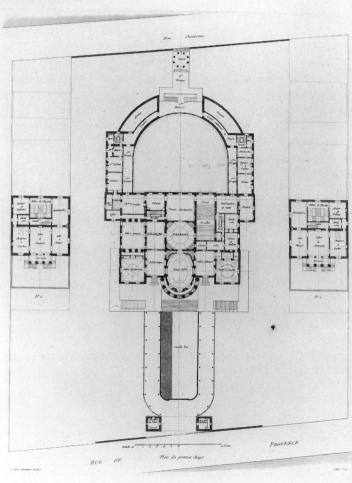

BATIMENT DE M. HOSTEIN
Executé d'Après les Ordres et desseins de M. le Doux Architecte de l'Académie
par M. de L'Arbre Entrepreneur de Batiment à Paris l'An 1792.

266 Claude-Nicolas Ledoux: Paris, Maisons Hosten, 1792–5, garden façade, watercolour (Paris, Musée Carnevalet).

Gymnasium'; just as the temple on the rock was probably inspired by Piranesi's engraving of the Temple of the Sibyl at Tivoli.[64] Ledoux always emphasized the pictorial content of his architecture;[65] and the arch of the Hôtel de Thélusson, which initially encountered some public disapproval, served to set his 'picture' in the right frame. The view through this 'monstrous archway', with its gloomy vault, enabled him to enhance the brilliance and depth of what was seen beyond. This pictorial effect commanded the admiration of his contemporaries, and the engravings of the arch from various angles are clear evidence of this.

The interior of the house was no less unusual. The vestibule, where carriages set down their passengers, was at ground level; from it, as in the Hôtel de Montmorency, a main staircase led up to the reception rooms and a *porte cochère* allowed coachmen to drive on into the court behind the house. From this vestibule, too, steps led down to the grotto beneath the salon and thence to the sunken garden. The planning of the main (first) floor was a work of genius, both in its compactness and its reconciliation of intimacy with grandeur (Plate 265). A central, longitudinal axis led

through a succession of larger and larger spaces: from the rectangular first antechamber through an octagonal, domed hall with four niches – the second antechamber – into the projecting oval of the grand salon, also domed and entirely lined with mirrors. The central domed space was lit by a lantern above; and the dome of the grand salon, too, was ringed by a balustrade that concealed ten window openings. This longitudinal axis was crossed by three transverse axes, of which the one at the front, on the garden side contained the principal enfilade of music room, library, grand salon, autumn salon, bedroom; the central enfilade contained the domed antechamber, with the servery and painted dining room to its left; and the rear one contained a private apartment to the left of the square antechamber. To the right of the main axis were the staircase and another private apartment.

To the rear of the house, the side wings of the court were joined by a semicircular range containing another gateway and a rooftop *tempietto* that afforded a view of the still-rural hills of Montmartre. On the completion of the house in 1781 there was such a flood of curious visitors that tickets of admission had to be issued. Paris has seen few buildings of such originality, and it is one of the great tragedies of Parisian architectural history that in 1824 it was demolished.

Ledoux's building career came to an end in 1792–5 with the Maisons Hosten, a residential development for a rich planter, J.B. Hosten, in the Faubourg de la Poissonnière. These marked the conclusion of an evolutionary process that had begun with the Hôtel de Thélusson and had led Ledoux

264 Claude-Nicolas Ledoux: Paris, Hôtel de Thélusson, 1777–81, garden façade, watercolour (London, British Library).

265 Claude-Nicolas Ledoux: Paris, Hôtel de Thélusson, 1777–91, plans of the ground and first floors.

further and further away from the traditional pattern of the urban hôtel. Here he strung identical houses together without reference to a central feature, separated their main façades with open-fronted courts, and thus created the modern concept of terraced or row housing. The majority of the houses were grouped in a large U around a garden in the English style (Plate 266); and this continued beneath one of the houses, which was supported on *pilotis*, and through to a second group. At one end of the U was the private residence of the owner, Hosten, a traditional design with court and wings of domestic offices. The houses were designed to be rented out as single-family units, with a kitchen and dining room on the ground floor, living rooms and bedrooms on the first and second floors and servants' rooms in the attic. The elevations were completely undecorated, except for a continuous arcade that linked them at first-floor level. This uniformity was in keeping with the modular tendency of Ledoux's late architecture. It was enlivened only by the rhythm of the masses – four bays for each façade three for each court – and by the alternation of light and shade. Hosten emigrated to London in 1794, and only six of the planned fifteen houses were built. They were an astonishing anticipation of the nineteenth-century architectural ideas that gave birth to terraced housing and garden cities.

CHAPTER 5
Revolutionary Architecture

After his withdrawal from public life in the early 1780s, Boullée began to work on designs for public buildings and monuments that left tradition behind and opened up entirely new prospects for architecture. With their harsh, geometric forms and bare, unadorned outer surfaces, these projects for palaces, city gates and memorials invoked a utopian world that had nothing whatever in common with the aristocratic society of the eighteenth century. It was a world of vast dimensions, full of a high-flown symbolism that caused human beings to appear tiny by comparison with the immensity of the State, or of Death, or of the Cosmos. At the same time, Ledoux was designing for the Saline de Chaux an ideal city based on an equally utopian scheme of symbolism, both moral and artisanal.

The social and moral aims of this architecture were those of the Revolution: a new and better society in which nature would be the great exemplar, social distinctions would be abolished, and everyone would enjoy the right to happiness and prosperity. The term 'revolutionary architecture', coined by Emil Kaufmann on the basis of this identity of aims, is now in general use,[66] logically unsustainable though it is. For the great ideas behind revolutionary architecture arose, almost without exception, under the Ancien Régime; the Revolution itself contributed practically nothing. It would make better sense to call it 'visionary architecture'.

The principal exponents of revolutionary architecture were Boullée and Ledoux, although it involved a whole generation: Poyet, Desprez, Combes, Girardin, Jean-Nicolas-Louis Durand, Jacques-Pierre Gisors and others. The pioneer role played by Boullée and Ledoux was duly recognized by contemporaries themselves;[67] indeed, it was denounced by Viel de Saint-Maux in his book *La Décadence de l'architecture à la fin du XVIIIe siècle* (1800).

Of the two, Boullée undoubtedly had the greater inventive gift. He was a member of the Academy and, after its dissolution, of the Ecole Centrale du Panthéon, and sat on numerous expert committees; he was a highly respected teacher, and his influence was extensive, not to say inescapable. His *Essai sur l'art* (1793) was the principal theoretical work of revolutionary architecture – together with Ledoux's *L'Architecture considérée sous le rapport de l'art, des moeurs et de la législation* (1804) – and simultaneously marked the demise of Neoclassicism.[68] His drawings of his own designs, intended as illustrations to his manuscript, are visions of a new world; they spring from a confrontation with the basic forms of architecture, the 'solids' (*les corps*), as he called them.

Boullée's earlier utopian designs – the Metropolitan Church (1781–2; Plate 267), the Museum (1783), the Palace of a Monarch at Saint-Germain (1785) – still bore some relationship to real projects. His Metropolitan Church (Plate 267) was a development of Contant d'Ivry's designs for the Madeleine, to which Couture had added peristyles; the Museum had been mooted for the royal collections; the Palace at Saint-Germain was a reflection of Boullée's own designs for Versailles. All exemplify the transition from traditional forms to an abstract architecture.

In the Metropolitan Church, the built mass has coalesced into a block; the colonnades are no more than quotations. The interior acquires a colossal scale from the way in which Boullée has chosen to make the columns small, so that their sheer repetition serves to magnify the scene. The colonnades in the drum no longer create openings to admit the light but serve merely as decorative bands. Boullée is less interested in architectural than in spiritual effect. This is achieved not only by the gigantic crossing arches that serve to expand the dome, or by the temple-like drum, to which wide flights of steps ascend from the nave, but by the magical abundance of light that pours down like the miracle of Pentecost.

In the Museum, the transition to purely geometrical forms is complete (Plates 268, 269); this is a building not so much intended to contain certain collections as to celebrate the wider definition of a museum as a place of remembrance, a 'Temple of Nature and Genius'.[69] It is a square composition, with large exedrae and an inscribed Greek cross; its centrepiece is a Temple of Fame. The vaults in the arms of the cross have become plain hemicylinders, which spring from behind the colonnades and thus demote these to the status of mere set-dressing; the Temple of Fame, which forms the 'crossing', is roofed by an absolutely plain hemisphere. Here, again, Boullée evokes a spiritual function through the ring of columns that encircle this inner temple, the wide flights of steps, crowded with human figures, that rise to it from the arms of the cross – as in his royal library design, he undoubtedly has Raphael's *School of Athens* in mind here – and the light that suffuses the space.

In Boullée's later designs, the link with reality disappears altogether. These are paraphrases of the absolute form of a building, models of the potentialities of architecture. From the outset, there is an evident and close reference to the Academy. Many of the themes that Boullée takes up and resolves are precisely those set a few years earlier to the Academy students as exercises – a Museum, a City Gate, a Cathedral, a Palace of Justice, a Memorial for the Monarch of a Great Kingdom, and the like. It is tempting to see this as a result of his teaching work and of discussions with his students: all the more so as some of his personal pupils – Gisors, Durand and others – produced designs of their own that are surprisingly close to his.

In these compositions of Boullée's, the antique precedent increasingly recedes into the background – as with the ranks of columns that have dwindled into bands of ornament – but always remains a latent presence. For instance, the lines of cypresses around his Cenotaph for Newton and his Broken Pyramid Cenotaph derive from the Mausoleum of Augustus (as does Lequeu's Tomb of the Most Illustrious and Learned Men (Plate 270)); his Tomb of Hercules (Plate 271), a

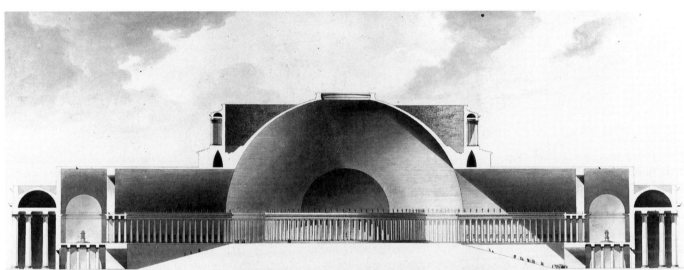

267 Etienne Louis Boullée:
Project for a Metropolitan Church
at the Feast of Corpus Christi,
1781–2 (Paris, Bibliothèque
Nationale).

268 Etienne-Louis Boullée:
Paris, design for a museum, 1783,
section (Paris, Bibliothèque
Nationale).

269 Etienne-Louis Boullée:
Paris, design for a Museum,
1785, interior (Paris, Bibliothèque
Nationale).

270   Jean-Jacques Lequeu:
Design for the Tomb of the Most
Famous and Most Learned Men,
c. 1785 (Paris, Bibliothèque
Nationale).

271   Etienne-Louis Boullée:
Design for the Tomb of Hercules,
c. 1785 (Paris, Bibliothèque
Nationale).

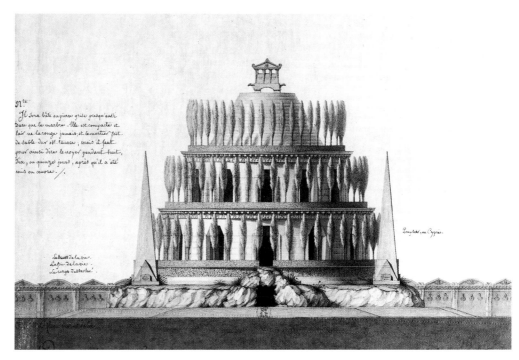

pyramid with a Doric peristyle, derives from the legendary Mausoleum of Halicarnassus; his Circus derives from the Colosseum (as does Bernard Poyet's drawing for a Hôtel Dieu) – not to speak of the Roman Pantheon, the idea of which underlies all Boullée's circular buildings, and which found its ultimate metamorphosis into revolutionary architecture in two of his designs in particular: the City of the Dead, with its truncated cone, and the Temple of Reason (1793–4) (Plate 272).[70] The same idea of antique monuments half-sunk in debris underlies the many examples of *architecture ensevelie* that appear in the cemetery designs.

Boullée also took an interest in preclassical cultures; and in this he was not alone among revolutionary architects. The pyramids of Egypt fascinated him, with their monumentality and 'immutability'; and the Tower of Babel, in Athanasius Kircher's engraving, supplied him with ideas for conical lighthouses and sepulchral monuments.

Against this classical background, which had lost its potential for formal definition and now appeared only by way of quotation, Boullée concentrated, like Ledoux and the other revolutionary architects, on the pure forms of nature, their sculptural and pictorial qualities. Diderot had already acknowledged the aesthetic value of the sheer surface and the undisguised cubic form; and under his influence Ledoux sought to fathom the basic elements of beauty in architecture. In a comparable effort to return to the sources of art, Boullée

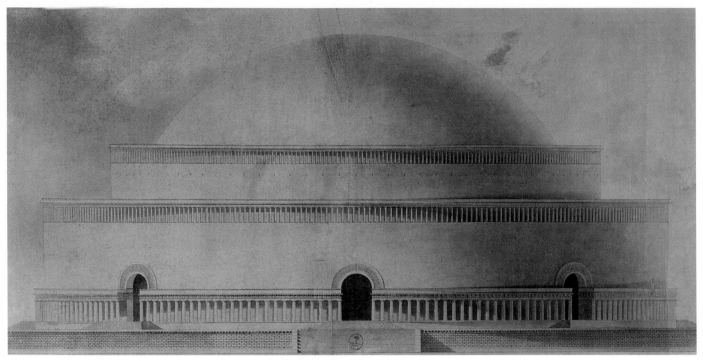

272 Etienne-Louis Boullée: Design for the Temple of Reason, 1793–4 (Florence, Uffizi).

developed his famous essay *La Théorie des corps*, in which he investigated the specific qualities of stereometric solids, in their effect on the senses and in their analogies with the human organism. By virtue of their inherent aesthetic and symbolic qualities, the cube, pyramid, cylinder and sphere became autonomous forms of architectural expression. Ledoux regarded the sphere in particular as the ideal form, not only because all points on its surface are equidistant from its centre, but also because it symbolizes eternity and infinity. The influence of Diderot was here joined by that of the steadily growing natural sciences. In particular, the *Cristallographie* of Romé de l'Isle (1783), which deals exhaustively with the properties of regular solids, must have exerted considerable influence on Boullée and his *Théorie des corps*.

One consequence of the crystalline compactness of the architectural unit was the change from vertical to horizontal articulation. The building now fell into a number of discrete horizontal layers that were no longer tied to any firm system of proportional relationship. Gondoin had been a pioneer in this respect: his Ecole de Chirurgie has a layered structure, with a continuous, unbroken cornice. Boullée elevated this principle into a rule. In his designs it is the endless, uninterrupted cornices that convey the impression of horizontality and monumentality.[71]

What counted in revolutionary architecture was not the articulation but the surface. This came to life through effects of light and shade, and through the contrasts created by the colonnades and by the sparse ornamentation. Both Boullée and Ledoux assigned great importance to shadow. Deep shadow seemed to provide the only way of bringing their planes and cubes to life. Boullée described himself as the inventor of this 'shadow architecture', of which he gave a striking example in a design for a funerary monument in the form of a temple seen against the sunlight.

This practice of painting with shadows underlines the pictorial elements that are intrinsic to Boullée's designs. In his eyes, pictorial presentation took precedence over mere execution; the prime task of the architect was stagecraft, the production of 'tableaux'. This was perfectly in keeping with his own dual talent, as an architect and as a painter. His designs are like paintings of architecture by a specialist in ruins. His cemeteries are seen against stormy skies; his interiors are never lit by windows but from above, by light that streams in through openings in domes.

The pictorial conception of architecture that he extols in the *Essai sur l'art* finds concentrated expression in what is probably his most celebrated work, the Cenotaph for Newton (Plates 273, 274).[72] This is a hollow sphere, the interior of which is filled in one version with sparkling light emitted by an astrolabium hanging from the top in the other one with profound darkness. In this version the surface of the sphere is perforated by tiny, carefully disposed apertures, so that the daylight penetrates as points of light, in a form that corresponds to the position of the stars in the heavens. At the very bottom stands the sarcophagus, lost in the immensity of space. One of the two drawings shows a starry night; the other shows daytime: it is a representation of the world in terms of the contrast between night and day. The impression on the viewer who enters the sphere through a long passageway is reinforced by the compulsion to remain in his allotted place, with the sarcophagus as his only substantive point of reference – so that, in Boullée's words, he has the sensation of being all alone in a vast plain or

273 Etienne-Louis Boullée:
Design for the Tomb of Newton
in daytime, 1784 (Paris,
Bibliothèque Nationale).

274 Etienne-Louis Boullée:
Design for the Tomb of Newton,
interior at night (Paris,
Bibliothèque Nationale).

far out at sea. Only the upper hemisphere is fully visible from
outside, the lower one being concealed by the cypress-lined
terraces of the podium – except on the entrance side, where the
terraces are interrupted to afford access.

The idea of this cenotaph (1784) sprang from the admiration that Boullée, along with all his contemporaries, felt for
Newton and his epoch-making discovery.[73] The spherical
form was, however, already known as a type of folly or
fabrique; Ledoux had used it in his House of the Rural
Constables at Maupertuis (*c.* 1780). But only with Boullée
does it unfold its full symbolic power. The idea was taken up
at once, albeit in different interpretations, by Antoine-Léon
Vaudoyer, Jean Sobre, Lequeu, Combes, Durand and others.
In Vaudoyer's House for a Cosmopolite (1785), the sphere
rests on a ring of Doric columns (Plate 275); in Lequeu's

Temple of the Earth, dedicated 'To the Supreme Wisdom',
it rests on a ring of piers; in Durand's Temple of the Ten-
Day Week (Temple Décadaire, 1795), it is set in a terraced
base; and Jean Houel has it borne upon clouds and supporting a chariot in which the French Republic rides with
Liberty as her charioteer (1800). In Sobre's Temple of
Immortality, the lower hemisphere is created by the reflection
of the upper hemisphere in water. In all these cases, as in
the giant globes of the Baroque, the dome of the upper
hemisphere displays a world map on the outside and a star
map on the inside;[74] Vaudoyer, Sobre, Combes and some
others add the circle of the Zodiac. Viel de Saint-Maux, in
his *Lettres sur l'architecture*, had given a reconstruction of the
oldest Greek temples and had suggested, in connection with
the astronomical significance of those buildings, that the

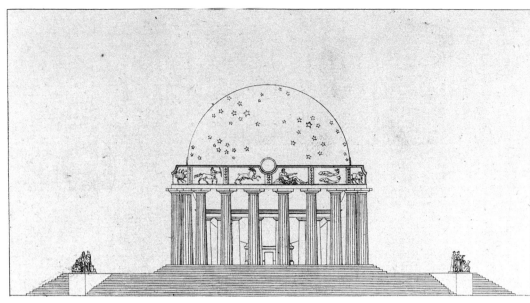

275 Antoine-Laurent-Thomas Vaudoyer: Design for the House of a Cosmopolite, 1785 (Landon, *Annales du Musée et de l'Ecole moderne des Beaux Arts*, Paris 1800–9, t.II p. 123).

276 Etienne-Louis Boullée: Design for a Fortress Gate, *c.* 1785 (Paris, Bibliothèque Nationale).

277 Etienne-Louis Boullée: Design for a Tomb in the Egyptian Manner, *c.* 1785 (Paris, Bibliothèque Nationale).

278 Pierre-François Fontaine: Mausoleum for a Monarch, 2nd prize at the Académie d'architecture in 1785 (Paris, Bibliothèque de l'Ecole des Beaux Arts).

entablature was originally intended for a display of zodiacal signs;[75] and this was the symbolic interpretation that architects had in mind.

In revolutionary architecture, with its finger-wagging didacticism, *architecture parlante* is ever-present. But with Boullée the language of symbol transcends all merely topical references to soar into the sublime. His monuments are designed for a race of men who place their faith, not in the immortality of the soul, but in individual survival in the memory of future generations.[76] The aim of his gigantic pyramids, his skittle-shaped lighthouses, his city gates and his triumphal arches was to convince posterity of the greatness of the age that could build them. Serried ranks of watchmen stand guard over the central arch of his fortress gates (Plate 276); his square fortress bears the shield of Achilles; and his Palais Municipal rests on four pedestal-like

guardhouses, to demonstrate how society is founded on the power of the state to maintain law and order. Similarly, Ledoux conceived his prison for Aix as a square, fortress-like block with sarcophagus roofs and sternly forbidding entrances. Every sign of stylistic individuality is swamped, so to speak, by the 'character' of the building.

The poetic content of these designs, remote as they are from practical life, is evident and entirely intentional.[77] Both Boullée and Ledoux shared the general emphasis on feeling that had been a sign of the times ever since it was first voiced by Jean-Jacques Rousseau. The first to introduce it into architecture had been Le Camus de Mézières, in his book *Le Génie de l'architecture* (1781), which had the significant subtitle 'The Analogy of that Art with Our Sensations'.

The most prevalent type in revolutionary architecture, and

one that embraces some of the most magnificent creations of Boullée and his school, is the sepulchre. Outstanding examples include Boullée's Cenotaph in the Form of a Frustum and Cenotaph in the Egyptian Manner (Plate 277); the respective designs of Fontaine (Plate 278) and Sobre for the Mausoleum of a Monarch (both 1785) and the stage designs of Desprez. Often these designs show pyramids in an expanse of what looks like desert, enclosed within a sacred precinct bounded by a ring of small pyramids; or massive, peripteral Doric rotundas on the lines of the Roman Pantheon.

The late eighteenth century was obsessed with the cult of the dead.[78] Since most of the best-preserved remains of antiquity were tombs, both archaeologists and architects – starting with the Rome scholars of the 1740s and 1750s – tended to regard these as the most important part of antique architecture; they also played a prominent part in the work of Piranesi, whose influence was as strong as ever.

To this was added a new conception, specific to Neoclassicism: that of the survival of human greatness after death. Shortly after he took office, Angiviller embarked on a set of statues of Frenchmen who had deserved well of their country. In 1791 the church of Sainte-Geneviève was converted into a Panthéon des Grands Hommes; in 1794 the Musée des Monuments Français was opened, and in it Alexandre Lenoir included a number of salvaged monuments of such great men of the past as Molière, Descartes and Turenne. Memorials in public places had hitherto been for monarchs only; but now the memory of 'men of genius' or 'men of virtue' became a public cult in its own right – to which the Cenotaph of Newton certainly belongs. In this, Boullée was continuing the tradition of the antique mausolea. The sphere, as the expression of perfection, was the ideal form, and the proposed installation of the sarcophagus in its vaulted interior was in keeping with the ancient custom of laying a hero to rest in a sarcophagus beneath the vault of heaven.

The tomb cult was also fostered by the closing of the old Parisian cemeteries, which had been demanded not only by Diderot in the *Encyclopédie* but, with increasing urgency, by the medical profession. The first to be closed, in 1785, was the Cimetière des Innocents; and when, in 1789, the cemeteries were removed from the jurisdiction of the Church, there was talk of new, out-of-town cemeteries, and of more individual initiative in the design and maintenance of graves – something that the Church had always resisted. This led to numerous necropolis designs, almost invariably with an Egyptian pyramid in the centre. In due course, when religion was abolished, there was even an opinion survey on the future design of cemeteries.[79]

Finally, in 1804, Napoleon ordered a large cemetery to be laid out in the northeastern part of Paris, and Brongniart supplied the design for what eventually became the Père-Lachaise. In the centre, once more, was to be a pyramid,

which was to be used for cremation; all around were private sepulchral monuments. The design was a blend, once more, of the hero cult, the invocation of history and the personal need for a pilgrimage to the ancestral resting-place.

With Ledoux, who had his patrons' wishes to take into account, the authority of classical models – and especially that of Palladio – prevailed for longer. Even his Barrières constituted a compendium of architectural styles, although what he made of this ring of tollbooths is without parallel in the history of architecture. In the designs for the ideal city of Chaux, on the other hand, we meet another Ledoux altogether: the philosophically minded author of *L'Architecture*. The expansion of Chaux – that is, the duplication of the semicircle of the Saline and the creation of a city for the workers all around – had been on his mind since 1775; we have it complete, in the form of engravings (Plate 279). Although he had an encouraging response from Turgot, the plan ultimately came to grief for financial reasons. Even so, he worked on it intensively until the Revolution.[80] There had been plans for ideal cities before Ledoux. But never yet had anyone drawn up so complete a programme for the life-style of the inhabitants, embracing their working conditions, education and leisure activities. Ledoux had thought of everything. The garden-city layout sprang from his own love of nature and his sentimental passion for rural life. The Hôtel de Thélusson, too, was set amid greenery; and the Maisons Hosten were laid out as a garden suburb.

With their Palladian forms, the buildings of Ledoux's first phase of planning for Chaux (before 1785) – the church, the

market, the public baths – belong within the context of the public projects on which Ledoux was working at the time. The church is an 'improved' form of the controversial Greek-cross design for Sainte-Geneviève, with its colonnaded ambulatories all round, but with a lighter dome and stouter abutments. By contrast, the designs of Ledoux's second phase (1785–9), after all hopes of execution had faded, represent a radical departure from tradition. They exemplify a purely functional and at the same time utopian architecture, in hard, stereometric forms, with no modelling of individual elements and without a trace of ornament.[81] This is an architecture dominated by the solids that Ledoux called 'the letters of his alphabet':[82] cube, cylinder and sphere, with the occasional addition of the pyramid, as in the Charcoal Kiln and the Cannon Forge. In many respects, Chaux shows the influence of Boullée, especially in the large cemetery, with its central sepulchre consisting of a sphere half-buried in the earth (Plate 280). This could never have been conceived without the precedent of the Cenotaph for Newton; and there is a reference to the Newtonian laws of gravitation in the representation of the solar system that is appended to the cemetery design (Plate 281).

All these buildings are prototypes, exemplars of a programmatic architecture. The whole city is a manifesto for the moral education of humanity, steeped in the nature cult of Rousseau. Life is to become a single path to virtue.[83] Everyone is to have sufficient space, sufficient air, light and water; everyone may live on the produce of his own garden. Conflicts are to be resolved by a judge sitting in the Court of

279 Claude-Nicolas Ledoux:
Arc et Senans, Saline de Chaux,
plan of the Ideal City, *c.* 1775.

280 Claude-Nicolas Ledoux:
Saline de Chaux, the Ideal City,
Cemetery.

281 Claude-Nicolas Ledoux:
Saline de Chaux, the Ideal City,
Cemetery, Homage to Newton.

282 Claude-Nicolas Ledoux:
Saline de Chaux, the Ideal City,
Temple of Memory.

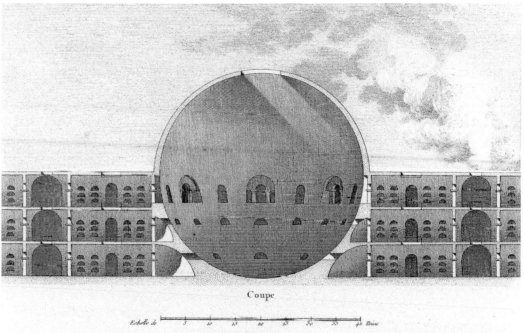

Coupe

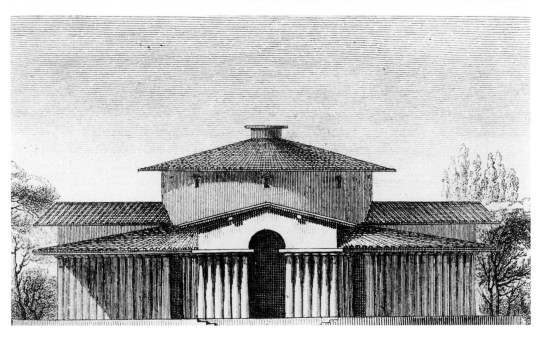

283 Claude-Nicolas Ledoux: Saline de Chaux, the Ideal City, House of the Hoop-Makers.

284 Claude-Nicolas Ledoux: Saline de Chaux, the Ideal City, House of the River Authority.

285 Claude-Nicolas Ledoux: Saline de Chaux, the Ideal City, House of the Sawyers.

286 Eienne-Louis Boullée: design for a Palais des Etats, 1792 (Paris, Bibliothèque Nationale).

Peace, the Pacifère; virtue is to be taught by example in the Panarétéon; women and their achievements as educators are commemorated in the Temple of Memory (Plate 282). There are also a Temple of Reconciliation, a phalliform Oikéma (House) for purposes of sexual initiation, a House of Education, and more besides, so that one is inclined to suspect that Ledoux belonged to one of the Orders of Illuminati that were so strong in his day.[84]

In the buildings set aside for the manual trades, the symbolism occasionally verges on the ludicrous. The House of the Coopers has concentric hoops on its outside walls (Plate 283); the House of the River Authority is shaped like a water pipe, through which the river Loue flows (Plate 284); the House of the Charcoal-Burners is a half-dome resting on untrimmed tree-trunks; that of the Gunsmiths is a square array of smoking pyramids. The interiors of all these buildings are highly impractical, and indeed barely usable. They show that Ledoux, for all his social ideals, had no real idea of the practical needs of the manual trades. Their forms are taken from the *fabriques* of landscape gardening and the buildings themselves were probably intended as such. The House of the Coopers, for example, derives from the Chinese pavilions with circular lateral openings built by Bélanger at Bagatelle, Saint-James and elsewhere; the House of the Sawyers (Plate 285) derives from another popular idea, that of the 'primal hut' of the origins of architecture, in which the columns are formed by tree trunks with their bark still on them, and the capitals and bases are plain planks of wood.[85] Ledoux himself had designed *fabriques* of this sort for the park at Maupertuis, the spherical House of the Rural Constables being the best known.

The inner transformation that Ledoux underwent, and his progression towards utopian architecture, are captured in the engravings that he commissioned, from 1773 onward, of everything he built and everything he dreamed of building. In these he consistently reworked and simplified the forms of his designs, moving further and further from the traditional canon of form.[86] He progressively replaced mansards with flat roofs, windows in the attic with blank walls; mouldings disappeared, and columns lost their fluting (Plate 214b). The resulting harsh, angular, unadorned forms amount at times to an unrecognizable travesty of his own previous work. In these engravings, which he published, with his own frequently esoteric commentaries, in his literary testament, *L'Architecture* (of which the first and only volume appeared in 1804), Ledoux sought to present himself to posterity as the creator of a new, functional architecture, tailored to the needs of a mass society.[87]

Revolutionary architecture was largely denied the chance to put its ideas into practice. During the disintegration of the monarchy and the subsequent Terror, both money and organizational capacity were lacking, and under the Directoire the country lacked the strong will that is needed to convert ideas into reality. The architectural dreams of the period remained confined to the splendid drawings produced for the Academy (until 1793) and to the ephemeral festival structures in which revolutionary uplift mingled with the Romantic enthusiasm for nature.

There was, however, no lack of high aspirations. In 1791 a member of the National Assembly, Kersaint, proposed the erection of public buildings 'in order to strengthen confidence in the new laws through the solidity of the buildings intended to maintain and perpetuate them'. In his *Discours sur les monuments publics* (published 1792), he was able not only to cite a succession of earlier proposals for a Palais des Etats, by Vaudoyer (1784), Combes (1789), Poyet (1790) and others, but also to present a string of new designs on a grand scale by Legrand, Molinos, Boullée and others.[88] The most impressive of these is Boullée's, with its combination of genuine monumental quality and symbolic content (Plate 286). The walls of his immense, block-like Palais National are inscribed with the text of the constitution; on the podium stand allegorical figures of the newly created Departments; the band of reliefs in the attic depicts the national festivals; on the parapet stands the triumphal car of Liberty. This revolutionary tableau is framed by two antique Trajanic columns.

None of this was ever built. The National Assembly had to content itself with the Salle des Machines in the Tuileries, as remodelled by Gisors. In 1794 a further competition was held for a Temple of Equality, in which the first prize went to Durand. His design, which employed piers instead of columns and women's heads instead of the traditional capitals – on the model of the temple of Denderah – and in which the piers themselves bore inscriptions that made them into representations of the Republican Virtues, was recom-

287 Jean-Jacques Lequeu: design for a cow-shed, c. 1792 (Paris, Bibliothèque Nationale).

288 Jean-Jacques Lequeu: design for the Symbolic Order of the Salle des Etats at the Palais National, 1789 (Paris, Bibliothèque Nationale).

289 Gisors-Leconte: Paris, design for the conference-room at the Palais Bourbon (Conseil des Cinq Cents), 1795–7, engraving.

290 Bernard Poyet: Paris, Chambre des Députés, façade, 1806.

mended for execution as a national monument; but this too was never built.

Some of the weirdest products of the prevailing symbolic mood were the works of Jean-Jacques Lequeu (1756–1825), who had worked as an architectural draughtsman for Le Brument in Rouen and for Soufflot in Paris, and who was employed from 1793 onwards in the government land survey office.[89] His designs for temples, villas, public monuments, city gates and the like are a bizarre mixture of technical bravura, naivety and self-conceit. The incongruity of his juxtapositions combines with his utter lack of stylistic sense to create an alienation effect that has traits which anticipate Surrealism and collage. His design for a cow-shed has a façade shaped like a cow (Plate 287); his Palais National (Plate 288) employs a 'symbolic' order in which the entablature is supported by busts of aristocrats – 'those fugitive despots', chained to antique columns – and of their 'subordinate accomplices'. By determinedly setting aside formal and aesthetic standards of the past he came close to early-nineteenth-century patterns; but his contribution to Revolutionary architecture was negligible.

The only building that the Revolution has bequeathed to Paris is the Salle des Cinq Cents, now the Chambre des Députés (Plate 289). The hemicyclic debating chamber that Gisors and Leconte, assisted by Hurtault and Gisors the Younger, built into the Palais Bourbon in 1795–7 for the newly created Council of the Five Hundred still breathes something of the spirit of revolutionary architecture. In form, it harks back to Gondoin's amphitheatre at the Ecole de Chirurgie; but the arc is lined by an Ionic colonnade, totally subordinated to the sober wall surface, and the straight wall and the over-sized proscenium arch in front of it are adorned with symbols of antique virtues and texts of laws.

This chamber, with its semicircular arrangement, its niche for the orator and the president, and its visitors' galleries (already present in the Salle des Machines) above the deputies' benches, has served as the model for numerous later parliamentary chambers.[90] The river front however (Plate 290) was started only in 1806, by Poyet, who wanted to hide the tall and unsightly roofs of the debating chamber. He therefore built a huge central dodecastyle portico and flanking wings that entirely screen the old Palais Bourbon from view. In the pediment relief he represented Napoleon on horseback, followed by his soldiers, and the Pope officiating at Napoleon's marriage. There is a strong resemblance here to the church of the Madeleine, as built by Vignon in the same year at the other end of the north-south axis through the Place de la Concorde (formerly Place Louis-XV); both have the frigidity, and the literal imitation of the antique, that are so typical of Napoleonic buildings.

The Napoleonic counter-revolution dismissed revolutionary architecture out of hand. The representatives of academic doctrine, Charles-François Viel among them, no doubt knew perfectly well how novel and forward-looking Boullée's and Ledoux's ideas were. But, far from accommodating them within the antique revival movement that created the Napoleonic buildings of Paris, they dismissed their audacities out of hand as mere political aberrations. The influence of revolutionary architecture is therefore not to be found so much as in France, in Germany (Friedrich Gilly, Peter Speeth) and in Russia (Thomas de Thomon, Andrey Dimitrievich Zakharov).

The custodian of the Neoclassical inheritance in France was Boullée's pupil Jean-Louis-Nicolas Durand (1760–1834), who moulded it into a functional architecture intended for daily use. As a professor at the Ecole Polytechnique, Durand had the task of training young engineers and architects, and he welded Boullée's aristocratic handling of the classical repertoire of forms, Ledoux's cubist mode of building by addition, and pure, academic classicism into a rational, eclectic functionalism appropriate to the new architectural needs of a mass society. His *Précis des leçons d'architecture* of 1802–5, which reconciled the opposing tendencies within late eighteenth-century architecture, was to become the manual of Romantic classicism in the nineteenth century.[91]

CHAPTER 6

Decoration

The trend towards austerity and sobriety that marked the true Louis XVI style – that of the last quarter of the eighteenth century – had little influence on decoration. It would be easy to be misled by those ever more rigorous Palladian façades; the decor behind them was hardly less opulent than that of the previous age. People had no intention of giving up the surroundings that they were used to, just for the sake of some antique precedent. In this, the hôtels of Boullée, Brongniart, Bélanger and Ledoux speak with one voice. What did change was above all the articulation of the wall surfaces. Panelling did not altogether disappear, but in state apartments it was largely replaced by an architectural decor of pilasters or columns. Contant d'Ivry had introduced fluted pilasters at the Palais-Royal, and they had been taken up by Boullée, Cherpitel, Brongniart and others. They remained fashionable until the 1780s, especially in small rooms and cabinets; but as early as 1770. Barré had used engaged columns in the interiors of Le Marais and in the room erected for the Dauphin's wedding festivities, Chalgrin had set free-standing columns, complete with architrave, in front of the walls. Pilasters were a native French inheritance; columns however were an element of antique origin, brought to France by the returning Rome scholars. At Åkerö, Le Lorrain painted a columnar decor on the walls; Peyre decorated the Duc de Nivernais's dining room with – probably engaged – Ionic columns; and columns accordingly featured in the antique decor of the Pavillon de Brancas. And so, as fashion turned towards the antique – but also in response to the colonnades of the newly built basilican churches – columns increasingly featured in the state rooms of houses, spreading from the vestibule and staircase to the grand salon and the ballroom or dining room, and relegating panels to the private apartments; at the same time, painted decor gave way to reliefs.

The three-dimensional possibilities of this system of articulation are brilliantly exploited in Antoine's grand salon at the Hôtel de la Monnaie, in Chalgrin's Salle des Actes at the Collège de France (1780) (Plate 291), in the vestibule of Etienne Legrand's Hôtel de Gallifet, where the intercolumniations are occupied by mirrors, and in Clérisseau's ballroom for the Maison Lenoir (c. 1780). In the 1780s the columnar decor freed itself from the surface of the wall. The Salle des Menus-Plaisirs, later the Salle des Etats, at Versailles (1787), was divided into a nave and aisles by Doric columns precisely imitated from the antique; the result was indistinguishable from a Roman basilica.

Along with this went niches for statues or – as at the Collège de France – for pedestals bearing busts of emperors. The fashion for adorning interiors with 'antique' statues was so universal that there were sculptors' workshops in Paris that did nothing but copy classical originals. Quality was not their prime concern. Where real pieces would have been too expensive, or would have occupied too much room, the sculptures were painted on the wall in grisaille.

All this, it is true, was only skin-deep; underneath, the love of luxury persisted. Behind a sober classical façade, the interior was often dominated by an utterly contrasting, feminine sensibility, with a preference for delicate colours and for the use of fabrics and draperies. One centre of this refined style of decoration was the court of Versailles, where the queen set the tone. While the king mostly contented himself with his predecessor's rooms and modernized very sparingly, in the queen's apartments alterations never ceased.[92] They began, almost as soon as Marie-Antoinette moved into Versailles, with the Petits Appartements on the first floor, spread to the second floor from 1776 onwards and had reached the ground floor by 1783. There, in the central corps de logis between the Cour de Marbre and the garden, adjoining the apartments of the royal children, a large apartment with three libraries gradually took shape.

Marie-Antoinette's improvements even extended to the state rooms themselves, the Grands Appartements. She showed no respect whatever for the architecture of J.H. Mansart; her sole aim was the complete modernization of the venerable Appartement de la Reine – including the Salon de la Paix, which served her as a card room and occasionally even as a theatre. Heurtier, the palace inspector of works, produced a plan providing for the removal of all the marble facing and bronze trophies and the insertion of a false ceiling beneath that painted by Le Brun. In a uniform rhythm, the room was to be lined with a blind arcade of wooden panelling to match the window openings. Absurdly enough, it was the Revolution that thwarted this plan and saved the Salon de la Paix. However, the other rooms, and the Cabinet des Nobles in particular, lost most of their marble facing and bronze ornaments and acquired fresh chimneypieces, cloth hangings, and a complete set of new furniture.

The men responsible for this work, after Gabriel's retirement in 1775, were Mique and the brothers Hugues-Jules and Jean-Siméon Rousseau.[93] In all essentials, however, the style was determined by the queen herself. This 'Marie-Antoinette style', unarchitectural and decorative but of extreme elegance, was marked by tranquil lines, classical profiles, rich gilding, overdoor reliefs and a certain transparency. The atmosphere of the rooms was set by glass doors (even on the bookcases), tall mirrors and light-coloured materials with a predominance of white. The straight lines of the walls were broken by alcoves, each with a mirror on its back wall and another in its soffit. According to contemporaries, the queen's ground-floor boudoir was nothing but a cabinet of mirrors, relying on Baroque effects to make its impression.[94] All this was complemented by a love of draperies, curtains, trimmings, fringes and tassels that was somewhat reminiscent of the taste of a modiste.

This style, which robbed courtly Neoclassicism of all its rigour, prevailed even in Pâris's festive rooms in the Baraques; and with it went the floral motif. Carvings, paint-

Décoration intérieure de
la grande Salle des Actes

291 Jean-François-Thérèse Chalgrin: Paris, design for the Salle des Actes at the Collège de France, 1780 (Paris, Bibliothèque Nationale).

292 The Rousseau brothers: Versailles, Appartements de Marie-Antoinette, La Méridienne, 1781.

ings, hangings, clothes, furniture: everything was swamped with flowers. Floral swags, fruit and flower still-lifes and cherubs playing with flowers, as popularized by the engravings of Gilles-Paul Cauvet, Pierre Ranson, Henri Salembier and the rest,[95] ousted the heavy, classical trophies of Delafosse's *Iconologie*. It was undoubtedly Marie-Antoinette's influence that attuned the decorations of the brothers Rousseau to this floral style. The best examples are to be found in the Méridienne (Plate 292), an octagonal cabinet with alcoves, fitted out in 1781 behind the Chambre de la Reine on the occasion of the Dauphin's birth; in the panelling on the ground floor, only partly preserved; in the murals of the Belvédère at the Petit Trianon; and in the Chaumière or thatched cottage (Plate 293) at Rambouillet (1772–8). In these, the naturalism of the Louis XVI style reached its zenith, though the delicate, symmetrical carvings of the panels and glass doors produce a somewhat schematic effect that falls far short of the exuberant fancy of the Louis XV style. Initially however the Neoclassical element was not very prominent. Where it did appear – in the Cabinet Doré, for example, or in the chimneypieces – it was modelled on Piranesi's engravings: sphinxes, incense burners, Roman eagles, caryatids and so forth.

A fundamental change in decorative practice came with the introduction of the grotesque, which replaced minutely subdivided ornament with coherent compositions. Ledoux had set an example with his much-admired and much-copied large arabesques in the Hôtel d'Hallwyl and Hôtel d'Uzès, derived from motifs by Le Brun. It was Clérisseau, however, who set the new fashion. He introduced a system derived from antique decorative painting and plasterwork; its principal constituents were arabesques and grotesques, in paint or plaster, interspersed with medallion-framed paintings or framing scenes of antique ruins. The accompanying friezes of tendrils were mostly copied from antique originals, as may be seen from Clérisseau's surviving drawings.

Clérisseau's pioneer work, as far as Paris was concerned, was the Hôtel Grimod de la Reynière (*c.* 1780),[96] the decor of which is known to us from the drawings of the Polish artist Jan Baptist Kamsetzer (Plate 294).[97] The salon walls were adorned with eight large, framed panels of grotesques – now in the Victoria and Albert Museum in London – of which two flanked the chimneypiece, two pairs flanked the doors on the end walls, and two separated the three windows on the remaining long wall. Narrow strips of tendril ornament served as frames.

The grotesque was by no means unknown in France: both Le Brun and Bérain had made use of it. But there was something special about these grotesques. They were lighter and livelier than those of Le Brun, closer to the antique than those of Bérain. The tendrils rising in strict symmetry from the floor were combined with sphinxes and other fabulous beasts and supported smoking sacrificial bowls, swers and half-moon-shaped shields. Coloured relief plaques, and medallions of historical subjects painted by Lavallée-Poussin, formed the centres of the compositions. Everything except the medallions was on a very small scale. The leaves of the doors, too, were painted with classical motifs, and above them were overdoor paintings. The copiousness of Clérisseau's imagination is illustrated by a different scheme

293 The Rousseau brothers: Rambouillet, La Chaumière, *c.* 1775, petit cabinet.

294 Charles-Louis Clérisseau: Paris, Hôtel Brimod de la Reynière, decoration, 1772–5.

295 Jean Dugourc: Paris, Bagatelle, 1777, decoration.

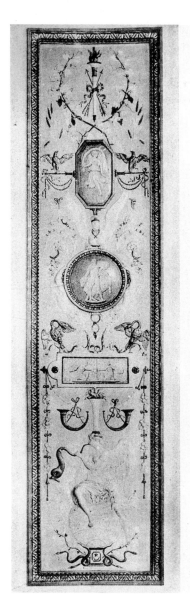

– constructed on the same principle and also filling the entire wall surface – that he used in 1773 in the Roman House for Catherine the Great. Here he divided the wall gridwise into four zones or registers, dominated by scenes of ruins in the second and third zones; grotesques appeared only in the central strip, which incorporated a pilaster-like upward continuation of the forward breaks in the dado zone.

The Hôtel Grimod de la Reynière became one of the sights of Paris. It was there, in 1782, that Clérisseau met Catherine's son, the heir to the Russian imperial throne: an encounter that produced not the expected praise and recognition but a public row.

The invention of this now decorative system can most probably be ascribed to Clérisseau himself; this is suggested not only by the extraordinarily similar early work of his pupil, Robert Adam – at Castle Ashby, Osterley Park and elsewhere – but also by the (purely literary) record of Clérisseau's own decor for the 'Café' of Cardinal Albani (1761). The only difference between this and the work of Robert Adam is that Adam sets white plaster ornament against a coloured ground, while Clérisseau makes the ground white and the motif coloured. The dissemination of the style was largely the work of Clérisseau's friend Piranesi, who was using a very similar formula as early as the 1760s (as at S. Maria del Priorato and the Villa Malta), and who introduced it to the public in his volume of engraving *Diverse maniere di adornare i cammini* (1769), which Lhuillier brought to France in the very year of its publication and no doubt used in his work at the Pavillon de Brancas. The historic impact of the new style is revealed by its almost simultaneous appearance at the Hôtel Grimod de la Reynière and at Bagatelle, as well as in the work of Robert Adam in England, of Erdmannsdorf at Wörlitz and of Cameron at Tsarskoe Selo.

The decor of the Hôtel Grimod de la Reynière was a spectacular success, although Cherpitel, himself probably imitating the Pavillon de Brancas, had already decorated the salon of the Hôtel du Châtelet in the same manner in 1771. Nevertheless, the court took its grotesque decoration not from Clérisseau but from the engravings of Camporesi and Volpato, published in 1776, and from those of Colombani, Pergolesi, Richardson and others.[98] These were immediately imitated, and the wall panel came to be seen no longer as a framed area but as a pictorial unit. As in the earlier grotesques of the school of Le Brun and in the arabesques of Ledoux, a central axis was formed out of several motifs one on top of the other, and these were framed – as on the mirrors in 'Napoleon's Bathroom' at Fontainebleau – by thin vases, slender female figures and vine tendrils. The composition consisted of a few large motifs: flower vases alternating with winged geniuses or sphinxes and relief medallions with ancient Greek or 'Etruscan' scenes. Etruscan motifs, derived from vases found in Italy, appeared for the first time in Jean Dugourc's decorations at Bagatelle (1777) (Plate 295) and the Folie Saint-James (1778). At court, the Etruscan fashion did not set in until the mid 1780s.[99]

The *Antichità d'Ercolano* served as a pattern for many of these relief scenes. They differed from seventeenth-century grotesques – such as those at Vaux-le-Vicomte – not so much in the motif as in the mode of execution, which resembled the Pompeian style in its lightness and elegance

296 Jean-François Chalgrin: Versailles, Pavillon de Musique de Madame, 1784, central salon.

and in the isolation of individual motifs. This style was already in evidence in the door panels of the Cabinet Doré at Versailles (1783), but it reached full flower in the Appartement de la Reine at Fontainebleau, redecorated in 1785. There, the Cabinet de Toilette may be regarded as the high-water mark of this Neo-Pompeian style (Plate 297).[100] The room is painted mother-of-pearl throughout, with plaster reliefs over the doors, and contains choice furniture inlaid with mother-of-pearl.

The Rousseau brothers' last arabesque decoration in this style – for Ledoux's Maison de Monsieur Hosten – was done in 1792; and the work itself makes it clear that the queen's taste was no longer a background influence. By then, this form of decoration had won universal popularity. Through improvements in wallpaper manufacture, which reached a very high standard from the 1770s onwards in the products of the firm of Réveillon, it brought radiant colours, Pompeian motifs and delicate festoons of flowers into every house. Only the tendency towards isolation and simplification into block-like shapes, which set in around 1790, put an end to this play of arabesques and ephemeral architecture.

Away from court, the work done in the 1780s by Chalgrin for the Comte de Provence and by Bélanger for the Comte d'Artois stands out particularly; Chalgrin's for its quality, Bélanger's for its bold inventiveness. At Versailles, the interior of the Pavillon de Musique de Madame (1784), by Chalgrin, looks like a continuation of the Petit Trianon. The cool, white paintwork and absence of gilding make the

297 The Rousseau brothers: Fontainebleau, Appartement de la Reine, Cabinet de Toilette, 1785.

articulation stand out more strongly than it does in Mique's work. There are overdoor panels in the classical style, and the octagonal salon, clad with mirrors up to the heads of the windows, is lined by arcading with a vigorous entablature. But even here the strictness of the profiles is balanced by a rich and graceful floral decor: there are flowers in the delicate relief of the carved door panels, plaster garlands of flowers on the upper part of the walls and acanthus fronds in the coving. Like the dining rooms of the Hôtel de Thélusson (1780) and the Pavillon Beaujon at Issy (*c.* 1775), the central, circular music room is decorated all round with views of a landscape (Plate 296). The spectator finds himself in the middle of all this, surrounded by the painted columns of a circular temple.

Bélanger, by contrast, carried on the line of Piranesi and Clérisseau. His decorations for Bagatelle (1777–8) and for the Folie Saint-James (1778) – grotesques in coloured plasterwork, linked with painted medallions and small relief panels – were a continuation of the Hôtel Grimod de la Reynière. For the plaster grotesques, he called in as his assistant the young ornamental designer Dugourc, who, like Clérisseau, had made a thorough study of antiquity in Rome. They are an exact imitation of Raphael's grotesques in the Vatican Logge. This first example at Bagatelle, where Lhuillier was responsible for the plaster modelling and Dusseaux and Hubert Robert for the painting – including that of the unstuccoed walls – was no whit inferior to its Roman model. It was a much-admired masterpiece;

Dugourc employed the same technique at the Folie Saint-James (1778), the Château de Brunoy (1780) and elsewhere. Bagatelle was celebrated for its furnishing: by way of allusion to the princely owner's office as grand master of artillery, his bedchamber was fitted out as a military tent, with hangings all round, even on the tent-like bed canopy, and gilt trim.[101]

In contrast to this, Bélanger's decoration at the Château de Maisons (*c.* 1780) perpetuates the architectural tendency of the Pavillon de Brancas, with its articulation of columns and niches; but such was the perfectionism and antiquarian expertise of Lhuillier, who was responsible for nearly all the three-dimensional decoration, that this involves no sacrifice of elegance or charm. The masterpiece here is the summer dining room, with its relief friezes, its plaster ceiling panels, the eagle inspired by the church of SS. Apostoli over the chimneypiece and the big figures in the niches. This Neo-classical atmosphere comes remarkably close to the classicism of François Mansart, as seen in the other, unchanged rooms of the same château.[102]

It was also through Bélanger – who, like the Comte d'Artois, was affected by the Anglomania of his time – that the English decorative influence made itself felt. The bearing

300 Berthault: Paris, Hôtel Récamier, decoration of the bedroom, 1798.

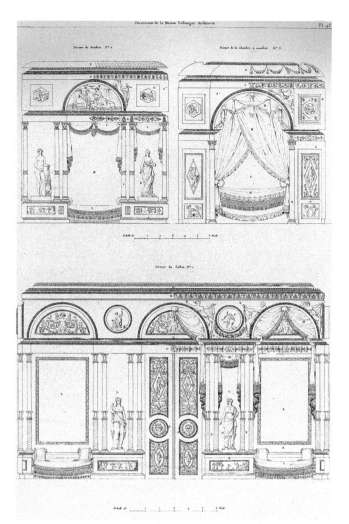

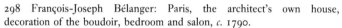

298 François-Joseph Bélanger: Paris, the architect's own house, decoration of the boudoir, bedroom and salon, c. 1790.

299 François-Joseph Bélanger: Paris, Hôtel Dervieux, decoration of the bathroom, 1788.

of this influence on the genesis of the Louis XVI style has been thoroughly discussed by scholars.[103] In the period before 1780 its role was negligible. Clérisseau and the Adam brothers, had drawn on the same sources: they had all been in Rome at the same time, had been friends with Piranesi, and had spent years studying the ancient grotesques. But when they returned home they applied these lessons in very different ways. The Adam style, which was based on a smooth expanse of wall, could never have more than a limited application to the French panel system. Again, French ornamentation rested on a naturalism constantly fed by painters and engravers; the Adam arabesques, which were not backed by any true painting, were bound to seem thin and bloodless by comparison. The French decoration of the 1770s therefore shows barely a trace of the influence of *The Works in Architecture of Robert and James Adam*, a collection of engravings that appeared in 1773.

The first signs of borrowings from England appeared at the Folie Saint-James and at Maisons; then, in the period after 1785 – starting with the Folie du Comte d'Artois, the Folie d'Adeline Colombes, the redecoration of the house of Mademoiselle Dervieux,[104] and his own house – Bélanger completed the change to a new style largely inspired by the Adam style (Plates 298, 299). The main element in the articulation of the room now consisted of slender wooden columns standing on wooden socles – such as still exist at Malmaison – in a style reminiscent of what is known as the Fourth Pompeian Style. The walls, unlike those of the Vatican Logge, were painted with separate scenes hovering loosely on the surface in the Pompeian way and framed by thin mouldings. The pilasters, painted in delicate colours, now acquired ornamental panels of their own, in white plaster, composed of numerous individual motifs taken from the grotesques. They thus lost their architectural function and instead supplied new, coloured accents to the articulation of the room. The ceiling decorations were also borrowed from England. Tent roofs, sail vaults, coffers filled with painted or plaster medallions or with arabesques of figured scenes based on ancient models, produced a bright, often somewhat overloaded effect, far removed from the light plaster ceilings of Gabriel.

This style, popularized not only by Bélanger but by Cellerier, Legrand, Molinos and Henry, by Percier and Fontaine – just returned from Rome – and by many other members of the younger generation, became the style of the Directoire and the early Empire. It is identical with the style of Malmaison (*c.* 1800) and Saint-Cloud (1802), decorated by Percier and Fontaine for Joséphine de Beauharnais.

English influence also found its way into France in another field. The apse screened by a pair of columns, as in the libraries of Syon House and Kenwood, reappeared in the gallery of the Petite Maison of the Prince de Soubise, by Cellerier (1786), in the gallery of the art dealer Lebrun, and in the Château de Saint-Gratien (Somme).

The Revolution caused no real break. Napoleon's court architects, Percier and Fontaine, continued in the same vein, though under the Directoire the English influence waned and Egyptian motifs became more frequent.[105] Just as a straight line leads from Pâris's Salle des Menus-Plaisirs at Versailles to Percier and Fontaine's Salle des Fêtes at Compiègne, so the same spirit prevails in the Hôtel Récamier, decovated by Berthault (1798), as in Bélanger's Maison Dervieux (1786). The Hôtel Récamier an early work of Fontaine was the most elegant house of the Consulat period and the model for early Empire decoration (Plate 300). It was permeated by a delicate Pompeian classicism that could hardly be distinguished from the refinement of the Ancien Régime.[106] Those who had survived the horrors of the Revolution were far from wanting to live a heroically socialist life; their efforts were directed to starting again as quickly as possible at the point where the sweet life of days gone by had come to an end.

Notes

Abbreviations used in the notes

AB	The Art Bulletin
BAAM	Bulletin de l'art ancien et moderne
BM	Bulletin monumental
BMag	Burlington Magazine
BSHAF	Bulletin de la Société d'Histoire de l'Art français
BSHPIF	Bulletin de la Société d'histoire de Paris et de l'Ile de France
CdA	Connaissances des arts
CA	Congrès archéologique
CAAAN	Cahiers alsaciens d'archéologie, d'art et d'histoire
GBA	Gazette des Beaux-Arts
JSAH	Journal of the Society of Architectural Historians
JWCI	Journal of the Warburg and Courtauld Institutes
MH	Les Monuments historiques de la France
RA	Revue de l'art
RAAM	La Revue de l'art ancien et moderne
SHAS	Société d'histoire et d'archéologie de Saverne et environs

PART I

1. On this see the description by Voltaire in *Le Siècle de Louis XIV* (Paris, 1751); also P. Verlet, *La Maison du XVIIIe siècle en France* (Paris, 1966).

2. G. Brice, *Description de Paris* (Paris, 1713), 2, 321.

3. On the *goût moderne* see also H. Sedlmayr's preface to the section 'Das Gesamtkunstwerk', in exh. cat. *Europäisches Rokoko* (Munich, 1958); also H. Bauer and H. Sedlmayr, *Rokoko: Struktur und Wesen einer europäischen Epoche* (Cologne, 1991).

4. The first volume appeared in 1727; vols. 2 and 3 followed several years later. The fourth volume, which appeared under the same title, does not really belong to the series; it is nothing other than a new edition of the *Grand Marot*. A further volume, published in 1738, in a larger format and with a slightly altered title, contains the royal châteaux, the stables at Chantilly and other comparatively large buildings; see A. Mauban, *L'Architecture française de Jean Mariette* (Paris, 1946). On Jacques-François Blondel's collaboration see E. Kaufmann, 'The Contribution of J.F. Blondel to Mariette's *Architecture française*', *AB* 31 (1949), 58.

5. See Jacques-François Blondel, *De la distribution des maisons de plaisance* (Paris, 1737–8), 1, 3, 2, 81ff.; also idem, *Cours d'architecture* (Paris, 1771–7), 4: 'La convenance doit être regardée comme la partie la plus essentielle de toute la production de l'Architecte.' Likewise G. Boffrand, *Livre d'architecture* (Paris, 1745): 'L'excellence du goût consiste dans une juste convenance.'

6. A. Röver, *Bienséance: Zur ästhetischen Situation im Ancien Régime* (Hildesheim, 1977). C.E. Briseux, in his *Architecture moderne* (1728), also provided specimen designs of modest and simple houses.

7. R.D. Middleton, 'The Abbé de Cordemoy and the Graeco-Gothic Ideal. A Prelude to Romantic Classicism', *JWCI* 25 (1962), 26 (1963).

8. Cf. the account given by Abbé Lambert, and in the *Mémoires* of the Duc de Saint-Simon, who accused J.H. Mansart of ignorance and lack of taste and alleged that he got all his ideas from Lassurance, whom he kept 'sous clef': P. Bourget and C. Cattaui, *Jules Hardouin-Mansart* (Paris, 1956).

9. B. Jestaz, *Jules Hardouin-Mansart: l'œuvre personnelle, les méthodes de travail et les collaborateurs* (Paris, Ecole des Chartes, 1962).

10. Comte P. Biver, *Histoire du château de Meudon* (Paris, 1923); L. Hautecoeur, *Histoire de l'architecture classique en France* (Paris, 1948–53), 2, 624.

11. F. Hamon, 'La Chapelle de la Vierge en l'église Saint-Roch à Paris', *BM* 1970, 229.

12. P. Marot, 'Jules Hardouin-Mansart et les plans de la Primatiale de Nancy', *Le Pays lorrain*, 1930; P. Simonin, 'La Cathédrale de Nancy', *Le Pays lorrain*, 1970, 107ff.

13. The identity of the designer of the third storey of the façade is not known for certain. The design is signed by the financial administrator of the Primatiale, Dumolard; but it is likely that Dumolard, who was anxious for a speedy end to the building works, made use of his relatively privileged access to the duchess regent by lending his name to an idea by the watchmaker Barbe, whom local sources invariably name as the designer.

14. R.M. Neumann, *Robert de Cotte, Architect of the Late Baroque* (Ann Arbor and London, 1980).

15. B. Jestaz, *Le Voyage en Italie de Robert de Cotte* (Paris, 1966).

16. B. Jestaz, 'Le Trianon de marbre ou Louis XIV architecte', *GBA* 74 (1969), 259.

17. 'C'est un homme actif, intelligent, capable d'imaginer de grandes choses et de les conduire', *Le Mercure galant*, May 1708, 299.

18. G. Brière and P. Vitry, *L'Abbaye de Saint-Denis* (Paris, 1948); R.M. Neumann (note 14); J. Mayer-Long, 'Les Projets de Robert de Cotte pour les bâtiments conventuels de l'abbaye de Saint-Denis', *BSHAF* 1981, 59.

19. A contemporary description in J.A. Piganiol de la Force, *Description de Paris* (Paris, 1742); see M. Vloberg, *Notre-Dame de Paris et le vœu de Louis XIII* (Paris, 1926). All this work, with the exception of the choir stalls, was destroyed in the course of Eugène Viollet-le-Duc's restoration of Notre-Dame.

20. J.D. Ludmann, 'Projets de Robert de Cotte et de l'agence des Bâtiments du Roi pour la Ville de Lyon', in *L'Art baroque à Lyon: Actes du colloque de Lyon, octobre 1972* (Lyon, 1975); G. Gardes, 'La décoration de la Place Royale de Louis-le-Grand à Lyon', *Bulletin des Musées et Monuments Lyonnais*, 5 (1975), 327.

21. The demolished façades were rebuilt, with some modifications, in the early nineteenth century; the equestrian monument was replaced with a new one by François Lemot in 1825.

22. The château was pulled down in 1823; see P. de Cossé-Brissac, *Châteaux de France disparus* (Paris, 1947); E. Schlumberger, 'Chanteloup, un destin glorieux et cruel', *CdA* (1962), 72.

23. M. Hauttmann, 'Die Entwürfe Robert de Cottes für Schloss Schleissheim', *Münchner Jahrbuch für Kunstgeschichte* 6 (1911), 256ff.

24. A detailed account of this in H.J. Kunst, *Die Stadtresidenz der Kölner Kurfürsten von den Anfängen bis zum Brand am 16.1.1777*, Die Bonner Universität: Bauten und Bildwerke (Bonn, 1968). A preliminary sketch by de Cotte leaving Zuccali's plan almost untouched indicates vaguely the extension of the palace towards the old fortifications.

25. The Elector was so delighted with this oval salon that he made a point of asking for another to be included in his new Schloss Brühl; see E. Renard and F. Graf Wolff-Metternich, *Schloss Brühl* (Berlin, 1934).

26. Y. Bottineau, 'Felipe V y el Buen Retiro', *Archivo español de arte*, 31 (1958), 117; idem, *L'Art de cour dans l'Espagne de Philippe V* (Bordeaux, 1961).

27. W. von Kalnein, *Das kurfürstliche Schloss Clemensruhe in Poppelsdorf* (Düsseldorf, 1956).

28. The Elector had applied to J.H. Mansart in 1704, and after Mansart's death the Duc d'Antin referred him to Robert de Cotte.

29. For a detailed account of the derivation of the round court, see W. von Kalnein (note 27).

30. A. Rauch-Elkan, 'Acht Pläne und ein Baumémoire Robert de Cottes für Schloss Tilburg in Brabant', *Brabantia*, 2, February 1958, 43ff.; the castle was demolished in 1755.

31. R. Sedlmaier and M. Pfister, *Die fürstbischöfliche Residenz zu Würzburg* (Munich, 1923); P. du Colombier, *L'Architecture française en Allemagne au XVIIIe siècle* (Paris, 1956).

32. K. Lohmeyer, *Die Briefe Balthasar Neumanns von seiner Pariser Studienreise 1723* (Düsseldorf, 1911); G. Brunel, 'Würzburg: les contacts entre Balthasar Neumann et Robert de Cotte', in *Actes du XXIIe Congrès international d'Histoire de l'Art* (Budapest, 1969), 2, 116–17.

33. F. Lübbecke, *Das Palais Thurn und Taxis zu Frankfurt am Main* (Frankfurt, 1955); P. du Colombier (note 31); see also U. Reinhardt, *Die bischöflichen Residenzen von Châlons-sur-Marne, Verdun und Strassburg* (Basel, 1972).

34. Dated 8 January 1727. De Cotte's major designs were routinely accompanied by explanatory *mémoires* of this kind. It makes mention of a first (now lost) design, on a French pattern, of unknown authorship.

35. On the Castelli family and C.P. Morsegno, see Baron Ludwig Döry, 'Die Stukkaturen der Mainzer Deutschordens-Kommende', *Mainzer Zeitschrift*, 1961–2, no. 56/57, 55.

36. In the course of building, the left-hand apartment on the first floor, that of the princess, was enlarged by a narrow gallery that projected beyond the garden front; for this it was necessary to purchase a neighbouring house. A direct access was also created between the vestibule and the garden salon. The Palais Thurn und Taxis remained the principal family seat until 1748; after that it was only in occasional use. In 1895 the furniture and fittings were transferred to the

new family residence in Regensburg, and the Palais Thurn und Taxis was sold. It was destroyed in the Second World War.

37. F. Thievaud-Le Hénand, 'La Reconstruction du château de Compiègne au XVIIIe siècle', in *Position de Thèses: Ecole des Chartes* (Paris, 1970).

38. For a detailed account see U. Reinhardt (note 33); R.M. Neumann (note 14).

39. This process of welding the whole house into a single block was already heralded in de Cotte's designs for Parisian hôtels – such as the Hôtel de Torcy or the Hôtel de Montesquiou – in which the court expanded sideways, carving a slice out of the side wings. In de Cotte's Pavillon d'Orly, the *corps de logis* itself was affected. J. Garms, 'Der Grundriss der Malgrange I von Boffrand', *Wiener Jhb. f. Kg.* XXII 1969, 184.

40. J. Duportal, 'Les Dessins de Robert de Cotte pour le palais de Saverne', *BAAM* 1921, 126; C. Grodecki, 'Travaux du premier cardinal de Rohan au château de Saverne 1704–1730', *CAAAH* 1967, 97.

41. H. Haug, 'L'Architecture Régence à Strasbourg', *Archives alsaciennes d'histoire d'art*, 1926; idem, *Le Château des Rohan et les grands hôtels du XVIIIe siècle à Strasbourg* (Strasbourg, 1953); U. Reinhardt (note 33); J.D. Ludmann, *Le Palais Rohan de Strasbourg* (Strasbourg, 1978–80).

42. U. Reinhardt (note 33) takes the view that the dome, too, is by de Cotte; but there is no sign of this in any of the drawings, and it seems too heavy for him. See J.D. Ludmann, 'L'Evolution des projets de Robert de Cotte pour le palais épiscopal de Strasbourg', *BSHAF* 1968, 23ff.

43. 'I have just been told that Mons. de Beaufrand is not the best, but Monsieur de Coti and his son.' K. Lohmeyer (note 32).

44. A detailed account in M. Gallet and J. Garms, eds, exh. cat. *Germain Boffrand 1667–1754* (Paris, 1986).

45. 'L'architecte qui en a donné les dessins nommé Boffrand, mérite des louanges et s'est acquis par cet ouvrage de la réputation chez les gens délicats.' G. Brice, *Description de Paris*. (Paris, 1713 ed.)

46. The Hôtel d'Argenton was unique among the works of the Mansart school in that it had a straight parapet, no pediment, and an arcade on the garden front with vigorous imposts inspired by the villas of Palladio. From 1726 onwards, as the Hôtel d'Argenson, it was the official residence of the Marquis d'Argenson who was chancellor to the Duc d'Orléans; it was pulled down in 1916. Boffrand had been recommended to the Elector by the latter's mistress, the Comtesse d'Arco, a friend of Madame d'Argenson's.

47. The Pagodenburg in the park of Nymphenburg, Munich (1716); Waghäusel, near Bruchsal (1724–9); Fürstenried, near Munich (1737); Clemenswerth, near Meppen (1736–7). The connection with the Elector continued: Boffrand built him a *château* at Saint-Cloud, where the site architect in charge was Joseph Effner; and Effner carried Boffrand's style to Bavaria. His staircase at the Dachauer Schloss (1716–17) is a copy of the château of the Duc d'Ovléaus at Saint-Cloud.

48. On this see J. Garms, 'Boffrand et la Lorraine', in M. Gallet and J. Garms (note 44).

49. According to the accounts, the remodelling of the old *corps de logis* was completed in 1705; how far it actually resembled the anonymous design mentioned here we do not know, but it is possible that the open loggia or vestibule was already present. Until 1706 the chief architect to the duke was Pierre Bourdiet. On this first phase of building work, see P. Simonin, 'Boffrand et la décoration de l'appartement ducal au château de Lunéville', *Le Pays lorrain*, 1975, 181; idem, 'Projets de Boffrand pour le château de Lunéville', *Le Pays lorrain*, 1985, 157.

50. On the various designs and the sequence of the planning process, see P. Simonin, 'Le Château de Lunéville', in M. Gallet and J. Garms (note 44).

51. The engravings in Boffrand's *Livre d'architecture* are not without their contradictions: they show the château sometimes with pitched roofs and sometimes with leads and balustrades. In either case, Boffrand's roof differed from the present one (by Héré) in presenting a simple rather than an animated skyline.

52. Building started at Rivoli in 1704, without reference to the French designs; see A.E. Brinckmann, *Theatrum novum Pedemontii* (Düsseldorf, 1931), 50ff.; J. Garms, 'Der Grundriss der Malgrange I von Boffrand', *Wiener Jahrbuch für Kunstgeschichte* 22 (1969), 181ff. The Malgrange I design was reused by Jadot for Mariemont.

53. L. Hautecœur, 'Le Plan en X à propos de Boffrand', *BSHAF* 1959, 166; J. Garms, *Studien zu Boffrand* (Vienna, 1962).

54. An echo of Bibbiena's work in Nancy is to be found in the staircase of the Hôtel Ferraris by Boffrand (*c.* 1722), the top floor of which is a magnificent piece of Baroque stagecraft by Bibbiena's pupil Giacomo Barilli: M. Antoine, 'L'Opéra de Nancy', *Le Pays lorrain*, 1965, 1ff. A.E. Brinckmann, followed by Wittkower, argues that La Malgrange II is an imaginary project, based on Juvarra's plan for Stupinigi; but this is disproved by the evidence of the tracings in the Recueil Piroux. The link with Vienna was first pointed out by L. Aurenhammer in the catalogue to the Fischer von Erlach exhibition (Vienna, 1956); it is also men-

tioned by H. Sedlmayr, *Johann Bernhard Fischer von Erlach* (Vienna and Munich, 1956), 92ff.

55. The preliminary drawings in the Recueil Piroux show that from the start Boffrand conceived La Malgrange II lengthways, i.e. looking towards the narrow side; the crosswise positioning in the *Livre d'architecture* gives a false impression.

56. In the Musée historique de Lorraine, there is an instructive drawing in which Boffrand's new building is shown superimposed on the still-existing old palace; see J. Garms, 'Les Projets de Mansart et de Boffrand pour le palais ducal de Nancy', *BM* 125 (1967), 231, with bibliography.

57. The similarity of the façade to that of Palazzo Chigi in Rome has already been pointed out more than once. Like the somewhat earlier Hôtel Amelot in Paris, it is a further illustration of Boffrand's closeness to Bernini However, Bernini's façade here appears translated into terms of Gallic elegance, and more tranquil in its rhythms; notably, the proportions and the window forms are different.

58. Despite all assertions to the contrary in the local literature, very few of the numerous hôtels built for the nobility in Nancy after 1715 are by Boffrand; nor do the remainder display any consistent evolutionary line.

59. See M. Gallet and J. Garms (note 44), 90 (Commercy), 94 (Haroué).

60. Illustrated and discussed by R. Sedlmaier and M. Pfister (note 31).

61. In this, the new hôtel type is described as 'moindre qu'un palais ... et aussi plus considérable que la maison d'un particulier'. Daviler had worked for five years under J.H. Mansart, from whom he took his use of long, uninterrupted corridors.

62. On the connection between domestic arrangements and social structure in French court society, see N. Elias, *Die höfische Gesellschaft* (Frankfurt, 1989), 68ff.

63. N. Elias (note 62) is clearly familiar only with the Blondel formula, and not with that of Daviler; his conclusions are therefore not applicable to the early part of the century.

64. In detail in B. Jestaz, 'L'Hôtel de Lorge, sa place dans l'œuvre d'Hardouin-Mansart', *BM* 1971.

65. The first to draw attention to the architectural symbolism of J.H. Mansart, and to the influence of the Hôtel de Lorge, was A. Corboz, 'Une œuvre méconnue de l'agence Mansart à Genave: l'Hôtel Buisson (1699)', *Genava*, n.s. 32 (1984).

66. Discussed in detail by R.M. Neumann, 'French Domestic Architecture of the Early Eighteenth Century: the Town House of Robert de Cotte', *JSAH* 39 (1980); A. Marie, *Inventaire manuscrit des dessins de Robert de Cotte* (Paris, 1941).

67. Jean-Baptiste Colbert, Marquis de Torcy, received designs from de Cotte and from Boffrand simultaneously. It is impossible to be sure whether these were for the same site; the larger design, by Boffrand, was ultimately chosen in preference to that of de Cotte. See R.M. Neumann (note 66).

68. According to Le Blond's new edition of Daviler's *Cours d'architecture* (1710), the minimum composition of an apartment was: vestibule – antechamber – salon – bedchamber (or *chambre de parade*) – cabinet. The *chambre de parade* or state bedchamber gradually lost its primary function and served only for display.

69. J. Boyer, 'Une œuvre inédite de Robert de Cotte à Aix-en-Provence: l'Hôtel de Caumont', *BSHAF* 1964, 55.

70. F. Laudet, *L'Hôtel de Toulouse, siège de la Banque de France* (Paris, 1960); J.D. Ludmann and B. Pons, 'Nouveaux documents sur la galerie de l'Hôtel de Toulouse', *BSHAF* 1979, 115. The decision to expand the Hôtel de Toulouse and the Arsenal into princely residences sprang from Louis XIV's desire, after the death of the Duc de Bourgogne, to safeguard the succession by legitimizing his sons by Madame de Montespan.

71. His hôtels are listed by M. Gallet and J. Garms (note 44).

72. In de Cotte's changes to Boffrand's designs, presumably made at the Duchess's behest, this is contracted into a single space, and the court in front is regularized by the addition of a continuous colonnade with an exedra. (De Cotte papers, Bibliothèque Nationale, Paris.)

73. Acquired by Eugène de Beauharnais in 1803 and extensively altered, notably by the addition of an Egyptian-looking doorway; it was purchased by the King of Prussia in 1814 and became the Prussian legation and eventually the German embassy.

74. For the Arsenal, and the oval pavilion on the left bank of the Seine, see M. Gallet and J. Garms (note 44).

75. Illustrated in Boffrand's *Livre d'architecture*; the originals in Nationalmuseet, Stockholm.

76. See note 4.

77. E. Langenskjöld, *Pierre Bullet, the Royal Architect* (Stockholm, 1959); R. Strandberg, 'Jean-Baptiste Bullet de Chamblain, Architecte du Roi', *BSHAF* 1963; idem, 'Le Château de Champs', *GBA* 1963, 81; idem, *Pierre Bullet et Jean-Baptiste Bullet de Chamblain* (Stockholm, 1971). For Poisson de Bourvalais, Bullet de Chamblain built a large town house on the Place Vendôme (later converted by Robert de Cotte into the Chancellerie de France).

78. The plan is by Bullet de Chamblain, the elevations by Pierre Bullet; on

the relationship between Issy and Palladio (the Villa Rotonda), see R. Strandberg (1971; as note 77).

79. A design by Pierre Bullet and Bullet de Chamblain has a projecting oval vestibule as well as the oval salon. The oval salon seems to have been Bullet de Chamblain's idea; it had been present in his earlier, more modest design for the same site (before 1701).

80. The oval mansard windows were added by the next owner, *c.* 1725 (after Poisson de Bourvalais had been arrested for embezzlement).

81. See the excellent account of the nature of the *maison de plaisance* in A. Schmarsow, *Barock und Rokoko* (Leipzig, 1897), 372ff.

82. According to Blondel the initial work was by Courtonne, and only the remodelling was by Le Blond.

83. B. Lossky, 'Le Blond, architecte de Pierre le Grand, son oeuvre en France', *Bulletin de l'Association russe pour les recherches scientifiques à Prague*, 3 (1936); L. Réau, 'L'Architecture française en Russie de Le Blond à Ricard de Montferrand', *Urbanisme et architecture*, 1954.

84. J.R. Babelon, *Musée de l'histoire de France, historique et description des bâtiments des Archives Nationales* (Paris, 1958); idem, 'Les Façades sur jardin du Palais Rohan-Soubise', *RA* 1969, 66.

85. It appears that the beauty of the princess, to which the king was not unsusceptible, was largely responsible for the family's new found wealth; the Duc de Saint-Simon even drew a comparison with Madame de Montespan.

86. His father, Jean Oppenord, was a native of Guelders (Geldern); he had become a naturalized Frenchman in 1679 and, as *ébéniste du Roi*, he had living quarters in the Louvre. The spelling varies between Oppenoordt, Oppenordt and Oppenord.

87. Mentioned as chief architect to the Duc d'Orléans in 1715, and appointed as his superintendent and surveyor of buildings and gardens in 1724: F. Kimball, 'Oppenordt au Palais-Royal', *GBA* 1936, 112; idem, *Le Style Louis-XV* (Paris, 1949), 100.

88. A.J. Dézallier d'Argenville calls him the French Borromini; C. Linfert, *Die Grundlagen der Architekturzeichnung* (Berlin, 1931).

89. *Grand Oppenord* (see following note), plates XCII–XCIV; they were intended for the Hofgarten in Bonn.

90. After his death almost 2,000 drawings came into the hands of the publisher Huquier, who had them engraved and published approximately 420 engravings in three series: *Moyen Oppenord* (1737–8), *Petit Oppenord* and *Grand Oppenord* (1748–51).

91. The idea came from François Mansart (gallery of the Hôtel de Toulouse) and ultimately from Philibert de l'Orme. In this salon hung the most celebrated paintings in the collection, which were those that had formerly belonged to Queen Christina of Sweden. V. Champier and R. Sandoz, *Le Palais Royal* (Paris, 1908).

92. The remodelling of the Hôtel du Temple (1720–1); a dwelling house built over the *porte cochère* of the Hôtel Crozat (1730); an orangery for Crozat's country seat at Montmorency; probably also the Château de Bôve-en-Laonnais (after 1719). M.G. Huart, in L. Dimier, ed., *Les Peintres français du XVIIIᵉ siècle* (Paris and Brussels, 1928–30).

93. J.R. Babelon, *Le Cabinet du Roi ou le Salon de Louis XV de la Bibliothèque Nationale* (Paris, 1927), J. Porcher, 'Deux projets de construction pour la Bibliothèque du Roi', *BSHAF* 1930, 100.

94. Begun in 1720 for Charles-Louis de Montmorency-Luxembourg, Prince de Tingry, but sold in 1723, while still unfinished, to Jacques de Matignon, who completed it and gave it his name: see L.H. Labande, 'L'Hôtel de Matignon à Paris', *GBA* 13 (1935), 257; L. Hautecoeur (note 10).

95. The house was illustrated by Mariette. For the same celebrated actress (formerly mistress to the regent, by whom she had a daughter), Hoguer also had a *folie* built at Châtillon, adjoining the Maison Regnault probably by Le Blond; no further biographical details are available for Aubry, who also designed the Hôtel de la Vrillière (later de Conti), listed by P.J. Mariette, *Architecture française* (Paris, 1737–8).

96. Marquis de Montmort, *Le Château de Beaumont-sur-Vingeanne* (Dijon, 1950); F. de Ganay, *Châteaux de France: Est* (Paris, 1953), who gives the wrong date of construction.

97. In 1709–10 he also worked on the Château de Saint-Maur; see G. Mâcon, *Les Arts dans la maison de Condé* (Paris, 1903); F. Souchal, 'Jean Aubert, architecte des Bourbon-Condé', *RA* 1969, no. 6, 29.

98. H. Lemonnier, 'Les Grandes Écuries de Chantilly et le style architectural des écuries aux XVIIᵉ et XVIIIᵉ siècles', *BSHAF* 1926, 7; planning work, in which the Augustinian friar Nicolas Bourgeois was also involved, started in 1719.

99. Here stood the horse fountain, in which figures of boys tendered water in seashells to two life-size horses.

100. The name of Jacques V Gabriel has been mentioned in this connection, by Mariette and others; but he was responsible only for interior decoration. As J.H. Mansart's cousin, Gabriel was well placed at court, and his name was often used as a signal of quality. See J.H. Contant, *Le Palais Bourbon au XVIIIᵉ siècle*

(Paris, 1905); F. Souchal (note 97).

101. The two courts are already in de Cotte's designs, which include both an antiquated-looking quadrangular plan and two U-shaped plans that seem to have inspired the pavilion-like entrances on the return façades of the side wings. (De Cotte papers, Bibliothèque Nationale, Paris.)

102. 'Ce bâtiment est le premier en France où l'on ait imaginé ces genres de commodité qui font tant honneur à nos Architectes François...' Jacques-François Blondel, *Architecture française* (Paris, 1752–6), I, 267; similarly P. Patte, *Monuments érigés en France à la gloire de Louis XV* (Paris, 1767), 6.

103. The attribution to Jacques V Gabriel derives from a misstatement in G. Brice (note 45), constantly repeated. The house was sold in 1736 to the Duchesse du Maine, and in 1753 to Maréchal de Biron, who gave it his name. It is now the Musée Rodin; see J. Vacquier, *L'Ancien Hôtel du Maine et Biron* (Paris, 1909); L. Hautecoeur (note 10).

104. R.A. Weigert, *Jean I Bérain* (Paris, 1937); F. Kimball (note 87), 78.

105. Copies of the chimneypiece designs were supplied to the Princesse de Conti and the Duchesse de Chartres, and copies of the Trianon designs were made available for the Château de Champs (Nationalmuseet, Stockholm, Cronstedt collection).

106. The Cabinet du Conseil was altered in 1755; the portions of its original decor that survive are the large piers (*trumeaux*) between the mirrors, the door panels, and the lowest tier of panelling.

107. A necessary precondition of the new 'verticality' was the introduction of flat ceilings in place of vaulted ones, and the associated heightening of the walls. For a full discussion of verticality as a governing factor, in internal and also in external design, see S. Giedion, *Spätbarocker und romantischer Klassizismus* (Munich, 1922).

108. L. Deshairs, *Le Château de Bercy* (Paris, 1911); F. Kimball (note 87). Removed when the house was torn down in 1860, the decorations have been reassembled, with some modern additions, in a new setting.

109. This multiple recession or 'layering' of relief is first seen at the Grand Trianon (1703).

110. On this see R. Sedlmaier, *Grundlagen der Rokokoornamentik in Frankreich* (Strasbourg, 1917).

111. These relief friezes first appear in the designs for the Ménagerie at Versailles (1698).

112. For a detailed account see B. Pons, 'Germain Boffrand et le décor intérieur', in M. Gallet and J. Garms (note 44).

113. Since the disappearance of the Recueil Piroux, the decorations for La Malgrange have been available only in the tracings by Morey in Nancy. The evidential value of these is admittedly limited, but they do not deserve to be dismissed out of hand as they were by Kimball.

114. For a detailed account, see P. Simonin, 'Le Château de Lunéville', in M. Gallet and J. Garms (note 44).

115. L. Hautecoeur (note 10); F. Kimball (note 87).

116. Toro was master sculptor at the Arsenal in Toulon from 1714 onwards; in Paris in 1716–17. J. Boyer, 'Une famille de sculpteurs bourguignons établis en Provence au XVIIIᵉ siècle: les Turreau ou Toro', *GBA* 69 (April 1967), 201.

117. In a letter to Carl-Gustaf Tessin, dated 15 March 1732, the Swedish architect Carl Härleman described two tendencies among carvers in Paris: one group working in Oppenord's manner and the other in Vassé's. P. Lespinasse, 'Le Voyage d'Härleman et de Tessin en France (1732–42)', *BSHAF* 1910, 279.

118. Oppenord's altar for Saint-Germain des Prés (of the same type, with baldachin, as that of Val-de-Grâce) was copied in 1710 for the altar of Sainte-Trinité, Caen (since transferred to Notre-Dame de Gloriette, also in Caen). On Oppenord's designs, see F. Kimball (note 87) and F. de Catheu, 'Les Marbres de Leptis Magna dans les monuments français du XVIIIᵉ siècle', *BSHAF* 1936, 51.

119. Some of them largely follow Borromini's cartouches at S. Giovanni in Laterano, of which Oppenord had made drawings.

120. Introduced as a motif by Lepautre, e.g., in the Versailles palace chapel; used in a secular context by de Cotte, in the chimneypiece designs for Bonn (1716). On this see P. Kjellberg, 'Ce qu'il faut regarder pour reconnaître le style Régence', *CdA* October 1962, 72.

121. The Galerie Dorée as it stands at present dates from 1870–5, when it was completely rebuilt. The decorative work was carefully preserved and reused; the paintings were moved to museums and replaced by copies. F. Laudet (note 70); J.D. Ludmann and J. Pons, 'Nouveaux documents sur la galerie de l'Hôtel de Toulouse', *BSHAF* 1979, 115.

122. Other work by Vassé: interior decoration of Château de Petitbourg for the Duc d'Antin, with a salon chimneypiece also inspired by the Galerie d'Énée; lady chapel in the south transept of Notre-Dame (1718–19).

123. The Hôtel d'Assy reflects the design illustrated in *Le Grand Oppenord*, plate LXIV. The cartouche shape of the upper wall panels, which becomes light and two-dimensional in execution, is characteristic of the evolution of Oppenord's formal ideas from the Italian to the French manner. J. Babelon, (note 84, Musée

de l'histoire de France).

124. Attributed by F. Kimball (note 87) to Oppenord, the attribution to Hardouin and Lange established by M. Gallet, 'Quelques étapes du Rococo dans l'architecture parisienne', *GBA* 67 (1966), 155.

125. R. Strandberg (1971; as note 77) detects the hand of Bullet de Chamblai, who had designed a similar coving for Poisson de Bourvalais in the music room at Champs (and a coving for the Cabinet du Chancelier, for which the design is now in Stockholm). As against this, however, the same coving reappears several times in the contemporaneous decorations for Bonn.

126. Built in 1723–5 by Jacques V Gabriel for Peyrenc de Moras, who had made his fortune by stock-speculations; it was sold to M. Boullongne in 1728. The corner-cabinet was famous for its paintings by Audran and Lancret. A. Thiry, 'L'Hôtel Peyrenc de Moras, puis de Boullongne', *BSHAF* 1979, 51.

127. The decorations, which are now at the Hôtel de Breteuil and Waddesdon Manor, are otherwise known only from Mariette's engravings and from one original drawing in Stockholm; they are among the most progressive of the period. Erroneous dating *c*. 1750 in Kimball (note 87); R. Strandberg (1971; as note 77).

PART TWO

1. E. and J. de Goncourt, *L'Art du XVIIIᵉ siècle* (Paris, 1873–4); H. Bauer and H. Sedlmayr, *Rokoko: Struktur und Wesen einer europäischen Epoche* (Cologne, 1991); E. Hubala, *Barock und Rokoko* (Stuttgart, 1971).

2. The word *rococo* was first used in literature by Stendhal, *Promenades dans Rome* (1828); it was included in the supplement to the *Dictionnaire de l'Académie Française* in 1842. Cf. H. Rose, *Spätbarock* (Munich, 1922), IX.

3. The word *pittoresque* was first defined in 1726 by Coypel, as 'un choix piquant et singulier des effets de la nature' (*Discours sur la peinture*, 1732); F. Kimball, *Le Style Louis-XV* (Paris, 1949), 146; idem, 'J.A. Meissonnier and the Beginning of the Genre Pittoresque', *GBA* 12 (1942), 27.

4. F. Kimball, *The Genesis of Rococo* (Philadelphia, 1942); R.A. Weigert, *L'Epoque Louis XIV* (Paris, 1962).

5. Ph. Minguet, *Esthétique du Rococo* (Paris, 1960).

6. 'Les décorations intérieures des appartements font à présent à Paris une partie considérable de l'Architecture; elles font négliger la décoration extérieure, non seulement des maisons particulières, mais encore des Palais et des Edifices publics.' G. Boffrand, *Livre d'architecture* (Paris, 1745), 41.

7. In retrospect, Jacques-François Blondel spoke of this as a time when the majority of architects had been out of their minds; *Les Amours rivaux* (Amsterdam, 1774).

8. Certain maçon, en Vitruve érigé,
   Lui trace un plan d'ornements surchargé;
   Nul vestibule, encore moins de façade;
   Mais vous aurez une longue enfilade;
   Vos murs seront de deux doigts d'épaisseur;
   Grands cabinets, salons sans profondeur,
   Petits trumeaux, fenêtres à ma guise,
   Que l'on prendra pour des portes d'église;
   Le tout boisé, verni, blanchi, doré, Et des badauds à coup sûr admiré.
Voltaire, *Le Temple du goût* (1735).

9. J. Lejeaux, 'Jacques-François Blondel, professeur d'architecture', *L'Architecture* 1927, 23; E. Kaufmann, *Architecture in the Age of Reason* (Cambridge, 1955), 131; E. Schlumberger, 'L'Art de bâtir à la campagne selon Jacques-François Blondel', *CdA* March 1967, 74.

10. Jean-François Blondel (1683–1756), a native of Rouen, was appointed to the Service des Bâtiments in 1707. In 1721–4 he was working in Geneva, and his buildings there were engraved in P.J. Mariette, *Architecture française* (Paris, 1737–8).

11. Written in French and in Latin, and equipped with parallels with Horace's *Ars poetica*, the *Livre d'architecture* (note 6) is a testimony to Boffrand's universal culture. The book includes all his major works, sometimes with later corrections, and additionally contains a detailed discussion of taste. E. Kaufmann (note 9), 130.

12. André's work is based on the *Traité du Beau* (1714) by the Lausanne professor of philosophy J.P. de Crousaz. There is an extract from this in the preface to the second edition (1759) of the *Essai sur le beau*. L. Hautecoeur, *Histoire de l'architecture classique en France* 3, 461 (Paris, 1950).

13. Voltaire (note 8).

14. Cited by M. Gallet, 'L'Architecte Pierre Vigné de Vigny 1690–1772', *GBA* 82 (1973).

15. M. Gallet and Y. Bottineau, *Les Gabriel* (Paris, 1982), 53.

16. R.A. Weigert and C. Hernmarck, *L'Art en France et en Suède: extraits d'une correspondance entre l'architecte Nicodème Tessin le jeune et Daniel Cronström* (Stockholm, 1964).

17. M. Gallet and Y. Bottineau (note 15), 123.

18. M. Gallet and Y. Bottineau (note 15), 44.

19. C. Nières, *La Reconstruction d'une ville au XVIIIᵉ siècle* (Rennes, 1972); R.P. Kain, 'The Rebuilding of Rennes', *The Connoisseur* 1975, no. 766, 249.

20. M. Gallet and Y. Bottineau (note 15), 56.

21. P. Courteault, *Bordeaux, cité classique* (Paris, 1932); F.G. Pariset, *Histoire de Bordeaux au XVIIIᵉ siècle* (Bordeaux, 1968); J.G. Avisseau, 'La Place Royale de Bordeaux', in M. Gallet and Y. Bottineau (note 15), 104.

22. M.L. de Grandmaison, 'André Portier de Leugny (1702–70), architecte-inspecteur des travaux à la Place Royale de Bordeaux', *BSHAF* 1934, 105.

23. The Estates had initially had Oppenord in mind, but de Cotte had intervened to replace him with Gabriel. The governor of the province, the Duc de Bourbon-Condé, resented Gabriel, and this made his work very much more difficult; Y. Beauvalot, 'Gabriel à Dijon', in M. Gallet and Y. Bottineau (note 15), 85, with further literature.

24. The wing was completed only in 1776–80, when the court behind was remodelled.

25. Another, unexecuted design of 1735 (Union centrale des Arts décoratifs) shows the large window arches containing smaller windows, each surmounted by a tympanum filled with a cartouche, and each flanked by voluminous pendant trophies of a kind used by Gabriel at Versailles from 1730 onwards. This is evidently a sketch by Gabriel, with instructions for the draughtsman in his office.

26. These niches were presumably intended for figures of the Four Seasons; under Louis XVI they were filled with copies after the antique.

27. It is possible that the idea came from Bourbon-Condé, who was also the owner of Chantilly; see Y. Beauvalot (note 23).

28. By 1785 this doorway had come to be regarded as a 'detestable example' of the Baroque style, and in that year Le Jolivet altered it into something more Neoclassically acceptable to match the new wing on the other side of the Palais des Etats. The tympanum with its sculptures was destroyed.

29. Le Mousseux had already worked under Gabriel in Rennes, where he had fallen out with him; however, he was summoned to Dijon in 1733 to supervise the construction of the staircase wing.

30. 'L'édifice qui fait le plus d'honneur à M. Boffrand est sans contredit l'hôpital des Enfants-Trouvés à Paris': J.C. Pigneron, *Vies des artistes anciens et modernes* (Paris, 1771). J. Garms, 'L'Aménagement du Parvis de Notre-Dame par Boffrand', *Art de France* 1967, 152ff.; M. Gallet and J. Garms, eds, exh. cat. *Germain Boffrand 1667–1754* (Paris, 1986), 120ff., 155ff.

31. This opinion is shared by J. Garms (note 30); the same motif is taken up in the grounds of Stowe.

32. 'Le centre de la ville obscur, resserré, représente le temps de la plus honteuse barbarie.' Voltaire, *Des embellissements de Paris* (Paris, 1749).

33. L. Duclaux, 'La Décoration de la chapelle des Enfants-Trouvés à Paris', *RA* 1971, 45; P. Violette, 'Natoire et Boffrand', in M. Gallet and J. Garms (note 30).

34. M. Gallet (note 14), 263.

35. P. Lejeaux, 'La Place de la Comédie', *Le Pays lorrain* 25 (1933), 1.

36. In 'Procuration curieuse du Sieur Pierre Alexis Delamair, architecte à Paris' (Bibliothèque Nationale, Paris). See also J. Garms, 'Projects for the Pont Neuf and Place Dauphine in the First Half of the XVIIIth Century', *JSAH* 1967, 104.

37. P.L. Moreau, *Plan Général de différents projets d'embellissement les plus utiles et les plus convenables à la commodité des citoyens et à la décoration de la ville de Paris* (Paris, 1759); this was the beginning of the transformation of Paris into a modern city.

38. P. Lavedan, *Histoire de l'urbanisme: Renaissance et temps modernes* (Paris, 1926–52); idem, *Les Villes françaises* (Paris, 1960), 128. See also the excellent analysis in S. Giedion, *Spätbarocker und romantischer Klassizismus* (Munich, 1922).

39. P. Courtault, *La Place Royale de Bordeaux* (Paris, 1923); P. Lavedan (note 38); P. Zucker, *Town and Square* (New York, 1959); J. Thuillier, 'Economie et urbanisme', *Art de France*, 1961, no. 1:31.

40. In his *Traité de police* (Paris, 1738), de la Mare mentions three kinds of public square: those for trade and commerce; those for public gatherings and the administration of justice; and finally the Places Royales. These thus already formed a special category in the contemporary mind. The royal statues in the present Place des Vosges and in the Place Dauphine had been erected retrospectively, and indeed imported from Italy – an important clue to the genesis of the Place Royale.

41. E. de Ganay, 'Le Jardin de la Fontaine à Nîmes', *RAAM* 59 (1931), 117; idem, *GBA* 54 (1955), 20.

42. On this see M. Gallet and Y. Bottineau (note 15), 10; a particularly instructive source is the diary of the Duc de Croÿ, *Journal inédit du duc de Croÿ 1718–1784* (Paris, 1906), I, 287.

43. Argenson wrote about this in 1752: 'On a calculé que depuis 1726 jusqu'au présent les bâtiments ont monté en dépenses à 350 millions, le tout pour ne faire que des nids à rats, à faire et à défaire. C'est le Château de Choisy

qui est le plus grand théâtre de ces variations. Il n'y a point d'année où l'on ne détruise pour rebâtir ce que l'on change l'année suivante.' R.L. de Voyer d'Argenson, *Journal et mémoires* (Paris, 1865), 7, 127.

44. H. Racinais, *La Vie inconnue des petits appartements de Versailles* (Versailles, 1951); P. Verlet, *Versailles* (Paris, 1961); M. Gallet and Y. Bottineau (note 15), 151.

45. M. Gallet and Y. Bottineau (note 15), 42.

46. Only the eastern half of the wing and the central pavilion were built under the supervision of Jacques, V Gabriel; the western half was completed along the same lines by his son Ange-Jacques in 1773–4. Y. Bottineau, *L'Art d'Ange-Jacques Gabriel à Fontainebleau* (Paris, 1962).

47. The idea of the Grand Projet first appeared in 1738 in a pencil sketch laid over the plan for the Cour du Cheval-Blanc, and early in 1739 it was mentioned in a letter from the surveyor of works at Fontainebleau, Louis de Cotte, to Orry; M. Gallet and Y. Bottineau (note 15), 39.

48. 'Le Roi fait continuellement dessiner devant lui, en particulier le jeune Gabriel, de ses Bâtimens'; Argenson (note 43), 2, 192. 'S.M. a beaucoup de bonté pour lui, et il travaille très souvent seul avec le Roi pour des plans et des projets'; Duc de Luynes, *Mémoires sur la cour de Louis XV (1735–1738)* (Paris, 1860). In 1739, at the king's behest, and in defiance of established custom, Gabriel was given the surveyorship at Choisy in addition to that at Versailles, which he already held.

49. C. Tadgell, *Ange-Jacques Gabriel* (London, 1978); Y. Bottineau, 'Ange-Jacques Gabriel: proposition pour un portrait', in M. Gallet and Y. Bottineau (note 15), 132.

50. M.C. Tadgell, 'L'Eglise royale et paroissiale de Choisy', *BSHAF* 1973, 171.

51. Listed by G. Poisson, 'Les Pavillons de chasse', in M. Gallet and Y. Bottineau (note 15), 252.

52. A variation on Le Butard is the Pavillon de la Muette (1764–75), originally planned likewise on a square plan with a portico; C. Tadgell (note 49), 164.

53. L. Hautecoeur (note 12), 3.564; *CdA* March 1956, 68; C. Tadgell (note 49), 43.

54. Ph. de Cossé-Brissac, *Châteaux de France disparus* (Paris, 1947), 105. Contemporaries already doubted whether Madame de Pompadour had financed the château unaided; it is more likely that the king himself was involved. C. Tadgell (note 49), 155; G. Poisson, 'Bellevue', in M. Gallet and Y. Bottineau (note 15), 249.

55. The following statements largely echoes the excellent and comprehensive study by J. Rau, Gräfin von der Schulenburg, *Emmanuel Héré* (Berlin, 1973).

56. E. Héré, *Recueil des plans, élévations et coupes, tant géométrales qu'en perspective des châteaux, jardins et dépendances que le Roy de Pologne occupe en Lorraine y compris les bâtimens qu'il y a fait élever...* (Paris, n.d.); idem, *Plans et élévations le la Place Royale de Nancy et des autres édifices qui l'environnent, bâtie par les ordres du Roy de Pologne, duc de Lorraine* (Paris, 1752). In 1753 Héré had the privilege of presenting the second of these two works to Louis XV; it was a special honour and the crowning moment of his career.

57. The lack of contemporary illustrations means that it is impossible to be absolutely sure of the shape of Boffrand's roof at Lunéville. However, the steep roofs and central dome shown in the *Livre d'architecture* are entirely corresponding with Boffrands habits and were also present in the contemporary and well-documented La Malgrange I. The restless outline of the present truncated pyramid would have been unthinkable for Boffrand. J. Rau-Schulenburg (note 55), 53.

58. He probably replaced the attic on the garden side with a full storey. As late as c. 1740, to judge by the existence of designs by Jadot, Duke Charles was still thinking of extending his mother's château for his own use and that of his wife, Maria Theresa, Queen of Hungary; J. Rau-Schulenburg (note 55), 73.

59. The same colonnade form appears on a façade design in the sketchbook of Boffrand's pupil Jadot, in the Bibliothèque Doucet, Paris; J. Schmidt, *Die Alte Universität in Wien und ihr Erbauer Jean-Nicolas Jadot* (Vienna and Leipzig, 1929).

60. The Croix de Mission, a large cross carried through Lorraine in 1739 by the first Jesuit mission instituted by Stanislas, was erected beneath a baldachin in the grounds of La Malgrange.

61. 'Là, en un mot, on trouve une foule de nouveautés, et partout c'est le riant et le gracieux qui dominent. Que nos artists illustres aillent à l'école du Grand Prince et ils apprendront mille manières nouvelles de nous surprendre, de nous plaire, de nous enchanter.' M.A. Laugier, *Essai sur l'architecture* (Paris, 1753), 293.

62. Stanislas sent the *Recueil* (note 56) to the King of Prussia in summer 1754; at Potsdam, after several months of planning, building began in 1755. The Teehaus at Sansssouci is externally richer and enlivened by a number of life-size figures of Chinese character; internally, however, it is simpler and more sober.

63. The most detailed of the contemporary accounts is 'Voyage d'un Bourguignon: observations faites au cours de mon voyage...' (Nancy, Bibl. mun. ms., 1753); also Duc de Luynes (note 48), 62.

64. Notably by P. Boyer in *Les Châteaux du roi Stanislas en Lorraine* (Nancy, 1910).

65. J. Rau-Schulenburg (note 55), 129, draws attention to a possible source: the late seventeenth-century castle of Mariemont, near Warsaw, which also had a central first-floor space in the shape of a Greek cross.

66. On a sheet of sketches in the Codex Montenuovo in Vienna the Tower of Babel appears in a three-storey form, as at Chanteheux; sketches of this kind by Fischer-possibly belonging to Boffrand might have reached Stanislas or Héré. H. Sedlmayr, *Johann Bernhard Fischer von Erlach* (Vienna and Munich, 1956), fig. 125.

67. 'Chanteheux, Einville, la Malgrange, le Château d'Eau de Commercy s'effacèrent bientôt comme de beaux rêves.' N. Durival, *Description de la Lorraine et du Barrois* (Nancy, 1778–83).

68. P. Marot, 'La Genèse de la Place Royale de Nancy', *Annales de l'Est*, 1954; idem, *La Place Royale de Nancy* (Paris, 1966); J. Rau-Schulenburg (note 55), 191; E. Héré, *Plans et élévations...* (note 56).

69. The king originally intended to transfer the Place Royale to the marketplace of the new quarter, but he changed his mind after objections from the merchants.

70. 'Le projet de S.M. fut dès son principe de réunir en Lorraine, dans un même-tems, deux Souverains qui n'y feraient que s'y succéder et de donner à tous les siècles le premier exemple d'un Roi qui dans ses propres Etats érige des statues à un autre Roi.' N.L. Michel, *Compte général de la dépense des édifices et bâtiments que le Roi de Pologne, Duc de Lorraine et de Bar, a fait construire pour l'embellissement de la ville de Nancy* (Lunéville, 1759).

71. The inscriptions on the medallions above the lateral arches give the tenor of the iconographical programme: *Principi pacifico* and *Principi victori*. The bronze figures in the attic are by Guibal.

72. The painted architectural prospect on the landing, by André Joly, was destroyed in the nineteenth century, and the wall is now covered by a curtain.

73. Jean Lamour, locksmith in ordinary to the King of Poland, was one of Héré's closest collaborators and worked almost exclusively for the king; R. Chavancé, *Jean Lamour et la ferronnerie d'art* (Nancy, 1942).

74. The statue was destroyed in 1792; a bronze *modello*, formerly at Chanteheux, is now in the Musée Lorrain, Nancy.

75. The chapel erected on the spot where Duke Charles the Bold was slain at the battle of Nancy (1477) had become a place of pilgrimage under the name of Chapelle des Bourguignons. Héré's church on the site contains the tombs of the king and queen, as well as those of the Duke and Duchess of Ossolinski. J. Rau-Schulenburg (note 55), 168.

76. See J. Marot, *Emmanuel Héré* (Nancy, 1954), J. Garms, *Studien zu Boffrand* (Vienna, 1962); J. Rau-Schulenburg (note 55), 179.

77. Jadot's design (Bibliothèque Doucet, Paris) bears the following legend: 'Projet que j'ai fait du Portail et des Tours des chanoines réguliers depuis le Dessus des niches en 1731'; the lower part of the façade would thus seem to have been already built at that date.

78. Fifteen signed drawings in the Musée des Arts Décoratifs in Paris, on a sheet dated 1734; L. Hautecoeur (note 12), 3:255; F. Kimball (note 3), 155; M. Gallet, 'Quelques étapes du Rococo dans l'architecture parisienne', *GBA* 67 (1966), 154.

79. The former arrangement now entirely obscured by subsequent development to house the Archives Nationales; J.R. Babelon, 'Les Façades sur jardin du Palais Rohan-Soubisc', *RA* 1969, 66.

80. A detailed account in M. Gallet (note 78), 146; idem, *Paris Domestic Architecture of the Eighteenth Century* (London, 1972).

81. M. Gallet (note 34), 263.

82. J.J. Gloton, 'Quatre hôtels aixois bâtis en 1757', *BSHAF* 1976, 185.

83. After working on the palace chapel at Versailles and on the choir of Notre-Dame, Lainée arrived in Avignon in 1714. In his *Livre de dessins d'ornements* he styled himself *architecte et sculpteur du Roi*; P. Lavedan, 'La chapelle des Pénitents noirs à Avignon' *CdA* 121 (1963).

84. P. Lavedan, 'Hôtels particuliers à Avignon', *CdA* 121 (1963).

85. Jacques-François Blondel says of the ground plan: 'Rien de si bien entendu que ce plan: beauté, proportion, variété, agrément, commodité, symétrie, relation des dedans aux dehors, tour s'y trouve réuni. En un mot, ce projet nous paraît un chef-d'œuvre.' *Encyclopédie, ou Dictionnaire raisonné des sciences, des arts et des métiers*, plate vol. 1 (1761), plate xxv.

86. Listed by E. Bonnel, 'La Chapelle Saint-Charles à Avignon', *CdA* 121 (1963).

87. After his appointment as *Trésorier de la Bourse*, Joseph Bonnier was created Baron de la Mosson. His son led a brilliant social life in Paris. The château is now a ruin; A. Bon, 'Châteaux et résidences d'été du XVIIIᵉ siècle dans la campagne montpelliéraine', *CA* 108 (1931); P. Castan, *La folie perdue de messieurs de la Mosson* (Montpellier, 1989).

88. Originally single-storeyed, with roof terrace and balustrades; upper storey added later. The façades are dominated respectively by the bowed projections of

the vestibule and of the oval garden room, which was flanked by two additional salons.

89. F. Lucet-Vivier, 'Asnières et son château', *Urbanisme et habitation*, 1955, 15.

90. J. Evans, *Monastic Architecture in France from the Renaissance to the Revolution* (Cambridge, 1964).

91. 'Les églises nouvellement bâties en France sont à quelque-chose près toutes faites sur le même modèle.' J.L. de Cordemoy, *Nouveau traité de toute l'architecture* (Paris, 1706), 108.

92. A detailed account in F. Hamon, 'Les Eglises parisiennes du XVIIIᵉ siècle', *RA* 1976, 32.

93. Published by Jean Pinard, 1748; J. Duportal, 'Le Cours d'architecture de Desgodets and the Académie Royale d'Architecture', *AB* 40 (1958); Th. Lunsing Scheurleer, 'Een exemplaar van Antonie Desgodets' "Traité de la commodité de l'architecture" in het Rijksprentenkabinett', in *Opus musivum*, Festschrift Ozinga (Assen, 1964), 285.

94. J. Garms (note 36), 104.

95. E. Langenskjöld, *Pierre Bullet, the Royal Architect* (Stockholm, 1959); R. Strandberg, 'Jean-Baptiste Bullet de Chamblain, Architecte du Roi', *BSHAF* 1963.

96. G. Lemesle, *L'Eglise Saint-Sulpice* (Paris, 1931); E. Malbois, 'Oppenord et l'église Saint-Sulpice', *GBA* 75 (1933): 1.34. The whole decor of the choir, with the exception of the marble floor, was destroyed in the Revolution; the present choir stalls come from Saint-Denis.

97. A preliminary design (Nationalmuseet, Stockholm), which Patte does not mention, has tall, slender towers, like the steeples of the City of London churches, and open loggias with round-headed arches on both levels; illustrated by F. Hamon (note 92).

98. Not mentioned in Jacques-François Blondel's *Architecture française* (1752), but shown in the medal struck in 1754 to commemorate the commencement of work on the Parvis; also visible in de Machy's painting *Ruines de la Foire Saint-Germain*, of 1763.

99. Servandoni's most important decorative works: the altar baldachins at Sens Cathedral and Saint-Bruno des Chartreux in Lyon; the illusionistic paintings at Condé-en-Brie (*c.* 1740); and festival decorations in Paris in 1729 (birth of a Dauphin) and 1739 (marriage of a daughter of the king). J. Bouché, 'Servandoni', *GBA* 1910, II, 121; R.D. Middleton, 'The Abbé de Cordemoy and the Graeco-Gothic Ideal. A Prelude to Romantic Classicism', *JWCI* 25 (1962) and 26 (1963), 278; E. Schlumberger, 'Un génie d'opéra: Servandoni', *CdA* August 1965, 14; H. Demoriane, 'La Décoration et l'apparat de Condé-en-Brie', *CdA* January 1967, 37.

100. On this see P. Patte, *Mémorial sur l'achèvement du grand portail de l'église Saint-Sulpice* (Paris, n.d.); idem, *Mémoires sur les objets les plus importants de l'architecture* (Paris, 1769). On Patte's role and his rivalry with Oudot de Mac Laurin, see M. Mathieu, *Pierre Patte* (Paris, 1940).

101. Chalgrin's façade is a long way removed from Servandoni's intentions. The look of the original façade is preserved to some extent in the façade of Saint-Eustache (1756), which Mansart de Jouy built on the model of Saint-Sulpice.

102. The project is illustrated on the medal by Joseph-Charles Roettiers (1754); E. Malbois, 'Projets de place devant Saint-Sulpice', *GBA* 64 (1922), 2.283.

103. P. Moisy, 'Deux cathédrales, Versailles et La Rochelle', *GBA* 39 (1952): 85; M. Gallet, 'La Cathédrale de La Rochelle', in M. Gallet and Y. Bottineau (note 15), 1982.

104. The post-medieval hall churches of Lorraine, beginning with Saint-Clément in Metz (1680–93), do not derive from Saint-Nicolas du Port but from the Gothic hall churches of the Eifel and the area around Trier; the point of contact is the Jesuit church in Luxembourg. P. Héliot, 'Eglises françaises de l'Est et du Midi influencées par l'art médiéval aux XVIIᵉ et XVIIIᵉ siècles', *GBA* 1919; R.D. Middleton (note 99), 311.

105. Moisy connects this group with the theories of Cordemoy and Laugier, although both of these are based on the lintel, not on the columnar arcade; Blunt correctly points to Flemish precedents. P. Moisy, *Les Eglises jésuites de l'ancienne assistance de France* (Rome, 1958); review by A. Blunt, *BMag* 101 (1959), 112.

106. R. Tournier, *Les Eglises comtoises* (Paris, 1954); idem, *L'Architecte Nicolas Nicole (1702–1784)* (Besançon, 1942).

107. C. Perret, 'L'Eglise Saint-Bruno des Chartreux', *CdA* 98 (1935), 146; M.F. Perez, 'Un ultime exemple de l'art baroque à Lyon, Saint-Bruno des Chartreux', *MH* 1979, 30; L. Mascoli, 'Le voyage de Naples de Ferdinand Delamonce', *Mémoires et documents sur Rome et l'Italie méridionale* N.S.1 1984.

108. J. Vallery-Radot, 'L'Eglise de l'Oratoire', *CA* 1963:119; J.J. Gloton, 'La Vieille Charité de Marseille', *Arts et livres de Provence*, 1970, no. 75, 52.

109. S. Conard, 'Beaucaire, Notre-Dame des Pommiers', *CA* 1976, 99.

110. M. Petzet, *Soufflots Sainte-Geneviève und der französische Kirchenbau des 18. Jahrhunderts* (Berlin, 1961).

111. G. Chenesseau, *Sainte-Croix d'Orléans* (Paris, 1921); P. Hélier, 'La Fin de l'architecture gothique en France durant les XVIIᵉ et XVIIIᵉ siècles', *GBA* 1951, 127; exh. cat. *Le Gothique retrouvé avant Viollet-le-Duc* (Paris, 1979).

112. F. Kimball (note 3), 164; idem, 'J.A. Meissonnier and the Beginning of the Genre Pittoresque', *GBA* 22 (1942), 27.

113. Jacques-François Blondel, *Cours d'architecture* (1772), 3:349; F. Kimball (note 3), 165; M. Roland-Michel, *Lajoue et l'art rocaille* (Paris, 1984). Meissonnier's style as a goldsmith survives only in the work of Benjamin Duvivier; but his inspiration is frequently visible in that of Thomas Germain.

114. S. Lorentz, 'Projets pour la Pologne de Juste-Aurèle Meissonnier', in *Actes du XIXᵉ Congrès international d'histoire de l'art* (Paris, 1958), 322.

115. Asymmetry had long been familiar in figured ornament, but it had been scrupulously avoided in the framing of panels; it was first discussed in mathematical terms in the *Essai sur le goût* of Montesquieu, who no longer equated symmetry with proportion but with a balance of weight on either side. The blame for the introduction of asymmetry was assigned by Cochin to Meissonnier, and by Blondel to Pineau.

116. Daviler (*Explication des termes de l'architecture*) describes rocaille as 'composition rustique qui imite la nature'; on the definition and origins of rocaille see H. Bauer, *Rocaille* (Berlin, 1962); P. Ward, 'Some Mainstreams and Tributaries in European Ornament 1500–1750', *Victoria and Albert Museum Bulletin*, October 1967, 3.

117. M. Roland-Michel (note 112); on Lajoue as an influence on Mondon see idem, 'François-Thomas Mondon, artiste "rocaille" méconnu', *BSHAF* 1979, 149.

118. Joseph Bonnier, owner of La Mosson, near Montpellier (see note 87), had bought the Hôtel de Lude in 1730 and had employed Courtonne and Leroux to remodel it to contain his collections.

119. L. Deshairs, *Nicole et Dominique Pineau* (Paris, n.d.); F. Kimball (note 3); M. Roland-Michel (note 112). Caustic characterizations of Pineau and Meissonnier in C.N. Cochin, *Supplication aux orfèvres* (Paris, 1754).

120. Most of this work is known from the engravings of Mariette and Blondel; C. Lamy-Lassalle, 'La Galerie de l'hôtel de Villars', *BSHAF* 1979. The decorations from Asnières are now at Cliveden.

121. An asymmetrical precedent in the decor of the Hôtel Dodun (1725, by Bullet de Chamblain), which Kimball erroneously assigned to the 1750s.

122. Jacques-François Blondel, *Discours sur la nécessité de l'étude de l'architecture* (Paris, 1754), 55.

123. M. Gallet, 'Oppenord au Château de la Grange-du-Milieu', *RA* 1968, 99.

124. F. Kimball (note 3), 190; J.R. Babelon (note 79); the scheme also included the Cabinet Vert, now installed in the Hôtel de Rohan, with its carvings of Aesop's fables. The Salon de la Princesse certainly influenced Schloss Amalienburg, in the grounds of Schloss Nymphenburg, Munich.

125. J.R. Babelon, *Le Cabinet du Roi ou le Salon de Louis XV de la Bibliothèque Nationale* (Paris, 1927).

126. B. Pons, 'Jacques Verberckt (1704–72), sculpteur des Bâtiments du Roi', *G.B.A.* 1992, I. 173.

127. Work on the Cabinet Intérieur began in 1738 with the building of a polygonal end (hence the alternative name of Cabinet à Pans) to adjoin the Arrière-Cabinet, the former Salon Ovale. The present wainscoting, with the exception of the mirrors, dates from 1753; the broken end wall was straightened in 1759.

128. The Appartement de Madame Adélaïde, which occupied the position of Mignard's Petite Galerie and of the vanished Escalier des Ambassadeurs, consisted of four rooms; its decor has survived in the Salon de Musique and, in part, in the dining room (now known as the Salle à Manger aux Salles Neuves).

129. Parts of this are installed in the so-called Petits Appartements de Napoléon; on the decor at Fontainebleau see Y. Bottineau (note 46); J.P. Samoyault, in M. Gallet and Y. Bottineau (note 15), 40.

130. They can be dated only on stylistic grounds, but probably bear some relation to the king's frequent visits to Rambouillet between 1727 and 1733; they certainly do not postdate the death of the Comte de Toulouse in 1736. F. Lorin, *Histoire de Rambouillet* (Paris, 1907); H. Longnon, *Le Château de Rambouillet* (Paris, n.d.); F. Kimball (note 3).

131. Surviving work from the Marquise's time (since 1747) includes, above all, the former bedchamber (now salon) and Huet's Cabinet des Singes; these retain the asymmetries that disappear from later work.

PART THREE

1. 'Entre le beau et l'utile il n'y a point à balancer quand on ne peut réunir les deux...Il faut subordonner et même sacrifier le beau à l'utile dès que les circonstances ne permettent pas que l'on concilie l'un avec l'autre.' Letter from Duverney to Gabriel, concerning the cutting back of the first design for the

Ecole Militaire; R. Laulan, *L'Ecole Militaire* (Paris, 1950), 20.

2. H. Honour, *Neo-Classicism* (Harmondsworth, 1968); F.G. Pariset, *L'Art néo-classique* (Paris, 1974); S. Eriksen, *Early Neo-Classicism in France* (London, 1974).

3. Quoted at length in W. Herrmann, *Laugier and 18th-Century French Theory* (London, 1962).

4. C.N. Cochin, *Voyage d'Italie* (Paris, 1758); H. Roujon, *Le Voyage du marquis de Marigny en Italie* (Paris, 1898); F. Kimball, *Le Style Louis-XV* (Paris, 1949).

5. Charles-Nicolas Cochin the Younger (1715–90) worked as a draughtsman and engraver for the Menus-Plaisirs from 1739 onwards; he was drawing-master and adviser to Madame de Pompadour, and a severe critic of the excavations at Herculaneum.

6. S. Eriksen, 'Marigny and the *goût grec*', *BMag* 1963, no. 4, 96; A. Braham, *The Architecture of the French Enlightenment* (London, 1980), ch. 2; D. Scott, 'The Marquis de Marigny: a Dispenser of Royal Patronage', *Apollo*, June 1973, 25.

7. *Encyclopédie, ou Dictionnaire raisonné des sciences, des arts et des métiers* (1751 onwards); the first volume of plates, in which architecture has an important place, did not appear until 1761.

8. L. Hautecoeur, *Rome et la renaissance de l'antiquité à la fin du XVIIIᵉ siècle* (Paris, 1912); F.J.B. Watson, 'Neo-Classicism on Both Sides of the Channel', *Apollo*, 1967, 239.

9. On this see Fernow's formulation: 'There is only one pure, exemplary style, just as there is only one good and correct taste.' C.L. Fernow, *Römische Studien* (Zürich, 1806–8), 1, 35.

10. S. Rocheblavc, *L'Age classique en France* (Paris, 1932); J. Seznec, 'Le Singe antiquaire', in idem, *Essais sur Diderot et l'antiquité* (Oxford, 1957).

11. '... le style antique, ou pour me servir du mot dont on abuse si fort actuellement, dans le goût grec'; A.L. La Live de Jully, *Catalogue historique* (1764).

12. M. Grimm, in M. Grimm and D. Diderot, *Correspondance littéraire, philosophique et critique... depuis 1752 jusqu'à 1790* (1829–91), 5, 282.

13. W. Herrmann (note 3); R.D. Middleton, 'The Abbé de Cordemoy and the Graeco-Gothic Ideal. A Prelude to Romantic Classicism', *JWCI* 25 (1962) and 26 (1963).

14. *CdA* 1958, 80; E. Kaufmann, *Architecture in the Age of Reason* (Cambridge, 1955), 151.

15. F. Kimball, 'Les Influences anglaises dans la formation du style Louis-XVI', *GBA* 5 (1931), 29; F.J.B. Watson (note 8), 22.

16. Continued and completed by his pupil, Patte (2 vols., 1773–7); J. Lejeaux, 'Jacques-François Blondel, professeur d'architecture', *L'Architecture* 1927, 23.

17. The west front of the cathedral was replaced by a Gothic Revival version in 1898. J. Lejeaux, *La Place d'Armes de Metz* (Strasbourg, 1927); L. Hautecoeur, *Histoire de l'architecture classique en France* (Paris, 1948–53), 3, 598.

18. L. Hautecoeur (note 17), 3, 603; J. Garms, 'Le Plan d'urbanisme de Strasbourg, dressé par Jacques-François Blondel en 1764–1769', *CAAAH* 12 (1978): 103.

19. V. Champier and R. Sandoz, *Le Palais Royal* (Paris, 1908); J. Kretzschmar, 'Pierre Contant d'Ivry' (Ph.D. diss., Cologne University, 1981).

20. H. Coutant, *Le Palais Bourbon au XVIIIᵉ siècle* (Paris, 1905).

21. Exh. cat. *Chevotet-Contant-Chaussard, un cabinet d'artistes au siècle des lumières* (Paris, 1987); C. Connolly and J. Zerbe, *Les Pavillons: French Pavilions of the Eighteenth Century* (London, 1962).

22. F. Vignier, 'L'Hôtel Bouhier de Lantenay et la Préfecture de la Côte-d'Or', *Les Cahiers du Vieux Dijon*, 1978, no. 7; *MH* December 1991, 38.

23. C. Martin, *Nantes au XVIIIᵉ siècle* (Paris, 1928); P. Lelièvre, *L'Urbanisme et l'architecture à Nantes* (Nantes, 1942).

24. N. Pevsner, 'The Doric Revival', in idem, *Studies in Art, Architecture and Design* (London, 1968), 197.

25. J. Harris, 'Legeay, Piranesi and International Neoclassicism in Rome, 1740–50', in *Essays on the History of Architecture Presented to Rudolf Wittkower* (London, 1967); exh. cat. *Piranesi et les français* (Rome, 1976).

26. G. Erouard, *L'Architecture au pinceau* (Milan and Paris, 1982). J.M. Pérouse de Montclos. *Etienne-Louis Boullée*, Paris 1969, 39.

27. On the Festa della Chinea see H. Tintelnot, *Barocktheater und barocke Kunst* (Berlin, 1939), 290; J. Harris (note 25).

28. Another member of the same circle, William Chambers, in his *Treatise on Civil Architecture* (London, 1749), used window forms from Michelangelo, Vignola and Ammanati, and chimneypiece designs by Scamozzi and Palladio on Challe see R.P. Wunder, 'Ch. M. 17, Challe A study of his life and work', *Apollo* Jan. 1968, 22.

29. J.M. Pérouse de Montclos, *Les Prix de Rome, concours de l'Académie Royale d'Architecture au XVIIIᵉ siècle* (Paris, 1984).

30. F.G. Pariset, 'L'Architecte Barreau de Chefdeville', *BSHAF* 1962.

31. S. Eriksen, 'La Live de Jully's Furniture *à la grecque*', *BMag* 1961, 340 on the chronological precedence of this work over comparable English pieces see R. Harris, J. Thornton and F.J.B. Watson in *Apollo*, 1968.

32. On Jardin's work in Denmark, see A. Braham (note 6), 56.

33. Il ne pouvait jamais se borner à la demande qu'on lui faisait, et le grand Mogol n'aurait pas été assez riche pour élever les bâtiments qu'il projetait.' Cochin, *Mémoires inédits*, ed. C. Henry (Paris, 1880), 143, 33. See G. Erouard (note 26).

34. J. Harris (note 25) and E. Kaufmann (note 14) ascribe these compositions, with their strong reminiscences of the 1740s, to Legeay's Roman period.

35. Voltaire, *Ce qu'on ne fait pas* (Paris, n.d. [before 1745]); idem, *Des embellissements de Paris* (Paris, 1749); La,Font de Saint-Yenne, *le Génie du Louvre* (Paris, 1748).

36. L. Hautecoeur, *Histoire du Louvre* (Paris, n.d.); C. Tadgell, *Ange-Jacques Gabriel* (London, 1978), 194.

37. E. Lambert, 'Un projet de Place Royale à Paris en l'honneur de Louis XV', *BSHAF* 1938, 85; P. Lavedan, 'Le IIᵉ Centenaire de la place de la Concorde', *La Vie Urbaine*, 1956; S. Granet, 'Images de Paris: la place de la Concorde', *Revue géographique et industrielle de France*, 61 (1963), N.S. no. 26; C. Tadgell (note 36), 175; J. Ducros, 'La Place Louis-XV', in M. Gallet and Y. Bottineau, *Les Gabriel* (Paris, 1982), 254; J. Gautier, 'Le garde-meuble de la Place Louis XV'. *Mon. Hist.* 190 (1993).

38. The more important projects were published in P. Patte, *Monuments érigés à la gloire de Louis XV* (Paris, 1765).

39. Fischer von Erlach's engraving in his *Entwurf einer historischen Architektur* was undoubtedly known to Boffrand; on similar projects for this site, see R. Josephson, 'Un projet de place à la pointe de la Cité', *BSHAF* 1928; M. Gallet and J. Garms, eds, exh. cat. *Germain Boffrand 1667–1754* (Paris, 1986), 122.

40. The designs returned to the entrants were published in *La Vie urbaine*, 1962; S. Granet, 'Le Livre de vérité de la place Louis-XV', *BSHAF* 1961, 107, catalogued the designs not published by Patte.

41. Behind all this there was a property speculation on a vast scale, involving high government officials who used Lassurance as a figurehead; see J. Ducros (note 37).

42. Laugier called this, accurately, 'l'image d'une esplanade embellie au milieu d'une campagne riante et d'où l'on aperçoit divers Palais dans l'éloignement'; M.A. Laugier, *Essai sur l'architecture* (Paris, 1753). There was no north-south axis until the Pont Louis-XVI (now Pont de la Concorde) was built in 1787–90.

43. 'This building is truly beautiful and dignified; for it is imbued with sound reflection, exact calculation and a simplicity from which the architect must never depart, even in the midst of the greatest opulence...'; E. Viollet-le-Duc, *Entretiens sur l'architecture* (Paris, 1872), 2, 199.

44. R. Laulan (note 1); C. Tadgell (note 36); M. Gallet and Y. Bottineau (note 37).

45. The Duverneys had been clients of François Poisson, the favourite's father, and after his condemnation and flight they had taken care of his family. Pâris-Duverney was to remain Madame de Pompadour's close confidant and adviser.

46. Antoine Le Roy's *Grand Prix* design of 1759, for a riding school, which Gabriel probably used, already contains the essentials of Gabriel's façade.

47. Described and illustrated in Perrault's Vitruvius translation, *Les Quatre Livres...* (1676); the interior is flanked by two-storey side-aisles that do not appear as spatial forms in their own right.

48. C. Tadgell (note 36), 151; G. Poisson, in M. Gallet and Y. Bottineau (note 37), 242.

49. C. Tadgell, 'L'Eglise royale et paroissiale de Choisy', *BSHAF* 1973, 171.

50. The pavilions and communicating ranges were demolished under Louis XVI, followed in 1835 by the *corps de logis* itself, so that nothing of the composition now remains; see C. Tadgell (note 36), 164; G. Poisson, in M. Gallet and Y. Bottineau (note 37), 246.

51. C. Tadgell (note 36), 140; J.M. Moulin, in M. Gallet and Y. Bottineau (note 37), 232.

52. The rectangular Cour Royale already appears on designs dating from the 1730s, probably by Jacques V Gabriel; these were available to Ange-Jacques, as was the design of 1745, which shows the composition open towards the town, with a Place d'Armes in front.

53. 'J'espère que Sa Majesté sera contente de la simplicité et noblesse de l'architecture en est belle et bonne et servira de modèle pour tout le Reste de la bâtisse.' Letter from Gabriel to Marigny, June 1752.

54. In plan, this pavilion resembled the Eremitage at Fontainebleau, but it consisted of a single storey; it was enlarged in succeeding years on the model of the Petit Château at Choisy.

55. In his memorandum of 1780, Le Dreux writes: 'Tous les bâtiments qui ont été faits au château de Compiègne ont été exécutés sur un projet général admis en 1752 et depuis ce tems on l'a suivi sans y rien changer, si ce n'est dans de petits objets de détails de distribution locale de peu de conséquence.' (J.M. Moulin, 'Compiègne', in M. Gallet and Y. Bottineau (note 37), 236).

56. Notably that of Campbell's Stourhead; F. Kimball (note 15) also cites Robert Morris's *Select Architecture* (1757).

57. A. Marie, 'Les Théâtres du Château de Versailles', *Revue d'histoire du théâtre*, 1951, no. 2; J. Feray, 'Les Théâtres successifs du Château de Versailles', *MH* 1957, no. 1; P. Verlet, *Versailles* (Paris, 1961), 438; R.M. Langlois, *L'Opéra de Versailles* (Paris, 1958); C. Tadgell (note 36), 119; T. Boucher, 'L'Opéra royal', in M. Gallet and Y. Bottineau (note 37), 199.

58. A detailed enumeration of the successive planning stages and designs in C. Tadgell (note 36).

59. On the Grand Projet see Comte de Fels, *Ange-Jacques Gabriel* (Paris, 1924), 145; P. Verlet (note 57), 358; C. Tadgell (note 36), 84; C. Baulez, in M. Gallet and Y. Bottineau (note 37), 182.

60. The idea of demolition surfaced as early as 1741, in a dated 'Mémoire concernant la dêmolition du grand degré des Ambassadeurs, degré provisionnel à faire et cabinet des médailles au château de Versailles', accompanied by two plans.

61. May be dated before 1742 on the strength of the spatial division and the agreement with Blondel's *Architecture française*; the accompanying façade designs (formerly attributed to J.H. Mansart) are probably initial sketches by Gabriel for the Grand Projet.

62. Tadgell links the planning phases of the Grand Projet with events in the royal family and the growing need for space.

63. Y. Bottineau, *L'Art d'Ange-Jacques Gabriel à Fontainebleau* (Paris, 1962); C. Tadgell (note 36), 127; J.P. Samoyault, in M. Gallet and Y. Bottineau (note 15), 214.

64. L. Hautecoeur (note 17), 4, 207ff.; idem, *BSHAF* 1924, 30–1.

65. A. Hachette, *Le Couvent de la Reine à Versailles* (Paris, 1923); L. Hautecoeur (note 17), 4, 78ff.

66. M. Mosser, 'L'Hôtel des Monnaies de Paris, œuvre de J.D. Antoine', *L'Information d'histoire d'art* 1971, 16; J.M. Darnis, 'Façade et locaux de l'Hôtel des Monnaies de Paris', *Le Club français de la Médaille* 1985, 89. Among Antoine's papers there is a design, unsigned but most probably by Boullée, that bears an astonishing resemblance to Antoine's final design; J.M. Pérouse de Montclos (note 29).

67. In an earlier design, the wings are further accentuated by projecting balconies and triangular pediments.

68. B. Sournia, 'La Place Louis-le-Grand de Montpellier', *MH* 1982, no. 20, 42.

69. Admitted to the Lyon Academy on the strength of a published study of St Peter's in Rome and Bernini's colonnades, 1739; D. Ternois, 'Soufflot et Lyon', in *Actes du Colloque 'Soufflot et l'architecture des lumières'* (Lyon, 1980); M. Gallet and D. Ternois, exh. cat. *Soufflot et son temps* (Paris, 1980).

70. J. Roubert, 'L'Hôtel-Dieu de Lyon au XVIIIe siècle', in *Actes du Colloque 'Soufflot...'* (note 69), 134; A. Charre, 'L'Hôtel-Dieu de Lyon', in M. Gallet and D. Ternois (note 69).

71. Illustrated in D. Ternois (note 69). A pupil of Cartaud's Lebon won the Prix de Rome in 1728 and worked for Cardinal de Rohan at Saverne.

72. Loyer flouted Soufflot's intentions by increasing the height of the dome; this led to vigorous protests. When the building was restored in 1944, the dome was returned to its original form.

73. Published by Dumont in 1764.

74. It was not until several years later that Cochin published his treatise *Projet d'une salle de spectacle pour un théâtre de comédie* (Paris, 1765), and the publisher Dumont brought out the comprehensive survey, *Parallèle des plans des plus belles salles de spectacle d'Italie et de France* (Paris, 1764–7).

75. Its appearance is preserved only in Dumont's engraving; two drawings, in the Kunstbibliothek in Berlin and in an English private collection, differ markedly from each other.

76. Another, larger oval chapel, based on the Charité, was that of the Hôtel-Dieu in Mâcon (1761–70), by Soufflot's pupil Munet.

77. In the same year he became director of the Manufactures Royales des Gobelins and of the Savonnerie.

78. J. Mondain-Monval, *Soufflot, sa vie, son œuvre, son esthétique* (Paris, 1918), 351; M.F. Poullet, 'Les Projets de Place Royale à Reims', in *Actes du Colloque 'Soufflot...'* (note 69), 69; idem, 'Les Places Royales et l'aménagement urbain sous Louis XV', *MH* 1982, no. 120, 10.

79. 'Heureusement ce projet a été rejeté, on a préféré les idées de l'ingénieur de la province. Celui-ci a pensé que dans une ville de commerce, il fallait un plan marchand.' D. Diderot, 'Le Monument de la Place Royale de Reims', cited by M.F. Poullet (note 78).

80. M. Petzet, *Soufflots Sainte-Geneviève und der französische Kirchenbau des 18. Jahrhunderts* (Berlin, 1961); idem, Soufflot et l'ordonnance de Sainte-Geneviève', in *Actes du Colloque 'Soufflot...'* (note 69), 13; M. Gallet and D. Ternois (note 69), 188; A. Braham (note 6), 32; P. Chevalier and D. Rabreau, *Le Panthéon* (Paris, 1977).

81. Only thus could it have happened that the project by the city architect of Paris, Laurent Destouches (1753), which anticipated crucial features of Soufflot's design, became publicly known only in 1772, after Destouches's death; see M.

Petzet (note 80), 58.

82. Gabriel also employed Corinthian columns: 'Vous ne trouverez plus aujourd'hui de corinthien chez aucun architecte...Du temps de Soufflot les ruines de Palmyre et de Baalbek étaient en vogue.' Quatremère de Quincy, *Rapport sur les travaux entrepris, continués ou achevés au Panthéon français* (Paris, Year II [1793]), 65. In the portico, Soufflot reverted to the precedent of Saint-Pierre, Geneva; at a session of the Academy in 1770 he cited other precedents including S. Agostino in Piacenza, S. Carlo al Corso in Rome and the Cappella Regia in Turin.

83. 'Le principal objet de M. Soufflot au bâtiment de son église a été de réunir sous une des plus belles formes la légèreté de la construction des édifices gothiques avec la pureté et la magnificence de l'architecture grecque.' M. Brebion, 'Mémoire à M. le Comte de la Billarderie d'Angiviller' (1780). (Arch. nat. O1 1694-43).

84. In the building as executed, these were replaced with squat Tuscan columns.

85. A prototype is to be found in the Mausoleum of Halicarnassus, of which Caylus advanced a conjectural reconstruction in 1753; however, the stepped pyramid or dome was a familiar theme in the architecture of Juvarra, and he was no doubt the source of Dumont's design, which was made on the occasion of his admission to membership of the Accademia dir San Luca. W. Oechslin, 'Pyramide et sphère', *GBA* 113 (1972), 201.

86. A full account of the polemic between Patte and Soufflot, which continued after the latter's death, is to be found in M. Mathieu, *Pierre Patte* (Paris, 1940).

87. Gauthey likened Soufflot's constructional scheme and the Toussaints, Angers, 'le monument le plus hardi que nous avons en ce genre'; on Gauthey see M. Petzet (note 80), 68.

88. M. Mosser, 'Monsieur de Marigny et les jardins', *BSHAF* 1973.

89. Soufflot disapproved of Marigny's authoritarian treatment of the Academy, and also of such eccentricities as his demand for a Chinese pavilion at Ménars. As a convinced Neoclassicist, he was bound sooner or later to find himself out of sympathy with the 'snobbery and caprice of this parvenu' (M. Gallet).

90. J. Catinat, *Le Château de Chatou et le Nymphée de Soufflot* (Paris, 1974).

91. Peyre the Younger – Antoine-François Peyre (1739–1823), brother to Marie-Joseph, and himself a winner of the Prix de Rome and a member of the Academy – came to the fore only in the last quarter of the century, initially through the Schloss in Koblenz, which he built for the Elector of Trier (1779–86).

92. J.F. Bélanger, *Notice nécrologique de Charles de Wailly* (Paris, 1798); J. Lavallée, *Notice historique sur Charles de Wailly* (Paris, 1800–1); A. Braham, 'Charles de Wailly and Early Neo-Classicism', *BMag* October 1972; exh. cat. *Charles de Wailly, peintre-architecte dans l'Europe des lumières* (Paris, 1979).

93. Note, for instance, the mixture of Neoclassicism and Lepautre in the motifs of the frame he designed for an engraved portrait of the Duc de Nivernais (1764); illustrated in A. Braham (note 6), 88.

94. He had won the third prize at the age of twenty, already in 1750, with a design for an orangery that was entirely in the spirit of the Mansart school.

95. Y. Beauvalot, 'Un château extraordinaire à Dijon: le Château de Montmusard', *Cahiers du Vieux Dijon*, 1978, no. 6; idem, 'A propos de documents inédits, la construction du Château de Montmusard à Dijon', *BSHAF* 1984, 119. The designs were shown at the Salon in 1771.

96. It was just at this time that Blondel's pupil Nicolas Lenoir (Lenoir-le-Romain) completed the Hôtel Bouhier de Lantenay, in Dijon (1756–60), a work of exceptional size and splendour (see note 22).

97. It was mediated by the Marquis de Voyer d'Argenson, a relative of the client's by marriage; and this induced both Hautecoeur and Braham to regard it as a subsequent, reduced design. We are indebted to Y. Beauvalot (note 95) for disposing of this hypothesis and proving that the design preceded the château which was actually completed.

98. M. Steinhammer and D. Rabreau, 'Le Théâtre de l'Odéon de Charles de Wailly et Marie-Joseph Peyre, 1767–1782', *RA* 1973, no. 19.; exh. cat. *Charles de Wailly* (Paris, 1979).

99. A cruel affront to De Wailly, who had shared his Prix de Rome with Moreau and had thus made it possible for him to spend time in Rome.

100. The present-day Odéon has nothing in common with De Wailly's and Peyre's building but the façade. The interior has been burnt out twice and totally remodelled, the proportions of the roof were lost when Chalgrin lowered it in 1808, and the lateral arches were torn down *c.* 1830.

101. X. Duquenne, *Le Château de Seneffe* (Brussels, 1978).

102. Shown in an engraving by Leprince; in the execution the portico was straightened.

103. From the first design (1773) onwards, the columns are not fluted (concave) but reeded (convex): a violation of every antique precedent.

104. D. Rabreau and M. Gallet, 'La Chaire de Saint-Sulpice', *BSHPIF* 98 (1971), 115.

105. '... et pour ceux qui n'ont point vu les églises de l'Italie, c'est à coup sûr

ce qu'on peut admirer de plus magnifique'; Pidansat de Mairobert, *L'Observateur anglais* (1777–8).

106. S. Pressouyre, 'Un ensemble néo-classique à Port-Vendres', *MH* October-November 1963, 199.

107. The foundation stone of the obelisk was laid in 1780.

108. After De Wailly's departure the building was crowned with a dome and used as a guardhouse.

109. H.C. Dittscheid, 'Charles de Wailly in den Diensten des Landgrafen Friedrich II. von Hessen-Kassel', *Kunst in Hessen und am Mittelrhein*, 1981, no. 20, 21.

110. J. Adhémar, 'L'Ecole de Médecine, sa place dans l'architecture française du XVIIIᵉ siècle, *L'Architecture*, 1934, 105; E. Kaufmann (note 14), 167; A. Braham (note 6), 137.

111. In his *Description des Ecoles de Chirurgie* (published 1780), Gondoin cited Turin University and the Collegio Elvetico in Milan; courts screened by open colonnades also in Neufforge 1, 43–5.

112. The words are those of Quatremère de Quincy; even Patte, Blondel's mouthpiece, called it 'a type of architecture superior to everything I have seen newly constructed in Paris'.

113. F.G. Pariset, 'Notes sur Victor Louis', *BSHAF* 1959, 41; A. Braham (note 6), 145.

114. S. Lorentz, 'Victor Louis à Varsovie', *Urbanisme et architecture*, 1954, 233; idem, 'Victor Louis à Varsovie', *Revue historique de Bordeaux* 1958, 38; idem, exh. cat. *Victor Louis et Varsovie* (Paris, 1958). It was after his return from Warsaw that Louis changed his first name from Nicolas to Victor.

115. E. de Ganay, 'Une œuvre de l'architecte Louis à Besançon, l'Hôtel de l'Intendance de Franche-Comté', *RAAM* 1926; I. Polti, Les Persiennes de l'Hôtel de l'Intendance de Franche-Comté à Besançon', *MH* 1939; *MH* 1991, no. 178, 45.

116. J. Lejeaux, 'Charles-Louis Clérisseau, architecte', *L'Architecture*, 1928, 115; T.J. McCormick and J. Fleming, 'A Ruin Room by Clérisseau', *The Connoisseur*, April 1962; T.J. McCormick, *Charles-Louis Clérisseau and the Genesis of Neo-Classicism* (Cambridge and London, 1990).

117. On Clérisseau's work in surveying ancient monuments in Provence, see his correspondence with Winckelmann in J.J. Winckelmann, *Briefe*, ed. N. Diepolder and W. Rehn (Berlin, 1952–6), vol. 3.

118. Born in 1721, died after 1793; he designed the Hôtel de Beauvau, now the ministry of the interior (c. 1769), and wrote a treatise, *Le Génie de l'architecture ou l'analogie de cet art avec nos sensations* (Paris, 1780; tr. as *The Genius of Architecture*, Santa Monica, 1992). Le Camus de Mézières is not to be confused with Louis-Denis Le Camus, the architect who enlarged Chanteloup for the Duc de Choiseul and built the pagoda in the grounds (1775–8).

119. M.K. Denning, *La Halle au Blé de Paris 1762–1813, cheval de Troie de l'abondance dans la capitale des lumières* (Brussels, 1984).

120. The same technique was used for the vault of the Halle aux Draps (1786), by Legrand and Molinos, and for that of Saint-Philippe du Roule (1784), by Chalgrin.

121. Laugier had high praise for the Hôtel de Chavannes: 'The architect... has shown the public that it is possible in a limited space to do great things' (M.A. Laugier, *Observations sur l'architecture*, Paris, 1765). The same façade formula appears in Moreau's design for the Comédie-Française.

122. M. Gallet, *Demeures parisiennes à l'époque Louis-XVI* (Paris, 1964); idem, *Paris Domestic Architecture of the Eighteenth Century* (London, 1972).

123. E. Kaufmann, 'Three Revolutionary Architects: Boullée, Ledoux, and Lequeu', *Transactions of the American Philosophical Society* (Philadelphia, 1952); idem (note 14); H. Rosenau, *Boullée's Treatise on Architecture* (London, 1953); J. Langner, 'Boullée und Ledoux', *Neue Zürcher Zeitung*, 22 March 1966; J.M. Pérouse de Montclos, *Etienne-Louis Boullée* (Paris, 1969).

124. Described by Dézallier d'Argenville in his *Voyage pittoresque* (1765). The decor of the Grand Salon is now in a private collection; the painted prospect probably inspired Ledoux's perspective at the Hôtel d'Hallwyl.

125. In this, Boullée largely used seventeenth-century decorative forms, as published by Jombert, *Répertoire des artistes* (Paris, 1764).

126. The Hôtel de Tessé in Paris (1764), by Pierre-Noël Rousset, is extraordinarily close both to Chaville and to the Hôtel Alexandre, but has no connection with Boullée.

127. Ledoux's falsification of his early style brilliantly analysed by J. Langner, 'Ledoux' Redaktion seiner eigenen Werke für die Veröffentlichung', *Zeitschrift für Kunstgeschichte* 23 (1960), 151; see also the simultaneous publication by W. Herrmann, 'The Problem of Chronology in Claude-Nicolas Ledoux's Engraved Work', *AB* 42 (1960), 191.

128. E. Kaufmann, *Von Ledoux bis Le Corbusier* (Vienna and Leipzig, 1933); M. Raval and J.C. Moreux, *Claude-Nicolas Ledoux 1756–1806* (Paris, 1945); E. Kaufmann (notes 14, 123); J. Langner, *Claude-Nicolas Ledoux, die erste Schaffenszeit 1762–74* (Freiburg, 1959); M. Gallet, *Ledoux à Paris*, Cahiers de la Rotonde (Paris, 1979); idem, *Claude-Nicolas Ledoux* (Paris, 1980).

129. F.G. Pariset (note 113).

130. See J. Langner (note 128), 26; W. Herrmann (note 127), 198; M. Gallet (1980; as note 128), figs. 13–14.

131. Jacques-François Blondel, *L'Homme du monde éclairé par les arts* (Paris, 1774).

132. The Maison Mannery at Salins, mentioned by Blunt ('Palladio e l'architettura francese', *Bolletino del centro internazionale di studi de'architettura'*, Vicenza, 1968) and also by Raval and Moreux, was probably never built; M. Gallet (1980; as note 128).

133. A successor to Bénouville is the staircase of the archbishop's palace in Paris, built by Pierre Desmaisons in 1772.

134. Jeanne Bécu (1743–94), a celebrated beauty and a *vendeuse* in an elegant dressmaker's shop, became the king's mistress in 1768 and, having been married off for form's sake to the Comte du Barry, made her court debut as Comtesse du Barry in 1769. In 1770 she was given an apartment on the second floor of the Petites Appartements at Versailles, but her favourite home was the small, early eighteenth-century Château de Louveciennes. B. Scott, 'Madame du Barry', *Apollo*, January 1973, 60.

135. Demolished in 1930 and replaced by a copy with an added attic; C. Connolly and J. Zerbe (note 21).

136. Pen and wash drawing of the original design at Sceaux (Musée de l'Ile de France); in Ledoux's engravings the château appears with flat roofs and a square-set attic over the centre.

137. When Madame du Barry was banished from court, her stable building passed to the Comte de Provence. It is now a police barracks; the former residence is the seat of the Versailles chamber of commerce.

138. Another design that probably stems from the 1780s is that for a palace for the Landgrave, which Ledoux published in *L'Architecture* (1804): the cylindrical lantern on the roof – to light the interior – and the monotonous array of *serliana*-like windows beneath monstrous pediments bring the design very close to the realm of utopian architecture.

139. See the list of new buildings in Hautecoeur (note 17), appendix, 4, 533.

140. On the reversion to Gothic see R.D. Middleton (note 13); W. Herrmann (note 3).

141. On this see the letter from Canon van der Driesch of Arras, 20 January 1744, in M. Petzet (note 80), 99.

142. Commemorative album, *L'Eglise et la paroisse Saint-Géry de Cambrai* (Cambrai, 1933).

143. On Couture see M. Gallet, in M. Gallet and D. Ternois (note 9).

144. A digest is to be found in M. Petzet (note 80).

145. J.P. Mouilleseaux, 'L'Eglise de la Madeleine à Rouen', in *Actes du Colloque 'Soufflot...'* (note 69), 168.

146. Y. Beauvalot, 'L'Eglise de Poncey-sur-l'Ignon', *Mémoires de la Commission des Antiquités de la Côte-d'Or*, 1970–1.

147. On this see R. Tournier, *Les Eglises comtoises* (Paris, 1954).

148. A. Braham (note 6), 123.

149. M. Gallet, 'Louis-François Trouard et l'architecture religieuse dans la région de Versailles au temps de Louis XVI', *GBA* 118 (1976).

150. Louis, Duc d'Orléans (1725–85), had left the Palais Royal in 1776 and moved to the Chaussée d'Antin, from which it was long way to the churches of central Paris; on the foundation and building of this friary, see M. Goutal, in exh. cat. *Alexandre-Théodore Brongniart* (Paris, 1986), 97.

151. Clodion's reliefs, 6.5 metres long and 1.5 metres wide, were executed in 1789, severely damaged in the Revolution, and plastered over in 1807; M. Goutal (note 150).

152. After the Revolution the cloister was closed off on the garden side by a fourth range, and the north and south wings were raised by one storey; the four niches on the central portion of the façade were replaced by windows, and four more windows were inserted above to coincide with the ends of the original relief plaques. Two upper windows were also added to the street end of the north (right-hand) wing.

153. M. Gallet (note 149).

154. Exh. cat. *Le Gothique retrouvé* (note 111).

155. S. Eriksen (note 2).

156. The actual furniture has not survived, but it was almost identical with the pieces supplied for the Palais Bernstorff in Copenhagen.

157. Cochin condemned sharply the uncritical copying of antique motifs as an abuse of antiquity.

158. The earliest chairs with Neoclassical legs were made for Marigny, as late as 1763; they were probably designed by Soufflot; S. Eriksen, 'Early Neo-Classicism in French Furniture', *Apollo*, November 1963, 344.

159. William Kent had already used griffins at Holkham Hall, which was begun by 1734.

160. The most celebrated piece of this kind is the *Bureau du Roi* at Versailles, begun in 1760 by François Oeben and completed in 1769 by Jean-Henri Riesener.

161. The arabesques appear in this form in Rousset's design for the Hôtel d'Uzès (1765), from which Ledoux presumably took them.

162. The garland ornament was already present in the Hôtel d'Uzès; on Marie-Antoinette's library, see M. Jallut, 'Cabinets intérieurs et Petits Appartements de Marie-Antoinette', *GBA* 63 (1964), 289.

163. Other publications: *Ordres d'architecture* (*c.* 1785), *Recueil d'ameublement* (*c.* 1787); the majority of his drawings are in the Musée des Arts Décoratifs, Paris. G. Levallet, 'L'ornemaniste Jean-Charles Delafosse', *GBA* 1929, I, 158; *CdA* January 1955, 26.

PART FOUR

1. J.M. Pérouse de Montclos, *Les Prix de Rome, concours de l'Académie Royale d'Architecture au XVIIIᵉ siècle* (Paris, 1984).

2. L. Hautecoeur, *Histoire de l'architecture classique en France* (Paris, 1948–53), 4, 21. Mariette's criticism appeared in the *Gazette littéraire*, and that of Le Roy in the *Observations sur les édifices* (1767); R. Wittkower, 'Piranesi's "Parere sull'architettura"', *JWCI* 2 (1938–9), 147.

3. A further example was the hothouse in the Jardin Botanique, by Molinos (1795), demolished in 1928; N. Pevsner, 'The Doric Revival', in idem, *Studies in Art, Architecture and Design* (London, 1968), 1, 196; idem, *Thomas Hope and the Neoclassical Idea* (London, 1968); N. Pevsner and S. Lang, *Apollo or Baboon* (London, 1948); on David, see R. Crozet in *GBA* 14 (1955), 211. By the late eighteenth century, instead of serving as a structural element within a larger whole, the column was increasingly assuming the value of a sculptural solid in its own right; see S. Giedion, *Spätbarocker und romantischer Klassizismus* (Munich, 1922).

4. J.M. Pérouse de Montclos, 'Charles-François Viel, architecte de l'Hôpital Général et Jean-Louis Viel de Saint-Maux, architecte, peintre et avocat au Parlement de Paris', *BSHAF* 1966, 257.

5. E. von Erdberg, *Chinese Influence on European Garden Structures* (Cambridge, 1936); L. Hautecoeur (note 2), 5, 33; H. Honour, *Chinoiserie* (London, 1961); H. Börsch-Supan, 'Landschaftsgarten und Chinoiserie', in exh. cat. *China und Europa* (Berlin, 1973).

6. L. Hautecoeur, *Rome et la renaissance de l'antiquité à la fin du XVIIIᵉ siècle* (Paris, 1912); N. Pevsner, 'The Egyptian Revival' in idem, *Studies . . .* (note 3), 1, 213.

7. Comte de Caylus, *Recueil d'antiquités égyptiennes, étrusques, grecques et romaines*, 'Avant-propos' to vol. 3 and vol. 5, 3.

8. On the Turkish influence see 'La Turquerie au XVIIIᵉ siècle', *CdA* February 1953, 52.

9. Examples collected by J.C. Krafft, *Plans des plus beaux jardins pittoresques de France, d'Angleterre et d'Allemagne* (Paris, 1809–10) and G.L. Le Rouge, *Jardins anglo-chinois*, Paris 1776–87.

10. J. Moulin, 'Le Château d'Aunoy et l'importation en France du jardin à l'anglaise', *BM* 1991, 4.

11. The layout of the park described in Marquis de Girardin, *De la composition des paysages* (Geneva, 1777).

12. T. Boelkin, 'Le Tombeau de Jean-Jacques Rousseau', *GBA* 16 (1936), 15; F. Kimball, 'Romantic Classicism in Architecture', *GBA* 25 (1944), 95; H.F. Clark, 'The Role of "Associations" in the Landscape Movement', *JWCI* 6 (1943), 65; L. Hautecoeur (note 2), 5, 15ff.

13. F. Folliot, in exh. cat. *Le Gothique retrouvé avant Viollet-le-Duc* (Paris, 1979), 133.

14. L. Hautecoeur (note 2), 5, 93ff.

15. He was awarded the title of *premier architecte honoraire* and retained the directorship of the Academy until his death; his influence on Versailles was maintained through the inspector-general there, who was his colleague of many years' standing, François Heurtier.

16. B. Scott, 'The Comte d'Angiviller', *Apollo*, January 1973.

17. As presented by H. Robert, 'Projet pour la Grande Galerie du Louvre', (Musée du Louvre, Paris).

18. The temple was intended to house Bouchardon's marble figure of *Cupid Fashioning Hercules' Club into a Bow*, which was then already on show in the Louvre; it was later replaced by a copy.

19. Following the example of the Duc d'Orléans at the Parc Monceau, she had already had a Chinese carousel erected next to the Pavillon Français at Trianon.

20. P. Gluth, 'La Laiterie de Rambouillet', *CdA* May 1958, 74; J. Langner, 'Architecture pastorale sous Louis XVI', *Art de France*, 1963, no. 3, 171, with important information on the origin and iconography of dairies.

21. Now in the Wildenstein collection; only the medallion over the entrance is still in situ.

22. In 1811, the designs were collected by Dufour in an album, now in the Service d'Architecture at Versailles. Peyre the Younger's designs are in his *Oeuvres d'architecture*, published by Percier and Fontaine in 1818; P. Verlet, *Versailles* (Paris, 1961), 643. According to another version, the competition did not take place until 1783; see J.M. Pérouse de Montclos, *Etienne-Louis Boullée* (Paris, 1969), 144.

23. A. Gruber, 'L'Oeuvre de Pierre-Adrien Pâris à la cour de France', *BSHAF* 1974, 273; his designs and executed buildings are recorded in his 'Etudes d'architecture' (Bibliothèque Municipale, Besançon).

24. A. Marie, 'Les Féériques Baraques qui se greffaient sur le château de Versailles', *CdA* January 1968, 68; for Marie-Antoinette's attitude to Versailles, see P. Verlet (note 22).

25. The Hôtel de Ville, Neuchâtel (1783), is in the same austere style. The contrast between the big pediments, supported by columns, and the bare walls recalls Peyre; the vestibule, with its Doric columns, recalls Ledoux. See H. Haug-Levallet, 'L'Hôtel de Ville de Neuchâtel', *BSHAF* 1933, 88; L. Hautecoeur (note 2), 4, 313.

26. On Lenoir-le-Romain see L. Hautecoeur (note 2), 3, 664; A. Braham, *The Architecture of the French Enlightenment* (London, 1980), 239.

27. J.M. Pérouse de Montclos (note 22), 128, 149ff.; J. Stern, *A l'ombre de Sophie Arnould: François-Joseph Bélanger* (Paris, 1930), 127.

28. This attribution in J. Mondain-Monval, *Soufflot, sa vie, son œuvre, son esthétique* (Paris, 1918), 173; a peristylar rotunda in conjunction with a rectangular block appears in Neufforge as a combination of a theatre with a villa.

29. J.M. Pérouse de Montclos (note 22), 165.

30. J.M. Pérouse de Montclos (note 22), 140.

31. De Laborde, *De l'organisation des bibliothèques dans Paris* (Paris, 1846). Boullée also published the *mémoire* that he had appended to his designs. 'M. Boullée a conçu une idée grande, neuve, ingénieuse et simple'; Louis Petit de Bachaumont et al, *Mémoires secrets* (London, 1777–89).

32. Not to be confused with his brother Jean-Louis Viel de Saint-Maux, whose theoretical work, and in particular the *Décadence de l'architecture à la fin du XVIIIᵉ siècle*, takes a rigidly conservative line against the anti-classical tendencies of Boullée and Ledoux.

33. Perronet's principles in bridge-building were: a level road surface, with no 'humpback'; piers uniformly wide, uniformly spaced and as streamlined as possible. His celebrated bridge-building achievements collected in *Description des projets de la construction des Ponts de Neuilly* (1782–3).

34. On this see the alternative project by Boullée (1787), in which the piers are designed in the form of ship's prows and a historical relief frieze runs along the parapet; the functional character of Perronet's engineering has been replaced by a monument of *architecture parlante*. J.M. Pérouse de Montclos (note 22), 170.

35. Exh. cat. *Mathurin Crucy 1749–1826* (Nantes, 1986).

36. Compare Crucy's verdict on Blondel: 'When I was set free from that pedant Blondel, my design for public baths, which I made at the Academy, took wing.' Exh. cat. *Mathurin Crucy* (note 35).

37. In keeping with Laugier's analogy of a *carrefour* in a forest, where the rides meet in a radiating pattern.

38. Compare the similar Academy designs of Le Roy's pupils, especially Percier's Prix d'Emulation entry of August 1782 for a princely *maison de plaisance* in a park. J.M. Pérouse de Montclos (note 1), 179.

39. It had a precedent in Palazzo Mancini, the home of the Académie de France in Rome, where Louis himself had lived for several years; F.G. Pariset, *Histoire de Bordeaux au XVIIIᵉ siècle* (Bordeaux, 1968), 5, 630; C. Taillard, *Bordeaux classique* (Toulouse, 1987), 137; *MH* 1991, no. 178, 94.

40. Both were Freemasons and had first met at a Masonic meeting in Bordeaux. The duke, grand master of the Order in France, had laid the foundation stone of the Grand Théâtre in Bordeaux.

41. P. du Colombier, *L'Architecture française en Allemagne au XVIIIᵉ siècle* (Paris, 1956); H. Heitz, 'Itinéraire d'histoire dans le Vieux Saverne', *SHAS* 1981, 14.

42. Salins worked in Alsace from 1776 onwards. He emigrated in 1792 and settled in Frankfurt am Main in 1797. He assumed the additional name of de Montfort only at a late stage; see P. du Colombier (note 41).

43. J. Langner, 'Claude-Nicolas Ledoux, die erste Schaffenszeit 1762–74' (unpublished diss., Freiburg University, 1959); M. Gallet, *Claude-Nicolas Ledoux* (Paris, 1980).

44. The chapel, which opened in large *serliane* towards the sanctuary and to either side, was the model for Legrand's church of Saint-Louis, Port-Marly (1778). The director's house was struck by lightning in 1918; in 1926 it was blown up, on the alleged grounds that it was an unsafe structure. It has been reconstructed after World War II.

45. Bertrand borrowed Ledoux's style for his own buildings. In particular, the beautiful Château de Moncley (Doubs), which he built in 1778 for President de Santans of the local Parlement, has pronounced Ledoux-like features.

46. Not present in the initial design.

47. In 1857 the theatre was radically altered, and in 1958 it was gutted by fire; all that remains of Ledoux's original building is the portico.

48. Above this level, the present buildings, by Penchant, are an approximation to Ledoux's intentions.

49. M. Gallet (note 43), 142.

50. 'Le mur murant Paris rend Paris murmurant.'

51. It was reintroduced in 1799. Most of the customs posts were demolished under Napoleon III. The suites of engravings are listed by M. Gallet (note 43).

52. 'Never did architects have such an opportunity to display their talents as in the last thirty years before the Revolution. A new city rose around the old Paris, and wide stretches of marshland became covered with stately buildings.' C.A. Guillaumot, *Considérations sur l'état des beaux-arts à Paris* (Paris, Year X [1802]).

53. C. Connolly and J. Zerbe, *Les Pavillons: French Pavilions of the Eighteenth Century* (London, 1962); E. Schlumberger, *CdA* March 1964, 88.

54. J. Silvestre de Sacy, *Alexandre-Théodore Brongniart* (Paris, 1940); exh. cat. *Alexandre-Théodore Brongniart* (Paris, 1986).

55. See M. Hébert, 'Les Demeures du duc d'Orléans et de Madame de Montesson à la Chaussée d'Antin', *GBA* 64 (1964), 161.

56. The singer Dervieux was a bitter rival of the dancer Guimard, and was keen to outdo her in everything. Her distinguished roster of lovers – the Prince de Soubise had paid for her house – included Bélanger, who remodelled her house (after his separation from the singer Sophie Arnould in 1789) and married her in 1795.

57. These reliefs, which are among Clodion's finest works, were taken down in 1921 and are now in the Metropolitan Museum, New York.

58. E. Terry, 'Le Palais abbatial de Royaumont', *Art et style*, no. 5, 41; J.C. Moreux, 'Louis Le Masson: château de Royaumont et église de Courbevoie', *RA* 1951, 31.

59. J. Stern (note 27); A. Braham (note 26), 7.

60. These consisted of the modernization of three rooms on the ground floor and the transformation of the French park into an 'English garden'.

61. J. Stern (note 27); G. Pascal, *Histoire du château de Bagatelle*. Friedrich Gilly visited Bagatelle in 1797; his excellent description, together with a plan and sketches of the interior, published by A. Rietdorf, *Gilly – Wiedergeburt der Antike* (Berlin, 1940), and in Friedrich Gilly, *Essays on Architecture* (Santa Monica, 1993).

62. M. Gallet (note 43), 199.

63. The identification with the arch at the Circus of Maxentius was established by O. Reutersvärd, 'De sjunkna bagarnaa hos Ledoux, Boullée, Cellerier och Fontaine', *Konsthistorisk Tidskrift* 29 (1960), 98; J. Langner, 'La vue pardessus le pont', in: *Piranèse et les Français* (Rom, 1976); the arch had been published in an engraving by Barbault.

64. The same bowed frontispiece, with columns, in Ledoux's Maisons Saisseval. He illustrated these in *L'Architecture* (note 65), but they are otherwise undocumented, and it is questionable whether they were ever built; M. Gallet (note 43), 212.

65. C.N. Ledoux, *L'Architecture* (Paris, 1804), 36.

66. The nature of 'revolutionary architecture' was first recognized and fully evaluated by Emil Kaufmann, 'Architektonische Entwürfe aus der Zeit der französischen Revolution', *Zeitschrift für bildende Kunst*, 1929–30, 38; idem, *Von Ledoux bis Le Corbusier* (Vienna, 1933); idem, 'Three Revolutionary Architects: Boullée, Ledoux, and Lequeu', *Transactions of the American Philosophical Society* (Philadelphia, 1952); idem, *Architecture in the Age of Reason* (Cambridge, 1955); idem, exh. cat. *Les architectes visionnaires à la fin du XVIII siècle* (Geneva, 1965).

67. A.L. Vaudoyer, in his *Etat de l'architecture en France* (1806), sets Ledoux and Boullée alongside Peyre the Younger and Pâris as the leaders of the dominant schools under Louis XVI; on Boullée's pupils see J.M. Pérouse de Montclos (note 22), 209.

68. In 1793 Boullée made it his legacy to the French nation, i.e., to the young republic. The *Essai sur l'art* was intended as a treatise, but never finished. Its mixture of royalist and republican ideas made it unpublishable under Napoleon, and it was published only in 1953, by H. Rosenau; a German edition with extensive commentary by A.M. Vogt followed in 1987. H. Rosenau, *Boullée's Treatise on Architecture* (London, 1953); A.M. Vogt, *Etienne-Louis Boullée, Architektur, Abhandlung über Kunst* (Zürich, 1987).

69. A.M. Vogt, *Boullées Newton-Denkmal, Sakralbau und Kugelidee* (Basel, 1969), 216ff.; The idea of a 'museum' of this kind also underlay the Musée des Monuments français.

70. A.M. Vogt (note 69); K. Lankheit, *Der Tempel der Vernunft* (Basel, 1973), with a detailed analysis of the statue of Artemis inside.

71. 'La non-interruption des lignes qui ne permettent pas que l'œil soit distrait par des accessoires nuisibles'; C.N. Ledoux (note 65). The new, block-like compactness of architecture, as opposed to the spatial idea of architectural unity, splendidly analysed by S. Giedion (note 3).

72. J.M. Pérouse de Montclos (note 22); A.M. Vogt (note 69); idem, 'Die französische Revolutionsarchitektur und der Newtonismus', *Die Kunst des Abendlandes*, 1967; H. Rosenau, 'The Sphere as an Element in the Montgolfier Monument', *AB* 1968, no. 1; K. Lankheit (note 70).

73. 'Esprit sublime! Génie vaste et profond! Etre divin! O Newton!' – and elsewhere, 'C'était dans le ciel que je voulais placer Newton.' E.L. Boullée, *Essai sur l'art* (see note 68).

74. There were two giant globes of this kind at the Hôtel de Nevers, which now forms the back wing of the Bibliothèque Nationale. The starry sky within the dome appears several times in the designs for a Palais des Etats; Louis Combes (1789) even arranged the heavens in the precise configuration for 14 July 1789, 'the memorable instant of our liberty'.

75. J.M. Pérouse de Montclos (note 22).

76. Diderot had already voiced this idea. See also C.I. Becker, *The Heavenly City of the Eighteenth-Century Philosophers* (New Haven, 1952); H. Sedlmayr, *Verlust der Mitte* (Salzburg, 1949), 25.

77. 'Nos édifices publics devraient faire en quelque façon de vrais poèmes. Les images qu'ils offrent à nos sens devraient exciter dans nos coeurs des sentiments analogues à la destination.' E.L. Boullée, *Essai sur l'art* (see note 68).

78. J. de Caso, 'Remarques sur Boullée et l'architecture funéraire à l'âge des lumières', *RA* 32 (1976), 15.

79. On this see P. Giraud, 'Les Tombeaux, ou Essai sur les sépultures' (n.d.) and J. de Cambry, 'Rapport sur les sépultures présenté à l'administration générale du Département de la Seine' (1799), both in exh. cat. *Alexandre-Théodore Brongniart* (note 54).

80. Ledoux's friend, the poet Delille, wrote: 'He was constantly improving his plans for an imaginary city in which all those buildings that were useful to the inhabitants and conducive to their edification were brought together in the best possible relationship to each other: temples, palaces, academies, factories, theatres, public baths ... It was a veritable architectural utopia; this work might have been intended for the Republic of Plato.' M. Gallet (note 43), 27.

81. 'Function' is to be understood here, in accordance with the *Encyclopédie*, as 'une action correspondante à sa destination'. This utilitarian tendency also occurs in the gigantic designs by Poyet, Vien and Bonnard for a new Hôtel-Dieu, and in Combes' design for the port of Bordeaux; see H. Rosenau, 'The Functional Element in French Neo-Classical Architecture', *Die Kunst des Abendlandes*, 1967, 226ff.

82. Cube: 'La forme d'un cube est la forme de l'immutabilité; on asseoit les dieux, les héros sur un cube.' Pyramid: 'C'est l'idée de la flamme qui s'effile par la pression de l'air et en détermine la forme.' Circle: 'L'atelier du monde n'est-il pas inscrit dans un cercle? ... Cercle éternel dont le centre est partout et la circonférence nulle part.' C.N. Ledoux (note 65).

83. The social and moral basis is the thread that runs through Ledoux's *L'Architecture*. His preface contains these words: 'Peuple! Unité si respectable par l'importance de chaque partie qui la compose, tu ne seras pas oublié dans les constructions de l'art.' And again: 'Rien de ce qui peut propager les bonnes moeurs, corriger les mauvaises, en punir et surtout en prévenir les effets, n'est négligé.' C.N. Ledoux (note 65).

84. See William Beckford's description of his drive with Ledoux to a mysterious house outside Paris. The occasion was probably an initiation ceremony of the Rosicrucians, to whom Ledoux belonged. M. Gallet (note 43), 26.

85. See the excellent study by J. Langner, 'Ledoux und die Fabriques', *Zeitschrift für Kunstgeschichte* 26 (1963), 1.

86. J. Langner, 'Ledoux' Redaktion seiner eigenen Werke für die Veröffentlichung', *Zeitschrift für Kunstgeschichte* 23 (1960), 151. The engravings were first circulated as individual sheets; hence the imitation of the Pavillon Guimard at the church of Badonviller and of the chapel of the Salines de Chaux at Saint-Louis, Port Marly. M. Gallet, 'Les Inédits de Claude-Nicolas Ledoux, un versant ignoré de son utopie', *GBA* 116 (1990), 9; idem, *Architecture de Ledoux: Inédits pour un tôme III* (Paris 1991).

87. Ledoux wrote the text in prison during the Revolution. He changed the title successively from *Architecture pratique*, by way of *Muséum architectural*, to *L'Architecture considérée sous les rapports de l'Art, des Moeurs et de la Législation*: that is, architecture interpreted as a educative and social force, in line with revolutionary ideology. The part that eventually appeared was planned as the first volume of a multi-volume work. By the time Ledoux died, most of the copper plates for the later volumes had already been prepared, or at any rate begun. Before his death, Ledoux handed them over for publication to his executor Pierre Vignon, the architect of the Madeleine; but no more were published until *Architecture de Claude-Nicolas Ledoux* appeared in 1847, with a preface by Daniel Ramée. The remaining plates have been published by M. Gallet (note 86).

88. F. Boyet, 'Projets de salles pour les assemblées révolutionnaires à Paris 1789–1792', *BSHAF* 1933, 170; idem, 'Notes sur les architectes Jacques-Pierre Gisors, Charles Percier et Pierre Vignon', *BSHAF* 1933, 256; idem, 'Les Tuileries sous la Convention', *BSHAF* 1932, 197; idem, 'Les Salles d'assemblée sous la Révolution française et leurs répliques en Europe', *BSHAF* 1952, 88.

89. H. Rosenau, 'Jean-Jacques Lequeu', *Architectural Review*, August 1949; G. Metken, 'Jean-Jacques Lequeu ou l'architecture rêvée', *GBA* 65–213 (1965); P. Duboy, *Lequeu, an Architectural Enigma* (London, 1986). J. Guillerme, 'Lequeu et l'invention du mauvais goût', *GBA* 66 (1965), 153. Ph. Duboy, *Lequeu, an*

architectural enigma, London, 1986. Kaufmann credits Lequeu with a powerful influence on revolutionary architecture as a whole, but such a thing is out of the question; he lacked the ability to be anything more than an architectural draughtsman.

90. F. Boyet, 'Le Conseil des Cinq Cents au Palais Bourbon', *BSHAF* 1935, 59; idem, 'Le Palais Bourbon sous le Premier Empire', *BSHAF* 1936, 91; idem, 'Six statues des législateurs antiques pour le Palais Bourbon sous le Directoire', *BSHAF* 1958, 91.

91. W. Szambien, *Jean-Nicolas-Louis Durand 1760–1834* (Paris, 1984).

92. See M. Jallut, 'Cabinets intérieurs et Petits Appartements de Marie-Antoinette', *GBA* 63 (1964), 289, and also P. Verlet (note 22), 681.

93. Both Rousseau brothers, Hugues-Jules as carver and Jean-Siméon, known as Rousseau de la Rottière, as painter, were enlisted by their father Antoine from 1774 onwards to assist in the decorative work at Versailles, where they subsequently succeeded him; see L. Hautecoeur (note 2), 4, 485.

94. M. Jallut (note 92), 349. The cabinet was described by Charles Constant, a citizen of Geneva, on the occasion of a visit in 1796.

95. 'L'Influence de Marie-Antoinette sur l'art de son temps', *CdA* May 1955, 44. In numerous designs for ornaments, Henri Salembier (1753–1820), in particular, decisively moved the Louis XVI style in the direction of elegance and grace.

96. Built in 1767 by Gabriel's pupil Nicolas Barré, and pulled down in 1928 to give way to the Embassy of the United States of America.

97. Warsaw University Library; L. Réau, in *BSHAF* 1937, no. 1, 7; F. Kimball, in *GBA* 5 (1931), 29. T.J. McCormick, *Charles-Louis Clérisseau and the Genesis of Neo-Classicism*, New York, 1990.

98. Pergolesi, *Designs for Various Ornaments* (London, 1777); Colombani, *A New Book of Ornaments* (London, 1775); T. Chippendale, *Sketches of Ornament* (London, 1779); C. Richardson, *A Book of Ceilings* (London, 1781).

99. In 1786–7, the Salon Frais of the dairy at Rambouillet acquired Etruscan furniture based on designs by Hubert Robert; see F.J.B. Watson, *Wallace Collection Catalogue: Furniture* (London, 1956). On Etruscology in the eighteenth century, see *CdA* May 1958, 74; M. Horster, 'Eine Elfenbeinpyxis mit Szenen aus der etruskischen Mythologie', in *Mouseion, Studien aus Kunst und Geschichte für O.H. Förster* (Cologne, 1959).

100. On the dating of the Cabinet de Toilette, see P. Verlet, 'Le Boudoir de Marie-Antoinette à Fontainebleau', *Art de France* 1 (1961), 159.

101. 'La chambre à coucher du Prince était à elle seule tout un poème.' Description of the bedroom in C. Gailly de Taurines, *Aventurières et femmes de qualité* (Paris, n.d.)

102. The original group of three rooms that Bélanger had to redecorate comprises the white summer dining room – with relief decoration and a chimneypiece in the manner of Piranesi by N.F. Lhuillier – the winter dining room and the Salon des Jeux, with green imitation marble covered with white plaster reliefs and arabesques, also by Lhuillier. H. Demoriane, 'Le Château de Maisons retrouve une vie brillante', *CdA* October 1967, 87.

103. F. Kimball, 'Les Influences anglaises dans la formation du style Louis-XVI', *GBA* 5 (1931), 29; P. Thornton, 'Proto-Neo-Classicism: the Battle of the Giants', *Apollo*, 1963, 130; M. Gallet, *Demeures parisiennes à l'époque Louis-XVI* (Paris, 1964), 53.

104. See J. Stern (note 27).

105. G. Janneau, 'Sur le Style Directoire', *RAAM* 71 (1937), 341.

106. R.G. and C. Ledoux-Lebard, 'La Décoration et l'ameublement de la chambre de Madame Récamier sous le Consulat', *GBA* 11 (1952), 175.

Bibliography

This bibliography does not include publications of architectural engravings without text. Such publications, as well as papers in journals and periodicals, are referred to in the notes. It goes without saying that such a bibliography as this is not complete. It is confined to the essential and the most recent publications, which in their turn as a rule carry their own bibliography.

A. SOURCES

ANDRÉ, P. *Essai sur le Beau.* Paris, 1741 and 1770.

ARGENSON, R.L. DE, VOYER DE PAULMY, MARQUIS D'. *Journal et Mémoires.* Paris, 1861–7.

BACHAUMONT, L.P. DE. *Mémoires secrètes pour servir à l'histoire de la République des Lettres en France depuis 1762 jusqu'à nos jours.* London, 1777–89.

BARBIER, E.J.F. *Journal historique et anecdotique du Régne de Louis XV.* Paris, 1866.

BLONDEL, J.-F. *De la distribution des maisons de plaisance et de la décoration des édifices en général.* Paris, 1756, 1773.

BLONDEL, J.-F. *Architecture française.* Paris, 1752, 1754, 1756.

BLONDEL, J.-F. *Cours d'architecture* (continued by Patte). Paris, 1771–7.

BLONDEL, J.-F. *Les amours rivaux.* Amsterdam, 1774.

BOFFRAND, G. *Livre d'architecture.* Paris, 1745.

BRICE, G. *Description de Paris.* Paris, 1702, 1715, 1723, 1725, 1752.

BRISEUX, C.E. *Traité du beau essentiel dans les arts appliqués particulièrement à l'architecture.* Paris, 1752, 1753.

COCHIN, N. *Supplication aux orfèvres.* Paris, 1754.

COCHIN, N. *Voyage d'Italie.* Paris, 1758.

CORDEMOY, L. DE. *Nouveau Traité de toute l'architecture.* Paris, 1706.

CROY, DUC DE. *Journal inédit du Duc de Croy.* Paris, 1906.

DANGEAU, MARQUIS DE. *Journal de la cour de Louis XIV depuis 1684 jusqu'à 1715.* 19 vols. London, 1774.

DAVILER, C. *Cours d'architecture.* Paris, 1691, 1710.

DELAFOSSE, C. *Nouvelle Iconologie historique.* Paris, 1768.

DÉZALLIER D'ARGENVILLE, A.J. *Vie des plus fameux architectes et sculpteurs.* Paris, 1787.

DÉZALLIER D'ARGENVILLE, A.J. *Voyage pittoresque de Paris,* 1749.

DÉZALLIER D'ARGENVILLE, A.J. *Voyage pittoresque des environs de Paris.* Paris, 1749, 1755, 1778.

DIDEROT, D. and D'ALEMBERT, J. *Encyclopédie, ou Dictionnaire raisonné des sciences, des arts et des métiers.* Paris-Amsterdam, 1751–77.

DURIVAL, N. *Description de la Lorraine et du Barrois.* Nancy, 1778–83.

GRIMM BARON. *Correspondance littéraire, philosophique et critique de Grimm et de Diderot, depuis 1752 jusqu'en 1790,* 15 vols. Paris, 1829–31.

GUIFFREY, J. *Comptes des Bâtiments du Roi 1644–1715.* Paris, 1881–1901.

JESTAZ, B. *Le voyage d'Italie de Robert de Cotte.* Paris, 1966.

LA FONT DE SAINT-YENNE. *L'Ombre du Grand Colbert, le Louvre et la ville de Paris.* The Hague, 1749.

LA FONT DE SAINT-YENNE. *Le Génie du Louvre aux Champs Elysées.* Paris, 1756.

LA MARE, DE. *Traité de la police.* Paris, 1738.

LAUGIER, M.A. *Essai sur l'architecture.* Paris, 1753.

LAUGIER, M.A. *Observations sur l'architecture.* Paris, 1765.

LEDOUX, C.N. *L'Architecture considérée sous le rapport de l'art, des moeurs et de la législation.* Paris, 1804.

LEMONNIER, H. *Procès verbaux de l'Académie d'Architeture.* Paris, 1911–26.

LOHMEYER, K. *Die Briefe Balthasar Neumanns von seiner Pariser Studienreise 1723.* Düsseldorf, 1911.

LUBERSAC, ABBÉ DE. *Discours sur les monuments publics.* Paris, 1775.

LUYNES, DUC DE. *Mémoires sur la cour de Louis XV* (1735–58). Paris, 1860.

MARCEL, P. *Inventaire des papiers manuscrits du Cabinet de Robert de Cotte.* Paris, 1906.

MARIE, A. *Inventaire manuscrit des dessins de Robert de Cotte.* Paris, n.d.

MARIETTE, J. (éd. P. de Chennevières and A. de Montaiglon). *Abécédario.* Paris, 1851–60.

MASCOLI, L. 'Le voyage de Naples de Ferdinand Delamonce', *Mémoires et documents sur Rome et l'Italie méridionale,* N.S. 1, 1984.

MONTAIGLON, A. DE, and GUIFFREY, J. *Correspondance des directeurs de l'Académie de France à Rome.* Paris, 1887–1908.

PATTE, P. *Monuments érigés à la gloire de Louis XV.* Paris, 1765.

PATTE, P. *Mémoires sur les objets les plus importants de l'architecture.* Paris, 1769.

PATTE, P. *Mémoires sur la construction de la coupole projetée pour couronner la nouvelle église de Ste. Geneviève à Paris.* Paris, 1770.

PATTE, P. *Mémoires sur l'achèvement du grand portail de l'église de St. Sulpice.* Paris, n.d.

PIGANIOL DE LA FORCE. *Description de Paris,* 1718, 1736, 1742, 1756.

PINGERON, J.C. *Vie des artistes anciens et modernes.* Paris, 1771.

POMPADOUR, MADAME DE (éd. A.P. Malassis). *Correspondance.* Paris, 1878.

QUATREMÈRE DE QUINCY, A.C. *Notices historiques.* Paris, n.d.

QUATREMÈRE DE QUINCY, A.C. *Vie des plus célèbres architectes.* Paris, n.d.

SAINT-SIMON, DUC DE. *Mémoires.* Paris 1830 ff.

THIÉRY. *Guide des amateurs et des étrangers voyageurs à Paris.* Paris, 1787.

VIEL DE SAINT-MAUX, C.F. *Décadence de l'architecture à la fin du XVIIIe siècle.* Paris, 1800.

VOLTAIRE. *Le Temple du goût.* Paris, 1733.

VOLTAIRE. *Des embellissements de Paris.* Paris, 1749.

VOLTAIRE. *Le siècle de Louis XIV.* Paris, 1751.

B. GENERAL WORKS

Les architectes visionnaires de la fin du XVIIIe siècle (Exh. Cat.). Paris, 1964.

BAUER, H. *Rocaille.* Berlin, 1962.

BAUER, H. and SEDLMAYR, H. *Rokoko.* Cologne, 1992.

BLOMFIELD, A. *A History of French Architecture 1661–1774.* London, 1921.

BÖRSCH-SUPAN, H., 'Landschaftsgärten und Chinoiserie', in *China und Europa,* Exh. Cat. Berlin, 1973.

BOTTINEAU, Y. *L'Art de Cour dans l'Espagne de Philippe V.* Bordeaux, 1961.

BOYÉ, P. *Les châteaux du Roi Stanislas en Lorraine.* Nancy, 1910.

BOYÉ, P. *Les Châteaux de Stanislas et les beaux arts.* Nancy, 1927.

BRAHAM, A. *The Architecture of the French Enlightenment.* London 1980.

BRINCKMANN, A.E. *Baukunst des 17. und 18. Jahrhunderts in den romanischen Ländern* (Handbuch der Kunstwissenschaft). Berlin, 1915.

BRINCKMANN. A.E. *Theatrum Novum Pedemontii.* Düsseldorf, 1931.

COLOMBIER, P. DU. *L'Art français dans les cours rhénanes.* Paris, 1930.

COLOMBIER, P. DU. *L'Architecture française en Allemagne au XVIIIe siècle.* Paris, 1956.

CONOLLY, C. and ZERBE, J. *Les Pavillons, French Pavilions of the Eighteenth Century.* London, 1962.

COSSÉ-BRISSAC, PH. DE. *Châteaux de France disparus.* Paris, 1947.

DIMIER, L. *Les Peintres français du XVIIIe siècle.* Paris-Brussels, 1928.

DUMOLIN, M. *Etudes de topographie parisienne.* Paris, 1929, 1931.

DUMOLIN, M. and OUTARDEL, G. *Les Eglises de France, Paris et la Seine.* Paris, 1936.

ERDBERG, E. VON. *Chinese influences on European Garden Structure.* Cambridge, 1936.

ERIKSEN, S. *Early Neo-Classicism in France.* London, 1974.

EVANS, J. *Monastic architecture in France from the Renaissance to the Revolution.* Cambridge, 1964.

GANAY, E. DE. 'Les Jardins à l'anglaise en France au XVIIIe siècle' (thesis). Paris, 1923.

GANAY, E. DE. *Châteaux de France.* Paris, 1948–50.

GANAY, E. DE. *Les Jardins de France et leur décor.* Paris, 1949.

GIEDION, S. *Spätbarocker und romantischer Klassizismus.* Munich, 1922.

GIEDION, S. *Space, Time and Architecture.* London, 1952.

GONCOURT, E. and J. *Portraits intimes du 18e siècle.* Paris, n.d.

Gothique retrouvé avant Viollet-le-Duc, Le. (Exh. Cat.). Paris, 1979.

HAROUEL, J.L. *L'embellissement des villes; l'urbanisme français au XVIIIe siècle.* Paris, 1993.

HARRIS, J., 'Legeay, Piranesi and international Neoclassicism in Rome 1740–1750'. *Festschrift Wittkower.* London, 1967.

HAUG, H. 'L'Architecture Régence à Strasbourg', *A.A.H.A.* 1926. Strasbourg, 1926.

HAUG, H. *Trois siècles d'art alsacien.* Strasbourg, 1948.

HAUTECOEUR, L. *L'Architecture classique à St. Pétersbourg à la fin du 18e siècle.* Paris, 1912.

HAUTECOEUR, L. *Rome et la renaissance de l'antiquité à la fin du XVIIIe siècle.*

Paris, 1912.
HAUTECOEUR, L. *Histoire de l'architecture classique en France*
II. *Le Règne de Louis XIV*, Paris, 1948.
Paris, 1950.
III. *Première moitié du XVIIIᵉ siècle – le style Louis XV*. Paris, 1950.
IV. *Seconde moitié du XVIIIe siècle – Le Style Louis XVI*. Paris, 1952.
  V. *Révolution et Empire*. Paris, 1953.
HÉLIOT, P. 'La Fin de l'architecture, gothique dans le nord de la France aux XVIIe et XVIIIe siècles', *Bull. de la Comm. Royale des monuments et des sites*, VIII, Brussels, 1957.
HERRMANN, W. 'Antoine Desgodets and the Académie Royale d'Architecture', *The Art Bulletin* XL, March, 1958.
HERRMANN, W. *Laugier and 18th century French theory*. London, 1962.
HONOUR, H. *Chinoiserie*. London, 1961.
HONOUR, H. *Neo-Classicism*. Harmondsworth, 1968.
HUBALA, E. *Barock und Rokoko*, Stuttgart, 1971.
KALNEIN, W. GRAF VON. *Schloss Clemensruhe in Poppelsdorf*. Bonn, 1956.
KAUFMANN, E. *Von Ledoux bis Le Corbusier. Ursprung und Entwicklung der autonomen Architektur*. Vienna-Leipzig, 1933.
KAUFMANN, E. 'Three Revolutionary Architects, Boullée, Ledoux and Lequeu', *Transactions of the American Philosophical Society*. Philadelphia, 1960.
KAUFMANN, E. *Architecture in the Age of Reason. Baroque and Post-baroque in England, Italy and France*. Cambridge, 1955.
KIMBALL, F. *Le Style Louis XV*. Paris, 1949.
LANG, S. 'The Early Publication of the Temples at Paestum', *J.W.C.I.*, XIII (1950).
LANGNER, J. 'Architecture pastorale sous Louis XVI', *Art de France* no. 3 (1963).
LANSON R. *Le Goût du moyen âge en France au XVIIIe siècle*. Paris, 1926.
LAVEDAN, P. *Histoire de l'urbanisme*. Paris, 1941.
LAVEDAN, P. *Les Places Louis XV*, Paris, 1958.
LAVEDAN, P. *Les Villes françaises*. Paris, 1960.
LÉON, P. *Les Monuments historiques*. Paris, 1917.
LÉON, P. *La Vie des monuments français*. Paris, 1951.
LESPINASSE, P. *L'Art français et la Suède de 1673 à 1816*. Paris, 1913.
LESTOCQUOY, J. 'L'Architecture gothique aux XVIIe et XVIIIe siècles', *L'Art sacré* (January–February 1948).
LINFERT, C. *Die Grundlagen der Architekturzeichnung*. Berlin, 1931.
MÂCON, S. *Les arts dans la maison de Condé*. Paris, 1903.
MARIE, A. *Jardins français classiques des XVIIe et XVIIIe siècles*. Paris, 1949.
MAUBAN, A. *L'Architecture française de Mariette*. Paris, 1946.
MIDDLETON, R.D. 'The Abbé de Cordemoy and the Graeco-Gothic Ideal', *J.W.C.I.*, XXV (1962), XXVI (1963).
MINGUET, PH. *Esthétique du Rococo*. Paris, 1960.
MOISY, P. *Les Eglises jésuites de l'Ancienne Assistance de France*. Rome, 1958.
PARENT, P. *L'Architecture des Pays-Bas méridionaux des XVIe, XVIIe et XVIIIe siècles*. Paris-Brussels, 1926.
PARISET, F.G. *L'art néo-classique*. Paris, 1974.
PÉROUSE DE MONTCLOS, J.B. *Les Prix de Rome*. Paris, 1984.
PETZET, M. *Soufflots Sainte-Geneviève und der französische Kirchenbau des 18. Jahrhunderts*. Berlin, 1961.
PEVSNER, N. *An Outline of European Architecture*. 7th ed. Harmondsworth, 1963.
PEVSNER, N. *Studies in Art, Architecture and Design*. London, 1968.
PLANTENGA, J.H. *L'Architecture religieuse de Brabant au XVIIe siècle*. The Hague, 1926.
POULLET, M.F. 'Les Places Royales et l'aménagement urbain sous Louis XV.' *Mon. Hist.* 1982 no. 120.
RÉAU, L. *L'Architecture Française en Russie de Le Blond à Ricard de Montferrand (Urbanisme et Architecture)*. Paris, 1954.
RÉAU, L. *Les Monuments détruits de l'art français*. Paris, 1959.
ROCHEBLAVE, S. *L'Art et le goût en France de 1600 à 1900*. Paris, 1930.
ROCHEBLAVE, S. *L'âge classique en France*. Paris, 1932.
RÖVER, A. *Bienséance. Zur ästhetischen Situation im Ancien Régime*. Hildesheim, 1977.
ROSE, H. *Spätbarock*. Murich, 1922.
ROSENAU, H., *The Ideal City*. London, 1959.
ROSENAU, H. 'The Functional Element in French Neo-Classical Architecture', *Die Kunst des Abendlandes*, 1967.
ROUJON, H. *Le voyage du Marquis de Marigny en Italie*. Paris, 1898.
SCHMARSOW, A. *Barock und Rokoko*. Leipzig, 1897.
SCHNEIDER, R. *Quatremère de Quincy et son intervention dans les arts*. Paris, 1910.
SEDLMAIER, R. *Grundlagen der Rokokoornamentik in Frankreich*. Strassburg, 1917.
SEZNEC, J. *Essai sur Diderot et l'antiquité*. Oxford, 1957.
TINTELNOT, F. *Barocktheater und barocke Kunst*. Berlin, 1939.
TOURNIER, R. *Les Eglises comtoises, leur architecture des origines au XVIIIe siècle*.

Paris, 1954.
Urbanisme et architecture (Etudes écrites et publiées en l'honneuer de Pierre Lavedan). Paris, 1954.
VALLERY-RADOT, J. *Le Recueil de plans d'edifices de la compagnie de Jésus, conservé à la D.N. en Paris*. Rome, 1960.
VERLET, P. *La Maison du XVIIIe siècle en France*. Paris, 1966.
VOGT, A.M. *Der Kugelbau um 1800 und die heutige Architektur*. Zürich, 1962.
VOGT, A.M. 'Die französische Revolutionsarchitektur und der Newtomismus'. *Die Kunst des Abendlandes*, 1967.
WEIGERT, R.A. *Le Style Louis XIV*. Paris, 1941.
WEIGERT, R.A. *L'époque Louis XIV*. Paris, 1962.
WEIGERT, R.A. and HERNMARCK, C. *L'art en France et en Suède, extraits d'une correspondance entre l'architecte Nicodème Tessin le jeune et Daniel Cronström*. Stockholm, 1964.
ZOLTAN, H. *La Cour de Léopold*. Paris, 1938.
ZUCKER, P. *Town and Square*. New York, 1959.

C. INDIVIDUAL ARCHITECTS

AUBERT
Souchal, F. *Jean Aubert, Architecte des Bourbon-Condé*, R.A. 1969 (6).

BELANGER
Stern, J. *A l'ombre de Sophie Arnould. Francois-Joseph Bélanger*. Paris, 1930.

BERAIN
Weigert, A.R. *Jean I Bérain*. Paris, 1937.

BERTRAND
Tournier, R. 'L'architecte Cl.J.A. Bertrand', *Mém. de l'Académie de Besançon*, 1943.

BETTO
Marot, P. *L'Architecte Jean Betto*. Nancy, 1944.

BLONDEL
Lejeaux, J. 'Jacques-François Blondel, professeur d'architecture', *L'Architecture*, XI, 1927.'

BOFFRAND
Garms, J. 'Studien zu Boffrand', thesis, Vienna, 1962.
Gallet, M. and Garms, J. *Germain Boffrand 1667–1754* (Exh. Cat.) Paris, 1986.
Garms, J. 'Les nouveaux dessins lorrains de Boffrand, leur place dans l'architecture de leur temps', *B.S.H.A.F.*, 1991, 81.

BOULLÉE
Kaufmann, E. 'Three Revolutionary Architects: Boullée, Ledoux and Lequeu', *Transactions of the American Philosophical Society*, Philadelphia, 2, 1960.
Lankheit, K. *Der Tempel der Vernunft*. Basel, 1973.
Pérouse de Montclos, J.M. *Etienne-Louis Boullée*. Paris, 1969.
Rosenau, H. *Boullée's Treatise on architecture*. London, 1953.
Vogt, A.M. *Boullées Newton-Denkmal, Sakralbau und Kugelidee*. Basel, 1969.
Vogt, A.M. *Russische und Französische Revolutionsarchitektur 1917, 1789*. Cologne, 1974.
Vogt, A.M. *Etienne-Louis Boullée, Architektur. Abhandlung über Kunst*. Zürich, 1987.

BRONGNIART
Alexandre-Théodore Brongniart (Exh. Cat.). Paris, 1986.
Lanney, L. de. *Les Brongniart*. Paris, 1944.
Silvestre de Sacy, J. *Alexandre-Théodore Brongniart*. Paris, 1940.

BULLET
Langenskjöld, E. *Pierre Bullet, The Royal Architect*. Stockholm, 1959.
Strandberg, R. *Pierre Bullet et Jean-Baptiste de Chamblain*. Stockholm, 1971.

CHALGRIN
Quatremère de Quincy, A.C. *Notice sur Chalgrin*. Paris, 1816.

CHALLE
Wunder, R.P. 'Ch. M.A. Challe, A study of his life and work', *Apollo* (Jan. 1968), 22.

CLERISSEAU
Lejeaux, J. 'Charles-Louis Clérisseau, architecte'. *L'Architecture*, 1928.
McCormick, T.J. *Charles-Louis Clérisseau and the Genesis of Neo-Classicism*. New York, 1990.

CONTANT D'IVRY
Kretzschmar, J. 'Pierre Contant d'Ivry' (thesis). Cologne, 1981.
Chevotet-Contant-Chaussard, un cabinet d'artistes au siècle des lumières. Paris, 1987.

DE COTTE
Brunel, G. 'Les contacts entre Balthasar Meumann et Robert de Cotte'. *Actes du XXIIe Congrès International d'Histoire de l'Art*, Budapest II, 1969.
Kalnein, W. Graf. *Das Kurfürstliche Schloss Clemensruhe in Poppelsdorf.* Düsseldorf, 1956.
Ludman, J.D. *Projets de Robert de Cotte et de l'Agence des Bâtiments du Roi pour la Ville de Lyon (L'art baroque à Lyon).* University of Michigan, 1978.
Neumann, R. 'French Domestic Architecture in the early 18th Century, The town house of Robert de Cotte'. *J.S.A.H.* vol. XXXIX, 1980.
Marcel, P. *Inventaire des papiers manuscrits du cabinet de R. de Cotte.* Paris, 1906.
Rauch-Elkan, A. *Acht Pläne und ein Bau-Mémoire Robert de Cottes für Schloss Tilburg in Brabant.* 's Hertogenbosch, 1958.
Reinhardt, U. *Die bischöflichen Residenzen von Châlons-s.-M.*, Verdun and Strassburg. Basel, 1972.

CRUCY
Mathurin Crucy 1749–1826 (Exh. Cat.). Nantes, 1986.

DELAFOSSE
Levallet, G. 'L'ornemaniste Jean-Charles Delafosse'. *G.B.A.* (1929) I.

DELAMONCE
Charvet, L. *Les Delamonce.* Paris, 1892.

DESPREZ
Wollin, N.G. *Desprez en Italie.* Malmö, 1934.
Wollin, N.G. *Desprez en Suède.* Stockholm, 1939.

DUGOURC
Trévise, Duc de. *La réapparition de Dugourc, Renaissance de l'art français.* Paris, 1925.

DURAND
Szambicn, W. *Jean-Nicolas-Louis Durand, 1760–1834.* Paris, 1984.

FISCHER VON ERLACH
Sedlmayr, H. *Johann Bernhard Fischer von Erlach.* Vienna, 1956.

GABRIEL
Bottineau, Y. *L'art d'Ange-Jacques Gabriel à Fontainebleau.* Paris, 1962.
Fels, Comte de. *Ange-Jacques Gabriel.* Paris, 1912.
Gallet, M. and Bottineau, Y. *Les Gabriel* (Exh. Cat.). Paris, 1982.
Gromort, G. *Ange-Jacques Gabriel.* Paris, 1933.
Tadgell, C. *Ange-Jacques Gabriel.* London, 1978.

HÉRÉ
Marot, P. *Emmanuel Héré.* Nancy, 1954.
Pfister, C. *Emmanuel Héré et la place Stanislas.* Nancy, 1905, 1906.
Rau, J. and Schulenburg, Gräfin. *Emmanuel Héré.* Berlin, 1973.

JADOT
Schmidt, J. 'Die alte Universität in Wien und ihr Erbauer J.N. Jadot'. *Wiener Forschungen zur Kunstgeschichte*, 1929.

KLEBER
Danis, R. *Kléber, architecte à Belfort (1789–92).* Strasbourg, 1926.

LAJOUE
Lossky, B. 'Le Blond, Architecte de Pierre le Grand, son œuvre en France'. *Bull. de l'ass. russe pour les recherches scientifiques à Prague* III, 1936.
Roland-Michel, M. *Lajoue et l'art Rocaille.* Paris, 1984.

LEDOUX
Christ, Y. *Ledoux, Architecte du Roi.* Paris, 1961.
Gallet, M. *Ledoux à Paris* (Exh. Cat.). Paris, 1979.
Gallet, M. *Claude-Nicolas Ledoux.* Paris, 1980.
Kaufmann, E. 'Three Revolutionary Architects: Boullée, Ledoux and Lequeu', *Transactions of the American Philosophical Society*, Philadelphia, 2, 1960.
Langner, J. 'Claude-Nicolas Ledoux. Die erste Schaffenszeit 1762–74' (thesis). Freiburg, 1959.
Levallet, G. and Haug, H. *Claude-Nicolas Ledoux.* Strasbourg, 1936.
Raval, M. and Moreux, J.C. *Ledoux.* Paris, 1945.

Rosenau, H. 'Claude-Nicolas Ledoux'. *Burl. Mag.* LXXXVIII, 1946.
Vidler, A. *Ledoux.* Paris, 1987.

LEGEAY
Erouard, G. *L'architecte au pinceau.* Milan-Paris, 1982.

LEQUEU
Duboy, Ph. *Lequeu, an architectural enigma.* London, 1986.
Rosenau, H. 'Jean-Jacques Lequeu'. *Arch Review* (August 1944).
Kaufmann, E. 'Three Revolutionary Architects: Boullée, Ledoux and Lequeu', *Transactions of the American Philosophical Society*, Philadelphia, 2, 1960.

LOUIS
Marionneau, C. *Victor Louis.* Bordeaux, 1881.
Victor Louis et Varsovie (Exh. Cat.). Bordeaux, 1958.
Taillard, Chr. 'Le Château de Bouilh'. *C.A.* 1990, 127.

MEISSONNIER
Kimball, F. 'J.A. Meissonnier and the beginning of the genre pittoresque'. *G.B.A.* XII 1942.
Kimball, F. *Le Style Louis XV.* Paris, 1949.

NICOLE
Tournier, R. *L'Architecte Nicolas Nicole 1702–84.* Besançon, 1942.

PÂRIS
De Ganay, E. 'Pierre-Adrien Pâris', *R.A.A.M.*, 1924.
Estignard, P. *Pierre-Adrien Pâris.* Paris, 1902.
Garcier, C. *L'Architecte Adrien Pâris. La Renaissance de l'art français.* Paris, 1920.

PATTE
Mathieu, M. *Pierre Patte, sa vie et son œuvre.* Paris, 1940.

PINEAU
Deshairs, N. *Nicolas et Dominique Pineau.* Paris, n.d.

PIRANESI
Focillon, H. *Giovanni-Battista Piranesi.* Paris, 1918.
Hindt, A.M. *Giovanni Battista Piranesi, a Critical Study.* London. 1992.
Piranèse et les Français (Exh. Cat.). Rome Dijon-Paris, 1976.
Scott, J. *Piranesi.* London, 1975.

SERVANDONI
Bouché, J. 'Servandoni'. *G.B.A.* IV, 1910.

SOUFFLOT
Actes du Colloque Soufflot et l'architecture des lumières. Lyon, 1980.
Catinat, J. *Le Château de Chatou et la Nymphée de Soufflot.* Paris, 1974.
Gallet, M. and Ternois, D. *Soufflot et son temps* (Exh. Cat.). Paris, 1980.
Mondain-Monval, J. *Soufflot, sa vie, son œuvre, son esthétique.* Paris, 1918.
Le Panthéon, Symbole des révolutions (Exh. Cat.) Paris-Montreal, 1989.

VIGNY
Gallet, M. 'L'architecte Pierre de Vigny 1690–1772'. *G.B.A.* LXXXII, 1973.

DE WAILLY
Charles de Wailly, peintre-architecte dans l'Europe des lumières (Exh. Cat.). Paris, 1979.
Dittscheid, H.C. 'Charles De Wailly in den Diensten des Landgrafen Friedrich II. von Hessen-Kassel'. *Kunst in Hessen und am Mittelrhein*, 1981.

D. INDIVIDUAL PLACES

PARIS: GENERAL
Colas, R. *Paris qui reste. Vieux Hôtels, Vieilles Demeures.* Paris, 1919.
Rochegude, Marquis de, and Dumolin, M. *Guide pratique à travers le vieux Paris.* Paris, 1923.
Gallet, M. *Demeures parisiennes à l'époque Louis XVI.* Paris, 1969.
Gallet, M. *Paris domestic architecture of the 18th century.* London, 1972.

PARIS: CHURCHES
Christ, Y. *Eglises parisiennes, actuelles et disparues.* Paris, 1947.
Krieger, A. *La Madeleine.* Paris, 1937.
Vloberg, M. *Notre Dame de Paris et le vœu de Louis XIV.* Paris, 1926.
Monval, J. *Le Panthéon.* Paris, 1928.

Chevalier, P. and Rabreau, D. *Le Panthéon*. Paris, 1977.
Petzet, M. *Soufflots Ste. Geneviève und der französischen Kirchenbau des 18. Jahrhunderts*. Berlin, 1961.
Nichaud, M.I. *L'Eglise de St. Roch*. Paris, n.d.
Lemesle, G. *L'église St. Sulpice*. Paris, 1931.

PARIS: HÔTELS
Contet and Vacquier. *Les Vieux Hôtels de Paris. Architecture et décoration*. Paris, 1910 ff.
Langlois, C. *Les Hôtels de Clisson, de Guise, de Rohan-Soubise au Marais*. Paris, 1922.
Babelon, J. *Musée de l'Histoire de France Historique et description des bâtiments des Archives Nationales*. Paris, 1958.
Babelon, J. *Le Cabinet du Roi ou le Salon Louix XV. de la Bibliothèque Nationale*. Paris-Brussels, 1927.
Laulan, R. *L'Ecole Militaire de Paris*. Paris, 1950.
Laudet, F. *L'Hôtel de la Vrillière*. Paris, n.d.
Laudet, F. *L'Hôtel de Toulouse, Siège de la Banque de France*. Paris, 1960.
Pillement, G. *Les hôtels de Paris*. Paris, 1945.
Vacquier, C. *L'ancien hôtel du Maine et de Biron*. Paris, 1909.

PARIS: PALACES
Hautecoeur, L. *Histoire du Louvre*. Paris, n.d.
Coutant, H. *Le Palais Bourbon au XVIIIe siècle*. Paris, 1905.
Marchand J. and Boulas, J. *Le Palais Bourbon*. Paris, 1962.
Champier, V. and Sandoz, R. *Le Palais Royal*. Paris, 1908.
Dupezard, E. *Le Palais Royal de Paris*. Paris, 1911.
Espezel, A.d'. *Le Palais Royal*. Paris, 1936.

PARIS: PUBLIC BUILDINGS
Denning M.K. *La Halle au blé de Paris 1762–1813*. Brussels, 1984.
Steinhauser, M. and Rabreau, D. 'Le Théâtre de l'Odéon de Charles de Wailly et Marie-Joseph Peyre 1767–82'. *R.A.* no. 19, 1973.
Gautier, J. 'Le garde-meuble de la Place Louis XV'. *Mon. Hist.* 190 (1993).

BELLEVUE
Biver, P. Comte. *Histoire du Château de Bellevue*. Paris, 1933.

BERCY
Deshairs, L. *Le Château de Bercy*. Paris, n.d.

BONN
Kunst, H.J. *Die Stadtresidenz der Kölner Kurfürsten von den Anfängen bis zum Brand am 16.1.1777 (Die Bonner Universität, Bauten und Bildwerke)*. Bonn, 1968.

BORDEAUX
Courteault, P. *La Place Royale de Bordeaux*. Paris, 1923.
Courteault, P. *Bordeaux, cité classique*. Paris, 1932.
Lhéritier, J. *Tourny intendant de Bordeaux*. Paris, 1920.
Pariset, F.G. *Histoire de Bordeaux an XVIIIe siècle*. Bordeaux, 1968.
Welles, J. de. *Le Palais Rohan, Hôtel de Ville de Bordeaux*. Bordeaux, 1954.

CAMBRAI
L'église et la paroisse St. Géry à Cambrai (Festschrift). Cambrai, 1933.

CHALONS-SUR-MARNE
CHAMPS Berland, J. *L'Hôtel de l'Intendance de Champagne*. Châlons-sur-Marne, 1938.
Cahen d'Anvers. *Le Château de Champs*. Paris, n.d.

CHANTILLY
Ganay, E. de. *Chantilly*. Paris, 1935.
Lemonnier, H. 'Les grandes Ecuries de Chantilly et le style architectural des Ecuries aux XVIIe et XVIIIe siècles. *B.S.H.A.F.*, 1926.
Malo, H. *Le Château de Chantilly*. Paris, 1948.

CHOISY
Chamchine, B. *Le Château de Choisy*. Paris, 1910.

COMPIÈGNE
Robiquet, J. *Pour mieux connaître le palais de Compiègne*. Compiègne, 1938.
Thiévaud, F. and Le Hénand. *La reconstruction du Château de Compiègne au XVIIIe siècle (Ecole des Chartes)*. Paris, 1970.

DIJON
Cornereau. *Le Palais des Etats à Dijon*. Paris, n.d.

FONTAINEBLEAU
Bottineau, Y. *L'Art d'Anges-Jacques Gabriel à Fontainebleau*. Paris, 1962.
Bray, A. *Les plus excellents bâtiments de France: le Château de Fontainebleau*. Paris, 1955.
Bray, A. *Le Château de Fontainebleau*. Paris, 1956.
Terrasse, C. *Le Château de Fontainebleau*. Paris, 1946.

FRANKFURT
Lübbecke, F. *Das Palais Thurn und Taxis zu Frankfurt am Main*. Frankfurt, 1955.

LYON
Charvet, E.L. *Lyon artistique*. Lyon, n.d.
Le Nail, R. *Lyon, architecture et décoration aux 17e et 18e siècles*. Paris, n.d.

MARSEILLE
Gloton, J.J. 'La vieille Charité de Marseille'. *Arts et Livres de Provence*, no. 75 (1970).

METZ
Lejeaux, J. *La Place d'Armes de Metz*. Strasbourg, 1927.
Lejeaux, J. *La Place d'Armes de Metz, un ensemble architectural du 18e siècle*. Paris, 1927.

MEUDON
Biver, P. Comte *Meudon*. Paris, n.d.

MONTMUSARD
Beauvalot, Y. *Un château extraordinaire à Dijon: Le Château de Montmusard. Cahiers du Vieux Dijon* no. 6. (1978).

MONTPELLIER
Fliche, A. *Montpellier*, Paris, 1935.
Sournia, B. 'La Place Louis-le-Grand de Montpellier'. *Mon. Hist.* no. 20, 1982.

NANCY
Antoine, M. *L'Opéra de Nancy*. Le Pays lorrain, 1965.
Chavancé, R. *Jean Lamour et la ferronnerie d'art*. Nancy, 1942.
Marot, P. *Le Vieux Nancy*. Nancy, 1935.
Marot, P. *La Place Royale de Nancy*. Paris, 1960.
Pfister, C. *Histoire de Nancy*. Paris-Nancy, 1902–9.
Simonin, P. *La Cathédrale de Nancy*. Le Pays lorrain, 1970.

NANTES
Lelièvre, P. *L'Urbanisme et l'architecture à Nantes*. Nantes, 1942.
Martin, C. *Nantes au XVIIIe siècle*. Nantes, 1928.

ORLÉANS
Chenesseau, G. *Ste. Croix d'Orléans*. Paris, 1921.

RAMBOUILLET
Longnon, H. *Le Château de Rambouillet*. Paris, n.d.
Lorin, F. *Histoire de Rambouillet*. Paris, 1907.

REIMS
Bazin, G. *Reims*. Paris, 1908.

RENNES
Banéat, P. *Le Vieux Rennes*. Rennes, n.d.
Nières, C. *La reconstruction d'une ville au XVIIIe siècle*. Rennes, 1972.
Nitsch, G. *L'Hôtel de Ville, La Tour de l'Horloge, Le Présidial de Rennes*. Rennes, 1928.

SAINT-DENIS
Brice, G. and Vitry, P. *L'Abbaye de Saint-Denis*. Paris, 1948.

SAINT-HUBERT
Maillard, J. *Le Château royal de St. Hubert*. Versailles, 1905.

SCHLEISSHEIM
Hauttmann, M. 'Die Entwürfe Robert de Cotte für Schloss Schleissheim', *Münchner Jhb.* VI, 1911.

SENEFFE
Duquenne, X. *Le Château de Seneffe*. Brussels, 1970.

STRASBOURG
Haug, H. *Le Château des Rohan et les grand hôtels du XVIIIe siècle à Strasbourg*. Strasbourg, 1953.
Ludman, J.D. *Le Palais Rohan de Strasbourg*. Strasbourg, 1978–80.

VERSAILLES
Hachette, A. *Le Couvent de la Reine à Versailles*. Paris, 1923.
Jallut, M. 'Cabinets intérieurs et Petits Appartements de Marie-Antoinette', *G.B.A.*, 63 (1964), 289.

Langlois, R.M. *L'Opéra de Versailles*. Paris, 1958.
Mauricheau-Beaupré, C. *Versailles, l'histoire et l'art*. Paris, 1949.
Nolhac, P. de. *Histoire du Château de Versailles*. Paris, 1911.
Nolhac, P. de. *Versailles au 18e siècle*. Paris, 1918.
Nolhac, P. de. *La Chapelle royale de Versailles*. Paris, n.d.
Racinais, *La Vie inconnue des petits appartements de Versailles*. Versailles, 1951.
Verlet, P. *Versailles*. Paris, 1961.

WÜRZBURG
Sedlmaier, R. and Pfister, M. *Die fürstbischöfliche Residenz zu Würzburg*. Munich, 1923.

Index

References to the notes are given to the page on which the note occurs, followed by the number of the note; thus 272[46] indicates page 272, note 46. Numbers in *italic* refer to plates.

Photographic Acknowledgements

Inventaire Général en Alsace (SPADEM 1968): 245; Service photographique des Archives Nationales, Paris: 97, 98, 146, 160, 169, 175, 177, 178, 189; James Austin: 53, 55, 64, 99, 100, 101, 119, 127, 164, 165, 167, 170, 172, 179, 181, 182, 190, 217, 225, 236, 237 (ext), 244, 255, 258, 259, 290; Mairie d'Avignon: 116; Tim Benton: 126; Marccllo Bertoni: 272; Bibliothèque Nationale: 8, 9, 10, 11, 13, 16, 18, 20, 45, 75, 95, 121, 125, 163, 166, 184, 185, 188, 209, 220, 224, 238, 240, 241, 267, 268, 269, 270, 271, 273, 274, 276, 277, 286, 287, 288, 291; By permission of the British Library: 216, 264; Bonn, Rheinisches Amt für Denkmalpflege: 15; Caen, Conseil généneral du Calvados: 214 (Jean-Yves Faulin); Paris, Caisse Nationale des Monuments Historiques: 147, 231, 293, 296; Cologne, Rheinisches Bildarchiv: 17; Copenhagen, Kunstindutrimuseet: 152, 155; London, Courtauld Institute of Art, Conway Library: 202, 203; Laurence Daniere: 131, 186; Bibliothèque de Dijon: 196 (François Perrodin); Mairie de Dijon: 91, 92; New York, Cooper-Hewitt Museum, Smithsonian Institution: 59; Frankfurt, Stadtarchiv: 19; French Government Tourist Office: 87; Giraudon: 81, 144, 151, 157; A F Kersting: 180; Photothèque Institut Claude-Nicolas Ledoux: 249 (Gilles Pernet); Eric de Maré: 38, 49, 112, 123, 129, 145, 150, 168, 201, 204, 223, 230; Daniel Martinage: 115; New York, Metropolitan Museum of Art, Gift of George D Pratt, 1933: 68; Office de Tourisme de Metz Cathédrale: 149; Vincent Monthiers: 205; Munich, Staatsbibliothek: 56; Paris, Serv. Commercial Monuments Historiques: 237 (int); Nantes, Musées du Château des Ducs de Bretagne: 242; Claude O'Sughrue: cover, 183; Paris, Bibliothèque d'Art et d'Archéologie: 82, 212, 254; Mairie de Paris: 215; Paris: Musée des Arts Decoratifs: 90, 206 (Laurent Sully Jaulmes); Photothèque des Musées de a Ville de Paris (SPADEM): 191, 197, 198, 208, 210, 256, 266; Pont-a-Mousson, Abbaye des Prémontrés: 128; Potsdam-Sanssouci, Stiftung Schlösser und Gärten: 158, 200; Nancy, Service regional de l'inventaire général en Lorraine: 29; Ville de Nancy: 5; Paris, Réunion des Musées Nationaux: 69, 114, 143, 195 (Musée de Dijon), 228, 229, 243, 292; Rennes, Archives départementales d'Ille-et-Villaine: 86; Roger-Viollet: 31, 67, 113; Roubier: 218; Paris, Service du Patrimoine mobilier et des achats, Sénat: 47, 73; Stockholm, Statens Konstmuseer: 122; Les Musées de la ville de Strasbourg: 23, 25; Christiohcr Tadgell: 110, 248; Tel: 32, 232; Warsaw, University Library: 294.